KNIVES 2015

EDITED BY
Joe Kertzman

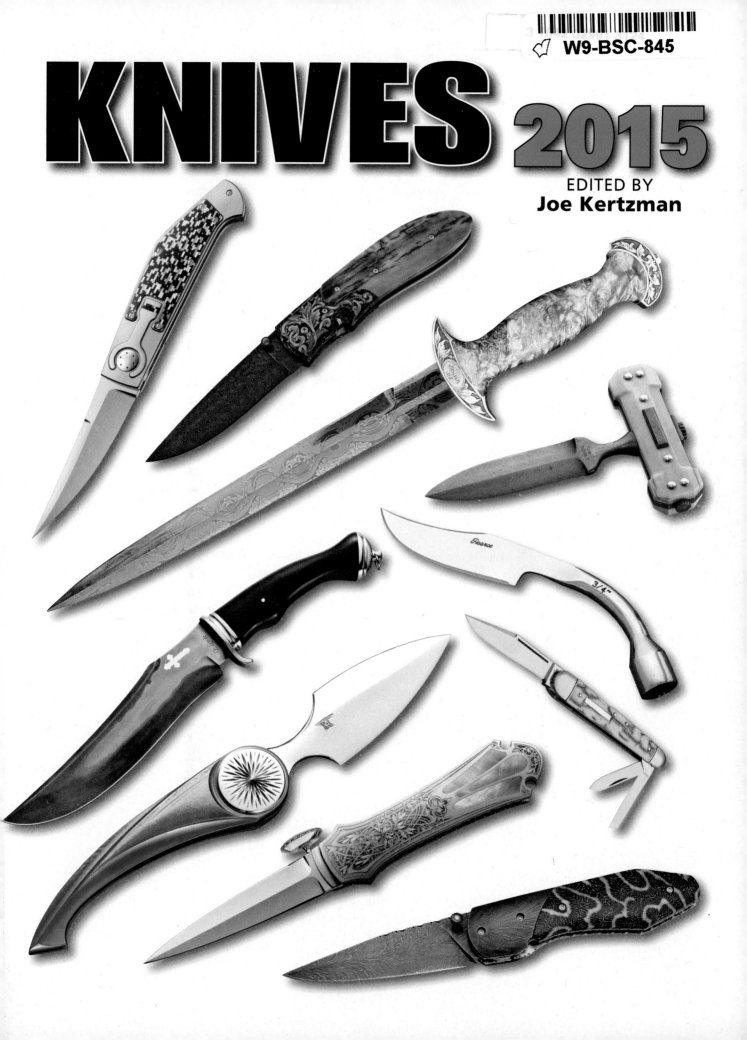

Published by

Krause Publications a division of F+W Media, Inc.
700 East State Street • Iola, WI 54990-0001
715-445-2214 • 888-457-2873
www.krausebooks.com

To order books or other products call toll-free 1-800-258-0929
or visit us online at www.shopblade.com

ISSN 0277-0725
ISBN-13: 978-1-4402-4073-7
ISBN-10: 1-4402-4073-6

Cover Design by Sharon Bartsch
Designed by Rachael Wolter
Edited by Corrina Peterson

Printed in United States of America

Dedication and Acknowledgments

For years the *KNIVES* annual book has laid claim to having the *world's greatest knife writers* contributing feature articles on a myriad of blade-related subjects. I acknowledge them and their contributions, and dedicate this, the *KNIVES 2015,* book to each of them. **Rod Halvorsen** has always been fascinated with indigenous and ethnographic cutting tools and weapons. Extensive travel has given him an appreciation for the blades of various cultures, designs he has been able to modify and explore through knifemaking in his own shop. **Greg Bean's** studies of writing and history went perfectly with his passion for sharp, pointy things. He began writing for *BLADE® Magazine* and the *KNIVES* book series while working for C.A.S Iberia. Accomplished custom knifemaker **Vince Evans'** interest in historical knives and swords keeps him traveling internationally to research and study original pieces in museums. He makes some of the most true-to-form reproductions of knives and swords extant. **Mike Haskew** has been writing for *BLADE* for 23 years, and has developed a great appreciation for the industry and its people. He is also an avid writer of military history and general interest articles, and is the author of more than a dozen books. **Michael Janich** is an accomplished author and recognized

expert on knives and all aspects of self-defense. A member of *Black Belt Magazine's* prestigious Hall of Fame, co-host of Outdoor Channel's "The Best Defense" TV show, and founder of Martial Blade Concepts, he is also a prolific knife designer. **Jordan Clary** is a freelance writer and professional blogger who became interested in knives while visiting a primitive tribe of knifemakers in Burma. **Pat Covert** started seriously collecting knives in the mid-80s and penning articles about them in 1996. He has been writing for *BLADE* and *KNIVES* since 2010. **James Morgan Ayres** has written over 50 articles for *BLADE,* as well as eight books—four of them on survival, firearms and knives. He served with the 82nd Airborne Division and the 7th Special Forces Group (Green Berets). Knife collector and purveyor **Don Guild** is a retired pharmacist who had a chain of 24 stores in California. He has written loads of articles on art knives for *BLADE* and *KNIVES*. **Evan Nappen** has dedicated his life to fighting for gun and knife rights. He has practiced law since 1988 and was one of the first attorneys to ever get a federal injunction against a state gun law. He has written and produced DVDs, and authored a number of gun rights books, as well as numerous articles that have appeared in national magazines. There, how's that for the world's greatest knife writers?!

Joe Kertzman

Contents

On The Cover

Fifty years working as a knifemaker, and when I contacted American Bladesmith Society master smith Joe Keeslar to ask him if he could send me a particular knife (far left, front cover) for possible inclusion on the *KNIVES 2015* book, he was excited to be considered. Now that's saying a lot, not only for the *KNIVES* annual, but also for Keeslar's humility, particularly considering the workmanship of this particular knife. The "Brut de Forge" clip-point fixed blade is forged from a 19th-century French file, and all work is that of the maker, including the vine file work, "dragon scales" engraving on the bolsters and silver wire inlay embellishing the curly maple handle. The 10-inch blade is left with file marks intact, and the knife also showcases a 50th year of knifemaking anniversary medallion on the reverse side of the handle. To the right of Keeslar's piece, spanning the bottom of the front cover is knifemaker Jason Fry's upswept bird-and-trout knife parading a stabilized spalted-pecan handle handsomely partnered with juniper-burl bolsters, a 3 3/8-inch 154CM blade and a tapered tang. It comes with a tooled-leather sheath in a basket-weave pattern. In the center is a completely sculpted and 18k-gold-inlaid Ronald Best art folder boasting a 4.25-inch Damasteel blade, a 416 stainless steel frame, lapis-lazuli handle inlays and more TNT Damasteel following the curve of the grip. All come together like the instruments of a symphony orchestra, and each of the knives is similarly well orchestrated, making for a fine cover at that. (cover photo by Kris Kandler)

Introduction

Welcome to one of the most fantastical worlds this side of Oz, Disney or Hogwarts. Scattered throughout the landscape are gemstones, ivory, pearl, gold, meteorite and other precious commodities. Edges keep watch, knife points unsheathed, little soldiers standing guard. The artists have left their marks, engraving enchanting images, scrimshawing ivory in brilliant hues, building bezels for diamonds and rubies, inlaying, overlaying and etching. Nothing is left to chance or left alone. The place is populated with only good-looking beings whose ancestry has been researched and recorded.

Population growth in knife fantasyland is the most miraculous aspect of the world's best place to live. Though there are some production pieces herein, most are handmade, and no assembly line or manufacturing plant churned out those little numbers. Instead they are one-of-a-kind creations, like snowflakes or fingerprints, with no two being alike. To keep up such a pace, propagating the population, producers work long hours, often in less-than-ideal conditions, pounding, grinding, churning until the finished products are made, sharpened, shined and oiled. Then the little numbers go to market where they are displayed, priced and sold. And new pieces take their places, building a market and satisfying the appetite of collectors who drink in this fantastical world as if it were filled with the lifeblood and nutrients their bodies need.

This is where knives are made, showcased and lauded, and the *Knives 2015* books captures them in glorious full color for all enthusiasts to see, drool over, covet. The makers are many, with 2,200 of them listed in the Custom Knifemaker Directory at the back of the publication, including their contact information, specialties, patterns, technical information, prices, remarks and descriptions of their tang stamps or marks.

They've left their marks in the Trends, State Of The Art and Factory Trends sections of the book, as well as in the feature articles penned by some of the world's best writers. Why the world's best writers, and who says so? Read the Dedication and Acknowledgements on page 3 for brief bios of the authors touting their qualifications. And besides, the *Knives* annual is known as The World's Greatest Knife Book. Then flip to pages 8-56 to get lost in illustrated articles covering such subjects as knife trading along early emigrant trails, one author's fixed-blade fixation, the popularity and quality of frame-lock folders, what features make an ideal survival knife, international art knives, blades used on tall ships, hidden or disguised knives, a sword for a warrior king, whether quality outdoors, camp and hunting knives are worth the extra cost and the first knives some makers ever built.

It's always fascinating to discover what Trends emerge each year in knife fantasyland, and the past year proved fruitful and ultimately fulfilling, with makers fashioning everything from technologically advanced folders to belt and boot knives. Some pieces are "Battle Honed," while others are "Picture-Perfect Pocketknives," "Cool as a Camp Cutter" and "Food Preppers." Many knifemakers find themselves in "A Bromance with the Bowie," and more fashion "Genteel Steel" and "Sweeping Uppercuts." There are utility knives and choppers, pieces inspired by the late Bob Loveless, blades with telltale temper lines, coffin-handle bowies, high-class hunters, push daggers and Western wares. Don't miss the "Animal-Printed Points" in the State of the Art section, as well as etched and engraved knives, gold inlaid pieces, damascus patterns, sculpted steel, ivory artistry, dyed wood, San Mai steel, mosaic damascus, dressed-up daggers, a "Sheathing Review," carved knives, and handle marquetry and mosaics.

Complementary Directories list Sporting Cutlers, Importers, Knifemaking Supplies, Organizations, and everyone from appraisers to custom grinders, handle makers, engravers, etchers, heat treaters, leather workers, photographers, sheath makers and scrimshaw artists.

Here's hoping you enjoy your stay in this fantastical knife world, where a feast has been prepared for you, spread out and served. While steely blades reflect the light, exotic materials make themselves known and embellishments pretty up the place, welcoming onlookers and soothing their senses.

Joe Kertzman

2015 WOODEN SWORD AWARD

How you even envision such a piece of functional art before creating it is beyond me. But then again, I'm not a true artisan as is the winner of the 2015 Wooden Sword Award, Donald Vogt. Vogt's "Shoot and Stab Gun Knife" is a combination single-action automatic knife and a .36-caliber powder percussion pistol (yes, it works). Let's start with the blade. The upswept, re-curved, almost Persian-looking folding blade is Rob Thomas damascus steel that Vogt meticulously en-graved. The sculpted, carved and engraved bolsters, gun trigger, gun hammer and gun barrel are also the same Thomas damascus steel, and the gun body is 303 stainless steel. Mammoth-ivory handle scales, carved by the maker in a floral/vine motif, flow into the bolsters, interlocking with them like puzzle pieces. The entire gun/knife, including such areas as the previously noted trigger and gun hammer, are carved using chisels and a chase hammer, and 14k-gold and ruby inlays are set smartly on the top, or spine, of the gun/ knife, as is a gold plate stating the caliber—"36 Cal." Oh, and while admiring the spine of the piece, note the vine and scroll file work on the titanium liners and steel spacer, respectively. The knife latch is carved and hardened 440C stainless steel. Blade length is 5.5 inches, the overall open length is over a foot long, at 12.25 inches, and the gun barrel stretches 4 inches. Because words can't even begin to describe the piece, Vogt had several images taken and sent to this *KNIVES 2015* book editor, who was smitten and impressed all at the same time, and thus the 2015 Wooden Sword Award goes to Donald Vogt. Thank goodness guys like him follow through on their incredible visions so the rest of us can enjoy the fruits of their labor.

Joe Kertzman

"The First Knife I Ever Made"

They're not all pretty, and their makers aren't always proud, but the "firstborns" remain special

By Mike Haskew

Everybody has to start somewhere. The greatest knifemakers the world has ever known, the up and coming, the dabblers in knife kits and the absolute novices all share a common experience—the first knife they ever made.

Looking back on that first knife, there are more smiles than regrets, there is pride in progress, and there is real history. Beginning with the basics and using everything from saw blades to old springs, that first knife has launched many a storied career in the custom knife industry.

"I guess everybody has made a knife in school, out of a piece of iron or something," reasoned Bob Dozier, who at age 73 has passed the half-century mark in his knifemaking journey. "My grandfather, Milton Bihm, made knives out of 14-inch files, and we called them

At the age of 23, Bob Dozier was out on an oilrig, rough-necking in the Gulf of Mexico. With time on his hands, he found a small file lying unattended on a bench. A nearby grinder drew him close like a magnet. In a few hours, he'd made his first knife.

saddle knives. The deer hunters would carry them on their saddles. They were big old choppers."

Dozier made his first knife at age 12 with his grandfather at his side. "I went to Grandpa and asked, 'Can you teach me how to do this?' We built a forge out of the bottom of a barrel and took my mother's canister vacuum cleaner and reversed the hose on it, put a damper in the pipe and controlled the fire. And I forged. I was the only grandson who showed interest in knifemaking," he continued, "and Grandpa showed me how to take a crosscut saw blade, break it up and make knives."

That knife had lead alloy bolsters and an old hickory handle taken from a hammer. Bob says he made seven or eight pieces with his grandfather and admits that they were "terrible looking."

For several years, Dozier's knifemaking went dormant. He had read an article in *True* magazine about Randall knives selling for the princely sum of $18, and that notion stayed in the back of his mind. At the age of 23, he was out on an oilrig, rough-necking in the Gulf of Mexico. With time on his hands, he found a small file lying unattended on a bench. A nearby grinder drew him close like a magnet.

"In a few hours, I had a knife blade," Bob grinned. "I had that knife for years, and my wife and I used it to open cans in the kitchen. Then it got lost for a while. I found it again six or seven years ago mixed in with a bunch of other knife stuff. I made that knife after I was a grown man, and my interest was rekindled, so I really call that one my first knife."

Functional, Usable Artwork

Michael Ruth Jr. learned custom knifemaking from a couple of the best teachers around. It all started when Jerry Fisk wanted some business cards and came into the Ruth family's print shop. Jerry happened to have a few of his handmade knives and laid them out for everyone to look at.

"That was in the late 1980s, and we were all fascinated by his work," said Michael. "These were clearly something more than just tools—they were artwork—fully functional, usable artwork. I don't think I've ever looked at knives the same way after that day."

Michael and his father, Michael Ruth Sr., made countless trips to Fisk's shop, and B.R. Hughes, who brought Jerry into the Ruth's print shop that day, was a guiding presence as well. "Jerry taught us the process of creating each piece from raw materials to the finished product. B.R. was always there to help us understand the concepts of design and the standards of performance that the ABS [American Bladesmith Society] teaches its students," Michael Jr. noted.

The first knife Michael Ruth Jr. fashioned is this hunter with a 5160 blade and an ironwood handle. He keeps it in a drawer in his shop and uses one side of the handle to experiment with new carving and cutting ideas. The side he keeps pristine is shown.

"Being a young guy with a hot bar of steel and a hammer, I usually had the nagging urge to make the world's finest 'Flying Klingon-Ninja Deathblade,' but B.R. was there to remind me that form follows function," he reflected. "If you're going to make something, make sure it serves its purpose first and foremost."

Michael's first knife was a hunter with a 5160 steel blade and ironwood handle. He keeps it in a drawer and takes it out from time to time, just to get focused again on the task at hand.

"From a design standpoint, it reminds me what not to do," he laughed. "The pins are off-centered, the handle is boxy and almost completely square. It's uncomfortable to hold, let alone use for any amount of time. The choil is a mess, and the differentially hardened area of the blade doesn't extend all the way back to the ricasso. The bottom of the guard is too thin. I could go on about its flaws for days.

"The knife really isn't as bad as it could be, I suppose," he allows. "The blade is in the center of the handle, and the transition between the guard and the handle is smooth. It's good to have something to look back on and remember where I was when I started."

Michael found success early, and his second knife, a hunter with a 5160 blade and spalted maple handle, was his first sale. He took it along to a show, just on a whim. After a collector bought a bowie from his father, he turned and asked young Michael what he wanted for the hunter. "The collector looked it over and inspected it for what felt like a lifetime," said Michael. "Then, he finally looked up and asked, 'How does $250 sound?' I was floored!"

From First Knife to Silver Screen

No other knifemaker's work has graced the silver screen like that of Gil Hibben. The Kentuckian has made knives that have appeared in more than 50 motion pictures, including the famed Sylvester Stallone Rambo knife, knives for Steven Seagal in films such as *Under Siege* and many others. His fantasy knives have been prized for years, and he recently completed several years of service as president of the Knifemakers' Guild.

"I made my first knife in high school, but I didn't finish it. So, I don't count that one," he said. "I got out of the Navy in 1956, and I was 21 years old. I saw the movie *The Iron Mistress* with Alan Ladd and had to have a bowie."

Gil made his first knife while he worked in Washington for the Boeing aircraft company. It was a bowie finished with his father-in-law's grinder, a ¼-inch drill and sandpaper.

"I made that knife with a piece of O1 tool steel I requisitioned from Boeing," Hibben grinned. "It has a leather-washer

Gil Hibben's first knife was a bowie fashioned with his father-in-law's grinder, a ¼-inch drill and sandpaper. It has a leather-washer handle, and after he and his brother, Fred, decided to go out and throw it a few times, they chipped the point. With the broken tip, the blade is about 9 3/4 inches long, and the knife stretches 16 inches overall.

The first knife Lucas Burnley made is this integral drop-point hunter now owned by knifemaker Tom Krein's son, Ben. Lucas fashioned it from O1 tool steel and cut the blade out with a hacksaw.

handle, and after my brother, Fred, and I decided to go out and throw it a few times we chipped the point. With the broken tip, the blade is about 9 3/4 inches, and the knife stretches 16 inches overall."

In the span of time since his business started booming, nearly 50 years ago, Gil nearly forgot the significance of that first bowie. "It is a heavy knife," he reflected. "I threw it away once, and my ex-wife got it out of the trash. After that, I decided I had better keep it. Now, it keeps me humble. I think about my passion for making knives and remember having so much fun working on it. I was so proud when I got it done, as humble as it is, but it was my baby and the thing that encouraged me to get better. I'm still trying to get better."

When Lucas Burnley delved into knifemaking in 2001, he had already learned quite a bit about steel, having been through trade school in welding and working in a machine shop as a teenager. His interest in knives, so his father says, actually goes back to his boyhood, walking, talking and chattering about making a knife.

"I'm not sure how I got that in my head," laughed Lucas, "but I guess the drive to make knives has been there for a while. The machine shop that employed me specialized in body-piercing jewelry. They had grinders, drill presses, buffers and stuff in a back room, and I decided to stay after work one day and make a knife out of a little file. That one didn't work out so well."

Lugging the Grinder Around

Lucas saved money and bought a Bader grinder that went with him from apartment to apartment until he rented a place with a one-car garage and set up shop. In the meantime, he met respected knifemaker Joe Cordova, who welcomed the young maker into his established shop.

"Joe helped me a lot in the beginning and would never begrudge me a visit," said Burnley. "I would approach him with a problem, and he would help me work it out. Joe has always impressed me because it seems like he can do anything, forging, stock removal, classic and contemporary. He has amazing range."

Burnley's first knife was an integral drop-point hunter of ¼-inch O1 tool steel. He cut the blade out with a hacksaw, shaped it with his grinder, and then did the heat-treating with a welding torch.

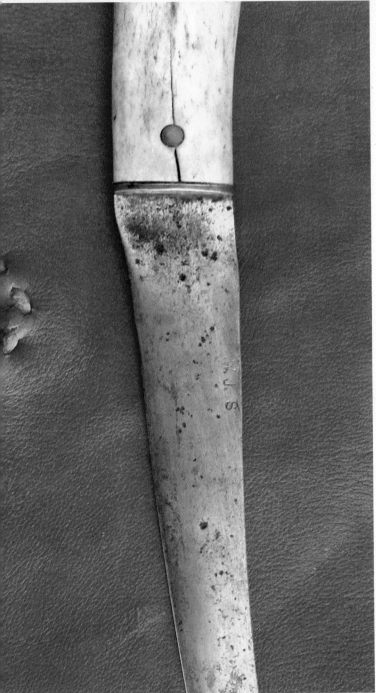

American Bladesmith Society master smith Steve Schwarzer made his first blade, a fillet knife, for his dad. He continued to make similar knives, calling them "ugly and crude." Still, there was a market for them, and they sold and kept selling at $15 to $20 each.

"I beat on it for a few years and then it ended up in a box in a closet," he said. "I couldn't bring myself to toss it out, and eventually gave it to Ben Krein, Tom Krein's 11-year-old son. I figured since his dad is a knifemaker he would be able to get some use out of it. The biggest challenge with it was grinding. I knew what I wanted it to look like, but I couldn't make it happen. It just takes time. Sharpening was another one. I got this knife done, and I realized that I had no idea how to sharpen it on the grinder. It scared the heck out of me."

Lucas sold his first knife to custom knifemaker Bob Terzuola and his wife, Susan, at a show in Scottsdale, Ariz. Susan still keeps the little scalpel with white Micarta® handle scales and silver pins on her workbench.

If the words "mosaic damascus" are mentioned in the knife industry, ABS master smith Steve Schwarzer comes to mind. Acknowledged by many to be one of the world's foremost forgers of mosaic damascus, Steve sold his first knife in 1976.

"I made two or three knives in the 1960s," Steve recalled, "but the first forged knife was a few years later. I got a book on blacksmithing and there was a little chapter on forging blades. So I got an anvil, some coal and crosscut saw blades. I cut the blades out with a coal chisel on top of the anvil, red hot. I didn't know anything about tempering. I cut them out, ground them and put them in oil, and the things would out-cut anything anybody had for filleting fish."

Ugly and Crude Knives

Schwarzer said the knives were "ugly and crude." "Buddy, these were homemade," he stressed. Still, there was a market for them. They sold and kept selling at $15 to $20 each. Then, he met a knifemaker named Bobby Tison.

"I had been making these knives, and my buddies thought I was wonderful," Steve smiled. "I thought I was too. I had three or four of these knives wrapped up in my hip pocket one day, and I said to Bobby, 'I hear you make knives.' He leaned against a sulfuric acid tank and pulled out a beautiful folding knife that walked and talked, made of D2 steel. I had never seen such a thing, and he made the mistake of letting me come to his shop and work with him."

Schwarzer has since become one of the world's most renowned custom knifemakers of his generation, and the vast majority of the mosaic-damascus blade patterning in vogue today was born in his shop.

"I've still got that first knife," he commented. "I made it for my dad. It was a fillet knife, and I used a coin for the bolster. The blades on those ran anywhere from seven to nine inches, and the knives were 11-13 inches overall. There was a guy named Eddie Delaney who used to sell my knives at a local hardware store, and when I upped the price to $30, you have never heard such crying and caterwauling. I have a knife with the same materials on the truck seat with me now, and it sells for $300."

Steve notes that, with the nostalgia surrounding all those old fillet knives, he plans to make a few new ones, crosscut saw blades and all. "It makes me feel good, and I like making them," he said. "It is the same joy of creation at one level or another."

One bit of advice that Schwarzer offers new knifemakers is to get to any seminar on knifemaking or bladesmithing they can attend. Forty years ago, there were few of them. "People can save themselves 10 years of digging through a mess on their own," he said. "That is why guys are so successful in a short time now. They have stood on the shoulders of giants."

Legendary or learning, gifted or practiced, for every knifemaker who hopes to succeed there is a price to pay in sweat and preparation. That first knife, though, in many ways, will always remain priceless.

Are Quality Knives Worth the Quid?

The "collector" took a backseat to the "user" as the author real-world tested Fällkniven knives

By Roderick T. Halvorsen

One of the grandest campfire knife debates involves the age-old question of whether costly, premium knives are worth the buck paid. Arguments rage one way or another, with the debate oftentimes stalling due to a dearth of experience with the real pricey ones. Truth is, who wants to plunk down the big dough just to treat a cutting tool like a farm implement in order to find out if it was worth all the quid? And, well, what if it isn't?

Mulling this over, I decided to dedicate myself to the exclusive use of a pair of "high enders" in order to see for myself. Where I use my knives in winter,

With rugged, suitable sheaths, the Fällkniven Tor and Frej models are true examples of the knifemaker's art straight from the factory box. It is hard to imagine a better combination for hard use in remote country.

I must have good faith they will serve well or I may be in it deep. Deep snow and ice that is, and far from home and hearth. I cannot afford failure, whatever the dollar price paid! My work and play take me into remote, high mountains where knives are not just helpful, they are essential.

So it was with a little trepidation I swore off my own handmade and well-proven knives in order to obtain a couple Fällkniven AB models. Fällkniven has earned high praise the world over, and is a thoroughly modern company. The finest Swedish iron is mined 140 miles from its headquarters in Norbotten, Sweden, whereupon it is shipped to Japan. There, Swedish iron becomes Japanese steel, and the knives are made. Some years ago, the company used Hitachi ATS-34 stainless steel, but now favors a VG-10 steel laminate for the toughest of its outdoors knives. Leather scabbards are made in Spain.

Fällkniven takes pride that, in 25 years of production, its knives have leapt to the forefront of the short list of world's best. Or so they say. Are they? My feeling was that I could not agree or disagree until I knew through my own experience.

Reality sneaks in with the fact that I have, until now, never used a Fällkniven knife under hard conditions, and many of the ones I know of owned by friends and acquaintances rest comfortably in such places as mantles and presentation cases where they are treasured, not used.

Before I went to work, I had to decide which of the company's knives I wanted to subject to Old Man Winter. That wasn't too difficult. Due to the nature of my backcountry skiing and snowshoeing, I have for many years carried a pair of knives for the gamut of needs I face. These include shelter building, and general camp and emergency survival challenges. I favor a medium-length bolo or parang (Malaysian or Indonesian knife similar to a machete) and a smaller general-purpose knife in tandem. The big one does what the little one can't, and the little one does better what the big one can. Put differently, there is no other way to get the service of one or the other than by carrying both. I've worked this all out over the years, and due to the stress added weight puts on me I wouldn't carry it if it weren't "worth the weight!"

Treat *These* Like Garden Tools?

When the Fällkniven knives I had ordered arrived in the mail, I opened the boxes and immediately understood the hesitation some have about using these knives hard. Close examination made

Seeing is believing—craftsmanship of the Fällkniven models is superb.

clear that my first impression was spot on about the knives being gorgeous and finely crafted, true pieces of art. I wish I could nitpick and sound like I am not fawning, but I can't. Every angle was straight; every edge grind ran true, every mating of parts, perfect. I admit, I had to rethink my intent to treat these things like garden tools, but eventually, curiosity overcame hesitation, and the collector in me took a back seat to the user.

Some similarities between the two knives are worth noting. First, both possess stacked-leather handles. Prior to my selection, discussion among several experts resulted in a recommendation to choose Kraton®-handle models, but I have decades-long experience with leather handles and I like them. In the end, no trouble whatsoever resulted in their exposure to five months of ice, snow and rain.

A stacked-leather grip is extremely tough, and the Fällkniven handles are superb examples of the type. Well fitted and tight from the start, neither demonstrated any tendency to absorb water. Regardless, my normal practice was applied, and a month or so into knife testing I soaked both in boiled linseed oil, and thereafter, when the knives were used repeatedly for fine dicing and meat cutting, I merely coated the blades in olive oil as I usually do with edged tools used around food. I allowed the oil to run down onto the grips where I rubbed it in.

Except for slight darkening caused by the oil, and some dents and a few rub marks from dropping the knives and bumping them in the field, they look and serve as good as new. Both handles have lanyard holes,

The combination of steel type, heat treat, edge grind and balance are all factors in heavy chopping, in this case using the Fällkniven Tor model.

and the pommels are secured with split spanner-type nuts, which likely could be tightened with a modified screwdriver should the handles ever require it.

The blades are VG-10 steel laminated between two layers of 420-J2 stainless steel, and what a sandwich this makes! While the Rockwell hardness is listed as 59 HRC, sharpening is a snap and edge holding marvelous. The former, for me, has always held some sway over the latter. All blades, no matter how hard, tough, well ground, shaped or heat treated, will dull. And though it may seem that dulling is a demon from which one must place first priority to flee, in a survival scenario, in fact it is sharpening that is the devil.

Some high-tech steels hold edges phenomenally, but become true liabilities in the field when they eventually dull because they require a machine shop of specialty tools to sharpen. Not so with the VG-10/420-J2 laminate. Though it took the skinning and cutting up of an elk and a deer, and then some camp chores, to remove the hairsplitting factory edge, a few strops on an old carving-set steel brought the edge back to true. Then much later, after hard use in the field, merely a few minutes work with a small, hard Norton stone honed each edge.

Time Spent with a Convex Edge

Large and small blades arrived from the factory sporting convex-ground edges. Some may take issue with the manufacturer concerning this. Not me. I suggest the critics hold their tongues till they have spent some time with a Fällkniven convex edge. Fällkniven notes that this form of edge requires skilled hand grinding, and asserts its superiority over other edges for hard use. In deference to those who might think of the convex edge as more suitable for an axe or cleaver than for knives to be used for fine cutting, the Fällkniven grind isn't your average hatchet edge.

It is the combination of the angle with the quality of steel that achieves sharpness and resistance to the forces of dulling. At first blush I myself might have been tempted to question the use of the convex grind on the smaller of the two, but in the field I found both knives to cut superbly, even for fine work. Cleaning a mess of small brook trout proved the theory.

The sheaths are made of leather. Leather put to hard use has been the subject of criticism in recent years due to the development, production and marketing of excellent synthetics. But as a leatherworker, I have always been a fan of the stuff.

Frej's excellent convex edge performed like a flat grind on small trout.

It is incredibly tough, and should it be damaged, it is repairable. Certainly use in the tropics has gained it a reputation for disintegration and rotting, but in the cold, wet conditions to which I subjected the knives and sheaths, both scabbards served admirably with no indication of problems, no breaking of stitching, no rotting.

Part of the reason Fällkniven knives were chosen was that the company offers a truly large knife, as well as smaller models, and it was their largest I chose to be my "big one." This is the bowie-styled NL1 Tor. It is named Tor (Thor) for a reason. The knife is worthy of the symbolic association with the mythical Norse god. With a blade thickness of .275 inch at the spine, a blade length of 10 inches and an overall length of 15 1/8 inches, this big knife represents a rarity in today's market. Few truly massive, high quality knives exist.

Tor stood up to the hammering. Noted in the company literature as a "strong chopper of world class quality" and a "thrill to use," it is both. I readily admit I generally do not favor bowies as my big knives. They often possess marginal chopping ability, forcing excessive muscling of the blade and, due to the lack of a positive stop for the hand on the pommel, consequently become dangerous to use as I become fatigued, risking slippage on the grip.

The NL1 is the best bowie-type blade I have ever used. The chopping properties of the knife are not just adequate, but rather excellent. Numerous small trees up to 8 inches or so in thickness were felled. It is fun to use. And the width of the NL1 is 1.75 inches, allowing choking up of the hand forward of the guard for fine work.

Finding Fault

I had to search for something to criticize. While the scabbard materials and workmanship are flawless, I did experience one problem. The belt loop has two hard snaps that allow it to be removed from a

In a remote, high mountain camp, the author's buddy appears to appreciate the security provided by a pair of truly excellent knives.

belt without stripping the belt of other tools. This is, of course, an excellent idea. However, in use, I found the snaps to detach from time to time. This occurred while skiing, when falling and occasionally when I tossed my gear belt on the ground. The solution was simply to wrap the loop with a leather thong.

The retention strap was on the same side as the edge, meaning that the edge could cut it when the knife was removed. On sheaths I make myself, I place the retention strap on the opposite side of a cross-guarded knife where the blade cannot cut it. Fällkniven's solution was to incorporate a small elastic cord that pulls the strap away from the edge. Curious, but ingenious, and effective! If anything on the knife itself could be changed, it might be to soften the edge of the guard just a little to add

comfort when the index finger rests over it for control in making fine cuts. Only a couple strokes with a file would round it over.

Tor's little brother, the second of the pair, is Frej, the NL4. Hearkening in general shape back to the ancient and effective Marble's Ideal, this knife too benefited from the stainless properties of the superb VG-10/420-J2 laminate. Blade length is a little over 5 inches, with a spine thickness of .197 inch and overall length of 9 5/8 inches. Balance is excellent and cutting properties are absolutely workhorse. Fine skinning and caping were easily accomplished, and for camp, kitchen and food prep chores it was a delight to use.

In practice, I tend to protect the littler knife when traveling in the backcountry since I want the

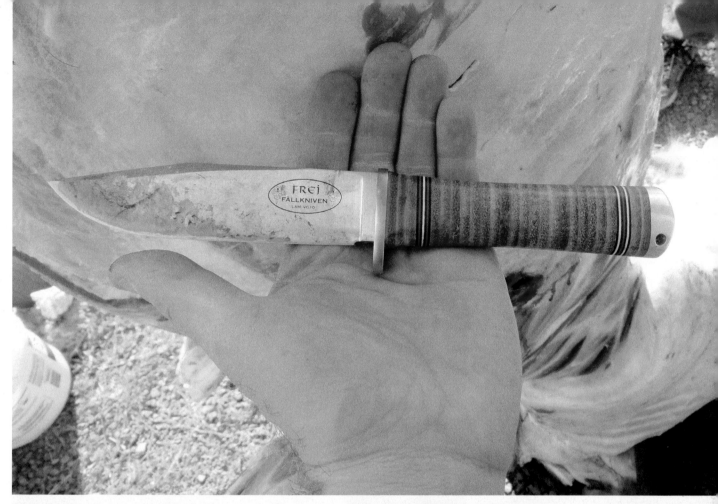

With a blade a little over 5 inches in length, the Frej is a nice hunting knife, well balanced, and handles skinning and caping chores well.

finest edge preserved for medical or other needs in the event of an emergency. Frej didn't get that favoritism. I hacked and worked it setting up camps and against bone in butchering, generally treating it poorly, and it served well. The point opens soup cans well. The fact that the blade is so easily sharpened tended to encourage its use, though the fact that it holds an edge well meant I rarely had to sharpen it! And when I did, it was back to shaving sharp, and though not a tiny knife, I found it served well even in the cleaning of small fish. This is one general-use knife that defies improvement. Around the ranch, every visitor who grabbed it had to be patted down before leaving … just to make sure they weren't absconding with my knife!

Value is a funny thing. Everyone has his or her own definitions of what it is. But I believe all would agree it exists in its highest form when art meets function, as exemplified by the Fällkniven knives. With a combined cost of around $1,375 for both knives, the question remains. Are they worth it? That is a question only an individual can possibly

The author says it is hard to conjure a better general-purpose knife than the Fällkniven Frej.

provide, but if the answer relies on getting the best of the best for actual hard use, that's easy—yes!

To order your Fällkniven knife or knives, contact the U.S. distributor, Moteng NA, 7220 Trade St., Ste. 100, San Diego, CA 92121 800-367-5900 or 858-715-2500 info@moteng.com.

Switching to Survival Knife Mode

The saying is true that the best survival knife is the one you have with you … so learn to use it!

By James Morgan Ayres
All images by ML Ayres

There's an old saying that the best survival knife is the one you have with you when you need to survive. When I was 10 years old, the Boy Scout knife in my jeans pocket enabled me to cut open a wet log to get to the dry wood inside and get a fire going after I had injured my ankle and fallen into an icy creek miles from home. I had to spend a night out in midwinter, soaking wet with temperatures below freezing and no camping gear. That fire probably saved my life. By any measure my Boy Scout folder qualified as a survival knife. That experience had a lot to do with my lifelong interest in survival and survival knives.

Jan Lisewsky, a kite surfer becalmed in the Red Sea, fought off attacking sharks for two days by stabbing them in the snout and eyes with his dive knife. During the tragedy of 911, a paramedic cut open a steel shipping container with his folding knife, using a steel flashlight as a baton, to rescue a trapped and injured woman.

The Fållkniven S1 proves up to the task of cutting a bow stave.

The author uses a tree branch as a baton, lightly but firmly tapping the blade spine of the Strider Knives folder to chop wood.

After a boulder crushed his arm and trapped him for five days, Aron Ralston cut off his own arm with the blade of a muti-tool to escape and survive. The driver of an 18-wheeler had his rig tossed and flipped upside down by a tornado in the Midwest. With the windshield crushed he was trapped and gas was leaking from the tank into the cab. He cut his way out of the cab with his belt knife. A customer of knifemaker Bud Nealy used one of his custom fixed blades to cut through the roof of a car that skidded off the road and into an icy lake during winter in Finland, trapping him underwater. There are many such stories, and they all have certain things in common: an endangered person survived through quick thinking and effective action, and with the aid of the knife they had with them.

During the past year I've been working on a book about survival knives, and doing extensive field-testing of dozens of knives in a wide variety of environments in support of that book. We've foraged and hunted for food with primitive tools and weapons we made, built shelters and performed other survival-related tasks from the Mojave Desert to the Stara Planina Mountains of Bulgaria. We also deconstructed parts of abandoned buildings, and cut through walls, sheet metal and auto bodies.

In addition to personally using many knives for survival related tasks, I recruited others to assist me, some with no outdoor experience or any expertise in knife handling. I have many years of field experience and taught survival for over two decades, and I wanted to see just how little instruction a novice needed to be able to effectively use a knife for survival. In addition to teaching survival skills with a knife during this past year, I also showed students how to build shelters and other critical outdoor skills without a knife. Doing this even once will quickly convince even the skeptical of the importance of the blade.

Certain things emerged from this yearlong exercise:

- The old saying that the best survival knife is the one that you have with you was confirmed. There is no doubt that a purpose-designed survival knife is a superior tool for its designated use. However, having any knife is better than having no knife by a wide margin, maybe a lifesaving one.
- Big knives, 7 to 9 inches in blade length, are the most efficient for most wilderness tasks, but they are too big to carry unless you live in the wilderness, and not the most efficient for small tasks.

©ML Ayres

Striking a flint stick with the back, or spine, of a knife blade works well for starting a fire.

This trio of fixed blades is suitable for extreme use and urban survival.

- Medium-sized knives, 5 to 7 inches in blade length, are highly efficient for most critical survival functions, and are a good compromise in carry convenience between the big blade and smaller ones. Smaller blades in the 4-inch range can be handier for fine woodworking, but lose out to the medium-sized blade for such wilder-ness tasks as *quickly* making a survival shelter, splitting wet wood to get to the dry wood inside, and for urban tasks such as digging out from a collapsed building.

- Smaller fixed blades, 3.5 to 4.5 inches in blade length, are good all-around utility knives, and although not as efficient as the medium-sized knife, will serve for most survival functions and are more convenient to carry than larger knives.

- A solid, well-made folder, a tactical folder in cur-rent terminology, can accomplish far more than many survival experts would have us believe. This is important because the most commonly carried knife is a folder.

- Many people lack basic knife handling skills. Without those skills it difficult, if not impossible, to take advantage of the lifesaving features of the knife. Basic knife handling skills can be learned with a few minutes of instruction and an hour's practice.

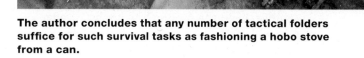

If your daily rounds and jurisdiction allow for regular fixed-blade carry, the Ontario Pilot Survival Knife (top) and Fållkniven F1 fixed blade would be ideal choices.

Given that we've established that the best survival knife is the one you have with you—that survival knife you have stored in your bug-out bag, the tree-chopping, zombie killing, urban knife of destruction with the ¼-inch-thick, 12-inch-long blade isn't going to do you any good if it's not on your person when fate comes calling. It's a good thing to have a big blade as a back up to your primary blade—the one you always have with you. But, like the people previously described, you will most likely find yourself in a survival situation when you least expect it.

Survival knife selection starts with deciding what knife you can have with you at all times. Can you carry a medium-sized fixed blade with you at all times? If so, do it. It's your best all-around choice. If, like most of us, you cannot carry a 5- to 6-inch blade on your daily rounds, a small fixed blade is the next best choice.

If legal restrictions and social custom prevent you from carrying any kind of fixed blade, tote a stout folder with a solid lock. If you know how to use your knife, and how to work within its limits, you can make any of these choices work for you and maybe save your life. However, keep in mind that in actual field practice, we have found that most tasks can be more rapidly accomplished with a medium fixed blade than a small one, and more rapidly with any fixed blade than with a folder due to the need of working around the folder's weak point—it folds. If it's a folder you have, which is likely, you should make allowances for the limitations of your tool.

The basic skills needed to make efficient use of a survival knife are these:

©ML Ayres

The author concludes that any number of tactical folders suffice for such survival tasks as fashioning a hobo stove from a can.

The author demonstrates a "press cut" through a sapling.

- **Edge and Point Awareness:** If you direct your attention to the cutting edge of your knife and use it, you will become familiar with how it cuts. This makes you more efficient and is a safety factor. If you know precisely how your knife cuts, you are less likely to injure yourself. This also builds blade awareness and makes it less likely you'll lose your knife. In the field, your knife belongs in your hand or in its sheath. Laying your knife down for "just a moment" is the most common cause of knife loss in the field.

- **The Draw Cut:** Place the edge of your blade on the material you want to cut, press down firmly and draw the edge across the material while maintaining downwards pressure. This is the most versatile cut and can be used for skinning, stripping bark, cutting meat, whittling and so on.

- **The Push or Press Cut:** Simply press down with a good bit of pressure with the edge of your blade on the material to be cut. This cut can be used, for example, to make notches in wood for, say, a survival bow. It can also be used to cut through a sapling with a small knife. In this instance, bend the sapling and apply the edge of your blade to the outside of the bend. As the blade cuts into the sapling, rock the edge back

and forth slightly. The point can also be used with a press cut. This is useful when you dig into a dead log to get to dry wood, or to start a hole you want to drill.

- **Drilling:** Press the point of your blade into the surface to be drilled, for instance, when making a notch in a fireboard, then twist the blade left or right toward the direction of the primary edge. After making some progress, reverse and turn the edge in the other direction. To continue, press down into the cavity and turn the blade, reversing the edge as needed.

- **Batoning:** It is futile to try and chop with a small knife. The necessary leverage simply isn't available. Batoning is the best technique for cutting large tree limbs, for example, with a small knife. Since most of us are equipped with only a small knife most of the time, I consider batoning to be a critical survival skill. A baton is anything solid—a chair or table leg, a steel flashlight or even a hard-soled shoe—that can be used to tap a blade (on its spine) to push the edge through a resistant medium. Place the edge onto the large-diameter cutting medium and lightly but firmly strike the spine of the blade directly over the cutting surface—I repeat, lightly. Do not

Survival tasks might include building a rough shelter from limbs/poles, grasses and leaves gathered in the woods, or a more refined abode covered in a reflective blanket. Adding a small hobo stove will heat the latter adequately, even in winter, by adjusting the reflective blanket.

hit your blade like you're going for a home run. Doing so could damage it. If using a folder, hold the knife with a loose but firm grip, so that the handle can pivot around the axis of your thumb and first and second finger. This prevents undue stress on the lock.

• **Scraping:** Scraping is moving the edge of your blade over the surface of an object with the edge held perpendicular to the work. Skins need to be scraped to cure them. The belly of a survival bow needs to be scraped to refine it. The shaft of a spear should be scraped to remove snags and smooth it. The back of a blade's point can be used to scrape away mortar between bricks or concrete blocks to escape a collapsed building.

The small Spyderco folder bones out a chicken thigh.

Practicing these skills in daily tasks will increase your expertise and better your odds in survival situations. Meat cutting in your kitchen is similar to dressing game; splitting wood for your fireplace can be done with your folder and a baton; making a hobo stove from a coffee can, and using it, will show you how easy it is and how effectively this simple device can heat a shelter; making a survival bow in your backyard will prepare you if you ever need to do so.

Using your survival knife for daily tasks makes good sense. With a good knife and these skills, you can make tinder, kindling and firewood, build a shelter, and make primitive tools and hunting weapons. Urban survival might also require the same skills, in the event of, say, an earthquake and the need to extricate yourself or another from a collapsed building. The key points are to practice these skills before you find yourself in a survival situation, and to select a good knife you can have with you at all times.

A Sword for a Warrior King

The 7th-century, pattern-welded sword was surely as stunning to behold as a king in full regalia

By Vince Evans

On a patch of heathland overlooking the estuary of the River Deben in Sutton Hoo, England, around the year 625 AD, a warrior king was laid to rest in his ship and a mound raised over it. In 1939, "Mound 1," which contained his ship and its treasures, was excavated. Amongst the many personal belongings the king was buried with was what later proved to be an intricately pattern-welded sword, including a hilt richly ornamented with gold and garnets. Although we may never know the identity of the man buried at Sutton Hoo, the most likely candidate is Raedwald, King of East Anglia.

It has been nearly 25 years since Scott Lankton did his pioneering work in the forging of a replica Sutton Hoo sword blade for the British Museum (see the full article in *KNIVES 1990)*. Mr. Lankton's work has inspired many bladesmiths to push their abilities in pattern welding beyond the simple folding of steel.

British author, Paul Mortimer, has long been interested in the Sutton Hoo find, but had no intention of replicating the king's many personal treasures when he first had the helmet replicated. Over time he had the king's ornate purse and belt buckle reproduced. The first sword that he had made was not intended to be an exact replica, but forged in the spirit of the original. As Mortimer's direction became more refined, he desired to have a new sword made based more closely on the original.

As he related to me, "My first attempt at recreating the sword and complete belt rig were becoming increasingly limited by the fact that my earlier replica was inaccurate in a number of important ways. I needed to go back to the original information from the grave and start again. I contacted Vince Evans to see if he would be interested in helping me with the project and I was very pleased when he accepted, especially as his approach was similar to mine in that we needed to consult all the work that had been carried out on the material from the tomb."

"I had already spoken to Dave Roper about making the sword hilt for

Shown is the original Sutton Hoo sword hilt as it was found detached from the blade. The Sutton Hoo burial mounds lie peacefully in the background.

(photo of the sword hilt by N. Robinson)

The man buried at Sutton Hoo must have been magnificent to behold.

me," Mortimer continued, "as he was familiar with the jewelry techniques employed by the craftsmen at Sutton Hoo, having replicated virtually all the garnet and gold jewelry for me already. Matt Bunker had been researching scabbard technologies and was keen to make a scabbard for the blade.

"Vince and I were given an opportunity by the British Museum to study the sword out of its case, and Vince was able to consult the actual X-rays of the find. The latter experience was to prove especially fortunate, in that Vince did not see some of the things that he was expecting to see."

Angela Care Evans, author of *The Sutton Hoo Ship Burial,* describes the sword as follows:

"The blade and its scabbard had corroded into one inseparable mass, but radiography has revealed that beneath the corrosion the iron of the blade has survived sufficiently well in restricted areas for an interpretation of its structure to be possible ... The radiographs sug-

gest that it was built up of four bundles of seven rods twist-forged in an alternating pattern and lying back to back with four more bundles of seven rods. The bundles of rods twist alternately to right and left, forming a double band of the characteristic herringbone pattern that is one of the most distinctive features of such blades. The twisted bands alternate with straight bands along the length of the blade." [1]

After Mortimer contacted me about helping replicate the sword, I made arrangements with Dr. Janet Lang at the British Museum to view the radiographs of the Sutton Hoo blade. While studying the original radiograph I realized that I was not seeing a complete twist in the twisted portions of the bars. When a layered bar of steel is twisted, the layers form a spiral, or a helix, through the centre of the bar. When viewed from the surface, the bar appears as a series of diagonal lines, but if you were to look *through* the bar, you would also see the backside

The finished replica sword blade is pattern welded as close to the original as possible.

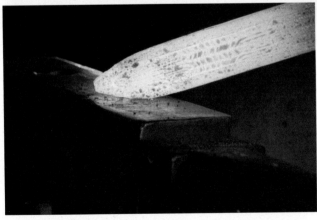

A replica of the Sutton Hoo sword blade is forged.

of the twist as an opposing set of diagonal lines that should form X's on a radiograph. The Sutton Hoo radiograph appears to show only one set of diagonal lines, leading me to believe that the back side of the twisted bars may have been removed, possibly by splitting the bars lengthwise.

By splitting one series of four core bars lengthwise, inverting one side—hilt to point—and welding the bars back together, the results are the offset twist and straight series that the radiograph shows.

The herringbone pattern points in the same direction on both faces of the blade.

Although one cannot conclude that this was the method that was used to forge the core of the original Sutton Hoo sword blade, it offers a plausible method that conserves materials and labor, as the bladesmith is only forging and twisting four core bars instead of eight.

Regarding a fuller in the blade, Lang commented, "I have no recollection of seeing any evidence of a fuller, but a careful examination might give more information on this point. And there isn't any indication that a fuller had been forged, either, because the radiographic film density does not increase along the blade axis, showing that the metal thickness had not been reduced along the middle of the blade."

Mortimer added, "On examining the Mound 1 sword, it became apparent that it didn't have a fuller, which was another departure from the established 'facts' about the sword; there was no sign of one in the cross-section of the blade at the top of the scabbard/blade mass. Conveniently, the handle ensemble broke away from the lower part of the sword, long before the grave was excavated, and we were able to view the top of the blade. In fact the blade appears to be lenticular [lens shaped] on both sides, if slightly flattened in the central sections."

He continued, "The original report states that the remnant grip was made from wood. However, there are a number of reasons for thinking that this is unlikely. First, the archaeologist, Esther Cameron, had re-examined the grip and believed that it was made of horn. Also, nearly all such grips on Anglo-Saxon swords of the period, where the material can be identified, are of horn. I therefore asked Dave Roper to make the grip of horn."

"The upper and lower guard were each composed of a sandwich of two gold plates, enclosing an unidentified organic material, so on the replica, we again used horn," Mortimer explained. "The material had to be very strong, because on the lower guard, where the top of the blade penetrates the lowest gold plate, it is the organic material, alone, that must take and absorb the stresses from the blade when the sword is in use."

Fine & Delicate to Make

"The two filigree clips were also made of solid gold on the original and are fine and delicate to manufacture," he concluded. "The garnet-jeweled pommel not only required slightly different patterning on each side, but also fine waffle-patterned gold foils behind the jewels in order to reflect the maximum amount of light back to the viewer. The jeweled pommel sits over an inner and separate pommel, and is then riveted firmly to the upper guard by ornamental, but strong rivets."

Many times much emphasis is placed on blade and handle details, and scabbards become no more than afterthoughts. Due to the historical nature of this sword, much research went into the scabbard that Bunker fashioned.

Bunker described the process: "Having been asked to make the scabbard for this important sword, I made the decision to try to fashion it using only materials and techniques that were known to exist at the time. It also gave me the opportunity to conduct an experiment to test a theory I have concerning the wooden elements of early English scabbards.

"Most reconstructions start with thick planks of wood that are then chiselled and carved down to provide the internal and external profile required," Bunker said. "Yet, no study has been carried out to examine the end-grain of the wood to see if this was the

The Sutton Hoo Sword replica, and in particular the hilt and pommel, showcases the jewels and fine woven linen tapes.

Fine waffle-patterned gold foils behind the garnets reflect the maximum amount of light back to the viewer, a similar effect to what is seen today in automobile lights to enhance visibility. *(Paul Mortimer photo)*

method used. I felt that it was entirely possible to start instead with laths that were already of the required thickness (usually 2-3mm) and form these to shape around the blade. Both methods of production were well within the skills of an Anglo Saxon woodworker."

"Having acquired some laths of freshly cut green poplar, 2mm in thickness, I cut them to shape and then lined them with beaver fur (the actual lining is, as yet, unidentified, but has been described as 'fur')," Bunker explained.

Snug Scabbard Fitting

"After this, I applied a casein glue (following the recipe written down by Theophilus Presbyter in the 12th century) to the edges of the lathes and then formed them around the blade, using a long linen bandage to bind them down tightly. I left it in a warm environment for a week. When I unbound the scabbard, not only did the laths stay together along the glued edges but also the scabbard retained its elliptical cross section when the blade was withdrawn. The fur had compressed slightly, resulting in a snug but not over-tight fit for the blade."

"The original scabbard shows no sign of surface decoration but is badly degraded to the extent that it's impossible to tell what, if any, decoration might have been present," Bunker added. "Many English scabbards of the period bear traces of decoration but this is usually confined to simple patterns of a few lines executed in cord-work beneath the surface of the leather cover."

"Looking further, some of the contemporaneous scabbards found in the Royal mounds of Vendel and Valsgarde in Sweden show the extent to which scabbards of the period could be decorated. As these scabbards belonged to leaders of the same social status as the man from Mound 1 at Sutton Hoo, and because there are Scandinavian elements in the burial, Paul chose something from one of the Swedish burials as the basis for the decoration for his scabbard, specifically the twin-serpent design from Valsgarde 6."

"The leather that I used for the cover was an oak-tanned calf skin, approximately 1.5mm in thickness, formed around the core, cut to shape, cased and then stitched up the back with linen thread," Bunker related. "Once dry, I re-cased the front of the scabbard and, using smooth bone and antler tine tools, I worked the leather into and around the design."

"The Mappae Clavicula (a collection of recipes thought to have been compiled originally in the 6th

The author (right) discusses the Sutton Hoo sword project at the British Museum with authors Steve Pollington (left) and Paul Mortimer (center).

century) gives instructions on how to dye leather red, green, yellow and purple. I thought that a deep red color would contrast well with the gold and garnet fittings of the sword and scabbard, so I examined the medieval recipes for anything that might indicate how to achieve this without resorting to cinnabar, which, being ore of mercury, is highly toxic," Bunker detailed.

"A few recipes mentioned kermes (a small insect similar to the Central American cochineal, which is found around the southern and eastern Mediterranean and reputedly the most expensive of medieval dyestuffs) and, as luck would have it, I had a small supply. After some experimentation, I was able to produce a good, strong dark red color using kermes, wood ash and water, which I used to dye the scabbard leather. This I then dressed with a mixture of beeswax and linseed oil, which not only sealed the leather and provided a degree of waterproofing, but also,

when buffed, gave a deep shine to the whole piece."

Mortimer exclaimed, "Many Anglo-Saxon swords have binding at the top of the scabbard. In the case of Sutton Hoo it was fine linen tape. Dariusz Wiewiorka made the tapes for me using two slightly different tapes so that the overlay could be seen. Although the weave can be detected on the original, the colors cannot, so I chose yellow as, together with the red scabbard, they would seem to reflect the predominant colors from the personal items from the grave."

The man buried at Sutton Hoo must have been magnificent to behold in his regalia, and new archaeological finds are giving us a clearer view of the splendor of these ancient warriors.

Rupert Bruce-Mitford, The Sutton Hoo Ship-Burial, Vol. 2, pg. 307, British Museum Publications Limited, 1978.

The Art Knife Goes International

First America and now the world seemingly has an insatiable appetite for art knives

By Don Guild

He dashed in, scratched his bid on a notepad just before deadline, and *voilà*, purveyor Steve D'Lack zapped my chance at buying that rare 6-inch Jurgen Steinau art knife. No problem, Steve is a good friend, and acquiring scarce knives is a competitive sport. At this three-hour extravaganza—the Art Knife Invitational (AKI)—175 collectors and buyers from the world over vie in an exclusive arena for knives that 25 of the planet's best makers

specially fashioned for the occasion.

Why did collector Daisy Zeng fly in from Chongqing, China, for a three-hour show? And how about Russian purveyor Anton Poseshchennyy of N-K Studio Knives, who won the "bid up" privilege of buying one knife? Serious art knife connoisseurs are drawn to the AKI like flies to a ripe mango.

They come from France, China, Italy, Russia, Canada, Germany and Indonesia to fork out $175 for an admission ticket and the "chance to win" (buy) a knife. Crazy, many would say. Others would call it stupid. Yet art knife collecting has driven the AKI to be the dream of international and U.S. buyers.

The brain behind the AKI, low-key, understated Phil Lobred, who experienced a slow take-off at his first show, recalls, "In my early days of knife collecting, I have to admit that I saw this oldest and most useful of all hand tools as a utility item only, certainly not art. But the art knife scene was only a flicker

Wolfgang Loerchner - AKI 2013
Francesco Pachi Photography

Wolfgang Loerchner had a flurry of bidders chasing his 8-inch art folder, driving the end price up to $41,000.

A renowned maker of art knives, Germany's own Jurgen Steinau draws a bid from one of his boxes at the Art Knife Invitational, while the author and his wife stand at attention. Famous knifemaker Ron Lake can be seen in the background, wearing red shirt and tie.

Juergen Steinau - AKI 2013
Francesco Pachi Photography

Italian collector Valter Somaschini was the high bidder ($33,333.33) for this Credit Card folder by Jurgen Steinau.

on the horizon back then. It seemed to me that what was needed was a show that catered to these special knives and to the collectors who wanted them."

"Get the right makers together with the right collectors," Lobred stresses. "It was such a new concept that the makers were not very committed, and even though it was free to the collectors (and completely catered), when I opened the doors only 18 people walked in. I was devastated. The show was financially successful, though, so I decided to try it again in 1984."

"We are now 20 years into the second phase of the AKI, and each show has done a bit better financially than the one before it. Our format is being copied by other shows. I will keep promoting it as long as my health holds up and the makers want me at the helm. As I wrote in 1983, 'Art Knives by important makers are rapidly gaining in popularity as unique collectables.'"

Every collector who pays the steep admission fee

to try their luck at "winning" a sought-after art knife from a renowned maker receives a book of personalized tickets for bidding or buying. Each maker, on the other hand, chooses how his three to eight knives are sold: via a fixed price, an open bid or a "bid-up."

Highest Bid Wins

At the AKI, a "bid-up" is an open notepad sitting next to a knife at a maker's table. Any time after 10 a.m., an interested party places his or her bidding price on the pad for all to see, and along comes another suitor, looks at the previous bid, and if so moved, dashes down a higher bid. The bidding closes between noon and 1 p.m.—no one knows exactly when in an effort to prevent shoving and fighting a minute or two before 1 p.m. An open bid is simply writing down a bid and putting it in a box "blindly" without knowing what others have bid. The highest bid wins the knife in either scenario.

After the frenzy starts at 10 a.m., the knives are

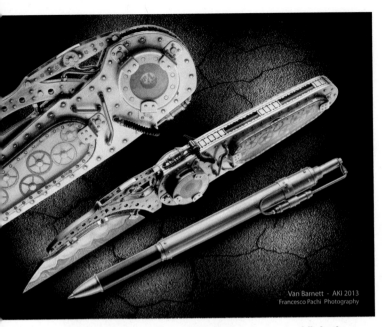
Van Barnett - AKI 2013
Francesco Pachi Photography

Maker Van Barnett is really into "steam punk" designs, and this complexity is a knockout.

chased until the whistle blows at 1 p.m. If all the makers' knives were evenly parceled out, each buyer would take home half a knife. Now that's competition!

Who in their right mind flies 15,000 miles to subject themselves to this pressure? Could it be the super open-bar lunch at the show, or the Saturday night awards banquet that is exquisitely presented? No! It's the excitement and expectation of acquiring a knife that would take 10 years to get directly from one of these prestigious makers.

Nordic Knives owner Dave Harvey, producer of the biennial Solvang Custom Knife Show, held opposite years to the AKI, paints this broad stroke of the art knife market: "The worldwide desirability of custom knives has seen solid growth over the past decade. Worldwide access to this wonder we call the 'Internet' is the main reason, of course. Beyond that we have seen many citizens of countries like China and Russia experiencing new wealth."

"The Internet and the relative ease of international shipping has now made the world a much smaller place, as reaching potential customers in the far corners is no longer an expensive or daunting task," Harvey adds. "What is all of this doing to the art knife collecting field? Well, of course it is driving up demand for these and other knives, which naturally results in higher prices/values, as the supply of art knives remains small, relatively speaking. It's important to note that all of this has not solely been

driven by international demand. Demand in the U.S. remains positive, and we have seen an increase in buyers of fine blades here also."

"The Solvang Show and AKI are seeing increased participation in international makers and buyers. This is a natural offshoot of our shrinking world and the true global economy that has developed over the past 20 years," he concludes. "Both shows have formats and collectors that drive the makers to create their best work. The result is those attending get to view an unprecedented number of outstanding works of art."

The talented young Italian knifemaker Emmanuel Esposito, who presented knives at his first AKI, observes, "I was nervous, too, for the show. It's an honor that you ask my opinion. To me the AKI is really the best art knife show on the planet. The quality of the knives is definitely at the top. The most important collectors are there, and everybody is looking forward to seeing what the best makers have created for the show. Having a three-hour show makes everything more exciting and creates a unique atmosphere. I also think the location is very important—everybody loves California!"

An Eastern Influx

"In the past seven years I've seen the knife market change a great deal," Esposito relates. "I think the same thing is happening that occurred a few years ago in the high-end watch market. It would seem the European market has changed more than any other market. Few new collectors come from 'old Europe,' but many new knife enthusiasts seem to be showing up from the East, such as from Russia and China."

"In the past few years at the Milan show, more collectors and dealers from eastern countries came to buy knives," he stresses. "I've seen the interest in European knifemakers grow a great deal. Now, I believe that attention is diverting. America still has some of the best knifemakers, but many other countries are improving the quality of their work and bringing new ideas to the knife world."

"I believe, in the next three or four years, the market will continue to expand, particularly where the world of knives is still new," Esposito predicts. "I've noticed an increase in the price of art knives. The tactical blades are also becoming increasingly popular, and I think they are replacing the market spot that art knives have lost in past years—the middle range."

A former Russian himself, knifemaker Zaza Revishvili, winner of the Lenin Award for art merit in his youth, is a purveyor of fine knives to Russian nobility. "The price of art knives is dependent on the buyers' financial status," he reasons. "And so far there are more wealthy people with high disposable income in the world than real masterpieces available."

Knife Legends' purveyor Paul Shindler reports, "The impact of wealthy new foreign collectors and dealers on the art knife market has pushed up retail prices on a small number of pieces by super-elite makers to new highs. It has also increased competition, since there are so few available. Foreign buyers account for only a small percentage of the super-elite knife purchases, while American collectors are still the primary buyers, leaving most of the foreign buyers to compete for the remaining few. That can elevate prices to even greater heights. Record prices were achieved at the most recent AKI, but those records were set by American collectors and not by foreign buyers alone.

"The boom in Chinese and Russian collectors today is primarily the result of a new, large wealthy class in those countries interested in all manner of luxury goods. It is not a stretch to see the collecting of high-end art knives as part of this trend. A number of serious art knife dealers in Russia and China, many with strong websites, showcase high-end knives, and there are monthly art knife magazines published in these countries. The final factor is the loss of confidence in the bond and equity markets. It seems people would rather buy goods they can hold in their hands and enjoy every day."

Poseshchennyy remarks, "That was my first AKI ever, and going there was like jumping into something I thought I knew but I really didn't. I did my homework, of course. I read reviews, comments and articles about the AKI, including the written experiences of other collectors. But, you know, one can read a thousand articles about how to ride a bike and only riding it can give you the expertise."

Emmanuel Esposito - AKI 2013
Francesco Pachi Photography

Lucky Anton Poseshchennyy won the Emmanuel Esposito art knife on a bid-up of $19,000, and then sold it to a fellow Russian.

Family Gathering

"I felt like I was invited to a big family gathering. Everybody is open and welcoming. They are of different ages, statuses and backgrounds, but during the show they are just one big gang. It all changes for three hours—rush hours. Every single collector/purveyor is solely on the hunt for that precious piece of art. Those are a frenzied few hours. I was lucky enough to get Emmanuel's dagger. Nothing from Steinau, but there were people who got nothing. Of course, serious collectors hunt for Steinau, [Wolfgang] Loerchner and [Michael] Walker, but prices for them just jumped up dramatically. Yes, Russian collectors and dealers are new to this world, and we have just

"Recently the upper echelon of art knife collectors has made confident purchases, convinced that the appreciation in value and aesthetic appeal will continue their upward trend, and knowing that true value has a rock-solid history. Since more and more collectors are chasing fewer and fewer top knives, this tends to reduce a collectors' financial risk," Favano reasons.

Zeng remarks, "Being Chinese, it endowed me with such an honor to be invited to attend the AKI, and then I truly realized the supreme significance of it. I started international knife collecting in a way that I guess is similar to the experience of many collectors, at first, being attracted by a picture on the Internet.

"I purchased my first art knife at age 27, and I can remember it was a fixed blade priced around $600. For me at that time it was a big amount of money but still affordable. And in fact, for about $300, there are still many pieces available that will allow you to get a good start in art knife collecting," she notes.

"Modern art knives have expanded my three main areas of discipline: design style, material and decoration, and

Juergen Steinau - AKI 2013
Francesco Pachi Photography

Collector Daisy Zeng of China paid a fixed price of $10,500 for this singular Jurgen Steinau 11-inch fixed blade. The resale value is estimated to be $24,000.

begun developing art knife culture in our country. It will take some time, but I am sure that Russians are able to appreciate truly unique craftsmanship."

Dan Favano, owner of I.Q. Knives, deals in the world's most desirable knives, and opines, "I am seeing a large increase at each AKI of overseas buyers, and it's due to new wealth around the globe, the AKI as the mother lode of the best, and the astonishing ongoing improvement of design and precise craftsmanship of the AKI's 25 makers. In the last 10 years, the attraction of the art knife has been greatly influenced by the continuum from utility to art."

structure and function," Zeng adds. "My collecting style changed in the past years, and those changes were all based on new experiences in my own life. Studying what I've collected over the last few years is like being able to see my inner self in a magical mirror. This is a fantastic experience to me.

"Most knife guys are straightforward and simple, but many have a good sense of the romantic. When we talk to each other about knives, the feeling evoked is as if we've been old friends for years despite differences in age and location."

Knives Hidden in Plain Sight

These everyday items are not as they appear, but rather knives in creative disguises

The decorative antler would look nice on a coffee table, desk or bar, and conceals a handy little fixed blade for household cutting chores.

By Evan F. Nappen, Attorney at Law

I suggest we bring some normality back to this country and say if you are carrying a knife, there must be zero tolerance. If it were up to me, everyone caught with a knife would get an automatic 10-year sentence.
—Simon Cowell

There are some people who irrationally hate knives. Sometimes it might be necessary to not offend them or to not bring undue attention to oneself. A secret knife is a hidden knife. Knives can be carried concealed on the body, and thus considered secret or hidden, but that's more commonly known as concealed carry.

This article focuses on knives that are hidden or disguised as something else—as items that don't offend the anti-knife crowd and avoid the suspicion of the law (though this may backfire if an officer discovers the disguised knife, and thus considers it illegally concealed). Many of these pieces are fascinating and clever in their design.

California has a number of laws that prohibit secret knives. The state's laws provide a lot of good ideas for knifemakers who want to build and sell secret knives in jurisdictions of the United States that still respect freedom and knife rights. Here are some of the secret knives that California thinks are intrinsically evil and require laws prohibiting them:

1. An "air gauge knife," which is a " … device that appears to be an air gauge but has concealed within it a pointed, metallic shaft that is designed to be a stabbing instrument and is exposed by mechanical action or gravity, and locks into place when extended."
2. A "belt buckle knife," or in other words "… a knife that is made an integral part of a belt buckle and consists of a blade with a length of at least 2 1/2 inches."
3. A "cane sword," which " … means a cane, swagger, stick, staff, rod, pole, umbrella or similar device, having concealed within it a blade that may be used as a sword or stiletto."
4. A "lipstick case knife," or " … a knife enclosed within and made an integral part of a lipstick case."

The pewter wizard holds something more than brains under his hat. Called the "Commanding Wizard" knife, it's a wall hanger complete with mounts.

these types of knives, particularly "hidden or disguised knives, such as air gauge knives, belt buckle knives, lipstick case knives or writing pen knives." Sound familiar? This policy is arbitrary. It would be one thing if eBay simply prohibited sales to persons in jurisdictions that barred these items, but instead everyone suffers for California's knife bigotry.

Let's take a closer look at what California has chosen to ban. Air gauge knives are apparently blades concealed in an air gauge that are " … exposed by mechanical action or gravity, and lock into place …" This is vague. What is "mechanical action?" Would a simple tool with a locking blade and an air gauge be prohibited? Mechanical action could arguably be opening a folding knife blade with two hands, or a thumbnail using a nail nick. California must have had rash of crimes committed with air gauge knives necessitating such a useless ban.

Belt buckle knives are also prohibited. Belt buckle knives have the practical advantage of being accessible by one's gun hand when carrying a gun on the belt. Normally, if a gun is on one's strong side, a knife must be carried on the weak side, but a belt buckle knife allows for strong-hand access. Additionally, fixed-blade belt buckle knives are usually carried horizontally. This is a safer carry, particularly for a hunter in a tree stand, to whom a fall might mean a fixed blade penetrating its sheath and jabbing into the hunter's leg. Some manufacturers of belt buckle knives include Bowen, Gerber, United and Valor.

Sword canes and sword umbrellas seem to have been around for as long as there have been canes and umbrellas. Many are quite collectable. I have an American sword cane dating to the late 1700's. The sword has a gold etching of 13 rings inter-locked, which was the symbol of the newly formed United States. Sword umbrellas were made famous by the old British *The Avengers* television show in which Daniel Patrick Macnee played the secret agent John Steed who carried his trademark sword umbrella. Of course a cane, or a sword for that matter, can be used as a weapon, but why let logic get in the way of a knife ban law?

A "shobi-zue" is a staff, crutch, stick, rod or pole concealing a blade that may be exposed by a flip of the wrist or by a mechanical action. Sword canes or sword umbrellas might qualify as shobi-zues. Again

5. A "*shobi-zue*," which " … means a staff, crutch, stick, rod or pole concealing a knife or blade within it, and that may be exposed by a flip of the wrist or by a mechanical action."

6. An "undetectable knife," or " … any knife or other instrument, with or without a hand guard, that satisfies all of the following requirements: (a) It is capable of ready use as a stabbing weapon that may inflict great bodily injury or death. (b) It is commercially manufactured for use as a weapon. (c) It is not detectable by a metal detector or magnetometer, either handheld or otherwise, which is set at standard calibration."

7. A "writing pen knife," which " … means a device that appears to be a writing pen but has concealed within it a pointed, metallic shaft that is designed to be a stabbing instrument and is exposed by mechanical action or gravity that locks it into place when extended or pointed. The metallic shaft is exposed by the removal of the cap or cover on the device."

California's "bad" knife list unfortunately seems to have had national influence. eBay bans many of the vague "mechanical action" term is used. Some ski poles or even scratch awls that have retracting spikes might meet the definition of being a shobi-zue.

The lipstick case knives I've seen require the caps to be removed, and when the bottom is twisted, a blade rises out of the case instead of lipstick. My good friend Rep. Jenn Coffey, who spearheaded with me the successful effort to repeal New Hampshire's knife laws, has a small business selling these knives and other cool items. Her book is called *Knives, Lipstick and Liberty*, and details her fight for knife rights. Her website is www.kniveslipstickandliberty.com.

She also sells writing-pen knives—pens that conceal blades. Could these knives end pointless writing?! They do provide one with a functional pen, if needed. The blade remains safely contained inside the metal pen tube until it is needed. Victorinox, the maker of Swiss Army Knives, manufactures a pen that has a Swiss Army Knife in it and a Swiss Army Knife that has a pen in it.

Poorly Worded Law

Undetectable knives are defined as " ... any knife or other instrument ... " that is capable of ready use as a stabbing weapon, and that may inflict great bodily injury or death. They are commercially manufactured to be used as weapons and not detectable by a metal detector or magnetometer. So therefore any knife solely made from titanium, plastic, ceramic, polymer, wood or any other material with no magnetic signature is banned in California, as long as it was made to be a weapon. If it was made to be a tool or a decoration, then apparently it's okay. In order to avoid arrest and conviction you must know the intent of the manufacturer. This is a poorly written law.

The infamous "CIA Letter Opener" is an "undetectable knife" commonly seen for sale at gun and knife shows. Lansky makes the LS17, which is a short, double-edged fixed blade fashioned from ABS plastic. An excellent executive carry method for these lightweight knives is behind one's necktie.

Cold Steel has a wide selection of "undetectable" knives that the company does not sell in the state of California. This includes their "Nightshade" series and knives like the Delta Dart—an 8-inch-long, ½-inch-diameter spike that weighs a half-ounce. Its handle is knurled and the butt is rounded and smooth. It boasts excellent piercing power and has been driven though a ½-inch-thick piece of leather.

Blackie Collins offered a "Personal Self Defense Knife." This was a folding, button-operated, non-metal-lic knife featuring a beryllium copper spring-assisted opening mechanism. It was 100 percent non-magnetic and could be easily sharpened. A thumb stud on the blade assisted in one-hand opening. The handle was made of virtually indestructible poly-resin, and the 2.75-inch blade came serrated or non-serrated. Overall length was 6.5 inches with a weight of 1.4 ounces.

"Coin knives" fortunately did not make California's ban list. A coin knife is a coin that conceals a knife blade. Often it consists of the obverse and reverse of a coin split in half down the edge, with two half-moon-shaped blades in between the coin halves. In 2001, the U.S. federal government sold a genuine U.S. silver

Member of a Masonic lodge, are you? Then you'll love the freemasonry symbol pendant, slung from around the neck via a bead chain, complete with hidden knife blade.

The Al Mar Knives "Wild Hair" is a metal comb on one end and a knife on the other. The knife end slides into a nylon pouch, and when so positioned, appears as if it's only a comb.

dollar that included a double-bladed hidden knife.

For just $75, an online shopper could have purchased this government-sanctioned secret knife, and had it shipped overnight. It weighed approximately one ounce and came in a black velvet box, the coin knife being "guaranteed for one year against any manufacturing defect." According to the Mint's online catalog, the coin featured a knife blade and nail file that opened from either side of the coin. The item was even antiqued to give it an aged appearance. Soon after 9/11, the Mint pulled the silver dollar knife from sale, making it one of the most desirable and collectable of secret coin knives.

During World War II the S.O.E. and O.S.S. (predecessor to today's CIA) provided covert knives for their agents. Various types of blades included lapel knives, thumb knives, sleeve daggers, shoe knives and even a bicycle pump knife. They were used in missions of sabotage, assassination and close combat in clandestine operations. Lapel knives, designed to be hidden and sewn-in behind jacket lapels, were easily withdrawn and brought into play. They had a small double-edged blade that was effective in hand-to-hand combat.

Wearable Wares

Thumb knives were larger than lapel knives and had sheaths made to be hidden in clothing. Sleeve daggers were steel spikes that had sheaths for strapping to an arm or sewing into a hidden clothing

spot. Shoe knives were made to fit under the sole of the foot or come out of a heel. Reproductions of these famous secret knives have been produced by a number of companies.

Money clip knives are a common hidden knife variation. Many are simple rectangular frames with a knife on one side and a nail file on the other. Stylish folks often get them engraved with their initials. Colonial, Imperial, Zippo and many others have all made them at one time or another. The Columbia River K.I.S.S. knife is a locking blade doubling as a money clip, and comes complete with a pocket clip.

Credit card knives have become popular. As their name implies, most resemble credit cards, some simply being fixed blades that slide into a wallet. The Boker Plus version is a locking folder resembling a credit card that is slim enough to fit into a wallet. The Iain Sinclair CardSharp Knife has a 2.6-inch blade and an ingenious design. The blade swings out from the credit-card-shaped frame, and the card frame becomes the handle.

Key ring knives have been around seemingly since the dawn of the automobile. EKA of Sweden made a nice key ring knife with a blade and bottle opener, and of course the Swiss Army "Classic" hangs on many a key ring but that, of course, is recognizable as a knife.

Combs that contain blades have been made in many variations. Al Mar Knives offered the "Wild Hair," which is a metal comb on one end and a knife on the other. The knife end slides into a nylon pouch, and when so positioned, it looks like it's only a comb. United Cutlery sells a plastic comb with a handle that pulls away to reveal a double-edge blade. This comb comes in pink, which eliminates even more suspicion.

Hold a toothbrush over a flame and pull each end, and it will create a sharp stabbing point as it stretches and cools. I guess at some point a do-gooder will try to outlaw toothbrushes. I own or have seen blades hidden in keys, crosses, rings, wall sculptures, pendants, antlers, bracelets, cartridges, shot shells, playing cards, rulers, lollipop sticks, letter openers, cell phones, watches, guns, gas tank caps, batons, billy clubs, dolls, lighters, cigarette packs and even dominoes. This list is by no means exhaustive. With imagination just about anything can conceal a knife.

Knife Trading Along Emigrant Trails

Essential to the settling and expansion of the West, the knife is rich in American history and lore

By Jordan Clary

The story of knives used during the westward expansion of the United States can tell us many things about the men and women who followed the emigrant trails west, settled there, the type of work they did, even the kind of people they were. Like the diversity of the country itself, early knives were a blend of techniques and materials taken from the indigenous tribes of the Americas as well as from immigrants to the country. Europe. Africa. Asia. All made their contribution to the knife, one of the most essential items on the western emigrant trails.

Tim Ridge of Swamp Fox Knives specializes in reproductions of hand-forged knives from frontier days. He said, "In the early years of the United States there were still a lot of imports coming over from England. Blades were shipped over by the barrel load. When shipments from England didn't arrive, local blacksmiths started making knives, which turned into a cottage industry throughout the country. A lot of what they used early on were trade knives. The sword makers and finer cutlers turned out some of the better knives, and it evolved into the 1800s."

The migration west began almost as soon as Europeans first stepped foot onto Plymouth Rock, but it wasn't until the 1800s that people began trickling into the Oklahoma Territory. With the California Gold Rush, that trickle grew, and waves of mostly men, but also some women, began flowing across the Mississippi River and on to the Pacific Coast.

African Americans escaping slavery and prejudice made up a small but significant percentage of early cowboys. Vaqueros and adventurers from Latin America also felt the lure of the Pacific Coast and came riding their horses north. And immigrants didn't just come overland. Ships brought arrivals from China, Japan, the Pacific Islands and elsewhere.

Western pioneers were highly dependent upon each other for survival. Access to markets for trade could sometimes mean a matter of life or death

The 5.5-inch blade and stag handle are typical of frontier knives during the years of the westward expansion of the United States. Ghosts of the early emigrants can still be felt today along the Emigrant Trail road, which leads to a rural neighborhood in Woodford, Calif. *(knife photo courtesy of Old West Antiques, www.oldwestantiques.biz)*

During the 1800s, shiploads of blades often arrived from England. This George Wostenholm, Sheffield, England, "hawkbill" pruning knife is a rare example of such pieces. *(photo courtesy of Old West Antiques)*

during the harsh winters. One westward expansion supply list advertised a knife with whetstone for $2.50, an axe for $3 and a hatchet for $2. A good blade was essential. While supply lists and early journals can give us clues about what life was like during the 1800s, there are still many holes.

Neven Gibbs, who defines himself as a cowboy, Native American and lay sociologist, said you have to know where to look for missing information. He noted, "All I have is a general knowledge passed down. Trade knives, goods and U.S. history have an interwoven past that has an applied knowledge effect on delving into the social behaviors of civilizations of the past."

Frontier Characters

Let's look at some of the characters that settled the West and how their knives can help fill in some of the holes.

The mountain man era was over by the time settlers began pouring across the Mississippi like spawning salmon, but the impact of these early traders was significant on the development of the West. Knives from this time were generally sturdy, inexpensive and practical—fixed blades with half tangs or stick tangs, some of the tangs as short as

one third of their overall handles.

Chuck Burrows, owner, maker and purveyor of handcrafted frontier leatherwork and knives at Wild Rose Trading Co., called frontier knives "Eastern blades that moved west." "The steel probably came from England or somewhere else in Europe," he surmised. "The handle could be from an eastern maple or a deer antler."

It would be impossible to name the hundreds of Native American civilizations peppered across the North American continent during the 1700s and 1800s, but their influence on the development the knife can't be disputed. The reverse is also true. Steel blades shipped from Europe quickly replaced bone and stone, while French and English trappers adapted some of the design and beadwork from indigenous tribes.

"Mountain men knives" are among the most popular reproductions for modern knifemakers. Burrows and others credit this to TV shows about Daniel Boone and Davy Crockett. "Every man of a certain

Reproductions of early frontier blades incorporate design influences from Native American and European sources. This custom "bear jaw dagger" and pipe tomahawk set is from Wild Rose Trading Co. The bladesmith was the late Gib Guignard and the leatherwork is by Chuck Burrows. *(photo courtesy of Chuck Burrows, Wild Rose Trading Co., http://www.wrtcleather.com/)*

The late Gib Guignard designed the blades and Chuck Burrows created the leatherwork on this frontier war club and knife set reproduction from Wild Rose Trading Co.

(photo courtesy Chuck Burrows, Wild Rose Trading Co.)

Tim Ridge, owner of Swamp Fox Knives, based this white bone-handle, French-style knife with 6-inch blade on pieces designed from 1750-1800. *(Scott Howard photo courtesy of Swamp Fox Knives, http://www.swampfoxknives.com)*

age probably grew up watching Daniel Boone on TV," Burrows reasoned.

J. Russell in Greenfield, Mass., first produced Green River knives. The factory began making butcher knives about 1832-'34 and shipping them west. However, the blades that have become closely associated with mountain men were probably not produced until sometime in the 1840s after the mountain man era had ended. Green River is a little like Shangri-La. The myth has gotten so tangled up with facts that much of its actual history has been lost.

Still, there is little doubt that Green River knives were some of the best the West had ever seen. A typical Green River full-tang hunter was considered a topnotch hunting knife, known for holding a sharp edge, yet sharpened easily if needed. The term "Green River" was soon being used for any knife of high quality on the trade routes. Merchants picked up on this, as well, and the Green River branding began.

Cowboy Up

Nothing evokes the romantic image of the American West like the cowboy. The cowboy is a cultural icon, a symbol of wide-open spaces and individualism. The reality was sometimes less charming. A few historical accounts (whether the generalizations are accurate or not), such as one in the *Cheyenne Daily Leader,* claimed cowboys were by and large "foulmouthed, blasphemous, drunken, lecherous, utterly corrupt." It went on, "Usually harmless on the plains when sober, they are dreaded in towns, for then liquor has an ascendancy over them."

In reality, and sans negative generalities, cowboys came from all walks of life, and with them came their knives. Some of the first American cowboys were Native American, *mestizo* (of European and Native American descent) and vaqueros. After the Civil War, a large number of African Americans headed west in search of lives where they would face less discrimination. Many of them became cowboys.

Dean Laner, who has been making knives for 21 years, said the basic cowboy knife has not changed

This reproduction of a large 1830-1850 era, Texas-style bowie sports a stag handle and 10-inch, clip-point blade. *(Scott Howard photo courtesy of Swamp Fox knives)*

that much since the 1800s. Early cowboy knives were 5- or 6-inch fixed blades with bone or wood handles, and could be carried in a boot or on a belt. With the rise of pocketknife manufacturing in the 1800s, folding cattle knives and stockman folders became preferred patterns. They would be needed for many things on the trail, from cutting rope to opening cans. And cowboy knives are by and large practical, light and fit well in one's hand.

As Laner said, "You could whittle wood, cut a rope, open a can, stir a stew, skin a fish or an animal. Everything was straight to the point."

Probably nothing contributed to the West Coast's amalgamation of cultures and characters like the

California Gold Rush. Dreams of fortune spurred even the unadventurous to take a chance at a new life in the relatively unexplored American West. For some, unrest at home combined with dreams of a new future helped push them into California. During this time, a new influence was added to the evolving western blade: Asia.

Asian Influence

Beginning about 1850, large numbers of Chinese, mostly from the Guangdong region in southern China, began sailing across the Pacific to San Francisco. They were part of a large migration of men and women fleeing political corruption and a poor economy for a more hopeful future in the United States. They called this new land *Gam Saan* or Gold Mountain.

Many went to work mining for gold, and for these miners, knives were crucial to their survival, as it was illegal for Chinese to own a gun. Some historical accounts tell of attacks on Chinese mining camps where the residents, armed only with knives, were murdered or driven into the hills. Not all these attacks were from Anglo miners, either. Disputes between *tongs* (Chinese societies) over claims were known to end in vicious knife battles. In fact, Chinese Camp, a Gold Rush mining town, in Tuolumne County, Calif., was the scene of some of the worst carnage of the era and is reputedly the spookiest ghost town in the West!

The Chinese Temple in Oroville, Calif., houses an extensive collection of artifacts from these early immigrants, including a selection of knives. Most common are the heavy cleavers that chop through bones with a single blow and are a mainstay in the Chinese kitchen. Like the earlier English blades, boxes of these cleavers were often shipped over at a time.

Other blades that show a more refined aesthetic than the cleaver are also in the museum. A Taoist ritual blade, with its handle wound in red twine for luck, indicates the importance of faith. A brass replica of a knife from the early years of the Qing Dynasty (about 1700) suggests someone's desire to hold onto his or her history. There's even a mini-beheading knife on display.

Every era has its outlaws, its opportunists and high fliers, and in the Old West, the gambler fit the bill. Gamblers liked to dress fine and their knives were more for show than practical use. Not that there was no thought of practicality. A gambler was far more likely to have a fixed blade that was easy to reach than a folding knife.

Bob Wood of Old West Antiques said, "Envision you are seated at a poker table in a saloon in Tombstone, Arizona Territory, 1882. The cowboy across the table from you has just lost all his money to you, and he wants it back. He jumps out of his chair and starts to climb across the table. You have two knives on you. One is a folding knife deep in your back pants pocket. The other is a straight-bladed knife, and since it doesn't fit in your pants pocket, you have it in a scabbard in your vest pocket. Which one can you get to quickest? These guys faced death daily, and the gun and knife were tools that allowed them to live another day."

The Bowie Blows Into Town

The bowie knife is named after Col. Jim Bowie, the 19th century soldier, mercenary and pioneer who gained fame in Louisiana at the Sandbar fight, a duel that turned into a brawl during which Bowie was pummeled, shot, stabbed, beaten, kicked and thrashed more severely than should have been humanly possible. But Bowie survived. His legend grew and the knife he reputedly used became the prototype for the bowie knife.

According to the Historic Arkansas Museum, the knife Bowie carried had been given to him by his brother who bought it from James Black, a blacksmith whose blades were copied by cutlers in Sheffield, England. These knives were then sold in America as Arkansas toothpicks. Before long the terms *Arkansas toothpicks* and *bowie knives* were being used interchangeably, sometimes for similar knives.

There are also some similarities between bowie knives and short Mexican swords, and Ridge said it's conceivable bowies evolved from Mexican pieces. "Knives were coming for trade from every country," he proposed. "A blacksmith might see a knife and make his version of it, but make it a little different, give it a different twist."

The bowie knife enjoyed a revival in the 1950s and continues to be popular today, with each bladesmith taking his or her own slant on the style. Ridge said, "Jim Bowie turned everyone into knife fanatics. It was like a craze descended on the whole country."

The bowie knife might be seen as both the ending and beginning of an era. Its origins were the Old West and the emigrant trails it traveled, but it has transcended time and evolved into one of today's most popular blades.

Feeding His Fixed-Blade Fixation

It all started when the author, as a teenager, bought a boot knife while at a store with his mom

The author's first boot knives include, clockwise from top, a vintage Gerber Mark I, a classic A.G. Russell Sting and a well-worn Bowen Belt Buckle Knife.

By Michael Janich

My interest in personal-defense knives began as a teenager in the mid 1970's, thanks primarily to my twisted but pragmatic circle of martial arts instructors and training partners. Although we all carried folders with aftermarket or jury-rigged one-hand opening devices, the era of the purpose-designed "tactical folder" had yet to dawn. For serious defensive use, the tool of choice at that time was a small fixed blade generically known as a "boot knife." Simpler, fast, and, at least at the time, more capable than a folder, boot knives ruled. And the more I learned about knife tactics, the more convinced I was

Another favorite was the Gerber Guardian, shown with a rare carry accessory kit and an even rarer original pencil drawing by the designer, R.W. Loveless.

The late Col. Rex Applegate had a keen eye for knife design. These prototypes, handmade by Bill Harsey, all have the matching serial number 002. From left to right they include the Applegate-Fairbairn Folder, a Mini Smatchet, two A-F Boot Knives and a downsized double-action automatic version of the A-F Folder made by Butch Vallotton.

that I had to have a boot knife.

My wish came true on my 15ᵗʰ birthday when I walked into a local gun shop with my mom and asked to see what was then regarded as the pinnacle of the breed—a Gerber Mark I. As I stared at it wide eyed, my mother explained to the shop owner that it was my birthday and that I had been saving for weeks to buy that specific knife.

Impressed by my determination, he thought about it a moment and asked, "Son, how much would you like to pay for that knife?" I pointed to the price tag and answered, "Sir, it says right here that it's $37.50." He laughed a bit and countered, "I know how much it's supposed to be, but how much do you want to pay?" A few minutes later I walked out of the store $30 lighter, but with a special memory and the seeds of a lifelong passion for fixed-blade personal-defense knives.

In today's world where even thinking about a knife in school could be grounds for expulsion, you might be wondering why a high school student would

need a boot knife. The honest answer is that I didn't need one—I *wanted* one. I also knew that if I wanted to carry it, I'd have to conceal it well and stay out of trouble. More importantly, if I did get in trouble, I needed to worry more about my parents' wrath than anything the school would do to me. It was a different time—one of accountability and personal responsibility—so I learned to be discreet.

Around that time, I also learned about the groundbreaking writings of the late David E. Steele in his "Steele on Knives" columns in *Soldier of Fortune* magazine and his book *Secrets of Modern Knife Fighting*. Steele's work was some of the only hardcore information available back then on self-defense knives, knife tactics, and carry and concealment methods. I read and reread everything he wrote and used it to steer the direction of my knife collecting and my carry methods.

My original Mark I typically rode inside my waistband at the small of my back. Since the sheath's

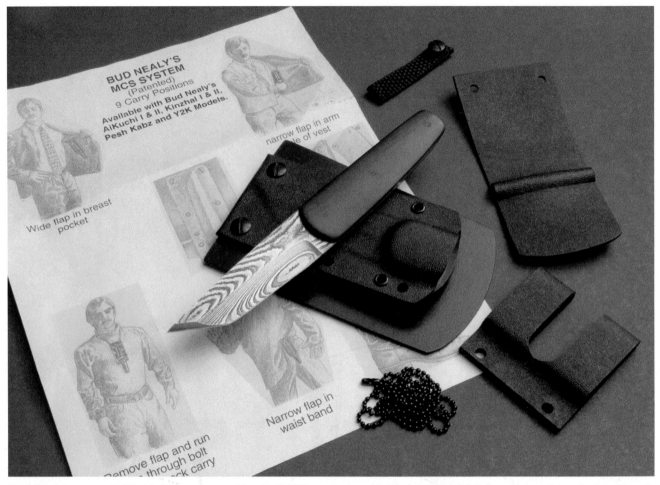

Bud Nealy's versatile Multi-Concealment Sheath (MCS) system revolutionized fixed-blade carry and concealment and featured rare-earth magnets for retention. It is shown here with one of his damascus Aikuchi knives.

spring clip only supported vertical carry and I was a relatively skinny kid, carrying the Mark I wasn't always pleasant. To solve that problem, I invested in another time-honored classic boot knife—an A.G. Russell "Sting." Its shorter length made it much more comfortable to carry, but the high-mouthed sheath left little of the handle exposed, hindering a quick draw.

Since this was back in the days before Kydex®, the only logical thing to do was to learn some leatherworking skills and start experimenting with carry and concealment positions. Although my early efforts were crude, I eventually turned out some pretty serviceable handmade sheaths, shoulder harnesses, forearm rigs and other carry hardware.

After graduating high school, I served nine years in the U.S. Army and five years as a Department of Defense civilian. During this period, my collection of compact fixed blades continued to grow. I also continued to tinker, exploring sheath design and carry systems and even making a few knives of my own.

Front Row Seat with the Colonel

In 1994, I left government service to start a video production department at Paladin Press. In that role, one of my primary responsibilities was to work with the late Col. Rex Applegate, the close-combat instructor for the OSS (Office of Strategic Services) during World War II and one of the world's leading experts in knife combat. Although nearly 80 when I first met him, Col. Applegate was still deeply involved in fighting knife design and appreciated my interest in that and other close-combat topics. At the time, he was working with custom knifemaker Bill Harsey on boot-knife-sized versions of his iconic designs, so I had a front-row seat to that development process and all the details it entailed.

Although my budget was limited, my boss at Paladin, Peder Lund, had a standing order with Harsey for exact duplicates of everything he made for Col. Applegate. Serial number 001 belonged to the Colonel; 002 belonged to Lund—at least initially. Years later, I

Cutlery Shoppe's Gryphon M-10 is a classic boot knife designed by Bob Terzuola. Shown here (from top to bottom) are original production pieces in ATS-34, AUS-8 and VG-10 blade steels, the latter still currently in production. Sheaths include an original Cutlery Shoppe production holster, a chest rig by Survival Sheath Systems and the current version by veteran Kydex wizard Mike Sastre.

purchased all the 002 models for my collection as lasting reminders of Col. Applegate and his mentorship.

One of the other perks of working at Paladin was attending *Soldier of Fortune*'s annual conventions in Las Vegas. That's where I met Bud Nealy, a talented custom knifemaker and an absolute genius in concealment sheath design. Nealy's patented Multi-Concealment Sheath (MCS) system pioneered the use of rare-earth magnets to hold the knife in the sheath, and came complete with Kydex hardware to support numerous carry styles and positions. Nealy's MCS system set a new standard in fixed-blade carry systems and I had the unique opportunity to feature it and his knife designs in a number of reviews for knife magazines and in my book *Street Steel*.

My network of friends in the knife industry grew steadily, and with those relationships came new knowledge, opportunities and a deeper understanding of high-performance fixed blades and conceal-

ment systems. Jeff Loffer of Cutlery Shop gave me an inside track on his Gryphon M-10 boot knife, designed by the legendary Bob Terzuola. The talented James Keating then taught the secrets of carry and reverse-grip application through his *Drawpoint* video series, while pioneering Kydex craftsman Mike Sastre provided custom sheaths for my personal M-10 knives. Life was indeed good.

In 2001 I wrote a review of several knives made by a then-unknown knifemaker named Mike Snody. The article kick started Snody's career as a full-time maker, and to show his gratitude he asked me to design my "ultimate neck knife." I had been doing a lot of live-blade testing and was convinced that the wharncliffe blade profile had potential as a personal-defense knife. Snody was skeptical of the design, but ultimately made one and did some test cutting of his own. That made him a believer, and my Ronin design was born. Originally produced only as a custom

The author's first fixed-blade design was the Ronin. Originally a custom knife made by Mike Snody, Spyderco later manufactured it. Shown here are a variety of Snody's custom pieces, including two "Rigger-Coated" versions hafted by James Piorek and a rare Ronin trainer. They are accompanied by a Spyderco production Ronin (right) engraved to commemorate the author's 2003 Martial Blade Camp event.

French knifemaker Fred Perrin pioneered the index finger hole and deep finger choil—brilliantly simple alternatives to a traditional guard. Perrin is the real deal and so are his blades.

design, it was later adopted by Spyderco and became my first production fixed blade.

Although manufacturing challenges limited the Spyderco Ronin to a single production run, shortly after its introduction I met Mickey Yurco. A veteran police officer, skilled martial artist and an extremely talented knifemaker, Yurco specializes in making small, concealable fixed blades housed in functional Kydex sheaths. We quickly became friends and my collection soon boasted many of Yurco's creations—including several interpretations of my Ronin design. Mickey's work is flawless, and the attention to detail he puts into the fit and finish of his knives and sheaths reflects the experience of a seasoned armed professional.

The release of the Ronin also led to my friendship with French knifemaker Fred Perrin. In addition to his skills as a knifemaker, Perrin is a highly sought-after close-combat instructor who was impressed with the logic behind the Ronin's design. Through our correspondence, he explained his philosophies on knife design, including the index finger hole and deep index finger choil that he developed to eliminate the need for a guard.

I soon added several of Fred's custom La Griffes to my collection and was blown away by their functional simplicity. I followed those purchases with the Spyderco Street Beat and Street Bowie of his designs, and later many mid-tech knives. Fred is a master of hardcore French *savate* (kickboxing) and old school street fighting, and his unique designs reflect a deep knowledge of practical, street-proven experience.

Holster Hardware

In 2004, I accepted an offer from BlackHawk Products Group to take charge of their knife brands, Masters of Defense and BlackHawk Blades. Black-Hawk's product line already included a variety of holsters and related hardware, so one of my first stops was the R&D department, where I promptly stocked up on every belt loop, paddle attachment, screw and snap I could afford as fodder for my sheath development.

Over the five years I worked for BlackHawk, I designed and engineered a number of different knives, including both large and small fixed blades. One of my absolute favorites was the Kalista and the sheath system that accompanied it, the TCCS (Total Concealed Carry Solution). The Kalista, meaning "a practitioner of kali" (a Filipino martial art renowned for its knife tactics), was intended to be a do-all concealable fixed blade large enough to rival a

Bud Nealy's concealment fixed blades are in a class by themselves. Of special interest is the knife on the lower right, which he made in limited numbers for members of an elite military unit. It is crafted exclusively from carbon fiber and its sheath has no metal components.

Mickey Yurco is a retired law enforcement officer, a talented martial artist and a skilled knifemaker with an exceptional understanding of fixed-blade carry and concealment. Here are a few of the author's Yurco knives, including outstanding expressions of the Ronin and Ronin2 designs.

traditional boot knife, but small enough to work as a neck knife. In addition to being flat and concealable, I wanted it to be comfortable in any grip, including edge-out and "reverse-edge" grips. Typically that requires a relatively neutral handle shape, which can make orienting the edge by feel challenging.

To achieve all this, the Kalista has offset scallops at the juncture of the handle and blade. The tang on the edge side of the handle also features *jimping* (texturing), while the back of the tang is smooth. Together, these features provide an asymmetrical feel that allows the user to immediately know which way the edge is facing by touch alone, yet enables the knife to be comfortably gripped with the edge facing in either direction.

The Kalista's TCCS sheath system was the culmination of years of thought and experimentation on fixed-blade carry methods. My original inspiration was Bud Nealy's MCS system, but I wanted even greater versatility and more options for angular adjustment. I started with the injection-molded belt and paddle platforms for BlackHawk's pistol holsters, which used a triangular three-hole pattern of mounting screws for five positions of angular adjustment. Durable and versatile, unfortunately the three-hole pattern did not work with knife sheaths because one of the holes would always be centered on the blade.

After a lot of thought and experimentation, I developed an "adapter plate" to interface between the three-hole pattern of the sheath hardware and a four-hole pattern in the sheath. The former gave me five angles of adjustment. The latter gave me four basic orientations. Together, they provided 20 degrees of angular adjustment around a full 360-degree range and worked equally well on both sides of the sheath.

Ultimately, the TCCS system included a paddle, a belt attachment, an inside-the-waistband loop, a ball chain, all the necessary screws and hardware, and complete illustrated instructions. Altogether, it provided more than 200 carry positions and was fully compatible with BlackHawk's other holster hardware, including shoulder harnesses and MOLLE attachments. The hardware package was also universal to several fixed-blade designs and is about as close to perfect as I've gotten when it comes to carrying concealable fixed blades.

Is that as good as it gets? I hope not, because my fixed-blade fixation is far from over.

Frame-Lock Fever!

It took time to catch on, but Chris Reeve's Integral Lock has been around over a quarter century

By Pat Covert

You're telling me the frame-lock folder is over a quarter century old? Where did the time go? There are several good reasons the frame-lock has floated under the radar, casually going about its business all those years. First off, unlike the Michael Walker LinerLock® folder from which it spun off, the frame-lock takes more machining capabilities to fabricate. A locking leaf on a LinerLock can be made using simple tools on thin sheet stock. The thick rear rail of a frame-lock folder, typically crafted from titanium, though other metals can be used, takes more machining.

The thick rear frame on most frame-lock folders is more expensive, especially when using titanium, than the thin liners of LinerLocks, and most knifemakers say titanium is much

The Chris Reeve Sebenza started out as a twist on a Michael Walker LinerLock, and over 25 years later the model has reached iconic status and is still the biggest seller in Reeve's line. *(Covert photo)*

harder to work than other metals. The bottom line is that frame-locks are difficult to craft.

Walker's locking-liner mechanism wasn't an overnight success; it took a radical twist in the knife market to catch fire. His early LinerLocks were designed in 1980 but didn't show up in any appreciable numbers until the late 1980s when custom knifemakers gradually started incorporating them into their folding knives, which were mostly fine gent's folders at the time.

Then, in the early 1990s, the combat folder—now referred to as the "tactical folder"—appeared on the scene in confluence with the Gulf War, and within no time Walker's LinerLock turned the folding knife market on its ears. Early tactical folder designers like Ernest Emerson, Bob Terzuola, Mel Pardue, Pat Crawford and Kit Carson became the hottest custom knifemakers on the market.

Sitting in the background watching from afar was a little known South African knifemaker named Chris Reeve. A machinist by trade who began making fixed-blade knives on the side in the mid-'80s, Reeve had seen and noted Walker's LinerLock and seized on a different way of using the basic design. Reeve tells *Knives 2015*, "In early 1987 I received a knife made by Michael Walker and was asked to fashion a knife like it. I didn't like the thinness of the LinerLock so I studied the mechanism, acquired some 3/16-inch titanium, and started to make what we now call a tactical [frame-lock] folder."

"I made a couple of prototypes in Africa," the knifemaker continues, "and then approximately 30 completely handmade knives, all almost identical to my Sebenza model, and sold them all. Next, 80 knives were made with machined handles, and they are stamped 'H' for 'handmade.' I was not pleased with them but they have become collectible. We moved to Boise, Idaho, in 1989, and I was so busy setting up my shop, I knew, to make the Sebenza properly, it needed to be done with CNC equipment. In 1991 we got our first CNC machine and went full speed with our production 'P' models."

A Lock of Many Callers

It should be noted that Reeve refers to his mechanism as an "Integral Lock®" and has the copyright on that name. It has also been replicated under other monikers such as "Mono Lock," but most enthusiasts call it a frame-lock because it is the most apt description of the lock itself.

Once Reeve's operation was up and running, the Sebenza folder started selling like hotcakes, and it's still the hottest model in his line today. His success with the Integral Lock caught the attention of other knifemakers, and some began to wade in. It was far from the landslide that accompanied the LinerLock, however. The custom knifemakers who embraced the frame-lock folder early were master machinists who could maneuver the testy waters of producing the mechanism.

Larry Connelley, proprietor of Knifeart.com, recalls, "It was the knifemakers with machining experience who were able to create the early frame-locking custom knives. Some of these makers include Allen Elishewitz, Rick Hinderer, Darrel Ralph, and Mick Strider and Duane Dwyer of Strider Knives. Making a quality frame-lock not only requires basic machining knowledge, but also an investment in the right equipment."

In 2003 the frame-lock took a big leap forward when Strider Knives adopted the mechanism for their SMF and SnG tactical folders. These models, with their unique angular handles, beefy blades and rock-solid construction, are still highly regarded by users and collectors today.

"Strider Knives makes a solid frame-lock on their pop-

The Strider Knives SnG and SMF tactical folders were a tremendous success right out of the chute and went a long way in popularizing the frame-lock mechanism. The SnG Gunner, identified by its heavily stippled grip, is pictured here. *(photo courtesy of KnifeArt.com)*

When Mike Grayman decided to add folders to his line-up of heavy-duty knives, he chose the frame-lock. The large Satu (at bottom) came first and was followed by its smaller sibling, the Dua (top). *(Covert photo)*

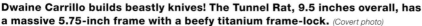

Dwaine Carrillo builds beastly knives! The Tunnel Rat, 9.5 inches overall, has a massive 5.75-inch frame with a beefy titanium frame-lock. *(Covert photo)*

for the frame-lock. Then, in 2006, their influence would be felt again when Zero Tolerance (ZT), the upscale tactical arm of Kershaw Knives, released its 300 series folders. A collaborative effort between Kershaw, Strider and noted custom knifemaker Ken Onion, the ZT 300 had features not previously seen in manu-factured knives. The backside featured a beautifully sculpted 3-D-machined lock design, mirrored on the front handle by the same pattern in G10. Onion's hallmark curves are easily evident in the bolo-inspired blade (with flipper no less!) and sculpted handle, and his assisted opening system was carried over from his rabidly successful designs in the Kershaw line. Not surprising, the 300 series is still a stalwart in the Zero Tolerance stable.

For the Brutally Tough

Knifemakers who build brutally tough knives often choose the frame-lock. Grayman Knives is known for extreme tank-like construction, and when it came to adding a folder to the line a few years back, Mike Grayman picked the frame-lock design. "We chose to go with a frame-lock design mainly for its strength, simplicity and proven reliability," he says. "There's just something about a locking system that includes the entire frame that inspires confidence. It's extremely robust."

Truth is Mike is being modest when he uses the word "robust." His Satu model is an absolute beast, and the smaller Dua—his second folder offering—doesn't fall far from the tree. Custom knifemaker Dwaine Carrillo tends to make oversized folding knives and some, like the Tunnel Rat, are downright huge. At 9.5 inches overall with a 5.75-inch handle, the Tunnel Rat is a force to be reckoned with and, you guessed it, it's a frame-lock!

Modifications geared to make the frame-lock more efficient have been made over the years. Most

ular SnG and SMF tactical folding knives," notes Connelly. "They utilize a variety of handle styles on these folders: a standard [flat] grip, a gunner [3-D machined, textured] grip and a concealed carry [contoured] handle. The SnG and SMF also utilize an ambidextrous oval hole and thumb studs as one-hand blade opening options. Strider Knives took the frame-lock into a distinctly tactical direction with a robust build and unique finish, which includes tiger-striped blades and flamed-titanium handles."

Strider's success with the frame-lock unquestion-ably broadened the awareness and consumer base notable is the Lockbar Stabilizer designed by custom knifemaker Rick Hinderer, who made his first frame-lock, the Firetac, in the year 2000. "The frame-lock is a strong mechanism," Hinderer remarks, "which lends itself well to one-hand usage. Also it is a very simplistic lock compared to a LinerLock. I feel that it is a safer lock mechanism."

But a near accident in 2001 caused him to rethink the locking mechanism and improve its design. "While using my frame-lock folder on an accident scene as a volunteer firefighter, I over extended the lock bar when I closed the knife due to a high amount of adrenalin. Of course, the blade could close but it rendered the knife useless. I knew then that I needed to come up with something that would prevent that from happening. I also wanted to incorporate a solution to the issue of lock movement toward the back

of the handle while gripping the knife tightly. This solution is the reason I call my invention the Lockbar Stabilizer and not just an over-travel stop."

Reeve never felt his Sebenza model needed a mechanism like the Lockbar Stabilizer. "It's a good innovation. I don't think it's always necessary, but in some cases I think it's an improvement to the knife," he allows. In fact, Reeve's Umnumzaan folder does include a modification to the frame-lock. "We included a 'lock stop' on the Umnumzaan to keep the tension on the locking leaf consistent."

In essence, this improvement keeps the leaf part of the frame-lock from being inadvertently bent outward or over-traveling by the user when disengaging the lock. Spyderco used an over-travel mechanism on several of its folders dating back to the early 1990s. Most recently the company incorporated it into their frame-lock design by knifemaker

The A.G. Russell Skorpions, available in large and small models, feature trim stainless steel frame-lock mechanisms. These are not your typical brawny frame-locks and their sleek frames make them lightweight and easy to conceal.

Brad Southard.

Another variation on Hinderer's Lockbar Stabilizer can be found on the Spyderco LionSpy frame-lock folder produced by LionSteel of Italy and based on the popular SR1 folder. Dubbed RotoBlock, this mechanism serves as an over-travel stop with an added benefit: by turning the top of the RotoBlock, it becomes a secondary lock and prevents the leaf from disengaging.

The LionSteel design also has another interesting feature on the lock itself. An R.I.L. insert on the forward area of the locking leaf contacts the blade and assures consistent wear on both components. It also guarantees the blade will not hang up should oil get between the contact area and blade tang. Frame-locks can jam when oil gets into the contact points between titanium and stainless steel. LionSteel's R.I.L. insert negates the chance of such problems.

The frame-lock took on a new look in 2008 when martial artist Chad Los Banos and Boker Knives teamed up to produce a series of small, easily concealed knives dubbed the Subcom models. Eschewing titanium or aluminum for their locks, the frames

of these super slim folders are made from stainless steel approximately 1/16-inch thick. The knives were an instant hit with consumers—so much so that Boker would add a handful of other Los Banos designs to its line-up, including the Trance and M Type folders, all featuring similar trim stainless steel frames. More recently A.G. Russell has adopted a similar design in his attractive Skorpion series, and Kershaw joined the fray with their Cryo I and II models. This frame-lock-on-a-diet concept seems here to stay.

If you want a glimpse into the future, look no further than the Zero Tolerance 777 introduced at the 2013 BLADE Show. This limited-edition folder has a dizzying array of features, among them a frame-lock mechanism comprised of a carbon fiber backing plate with a titanium sub-frame.

The frame-lock folder has proven it is no overnight fling in the knife industry. It remains today one of the strongest locking mechanisms. As long as the custom knifemakers and production facilities continue to add interesting twists and turns to the proven lock there's no end in sight!

TRENDS

I t takes a nation or a tight-knit community for a trend to start. People within the population have to be tuned into each other, aware of what's happening around them and connected in some way. Trends in fashion, movies, music and art occur when artists begin emulating each other, or adopting methods, materials and styles from around them. Movements are started, and soon a commonality emerges from a variety of sources.

The knife community is so close knit, like a family, that trends seem to be born daily. Sure, there are those that come and go quickly, lasting little longer than they took to arise in the first place, but some have staying power and soon become adopted or standard knife patterns, models or materials. What sparks the trends initially? The answer is innovation and creativity. A trend isn't born in a bubble. Outside sources inspire it, and then it is nurtured until it is unlike anything around it, but a new notion, a unique being and an anomaly. If it's a good anomaly, or at least attractive, endearing or likeable in some way, even sinfully sinister, then it might just catch on.

The knife community might be perfectly fine without any trends, providing cutting tools for those who need them, supplying our soldiers, chefs, farmers, electricians, sportsmen and outdoorsmen with the edges they desire, but it wouldn't grow and evolve. It's a business of sustained growth, after all, and trends help keep this tight-knit knife community growing right out of its little boy britches. Enjoy those that emerged this year and might just stick around into the future.

Sweeping Uppercuts

It's no secret or mystery why knifemakers enjoy fashioning long, sweeping-blade fighters and bowies. They get to stretch that steel out, and expand their minds and horizons, all at the same time. Pound that steel, boys, stretch, stretch, stretch it. And then hone it true, put that long edge on it, the bevel perfectly even, thinning to molecule-like thickness. Oil the blade and gleam it up, let it shine. The collectors love the long blades, too, especially if they curve and re-curve, sweeping upwards for that one last uppercut.

These are no sissy blades by any means. They're choppers, cutters and camp knives, bowies, like Col. James carried, ready at the hip, the sheath banging the thigh and kneecap when one strolls down Main Street. Still, these "sweeping uppercuts" aren't as heavy as bricks or anvils, either. Many have tapered tangs to lessen the weight, and most featured here ave fine balancing points, "sweet spots," if you will, where the hand and forefinger beg for the balance to be for cutting rope or whacking weeds.

There's a reason so many folks gravitate toward the long blades, the lengthy choppers, the sweeping uppercuts, it's because they're appealing, intriguing, mysterious and even dangerous all at once. And that, my friends, is what draws them in and pulls them toward the edge.

◄ **JUSTIN CHENAULT: Two 10-inch blades, one handled in giraffe bone, the other in stag, are accompanied by mokumé bolsters and smoky temper lines.** *(PointSeven photo)*

▲ **WAYNE HENSLEY: The upsweeping damascus blade could only be upstaged by a stabilized-pine-cone grip, and even then they vie competitively for attention.** *(PointSeven photo)*

JIM HAMMOND: With a name like the "Flesheater 5 Utility Bolo," it better have a 13-inch 440C blade to back it up. The Flesheater series was developed with Arcenio James Advincula, creator of the martial arts training program for the U.S. Marine Corps. *(SharpByCoop.com photo)*

JERRY HOSSOM: The "Vengeance Tanto" wreaks its havoc via a wickedly shaped, multi-ground 10.5-inch CPM 154 blade, accompanied by ivory Micarta and mosaic handle pins. *(PointSeven photo)*

RICARDO VELARDE: The long, sweeping sub-hilt fighter employs an 8-inch, re-curved blade, and a fossil-mastodon-ivory handle. *(PointSeven photo)*

BENONI BULLARD: There's an endearing dip to the 10-inch damascus blade of the stag-handle bowie. *(Ward photo)*

JAMES BATSON: Done in D-guard style, the whopping 16-inch 1084 blade extends the reach, while a walnut grip anchors the piece. James says it's an Alabama woman's bushwhacker. *(PointSeven photo)*

▶ **JERRY FISK:** Dizzying damascus and age-lined ivory define the 11-inch fighter forged by a master. *(Ward photo)*

▲ **TAD LYNCH:** In full fighter mode is an ironwood and damascus piece stretching 13 inches overall. *(Ward photo)*

▶ **RON WELLING:** Between walrus ivory and an 11-inch damascus blade is a slab of ironwood for which to place a finger and choke up on the handsome fighter. *(Ward photo)*

▲ **MICHAEL RUTH SR.:** The *swedge* along the spine of the 9-inch damascus blade further enhances the upswept look of the stag-handle fighter. *(Ward photo)*

▶ **RON NEWTON:** The first thing you notice is the fleur-de-lis ferrule wrap, and then that long "W's feather"-pattern damascus blade and fossil-walrus-ivory handle. It comes with a Paul Long leather sheath. *(SharpByCoop.com photo)*

▶ **DAVID SHARP:** Practically impenetrable black-linen-Micarta® gives one a reassuring handhold on the long CPM 154 fighter. *(SharpByCoop. com photo)*

Utility Knives & Choppers

These are the go-to knives, the axes and big, bodacious blades that whack, chop and slice without remorse—those that are kept in the garage, shed or on the workbench, handy, within reach. They are utility pieces, not all overly huge, but some small and handy, called to action when something needs to be cut. They have a purpose. They're tools, sharp edges, and nothing else will do when a cutting chore arises.

The genre is nothing new to handymen and women, blue-collar workers, those who build and fix things. It might even be the oldest category of knives, yet humble beginnings often produce extraordinary results, and such is the case with many of the models featured herein. Fashioning something exquisitely is not reserved solely for the handcrafting of art knives, or highly embellished pieces and fine cutlery.

In fact, sometimes more care goes into the making of utility tools than with those destined to reside on shelves and in display cases. The cutting ends must perform tasks without unnecessary maintenance, and the handle ends have to hold their own. To be used is not to be mistreated in the case of utility knives and choppers, but rather to be called to duty with honor and respect.

◀ **EDMUND DAVIDSON: At 7/8-inch thick and one solid piece of 154CM steel, you could chop until you drop.** *(PointSeven photo)*

▼ **ERIC EDQUIST: The rasp from which the knife was fashioned leaves its marks, while a Missouri walnut handle with mosaic pins pretties up the piece.** *(Ward photo)*

◀ **CHARLES VESTAL: In the style of the late Bob Loveless, the "Lamb Utility" is an evergreen design that's not too big or too small to handle chores via the CPM 154 blade and buffalo horn handle.** *(PointSeven photo)*

▲ **WAYNE HENSLEY: The trailing-point utility knife boasts a Bocote-wood handle, an ATS-34 stainless steel blade and a tooled leather sheath.** *(PointSeven photo)*

◀ LOGAN PEARCE: Talk about a utility tool, how's one that is able to cut a plug of tobacco and change a tire with equal aplomb? *(Ward photo)*

▶ LEE GENE BASKETT: The 10-inch CPM 154 blade will wallop what you need it to wallop, and the horse-matt-rubber handle will hold tight. *(PointSeven photo)*

▼ SCOTT HALL: Going by the blade grinds, serrations, secondary edge and bead-blasted finish, you know this ATS-34 fixed blade is meant to chop. *(Cory Martin Imaging)*

▶ JAMIN BRACKETT: Dyed, stabilized maple handle scales offer four finger grooves for the holding and manipulating of the cryogenically treated ATS-34 blade.

▲ BUD NEALY: Designed for defensive use and equally at home as a utility blade, the Beladau features a hollow-ground, modified-wharncliffe CPM 154 blade, thumb notches, an Australian she-oak handle and mosaic pins. *(PointSeven photo)*

LIN RHEA: A haft and a head, such a simple combo, but one that is beautifully orchestrated in mild steel and hickory. *(Ward photo)*

MIKE DEIBERT: In full chopping mode is a 14-inch 1095 model with wispy temper line, blued mild steel guard and a substantial ironwood handle. *(Ward photo)*

T.R. OVEREYNDER: The wharncliffe folder is done up in Dietmar Kressler's high-carbon stainless steel boasting 1.2 percent carbon, 15 percent chromium and .3 percent vanadium, not to mention a "lightning strike" carbon fiber handle and a stainless steel pivot that's textured on both sides. *(PointSeven photo)*

JAMES SCROGGS: A lightweight, full-tang spear-point utility knife features a black-walnut handle for a comfortable three-finger grip. The CPM 154 blade is flat ground and satin finished, and delivered in a Kenny Rowe leather sheath. *(PointSeven photo)*

TIM TABOR: Winner of the "Best Performance Bowie" award at the 2013 Arkansas Custom Knife Show, the maple-handle 52100 bowie needs no further introduction. *(Ward photo)*

▶ **LANDON ROBBINS:** "Wow" might be an appropriate word for the full-tang W2 bowie and its maple grip. *(Ward photo)*

▶ **MAX HARVEY:** The finger groove might be black Micarta, but the grip is all California buckeye burl on this big, handsome utility knife. *(R.V. Adams photo)*

◀ **CHRIS MONTGOMERY:** In the utility knife genre comes a clean W2 and Micarta® piece that'll cut the mustard. *(Ward photo)*

▲ **RAY KIRK:** It's a Bois d'arc (Osage orange wood) handle that the boys can use to arch the 52100 blade. *(Ward photo)*

▼ **DENNIS BRADLEY:** The nice little Tim Zowada damascus wharncliffe blade is a pointy enterprise anchored by pre-ban elephant ivory handle scales and stainless bolsters.

▶ **CALEB WHITE:** The "Big Grunt" produces guttural noises via a differentially hardened 1084 blade with a hand-rubbed finish and dark-brown Micarta handle scales.

▶ **SEVE RANDALL:** A hand-forged bowie-style chopper comes in a flat-ground W2 steel blade that's clay quenched with an active *hamon* or temper line, a contoured maple-burl handle and red liners that highlight the wood textures. *(PointSeven photo)*

▲ **JOHN PARKS:** A wrought iron grip is nothing to sneeze at, nor is the flat-ground 5160 blade. *(SharpByCoop.com photo)*

▼ **FRANCESCA WILBURN:** The second knife fashioned by Aaron Wilburn's daughter, this puppy has a satin-finished 52100 utility blade and an ironwood handle with grains that won't stop. *(BladeGallery.com photo)*

The Folds of Technology

▶ **POHAN LEU: A frightfully robust flipper folder is constructed of carbon fiber, titanium and a 3-inch modified-tanto blade.** *(Ward photo)*

◀ **DARREL RALPH: The largest of Darrel's "MADD MAXX" folders, the "Ultra MAXX" employs a Chad Nichols stainless damascus blade, a MAXX Glide pivot bearing system and mother-of-pearl handle inlays.** *(Ward photo)*

▶ **BUDDY GAINES: Rounded damascus handle overlays do the palm good, please the eyes and allow them to focus on the cutting task.**

▲ **TOM WATSON: The locking-liner folder's suit of armor includes a brown G-10 handle, clip-point ATS-34 blade, stainless steel bolsters, and titanium liners and pocket clip.**
(PointSeven photo)

▶ **DANIEL FAIRLY: The RF-1 frame-lock folder has the sculpted titanium and steel coolness factor down.**

▶ **JOE CASWELL:** Among other amenities, the pocket clip of the EDX folder retracts into the handle spine when not in use. *(SharpByCoop.com photo)*

◀ **BILL COYE:** Collectors just might flip out over the flipper folder in lightning-strike carbon fiber and CPM S35VN steel. *(PointSeven photo)*

▶ **RON APPLETON:** Despite its name, you don't have to be ultra intelligent to open the High-IQ button mechanism—decorated in a three-ring starburst pattern—for releasing the A2 tool steel blade from its home among anodized titanium. *(SharpByCoop.com photo)*

▼ **JENS ANSO:** A sharp RWL-34 appendage juts outs out from the grooved and arching armadillo-shell-like titanium handle. *(PointSeven photo)*

▶ **BOB TERZUOLA:** The tri-ground folding fighter is the stealth jet of frame-lock folders. *(PointSeven photo)*

THE FOLDS OF TECHNOLOGY

▶ **PHILIP BOOTH:** Though it's a "Twerp," the flipper folder stands on its own in a "toxic green" G-10 handle with an orange stripe, orange lanyard and skull bead, and a 154CM blade.

▶ **JOHN BARKER:** He could have stopped at the MokuTi handle, and we would have been happy, but the frame-lock folder also features a San Mai damascus blade with an AerMet 100 core. *(PointSeven photo)*

▲ **STEVE JERNIGAN:** Ball bearing pivots and elliptical thumbholes allow for quick blade opening of folders in 12C27 steel, and Micarta® and titanium handles. *(PointSeven photo)*

◀ **SEAN O'HARE:** The "Orion" locking-liner folder is dressed in layers of blue-anodized titanium, carbon fiber, Timascus and CPM 154 steel.

▲ **ERIC OCHS:** The folds of technology integrated into the "Tatsu Tanto Flipper" model are a chute-ground CPM S35VN blade, hand-hammered copper bolsters, floating spacers, a titanium pocket clip, lighting-strike carbon fiber handle scales and ceramic bearings.

▶ **AARON FREDERICK:** Geometric grind lines get things moving toward the chiseled points of two locking-liner folders in carbon fiber grips. *(PointSeven photo)*

▶ **ALLEN ELISHEWITZ:** The next best thing to a Chad Nichols damascus blade is grooved and sculpted carbon fiber.

▼ **RICHARD WRIGHT:** A grid crisscrosses the bronze bolsters of an Elmax flipper folder with ball bearing pivot system and carbon fiber handle scales.

▶ **LARRY AND RICHARD HARLEY:** The first folder from the father-and-son team of Larry and Richard, the "Cumberland" is done up in ATS-34 and canvas Micarta. *(PointSeven photo)*

▲ **STAN MOIZIS:** Lights, camera, double-action auto, out-the-front, mind you, in CPM 154 blade steel, bronze liners and G-10 handle scales.

► PETE CAREY:
Look closely at the
end of the carbon fiber handle
to see the rat-tail spike, perhaps
complementing the determinedly
pointed CPM 154 blade of the "Nitro"
flipper folder.

► KEN ONION: The only sharp
edge on the "Relay" flipper
folder is exactly where it's
supposed to be. *(SharpByCoop.
com photo)*

◄ JASON CLARK: The
long, sleek look of the
flipper folder isn't even
half the fun. *(Ward photo)*

► BUTCH BALL: Designed
by Rick Empson, mother-
of-pearl dragons highlight
the Masecraft Supply Micarta
handle scales of the folder, while
a 154CM blade gives it some bite.
(PointSeven photo)

▼ THINUS HERBST: The minimalist
design is ultimately fulfilling,
involving a skeletonized titanium
handle and 12C27 blade.
(Cones-Stuff photo)

▶ **SCOT MATSUOKA:** This one's about the speed (Ikoma Korth Bearing System), the lockup (Rick Hinderer Lock-bar Stabilizer) and the sharpness (hollow-ground CPM 154 blade steel.) *(SharpByCoop.com photo)*

▼ **STEVEN SKIFF:** The "Dauntless" tactical folder blends a Damasteel bolster with carbon fiber handle scales in a most pleasing pair-up. *(SharpByCoop.com photo)*

▼ **OLAMIC CUTLERY:** The mean-looking CPM S35VN "Wayfarer" is sweetened up by a honeycomb-pattern C-Tek handle. *(SharpByCoop. com photo)*

▶ **ALAN FOLTS:** Rob Thomas damascus gets color highlights via blued carbon fiber, blued titanium liners and a purplish pivot head. *(Ward photo)*

▶ **KEITH OUYE:** The dress tactical folder can back up its good looks. *(SharpByCoop.com photo)*

Belt and Boot Knives

You need a sheath with these. You wouldn't want to slide one of the pointed pieces into a boot without something between the blade and the bare foot, toes or stocking. And the belt, well, there are way too many internal, and in some cases external, organs close to the waist area not to sheath it if you've got it. Belt and boot knives aren't blunt-tip rescue blades. Most aren't big-bellied skinners, and few have sheepsfoot blades.

The knives are meant for cutting, utility, self-defense and ease of access. Where do your hands reach? The belt area is a natural place for the hand to reference, and with a slight bend of the knee, the boot area is easily accessible. How about the chest, small of the back, over the shoulder or under the arm? Yes, yes, yes and yes, they're all good places for concealed or open carry of a knife. But that's not where belt and boot knives are stored. Their name pretty much reveals where they reside.

Why make belt and boot knives today? Aren't they an outdated art form? I don't know, is hunting outdated, or fishing, skiing, winter camping, hiking or snowshoeing? I guess only if playing video games, eating dinner out and staying in hotels is your thing. Then you probably don't wear belt and boot knives—not a lot of places to stash them on the beach. But these aren't beach blades. They're belt and boot knives, and they're prepared for whatever comes their way, in the wild or on the streets, not necessarily at the spa.

◀ **ERIC EDQUIST:** The mammoth-ivory coffin handle, with ebony inlays, mosaic pins and nickel silver bolsters, is a hot grip to grab hold of, in order to use the damascus edge for a little blade play. *(Ward photo)*

▼ **RICK "BEAR BONE" SMITH:** A classically styled S-guard boot knife, it dons a 6.5-inch O1 tool steel blade in a hand-rubbed, antiqued finish, and a curly maple coffin-type handle secured by eight pins.

▲ **BILL BEHNKE:** The ox-horn handle with mosaic pin is smooth as silk, and the clip-point, ladder-pattern-damascus blade of the belt knife is sharp as all get-out. *(PointSeven photo)*

▶ **RALPH TURNBULL:** You might take a liking to the mother-of-pearl handle, the Doug Ponzio damascus or the rubies inlaid in the form of a cross, but if you don't, I wouldn't tell the maker.

▲ **GARY MARTINDALE SR.:** This one might belong in the boot, but it's easier to appreciate the CPM 154 blade and amber stag handle when it's unsheathed and in the hand. *(SharpByCoop.com photo)*

▼ **MIKE MCCLURE:** The mammoth-bone boot knife gets the 154CM blade steel treatment and some Jim Sornberger engraving on the dovetailed bolster. *(BladeGallery.com photo)*

▶ **DENNIS BRADLEY:** Break out the integral boot dagger with imitation tortoise shell handle and 440C blade when precision cutting becomes necessary.

▶ **JOHN HEGE:** The damascus dagger is a boot knife if I've ever seen one, anchored by an ironwood handle, copper fittings, and the shaft of the boot, of course.

Genteel Steel

The knifemakers might not sport manicured fingernails, but some of the collectors and buyers of these classy pocket cutters could have taken a trip to the spa lately. Many, of course, have not. It doesn't take a sophisticate to appreciate the finer things in life, and in some respects, those who have not, or work hard for what they do have, tend to appreciate quality tools just as much as the privileged few.

Regardless, it's not difficult to fall for the genteel steel shown here, to be drawn in by the translucent mother-of-pearl, the damascus patterning, engraved guards and bolsters, genuine Sambar stag, gold inlays, mammoth ivory handle scales and jewel inlays. You might feel so prim and proper that you take that trip to the manicurist after all, and surely one wouldn't be shy about extracting one of these beauties from a pants or vest pocket in the company of churchgoers or townsfolk.

That's the appeal of genteel steel—you can use one of these handmade blades to cut string off the fishing reel, slice a little sausage for a midday meal or give a Red Delicious apple a peel.

◀ DON HANSON III: The dress slip-joint folder makes a public appearance in amber-colored stag, and the maker's own damascus blade and bolster steel. *(SharpByCoop. com photo)*

▼ MICHAEL WALKER: Is it the gold, the blued pivot, damascus or titanium that trips your trigger finger? *(SharpByCoop.com photo)*

▲ KEVIN CASEY: Gazing at the ocean-fresh mother-of-pearl, or lost in the feather damascus pattern, one might overlook the moonstone thumb stud. *(SharpByCoop.com photo)*

▼ DANIEL STUCKY: The mammoth ivory is so clean, I had to determine if was real, and it is the authentic deal, as is the rest of the dress locking-liner folder with damascus bolster steel. *(SharpByCoop.com photo)*

▼ **MICHAEL VAGNINO:** One of the maker's convertible folders that transforms from a fixed blade to a push dagger, the forged damascus blade steel appeals to the sophisticate in all of us, and the bolster engraving brings some more class to the cut. It comes with a Paul Long sheath.

▲ **JOE SANGSTER:** The gent's everyday locking-liner folder is a fine example of its kind, in an ancient Kauri wood handle recovered from New Zealand, set off with damascus bolsters and blade, file work on the brass back spacer and brass screws. *(PointSeven photo)*

▲ **DES HORN:** Deep inlays of lapis lazuli and Gibeon meteorite share folding knife space with Damasteel and little gold dots along the blade spine. *(Francesco Pachi photo)*

▲ **CHICCI YONEYAMA:** The mammoth tooth isn't ivory white, but colorful hues that please the palate, and complemented by damascus blade steel, cementing the genteel deal. *(SharpByCoop.com photo)*

▶ **GRACE HORNE:** Gold dots simultaneously blend in and contrast with the stingray-skin handle of the double-blade damascus folder. *(PointSeven photo)*

▲ **STEVE HILL:** The maker's buffer caught and threw the blade of the "not so genteel steel" knife, and it skewered his leg, thus his model name "Curse of the Black Pearl" for the damascus folder with black-lip-pearl handle scales and heat-colored mosaic-damascus bolsters. *(Chas Freiburg photo)*

▼ **KEITH OUYE:** The "Chongming" flipper folder, engraved by C.J. Cai, is indeed reminiscent of Shanghai's secret island paradise and its watery gray wetlands where exotic migrant birds are spotted. *(Francesco Pachi photo)*

▶ **JOE KIOUS:** The exquisite folder features a CPM 154 modified-wharncliffe blade, a polished stainless steel frame, black-lip-pearl handle inlays and rope file work along the spine. *(PointSeven photo)*

▶ **ALAIN and JORIS CHOMILIER:** Patined bronze is carved into a fibrous exterior in gold, sculpted and blued, and then blown out with a damascus blade.

▶ **THOMAS HASLINGER:** The dovetailed mosaic-damascus bolsters of the compact gent's folders mate up with black-lip-pearl and snakewood handle scales, and complement damascus blades. The sapphire-inlaid titanium thumb studs are "flower file worked."

▶ **CALVIN ROBINSON:** "Pappy's Jack Knife" parades mother-of-pearl and Sandvik 14C28N steel. *(Ward photo)*

▲ **ROBERT MERZ:** With engraved bolsters by Alice Carter, the stag-handle lock-back folder fits in fashionably and equally well at the hardware store or church basement. *(PointSeven photo)*

▶ **DAVID TABER:** The teardrop-shaped handle, into which the ATS-34 blade silently slips, is mammoth ivory that has aged gracefully.

▲ **SCOTT SAWBY:** Bloodstones and agates from one of Buster Warenski's rocks adorn the CPM 154 folder. *(PointSeven photo)*

▶ **MEL NISHIUCHI:** The one-two color combination includes Devin Thomas mokumé bolsters and Labradorite handle scales, the latter a semi-precious stone from Paul's Island, Canada. *(PointSeven photo)*

▼ **KEN STEIGERWALT:** The pleasing, geometrically shaped Damasteel folders flex their mollusk-cles, one in black-lip pearl, the other in Pinnidae or pen shell (saltwater clam shell). *(SharpByCoop.com photo)*

▶ **TED MOORE:** Make mine a mammoth-tooth and Mike Norris damascus knife in a wharncliffe pattern. *(SharpByCoop.com photo)*

▶ **JOHNNY STOUT:** The feather-pattern damascus blade, engraved and gold-inlaid bolsters in a leaf motif, and "crackle"-mammoth-ivory handle scales all snap, crackle and pop. Jim Small engraved the piece.

▼ **PHILIP BOOTH:** The way the maker married ancient ivory, blued bolsters and Kevin Cashen twist-damascus proved a well-coordinated effort. *(Cory Martin Imaging)*

▶ **ALLEN ELISHEWITZ:** Mokumé and walrus ivory are equally fluid in a molten/milky kind of way. The flipper folder blade is Chad Nichols damascus.

▼ **BRIAN TIGHE:** Grooved and anodized titanium, even more groovy Damasteel and some STBS bearings make up the "Tighe Rade" button-lock flipper folder. *(PointSeven photo)*

▶ **MIKE "WHISKERS" ALLEN:** From the tip of the Rob Thomas damascus blade to the engraved bolsters, colorful Kirinite® handle scales and even the skull lanyard bead, this one sings a sweet tune. *(PointSeven photo)*

▶ **STEVE CULVER:** To properly settle any gentleman's feud, take 10 paces, turn and fire the damascus flint-lock pistol with spiral-welded barrel and highly figured wood grip. If you need to cut a plug of tobacco after the affair, a clip-point blade will do the favor. *(SharpByCoop.com photo)*

▶ **TOM HEARD:** Alabama damascus, titanium, mammoth tooth and silicon bronze are all in the fold.

▶ **GLEN MIKOLAJCZYK:** Buying a slab of the brain coral didn't take a brain surgeon, but putting it together with the tight feather pattern of the damascus blade and bolsters, and anodized titanium liners, was masterful. *(Cory Martin Imaging)*

▼ **R.B. JOHNSON:** A horn-handle gent's folder forges ahead in Damasteel and Robert Eggerling damascus. *(Cory Martin Imaging)*

▶ **CLIFF PARKER:** His "Butterflies & Flowers Spring Fever" mosaic-damascus folder is further awash in abalone handle scales. *(SharpByCoop.com photo)*

▼ **WILLIAM TUCH:** The maker takes us to sculpture school, with his example done completely in stainless steel. *(PointSeven photo)*

▶ **C. GRAY TAYLOR:** With 12 tools in CPM 154 steel, plus inserts that include a scissors, tweezers, ruler and pick, this is not only an art piece, but a useable multi-blade folder that just so happens to have an antique-tortoise-shell handle, gold liners and bolsters, and engraving by Lisa Tomlin. *(PointSeven photo)*

▲ **RICK BARRETT:** A proper gentleman avoids 5 o'clock shadows by using a damascus straight razor with "lightning strike" carbon fiber handle scales. *(Cory Martin Imaging)*

▶ **CRAIG BREWER:** His version of a Tony Bose "Lanny's Clip" slip-joint folder is favorably fashioned in CPM 154 steel, stag handle scales and a bomb shield.

▶ **EDDIE STALCUP:** You'd feel swell pulling the damascus spear-point folder from your pocket, running a thumb over the elephant-bark handle scales before opening the blade via the ruby-inlaid thumb stud. *(Hoffman photo)*

◀ **SCOTT SAWBY:** The stems of art Nouveau tulips, engraved and gold inlaid by Marian Sawby, seemingly extend onto the black jade handle of an art folder featuring a Mike Norris ladder-pattern-damascus blade.

▲ **LEE FERGUSON:** Pull out the Damasteel folder to trim a fingernail, and those who see the engraved and anodized titanium handle, not to mention the sapphire-inlaid thumb stud, will stand with mouths agape.

Cool as a Camp Cutter

► **ALLEN NEWBERRY:** After foraging for food, a guy needs a big 12-inch camp cutlass, preferably one with a blackwood handle, a clay-hardened 1095 blade and all kinds of smoky lines running across the steel. *(Ward photo)*

▼ **SCOTT GOSSMAN:** At camp two knives are better than one, for big and small tasks, putting the A2 blades and desert-ironwood and rosewood grips to good use.

► **MARCUS LIN:** Whoever "Ito" is, he's one lucky guy, this being "Ito's Camp Knife" in a stonewashed Elmax™ blade, canvas-Micarta® handle scales and thin red liners. *(Hiro Soga photo)*

▼ **HARVEY KING:** A big-old D2 blade with a bulbous fore end makes a fine camp knife, this one in giraffe-bone handle scales and mosaic pins. *(Ward photo)*

► **BEN SEWARD:** Winner of the Camp Knife Award at the 2013 Arkansas Knifemakers Association Show, the "Foggy Bayou Chopper" works equally as well on camp wood and tent stakes as it does on alligators. That's a 10-inch, re-curved W2 blade for those who want to know, and a blackwood handle. *(Ward photo)*

Forever In Loveless

▶ **JOHN YOUNG:** The horn of a bighorn sheep was an inspired handle choice for a Bob Loveless-style New York Special in Carpenter CTS 40CP stainless steel. *(PointSeven photo)*

▼ **CHARLES VESTAL:** The reach of the Loveless-style Big Bear is universal, and about 14 inches in the case of this piece in mammoth ivory and CPM 154 steel.
(SharpByCoop.com photo)

▶ **ROBERT NELSON PARKER:** Elephant ivory and Dave Lark engraving glitz up a Loveless-style chute knife with a blade of Bob's favorite—ATS-34 stainless steel.

▼ **STEVEN RAPP:** A parachutist would almost hope to get tangled upon landing just to use the stag-handle 154CM chute knife.
(PointSeven photo)

▶ **DAVID SHARP JR.:** The Loveless-pattern "Dixon" with a chute-style grind is 11 inches overall, much of which is rings of curly Koa that send shivers up the spine—the knife's, yours and mine.
(SharpByCoop.com photo)

Battle Honed

▶ **RON BEST:** Blade and handle carving elevates the CPM 154 *karambit* (curved Filipino fighting knife), with carbon fiber grips, above the ordinary. *(SharpByCoop.com photo)*

▶ **DARRIN SIROIS:** Textured G-10 and semi-serrated 154CM steel propel it into the realm of tactical knife. *(JZW Photography)*

▼ **LES GEORGE:** The M12 EOD (Explosive Ordinance Disposal) knife is designated as a suitable substitute for the official U.S. Marine Corps EOD technician's kit knife. *(PointSeven photo)*

▼ **GIL HIBBEN:** Outfitted in Macassar ebony and 440C stainless steel, this is the new, limited edition, full-size version of the knife carried by Sylvester Stallone in the movie *Rambo III.* *(PointSeven photo)*

▶ **JERRY BROUWER:** Grooves along the G10 handle cut right into the pinheads, and shimmy their way up to a CPM 3V blade heat-treated by Paul Bos.

▶ **JIM HAMMOND:** The third model in the "Flesheater" series, developed with Arcenio James Advincula, creator of the U.S. Marine Corps martial arts training program, it boasts stealth green linen Micarta and a bead-blasted 440C blade. *(SharpByCoop.com photo)*

▶ **JERRY HOSSOM:** Sometimes a sculpted body means just that, here in maroon Micarta® and CPM 154 steel. *(PointSeven photo)*

▼ **NATHAN CAROTHERS:** One piece of A2 steel extends from tip to full-tang grip, complete with blood groove, and handled in checkered Micarta. *(SharpByCoop.com photo)*

▶ **STEVE LELAND:** Battle honed and double edged is a 10.5-inch full-tang fixed blade interrupted only by black canvas Micarta and nickel silver thong tubes. *(PointSeven photo)*

▲ **ALAN FOLTS:** The "Small Desert Field Knife" is all 1095 blade and tan G-10. *(Ward photo)*

▶ **DANIEL WINKLER:** The all-black, double-edge dagger takes no prisoners. *(PointSeven photo)*

▼ **DAVID SHARP:** The big, double-hollow-ground blade of the battle knife would be unwieldy if not for the carbon fiber handle scales. *(SharpByCoop.com photo)*

◀ **LEE GENE BASKETT:** The telescoping rubber handle of the hatchet offers more reach, or less, depending on your tactical needs. *(PointSeven photo)*

▼ **LEVI GRAHAM:** A desert-camo-Cerakote™ finish covers the "Shadow" belt knife and "Ambush" tactical tomahawk, including the sculpted G-10 handles and high-carbon-steel edges. Levi worked with his brothers Christian and Tanner on the package. *(Ward photo)*

A.B. Schaller
Albuquerque,N.M.
Handmade

▲ **ANTHONY B. SCHALLER:** Blue and black G-10 add some color and depth to the CPM 154 "Shadow" fighter. *(SharpByCoop.com photo)*

Telltale Temper Lines

In any handcrafted item, there are telltale signs of quality workmanship. With furniture, it's tongue-and-groove joints; pegged drawers; dovetailed fronts; heavy, not light, solid wood; straight, tight stitching in the fabric; adjustable drawer glides and smooth overall finishes. Just like with furniture, weight is a consideration when judging a quality wristwatch, as is movement, brand name and tradition, Swiss branding and accuracy.

Similar to furniture, dovetailing is a sign of a quality knife, but in the case of cutlery, through dovetailed bolsters, not drawers or fronts. Tight fits and finishes wherever handle material meets bolster or blade material would qualify as good signs, as are the absence of gaps, no loose screws or parts, no jangling of a folding blade in a handle, strong folding knife springs and well-honed blades.

And then there's the blade-smith's favorite telltale sign—a temper line. Those who forge often take the extra and important step of differentially tempering a blade so it has a hard edge for better edge holding, and a soft spine, and thus less chance of breaking. By etching the blade after it is forged, differentially heat-treated and finished, a "temper line" is revealed, and not just any temper line, but a telltale temper line, one that denotes the quality of a forged blade.

▼ **RICK BARRETT:** The forged W2 blade of the "Tengu" cleaver showcases a "Choji" *hamon* (temper line) complemented by a bright-blue and purple Timascus guard and pommel, and a carbon fiber handle with a meteorite inlay. *(Cory Martin Imaging)*

◄ **DON HANSON III:** Mammoth ivory, left non-shaped or natural at the pommel end of the "Artifact Fighter" is combined with a forged-W2 blade parading a lively temper line. *(SharpByCoop.com photo)*

▼ **BEN TENDICK:** The polished hamon of the W2 blade undoubtedly helped the stag bowie land the "Best Bowie Knife" award at the 2013 Oregon Knife Collectors Assoc. Show.

▼ **MICHAEL RADER:** Whether you are a sushi chef or amateur cook, the hand-forged, differentially heat-treated W2 blade will cut the cabbage while the curly koa and box elder burl grip impresses the guests. *(BladeGallery.com photo)*

► MICHAEL BURCH: A "Dao" flipper folder can certainly carry off a differentially tempered 1095 blade with squiggly temper line. The handle is G-10 and Westinghouse Micarta®. *(SharpByCoop.com photo)*

◄ E. SCOTT MCGHEE: The "Puma" is a sleek cat in a forged W2 blade and ironwood body. *(PointSeven photo)*

▼ JON CHRISTENSEN: Follow the lines of the fighter blade from tip to choil, then wrap the hand around the sculpted blackwood grip. *(Ward photo)*

▼ JOHN DOYLE: Hand forged for his own wedding, and black and white—the wedding colors—the bowie boasts a white G-10 handle, a black G-10 frame and bolster, carbon fiber handle pins inlaid in joined and twisted "J's" (the bride-and-groom's first initials) and a 1075 blade used to cut the cake. *(SharpByCoop. com photo)*

▼ SCOTT MACCAUGHTRY: Some folks form lines, and others forge them, the latter being the case on the 8.75-inch W2 blade of the blackwood-handle fighter. *(SharpByCoop.com photo)*

▶ BRUCE BINGENHEIMER: Behold the bowie with forged blade and burly grip. *(SharpByCoop.com photo)*

▼ KYLE ROYER: It's true that every cloudy temper line has a silver lining, and in this case, deep-relief engraving and rings of beautiful curly **Koa wood.** *(Caleb Royer Studio Photography)*

▼ BEN SEWARD: The forge fire left beauty marks all along the 1075 blade of the ironwood-handle "Red River Bowie," and David Seward fashioned a leather sheath for the occasion. *(Caleb Royer Studio Photography)*

▲ KARL B. ANDERSEN: Of takedown construction, the hunter looks distinguished in a W2 blade, wavy temper line, a Ringed-Gidgee wood handle and a stainless steel guard.

Picture Perfect Pocketknives

People say, "Look at that sunset. It's like a postcard." Or, "My goodness, the scenery is breathtaking. Just give me a minute to take it all in." Other folks remark, "You couldn't paint those gardens better than that," or, "Look out on the horizon. Have you ever seen anything so beautiful?" They are affected by the landscape laid out before them. They are in awe, and who could blame them? If nature is nothing else, it is affecting in deep-seated ways.

The truth is, though, that pictures, paintings or postcards are seldom, if ever, as impressive as the real deals. And the picture perfect, or superior-to-photography, pocketknives on this and the following pages might just have that same awing effect on you, just by looking at the photographic images.

Some of the pocketknives incorporate nature right into their beings, with mammoth-ivory, pearl or stag grips, exotic wood handles or non-synthetic inlays and spacers. It's their manufacture, not natural makeup, though, that's picture perfect. The craftsmanship is what makes you stand in wide wonder. So go ahead, give yourself a moment to take it all in.

◄ **JOEL CHAMBLIN:** The premium mammoth ivory handle scales are bookended by stainless steel bolsters, embellished with a gold handle shield and pins, and guarded by three sharp blades. *(Ward photo)*

▲ **HARVEY DEAN:** Look closely and you'll see the handle shield is not metal, but black-lip pearl inlaid into the mother-of-pearl grip of a two-blade pocketknife. *(SharpByCoop.com photo)*

▶ **BRET DOWELL:** A stag-handle trapper is presented with a stainless steel blade and proper bow-tie-style shield. *(Ward photo)*

▲ **DAVID TABER:** Like the lined face of an elderly gentleman, bark-elephant-ivory handle scales give the swayback jack some character.

JEFF CLAIBORNE: A swell-center elephant toenail pattern, the main 52100 blade features a choice of a long-pull or eyelash nail nick, and, of course, the knife sports stag handle scales to grip. *(Hoffman photo)*

ENRIQUE PENA: The maker jigged the bone of the handle scales himself, outfitting the piece with five CPM 154 blades, and stainless steel liners and bolsters, no small feat. *(SharpByCoop.com photo)*

YOSHIO SAKAUCHI: The sportsman's knife has a wharncliffe main blade, a pen blade, saw, horse-hoof pick and corkscrew. The handle scales are stag with an acorn-style shield. Sweet! *(PointSeven photo)*

BILL RUPLE: Rope file work adorns the CTS-XHP blades, and stag covers the handle nicely. *(PointSeven photo)*

GRACE HORNE: What better to anchor a laminated silver-and-steel blade with than a sterling silver handle for a high-grade effect? *(PointSeven photo)*

▶ **CALVIN ROBINSON:** Red linen Micarta® is the rouge upon the pretty face of a single-blade Sandvik 14C28N trapper. *(Ward photo)*

▶ **STANLEY BUZEK:** Green jigged bone gets jiggy on the two-blade Texas jackknife in CPM 154 steel. *(Ward photo)*

▼ **DON HANSON III:** Talk about picture perfect check out the blue mammoth ivory handle scales, not to mention the sweet 440C blade. *(Ward photo)*

▶ **KEN ERICKSON:** The congress whittler is a dress slip-joint folder in CPM D2 blade steel, integral 416 stainless steel bolsters and frame, an antique tortoise shell handle and a coined center liner. Check out the manicure blade with file, in case you are in need of a "mani-pedi." *(SharpByCoop. com photo)*

▼ **KEITH R. JOHNSON:** A Tony Bose-style "Lanny's Clip" pocketknife, the highly figured, amber stag handle scales lend depth to the piece, while a CPM 154 blade with bronze pivot bushing takes it a good deal further. The federal shield in stainless steel is a nice touch. *(Hoffman photo)*

► **JUKKA HANKALA:** Ah, finally, a piece to cut the foil off the wine bottle and pull the cork out for a little tasting of the fermented juices. Black-lip pearl was an appropriate handle choice for the RWL-34 folder.

◄ **JAMES BATSON:** Seldom does a classically styled pocketknife look so authentic, here in mastodon ivory, German silver and high-carbon steel. *(PointSeven photo)*

▼ **CRAIG BREWER:** The jigged-bone cattle knife comes with three hand-ground and finished CPM 154 blades and some stainless steel liners and bolsters.

► **TONY BOSE:** The teardrop-style pre-ban elephant ivory handle feels as good as it looks, and the W2 high-carbon steel blade is fashioned with a long "match-strike pull" nail nick.

(SharpByCoop.com photo)

Splayed in Their Coffins

I t doesn't matter where these knives are splayed, or displayed, passersby will gawk like Western townsfolk looking at the open coffin of a hanged cattle rustler or stagecoach robber. Their mouths won't hang agape in horror or disgust, though, but in admiration and astonishment, at how beautiful coffin-handle bowies can truly be.

Why coffin shapes to the handles of these bowies? Well, maybe in recognition of the open coffins on Western boardwalks where rightfully or wrongly convicted killers and thieves were displayed for all to see. Or maybe it's in honor of the coffin makers themselves, who handcrafted folks' final resting boxes, just like knifemakers today hand forge and fashion edged tools and weapons. Handcrafters have to stick together, after all, and tout their wares.

In this case, the wares are coffin-handle bowies, the type collectors like to admire and purchase for their singularity, novelty and endearing shapes, even if they do evoke imagery of coffins and death. The blades are splayed in their coffins, so please pay your respects.

◄ **MIKE MOONEY:** The big upswept CPM 154 blade and coffin-style mammoth ivory handle give this piece a classic Southwest bowie profile.

▲ **BRUCE BINGENHEIMER:** Not only is the ironwood handle shaped like a coffin, but the guard of the bowie is also formed like a pine box, or in this case, a damascus box. *(SharpByCoop.com photo)*

▼**GARTH HINDMARCH:** As far as personal effects go, you could do worse than placing the coffin-handle damascus bowie with a giraffe-bone grip, an engraved ferrule and fancy file work in your coffin.

MAX HARVEY: The coffin-shaped handle is composed of a one-piece stainless steel frame with an Arizona ironwood handle overlay, one that likely won't decompose. *(R.V. Adams photo)*

JOHN DAVIS: A visual feast of a bowie, it sports a coffin-shaped copper handle with desert ironwood inserts, copper pins, black-lip pearl inlays, oh, and an 8-inch 52100 blade. *(PointSeven photo)*

FOREST "BUTCH" SHEELY: An antique bowie repro parades a comely coffin-shaped curly maple handle, domed sterling silver pins and a 5.5-inch 5160 blade. *(Cory Martin Imaging)*

J. NEILSON: A lacy she oak handle gets the coffin treatment, and is, in turn, treated to a 10.5-inch two-bar twist-damascus blade, as well as an antiqued high-carbon-steel guard. *(Ward photo)*

DOUG CAMPBELL: If the dark damascus blade, wrought iron guard and coffin-shaped ebony handle foreshadow what's to come, let's hope there's an afterlife. *(Ward photo)*

A Higher Class of Hunters

▶ **NESTOR LORENZO RHO:** Helped along by ebony, hardwood and bronze, the "Jaguar" 420 stainless steel fixed blade is bitingly beautiful. *(Federico Koch photo)*

▶ **MIKE MOONEY:** Calling it "sophisticated simplicity," the maker's "Voyager" model sports a 3.5-inch CPM S30V blade with a tapered tang, dovetailed 416 stainless steel bolsters, mammoth ivory handle scales, Micarta® spacers and a mosaic pin.

▼ **NORMAN SANDOW:** This higher class of hunter has a ringed Gidgee wood handle, mosaic pins and a stainless steel blade and bolsters.

▶ **MARK KNAPP:** Two knives are better than one, particularly those in damascus blades and fossil-walrus-ivory handles. *(SharpByCoop.com photo)*

▶ **ROBERT KOVACIK:** A pronged one looks out from a thicket of damascus steel and stabilized wood.

▶ **STEVE DAVIS:** The stabilized ash burl handle displays a galaxy of formations, while the twist-damascus blade showcases some patterns of its own.
(PointSeven photo)

▼ **SERGIO RAMONDETTI:** Of the drop-point hunter variety, it hits the field in desert ironwood and mosaic handle pins.

▶ **J.P. MILLER:** A polished brass guard beckons, a stag grip adds allure and the damascus blade seals the deal.
(PointSeven photo)

▶ **DENNIS BRADLEY:** The maker's trailing-point hunter displays a bulbous box-elder-wood handle, a flat-ground 440 stainless steel blade, stainless guard and butt cap, and a tooled leather sheath.

▶ **ROB HUDSON:** Maple and walrus ivory might sound like strange bedfellows, until, of course, they're paired up for a CPM 154 drop-point hunter in such a winsome manner.

▶ **RANDY LEE:** The coordinated handle of the CPM 154 drop-point hunter includes alternate ivory, ironwood, amber, black polyester resin, red fiber and nickel silver. *(PointSeven photo)*

▶ **DOUG CAMPBELL:** For his hand-forged 1084 drop-point hunter, the maker salvaged a rare True Kamani hardwood handle from old stock collected many years ago by a native Hawaiian friend of his. *(PointSeven photo)*

▶ **MIKE TYRE:** The forged 52100 blade and bolster are one, integral piece prettied up by a highly patterned lace-redwood-burl handle. *(PointSeven photo)*

▲ **SCOTT DAVIDSON:** With file work on the spine and a large finger choil, an oosic-handle hunter just begs you to choke up on it and tackle the cutting chore. *(PointSeven photo)*

▶ **JAMES SCROGGS:** Lest we forget the utility hunter, here's one in maple burl and a 5160 blade. *(Ward photo)*

◀ **ALAN HUTCHINSON:** The butt of the handle flares out like the base of the ironwood branch probably did at one time, while the 1084 blade comes to a distinctive dropped point.
(PointSeven photo)

◀ **FRED CARTER:** Like a fine engraved shotgun, the CPM 154 hunter is a highly embellished piece.

▶ **EUGENE SHADLEY:** A bird-and-trout knife dresses up the duck blind in green jigged bone and stainless steel.
(PointSeven photo)

▶ **BOB FISCHER:** Flint-knapped and naturally cool is the little stone hunter that could. *(Cory Martin Imaging)*

▶ **JASON FRY:** Named after the Llano, Texas, area where the knifemaker hunts, the "Llano Legend" has an appropriate Texas mesquite wood handle and dovetailed New Mexico juniper bolsters.

▶ **ROBERT NELSON PARKER:** Natural abalone is a brilliant choice for a D2 drop-point hunter. Paul Bos did the blade heat-treating honors.

▼ **ALBERT TRUJILLO:** The nice thing about stabilized box elder is that you can dye it the color you want for a pair of ATS-34 hunters. *(PointSeven photo)*

▼ **PEKKA TUOMINEN:** The lines of the multi-faceted white paper Micarta handle and multi-ground RWL-34 blade have just a snippet of sex appeal.

▼ **ED BRANDSEY:** The CPM 154 "Backhunter" features a round turquoise-pyrite inlay above the thong hole on each side of the desert ironwood handle. *(Cory Martin Imaging)*

▶ **GEOFF HAGUE:** Adjectives like "vulcanized," "stabilized" and "mosaic" describe the red fiber liners, spalted maple grip and two handle pins, respectively, of the RWL-34 drop-point hunter.

▼ **VASYL GOSHOVSKYY:** A hollow-ground ATS-34 blade affixed to a giraffe-bone handle procures a pretty drop-point hunter. *(SharpByCoop.com photo)*

▶ **JEFF BUSBIE:** The "Dark Hunter" is accomplished in Alabama Damascus and impala horn. *(PointSeven photo)*

▲ **WAYNE HENSLEY:** Mokumé gane and tiger coral lend alluring hues to a ladder-pattern damascus skinner. *(PointSeven photo)*

▶ **BRION TOMBERLIN:** The functional "Little River Hunter" is outfitted in a forged 1084 blade, desert ironwood handle and a Larry Parsons fitted pouch sheath.

(PointSeven photo)

101

▶ **JERRY MOEN:** The stainless steel bolsters of a drop-point hunter proved a proper palette for Nathan Dickinson gold inlay and engraving, butted up against mammoth ivory handle scales and stars for **pins.** *(PointSeven photo)*

▲ **STEVE LELAND:** The elk-horn-handle hunter is a welcome addition, here stretching a full 10.75 **inches.** *(PointSeven photo)*

▶ **KEVIN CASHEN:** The twist-damascus steel shows off the clip point or swedge of the hunter well, looking oh so sensational in a Sambar stag handle.

▶ **BILL BUXTON:** The "Mosaic W's" damascus is a nice, tight ladder pattern that plays to the blade shape and complements an amber-stag handle with a pommel shaped to match its grooves.
(Ward photo)

▶ **DANIEL ZVONEK:** With a tapered tang for balance, the CPM 154 skinner boasts maple burl handle scales, mosaic pins, stainless bolsters and a molded-lizard-skin sheath.
(PointSeven photo)

▼ **FRED OTT:** Japanese influences are evident on the three-bar-damascus hunter in a Thuya-burl handle and a stellar-sea-cow-bone spacer. *(BladeGallery.com photo)*

▶ **STEVE RANDALL:** That mesquite burl grip just screams class, as does the coined nickel silver spacer within a bronze ferrule, and the way the 52100 blade has equal amounts of shine and attitude. *(JZW Photography)*

▼ **VASYL GOSHOVSKYY:** Giraffe bone hugs the tapered tang of an ATS-34 drop-point hunter, and massages the palm of the outdoorsman who employs it. *(SharpByCoop.com photo)*

◀ **JOHN COHEA:** It didn't take pearl or gold, but walnut, copper and damascus to build a higher class of hunter. *(Ward photo)*

▶ **MARCUS LIN:** A Bob Loveless-style "Crooked Skinner" is orchestrated in the master's staples—a mirror-polished ATS-34 blade and a black-canvas-Micarta handle. *(Hiro Soga photo)*

▶ **DANA HACKNEY:** Presentation-grade curly Koa wood greases the palm of the happy hunter who owns this damascus piece with silica-bronze guard and pommel. *(BladeGallery.com photo)*

TRENDS **103**

A HIGHER CLASS OF HUNTERS

▶ **ROGER CLARK:** Garnering the "Hunter Award" at the 2013 Branson Hammer-In & Knife Show, this piece in an ironwood handle and ATS-34 blade curves in all the right places.
(Ward photo)

▶ **GARY WHEELER:** An upswept skinner gets the 324-layer random-pattern-damascus treatment, as well as a nickel silver guard and vintage Westinghouse ivory Micarta handle.
(PointSeven photo)

▶ **RICARDO VELARDE:** The stag-handle drop-point hunter, gorgeously engraved by Lucie Bandikova, would be a fine counterpart to an embellished shotgun. Or you could take it hunting and be the envy of the party.
(PointSeven photo)

◀ **KURT SWEARINGEN:** The upswept blade of the semi-skinner is appealing and utilitarian, stylishly handled in amber elk horn. *(Ward photo)*

▼ **DAVID ANDERS:** Like many of the more disciplined makers do today, the stainless steel pommel is file worked to match the contours of the stag handle on a 5160 drop-point hunter. *(PointSeven photo)*

▶ **MIKE DEIBERT:** A hunter and bird-and-trout knife combo fills the needs of the outdoorsman, parading maple-burl handles and 1095 blades with distinct temper lines. *(Ward photo)*

Push Dagger Presentation

▲ JOHN WHITE: There are very few "firsts" in the world, but a dog-bone push dagger in ancient walrus ivory might be one of them, also including a "Turkish twist" damascus blade, escutcheon plate, frame and finials, and domed sterling silver pins. *(Mitch Cohen & Prairie Digital photo)*

◄ CHAD NELL: All the push dagger is missing is blue, considering the white mother-of-pearl and red liners. Regardless, it's a fine presentation. *(SharpByCoop.com photo)*

▶ J. NEILSON: At 4 inches in length, the push dagger is the perfect size for slung-from-the-neck carry, and the chisel-ground ball-bearing-damascus blade a fashion accessory on its own, not to mention the Westinghouse Micarta® handle.

▶ LARRY MENSCH: The alternative ivory handle is sculpted to fit the hand, and the blade a leaf shape that's equally easy on the eyes.

▶ MICHAEL O'MACHEARLEY: If this were the only push dagger he ever made, it would be a successful endeavor, considering its mammoth ivory and damascus splendor. *(PointSeven photo)*

Worldwide Weaponry

Exoticism is rarely bad. It's never an insult to refer to someone as an exotic beauty. Exotic locales bring to mind beaches, coral reefs and the blue-green Caribbean Ocean. Exotic foods can tempt the taste buds, exotic plants add beauty to a room, and even exotic dancers, though not meeting the approval or lifestyle choices of everyone, hold a certain allure and mysticism.

Exotic weaponry, now that's a tasty cup of tea. Weaponry the world over takes on the characteristics and charms of the nation it represents. Each country has its own forms, patterns and styles of knives, swords, arms and armor. Many pieces are embellished for kings, queens and generals, and others boast purpose-driven designs that can punch their way through Volkswagens or Lamborghinis, depending, of course, on whether you're on the Autobahn or the Autostrade.

Like the planet itself, diversity reigns in the world of edged weapons. No two edges are alike, no handles the same, the guards ultimately twisted and turned in appealing ways, the blades pointed just so. Swords and daggers across the planet are as different as the people who hone and hold them, and isn't that refreshing? No, exoticism does not hold negative connotations, nor is it an insult to the senses, but rather a driver of diversity, and thanks to it, the world has a welcome place to parade its wares.

▶ **GEORGE YOUNG: They say the tanto tip may have begun as a broken sword blade, and the shape of this Samurai sword, exotically executed in a 6K Stellite™ blade and stabilized-wood handle, is a prime example.** *(PointSeven photo)*

▶ **TAD LYNCH: The "Irish Traveler" gets from place to place in ironwood, steel and wrought iron. Check out the temper line on that W2 blade.** *(Ward photo)*

◀ **E. SCOTT MCGHEE: A worldwide weapon of choice for 18th-century Europeans, the sword cane gets a remake here in damascus, Koa wood and copper.** *(SharpByCoop.com photo)*

▶ **CESARE TONELLI: The Italian knifemaker offers up an integral horn-handle RWL-34 knife with a blade shaped in the form of a Khanjar—Arab knife or dagger used in Turkey, India, the Balkans and Persia.** *(Francesco Pachi photo)*

► FRED OTT:
Combining Japanese
and Persian influences, the damascus
fixed blade is hafted in ironwood and outfitted in antiqued
and textured bronze fittings that hearken back to another
era. *(BladeGallery.com photo)*

▼ THINUS HERBST: A "Tizona Del Cid Sword"
(Tizona is the ancient sword carried by El Cid
to fight the Moors in Spain) parades an N690
blade, a sculpted bronze guard and pommel,
and a bird's-eye-maple handle.

▼ WALLY HOSTETTER: His Japanese Daisho,
or katana, is forged from 1084 high-carbon
steel with a wrapped Ho wood (magnolia from
the Honoki tree) handle. *(PointSeven photo)*

► ANSSI
RUUSUVUORI:
Is there anything
more exotic than
a mammoth-tooth-
handle Finnish
puukko with a hand-
forged blade? Maybe
a snow leopard lost in
Australia or something.

► RON NEWTON:
The Persian influence
on the upswept damascus
blade of the integral dagger
is undeniable, and black-lip pearl
intertwining amongst the frame also
cannot be denied. *(Ward photo)*

▶ **BRION TOMBERLIN:** The Filipino machete with "Janap"-style blade is hafted in ironwood and polished to show the blade's differentially heat-treated *hamon*, or temper line. Bronze fittings complete the **piece.** *(SharpByCoop.com photo)*

◀ **SCOTT GOSSMAN:** The Filipino-style CPM 3V bolo with black-and-green canvas Micarta handle scales will clear the vegetation in whatever jungle you've chosen to traverse.

▲ **PEKKA TUOMINEN:** A *puukko* (small Finnish belt knife) and *leuku* (big Sami/Lapland knife) combo comes in RWL-34 blade steel, birch bark and German silver.

▲ **ED BRANDSEY:** Named "The African," the damascus knife sports a gazelle-horn handle and elephant ivory, African blackwood and nickel silver spacers. The sheath is covered with **elephant hide.** *(Cory Martin Imaging)*

▶ **TIM TABOR:** Wickedly curved is all you can say about the blade of a Japanese-style piece with a cord-wrapped stingray-skin handle. *(Ward photo)*

◀ **DAVID MIRABILE:** Winner of the "Best Sword" at the 2013 BLADE Show, the wakizashi is executed in San Mai damascus, a titanium *tsuba,* or guard, a hilt of carbon fiber over Alaskan yellow cedar and an ancient walrus pommel. The handle ornament is a harpoon point **artifact.** *(SharpByCoop.com photo)*

▲ **JOHN WHITE:** Edged exoticism takes the shape of a 15-inch Persian dagger showcasing a four-bar-damascus blade, bolster and pommel, and a pre-ban-ivory handle. *(PointSeven photo)*

▲ **BRUCE NORRIS:** Apparently a classic "Roman Gladius Hispaniensis" sports a 25-inch W2 blade, a carved-bone hilt, Padauk-wood guard and pommel, and bronze fittings, because this beauty certainly does. *(Ward photo)*

◀ **J-T PALIKKO:** A fine example of a traditional Indian sword, the "Sosun Pattah II" is accomplished via a forged 28-inch T-ribbed blade, a cast-bronze hilt, etched and engraved decoration, and surface patina.

▶ **DIETRICH PODMAJERSKY:** Saxons didn't carry knives, but *seaxes,* and this is the maker's version in a W2-and-wrought-iron blade with wispy temper line, sterling silver bolsters and a Claro-walnut handle. *(SharpByCoop.com photo)*

▲ **KEVIN and HEATHER HARVEY:** The hot-gun-blued "Persian ribbon pattern"-damascus blade gets things rolling on a Swiss Baselard (short sword of the Late Middle Ages), while a box elder hilt and engraved guard and pommel further the presentation.

▶ **LOGAN PEARCE:** The decision to enlist Debbie Trotter to burn an image of a dragon onto the curly maple handle of the damascus tanto proved enlightened. *(Ward photo)*

▲ **ERIC EDQUIST:** Bronze-infused obsidian, a fluid damascus blade and bronze furniture define the "Swede Fighter." *(Ward photo)*

▲ **JONATHAN WICK:** A Roman-style dagger with what the maker calls a "Joe Keeslar twist," the piece sports an 11.5-inch differentially hardened 5160 blade, a forged integral guard, mesquite-burl handle, copper liners and nickel-silver pins. The sheath is leather-lined "fold-formed" copper.

◀ **JASON KNIGHT:** The "Raj Kukuri" features a "Dark Star"-pattern damascus blade with integral bolster that locks onto the African blackwood handle like a key hole fits over a key.
(SharpByCoop.com photo)

▶ **ANDERS HOGSTROM:** Wrap your mind, and fingers, if you'd like, around the Celtic-styled "Druid Sickle," also called a crescent sickle, with a claw-like, hand-ground Damasteel blade and "North Sea mammoth"-ivory handle.

▶ **VINCE EVANS:** If historic accuracy is what you're after, look no further than Vince's damascus Turkish Shamshir (curved saber) with fossil walrus ivory hilt, engraved blade, back strap and fittings, welded steel guard and gold and silver inlays.
(PointSeven photo)

▶ **ALAN FOLTS:** In the Spanish bowie realm comes a 15-inch piece with a differentially hardened blade, smoky temper line, Mokumé-and-copper guard and a cord-wrapped stingray-skin handle. *(Ward photo)*

◀ **VINCE EVANS:** An Italian Cinquedea (civilian short sword) gets its due, sashaying a grooved 16.5-inch pattern-welded blade, fossil ivory hilt, engraved steel guard, and engraved brass pommel cap and tang band.
(PointSeven photo)

Western Wares

Much of America's identity and culture was born in the West, where land was difficult to settle and those who conquered it were hardscrabble explorers, miners, farmhands and buckaroos. They didn't let the land beat them, but instead learned to live in harmony with the earth, to farm and ranch it, plant it, then cultivate, tend and harvest the fruits that it offered. They dug their fingers in the dirt.

It wasn't for the faint of heart, and the tools born from that era create a fabric that runs through the American spirit. Knives, tomahawks, daggers and axes helped fell trees, carve them into furniture, build fires, cook food, make saddles, skin game and defend oneself and family from enemies and all harm.

There is a look and a feel to the edged tools and weapons that populated the West. Those Western Wares tell stories of their own, having taken on a personality and look that conjures up images of cowboys, Indians and settlers of the sturdiest stock. They are distinctly American, weathered wares that won the West and made it their own. And a few— those who take kindly to strangers—have graced us with their presence.

▶ **JOHN COHEA: The handle material of choice for a big damascus bowie is mammoth ivory, which interestingly enough matches the jasper inlay of the leather sheath, with the knife and sheath also sporting wrought iron fittings.** *(Ward photo)*

▼ **GLEN MIKOLAJCZYK: The carved tiger maple haft of a pipe tomahawk is complemented by buckskin, feathers, a pierced damascus head and a damascus bowl.**
(Cory Martin Imaging)

▲ **ALAN TIENSVOLD: The maker had access to the original when creating this replica of an early 19th-century Henry Schively dirk, treating the 5160 high-carbon steel blade to an antique patina, tea staining and checkering the pre-ban elephant ivory handle and adding nickel silver fittings.**

▼ R.W. WILSON: Curly maple and mild steel are carved and engraved for the haft and head of a puff-ready pipe tomahawk. *(Cory Martin Imaging)*

▲ HEATHER HARVEY: A damascus steel spring has to be overcome in order to close the blade of the stag-handle mountain man folder with Mokumé-gane fittings. What patterning on the "paisley" damascus blade!

▶ LEVI GRAHAM: A bone handle and rawhide wrap add frontier flair to the handle and bolster of a high-carbon fixed blade. Cindy Morger did the quillwork for the band on the fringed leather sheath, which is further embellished by cones, horsehair and snake vertebrae. *(SharpByCoop.com photo)*

▶ LIN RHEA: A 5160 bit is laminated to the mild steel head of a maple-hafted tomahawk. *(Ward photo)*

▲ ED BRANDSEY: It doesn't get more western than a "scalping knife" in elk horn, turquoise, file-worked nickel silver, carved pipestone, and even a bison-horn inlay in the blade. *(Cory Martin Imaging)*

A Bromance with the Bowie

Guys and knives—it's a lot like guys and guns, or guys and cars or even guys and girls, well, not quite like guys and girls. Yet, there is a bromance going on, and a serious one, between knifemakers, collectors, enthusiasts and the bowie knife. It's a sordid affair that involves lovers and haters, an Iron Mistress, fakes, copies and reproductions, licensing, scandals, corruption, trademarks, historians and gentlemen callers.

Despite all the historical documentation, no one, it seems, really knows exactly what the very first bowie knife looked like, who made it or who owned it. It's named after Col. James Bowie, of course, and there was a guy named James Black involved, as well as James' brother, a Sandbar Fight and the Alamo. And ever since, guys who love knives have had a bromance with the bowie. They've forged their own versions, shaped them, honed them, manipulated them, changed them and rebuilt them all over again. They've been resized, redeveloped, retooled and reworked.

Yet the spark has never left the eye, the love never lost, the flame never snuffed. Maybe it's the mystery that is the ultimate allure. After all, it's usually the exotic ones who attract the most suitors. And perhaps it's good old American pride and patriotism. There's nothing quite like a hot model wrapped up in red, white and blue, and no one, and I mean no one, has ever been immune to the lure of the bowie knife.

▶ **NICK WHEELER:** The damascus bowie dances in the hand as well as in the moonlight. *(SharpByCoop.com photo)*

◀ **RALPH RICHARDS:** The maker delivers the goods in damascus and ironwood. *(Ward photo)*

▼ **BILL KIRKES:** Blackwood just seems fitting for the grip of a bowie honoring an original built by James Black. *(Ward photo)*

▲ **MICHAEL GREGORY:** With 10 inches of blade to work with, the maker used the space well, filling it with stag, stainless steel and the care of a craftsman.

JERRY VAN EIZENGA: No stops were pulled in fashioning the 19 5/8-inch "Confederate Bowie" with an oak handle and a lot of blood, sweat and tears. *(Ward photo)*

LIN RHEA: The "Gibeon Bowie" is a shapely damascus model forged from 15N20, 1084 and meteorite, handled in blackwood and guarded in stainless. *(Ward photo)*

LYLE SCHOW: From its fossil walrus ivory handle to the seashell "S"-guard and 41-layer damascus blade, this one whispers sweet nothings in your ear. *(Ward photo)*

SEAN O'HARE: A small copper spacer sandwiched by stainless steel in the ferrule helps highlight the brown hues of maple burl that, in turn, anchors the 1095 bowie blade.

JOE ZEMITIS: Such unusual amenities as a copper-and-silver ferrule wrap and brass fittings define the stag-handle 5160 bowie knife.

▶ **JOSEPH KEESLAR:** The maker's distinctive rustic style is evident in the southwestern bowie forged from 1084 high-carbon steel and given an amboyna burl handle with copper pins.
(PointSeven photo)

▼ **JAMES BATSON:** A Rees Fitzpatrick D-Guard bowie reproduction is an alluring combination of high- and low-carbon steels mated to a walnut handle.
(JZW Photography)

▶ **ROGER MASSEY:** Not only is the curly maple handle of the 1084 bowie knife checkered, but also the forged and heat-blued O1 double guard to match.
(PointSeven photo)

▶ **STEVEN RAPP:** The horse-head-pommel bowie might be a mainstay, but few are orchestrated like this CPM 154 steed in a stag saddle. *(PointSeven photo)*

▲ **JOSH FISHER:** The checkered ebony handle gives it a gun-grip feel, yet the Spanish notch and blued frame and fittings lend some exoticism to the piece.
(PointSeven photo)

STEVE RANDALL: The Cru Forge V bowie bends in all the right places, including the desert ironwood handle and hot-blued, mild-steel "S"-guard. *(JZW Photography)*

GARY MULKEY: Waves of damascus patterning washed up a clamshell pommel. *(Ward photo)*

BRION TOMBERLIN: Differentially tempered for a hard edge and soft spine, the smoky temper line denotes a job well done on the W2 blade of a stag-handle Southwest bowie. *(Ward photo)*

JOHN DAVIS: When fossils like oosic and mammoth tooth inhabit the handle of a damascus bowie, the historic significance of the package becomes apparent. *(PointSeven photo)*

FRED CARTER: French gray engraving and gold inlay enliven the ivory-handle bowie with flat-ground 440C blade.

▶ **BILL HERNDON:** His version of the original Iron Mistress from the 1952 Warner Bros. film parades an ebony handle and an ivory-backed "Jim Bowie" cutout. No two pins were alike on the original, or on the repro.

▶ **JOHN HORRIGAN:** Keep the elephant-ivory-handle vest bowie close to the vest or one might do more than covet those 24k-gold inlays or swirling damascus steel. *(PointSeven photo)*

▶ **MICHAEL RUTH SR.:** If 13 1/8 inches of damascus bowie blade aren't enough to send you into sensory overload, set your sights on the damascus clamshell guard and the pure-white elephant ivory grip. *(Ward photo)*

▼ **FOREST "BUTCH" SHEELY:** A crown-stag-pommel bowie with quillions on the guard gets the juices flowing. *(PointSeven photo)*

▼ **BRIAN THIE:** In a dog-bone style with domed pins, pre-ban-ivory handle and mosaic-damascus blade, just try to break up the bowie bromance. *(Cory Martin Imaging)*

► RICK MARCHAND: Hemp rope wraps around the handle of a 20-inch bowie with a forged O1 blade and copper strip on the spine. *(PointSeven photo)*

◄ JOHN WHITE: Follow the quill-like line of the feather damascus on up to the ivory haft. *(Ward photo)*

▼ PHIL EVANS: Dyed in a smoke black color with flame-like amber and yellow flats, the crown stag handle hints at the forge that fired the damascus bowie blade. *(Ward photo)*

► ALAN HUTCHINSON: Damascus and silver send shockwaves up the spines of all bowie detractors. *(Ward photo)*

▲ SAMUEL STONER JR.: The 5160 bowie blade is coal forged in old-order Menonite tradition using two horses on a treadmill to power the line shaft and all the shop tools! *(Cory Martin Imaging)*

▶ **LON HUMPHREY:** Curly maple clings on to the 10-inch bowie blade like a teenage girl with a crush. *(SharpByCoop.com photo)*

▼ **BILL BURKE:** Fossil walrus ivory and damascus are the two that tango before an appreciate audience of bowie lovers. *(Ward photo)*

▶ **MIKE DEIBERT:** The temper line on the 9-inch 1095 blade is so telling of the quality and workmanship that went into the maple-handle bowie. It also sports a blued mild steel guard, and quite dapperly at that. *(Ward photo)*

▶ **STEPHAN FOWLER:** Rosewood burl looks right as rain for the grip of a forged 52100 bowie/fighter. *(SharpByCoop.com photo)*

◀ **DOUG CAMPBELL:** The sinister look and feel of the damascus bowie with blackwood handle, otherworldly pin patterning and wrought-iron guard is spot on bad-to-the-bone bowie. *(Ward photo)*

▶ **JERRY FISK:** The eye-popping patterning of the 10-inch damascus blade is properly accompanied by an engraved guard and pommel, and a walrus ivory handle. *(Ward photo)*

▶ **D'ALTON HOLDER:** A vintage linen-Micarta® handle gives the highly polished 440C bowie a retro look. *(PointSeven photo)*

▼ **DANA HACKNEY:** The tight "twist" pattern of the damascus blade, guard and ferrule is a fitting match for the tight overall pattern of the stag-handle bowie itself. *(BladeGallery.com photo)*

◀ **BEN SEWARD:** The 9-inch W2 blade of the "Leatherman bowie" proudly displays its temper line like a buck parading a rack, possibly even the trophy animal that left us the stag handle. *(Ward photo)*

Food Preppers

A person's gotta eat. It doesn't matter if you're chopping carrots and potatoes for a tin foil meal over the campfire, or following a frou-frou recipe like those Emeril Lagasse, Rachael Ray and Paula Deen dish out (and there's nothing wrong with gourmet cooking on occasion), food prep is a big part of modern living. As one knife professional noted, families are spending more time in the kitchen, and thus spending more money upgrading not only their kitchens, but also appliances, tableware and tools, like cutlery.

One look at the edged "food preppers" on this and the following two pages, and you'll realize these aren't your mom's kitchen knives from the catchall silverware drawer. The best steels, most exotic handles and user-friendly shapes and sizes are reserved for the company of knife and food lovers alike.

With such food preppers, you'd expect white linen tablecloths, fine china and crystal glassware, but it's not necessary to get out Grandma's silver when preparing a nice meal for family and friends. The tools may be high-end, but there's no snobbery in this eatery. The makers of such fine cutlery stress only that the right tools make the job easier. So go ahead, food preppers, splurge a little. There's nothing like a chef's knife at hand when cutting pasta dough into thin slices for homemade noodles. Mmmm!

▲ **THOMAS HASLINGER:** The 9-inch blade of the "New Generation Chef" knife has a strong distal taper for balance, edge geometry and perfect cutting, and, oh, an ironwood grip for handling.

▼ **BILL BURKE:** Only Honduran rosewood would suffice as a counterpart to the 9.5-inch laminated damascus blade. *(PointSeven photo)*

▶ **JOHN HORRIGAN:** Each blade is a 1095-and-416-steel laminate anchored by stabilized-bird's-eye-maple grips, resulting in a trio of household helpers. *(Steve Woods photo)*

► **RAMON HUNT:** The 7-inch kitchen knife has a traditional German profile complemented by a stunning Brazilian rosewood handle. The O1 high-carbon-steel blade is flat ground and hand finished.
(PointSeven photo)

▼ **BEN TENDICK:** One chef's knife in carbon fiber, one in cocobolo, and a couple blades for slicing and dicing.

▼ **MICHAEL RADER:** The recipe for the wood grip of the 18-inch mar-quenched, hand-forged 52100 high-carbon-steel slicing knife calls for a pinch of curly mango, a dash of Hawaiian Koa and just a dab of box elder burl. *(BladeGallery.com photo)*

► **DON CARLOS ANDRADE:** Chef and bladesmith Don Carlos Andrade forged the small, full-tang Gyoto-style kitchen knife from 1095 high-carbon steel, adding a desert-ironwood handle with carved ridges for a firm grip when wet.
(PointSeven photo)

◄ **MARVIN WINN:** The maker fashioned a set of similar chef's knives for a customer, but his own wife fell in love with them, so here's the set he made for his sweetie, with buckeye burl handles, 154CM blades and cactus cellophane bolsters.

▲ **GLEN MIKOLAJCZYK:** If a forged-to-shape, 160-layer damascus blade doesn't cut the cauliflower, nothing will. Note the dyed-giraffe-bone grip and nickel silver bolster. *(Cory Martin Imaging)*

► **MIKE MOONEY:** East meet West within the confines of a CPM S30V carving set handled in African blackwood and Hawaiian curly Koa wood. The duo comes in a cedar wood box.

▼ **DAVID BRODZIAK:** And the carving commences via the full 8.75 inches of a Sandvik 12C27 blade anchored by a "snap and rattle" handle fashioned from the same piece of timber as the scabbard.

▼ **ERIK FRITZ:** Fitted with a rare, highly figured Afzelia-burl handle, the 52100 blade of the Gyoto chef's knife is triple quenched and tempered for a prime-rib-shaving sharp edge. *(PointSeven photo)*

► **NESTOR LORENZO RHO:** From the ebony-and-Alpataco-wood handles to the ducks engraved on the 420 stainless steel blade, the knife and fork set will tempt your taste buds. *(Frederico Koch photo)*

Natural-Handle Fighters

▲ KEVIN CASHEN: Damascus patterning dots and charts the multiple grind lines of an 11.5-inch stag-handle fighter.

▲ BEN SEWARD: An ironwood-handle "Equinex Fighter" boasts 5160 blade steel on the business end. *(Ward photo)*

► CHAD NELL: A Bob Loveless-style "Big Bear" demanded a slab of mammoth ivory and some CPM 154 steel. The knife is delivered in a Zac Buchanan sheath.
(SharpByCoop.com photo)

▼ JERRY MCCLURE: A crooked finger of a bowie/fighter, this one is handsome in its own right, parading damascus, copper and stag. *(Ward photo)*

▼ WILLIAM C. "BILL" JOHNSON: You can just feel the coolness of the blue brain coral cupped in your hand, can't you? *(Hoffman photo)*

▶ **JIM COFFEE:** Edged on top and bottom, the stag-handle damascus fighter ducks right, jabs left and finishes with a jaw-jarring uppercut. *(PointSeven photo)*

◀ **ED SCHEMPP:** Clad damascus never looked so clean or curvaceous as on this 15N20-and-52100 fighter with matching guard and butt cap, and a substantial stag grip. *(PointSeven photo)*

▼ **STEVE KOSTER:** One hand-forged 5160 blade, an elk-horn handle and a stainless guard and butt cap, and you've got yourself a fighter ... with a temper. *(PointSeven photo)*

▼ **BILL LUCKETT:** When the hand arrives at the ironwood grip, the finger rests against a stainless guard and acknowledges the wickedly re-curved CPM 154 blade before it.

▼ **KEVIN KLEIN:** Bloodwood is the hoof-shaped hilt at the end of the long, slender damascus fighter blade. *(SharpByCoop.com photo)*

▶ **DAN C. RAFN:** The uninterrupted flow includes an RWL-34 blade, 416 stainless steel bolsters and a mammoth-molar handle.

▼ **KEN HALL:** Grab hold and unlock the mysteries of the "African Blackwood Keyhole Fighter." *(JZW Photography)*

▶ **ERIK FRITZ:** Blackwood has a sobering effect on the "bloodshot eyes"-pattern damascus blade of a 14.5-inch fighter. *(PointSeven photo)*

▶ **PATRICE LEMEE:** From tip to rounded grip, the 1095 fighter is shrouded in darkness from its smoky temper line to an African blackwood handle and stark sign of the cross.
(SharpByCoop.com photo)

◀ **DERRICK WULF:** Rings of Koa wood introduce the 1095 fighter. *(PointSeven photo)*

NATURAL HANDLE FIGHTERS

▶ **GEORGE TROUT:** Ironwood, A2 steel and mosaic pins are transformed into a sub-hilt fighter. *(PointSeven photo)*

▼ **ALAN HUTCHINSON:** A bronze guard contrasts nicely with the sea-cow-rib-bone handle, and transitions into a length of 5160 fighter blade. *(Ward photo)*

▲ **BILL BUXTON:** If they all had swedges along their spines, like that along the "Turkish twist"-damascus blade, they'd be as tough as a Rhodesian Ridgeback, and the color of the fossilized-walrus-ivory grip. *(Ward photo)*

▲ **OLE PEDERSEN:** The "Sharkbird" takes flight via stabilized Moroccan Thuya burl and a beak of a CPM 154 stainless steel blade. *(BladeGallery.com photo)*

▶ **TONY HUGHES:** Damascus, mastodon ivory and gun-blued fittings give the bowie more character than Colonel James himself. *(SharpByCoop.com photo)*

▼ **DAVID LISCH: Put this one on your ring finger, and grip some stag.**
(SharpByCoop.com photo)

▲ **BILL MILLER: Say "fossil walrus ivory and 'W's'-pattern damascus" 10 times real fast.**
(PointSeven photo)

▶ **SHAWN KNOWLES: With this stag-handle fighter in hand, cutting is more pleasure, less chore.**
(SharpByCoop.com photo)

▶ **DAVID SHARP: The maker says the positioning of the guard close to the sub hilt on this Bob Loveless-style "Big Bear," along with hidden fasteners, allow for a neutral feel for the fighter, rather than the fingers and hand stretching.**
(SharpByCoop.com photo)

▲ **DON HANSON III and ANDERS HOGSTROM: The "H&H Subhilt" fixed fighter is outfitted in double-edged damascus, antiqued bronze, green fossil walrus ivory and ebony.** *(SharpByCoop.com photo)*

▶ **HARVEY KING:** The ensemble includes a stag handle, red liners, amber spacer, D2 blade and a brass guard and butt cap. *(Ward photo)*

◀ **BILL KIRKES:** It's the little things like vine file work along the spine of the 7.5-inch 5160 blade and dimpling on the ironwood handle that elevate the fighter to world-class status. *(Ward photo)*

◀ **EDMUND DAVIDSON:** Only stabilized box elder interrupts the flow of the one-piece/integral 440C blade, guard and pommel. *(PointSeven photo)*

▼ **DOUG CAMPBELL:** Mammoth ivory has a soothing effect on the damascus fighting blade with wrought iron guard. *(Ward photo)*

▲ **WAYNE HENSLEY:** Red liners highlight the stag-handle fighter in ATS-34 blade steel. *(PointSeven photo)*

► KEVIN HARVEY:
The fighter with random-"chaos"-pattern damascus blade and African blackwood handle was raffled successfully to raise money for the maker's niece and her cancer treatment. The engraved guard had to have helped.

► RONALD WELLING: The jury is no longer out on whether or not mammoth ivory, brass, wood and damascus can be combined into a ferociously handsome sub-hilt fighter. *(Ward photo)*

◄ STEVE RANDALL: The "S" guard curves toward the ironwood grip on one end and the CruForge V blade on the other. *(SharpByCoop.com photo)*

▼ TAD LYNCH: Wow does that W2 blade have a smoky temper line, and the fighter a mean demeanor appropriate for the genre. *(Ward photo)*

▲ SHAYNE CARTER: Damascus and ironwood prepare for the fight. *(SharpByCoop.com photo)*

STATE OF THE ART

Always leave a lasting impression. You don't have to tell knifemakers that twice. People who've never experienced the world of handmade knives are often left speechless after seeing quality pieces at shows, in magazines, or in this case, in a book. Very seldom does one witness truly handcrafted, quality items anywhere but at an art festival, craft show or in a handmade furniture or jewelry store. An individual certainly isn't getting the experience at a strip mall or big box store.

The art techniques knifemakers incorporate into their models have expanded over the years, and are no longer limited to scrimshaw, engraving, carving, sculpting and damascus pattern welding. In the not too distant past mosaic damascus made headway, and new to the mix this year are handle marquetry and mosaics, or handle inlays pieced together in patterns much like mosaic tiles.

There's a "Dyed in the Wood" section, a page reserved for "Animal-Printed Points," knives that are "Gold Inlaid and Bladed," some "San Mai Warriors" with San Mai or laminated-steel blades and "Dressed-Up Daggers" to complete a nice batch of offerings. A custom fixed blade without a handmade sheath is like a sundae without a cherry top, so a "Sheathing Review" seemed a fine choice to round out the "State Of The Art" section, and a good way, of course, to leave a lasting impression.

Handle Marquetry and Mosaics

▶ TOM LEWIS: The pins and handle are all mosaics, the latter in African blackwood and **Chakte Viga** *(Brazilwood).*

▶ ELIZABETH LOERCHNER: Cloisonné inlays are like the scales of a sculpted and dimpled amphibian that is ultimately the RWL-34 lock-back folder. *(Francesco Pachi photo)*

◀ VASYL GOSHOVSKYY: Mammoth ivory suspended in resin creates a mosaic of tile-like figures for the handle of a drop-point hunter. *(SharpByCoop.com photo)*

◀ EMMANUEL ESPOSITO: The C-Lock automatic prototype folder is fitted with an RWL-34 blade, and a stainless steel handle wearing a mosaic of black-lip pearl and old Bakelite™ inlays. *(Francesco Pachi photo)*

▲ BILL DUFF: Four woods zigzag across the handle of a 440C upswept bowie, creating masterful handle marquetry as they go. *(Ward photo)*

Animal-Printed Points

Maybe it's animal tracks etched on a blade or carved into a handle. Perhaps it's an elk deeply engraved into the bolster steel, a scrimshawed wildebeest or a snakeskin-covered handle. It could simply be a zebrawood handle with natural wood grains displaying stripes like those of a zebra or gazelle. Regardless, animal-printed points are knives outfitted in materials that pay homage to the animal kingdom.

Nature provides knifemakers with much of their inspiration, forms, shapes and materials. Talk to any knifemaker who's been plying his or her trade for a while, and they'll tell you that they often gain inspiration for blade shapes from tree leaves or blades of grass, and handle shapes from horns, branches or tusks. They use pearl, wood and precious stones in the makeup of their knives, while ivory, bone and stag remain popular choices.

Some embellish their knives with images of animals, like the "big five"—lion, elephant, cape buffalo, leopard and rhinoceros—of the African continent. Others use gemsbok horn and whale's-tooth handles. Mother Nature provides. And animal-printed points parade her glorious offerings for the world to see.

▶ **DAVID BRODZIAK:** A Tasmanian tiger (thylacine), hand painted by Carol Ann O'Connor, graces the handle of a damascus hunter, with the blade steel forged from an old shearing comb to achieve an animal print mimicking that of the thylacine.

▼ **CHARLES HAWKINS:** Yes, you're reading this correctly, that's an alligator-gar-skin (ray-finned fish) handle, complemented by a random-pattern-damascus blade, onyx/gold bolsters and mosaic pins.

▶ **JOE ZEMITIS:** Imagine pulling out the snakewood-handle straight razor and applying the damascus blade to lathered skin in the morning.

▲ **ROBERT KOVACIK:** The Swedish "Odin's Eye"-damascus blade is engraved with the image of a bugling elk, just to the right of an Australian goldfield wood handle with 14k-gold pattern numbers.

134

▲ T.R. LEWIS: Why wouldn't one think to crush turquoise, shape it into a roadrunner and inlay it into a maple-burl knife handle?

▲ THINUS HERBST: The knifemaker actually pierced images of the African "big five" through the 12C27 blade of his giraffe-bone-handle hunter. Amazing.

▲ T.C. ROBERTS: Darkened silver inlays depict a raven in flight and standing on the titanium bolsters of a gemsbok-horn-handle, mosaic-damascus folder. *(Ward photo)*

▲ MIKE PELLEGRIN: The 440C lock-back folder wears its spalted oak handle like a tiger wears its stripes. *(PointSeven photo)*

Ivory Artistry

White paper can't hold up to the milky, pure, solid, aged exterior of ivory. Not even oil on canvas can convey the deeply inked imagery of scrimshaw in ivory, where liquid dyes are poked into the pores via needles or hand-held gravers, scratched, embedded, painted into palatable pictures in living color. It's a singular art form with a fascinating history. Whalers on ships, out to sea for months at a time, rolling amid waves, rollicking, sitting down with pocketknives, needles, scrapers and sharpened marlinspikes, creating imagery in whale teeth and walrus tusks. You can't make this stuff up.

Modern scrimshaw is a far cry from early black-and-white whale tooth renderings, but the methods have changed little. These are not machined images, copies or transfers. Artists looked at natural forms and pictures popped into their heads. They had the skill to translate those mental images onto ivory, or into its pores, and in this case, the knife handles came alive, took on a life of their own.

Imagine picking one up, or better yet, use the Directory in the back of the book to look up one of the scrimshaw artists or knifemakers and purchase one of your own. Once you hold the utilitarian art in your hand, you'll be taken in. Don't fear using the knife—the painting won't wear off easily. You may even be inspired to take an ocean cruise, or at least paddle a dinghy around a lake for a while, after having gazed at the paintings, the incredible etchings, the ivory artistry.

◄ **GARY "GARBO" WILLIAMS:** Characters straight out of a Western adorn the ivory handle of a Ron Newton damascus dagger that also showcases Julie Warenski engraving, a damascus blade and gold beading. *(Ward photo)*

► **MIRELLA PACHI:** If the big cats and water buffalo don't engross you, how about the Gianfranco Pedersoli engraving on Paolo Brignone's RWL-34 fixed blade? *(Francesco Pachi photo)*

▲ **MARY BAILEY:** The Kim Breed ivory-handle ATS-34 folder isn't just talking turkey. *(PointSeven photo)*

► **LINDA KARST STONE:** The ivory-handle Jerry Moen knife with Nathan Dickenson engraving will provide you with a wagonload of memories. *(PointSeven photo)*

► **NICK FINOCCHIO:** The nude is as easy to embrace as the mammoth ivory handle of the Kevin Casey locking-liner folder in a feather-damascus blade. *(SharpByCoop.com photo)*

► **LAURIA TROUT:** The eagle profile and mammoth ivory have equal amounts of character, and Schuyler Lovestrand's fixed-blade fighter is the bladed beneficiary. *(SharpByCoop.com photo)*

◄ **DR. PETER JENSEN:** A Sioux in full regalia stares out from the mammoth ivory handle of a Johannes Ebner damascus fixed blade that also parades Kati Mau leaf engraving. *(Francesco Pachi photo)*

◄ **LINDA KARST STONE:** A specialist first class, Special Forces Afghanistan veteran and his awards and units are immortalized on the ancient-ivory handle of Bill Luckett's "American Warrior" fighter.

Etchings & Engravings

▶ **C.J. CAI:** The engraved, golden and copper Leonardo Da Vinci theme gracing the Joe Kious dress automatic folder is no less a masterpiece than the original paintings.
(SharpByCoop.com photo)

▲ **DAVID LARK:** Stay tuned to find out of the big cat gets the deer on the bolsters of a feather-pattern damascus hunter with a file-worked spine, mosaic pins and a burl oak handle.
(SharpByCoop.com photo)

▶ **JULIEN MARCHAL:** A pronounced scroll pattern adorns the bolter of an Andre Thorburn flipper folder in fiddleback Koa wood handle scales.
(PointSeven photo)

▼ **ROBERT KOVACIK:** Though the handle is Turkish walnut, attached with some cool mosaic pins, the engraving is all oak leaf, and deep and shaded, like the sanctuary an oak would provide.

▼ **ANTONIO MONTEJANO:** An RWL-34 stainless steel locking-liner folder by Leonardo Frizzi is gorgeously engraved and gold plated, depicting the seal of the Grand Masters of the Knights Templar.

► **PAUL MARKOW:** Bronze engraving not only enlivens the bolster area of a Kevin Casey locking-liner folder, but also brings out the colors of the little wires running through the "lighting strike" carbon fiber handle scales, and complements the feathery damascus blade pattern. *(SharpByCoop.com photo)*

▲ **FRED CARTER:** If cleanliness is next to godliness, then the engraved ivory-handle fighter is heavenly.

► **JULIE WARENSKI:** Engraving pierces the basket hilt and the heart of any sword lover who beholds the piece. Precious jewel and gold inlays, a thumb print bolster and damascus blade further the cause. *(PointSeven photo)*

► **JACK LEVIN:** The engraved pattern is modeled after the painting "Water" by medieval artist Giuseppe Arcimboldo, here embellishing a folding art knife with a Bertie Rietveld damascus blade and an artistic shield that opens automatically when the blade is unfolded. *(Francesco Pachi photo)*

▲ **LEE GRIFFITHS:** Bolster engraving on a pair of Mark Bair drop-point hunters represents the four species of big horn sheep in North America, while mammoth tooth handles and San Mai blades complete the pieces. *(PointSeven photo)*

▶ **FRED HARRINGTON:** Super scrollwork embellishes the hilt, sub-hilt and blade of a Bob Loveless-style "Big Bear" fashioned by William C. "Bill" Johnson. *(SharpByCoop.com photo)*

◀ **BARRY LEE HANDS:** There's raised engraving and gold overlays, there's inlaid engraving in the black-lip-pearl handle scales, and there's engraving on the blade of the gorgeous Tore Fogarizzu "T-Lord 1/7" art folder. *(Francesco Pachi photo)*

▼ **BARRY LEE HANDS:** Knifemaker Ron Lake told Barry to cover the thing in golden engraving, including the pearl handle and drop-point blade, and the engraver struck a vein, alright. *(SharpByCoop.com photo)*

◀ **VALERIO PELI:** It's not difficult to really dig this Salvatore Puddu dagger in vine and leaf engraving, black-lip pearl inlays, and golden touches all over the place. *(Francesco Pachi photo)*

▲ **KATI MAU:** "I'm a lion, hear me roar," and roar the Michael Jankowsky drop-point hunter does, outfitted in Elmax blade steel and an Arizona desert ironwood handle. *(Francesco Pachi photo)*

TOM FERRY: Skulls are trapped inside the carbon fiber handle scales of a "firestorm" damascus flipper folder that works off a full "Atomic bearing system." *(SharpByCoop.com photo)*

C.J. CAI: A sword-wielding Samurai warrior wears a golden hat and kimono, and Kanji characters spell out "must die sword" on the handle of a Keith Ouye CPM 154 flipper folder. *(Francesco Pachi photo)*

MICHAEL VAGNINO: Textured urethane handle scales resemble the scaly body of the serpent entwined on the bolsters of the locking-liner folder. *(SharpByCoop.com photo)*

LEE BERG: A compound, completely engraved kard (straight-bladed Persian knife) is put together like a classic Boy Scout knife-and-fork kit, but finely fit, finished and adorned in ivory, silver, nephrite jade, gold and rubies. *(Ward photo)*

CREATIVE ART: Raised golden and gray engraving gets things going on the guard of a Fabrizio Silvestrelli fantasy dagger that also sports a fluted mammoth ivory handle and an RWL-34 blade. *(Francesco Pachi photo)*

JULIEN MARCHAL: It took heat-colored "dragonskin" damascus along the edge of an otherwise mosaic-damascus blade of Bertie Rietveld's "Makiti" folder to compete with the engraved frame and black jade handle scales. *(Francesco Pachi photo)*

ETCHINGS & ENGRAVINGS

◀ **DENNIS FRIEDLY:** An owl with folded wings graces one side of the fully engraved folder, while game birds in flight adorn the other. *(PointSeven photo)*

▼ **JON CHRISTENSEN:** Reminiscent of Celtic engraving, let the artwork ease you into the mammoth-ivory-handle folder and its mosaic damascus blade. *(SharpByCoop.com photo)*

▶ **JOE MASON:** Leaf engraving with 18k-gold veins highlights the bolsters of a Mike Tyre damascus folder featuring mammoth ivory handle scales, blued titanium liners and vine file work along the spine. *(PointSeven photo)*

▼ **JON ROBYN:** Luck be a lady tonight, color engraved on the bolsters of a Warren Osborne lock-back folder in a Mike Norris damascus blade and black-lip-pearl handle scales. *(Cory Martin Imaging)*

▼ **LEE FERGUSON:** Vine and leaf engraving spreads along the brilliantly anodized titanium handle of a Damasteel locking-liner folder.

► **GARTH HINDMARCH:** Bark mammoth ivory is book-ended by engraved nickel silver bolsters like a portrait in a fancy frame.

► **DAVID RICCARDO:** Ancient scrolls have nothing over the engraving and 24k-gold inlay of a Jerry Halfrich lock-back folder. *(SharpByCoop.com photo)*

► **ROGER MASSEY:** Leaf engraving fans the piping-hot damascus folder like palm fronds cooling the king. *(Ward photo)*

▲ **TONY PITTS:** This Pete Truncali lock-back folder hums, complete with golden humming bird and some scrolls, leaves and other artistic amenities. *(Ward photo)*

▼ **MARIAN SAWBY:** An engraved hibiscus and butterfly theme is the sweet nectar of a Scott Sawby "Shearwater" folding dagger with jasper handle inlays.

▲ **DAMON SOILEAN:** Graciously engraved and gold inlaid is a Peter Martin black-lip-pearl girl in a Devin Thomas stainless damascus blade. *(Cory Martin Imaging)*

► **JIM SORNBERGER:** With more than one koi fish to color anodize and engrave, the maker needed two locking-liner folders to fit it all in.

► **TINUS OELOFSE:** The maker engraves a pair of 12C27 locking-liner folders in mammoth-ivory and mammoth-bark-ivory handle scales. *(PointSeven photo)*

► **JODY MULLER:** The engraved handle of a damascus locking folder depicts a bone yard of flag-waving skulls. *(SharpByCoop.com photo)*

► **JERE DAVIDSON:** Edmund Davidson's solid CPM 154 integral drop-point hunter is cloaked in wrap-around engraving of the finest kind. *(PointSeven photo)*

▲ **JOE MASON:** Engraved battle scenes create a colorful and touching tribute to POW's and those missing in action, all within the confines of a Tom Overeynder damascus lock-back folder. *(SharpByCoop.com photo)*

► **LISA TOMLIN:** Engraving surrounds a jade grip like a bezel grasping a gemstone and parading it before a royal court, and, of course, the Howard Hitchmough Damasteel folder is worthy of the king. *(PointSeven photo)*

◄ **ANTONIO MONTEJANO:** It's a testament to knifemaker Vasyl Goshovskyy that the engraver chose to depict Pablo Picasso's "Guernica" painting on the RWL-34 drop-point blade of a sheep-horn-handle hunter. The original painting was done in response to the bombing of Guernica, and has come to symbolize the suffering that war inflicts upon individuals, particularly innocent civilians. *(SharpByCoop.com photo)*

▼ **PIERRE LE BLANC:** Fleur-de-lis engraving decorates the guard of a James Glisson drop-point skinner. And completing a theme, the piece showcases a mammoth-ivory handle scrimshawed by Kurtz Miller to depict the alligators of our swampy waters once settled by the French. *(Ward photo)*

► **NATHAN DICKINSON:** Honoring Texas Governor Rick Perry, including the State of Texas seal, Jerry Moen's engraved ivory-handle folder in a CTS-XHP blade is already enjoying a warm reception. *(PointSeven photo)*

▲ **JODY MULLER:** Such a fantastic Frankenstein theme has to help sell the Pete Carey "Nitro" flipper folder in a Chad Nichols "Blackout" damascus blade.

Gold Inlaid and Bladed

Gold is a commitment. If you're afraid of commitments, you should pretty much stay away from gold. You don't want to sell your house and all your belongings, and buy a pack mule, a pickaxe, sluice box and a trommel if you're not serious about panning for gold. You shouldn't purchase that wedding ring after one fun, riotous night of dancing, singing, drinking and lovemaking unless you're just as sure you are in love months later as you were the night of.

As Beyoncé sings, "If you like it then you should have put a ring on it," meaning, if you're sure you love her, then you should have purchased the gold ring, but don't expect any lovin' until you do. So, are you ready to make the gold commitment? The makers of these knives sure were.

When figuring profits, losses, investments and potential earnings, custom knifemakers must determine if the return on their investments will be greater than the upfront costs, and of all the materials purchased, gold, silver, gemstones and exotic materials like platinum and meteorite are the most costly. But oh, what gold does to a knife! It bespeaks class, style and grace. It adds color and allure. Gold inlaid and bladed knives appeal to a higher class of clientele, more discerning, with more disposable income, and they're not afraid to make a commitment. So if you like it, put some gold on it.

▶ **S.R. JOHNSON:** A Bob Loveless-style sub-hilt fighter gets the Barry Lee Hands gold inlay, overlay and engraving treatment, from the flats of its CPM 154 blade to the stainless guard, mother-of-pearl handle and even the rear bolster. The design elements are set with more than 100 green and white diamonds, oh, and pink **sapphires.** *(PointSeven photo)*

◀ **JOHANNES EBNER:** Like bark on a tree branch, the textured gold bolster cleverly covers and mimics the natural exterior of the hematite handle, and spruces up an already remarkable damascus fixed blade.

▶ **STEVE HOEL:** Gold leaves didn't just fall on the folder, but were planted there by engraver Barry Lee Hands, with some diamond inlays for good measure. *(PointSeven photo)*

▲ **JERRY MCCLURE:** If a gold moon face on brilliant Mokuti handle material doesn't make you smile, maybe flipping open the "dot matrix" damascus blade will do the **trick.** *(SharpByCoop.com photo)*

LEONARDO FRIZZI: The file work and screws are 24-karat gold, the damascus of the Devin Thomas ilk, and the titanium handle engraved by Antonio Montejano of Spain.

RODRIGO SFREDDO: Gold and copper leaves softly land on the damascus blade and puzzle-piece-like bolster of an ironwood-handle fixed blade. Even the maker's mark is in gold. *(SharpByCoop.com photo)*

RONALD BEST: Sculpted into one hellacious auto folder are abalone, gold and damascus steel. *(SharpByCoop.com photo)*

LEE FERGUSON: Gold and gold-filled twisted wire make up only one redeeming quality of the fixed blade, which also enlists a Kevin Casey feather-pattern damascus blade and a buffalo-horn grip carved into a calla lily. *(Ward photo)*

JOHNNY STOUT: The "Aristocrat" locking-liner folder parades a crackle-mammoth-ivory handle, a Turkish-twist damascus blade and some golden vine and scroll engraving by Alice Carter.

▼ **BILL HERNDON:** Bill's interpretation of a Herman Schneider "De Santis Dagger" sports a black-oxide-treated 1060 high-carbon-steel blade, mother-of-pearl handle scales and Gil Rudolph's gold inlay and logo work.

▶ **JOHN HORRIGAN:** Gold vines creep along the "firecracker"-pattern damascus blade and the stainless steel rear bolster, framing a carved pre-ban elephant ivory handle. *(Steve Woods photo)*

▶ **REINHARD TSCHAGER:** Simple touches like file work and a gold border and pins enhance the pearl-handle damascus pieces. Anthony Metsala forged the blade steel.

▲ **C. GRAY TAYLOR:** The pheasant and golden retriever are truly golden, with kudos to Lisa Tomlin for the artwork, complemented by antique-tortoise-shell handle scales, 19 blades and implements, and a heavy dose of knifemaking wizardry. *(PointSeven photo)*

Dyed in the Wood

▶ **CHARLES HAWKINS:** In this particular case the colorful grip is dyed and stabilized box elder matched up with onyx/gold bolsters, black fiber spacers, mosaic pins and a raindrop-damascus blade.

▲ **BILL LYONS:** Silver wire cordons off sections of dyed curly maple for an array of color and shape, further emphasized by the lines and shapes of a twist-damascus blade. *(PointSeven photo)*

▶ **J.P. MILLER:** Painted for an authentic look, the antiqued 1095 blade and brass tacks further the theme of a gunstock war club. *(Cory Martin Imaging)*

◀ **EDMUND DAVIDSON:** Stabilized black-ash and box elder burls bring notes of color to a shapely pair of CPM 154 full-integral fixed blades. *(PointSeven photo)*

▲ **MIKE MOONEY:** Dyed redwood burl handle scales attached with mosaic pins adorn the damascus Santoku knife.

Damascus Patterns Parade

▶ **STEVE HILL:** Inspired by the wedding of Col. James Bowie and Ursula Veramendi, a Cupid's arrow pierces a pair of hearts on the tiger maple handle of the endearing damascus fixed blade.

▶ **STEVE MILLER:** A little blade bluing goes a long way on the full-integral Alabama Damascus drop-point skinner with a stabilized Amboyna burl handle and gold-plated Torx™-head screws. *(PointSeven photo)*

◀ **MIKE CRADDOCK:** The feather-like pattern of a damascus gent's bowie, as well as the buffalo horn handle, tickles the fancy. *(SharpByCoop.com photo)*

▶ **LIN RHEA:** A scintillating damascus blade makes up the business end of a blackwood-handle sub-hilt fighter showcasing guard and pin engraving by Jim Small. *(Caleb Royer Studio photo)*

▶ **MARK KNAPP:**
Spot on damascus blade
patterning by Mike Norris
shares billing with a Mokumé
guard, and a mammoth tooth
and blue amber handle.
(SharpByCoop.com photo)

◀ **RICK "BEAR BONES"
SMITH:** The steep ladder pattern
of the cutlass-style bowie would
make a pirate weep, as might the
sweet stag grip.

▼ **KEVIN HARVEY:** Where
the damascus pattern stops,
the Mokumé and box elder burl take over.
(Connie van der Merwe/Cornelius Photography photo)

▲ **J. NEILSON:** Not all three-bar twist
damascus blades looks this good, just
the stuff the smiths really work at, in this
case accompanied by a walnut handle and
brass guard and pins. *(Ward photo)*

▶ **KEVIN CASEY:**
The maker's own
feather damascus
dresses up the
locking-liner folder
handled in mammoth
ivory, and with care.
(SharpByCoop.com photo)

◀ **LOGAN PEARCE:** The 17.5-inch blade
of the "Tenkai" model rolls with "wave"
damascus splashing up against textured
and blued brass, and a leather-wrapped,
blue sting-ray-skin handle. *(Ward photo)*

▶ **DAVID LOUKIDES:** A 10.75-inch length of damascus is well anchored in sambar stag. *(SharpByCoop.com photo)*

◀ **ANDERS HOGSTROM:** As straight as the dagger is, the twist-damascus blade and snakewood handle slither their way along the pointed path. *(SharpByCoop.com photo)*

▼ **W.D. PEASE:** A lively lock-back folder rocks a Robert Eggerling damascus blade, integral G-10 bolsters and frame, ivory handle scales and nickel silver pin work. *(PointSeven photo)*

▼ **MIKE FELLOWS:** He calls it a "ripple twist"-pattern damascus blade, and who's to argue, complemented by file-worked titanium liners, engraved mild steel bolsters and green-mammoth-ivory handle scales?

▼ **ROB HUDSON:** The coordinated drop-point hunter dons a ladder-pattern Damasteel blade, an ironwood handle, stainless guard and pommel, and yellow and orange maple spacers.

▲ **MARK NEVLING:** If a knife is going to sport a "Super Nova" damascus blade and bolsters, it might as well be a "First Responder," and then one should probably outfit it in brown and blue mammoth ivory.

▶ **KYLE ROYER:** There's a lot going on within the mosaic-feather-pattern damascus blade of an ebony-handle art knife with silver line inlays. *(Caleb Royer Studio photo)*

▶ **OWEN WOOD:** Chevrons run through the "New Boston Dagger," done up in composite damascus, and a stainless steel handle with gold, pearl and Ettore Gianferrari damascus inlays.
(Francesco Pachi photo)

▶ **SERGIO RAMONDETTI:** The folder sports a Robert Eggerling high-carbon damascus blade and blued damascus bolsters, along with fossil mammoth ivory handle scales.

▼ **KEVIN CROSS:** It's a "Star Fighter," need we say more? Well, I guess we could credit Doug Ponzio with the damascus, and an ancient walrus for the handle.
(SharpByCoop.com photo)

▶ **DAN CHINNOCK:** A mammoth ivory handle with lots of character was necessary to absorb the shock of the Chad Nichols damascus blade and bolsters. *(Ward photo)*

▶ **BRUCE BARNETT:** The galaxy may not be ready for these two starburst-pattern damascus slip joint folders in mammoth ivory grips. *(PointSeven photo)*

▶ **TOM PLOPPERT:** This ivory-handle slip-joint folder has two sharp, pointed feathers in its cap. *(SharpByCoop.com photo)*

▼ **LANDON ROBBINS:** Did the damascus drip down that way, or did the talented blade smith plan such prized patterning? *(Ward photo)*

▶ **BRUCE BUMP:** "Zebra herd" damascus might just cause a stampede of knife collectors, particularly considering the pre-ban ivory handle and Brian Hochstrat engraving. *(Ward photo)*

▶ **ALLEN ELISHEWITZ:** Lines enliven the Chad Nichols damascus blade that pops out from within the black Moku-Ti handle scales and zirconium bolsters via a flipper mechanism.

▶ **BUTCH BALL:** A blistering Larry Donnelly damascus blade pattern was handpicked and forged for the blue-mammoth-ivory-handle folder.
(PointSeven photo)

▶ **BILL BEHNKE:** Eye candy includes a keen damascus blade, amber spacer and ironwood handle.
(Ward photo)

▶ **LEE GENE BASKETT:** A locking-liner folder is draped in Mike Norris damascus, blue mammoth ivory, gold and Paul Markow engraving.
(PointSeven photo)

▲ **AARON WILBURN:** A "serpentine feather" pattern is paraded before a crowd of fightin' knives fans.
(PointSeven photo)

▶ **JOEL WORLEY:** Feathery light damascus ingratiates one to the mammoth-ivory-handle bowie.
(Ward photo)

▼ **JOHN WHITE:** The "Blackheart" dagger shows it has a good side, considering a composite-damascus blade of Turkish twist and explosion patterns, and a carved African blackwood handle.
(Ward photo)

► **TERRY SCHREINER:** The 20-twist Damasteel blade of the "Boxer" shares the ring with an American bison-horn handle and mosaic-damascus fittings. *(Ward photo)*

► **DAVID LISCH:** A stag-handle "ring D-guard bowie" dresses in "dragon feather damascus" for its big day in the spotlight. *(Ward photo)*

▼ **PETER MARTIN:** Feather damascus fulfills its duty in dressing up the gemsbok-horn-handle bowie. *(Cory Martin Imaging)*

► **CRAIG STEKETEE:** So patterned is the sharp damascus blade, it almost looks slinky, perhaps emphasized by the "S"-guard and highly figured stag. *(Ward photo)*

▼ **GEOFF HAGUE:** Damasteel "Vinland" and "Heimskringla" patterns cover the blade, bolsters and even the back spring of a giraffe-bone-handle slip joint folder.

▶ **PETE CAREY:** One pattern is straight and black-and-white, while the other is colorful and curvy. Chad Nichols is credited for the blade steel.

▲ **RALPH RICHARDS:** Like rungs of a ladder, the damascus patterning ascends the blade from guard to tip, and back down again to the ironwood handle of the big, bad bowie. *(Ward photo)*

▲ **RON NEWTON:** For a knife in the style of a Michael Price bowie, Newton's own Wootz steel is forged in a Second Amendment theme, including a 9mm handgun and AR-15 rifle, each surrounded by tight Turkish-twist-damascus bars. The two phrases in the core are "Right to keep and bear arms," and "Just try to take them!"
(Ward photo)

▲ **JERRY FISK:** Adding anything other than a perfectly-pattern damascus blade to the engraved, mammoth-ivory-handle hunter would have been "Fisk-ally" irresponsible. *(Ward photo)*

▲ **LARRY COX:** I'm not sure if the "385 Damascus Bowie" has a 385-layer blade, or if that's how many days there would need to be in a year to fully appreciate it and its giraffe-bone handle. *(Ward photo)*

Carving Out a Knife

Some people carve out pretty good lives for themselves. Others carve out a knife or two for themselves. The two don't have to be mutually exclusive, and honestly, I'm sure they're usually not. Those who have chosen to fashion knives for a living, or at least part time after returning home from the day or night job, are cut from sturdy stock. They are chiseled from fine stone, have good genetics, come from good bloodlines. They're hard working, self sufficient, unwavering and don't ask for a lot … no handouts.

They are good people, know what they're made of, and what's inside is really what counts, much like the knives they carve out. At the heart of each one is a blade that cuts, is easy to hone and holds an edge. Then they add embellishment, in this case a carving, chipping away at handle, blade, guard or bolster material, getting to its core, and then forming objects, animals, skulls, flowers or beings, and bringing them to life.

It takes a good egg to know one. When you're carving out a life for yourself, it's nice to also have the ability to carve out a knife for yourself. And these guys and gals really know how to carve out a knife.

VLADIMIR BURKOVSKI: Fossil ivory is carved into "Lucky Bamboo and Frogs," but the onlookers are the lucky ones, also gazing at a Roger Bergh damascus blade and stabilized blue coral inlays. *(Francesco Pachi photo)*

TOMMY MCNABB: The outdoor scene carved from elk antler includes a bear looking to ascend a tree, mushrooms growing on the ground below him. The damascus dagger bears a couple turquoise spacers, too. *(JZW photo)*

BILL MILLER: Carved stag is "skullicious," making up the handle end of "The Nail" damascus fixed blade, complete with coffin display box. *(Ward photo)*

► **RICK LALA:** Titanium is anodized and cleverly carved into a Samurai warrior theme for the handle frame of a Damasteel flipper folder. *(PointSeven photo)*

► **ANDREA PULISOVA:** Hippo tooth changes its looks like a chameleon, or I guess the talented knifemaker carved it into a chameleon, adding a mosaic damascus blade and a buffalo horn spacer.

◄ **ARPAD BOJTOS:** "Ariel" the Little Mermaid comes to life on a damascus art knife with gold and black-lip-pearl inlays, and carving galore of the precious and semi-precious metals. *(SharpByCoop.com photo)*

► **MICHAEL BURCH** and **JODY MULLER:** That's some sea monster cast, or carved, in the bronze grip of the "Deep Sea" dress locking folder with a CPM 154 blade and black-lip-pearl inlays. *(SharpByCoop.com photo)*

▲ **ANDERS HOGSTROM:** There was only one person who knew what the buffalo bone was going to look like when done—he who built the Damasteel cleaver and carved a grip for it. *(SharpByCoop.com photo)*

▶ **KAJ EMBRETSEN:** Few arches, colonnades, columns or Baroque architectural features are fancier or finer than the carved grip of the damascus art folder with gold bail, pins and dots. *(SharpByCoop.com photo)*

▶ **WILLIAM LLOYD:** Is it safe to say this one is skulled and cross-honed? Carved bone comes back to life in a skull theme, highlighting a dagger blade with deep fullers and precious stone inlays. *(PointSeven photo)*

▲ **JOEL WORLEY:** Sculpted walrus ivory is the chocolaty sweet substance that makes up the handle of a damascus fixed blade with bronze guard. *(PointSeven photo)*

▲ **TERRY LEE RENNER:** Pierced and carved Alabama Damascus overlaid onto an anodized titanium frame gives the CPM S30V flipper folder an exotic—crane among bamboo—feel. *(SharpByCoop.com photo)*

▲ **MIKE FELLOWS:** Hippo tooth handle scales are deep relief carved with a full rose on the front and a bud on the reverse side, sprouting a ladder-pattern damascus blade and titanium liners.

San Mai Warriors

▲ **KARL B. ANDERSEN:** Having his hands on a 5,000-year-old piece of bog oak, the maker decided to fashion a San Mai blade for the piece, using 1095 tool steel for the edge with 420 stainless outer layers.

▲ **CLAUDIO SOBRAL and RYAN WEEKS:** The blade, by Claudio, is of San Mai construction with a stainless steel core and stunning O1 edge, complemented by Ryan's bog oak handle, steel guard and G10 liner. *(SharpByCoop.com photo)*

▶ **LARRY COX:** Licking the edge of the "Ghost Flame Damascus Hunter" is fiery damascus patterning laminated to 5160 outer layers of blade steel, all anchored by an English walnut handle. *(Ward photo)*

◀ **JERRY FISK:** The San Mai, or laminated, blade is W2 tool steel with a distinct damascus core that dazzles, doesn't it? *(Ward photo)*

◀ **JOHN HORRIGAN:** The laminated blade is 1095 and 416 stainless, while the guard is 24k-gold inlaid, and the handle of the carved and checkered elephant ivory variety. *(Steve Woods photo)*

Sculpted Steel

▶ **RON BEST:** The stepped terraces of Southeast Asia have nothing over the sculpted 416 stainless steel frame of the automatic lock-back folder, which also showcases a Damasteel blade, and handle inlays of gold and lapis lazuli. *(SharpByCoop.com photo)*

▼ **SUCHAT JANGTANONG:** Even the damascus blade is pierced and shaped, adding to the overall theme of a scroll-sculpted art folder with black-lip pearl inlays, and file-worked and anodized titanium liners and back spacer. *(SharpByCoop.com photo)*

▶ **JERRY MCCLURE:** The pull of the moon created a high tide of gold and stainless steel waves along the handle of the stainless-damascus "Duce" folder. *(Ward photo)*

▶ **WOLFGANG LOERCHNER:** The winged bird is one hot, chiseled model, all in stainless steel and stainless damascus. *(SharpByCoop.com photo)*

▲ **BRIAN TIGHE:** A fluted, re-curved Damasteel blade complements a sculpted and heat-colored Timascus handle. *(PointSeven photo)*

◀ **RON APPLETON:** The dress, locking folder is sculpted and grooved in all the right places. I believe that's a Mokumé handle inlay. *(SharpByCoop.com photo)*

◀ **MARK DALETZKY:** We can thank Luis Chavez for the chase and repoussé work, bringing flora and fauna to life on the silver handle and sheath of a damascus art knife.
(SharpByCoop.com photo)

▶ **RICK LALA:** The pirate skull theme is more than evident on the carved and purple-anodized titanium handle of a CPM S30V folder. *(PointSeven photo)*

▶ **ELIZABETH LOERCHNER:** It truly is sculpture when it's an all-steel piece, in this case RWL-34 and 416 stainless. *(Francesco Pachi photo)*

▲ **LIBOR TOBOLAK:** The claws of "The Sibyl" present an emerald at the pommel of a sculpted art knife in a solid tropical-hardwood handle and a pierced damascus blade.

Mosaic Makers Union

I f it were a true worker's union, there would be benefits other than job satisfaction. Wage increases would be factored into a contract, as would a retirement savings match, short- and long-term disability, conditions on firing or layoffs and some sort of medical and dental insurance carrying over after retirement and into the waning years of one's life.

There's none of that with the Mosaic Makers Union (MMU). It's not really a labor union, as such, but a union of men and women who are passionate about forging mosaic-damascus steel into repeating patterns, whether whimsical, natural, geometric or picturesque. They have the ability to envision what canister steel, bars or billets will look like after being cut into shapes, forge welded together, bent, twisted, hammered, flattened, smoothed and etched.

They make images in steel, not digitally, or on film, canvas, paper or plates, but within one of the hardest substances known to man—steel alloys that, when forged together, heat treated and etched, contrast with each other and create forms and shapes, even letters of the alphabet. No one watches out for the well being of the MMU. They are not insured, contracted, guaranteed or salaried. They are artists who have communed for a common cause, and what a creative endeavor it has become!

◀ **JOSH SMITH:** A sea of blue and mother-of-pearl, the maker forged the twisted mosaic damascus from steel scraps, and if you look close you can see his "JS" initials in the blade. *(PointSeven photo)*

▼ **DON HANSON III:** The maker scared up some mosaic damascus for the bolsters of his dress tactical folder in a W2 blade and mammoth ivory handle scales. *(SharpByCoop.com photo)*

▼ **GLEN MIKOLAJCZYK:** The mosaic makers union busied itself forging bars of steel for a mosaic-damascus blade and W's-pattern-damascus bolsters. *(Cory Martin Imaging)*

▲ **CLIFF PARKER:** A stag like the one forged into the steel left some highly figured antler for the handle of the fine folder. *(Cory Martin Imaging)*

► **MARK NEVLING:** Skull bolsters add a touch of whimsy to the "Harpoon" folder in a San Mai damascus blade and "lightning strike" carbon fiber handle scales.

◄ **BILL BURKE:** Mosaic damascus and Ziricote burl prove to be a food prepping dream team. *(PointSeven photo)*

▲ **MIKE TYRE:** While the maker forged the damascus bolsters, Robert Eggerling did the mosaic-damascus blade honors, all combined with mammoth ivory handle scales and an opal thumb stud. *(PointSeven photo)*

► **RICK DUNKERLEY:** The "dry flies and winding river" mosaic-damascus blade and bolsters do the Montana maker proud, and the mother-of-pearl handle scales are a nice catch, too. *(PointSeven photo)*

◄ **STEVE NOLTE:** It took a wide skinner blade to fit in all the images the mosaic maker had in mind, and for his hand he envisioned an ironwood grip with an Al Frisillo-engraved guard and bolsters. *(Ward photo)*

▶ **BARBIE NOLTE:** Between the blue mammoth ivory, the Al Frisillo engraving and the mosaic-damascus blade, it's a beauty, for sure.

▶ **MICHAEL CHRISTENSON:** The 1084-and-15N20 mosaic-damascus blade might be squares of steel, but it's got plenty of curve and a nicely rounded ironwood grip. *(JZW photo)*

◀ **KYLE ROYER:** No two mosaic-damascus blades are alike, nor would many makers attempt this 19-inch fighter showcasing a mammoth-ivory handle and 18k-gold inlays. *(Caleb Royer Studio photo)*

◀ **J.W. RANDALL:** The "Saddle Bronc Bowie" bucks any previous forging trends, taking a wild ride via mosaic damascus, fossil walrus ivory and 24-karat gold.

▲ **JUKKA HANKALA:** A steel steed holds his head high on the heat-colored mosaic-damascus bolsters of a flavorful folder in a mammoth-ivory grip.

► **ATTILIO MOROTTI:** The "Unicorns" mosaic damascus blade by Luca Pizzi called for a fluted antique narwhal tusk handle and carved gold spacer rings. *(Francesco Pachi photo)*

▲ **RON NEWTON:** The "Window Of China" model is a mosaic-damascus masterpiece, and handled in mammoth ivory no less. *(Ward photo)*

▲ **MIKE FELLOWS:** The miniature inter-frame folder benefits from a heat-blued powder-mosaic-damascus blade in a "Duchess" pattern, file-worked 9k-gold liners and black-lip-pearl inlays.

► **REINHARD TSCHAGER:** Stars in black-as-night steel make a lasting impression, trailing toward engraved gold inlays and pins and a giraffe bone handle.

Dressed-Up Daggers

▶ **JOHN HORRIGAN:** The "Kings Crown Dagger" indeed has a crown-shaped pommel parading ruby, sapphire, amethyst and emerald inlays, with the flashy piece also donning a 24k-gold-inlaid "firecracker"-pattern damascus blade, a fluted-ivory handle and a hot-blued **guard.** (SharpByCoop.com photo)

▼ **MIKE FELLOWS:** The composite mosaic-damascus blade is exquisite, matched up with a carved, engraved and heat-blued guard and pommel, and a carved elephant ivory grip.

▶ **MARDI MESHEJIAN:** A pierced-damascus blade dipsy-doodles its way down to a carved rosewood grip with a recessed sterling silver mark. (PointSeven photo)

▲ **JIM SORNBERGER:** An engraved silver handle holds inlays of coral and tortoise, tempting one nearer the ATS-34 dagger blade.

▲ **J.W. RANDALL:** Playful damascus patterning softens the look of the pointed dagger blade, an effect furthered by the abalone-inlaid mammoth ivory handle.

▶ **JEFF BUSBIE:** The "Skull Dagger" is all Alabama damascus but for the giraffe-bone handle, mosaic pins and fancy file work. *(PointSeven photo)*

▼ **STUART SMITH:** A bronze guard, ferrule and pommel bookend the ironwood handle of the "W's"-pattern damascus dagger.
(image by erinphoto.co.za)

▶ **BRUCE BUMP:** Dice are loaded into pommel of the damascus "Gambler's Dagger," which is also treated to Joe Mason engraving and gold inlay work.
(SharpByCoop.com photo)

▶ **BILL JOHNSON:** The snakewood grip is spiral fluted with a twisted wire overlay that plays off the damascus pattern of the dressed-up dagger. *(Cory Martin Imaging)*

▲ **ANDERS HOGSTROM:** Get a load of the gambler's dagger in a fossil-walrus-ivory grip, dimpled bronze guard and twist-pattern damascus blade.

▶ **KYLE ROYER:** What master smiths are doing with damascus these days—in this case a 14-inch mosaic-damascus blade with twist-mosaic outer edges—is as incredible as what they're doing with pre-ban elephant ivory and Argentium sterling silver. *(Caleb Royer Studio Photography)*

▼ **RICHARD WRIGHT:** Turkish-twist damascus forged by Jerry Rados boosts its swagger, as does the cape buffalo horn handle.

▲ **BILL DUFF:** Just as impressive as the 10-inch 440C blade and 416 stainless steel guard is the fluted maple burl handle with wire wrap. *(Ward photo)*

▼ **FRED OTT:** From the tip of the three-bar, twist-damascus blade to the antiqued bronze fittings, the wire-inlaid curly maple handle and the stag butt end, this dagger is a doozie (like a Duesenberg). *(BladeGallery.com photo)*

▶ **MIKE O'BRIEN:** A couple curvaceous daggers exhibit mortised-tang construction, as well as African blackwood and black ash burl handles, and ATS-34 and CPM 154 blades. *(SharpByCoop.com photo)*

▶ **JOHN WHITE:** Engraved and overlaid gold leaves, compliments of Joe Mason, embellish the damascus art dagger in a carved pre-ban ivory handle. That's a 12-inch "explosion-wrapped W's feather-pattern" damascus blade for inquiring minds who want to know. *(SharpByCoop.com photo)*

◀ **MIKE QUESENBERRY:** This one's long and pointy, with a coffin-shaped pre-ban elephant ivory handle, coined liners, an 11-inch ladder-pattern-damascus blade and nearly a full fuller. *(SharpByCoop. com photo)*

◀ **DON LOZIER:** Like soldiers standing guard are the CPM 154 daggers in nickel silver guards and Nicholas Impregnated Wood handles. *(PointSeven image)*

▶ **KEVIN CASHEN:** An iron wire wrap anchors the 16th-century-style damascus dagger, like chain-mail protects a person of knightly intentions. *(PointSeven photo)*

◀ **DAVID BRODZIAK:** Like rubies, do you? Then the ivory-handle, raindrop-damascus-pattern dagger with sterling silver fittings might be for you. It comes in an ebony sheath with carved ivory and ruby inlays.

STATE OF THE ART **171**

Sheathing Review

▼ **BILL REDD:** For his hand-forged, deep-etched "snake skin"-damascus fixed blade, the maker fashioned a fold-over friction sheath of leather, alligator skin, and patterned cowhide with a rattlesnake-skin window.

▶ **ANSSI RUUSUVUORI:** The 1080 puukko (Finnish belt knife) is handled in olivewood to match the sheath, the latter also with a vegetable-tanned leather throat and belt loop.

◀ **KEVIN HOFFMAN:** A damascus neck knife fits snugly into a walnut, ebony, oak, birch and bloodwood sheath with copper and glass-bead neck lanyard. It's utilitarian jewelry at its finest.

▶ **KENNY ROWE:** The epitome of a finely crafted, tooled leather sheath, this belt version includes an engraved silver concho and a carved floral motif.
(Ward photo)

▶ **GARY ROOT:** What better place for a crown-stag-handle fighter than in a traditional fringed-leather sheath with Native American-style beadwork by Heidi Rybar, the wife of knifemaker Ray Rybar Jr., who happened to forge the damascus blade for the piece?
(Kris Kandler photo)

FACTORY TRENDS

If you don't like the knives a company offers, do a Google search for another company, visit a knife show or big-box retailer, or pick up any outdoor retail catalog. The competition is stiff, the blade steels are varied, the styles of knives more varied than ever, and the innovations astounding. There are fixed-blade hunting knives, folders, skinning blades, replaceable-blade hunters, bird-and-trout knives, multi-knife packs and sheath systems, gut hooks, saws, pelvic bone splitters and more edges for the woods or outdoorsman than a guy or gal could carrying in 10 packs.

If tactical folders are your thing, then the choices multiply a thousand-fold, and the mechanisms, locks, blade assisted openers, one-hand openers, safeties, pivots, cams and bushings start coming out the woodwork. The synthetic bullet- and seemingly tank-proof handles have gotten stronger, lighter and more malleable. If you prefer real wood, don't worry the number of available domestic and exotic burls are in the hundreds.

Knife companies have experienced not only a renaissance of manufacturing, but steep global and stateside competition. Price wars resulted in outsourcing, and customer demand and high unemployment rates brought much of the manufacturing back to the good old U.S. of A. It was a vicious circle with one resounding winner—the customer, who has more choices of manufactured and factory knives than ever. Hallelujah!

Blunt Tips Rule Tall Ships

It is an ingrained habit for the chief mate of this tall ship to carry his knife at all times

By Greg Bean

"The only solution was a knife," said Jon Cook, chief mate on the tall ship *Liberty Clipper*. We were mid-voyage sailing from the Bahamas to Charleston, S.C., when he started telling sailing stories. Cook was describing two serious problems, potentially life threatening, he's encountered while sailing.

The first high-risk situation happened while raising a sail that had been *reefed* incorrectly in a storm. *Reefing* shortens a sail when the wind is too strong for a full sail. The sails are folded over themselves and tied to the boom, lowering the sail part way in the process. Following the storm, when the sail was being raised, the reef knot jammed.

Sails are raised by muscle power with the whole crew participating. It's high intensity, and getting a sail up quickly is a high priority. With the knot jammed, the sail was held up by the crew's strain, which is not a secure situation. Seeing the problem, Cook moved quickly to cut the reef line, releasing the sail before the crew's muscles gave out causing a crash of sail, wood and rigging.

The second moment of drama occurred on a 26-foot sloop when the forward sail was rigged so it was secured on only one side of the boat. When the boat tacked, which includes shifting the sails to the other side of the ship, the sail would have been loose and able to flap back and forth, called flogging. With a 20-knot wind anyone at the front would be in danger of being flogged by the sail and its ropes with a good chance of injury. As the crew started the tacking maneuvers, Cook saw the problem, and with little time to spare, cut the line that was rigged wrong so he could correct the rigging. All went well, but keeping his knife with him became an ingrained habit.

Engineer Mike McVeigh's "sailor's rig" includes a Cold Steel True Flight Thrower with a cut-off tip and a homemade marlin spike salvaged from a World War II boat. The sheaths and belt look like salvage items, too.

These two instances could have damaged the boat, the people or both, but fortunately such cases are rare. "You don't want to have to use a knife in an emergency, but it's available if you carry it on your person," he reasons, and Cook has a lot more to say about the everyday need for a knife. Daily knife use on a tall ship mostly relates to rope, which makes sense since rope is everywhere, from coils all over the deck to the top of the masts at a hundred feet above deck.

Knives are essential tools used for cutting cord to tie coiled rigging, shortening rope to take out damaged sections, preparing rope for splicing, as well as making gaskets, trimming splinters, and carving and cutting anything made of wood. And wood is also everywhere since it's essentially a wooden ship.

One thing should be mentioned about rope—it isn't the proper term. On board all ropes have specific purposes and are called *sheets*. No mention was made as to what the men use to cover the mattresses of their bunk beds.

Elijah Collins' Cold Steel Recon Tanto stands watch between the compass and the binoculars. All three are essential tools of the trade.

Blunt Tip on Ship

Cook uses an Italian-made dive knife with a stainless steel blade and a blunt tip. One of the leading causes of death on sailing ships is self-stabbing, and most of the crew's knives have blunt tips. He likes saying it's an Italian knife as if it were a pair of shoes or a suit, but it still rusted. Most of the knife blades are stainless steel due to the wet, salty environment. There are members of the crew who prefer high-carbon-steel knives and are willing to clean and oil the blades for the advantage of the tougher steel.

Mike McVeigh, the ship's engineer relies on a Cold Steel True Flight Thrower. He says the 1055 carbon steel blade has a sharp working edge, and he likes the thick spine. He used a hacksaw to cut the blade tip into a sheepsfoot shape, citing the danger to himself of the original point.

McVeigh made his own sheath and paired the knife with a marlinspike, which is used to splice rope and loosen knots. Ropes are spliced to repair damage, make short ropes into long ropes or to form specialized knots such as a marlinspike hitch or belaying pin splice. Marlinspikes can be as simple as a landscaping spike from a hardware store, but are usually specialty items from marine suppliers. McVeigh made his own spike from a random bolt off of a fuel injector on a World War II boat that he was salvaging. The knife and spike combination is called a *sailor's rig*, and when he worked as a deck hand, he always carried his rig with him. As the ship's engineer, he's responsible for mechanics and electronics instead of wood and rope, and his rig has given way to a flashlight and multi-tool.

Another sailor preferring high-carbon steel over stainless is Elijah Collins, one of the deck hands.

Chief mate Jon Cook's rusty stainless steel Italian-made dive knife is with him at the helm and at the ready.

Collins has knifemaking as well as seawater in his blood. He apprenticed under J.D. Smith of Hammersmith Knives in Boston, and plans to make his own knife by forging 1420-based damascus blade steel. He has the pattern and folds worked out; standing watch leaves plenty of time for thinking through

Multi-tools such as this Leatherman pull their share of duty.

Working when wet is part of the job for deck hand Tony Disanto's Gerber Paraframe folder.

the process. Although, the ship is now his home, the project is on hold until he can get back to Boston and take enough time to make the knife.

In the meantime Collins uses a Cold Steel Recon Tanto, which has been his personal knife since joining the U.S. Marines in 2001. He prefers the Cold Steel knife instead of the Marines standard-issue KA-BAR because of its thicker blade, and he says the point can endure more abuse. One story he enjoys telling is about jungle warfare training he undertook on Okinawa, with an obstacle course that included a rock face. He pounded the Tanto blade into a crack and used it as a piton, first pulling himself up and then using it as a step to get over the top of the rock face. He didn't say if he was able to get the knife loose or had to recover it later, but either way he's impressed that it endured the punishment.

When Collins left the Marines for sailing, he kept the Cold Steel Recon Tanto as a rig knife, and says he prefers it for the same reasons he liked it as a tactical knife—the blade holds its edge well and the thicker spine withstands considerable abuse. He's taken a hammer to the blade spine for splitting planks and for cutting wire cables, and it has held up just fine. He keeps the knife tethered to his belt, a habit he picked up in the Marines where soldiers tether everything they need to themselves.

Deck hand Tony Disanto's first sailing job was as an engineer. On land he's a mechanical engineer and rock climber and moves to different places around the country for climbing. One advantage to being an engineer is the ease of finding work wherever he

moves. He wanted to try sailing and was hired as an engineer on a boat headed to South America. The boat lost its engine south of Cuba and they had to make their way into the country for repairs using sail power alone.

Regardless of the poor relations between the U.S. and Cuba, both countries allow for emergencies. Getting home from Cuba was not as easy as getting there, though. In Cuba the knife he used was confiscated, or he lost it; he was a little hazy on that detail, possibly having to do with Cuban rum. His knife was a titanium dive knife, which he reports was not a good sailing knife. The blade had a sharp point and was edged on both sides, so he couldn't press down on the blade spine with his thumb.

A Suds Blade

With the dive knife left in Cuba, he replaced it with a Gerber Paraframe folder. Disanto says he's never needed a knife for anything dramatic on board, but he fishes and has opened a lot of beer by prying caps off with the back of the blade.

Everyone on board mentioned opening beer with knives. It makes you question if they only drink craft beer that is bottled without twist-off caps. Probably they just like saying it. What isn't in question is the everyday use of knives. Maintenance is constant, and knives are part of every tool collection. Fixed blades are the most common; opening a folder in harsh weather is difficult, even those with one-hand-opening blades.

"One hand for yourself, one for the ship" is the rule in storms. Anyplace you see a screwdriver or

For mechanical and electrical problems on the Liberty Clipper, engineer Mike McVeigh relies on a multi-tool and flashlight.

Filleting the mahi-mahi was done with a standard kitchen knife under the watchful supervision of the captain's pup.

wrench you also see a knife. The work area in front of the wheel, where the ship's compass and navigation equipment is housed, always has coffee mugs and a knife as standard equipment. Curiously the mugs never tip. There seems to be some kind of attraction between coffee mugs and wood.

Research for this article was conducted in May 2013 while on a transit from the *Liberty Clipper's* wintering grounds in Nassau to Charleston, S.C., on the way to the homeport in Boston for the warm season. This was blue water sailing, out of sight of land and over water too clear and deep to reflect anything but blue, a tough gig certainly, but no sacrifice is too great for a good knife story. An element of realism was injected into the article by volunteering as a crewmember, working the noon till 4 p.m. and midnight till 4 a.m. shifts.

A notably somber event occurred while in Charleston, but one that should be mentioned out of respect for those involved—a burial at sea. In the Bahamas two of the crew were returning after an evening off-ship when they encountered two women being robbed at gun point. One of the crew tried to stop the robbery and was shot and killed. He was cremated in the Bahamas and his remains brought back to the U.S. on the ship. His family flew in to Charleston for the memorial service held on the deck of the *Liberty Clipper*. His ashes were given to the sea in Charleston Harbor.

On a much lighter note, Disanto, as a snorkeling enthusiast and spear fisherman, had a spear gun with him, which turned into an amusing episode. Fishing

lines were constantly out, but very few fish were ever caught. Mahi-mahi tuna would swim along with the boat, but showed no interest in the bait. The crew became impatient and took a more aggressive approach and crafted a harpoon. The spear from the spear gun was lashed to a spar along with a retrieval line. Their luck didn't improve but they had fun trying.

On the last day at sea a mahi-mahi was finally caught. Capt. Chris Shaw did the honors of cleaning the fish, needing three different blades before he was through. The fish was dispatched with Collins' Cold Steel Tanto, the tail hacked off with a meat cleaver and completely filleted with a highly specialized knife raided from the galley and used for nothing else but food prep—a standard kitchen knife. The grilled mahi-mahi served that night was a fitting end to the trip.

The Liberty Fleet can be reached at 617-742-0333, or visit www.libertyfleet.com.

Fly-Open Factory Folders

▲ Hand Tech Made's "ZHammer" flies open via a flipper mechanism and "DDR-SAO" assisted opener, delivered in a radian-re-curved CPM-S35VN stainless steel blade and a green 6061-aluminum handle.

▼ The Famars USA SRT Tactical assisted-opening folder is fashioned for police, firemen and rescue, sporting a 3.5-inch 154CM modified tanto blade, and an aluminum handle with a glass breaker and seat belt cutter.

► The CRKT "Fire Spark" combines an Outburst assisted-opening mechanism, CRKT's "Fire Safe" to keep the blade closed until needed and the Lake And Walker Knife Safety (LAWKS) to lock the blade open.

► The Heckler & Koch Knives "Nitrous Blitz" features the "Nitrous Assist" blade-opening mechanism, a 3.4-inch 154CM blade, black G-10 handle scales and dual titanium liners.

▼ So many companies offer assisted-opening folders, including SOG Specialty Knives & Tools with its SOG Assisted Technology, here on the Twitch XL flipper folder in stainless AUS-8 blade steel and a rosewood handle.

▶ Featuring Buck's "ASAP" assisted-opening technology, the Buck Impulse has a 2.5-inch blade of 420HC stainless steel and an aluminum handle anodized pink—the ladies might like this one!

▼ Everyone seems to know the Ken Onion-designed "SpeedSafe" assisted opener, here on the Kershaw "Dimension" folder showcasing a 3-inch 8Cr13MoV blade and a machine-textured titanium handle.

▼ Blackie Collins designed the assisted-opening mechanism of the Puma "Swoop," also featuring a black-titanium-coated 440A stainless steel blade and G-10 handle scales.

In the Hunt

▼ The KA-BAR "Adventure Gamestalker" parades an orange pebble-textured grip for good hand purchase, as well as lots of blade belly for skinning work.

▲ The no-slip, textured fiberglass-reinforced handle scales, along with handle swell that fills the palm, are benefits of the Spyderco "Enuff Leaf" drop-point hunter (with leaf-shaped blade).

▲ An orange-and-black over-molded handle that provides enhanced control and feel is among the best features of the SOG Huntspoint.

▶ The design of the Buck Waterfowler is smart, with more handle than blade—most hunting knives being vastly over-bladed anyway—and nice and lean.

Tomahawk Chop!

▼ Condor Tool & Knife offers a "Tactical Rescue Tomahawk" in a 7-inch forged, epoxy powder coated 1075 high-carbon-steel head, and a Paracord-wrapped handle.

The TOPS Knives "Hoffman Hawkin' Stick," designed by Terrill Hoffman, makes use of a black-traction-coated 1095 high-carbon-steel head with a 2-inch cutting edge and a chromium/molybdenum 4130 haft.

United Cutlery's "M48 Apocalypse Tactical Tomahawk" has an upswept, oxide-coated 2Cr13 stainless steel head and a Paracord-wrapped, fiberglass-reinforced-nylon haft.

Knives Marketplace

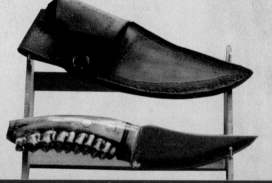
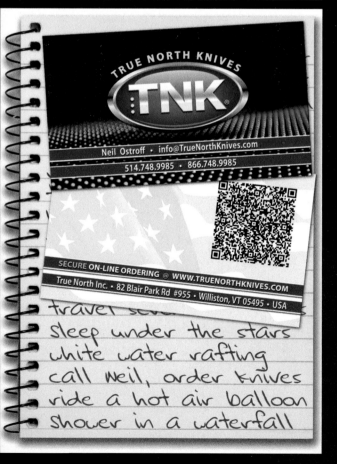
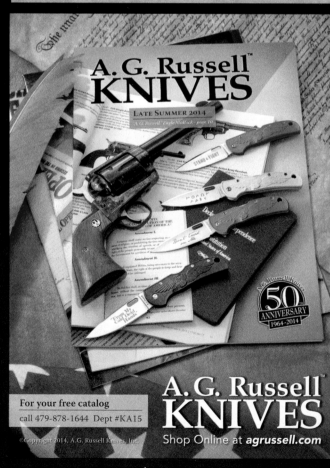

A CONCISE DICTIONARY OF Busseisms ...AND OTHER PECULIARITIES

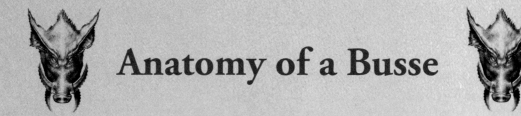

Anatomy of a Busse

Skull crusher, butt, pommel

Rear talon

Handle fasteners

Nuclear Meltdown
Fusion Steel Heart
(Satin + Black Paper)

Ricasso

Plunge line

BUSSE COMBAT
KNIFE COMPANY

Front guard
(aka Talon hole)

This design feature is a
registered trademark of
the Busse Combat
Knife Company

Choil

#882

Spine

Nuclear
meltdown
treatment

On selected models only

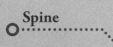

Sweep

Anatomy of a Busse Custom

Special Forces
Natural Outlaw

Skull crusher, butt, pommel

Rear talon

Mosaic handle pins

Multiple
handle materials

Natural materials,
G10 & micartas

Ricasso

Plunge line

Multiple
blade finishes

Satin, double cut
or custom colors

Spine

BUSSE
CUSTOM SHOP

Front guard
(aka Talon hole)

This design feature is a
registered trademark of
the Busse Combat
Knife Company

Choil

Custom blade shapes

G-Rex bolsters & integral liners

Sweep

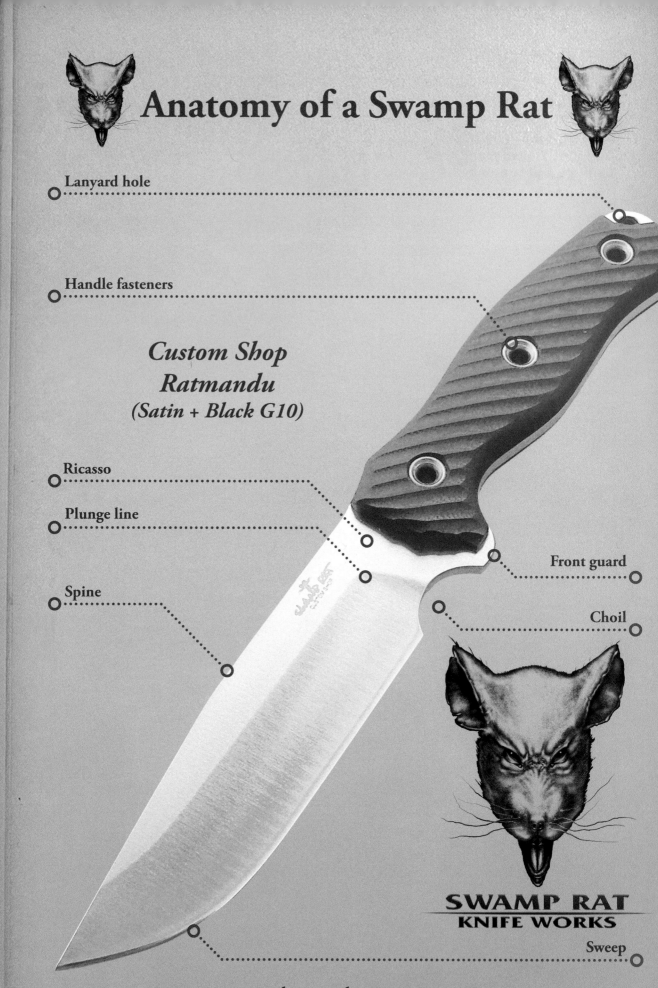

Anatomy of a Swamp Rat

Lanyard hole

Handle fasteners

Custom Shop
Ratmandu
(Satin + Black G10)

Ricasso

Plunge line

Spine

Front guard

Choil

SWAMP RAT
KNIFE WORKS

Sweep

Anatomy of a Scrap Yard

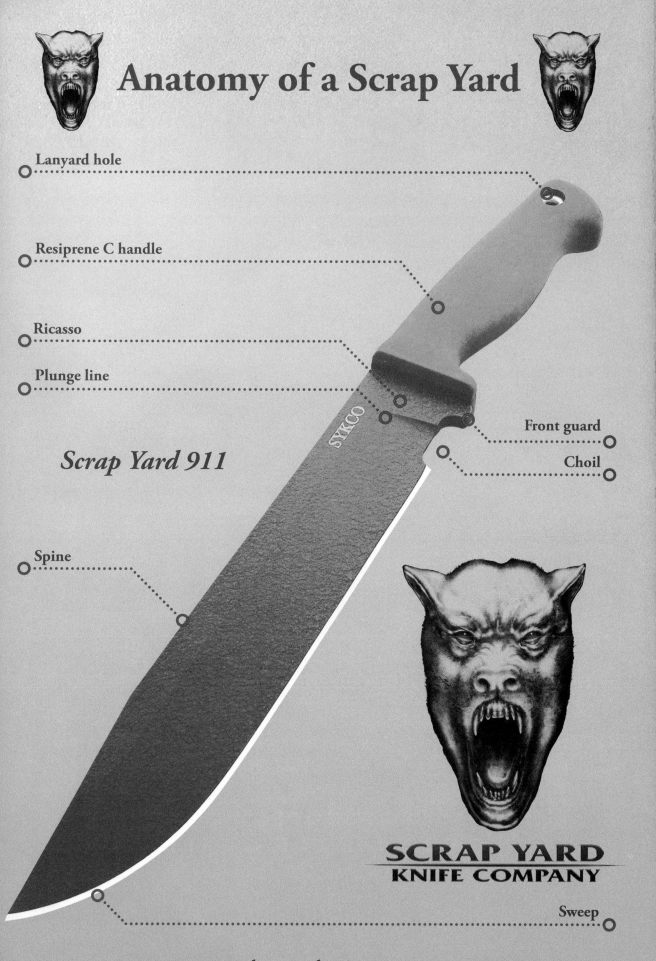

Lanyard hole

Resiprene C handle

Ricasso

Plunge line

Scrap Yard 911

Front guard

Choil

Spine

Sweep

SCRAP YARD
KNIFE COMPANY

DIRECTORY

A

ABEGG, ARNIE
5992 Kenwick Cr, Huntington Beach, CA 92648, Phone: 714-848-5697

ABERNATHY, LANCE
Sniper Bladeworks, 15477 N.W. 123rd St., Platte City, MO 64079, Phone: 816-585-1595, lanceabernathy@sbcglobal.net; Web: www.sniperbladeworks.com
Specialties: Tactical frame-lock and locking-liner folding knives.

ACCAWI, FUAD
131 Bethel Rd, Clinton, TN 37716, Phone: 865-414-4836, gaccawi@comcast.net; Web: www.acremetalworks.com
Specialties: I create one of a kind pieces from small working knives to performance blades and swords. **Patterns:** Styles include, and not limited to hunters, Bowies, daggers, swords, folders and camp knives. **Technical:** I forge primarily 5160, produces own Damascus and does own heat treating. **Prices:** $150 to $3000. **Remarks:** I am a full-time bladesmith. I enjoy producing Persian and historically influenced work. **Mark:** My mark is an eight sided Middle Eastern star with initials in the center.

ACKERSON, ROBIN E
119 W Smith St, Buchanan, MI 49107, Phone: 616-695-2911

ADAMS, JIM
1648 Camille Way, Cordova, TN 38016, Phone: 901-326-0441, jim@JimAdamsKnives.com Web: www.jimadamsknives.com
Specialties: Fixed blades in classic design. **Patterns:** Hunters, fighters, and Bowies. **Technical:** Grinds Damascus, O1, others as requested. **Prices:** Starting at $150. **Remarks:** Full-time maker. **Mark:** J. Adams, Cordova, TN.

ADAMS, LES
6413 NW 200 St, Hialeah, FL 33015, Phone: 305-625-1699
Specialties: Working straight knives of his design. **Patterns:** Fighters, tactical folders, law enforcing autos. **Technical:** Grinds ATS-34, 440C and D2. **Prices:** $100 to $500. **Remarks:** Part-time maker; first knife sold in 1989. **Mark:** First initial, last name, Custom Knives.

ADAMS, WILLIAM D
PO Box 439, 405 Century Farms Rd, Burton, TX 77835, Phone: 979-289-0212, Fax: 979-289-6272, wd4adams@broadwaves.net
Specialties: Hunter scalpels and utility knives of his design. **Patterns:** Hunters and utility/camp knives. **Technical:** Grinds 1095, 440C and 440V. Uses stabilized wood and other stabilized materials. **Prices:** $100 to $200. **Remarks:** Part-time maker; first knife sold in 1994. **Mark:** Last name in script.

ADDISON, KYLE A
588 Atkins Trail, Hazel, KY 42049-8629, Phone: 270-492-8120, kylest2@yahoo.com
Specialties: Hand forged blades including Bowies, fighters and hunters. **Patterns:** Custom leather sheaths. **Technical:** Forges 5160, 1084, and his own Damascus. **Prices:** $175 to $1500. **Remarks:** Part-time maker, first knife sold in 1996. ABS member. **Mark:** First and middle initial, last name under "Trident" with knife and hammer.

ADKINS, RICHARD L
138 California Ct, Mission Viejo, CA 92692-4079

AIDA, YOSHIHITO
26-7 Narimasu 2-chome, Itabashi-ku, Tokyo, JAPAN 175-0094, Phone: 81-3-3939-0052, Fax: 81-3-3939-0058, Web: http://riverside-land.com/
Specialties: High-tech working straight knives and folders of his design. **Patterns:** Bowies, lockbacks, hunters, fighters, fishing knives, boots. **Technical:** Grinds CV-134, ATS-34; buys Damascus; works in traditional Japanese fashion for some handles and sheaths. **Prices:** $700 to $1200; some higher. **Remarks:** Full-time maker; first knife sold in 1978. **Mark:** Initial logo and Riverside West.

ALBERT, STEFAN
U Lucenecka 434/4, Filakovo 98604, SLOVAKIA, albert@albertknives.com Web: www.albertknives.com
Specialties: Art Knives, Miniatures, Scrimshaw, Bulino. **Prices:** From USD $500 to USD $25000. **Mark:** Albert

ALCORN, DOUGLAS A.
14687 Fordney Rd., Chesaning, MI 48616, Phone: 989-845-6712, fortalcornknives@centurytel.net
Specialties: Gentleman style and presentation knives. **Patterns:** Hunters, miniatures, and military type fixed blade knives and axes. **Technical:** Blades are stock removal and forged using best quality stainless, carbon, and damascus steels. Handle materials are burls, ivory, pearl, leather and other exotics. **Prices:** $300 and up. **Motto:** Simple, Rugged, Elegant, Handcrafted **Remarks:** Knife maker since 1989 and full time since 1999, Knife Makers Guild (voting member), member of the Bladesmith Society. **Mark:** D.A. Alcorn (Loveless style mark), Maker, Chesaning, MI.

ALDERMAN, ROBERT
2655 Jewel Lake Rd., Sagle, ID 83860, Phone: 208-263-5996
Specialties: Classic and traditional working straight knives in standard patterns or to customer specs, his design; period pieces. **Patterns:** Bowies, fighters, hunters and utility/camp knives. **Technical:** Casts, forges and grinds 1084; forges and grinds L6 and O1. Prefers an old appearance. **Prices:** $100 to $350; some to $700. **Remarks:** Full-time maker; first knife sold in 1975. Doing business as Trackers Forge. Knife-making school. Two-week course for beginners; covers forging, stock removal, hardening, tempering,

case making. All materials supplied; $1250. **Mark:** Deer track.

ALEXANDER, EUGENE
Box 540, Ganado, TX 77962-0540, Phone: 512-771-3727

ALEXANDER,, OLEG, AND COSSACK BLADES
15460 Stapleton Way, Wellington, FL 33414, Phone: 443-676-6111, Web: www.cossackblades.com
Technical: All knives are made from hand-forged Damascus (3-4 types of steel are used to create the Damascus) and have a HRC of 60-62. Handle materials are all natural, including various types of wood, horn, bone and leather. Embellishments include the use of precious metals and stones, including gold, silver, diamonds, rubies, sapphires and other unique materials. All knives include hand-made leather sheaths, and some models include wooden presentation boxes and display stands. **Prices:** $395 to over $10,000, depending on design and materials used. **Remarks:** Full-time maker, first knife sold in 1993. **Mark:** Rectangle enclosing a stylized Cyrillic letter "O" overlapping a stylized Cyrillic "K."

ALLAN, TODD
TODD ALLAN KNIVES, 6525 W. Kings Ave., Glendale, AZ 85306, Phone: 623-210-3766, todd@toddallanknives.com; www.toddallanknives.com
Patterns: Fixed-blade hunters and camp knives. **Technical:** Stock-removal method of blade making using 154CM, high-carbon damascus, stainless damascus, 5160 and 1095 blade steels. Handle materials include various Micartas, stabilized woods and mammoth ivory. **Prices:** $175 to $1,000. **Remarks:** Full-time maker.

ALLEN, MIKE "WHISKERS"
12745 Fontenot Acres Rd, Malakoff, TX 75148, Phone: 903-489-1026, whiskersknives@aol.com; Web: www.whiskersknives.com
Specialties: Working and collector-quality lockbacks, liner locks, automatic folders and assisted openers of his own proprietary mechanisms. **Patterns:** Folders and fixed blades. **Technical:** Makes Damascus, 440C and ATS-34, engraves. **Prices:** $200 and up. **Remarks:** Full-time maker since 1984. **Mark:** Whiskers and month and year.

ALLRED, BRUCE F
1764 N. Alder, Layton, UT 84041, Phone: 801-825-4612, allredbf@msn.com
Specialties: Custom hunting and utility knives. **Patterns:** Custom designs that include a unique grind line, thumb and mosaic pins. **Technical:** ATS-34, 154CM and 440C. **Remarks:** The handle material includes but not limited to Micarta (in various colors), natural woods and reconstituted stone.

ALLRED, ELVAN
31 Spring Terrace Court, St. Charles, MO 63303, Phone: 636-936-8871, allredknives@yahoo.com; Web: www.allredcustomknives.com
Specialties: Innovative sculpted folding knives designed by Elvan's son Scott that are mostly one of a kind. **Patterns:** Mostly folders but some high-end straight knives. **Technical:** ATS-34 SS, 440C SS, stainless Damascus, S30V, 154cm; inlays are mostly natural materials such as pearl, coral, ivory, jade, lapis, and other precious stone. **Prices:** $500 to $4000, some higher. **Remarks:** Started making knives in the shop of Dr. Fred Carter in the early 1990s. Full-time maker since 2006, first knife sold in 1993. Take some orders but work mainly on one-of-a-kind art knives. **Mark:** Small oval with signature Eallred in the center and handmade above.

ALVERSON, TIM (R.V.)
209 Spring Rd. SE, Arab, AL 35016, Phone: 256-224-9620, alvie35@yahoo.com Web: cwknives.blogspot.com
Specialties: Fancy working knives to customer specs; other types on request. **Patterns:** Bowies, daggers, folders and miniatures. **Technical:** Grinds 440C, ATS-34; buys some Damascus. **Prices:** Start at $100. **Remarks:** Full-time maker; first knife sold in 1981. **Mark:** R.V.A. around rosebud.

AMERI, MAURO
Via Riaello No. 20, Trensasco St Olcese, Genova, ITALY 16010, Phone: 010-8357077, mauroameri@gmail.com
Specialties: Working and using knives of his design. **Patterns:** Hunters, Bowies and utility/camp knives. **Technical:** Grinds 440C, ATS-34 and 154CM. Handles in wood or Micarta; offers sheaths. **Prices:** $200 to $1200. **Remarks:** Spare-time maker; first knife sold in 1982. **Mark:** Last name, city.

AMMONS, DAVID C
6225 N. Tucson Mtn. Dr, Tucson, AZ 85743, Phone: 520-307-3585
Specialties: Will build to suit. **Patterns:** Yours or his. **Prices:** $250 to $2000. **Mark:** AMMONS.

AMOS, CHRIS
PO Box 1519, Riverton, WY 82501, Phone: 520-271-9752, caknives@yahoo.com
Specialties: HEPK (High Endurance Performance Knives). **Patterns:** Hunters, fighters, bowies, kitchen knives and camp knives. **Technical:** Hand-forged, high rate of reduction 52100 and 5160 steel. **Prices:** $150 to $1,500. **Remarks:** Part-time maker since 1997, full time since 2012. Coach/instructor at Ed Fowler's Knifemaking School. HEPK mastersmith rating, 2013. **Mark:** Early mark: CAK stamped; current mark: Amos on right side.

AMOUREUX, A W
PO Box 776, Northport, WA 99157, Phone: 509-732-6292
Specialties: Heavy-duty working straight knives. **Patterns:** Bowies, fighters, camp knives and hunters for world-wide use. **Technical:** Grinds 440C, ATS-34 and 154CM. **Prices:** $80 to $2000. **Remarks:** Full-time maker; first knife sold in 1974. **Mark:** ALSTAR.

ANDERS, DAVID
157 Barnes Dr, Center Ridge, AR 72027, Phone: 501-893-2294
Specialties: Working straight knives of his design. **Patterns:** Bowies, fighters and

hunters. **Technical:** Forges 5160, 1080 and Damascus. **Prices:** $225 to $3200. **Remarks:** Part-time maker; first knife sold in 1988. Doing business as Anders Knives. **Mark:** Last name/MS.

ANDERS, JEROME
14560 SW 37th St, Miramar, FL 33027, Phone: 305-613-2990, web:www.andersknives.com
Specialties: Case handles and pin work. **Patterns:** Layered and mosiac steel. **Prices:** $275 and up. **Remarks:** All his knives are truly one-of-a-kind. **Mark:** J. Anders in half moon.

ANDERSEN, HENRIK LEFOLII
Jagtvej 8, Groenholt, Fredensborg, DENMARK 3480, Phone: 0011-45-48483026
Specialties: Hunters and matched pairs for the serious hunter. **Technical:** Grinds A2; uses materials native to Scandinavia. **Prices:** Start at $250. **Remarks:** Part-time maker; first knife sold in 1985. **Mark:** Initials with arrow.

ANDERSEN, KARL B.
20200 TimberLodge Rd., Warba, MN 55793, Phone: 218-398-4270, Karl@andersenforge.com Web: www.andersenforge.com
Specialties: Hunters, Bowies, Fighters, Camp knives forged from high carbon tool steels and Andersen Forge Damascus. **Technical:** All types of materials used. Exotic inlay materials and silver wire embellishments utilized. **Prices:** Starting at $450 and up. **Remarks:** Full-time maker. ABS Journeyman Smith. All knives sole authorship. Andersen Forge was instrumental in paving the way for take-down knife construction to be more recognized and broadly accepted in knife making today. **Mark:** Andersen in script on obverse. J.S. on either side, depending on knife.

ANDERSON, GARY D
2816 Reservoir Rd, Spring Grove, PA 17362-9802, Phone: 717-229-2665
Specialties: From working knives to collectors quality blades, some folders. **Patterns:** Traditional and classic designs; customer patterns welcome. **Technical:** Forges Damascus carbon and stainless steels. Offers silver inlay, mokume, filework, checkering. **Prices:** $250 and up. **Remarks:** Part-time maker; first knife sold in 1985. Some engraving, scrimshaw and stone work. **Mark:** GAND, MS.

ANDERSON, MARK ALAN
1176 Poplar St, Denver, CO 80220, mcantdrive95@comcast.net; Web: www.malancustomknives.com
Specialties: Stilettos. Automatics of several varieties and release mechanisms. **Patterns:** Drop point hunters, sub hilt fighters & drop point camp knives. **Technical:** Almost all my blades are hollow ground. **Prices:** $200 to $1800. **Remarks:** Focusing on fixed blade hunting, skinning & fighting knives now. **Mark:** Dragon head.

ANDERSON, MEL
29505 P 50 Rd, Hotchkiss, CO 81419-8203, Phone: 970-872-4882, Fax: 970-872-4882, artnedge@tds.net, melsscratchyhand@aol.com; Web: www.scratchyhand.com
Specialties: Full-size, miniature and one-of-a-kind straight knives and folders of his design. **Patterns:** Tantos, Bowies, daggers, fighters, hunters and pressure folders. **Technical:** Grinds 440C, 5160, D2, 1095. **Prices:** Start at $175. **Remarks:** Knifemaker and sculptor; full-time maker; first knife sold in 1987. **Mark:** Scratchy Hand.

ANDERSON, TOM
955 Canal Rd. Extd., Manchester, PA 17345, Phone: 717-266-6475, andersontech1@comcast.net Web: artistryintitanium.com
Specialties: Battle maces and war hammers.

ANDRADE, DON CARLOS
CALIFORNIA CUSTOM KNIVES, 1824 Sunny Hill Ave., Los Osos, CA 93402, Phone: 805-528-8837 or 805-550-2324, andradeartworks@gmail.com; www.californiacustomknives.com
Specialties: Chef knife specialist, also integrally forged personal knives and camp knives. **Technical:** Forges to shape, and a small number of stain-resistant, stock-removal blades. All heat-treating in house. Uses 1095, W2, W1, 1084, 52100, 1065, 1070 and 13C26 blade steels. **Prices:** $250 to $1,650. **Remarks:** Full-time maker; first knife made in 2006 under tutorship of mentor Tai Goo. **Mark:** Initials "DCA" and two circles with a strike running through them (maker's version of infinity/continuity.)

ANDREWS, ERIC
132 Halbert Street, Grand Ledge, MI 48837, Phone: 517-627-7304
Specialties: Traditional working and using straight knives of his design. **Patterns:** Full-tang hunters, skinners and utility knives. **Technical:** Forges carbon steel; heat-treats. All knives come with sheath; most handles are of wood. **Prices:** $80 to $160. **Remarks:** Part-time maker; first knife sold in 1990. Doing business as The Tinkers Bench.

ANDREWS, RUSS
PO Box 7732, Sugar Creek, MO 64054, Phone: 816-252-3344, russandrews@sbcglobal.net; Web:wwwrussandrewsknives.com
Specialties: Hand forged bowies & hunters. **Mark:** E. R. Andrews II. ERAII.

ANGELL, JON
22516 East C R1474, Hawthorne, FL 32640, Phone: 352-475-5380, syrjon@aol.com

ANKROM, W.E.
14 Marquette Dr, Cody, WY 82414, Phone: 307-587-3017, weankrom@hotmail.com
Specialties: Best quality folding knives of his design. Bowies, fighters, chute knives, boots and hunters. **Patterns:** Lock backs, liner locks, single high art. **Technical:** ATS-34 commercial Damascus, CPM 154 steel. **Prices:** $500 and up. **Remarks:** Full-time maker; first knife sold in 1975. **Mark:** Name or name, city, state.

ANSO, JENS
GL. Skanderborgvej 116, Sporup, DENMARK 8472, Phone: 45 86968826, info@ansoknives.com; Web: www.ansoknives.com
Specialties: Working knives of his own design. **Patterns:** Balisongs, swords, folders, drop-points, sheepsfoots, hawkbill, tanto, recurve. **Technical:** Grinds RWL-34 Damasteel S30V, CPM 154CM. Handrubbed or beadblasted finish. **Price:** $400 to $1200, some up to $3500. **Remarks:** Full-time maker since January 2002. First knife sold 1997. Doing business as ANSOKNIVES. **Mark:** ANSO and/or ANSO with logo.

APELT, STACY E
8076 Moose Ave, Norfolk, VA 23518, Phone: 757-583-5872, sapelt@cox.net
Specialties: Exotic wood and burls, ivories, Bowies, custom made knives to order. **Patterns:** Bowies, hunters, fillet, professional cutlery and Japanese style blades and swords. **Technical:** Hand forging, stock removal, scrimshaw, carbon, stainless and Damascus steels. **Prices:** $65 to $5000. **Remarks:** Professional Goldsmith. **Mark:** Stacy E. Apelt - Norfolk VA.

APLIN, SPENCER
5151 County Rd. 469, Brazoria, TX 77422, Phone: 979-964-4448, spenceraplin@aol.com; Web: www.stacustomknives.com
Specialties: Custom skinners, fillets, bowies and kitchen knives. **Technical:** Stainless steel powder metals, stainless damascus. Handles include stabilized woods, various ivory and Micarta. Guard and butt-cap materials are brass, copper, nickel silver and Mokume. **Prices:** $250 and up. **Remarks:** First knife sold in 1989. Knives made to order only, nothing is pre-made. All blades are hand drawn, then cut from sheet stock. No two are exactly the same. **Mark:** Signature and date completed.

APPLEBY, ROBERT
746 Municipal Rd, Shickshinny, PA 18655, Phone: 570-864-0879, applebyknives@yahoo.com; Web: www.applebyknives.com
Specialties: Working using straight knives and folders of his own and popular and historical designs. **Patterns:** Variety of straight knives and folders. **Technical:** Hand forged or grinds O1, 1084, 5160, 440C, ATS-34, commercial Damascus, makes own sheaths. **Prices:** Starting at $75. **Remarks:** Part-time maker, first knife sold in 1995. **Mark:** APPLEBY over SHICKSHINNY, PA.

APPLETON, RON
315 Glenn St, Bluff Dale, TX 76433, Phone: 254-728-3039, ron@helovesher.com or ronappleton@hotmail.com; Web: http://community.webshots.com/user/angelic574
Specialties: One-of-a-kind folding knives. **Patterns:** Unique folding multi-locks and high-tech patterns. **Technical:** All parts machined, D2, S7, 416, 440C, 6A14V et.al. **Prices:** Start at $12000. **Remarks:** Full-time maker; first knife sold in 1996. **Mark:** Initials with anvil or initials within arrowhead, signed and dated. Usually only shows at the Art Knife Invitational every 2 years in San Diego, CA.

ARBUCKLE, JAMES M
114 Jonathan Jct, Yorktown, VA 23693, Phone: 757-867-9578, a_r_buckle@hotmail.com
Specialties: One-of-a-kind of his design; working knives. **Patterns:** Mostly chef's knives and hunters. **Technical:** Forged and stock removal blades using exotic hardwoods, natural materials, Micarta and stabilized woods. Forge 5160 and 1084; stock removal D2, ATS-34, 440C and 154CM. Makes own pattern welded steel. **Prices:** $195 to $700. **Remarks:** Forge, grind, heat-treat, finish and embellish all knives himself. Does own leatherwork. Part-time maker. ABS Journeyman smith 2007; ASM member. **Mark:** J. Arbuckle or J. ARBUCKLE MAKER.

ARCHER, RAY AND TERRI
4207 South 28 St., Omaha, NE 68107, Phone: 402-505-3084, archerrt@cox.net Web: www.archersknives.com
Specialties: Basic high-finish working knives. **Patterns:** Hunters, skinners camp knives. **Technical:** Flat grinds various steels like 440C, ATS-34 and CPM-S30V. **Prices:** $75 to $500. **Remarks:** Full-time maker. Makes own sheaths; first knife sold 1994. **Mark:** Last name over knives.

ARDWIN, COREY
4700 North Cedar, North Little Rock, AR 72116, Phone: 501-791-0301, Fax: 501-791-2974, Boog@hotmail.com

ARM-KO KNIVES
PO Box 76280, Marble Ray , KZN, SOUTH AFRICA 4035, Phone: 27 31 5771451, arm-koknives.co.za; Web: www.arm-koknives.co.za
Specialties: They will make what your fastidious taste desires. Be it cool collector or tenacious tactical with handles of mother-of-pearl, fossil & local ivories. Exotic dye/stabilized burls, giraffe bone, horns, carbon fiber, g10, and titanium etc. **Technical:** Via stock removal, grinding Damasteel, carbon & mosaic. Damascus, ATS-34, N690, 440A, 440B, 12C27, RWL34 and high carbon EN 8, 5160 all heat treated in house. **Prices:** From $200 and up. **Remarks:** Father a part-time maker for well over 10 years and member of Knifemakers Guild in SA. Son full-time maker over 3 years. **Mark:** Logo of initials A R M and H A R M "Edged Tools."

ARMS, ERIC
11153 7 Mile Road, Tustin, MI 49688, Phone: 231-829-3726, ericarms@netonecom.net
Specialties: Working hunters, high performance straight knives. **Patterns:** Variety of hunters, scagel style, Ed Fowler design and drop point. **Technical:** Forge 52100, 5160, 1084 hand grind, heat treat, natural handle, stag horn, elk, big horn, flat grind, convex, all leather sheath work. **Prices:** Starting at $150 **Remarks:** Part-time maker **Mark:** Eric Arms

custom knifemakers

ARNOLD, JOE
47 Patience Cres, London, ON, CANADA N6E 2K7, Phone: 519-686-2623, arnoldknivesandforge@bell.net
Specialties: Traditional working and using straight knives of his design and to customer specs. **Patterns:** Fighters, hunters and Bowies. **Technical:** Grinds 440C, ATS-34, 5160, and Forges 1084-1085 **Prices:** $75 to $500; some to $2500. **Remarks:** Full-time maker; first knife sold in 1988. **Mark:** Last name, country.

ARROWOOD, DALE
556 Lassetter Rd, Sharpsburg, GA 30277, Phone: 404-253-9672
Specialties: Fancy and traditional straight knives of his design and to customer specs. **Patterns:** Bowies, fighters and hunters. **Technical:** Grinds ATS-34 and 440C; forges high-carbon steel. Engraves and scrimshaws. **Prices:** $125 to $200; some to $245. **Remarks:** Part-time maker; first knife sold in 1989. **Mark:** Anvil with an arrow through it; Old English "Arrowood Knives."

ASHBY, DOUGLAS
10123 Deermont Trail, Dallas, TX 75243, Phone: 214-929-7531, doug@ashbycustomknives.com Web: ashbycustomknives.com
Specialties: Traditional and fancy straight knives and folders of his design or to customer specs. **Patterns:** Skinners, hunters, utility/camp knives, locking liner folders. **Technical:** Grinds ATS-34, commercial Damascus, and other steels on request. **Prices:** $125 to $1000. **Remarks:** Part-time maker; first knife sold in 1990. **Mark:** Name, city.

ASHWORTH, BOYD
1510 Bullard Place, Powder Springs, GA 30127, Phone: 770-422-9826, boydashworth@comcast.net; Web: www.boydashworthknives.com
Specialties: Turtle folders. Fancy Damascus locking folders. **Patterns:** Fighters, hunters and gents. **Technical:** Forges own Damascus; offers filework; uses exotic handle materials. **Prices:** $500 to $2500. **Remarks:** Part-time maker; first knife sold in 1993. **Mark:** Last name.

ATHEY, STEVE
3153 Danube Way, Riverside, CA 92503, Phone: 951-850-8612, stevelonnie@yahoo.com
Specialties: Stock removal. **Patterns:** Hunters & Bowies. **Prices:** $100 to $500. **Remarks:** Part-time maker. **Mark:** Last name with number on blade.

ATKINSON, DICK
General Delivery, Wausau, FL 32463, Phone: 850-638-8524
Specialties: Working straight knives and folders of his design; some fancy. **Patterns:** Hunters, fighters, boots; locking folders in interframes. **Technical:** Grinds A2, 440C and 154CM. Likes filework. **Prices:** $85 to $300; some exceptional knives. **Remarks:** Full-time maker; first knife sold in 1977. **Mark:** Name, city, state.

AYARRAGARAY, CRISTIAN L.
Buenos Aires 250, Parana, Entre Rios, ARGENTINA 3100, Phone: 043-231753
Specialties: Traditional working straight knives of his design. **Patterns:** Fishing and hunting knives. **Technical:** Grinds and forges carbon steel. Uses native Argentine woods and deer antler. **Prices:** $150 to $250; some to $400. **Remarks:** Full-time maker; first knife sold in 1980. **Mark:** Last name, signature.

B

BAARTMAN, GEORGE
PO Box 1116, Bela-Bela, LP, SOUTH AFRICA 0480, Phone: 27 14 736 4036, Fax: 086 636 3408, thabathipa@gmail.com
Specialties: Fancy and working LinerLock® folders of own design and to customers specs. Specialize in pattern filework on liners. **Patterns:** LinerLock® folders. **Technical:** Grinds 12C27, ATS-34, and Damascus, prefer working with stainless damasteel. Hollow grinds to hand-rubbed and polished satin finish. Enjoys working with mammoth, warthog tusk and pearls. **Prices:** Folders from $380 to $1000. **Remarks:** Part-time maker. Member of the Knifemakers Guild of South Africa since 1993. **Mark:** BAARTMAN.

BACHE-WIIG, TOM
N-5966, Eivindvik, NORWAY, Phone: 475-778-4290, Fax: 475-778-1099, tom.bache-wiig@enivest.net; Web: tombachewiig.com
Specialties: High-art and working knives of his design. **Patterns:** Hunters, utility knives, hatchets, axes and art knives. **Technical:** Grinds Uddeholm Elmax, powder metallurgy tool stainless steel. Handles made of rear burls of Nordic woods stabilized with vacuum/high-pressure technique. **Prices:** $430 to $900; some to $2300. **Remarks:** Part-time maker; first knife sold 1988. **Mark:** Etched name and eagle head.

BACON, DAVID R.
906 136th St E, Bradenton, FL 34202-9694, Phone: 813-996-4289

BAGLEY, R. KEITH
OLD PINE FORGE, 4415 Hope Acres Dr, White Plains, MD 20695, Phone: 301-932-0990, keithbagley14@verizon.net; Web: www.oldpineforge.com
Specialties: Folders. **Technical:** Use ATS-34, 5160, O1, 1085 and 1095. **Patterns:** Ladder-wave lightning bolt. **Prices:** $275 to $750. **Remarks:** Farrier for 37 years, blacksmith for 37 years, knifemaker for 25 years. **Mark:** KB inside horseshoe and anvil.

BAILEY, I.R.
Lamorna Cottage, Common End, Colkirk, ENGLAND NR 21 7JD, Phone: 01-328-856-183, admin@grommitbaileyknives.com; Web: www.grommitbaileyknives.com
Specialties: Hunters, utilities, Bowies, camp knives, fighters. Mainly influenced by Moran, Loveless and Lile. **Technical:** Primarily stock removal using flat ground 1095, 1075, and 80CrV2. Occasionally forges including own basic Damascus. Uses both native and exotic hardwoods, stag, Leather, Micarta and other synthetic handle materials, with brass or 301 stainless fittings. Does some filework and leather tooling. Does own heat treating. **Remarks:** Part-time maker since 2005. All knives and sheaths are sole authorship. **Mark:** Last name stamped.

BAILEY, JOSEPH D.
3213 Jonesboro Dr, Nashville, TN 37214, Phone: 615-889-3172, jbknfemkr@aol.com
Specialties: Working and using straight knives; collector pieces. **Patterns:** Bowies, hunters, tactical, folders. **Technical:** 440C, ATS-34, Damascus and wire Damascus. Offers scrimshaw. **Prices:** $85 to $1200. **Remarks:** Part-time maker; first knife sold in 1988. **Mark:** Joseph D Bailey Nashville Tennessee.

BAIR, MARK
386 E. 475 N, Firth, ID 83236, Phone: 208-681-7533, markbair@gmail.com
Specialties Fixed blades. Hunters, bowies, kitchen, utility, custom orders. **Technical:** High-end damascus, San Mai steel, stainless steel and 52100. Also mammoth ivory and other exotic handles, custom hand filework, and works with high-end custom engravers. **Prices:** $300 to $7,500. **Remarks:** Part-time maker; first knife made in 1988. **Mark:** MB Custom Knives.

BAKER, HERB
14104 NC 87 N, Eden, NC 27288, Phone: 336-627-0338

BAKER, RAY
PO Box 303, Sapulpa, OK 74067, Phone: 918-224-8013
Specialties: High-tech working straight knives. **Patterns:** Hunters, fighters, Bowies, skinners and boots of his design and to customer specs. **Technical:** Grinds 440C, 1095 spring steel or customer request; heat-treats. Custom-made scabbards for any knife. **Prices:** $125 to $500; some to $1000. **Remarks:** Full-time maker; first knife sold in 1981. **Mark:** First initial, last name.

BAKER, TONY
707 Lake Highlands Dr, Allen, TX 75002, Phone: 214-543-1001, tonybakerknives@yahoo.com
Specialties: Hunting knives, integral made **Technical:** 154cm, S30V, and S90V **Prices:** Starting at $500. **Prices:** $200-$1200 **Remarks:** First knife made in 2001

BAKER, WILD BILL
Box 361, Boiceville, NY 12412, Phone: 914-657-8646
Specialties: Primitive knives, buckskinners. **Patterns:** Skinners, camp knives and Bowies. **Technical:** Works with L6, files and rasps. **Prices:** $100 to $350. **Remarks:** Part-time maker; first knife sold in 1989. **Mark:** Wild Bill Baker, Oak Leaf Forge, or both.

BALBACH, MARKUS
Heinrich Worner Str.1-3, WeilmŸnster, GERMANY 35789, Phone: +49 (0) 6475-8911, Fax: 912986, Web: www.schmiede-balbach.de
Specialties: High-art knives and working/using straight knives and folders of his design and to customer specs. **Patterns:** Hunters and daggers. **Technical:** Stainless steel, one of Germany's greatest Smithies. Supplier for the forges of Solingen. **Remarks:** Full-time maker; first knife sold in 1984. Doing business as Schmiedewerkstatte M. Balbach. **Mark:** Initials stamped inside the handle.

BALL, BUTCH
2161 Reedsville Rd., Floyd, VA 24091, Phone: 540-392-3485, ballknives@yahoo.com
Specialties: Fancy and Tactical Folders and Automatics. **Patterns:** Fixed and folders. **Technical:** Use various Damascus and ATS34, 154cm. **Prices:** $300 - $1500. **Remarks:** Part-time maker. Sold first knife in 1990. **Mark:** Ball or BCK with crossed knives.

BALL, KEN
127 Sundown Manor, Mooresville, IN 46158, Phone: 317-834-4803
Specialties: Classic working/using straight knives of his design and to customer specs. **Patterns:** Hunters and utility/camp knives. **Technical:** Flat-grinds ATS-34. Offers filework. **Prices:** $150 to $400. **Remarks:** Part-time maker; first knife sold in 1994. Doing business as Ball Custom Knives. **Mark:** Last name.

BALLESTRA, SANTINO
via D. Tempesta 11/17, Ventimiglia, ITALY 18039, Phone: 0184-215228, ladasin@libero.it
Specialties: Using and collecting straight knives. **Patterns:** Hunting, fighting, skinners, Bowies, medieval daggers and knives. **Technical:** Forges ATS-34, D2, O2, 1060 and his own Damascus. Uses ivory and silver. **Prices:** $500 to $2000; some higher. **Remarks:** Full-time maker; first knife sold in 1979. **Mark:** First initial, last name.

BALLEW, DALE
PO Box 1277, Bowling Green, VA 22427, Phone: 804-633-5701
Specialties: Miniatures only to customer specs. **Patterns:** Bowies, daggers and fighters. **Technical:** Files 440C stainless; uses ivory, abalone, exotic woods and some precious stones. **Prices:** $100 to $800. **Remarks:** Part-time maker; first knife sold in 1988. **Mark:** Initials and last name.

BANAITIS, ROMAS
84 Winthrop St., Medway, MA 02053, Phone: 774-248-5851, rbanaitis@verizon.net
Specialties: Designing art and fantasy knives. **Patterns:** Folders, daggers and fixed blades. **Technical:** Hand-carved blades, handles and fittings in stainless steel, sterling silver and titanium. **Prices:** Moderate to upscale. **Remarks:** First knife sold in 1996. **Mark:** Romas Banaitis.

BANKS, DAVID L.
99 Blackfoot Ave, Riverton, WY 82501, Phone: 307-856-3154/Cell: 307-851-5599
Specialties: Heavy-duty working straight knives. **Patterns:** Hunters, Bowies and camp

knives. **Technical:** Forges Damascus 1084-15N20, L6-W1 pure nickel, 5160, 52100 and his own Damascus; differential heat treat and tempers. Handles made of horn, antlers and exotic wood. Hand-stitched harness leather sheaths. **Prices:** $300 to $2000. **Remarks:** Part-time maker. **Mark:** Banks Blackfoot forged Dave Banks and initials connected.

BAREFOOT, JOE W.
1654 Honey Hill, Wilmington, NC 28442, Phone: 910-641-1143
Specialties: Working straight knives of his design. **Patterns:** Hunters, fighters and boots; tantos and survival knives. **Technical:** Grinds D2, 440C and ATS-34. Mirror finishes. Uses ivory and stag on customer request only. **Prices:** $50 to $160; some to $500. **Remarks:** Part-time maker; first knife sold in 1980. **Mark:** Bare footprint.

BARKER, JOHN
5725 Boulder Bluff Dr., Cumming, GA 30040, Phone: 678-357-8586, barkerknives@bellsouth.net Web: www.barkerknives.com
Specialties: Tactical fixed blades and folders. **Technical:** Stock removal method and CPM and Carpenter powdered technology steels. **Prices:** $150 and up. **Remarks:** First knife made 2006. **Mark:** Snarling dog with "Barker" over the top of its head and "Knives" below.

BARKER, REGGIE
603 S Park Dr, Springhill, LA 71075, Phone: 318-539-2958, wrbarker@cmaaccess.com; Web: www.reggiebarkerknives.com
Specialties: Camp knives and hatchets. **Patterns:** Bowie, skinning, hunting, camping, fighters, kitchen or customer design. **Technical:** Forges carbon steel and own pattern welded steels. **Prices:** $225 to $2000. **Remarks:** Full-time maker. Winner of 1999 and 2000 Spring Hammering Cutting contest. Winner of Best Value of Show 2001; Arkansas Knife Show and Journeyman Smith. Border Guard Forge. **Mark:** Barker JS.

BARKER, ROBERT G.
2311 Branch Rd, Bishop, GA 30621, Phone: 706-769-7827
Specialties: Traditional working/using straight knives of his design. **Patterns:** Bowies, hunters and utility knives, ABS Journeyman Smith. **Technical:** Hand forged carbon and Damascus. Forges to shape high-carbon 5160, cable and chain. Differentially heat-treats. **Prices:** $200 to $500; some to $1000. **Remarks:** Spare-time maker; first knife sold in 1987. **Mark:** BARKER/J.S.

BARKER, STUART
51 Thorpe Dr., Wigston, Leicester, ENGLAND LE18 1LE, Phone: +447887585411, sc_barker@hotmail.com Web: www.barkerknives.co.uk
Specialties: Fixed blade working knives of his design. **Patterns:** Kitchen, hunter, utility/camp knives. **Technical:** Grinds O1, Rw134 & Damasteel, hand rubbed or shot blast finishes. **Prices:** $150 - $1,000. **Remarks:** Part-time maker; first knife sold 2006. **Mark:** Last initial or last name.

BARKES, TERRY
14844 N. Bluff Rd., Edinburgh, IN 46124, Phone: 812-526-6390, knifenpocket@sbcglobal.net; Web:http://my.hsonline.net/wizard/TerryBarkesKnives.htm
Specialties: Traditional working straight knives of his designs. **Patterns:** Drop point hunters, boot knives, skinning, fighter, utility, all purpose, camp, and grill knives. **Technical:** Grinds 1095 - 1084 - 52100 - 01, Hollow grinds and flat grinds. Hand rubbed finish from 400 to 2000 grit or High polish buff. Hard edge and soft back, heat treat by maker. Likes File work, natural handle material, bone, stag, water buffalo horn, wildbeast bone, ironwood. **Prices:** $200 and up **Remarks:** Full-time maker, first knifge sold in 2005. Doing business as Barkes Knife Shop. **Marks:** Barkes - USA, Barkes Double Arrow - USA

BARLOW, JANA POIRIER
3820 Borland Cir, Anchorage, AK 99517, Phone: 907-243-4581

BARNES, AUBREY G.
11341 Rock Hill Rd, Hagerstown, MD 21740, Phone: 301-223-4587, a.barnes@myactv.net
Specialties: Classic Moran style reproductions and using knives of his own design. **Patterns:** Bowies, hunters, fighters, daggers and utility/camping knives. **Technical:** Forges 5160, 1085, L6 and Damascus, Silver wire inlays. **Prices:** $500 to $5000. **Remarks:** Full-time maker; first knife sold in 1992. Doing business as Falling Waters Forge. **Mark:** First and middle initials, last name, M.S.

BARNES, GARY L.
Box 138, New Windsor, MD 21776-0138, Phone: 410-635-6243, Fax: 410-635-6243, mail@glbarnes.com; Web: www.glbarnes.com or www.barnespneumatic.com
Specialties: Ornate button lock Damascus folders. **Patterns:** Barnes original. **Technical:** Forges own Damascus. **Prices:** Average $2500. **Remarks:** ABS Master Smith since 1983. **Mark:** Hand engraved logo of letter B pierced by dagger.

BARNES, GREGORY
266 W Calaveras St, Altadena, CA 91001, Phone: 626-398-0053, snake@annex.com

BARNES, JACK
PO Box 1315, Whitefish, MT 59937-1315, Phone: 406-862-6078

BARNES, MARLEN R.
904 Crestview Dr S, Atlanta, TX 75551-1854, Phone: 903-796-3668, MRBlives@worldnet.att.net
Specialties: Hammer forges random and mosaic Damascus. **Patterns:** Hatchets, straight and folding knives. **Technical:** Hammer forges carbon steel using 5160, 1084 and 52100 with 15N20 and 203E nickel. **Prices:** $150 and up. **Remarks:** Part-time maker; first knife sold 1999. **Mark:** Script M.R.B., other side J.S.

BARNES, WENDELL
PO Box 272, Clinton, MT 59825, Phone: 406-825-0908

Specialties: Working straight knives. **Patterns:** Hunters, folders, neck knives. **Technical:** Grinds 440C, ATS-34, D2 and Damascus. **Prices:** Start at $75. **Remarks:** Spare-time maker; first knife sold in 1996. **Mark:** First initial, split heart, last name.

BARNES JR., CECIL C.
141 Barnes Dr, Center Ridge, AR 72027, Phone: 501-893-2267

BARNETT, BRUCE
PO Box 447, Mundaring, WA, AUSTRALIA 6073, Phone: 61-4-19243855, bruce@barnettcustomknives.com; web: www.barnettcustomknives.com
Specialties: Most types of fixed blades, folders, carving sets. **Patterns:** Hunters, Bowies, Camp Knives, Fighters, Lockback and Slipjoint Folders. **Prices:** $200 up **Remarks:** Part time maker. Member Australian Knifemakers Guild and ABS journeyman smith. **Mark:** Barnett + J.S.

BARNETT, VAN
BARNETT INT'L INC, 1135 Terminal Way Ste #209, Reno, NV 89502, Phone: 304-727-5512; 775-513-6969; 775-686-9084, ImATimeMachine@gmail.com & illusionknives@gmail.com; Web: www.VanBarnett.com
Specialties: Collector grade one-of-a-kind / embellished high art daggers and art folders. **Patterns:** Art daggers and folders. **Technical:** Forges and grinds own Damascus. **Prices:** Upscale. **Remarks:** Designs and makes one-of-a-kind highly embellished art knives using high karat gold, diamonds and other gemstones, pearls, stone and fossil ivories, carved steel guards and blades, all knives are carved and or engraved, does own engraving, carving and other embellishments, sole authorship; full-time maker since 1981. Does one high art collaboration a year with Dellana. Member of ABS. Member Art Knife Invitational Group (AKI) **Mark:** VBARNETT

BARR, JUDSON C.
1905 Pickwick Circle, Irving, TX 75060, Phone: 214-724-0564, judsonbarrknives@yahoo.com
Specialties: Bowies. **Patterns:** Sheffield and Early American. **Technical:** Forged carbon steel and Damascus. Also stock removal. **Remarks:** Journeyman member of ABS. **Mark:** Barr.

BARRETT, RICK L. (TOSHI HISA)
18943 CR 18, Goshen, IN 46528, Phone: 574-533-4297, barrettrick@hotmail.com
Specialties: Japanese-style blades from sushi knives to katana and fantasy pieces. **Patterns:** Swords, axes, spears/lances, hunter and utility knives. **Technical:** Forges and grinds Damascus and carbon steels, occasionally uses stainless. **Prices:** $250 to $4000+. **Remarks:** Full-time bladesmith, jeweler. **Mark:** Japanese mei on Japanese pieces and stylized initials.

BARRON, BRIAN
123 12th Ave, San Mateo, CA 94402, Phone: 650-341-2683
Specialties: Traditional straight knives. **Patterns:** Daggers, hunters and swords. **Technical:** Grinds 440C, ATS-34 and 1095. Sculpts bolsters using an S-curve. **Prices:** $130 to $270; some to $1500. **Remarks:** Part-time maker; first knife sold in 1993. **Mark:** Diamond Drag "Barron."

BARRY, SCOTT
Box 354, Laramie, WY 82073, Phone: 307-721-8038, scottyb@uwyo.edu
Specialties: Currently producing mostly folders, also make fixed blade hunters & fillet knives. **Technical:** Steels used are 440/C, ATS/34, 154/CM, S30V, Damasteel & Mike Norris stainless Damascus. **Prices:** Range from $300 $1000. **Remarks:** Part-time maker. First knife sold in 1972. **Mark:** DSBarry, etched on blade.

BARRY III, JAMES J.
115 Flagler Promenade No., West Palm Beach, FL 33405, Phone: 561-832-4197
Specialties: High-art working straight knives of his design also high art tomahawks. **Patterns:** Hunters, daggers and fishing knives. **Technical:** Grinds 440C only. Prefers exotic materials for handles. Most knives embellished with filework, carving and scrimshaw. Many pieces designed to stand unassisted. **Prices:** $500 to $10,000. **Remarks:** Part-time maker; first knife sold in 1975. Guild member (Knifemakers) since 1991. **Mark:** Branded initials as a J and B together.

BARTH, J.D.
101 4th St, PO Box 186, Alberton, MT 59820, Phone: 406-722-4557, mtdeerhunter@blackfoot.net; Web: www.jdbarthcustomknives.com
Specialties: Working and fancy straight knives of his design. LinerLock® folders, stainless and Damascus, fully file worked, nitre bluing. **Technical:** Grinds ATS-34, 440-C, stainless and carbon Damascus. Uses variety of natural handle materials and Micarta. Likes dovetailed bolsters. Filework on most knives, full and tapered tangs. Makes custom fit sheaths for each knife. **Mark:** Name over maker, city and state.

BARTLOW, JOHN
14 Red Fox Dr., Sheridan, WY 82801, Phone: 307-673-4941, 2jbartlow@gmail.com
Specialties: Skinner/caper sets, classic working patterns, and known for bird-and-trout classics. **Technical:** ATS-34, CPM-154, damascus available on all LinerLocks. **Prices:** $400 to $2,500. **Remarks:** Full-time maker, Guild member from 1988. **Mark:** Bartlow Sheridan, Wyo.

BASKETT, BARBARA
427 Sutzer Ck Rd, Eastview, KY 42732, Phone: 270-862-5019, baskettknives@windstream.net
Specialities: Hunters and LinerLocks. **Technical:** 440-C, CPM 154, S30V. **Prices:** $250 and up. **Mark:** B. Baskett.

BASKETT, LEE GENE
427 Sutzer Ck. Rd., Eastview, KY 42732, Phone: 270-862-5019, Fax: Cell: 270-766-

BASSETT—BENNETT

8724, bassettknives@hotmail.com Web: www.baskettknives.com
Specialties: Fancy working knives and fancy art pieces, often set up in fancy desk stands. **Patterns:** Fighters, Bowies, and Surival Knives; lockback folders and liner locks along with traditional styles. Cutting competition knives. **Technical:** Grinds O1, 440-c, S30V, power CPM154, CPM 4, D2, buys Damascus. Filework provided on most knives. **Prices:** $250 and up. **Remarks:** Part-time maker, first knife sold in 1980. **Mark:** Baskett

BASSETT, DAVID J.
P.O. Box 69-102, Glendene, Auckland, NEW ZEALAND 0645, Phone: 64 9 818 9083, Fax: 64 9 818 9013, david@customknifemaking.co.nz; Web:www.customknifemaking.co.nz
Specialties: Working/using knives. **Patterns:** Hunters, fighters, boot, skinners, tanto. **Technical:** Grinds 440C, 12C27, D2 and some Damascus via stock removal method. **Prices:** $150 to $500. **Remarks:** Part-time maker, first knife sold in 2006. Also carries range of natural and synthetic handle material, pin stock etc. for sale. **Mark:** Name over country in semi-circular design.

BATLEY, MARK S.
PO Box 217, Wake, VA 23176, Phone: 804 776-7794

BATSON, JAMES
176 Brentwood Lane, Madison, AL 35758, Phone: 256-971-6860
Specialties: Forged Damascus blades and fittings in collectible period pieces. **Patterns:** Integral art knives, Bowies, folders, American-styled blades and miniatures. **Technical:** Forges carbon steel and his Damascus. **Prices:** $150 to $1800; some to $4500. **Remarks:** Semi retired full-time maker; first knife sold in 1978. **Mark:** Name, bladesmith with horse's head.

BATSON, RICHARD G.
6591 Waterford Rd, Rixeyville, VA 22737, Phone: 540-937-2318, mbatson6591@comcast.net
Specialties: Military, utility and fighting knives in working and presentation grade. **Patterns:** Daggers, combat and utility knives. **Technical:** Grinds O1, 1095 and 440C. Etches and scrimshaws; offers polished, Parkerized finishes. **Prices:** $400 to $1,750. **Remarks:** Very limited production to active-dute military and vets only. First knife sold in 1958. **Mark:** Bat in circle, hand-signed and serial numbered.

BATTS, KEITH
500 Manning Rd, Hooks, TX 75561, Phone: 903-277-8466, kbatts@cableone.net
Specialties: Working straight knives of his design or to customer specs. **Patterns:** Bowies, hunters, skinners, camp knives and others. **Technical:** Forges 5160 and his Damascus; offers filework. **Prices:** $245 to $895. **Remarks:** Part-time maker; first knife sold in 1988. **Mark:** Last name.

BAUCHOP, ROBERT
PO Box 330, Munster, KN, SOUTH AFRICA 4278, Phone: +27 39 3192449
Specialties: Fantasy knives; working and using knives of his design and to customer specs. **Patterns:** Hunters, swords, utility/camp knives, diver's knives and large swords. **Technical:** Grinds Sandvick 12C27, D2, 440C. Uses South African hardwoods red ivory, wild olive, African blackwood, etc. on handles. **Prices:** $200 to $800; some to $2000. **Remarks:** Full-time maker; first knife sold in 1986. Doing business as Bauchop Custom Knives and Swords. **Mark:** Viking helmet with Bauchop (bow and chopper) crest.

BAXTER, DALE
291 County Rd 547, Trinity, AL 35673, Phone: 256-355-3626, dale@baxterknives.com
Specialties: Bowies, fighters, and hunters. **Patterns:** No patterns: all unique true customs. **Technical:** Hand forge and hand finish. Steels: 1095 and L6 for carbon blades, 1095/L6 for Damascus. **Remarks:** Full-time bladesmith and sold first knife in 1998. **Mark:** Dale Baxter (script) and J.S. on reverse.

BEAM, JOHN R.
1310 Foothills Rd, Kalispell, MT 59901, Phone: 406-755-2593
Specialties: Classic, high-art and working straight knives of his design. **Patterns:** Bowies and hunters. **Technical:** Grinds 440C, Damascus and scrap. **Prices:** $175 to $600; some to $3000. **Remarks:** Part-time maker; first knife sold in 1950. Doing business as Beam's Knives. **Mark:** Beam's Knives.

BEASLEY, GENEO
PO Box 339, Wadsworth, NV 89442, Phone: 775-575-2584

BEATTY, GORDON H.
121 Petty Rd, Seneca, SC 29672, Phone: 867-723-2966
Specialties: Working straight knives, some fancy. **Patterns:** Traditional patterns, mini-skinners and letter openers. **Technical:** Grinds ATS-34; makes knives one-at-a-time. **Prices:** $185 and up. **Remarks:** Part-time maker; first knife sold in 1982. **Mark:** Name.

BEATY, ROBERT B.
CUTLER, 1995 Big Flat Rd, Missoula, MT 59804, Phone: 406-549-1818
Specialties: Plain and fancy working knives and collector pieces; will accept custom orders. **Patterns:** Hunters, Bowies, utility, kitchen and camp knives; locking folders. **Technical:** Grinds D-2, ATS-34, Dendritic D-2, makes all tool steel Damascus, forges 1095, 5160, 52100. **Prices:** $150 to $600, some to $1100. **Remarks:** Full-time maker; first knife sold 1995. **Mark:** Stainless: First name, middle initial, last name, city and state. Carbon: Last name stamped on Ricasso.

BEAUCHAMP, GAETAN
125 de la Rivire, Stoneham, QC, CANADA G3C 0P6, Phone: 418-848-1914, Fax: 418-848-6859, knives@gbeauchamp.ca; Web: www.gbeauchamp.ca

Specialties: Working knives and folders of his design and to customer specs. **Patterns:** Hunters, fighters, fantasy knives. **Technical:** Grinds ATS-34, 440C, Damascus. Scrimshaws on ivory; specializes in buffalo horn and black backgrounds. Offers a variety of handle materials. **Prices:** Start at $250. **Remarks:** Full-time maker; first knife sold in 1992. **Mark:** Signature etched on blade.

BECKER, FRANZ
AM Kreuzberg 2, Marktl, GERMANY 84533, Phone: 08678-8020
Specialties: Stainless steel knives in working sizes. **Patterns:** Semi- and full-integral knives; interframe folders. **Technical:** Grinds stainless steels; likes natural handle materials. **Prices:** $200 to $2000. **Mark:** Name, country.

BEERS, RAY
2501 Lakefront Dr, Lake Wales, FL 33898, Phone: 443-841-4143, rbknives@copper.net

BEETS, MARTY
390 N 5th Ave, Williams Lake, BC, CANADA V2G 2G4, Phone: 250-392-7199
Specialties: Working and collectable straight knives of his own design. **Patterns:** Hunter, skinners, Bowies and utility knives. **Technical:** Grinds various steels-does all his own work including heat treating. Uses a variety of handle material specializing in exotic hardwoods, antler and horn. **Price:** $125 to $400. **Remarks:** Wife, Sandy does handmade/hand stitched sheaths. First knife sold in 1988. Business name Beets Handmade Knives.

BEGG, TODD M.
1341 N. McDowell Blvd., Ste. D, Petaluma, CA 94954, Phone: 707-242-1790, info@beggknives.com; Web: http://beggknives.net
Specialties: High-grade tactical folders and fixed blades. **Patterns:** Folders, integrals, fighters. **Technical:** Specializes in flipper folders using "IK135" bearing system. **Price:** $400 - $15,000. **Remarks:** Uses modern designs and materials.

BEHNKE, WILLIAM
8478 Dell Rd, Kingsley, MI 49649, Phone: 231-263-7447, bill@billbehnkeknives.com Web: www.billbehnkeknives.com
Specialties: Hunters, belt knives, folders, hatchets, straight razors, high-end letter openers and tomahawks. **Patterns:** Traditional styling in moderate-sized straight and folding knives. **Technical:** Forges own damascus, prefers W-2. **Prices:** $150 to $2,000. **Remarks:** Part-time maker. **Mark:** Bill Behnke Knives.

BELL, DON
Box 98, Lincoln, MT 59639, Phone: 406-362-3208, dlb@linctel.net
Patterns: Folders, hunters and custom orders. **Technical:** Carbon steel 52100, 5160, 1095, 1084. Making own Damascus. Flat grinds. Natural handle material including fossil. ivory, pearl, & ironwork. **Remarks:** Full-time maker. First knife sold in 1999. **Mark:** Last name.

BELL, DONALD
2 Division St, Bedford, NS, CANADA B4A 1Y8, Phone: 902-835-2623, donbell@accesswave.ca; Web: www.bellknives.com
Specialties: Fancy knives: carved and pierced folders of his own design. **Patterns:** Locking folders, pendant knives, jewelry knives. **Technical:** Grinds Damascus, pierces and carves blades. **Prices:** $500 to $2000, some to $3000. **Remarks:** Spare-time maker; first knife sold in 1993. **Mark:** Bell symbol with first initial inside.

BELL, GABRIEL
88321 North Bank Lane, Coquille, OR 97423, Phone: 541-396-3605, gabriel@dragonflyforge.com; Web: www.dragonflyforge.com & tomboyama.com
Specialties: Full line of combat quality Japanese swords. **Patterns:** Traditional tanto to katana. **Technical:** Handmade steel and welded cable. **Prices:** Swords from bare blades to complete high art $1500 to $28,000. **Remarks:** Studied with father Michael Bell. Instruction in sword crafts. Working in partnership with Michael Bell.**Mark:** Dragonfly in shield or kunitoshi.

BELL, MICHAEL
88321 N Bank Lane, Coquille, OR 97423, Phone: 541-396-3605, michael@dragonflyforge.com; Web: www. Dragonflyforge.com & tomboyama.com
Specialties: Full line of combat quality Japanese swords. **Patterns:** Traditional tanto to katana. **Technical:** Handmade steel and welded cable. **Prices:** Swords from bare blades to complete high art $1500 to $28,000. **Remarks:** Studied with Japanese master Nakajima Muneyoshi. Instruction in sword crafts. Working in partnership with son, Gabriel.**Mark:** Dragonfly in shield or tombo kunimitsu.

BELL, TONY
PO Box 24, Woodland, AL 36280, Phone: 256-449-2655, tbell905@aol.com
Specialties: Hand forged period knives and tomahawks. Art knives and knives made for everyday use.**Technical:**Makes own Damascus. Forges 1095, 5160,1080,L6 steels. Does own heat treating. **Prices:**$75-$1200. **Remarks:**Full time maker. **Mark:**Bell symbol with initial T in the middle.

BENDIK, JOHN
7076 Fitch Rd, Olmsted Falls, OH 44138

BENJAMIN JR., GEORGE
3001 Foxy Ln, Kissimmee, FL 34746, Phone: 407-846-7259
Specialties: Fighters in various styles to include Persian, Moro and military. **Patterns:** Daggers, skinners and one-of-a-kind grinds. **Technical:** Forges O1, D2, A2, 5160 and Damascus. Favors Pakkawood, Micarta, and mirror or Parkerized finishes. Makes unique para-military leather sheaths. **Prices:** $150 to $600; some to $1200. **Remarks:** Doing business as The Leather Box. **Mark:** Southern Pride Knives.

BENNETT, BRETT C
420 Adamstown Rd., Reinholds, PA 17569, Phone: 307-220-3919, brett@

bennettknives.com; Web: www.bennettknives.com
Specialties: Hand-rubbed satin finish on all blades. **Patterns:** Mostly fixed-blade patterns. **Technical:** ATS-34, D-2, 1084/15N20 damascus, 1084 forged. **Mark:** "B.C. Bennett" in script or "Bennett" stamped in script.

BENNETT, GLEN C
5821 S Stewart Blvd, Tucson, AZ 85706

BENNETT, PETER
PO Box 143, Engadine, NSW, AUSTRALIA 2233, Phone: 02-520-4975 (home), Fax: 02-528-8219 (work)
Specialties: Fancy and embellished working and using straight knives to customer specs and in standard patterns. **Patterns:** Fighters, hunters, bird/trout and fillet knives. **Technical:** Grinds 440C, ATS-34 and Damascus. Uses rare Australian desert timbers for handles. **Prices:** $90 to $500; some to $1500. **Remarks:** Full-time maker; first knife sold in 1985. **Mark:** First and middle initials, last name; country.

BENNICA, CHARLES
11 Chemin du Salet, Moules et Baucels, FRANCE 34190, Phone: +33 4 67 73 42 40, cbennica@bennica-knives.com; Web: www.bennica-knives.com
Specialties: Fixed blades and folding knives; the latter with slick closing mechanisms with push buttons to unlock blades. Unique handle shapes, signature to the maker. **Technical:** 416 stainless steel frames for folders and ATS-34 blades. Also specializes in Damascus.

BENSINGER, J. W.
583 Jug Brook Rd., Marshfield, VT 05658, Phone: 802-917-1789, jwbensinger@gmail.com Web: www.vermontbladesmith.com
Specialties: Working hunters, bowies for work and defense, and Finnish patterns. Occasional folders. **Technical:** High performance handforged knives in 5160, 52100, 1080, and in-house damascus. **Prices:** Range from $130 for simple bushcraft knives to $500 for larger knives. Damascus prices on request. **Remarks:** First knife made in 1980 or so. Full-time maker. Customer designs welcome. **Mark:** "JWB" and year in cursive.

BENSON, DON
2505 Jackson St #112, Escalon, CA 95320, Phone: 209-838-7921
Specialties: Working straight knives of his design. **Patterns:** Axes, Bowies, tantos and hunters. **Technical:** Grinds 440C. **Prices:** $100 to $150; some to $400. **Remarks:** Spare-time maker; first knife sold in 1980. **Mark:** Name.

BENTLEY, C L
2405 Hilltop Dr, Albany, GA 31707, Phone: 912-432-6656

BER, DAVE
656 Miller Rd, San Juan Island, WA 98250, Phone: 206-378-7230
Specialties: Working straight and folding knives for the sportsman; welcomes customer designs. **Patterns:** Hunters, skinners, Bowies, kitchen and fishing knives. **Technical:** Forges and grinds saw blade steel, wire Damascus, O1, L6, 5160 and 440C. **Prices:** $100 to $300; some to $500. **Remarks:** Full-time maker; first knife sold in 1985. **Mark:** Last name.

BERG, LEE
PO Box 267, Ketchum, OK 74349, kilatstrike@wavelinx.net
Specialties: One-of-a-kind and investment-quality straight knives of his own design, incorporating traditional, period, Near East and Asian influence. **Patterns:** Daggers, fighters, hunters, bowies, short swords, full size and miniature. **Technical:** Stock removal with file, damascus, meteorite, O1, D2 and ATS-34. **Prices:** $200 and up. **Remarks:** Part-time maker; first knife sold in 1972. **Mark:** Full name.

BERG, LOTHAR
37 Hillcrest Ln, Kitchener ON, CANADA NZK 1S9, Phone: 519-745-3260; 519-745-3260

BERGER, MAX A.
5716 John Richard Ct, Carmichael, CA 95608, Phone: 916-972-9229, bergerknives@aol.com
Specialties: Fantasy and working/using straight knives of his design. **Patterns:** Fighters, hunters and utility/camp knives. **Technical:** Grinds ATS-34 and 440C. Offers fileworks and combinations of mirror polish and satin finish blades. **Prices:** $200 to $600; some to $2500. **Remarks:** Part-time maker; first knife sold in 1992. **Mark:** Last name.

BERGH, ROGER
Dalkarlsa 291, Bygdea, SWEDEN 91598, Phone: 469-343-0061, knivroger@hotmail.com; Web: www.rogerbergh.com
Specialties: Collectible all-purpose straight-blade knives. Damascus steel blades, carving and artistic design knives are heavily influenced by nature and have an organic hand crafted feel.

BERGLIN, BRUCE
17441 Lake Terrace Place, Mount Vernon, WA 98274, Phone: 360-422-8603, bruce@berglins.com
Specialties: Working fixed blades and folders of his own design. **Patterns:** Hunters, boots, bowies, utility, liner locks and slip joints some with vintage finish. **Technical:** Forges carbon steel, grinds carbon steel. Prefers natural handle material. **Prices:** Start at $300. **Remarks:** Part-time maker since 1998. **Mark:** (2 marks) 1. Last name; or 2. First initial, second initial & last name, surrounded with an oval.

BERTOLAMI, JUAN CARLOS
Av San Juan 575, Neuquen, ARGENTINA 8300, fliabertolami@infovia.com.ar
Specialties: Hunting and country labor knives. All of them unique high quality pieces and supplies collectors too. **Technical:** Austrian stainless steel and elephant, hippopotamus and orca ivory, as well as ebony and other fine woods for the handles.

BERTUZZI, ETTORE
Via Partigiani 3, Seriate, Bergamo, ITALY 24068, Phone: 035-294262, Fax: 035-294262
Specialties: Classic straight knives and folders of his design, to customer specs and in standard patterns. **Patterns:** Bowies, hunters and locking folders. **Technical:** Grinds ATS-34, D3, D2 and various Damascus. **Prices:** $300 to $500. **Remarks:** Part-time maker; first knife sold in 1993. **Mark:** Name etched on ricasso.

BESEDICK, FRANK E
1257 Country Club Road, Monongahela, PA 15063-1057, Phone: 724-292-8016, bxtr.bez3@verizon.net
Specialties: Traditional working and using straight knives of his design. **Patterns:** Hunters, utility/camp knives and miniatures; buckskinner blades and tomahawks. **Technical:** Forges and grinds 5160, O1 and Damascus. Offers filework and scrimshaw. **Prices:** $75 to $300; some to $750. **Remarks:** Part-time maker; first knife sold in 1990. **Mark:** Name or initials.

BESHARA, BRENT (BESH)
PO BOX 557, Holyrood, NL, CANADA A0A 2R0, BESH@beshknives.com Web: www.beshknives.com
Specialties: Fixed blade tools and knives. **Patterns:** BESH Wedge tools and knives. **Technical:** Custom design work, grinds 0-1, D-2, 440C, 154cm. Offers kydex sheathing **Prices:** Start at $250. **Remarks:** Inventor of BESH Wedge geometry, custom maker and designer since 2000. Retired (24yrs) Special Forces, Special Operations Navy bomb disposal diver. Lifelong martial artist. **Mark:** "BESH" stamped.

BEST, RON
1489 Adams Lane, Stokes, NC 27884, Phone: 252-714-1264, ronbestknives@msn.com; Web: www.ronbestknives.com
Specialties: Folders and automatics. **Patterns:** Everything including butterfly knives. **Technical:** Grinds 440C, D-2 and ATS-34. **Prices:** $600 to $8000.

BETANCOURT, ANTONIO L.
5718 Beefwood Ct., St. Louis, MO 63129, Phone: 314-306-1869, bet2001@charter.net
Specialties: One-of-a-kind fixed blades and art knives. **Patterns:** Hunters and Bowies with embellished handles. **Technical:** Uses cast sterling silver and lapidary with fine gemstones, fossil ivory, and scrimshaw. Grinds Damascus and 440C. **Prices:** $100 to $800. **Remarks:** Part-time maker, first knife sold in 1974. **Mark:** Initials in cursive.

BEUKES, TINUS
83 Henry St, Risiville, Vereeniging, GT, SOUTH AFRICA 1939, Phone: 27 16 423 2053
Specialties: Working straight knives. **Patterns:** Hunters, skinners and kitchen knives. **Technical:** Grinds D2, 440C and chain, cable and stainless Damascus. **Prices:** $80 to $180. **Remarks:** Part-time maker; first knife sold in 1993. **Mark:** Full name, city, logo.

BEVERLY II, LARRY H
PO Box 741, Spotsylvania, VA 22553, Phone: 540-846-5426, beverlyknives@aol.com
Specialties: Working straight knives, slip-joints and liner locks. Welcomes customer designs. **Patterns:** Bowies, hunters, guard less fighters and miniatures. **Technical:** Grinds 440C, A2 and O1. **Prices:** $125 to $1000. **Remarks:** Part-time maker; first knife sold in 1986. **Mark:** Initials or last name in script.

BEZUIDENHOUT, BUZZ
PO BOX 28284, Malvern, KZN, SOUTH AFRICA 4055, Phone: 031-4632827, Fax: 031-4632827, buzzbee@mweb.co.za
Specialties: Working and Fancy Folders, my or customer design. **Patterns:** Boots, hunters, kitchen knives and utility/camp knives. **Technical:** Use 12-C-27 + stainless damascus, some carbon damascus. Uses local hardwoods, horn: kudu, impala, buffalo, giraffe bone and ivory for handles.
Prices: $250 to upscale. **Remarks:** Part-time maker; first knife sold in 1985. Member S.A. Knife Makers Guild **Mark:** First name with a bee emblem.

BILLGREN, PER
Stallgatan 9, Soderfors, SWEDEN 81576, Phone: +46 293 30600, Fax: +46 293 30124, mail@damasteel.se Web:www.damasteel.se
Specialties: Damasteel, stainless Damascus steels. **Patterns:** Bluetongue, Heimskringla, Muhammad's ladder, Rose, Twist, Odin's eye, Vinland, Hakkapelliitta. **Technical:** Modern Damascus steel made by patented powder metallurgy method. **Prices:** $80 to $180. **Remarks:** Damasteel is available through distributors around the globe.

BINGENHEIMER, BRUCE
553 Tiffany Dr., Spring Creek, NV 89815, Phone: 775-934-6295, mbing@citlink.net
Specialties: Forging fixed blade hunters, bowies, fighters. **Technical:** Forges own Damascus. Steel choices 5160, 1084. Damascus steels 15N20, 1080. **Prices:** $300 and up. **Remarks:** ABS Journeyman Smith 2010. Member of Montana Knife Makers Association and Oregon Knife Collector's Association. **Mark:** Bingenheimer (arched over) M B.

BIRDWELL, IRA LEE
PO Box 1448, Congress, AZ 85332, Phone: 928-925-3258, heli.ira@gmail.com
Specialties: Special orders. **Mark:** Engraved signature.

BISH, HAL
9347 Sweetbriar Trace, Jonesboro, GA 30236, Phone: 770-477-2422, hal-bish@hp.com

BISHER, WILLIAM (BILL)
1015 Beck Road, Denton, NC 27239, Phone: 336-859-4686, blackturtleforge@wildblue.net;Web: www.blackturtleforge.com
Specialties: Period pieces, also contemporary belt knives, friction folders. **Patterns:** Own design, hunters, camp/utility, Bowies, belt axes, neck knives, carving sets. **Technical:**

Forges straight high carbon steels, and own Damascus, grinds ATS34 and 154CM. Uses natural handle materials (wood, bone, stag horn), micarta and stabilized wood.**Prices:** Starting at $75 - $2500. **Remarks:** Past president of North Carolina Custom Knifemakers Guild, member ABS, Full-time maker as of 2007, first knife made 1989, all work in house, blades and sheaths **Mark:** Last name under crown and turtle

BIZZELL, ROBERT
145 Missoula Ave, Butte, MT 59701, Phone: 406-782-4403, patternweld@yahoo.com
Specialties: Damascus Bowies. **Patterns:** Composite, mosaic and traditional. **Technical:** Fixed blades & LinerLock® folders. **Prices:** Fixed blades start at $275. Folders start at $500. **Remarks:** Currently not taking orders. **Mark:** Hand signed.

BLACK, EARL
3466 South, 700 East, Salt Lake City, UT 84106, Phone: 801-466-8395
Specialties: High-art straight knives and folders; period pieces. **Patterns:** Boots, Bowies and daggers; lockers and gents. **Technical:** Grinds 440C and 154CM. Buys some Damascus. Scrimshaws and engraves. **Prices:** $200 to $1800; some to $2500 and higher. **Remarks:** Full-time maker; first knife sold in 1980. **Mark:** Name, city, state.

BLACK, SCOTT
27100 Leetown Rd, Picayune, MS 39466, Phone: 601-799-5939, copperheadforge@telepak.net
Specialties: Friction folders; fighters. **Patterns:** Bowies, fighters, hunters, smoke hawks, friction folders, daggers. **Technical:** All forged, all work done by him, own hand-stitched leather work; own heat-treating. **Prices:** $100 to $2200. **Remarks:** ABS Journeyman Smith. Cabel / Damascus/ High Carbone. **Mark:** Hot Mark - Copperhead Snake.

BLACK, TOM
921 Grecian NW, Albuquerque, NM 87107, Phone: 505-344-2549, blackknives@comcast.net
Specialties: Working knives to fancy straight knives of his design. **Patterns:** Drop-point skinners, folders, using knives, Bowies and daggers. **Technical:** Grinds 440C, 154CM, ATS-34, A2, D2, CPM-154 and damascus. Offers engraving and scrimshaw. **Prices:** $250 and up; some over $8500. **Remarks:** Full-time maker; first knife sold in 1970. **Mark:** Name, city.

BLACKWELL, ZANE
PO BOX 234, Eden, TX 76837, Phone: 325-869-8821, blackwellknives@hotmail.com; Web: www.blackwellknives.com
Specialties: Hunters, slip-joint folders and kitchen knives. **Patterns:** Drop-point and clip-point hunters, and classic slip-joint patterns like single-blade trappers. **Technical:** CPM 154, ATS-34, 440C and D2 blade steels, and natural handle materials. **Prices:** Hunters start at $325, single-blade folders at $350. **Remarks:** Six-month back log. **Mark:** Zane Blackwell Eden Texas.

BLACKWOOD, NEIL
7032 Willow Run, Lakeland, FL 33813, Phone: 863-812-5588, nblackwood4@gmail.com; Web: www.blackwoodcustomknives.blogspot.com
Specialties: Fixed blades and tactical folders. **Technical:** Blade steels D2 Talonite, Stellite, CPM S30V and RWL 34. Handle materials: G-10 carbon fiber and Micarta in the synthetics: giraffe bone and exotic woods on the natural side. **Prices:** $1000 to $1500. **Remarks:** Makes everything from the frames to the stop pins, pivot pins: everything but the stainless screws; one factory/custom collaboration (the Hybrid Hunter) with Outdoor Edge is in place and negotiations are under way for one with Benchmade. Collaborations with Boker.**Mark:**Blackwood

BLANCHARD, G R (GARY)
PO BOX 292, Dandridge, TN 37725, Phone: 865-397-9515, blanchardcustomknives@yahoo.com; Web: www.blanchardcustomknives.com
Specialties: Fancy folders with patented button blade release and high-art straight knives of his design. **Patterns:** Boots, daggers and locking folders. **Technical:** Grinds 440C and ATS-34 and Damascus. Engraves his knives. **Prices:** $1000 to $15,000 or more. **Remarks:** Full-time maker; first knife sold in 1989. **Mark:** First and middle initials, last name or last name only.

BLAUM, ROY
ROY'S KNIFE & ARCHERY SHOP, 319 N Columbia St, Covington, LA 70433, Phone: 985-893-1060
Specialties: Working straight knives and folders of his design; lightweight easy-open folders. **Patterns:** Hunters, boots, fishing and woodcarving/whittling knives. **Technical:** Grinds A2, D2, O1, 154CM and ATS-34. Offers leatherwork. **Prices:** $40 to $800; some higher. **Remarks:** Full-time maker; first knife sold in 1976. **Mark:** Engraved signature or etched logo.

BLOODWORTH CUSTOM KNIVES
3502 W. Angelica Dr., Meridian, ID 83646, Phone: 208-888-7778
Patterns: Working straight knives, hunters, skinners, bowies, utility knives of his designs or customer specs. Scagel knives. Period knives and traditional frontier knives and sheaths. **Technical:** Grinds D2, ATS34, 154CM, 5160, 01, Damascus, Heat treats, natural and composite handle materials. **Prices:** $185.00 to $1,500. **Remarks:** Roger Smith knife maker. Full-time maker; first knife sold in 1978 **Mark:** Sword over BLOODWORTH.

BLOOMER, ALAN T
PO Box 154, 116 E 6th St, Maquon, IL 61458, Phone: 309-875-3583 Cell: 309-371-8520, alant.bloomer@winco.net
Specialties: Folders & straight knives & custom pen maker. **Patterns:** All kinds. **Technical:** Does own heat treating. **Prices:** $400 to $1000. **Remarks:** Part-time maker. No orders. **Mark:** Stamp Bloomer.

BLUM, KENNETH
1729 Burleson, Brenham, TX 77833, Phone: 979-836-9577
Specialties: Traditional working straight knives of his design. **Patterns:** Camp knives, hunters and Bowies. **Technical:** Forges 5160; grinds 440C and D2. Uses exotic woods and Micarta for handles. **Prices:** $150 to $300. **Remarks:** Part-time maker; first knife sold in 1978. **Mark:** Last name on ricasso.

BLYSTONE, RONALD L.
231 Bailey Road, Creekside, PA 15732, Phone: 724-397-2671, taxibly@hotmail.com
Specialties: Traditional forged working knives. **Patterns:** Hunting utility and skinners of his own design. **Technical:** Forges his own pattern welded Damascus using carbon steel. **Prices:** Starting at $150. **Remarks:** Spare-time maker.**Mark:** Initials - upsidedown R against the B, inside a circle, over the word FORGE

BOARDMAN, GUY
39 Mountain Ridge R, New Germany, KZN, SOUTH AFRICA 3619, Phone: 031-726-921
Specialties: American and South African-styles. **Patterns:** Bowies, American and South African hunters, plus more. **Technical:** Grinds Bohler steels, some ATS-34. **Prices:** $100 to $600. **Remarks:** Part-time maker; first knife sold in 1986. **Mark:** Name, city, country.

BOCHMAN, BRUCE
183 Howard Place, Grants Pass, OR 97526, Phone: 541-471-1985, 183bab@gmail.com
Specialties: Hunting, fishing, bird and tactical knives. **Patterns:** Hunters, fishing and bird knives. **Technical:** ATS34, 154CM, mirror or satin finish. Damascus. **Prices:** $250 to $350; some to $750. **Remarks:** Part-time maker; first knife sold in 1977. **Mark:** Custom Knives by B. Bochman

BODEN, HARRY
Via Gellia Mill, Bonsall Matlock, Derbyshire, ENGLAND DE4 2AJ, Phone: 0629-825176
Specialties: Traditional working straight knives and folders of his design. **Patterns:** Hunters, locking folders and utility/camp knives. **Technical:** Grinds Sandvik 12C27, D2 and O1. **Prices:** £70 to £150; some to £300. **Remarks:** Full-time maker; first knife sold in 1986. **Mark:** Full name.

BODOLAY, ANTAL
Rua Wilson Soares Fernandes #31, Planalto, Belo Horizonte, MG, BRAZIL MG-31730-700, Phone: 031-494-1885
Specialties: Working folders and fixed blades of his design or to customer specs; some art daggers and period pieces. **Patterns:** Daggers, hunters, locking folders, utility knives and Khukris. **Technical:** Grinds D6, high-carbon steels and 420 stainless. Forges files on request. **Prices:** $30 to $350. **Remarks:** Full-time maker; first knife sold in 1965. **Mark:** Last name in script.

BOEHLKE, GUENTER
Parkstrasse 2, GERMANY 56412, Phone: 2602-5440, Boehlke-Messer@t-online.de; Web: www.boehlke-messer.de
Specialties: Classic working/using straight knives of his design. **Patterns:** Hunters, utility/camp knives and ancient remakes. **Technical:** Grinds Damascus, CPM-T-440V and 440C. Inlays gemstones and ivory. **Prices:** $220 to $700; some to $2000. **Remarks:** Spare-time maker; first knife sold in 1985. **Mark:** Name, address and bow and arrow.

BOHRMANN, BRUCE
61 Portland St, Yarmouth, ME 04096, Phone: 207-846-3385, bbohr@maine.rr.com; Web: Bohrmannknives.com
Specialties: Fixed-blade sporting, camp and hunting knives. **Technical:** Stock-removal maker using 13C26 Sandvik stainless steel hardened to 58-60 Rockwell. **Prices:** $499 for each model. Also, special "Heritage" production using historic certified woods (from Washington's, Jefferson's, Madison's and Henry's Plantations) - $1,250. **Remarks:** Full-time maker; first knife made in 1955. Always developing new models and concepts, such as steak knives, fixed blades and miniatures with special pocket sheaths. All knives serial #'d and can be personalized by etching initials into blades. **Mark:** The letter "B" connected to and lying beneath deer antlers.

BOJTOS, ARPAD
Dobsinskeho 10, 98403 Lucenec, SLOVAKIA, Phone: 00421-47 4333512; Cell: 00421-91 5875066, bojtos@stonline.sk; Web: www.arpadbojtos.sk
Specialties: Art knives, including over 100 folders. **Patterns:** Daggers, fighters and hunters. **Technical:** Grinds ATS-34 and stainless damascus. Carves on steel, handle materials and sheaths. **Prices:** $5000 to $10,000; some over. **Remarks:** Full-time maker; first knife sold in 1990. **Mark:** AB.

BOLDUC, GARY
1419 Tanglewood Dr., Corona, CA 92882, Phone: 951-739-0137, gary@stillwaterwoods.com; Web: www.bolducknives.com
Specialties: Fish fillet knives (larger sizes), medium 8" to large 10"-plus. Replica making of primitive Native Alaskan hunting and cutting tools, kitchen cutlery. **Patterns:** Hunters, skinners, fillet, boning, spear points and kitchen cutlery. **Technical:** High-quality stainless steel, mainly CTS-XHP, CPM-154 and CPM-S35VN for improved edge design. **Prices:** $200-$400 and up. **Remarks:** Full-time maker; first knife sold in 2007. **Mark:** First initial, last name with USA under, or grizzly bear with Bolduc Knives underneath.

BOLEWARE, DAVID
PO Box 96, Carson, MS 39427, Phone: 601-943-5372
Specialties: Traditional and working/using straight knives of his design, to customer specs and in standard patterns. **Patterns:** Bowies, hunters and utility/camp knives. **Technical:** Grinds ATS-34, 440C and Damascus. **Prices:** $85 to $350; some to $600. **Remarks:** Part-time maker; first knife sold in 1989. **Mark:** First and last name, city, state.

BOLEY, JAMIE
PO Box 477, Parker, SD 57053, Phone: 605-297-0014, jamie@polarbearforge.com
Specialties: Working knives and historical influenced reproductions. **Patterns:** Hunters, skinners, scramasaxes, and others.**Technical:** Forges 5160, O1, L6, 52100, W1, W2 makes own Damascus. **Prices:** Starts at $125. **Remarks:** Part-time maker. **Mark:** Polar bear paw print with name on the left side and Polar Bear Forge on the right.

BONASSI, FRANCO
Via Nicoletta 4, Pordenone, ITALY 33170, Phone: 0434-550821, frank.bonassi@alice.it
Specialties: Fancy and working one-of-a-kind folder knives of his design. **Patterns:** Folders, linerlocks and back locks. **Technical:** Grinds CPM, ATS-34, 154CM and commercial Damascus. Uses only titanium foreguards and pommels. **Prices:** Start at $350. **Remarks:** Spare-time maker; first knife sold in 1988. Has made cutlery for several celebrities; Gen. Schwarzkopf, Fuzzy Zoeller, etc. **Mark:** FRANK.

BOOCO, GORDON
175 Ash St, PO Box 174, Hayden, CO 81639, Phone: 970-276-3195
Specialties: Fancy working straight knives of his design and to customer specs. **Patterns:** Hunters and Bowies. **Technical:** Grinds 440C, D2 and A2. Heat-treats. **Prices:** $150 to $350; some $600 and higher. **Remarks:** Part-time maker; first knife sold in 1984. **Mark:** Last name with push dagger artwork.

BOOS, RALPH
6018-37A Avenue NW, Edmonton, AB, CANADA T6L 1H4, Phone: 780-463-7094
Specialties: Classic, fancy and fantasy miniature knives and swords of his design or to customer specs. **Patterns:** Bowies, daggers and swords. **Technical:** Hand files O1, stainless and Damascus. Engraves and carves. Does heat bluing and acid etching. **Prices:** $125 to $350; some to $1000. **Remarks:** Part-time maker; first knife sold in 1982. **Mark:** First initials back to back.

BOOTH, PHILIP W
301 S Jeffery Ave, Ithaca, MI 48847, Phone: 989-875-2844, pbooth@charter.net; Web: www.philipbooth.com
Specialties: Folding knives of his design using various mechanisms. **Patterns:** New "Twerp" ball-bearing flipper knife. "Minnow" folding knives, a series of small folding knives started in 1996 and changing yearly. One of a kind hot-rod car themed folding knives. **Technical:** Grinds ATS-34, CPM-154 and commercial damascus. Offers gun blue finishes and file work. **Prices:** $200 and up. **Remarks:** Part-time maker, first knife sold in 1991. **Mark:** Last name or name with city and map logo.

BORGER, WOLF
Benzstrasse 8, Graben-Neudorf, GERMANY 76676, Phone: 07255-72303, Fax: 07255-72304, wolf@messerschmied.de; Web: www.messerschmied.de
Specialties: High-tech working and using straight knives and folders, many with corkscrews or other tools, of his design. **Patterns:** Hunters, Bowies and folders with various locking systems. **Technical:** Grinds 440C, ATS-34 and CPM. Uses stainless Damascus. **Prices:** $250 to $900; some to $1500. **Remarks:** Full-time maker; first knife sold in 1975. **Mark:** Howling wolf and name; first name on Damascus blades.

BOSE, REESE
8810 N. County Rd. 375 E, Shelburn, IN 47879, Phone: 812-397-5114
Specialties: Traditional working and using knives in standard patterns and multi-blade folders. **Patterns:** Multi-blade slip-joints. **Technical:** ATS-34, D2, 154CM and CPM 440V. **Prices:** $600 to $3,000. **Remarks:** Full-time maker; first knife sold in 1992. Photos by Jack Busfield. **Mark:** R. Bose.

BOSE, TONY
7252 N. County Rd, 300 E., Shelburn, IN 47879-9778, Phone: 812-397-5114
Specialties: Traditional working and using knives in standard patterns; multi-blade folders. **Patterns:** Multi-blade slip-joints. **Technical:** Grinds commercial Damascus, ATS-34 and D2. **Prices:** $400 to $1200. **Remarks:** Full-time maker; first knife sold in 1972. **Mark:** First initial, last name, city, state.

BOSSAERTS, CARL
Rua Albert Einstein 906, Ribeirao Preto, SP, BRAZIL 14051-110, Phone: 016 633 7063
Specialties: Working and using straight knives of his design, to customer specs and in standard patterns. **Patterns:** Hunters, fighters and utility/camp knives. **Technical:** Grinds ATS-34, 440V and 440C; does filework. **Prices:** 60 to $400. **Remarks:** Part-time maker; first knife sold in 1992. **Mark:** Initials joined together.

BOST, ROGER E
30511 Cartier Dr, Palos Verdes, CA 90275-5629, Phone: 310- 541-6833, rogerbost@cox.net
Specialties: Hunters, fighters, boot, utility. **Patterns:** Loveless-style. **Technical:** ATS-34, BG-42, 440C, 59-61RC, stock removal and forge. **Prices:** $300 and up. **Remarks:** First knife sold in 1990. Cal. Knifemakers Assn., ABS. **Mark:** Diamond with initials inside and Palos Verdes California around outside.

BOSWORTH, DEAN
329 Mahogany Dr, Key Largo, FL 33037, Phone: 305-451-1564, DLBOZ@bellsouth.net
Specialties: Free hand hollow ground working knives with hand rubbed satin finish, filework and inlays. **Patterns:** Bird and Trout, hunters, skinners, fillet, Bowies, miniatures. **Technical:** Using 440C, ATS-34, D2, Meier Damascus, custom wet formed sheaths. **Prices:** $250 and up. **Remarks:** Part-time maker; first knife made in 1985. Member Florida Knifemakers Assoc. **Mark:** BOZ stamped in block letters.

BOURBEAU, JEAN YVES
15 Rue Remillard, Notre Dame, Ile Perrot, QC, CANADA J7V 8M9, Phone: 514-453-1069
Specialties: Fancy/embellished and fantasy folders of his design. **Patterns:** Bowies, fighters and locking folders. **Technical:** Grinds 440C, ATS-34 and Damascus. Carves precious wood for handles. **Prices:** $150 to $1000. **Remarks:** Part-time maker; first knife sold in 1994. **Mark:** Interlaced initials.

BOWLES, CHRIS
PO Box 985, Reform, AL 35481, Phone: 205-375-6162
Specialties: Working/using straight knives, and period pieces. **Patterns:** Utility, tactical, hunting, neck knives, machetes, and swords. **Grinds:** O-1, 154 cm, BG-42, 440V. **Prices:** $50 to $400 some higher. **Remarks:** Full-time maker. **Mark:** Bowles stamped or Bowles etched in script.

BOYD, FRANCIS
1811 Prince St, Berkeley, CA 94703, Phone: 510-841-7210
Specialties: Folders and kitchen knives, Japanese swords. **Patterns:** Push-button sturdy locking folders; San Francisco-style chef's knives. **Technical:** Forges and grinds; mostly uses high-carbon steels. **Prices:** Moderate to heavy. **Remarks:** Designer. **Mark:** Name.

BOYE, DAVID
PO Box 1238, Dolan Springs, AZ 86441, Phone: 800-853-1617, Fax: 928-767-4273, boye@cltlink.net; Web: www.boyeknives.com
Specialties: Folders and Boye Basics. Forerunner in the use of dendritic steel and dendritic cobalt for blades. **Patterns:** Lockback folders and fixed blade sheath knives in cobalt. **Technical:** Casts blades in cobalt. **Prices:** From $129 to $360. **Remarks:** Part-time maker; author of Step-by-Step Knifemaking. **Mark:** Name.

BOYES, TOM
2505 Wallace Lake Rd., West Bend, WI 53090, Phone: 262-391-2172
Specialties: Hunters, skinners and fillets. **Technical:** Grinds ATS-34, 440C, O1 tool steel and Damascus. **Prices:** $60 to $1000. **Remarks:** First knife sold in 1998. Doing business as R. Boyes Knives.

BOYSEN, RAYMOND A
125 E St Patrick, Rapid Ciy, SD 57701, Phone: 605-341-7752
Specialties: Hunters and Bowies. **Technical:** High performance blades forged from 52100 and 5160. **Prices:** $200 and up. **Remarks:** American Bladesmith Society Journeyman Smith. Part-time bladesmith. **Mark:** BOYSEN.

BRACH, PAUL
4870 Widgeon Way, Cumming, GA 30028, Phone: 770-595-8952, Web: www.brachknives.com
Specialties: Standard and one-of-a-kind straight knives and locking folders. Nickel silver sheath fittings and gemstone settings used on high-end pieces. **Patterns:** Hunters, bowies, daggers, antique bowies and titanium-frame folders. **Technical:** Grinds CPM-154 and forges high-carbon steel. Usually flat or full convex grinds. **Prices:** $150 to $1,000+. **Remarks:** Part-time maker; first knife sold in 1984. **Mark:** Etched "Paul Brach maker Cumming, GA" or "Brach" stamped.

BRACKETT, JAMIN
PO Box 387, Fallston, NC 28042, Phone: 704-718-3304, jaminbrackett@bellsouth.net; Web: brackettknives.com
Specialties: Hunting, camp, fishing, tactical, and general outdoor use. Handmade of my own design or to customer specs. **Patterns:** Drop point, tanto, fillet, and small EDC the "Tadpole," as well as large camp and tactical knives. **Technical:** Stock removal method, ATS-34 steel cryogenically treated to HRC 59-61. Mirror polish and bead blasted finishes. Handle materials include exotic woods, stag, buffalo horn, colored laminates, Micarta, and G-10. Come hand stitched 8-9 OZ leather sheaths treated in beeswax saddle oil mixture. Tactical models include reinforced tactical nylon sheaths Mollie system compatible. **Prices:** Standard models $150-$325. Personalized engraving available, for gifts and special occasions. **Remarks:** Part-time maker. First knife made in 2009. Member of NC Custom Knifemakers Guild.**Mark:** "Brackett", in bold. Each knife and sheath numbered.

BRADBURN, GARY
BRADBURN CUSTOM CUTLERY, 1714 Park Place, Wichita, KS 67203, Phone: 316-640-5684, gary@bradburnknives.com; Web:www.bradburnknives.com
Specialties: Specialize in clay-tempered Japanese-style knives and swords. **Patterns:** Also Bowies and fighters. **Technical:** Forge and/or grind carbon steel only. **Prices:** $150 to $1200. **Mark:** Initials GB stylized to look like Japanese character.

BRADFORD, GARRICK
582 Guelph St, Kitchener, ON, CANADA N2H-5Y4, Phone: 519-576-9863

BRADLEY, DENNIS
178 Bradley Acres Rd, Blairsville, GA 30512, Phone: 706-745-4364, bzbtaz@brmemc.net Web: www.dennisbradleyknives.com
Specialties: Working straight knives and folders, some high-art. **Patterns:** Hunters, boots and daggers; slip-joints and two-blades. **Technical:** Grinds ATS-34, D2, 440C and commercial Damascus. **Prices:** $100 to $500; some to $2000. **Remarks:** Part-time maker; first knife sold in 1973. **Mark:** BRADLEY KNIVES in double heart logo.

BRADLEY, GAYLE
1383 Old Garner Rd., Weatherford, TX 76088-8720, Phone: 817-504-2262, bradleysblades@aol.com; Web: www.bradleysblades.com
Specialties: High-end folders with wedge locks of maker's own design or lock backs, and work/utility knives. Uses high-end materials, including lapidary work and black-lip-pearl handle inlays. **Technical:** Grinds blades from bar stock, performs own heat treating. **Remarks:** Full-time maker; first knife made in 1988.

BRADLEY, JOHN
PO Box 33, Pomona Park, FL 32181, Phone: 386-649-4739, johnbradleyknives@yahoo.com

BRANDSEY—BROTHERS

Specialties: Fixed-blade using and art knives; primitive folders. **Patterns:** Skinners, Bowies, camp knives and primitive knives. **Technical:** Forged and ground 52100, 1095, O1 and Damascus. **Prices:** $250 to $2000. **Remarks:** Full-time maker; first knife sold in 1988. **Mark:** Last name.

BRANDSEY, EDWARD P
4441 Hawkridge Ct, Janesville, WI 53546, Phone: 608-868-9010, ebrandsey@ centurytel.net
Patterns: Large bowies, hunters, neck knives and buckskinner-styles. Native American influence on some. An occasional tanto, art piece. Does own scrimshaw. See Egnath's second book. Now making locking liner folders. **Technical:** ATS-34, CPM154, 440-C, O-1 and some damascus. Paul Bos heat treating past 20 years. **Prices:** $350 to $800; some to $4,000. **Remarks:** Full-time maker; first knife sold in 1973. **Mark:** Initials connected - registered Wisc. Trademark since March 1983.

BRANDT, MARTIN W
833 Kelly Blvd, Springfield, OR 97477, Phone: 541-747-5422, oubob747@aol.com

BRANTON, ROBERT
PO BOX 807, Awendaw, SC 29429, Phone: 843-928-3624, www.brantonknives.com
Specialties: Working straight knives of his design or to customer specs; throwing knives. **Patterns:** Hunters, fighters and some miniatures. **Technical:** Grinds ATS-34, A2 and 1050; forges 5160, O1. Offers hollow- or convex-grinds. **Prices:** $25 to $400. **Remarks:** Part-time maker; first knife sold in 1985. Doing business as Pro-Flyte, Inc. **Mark:** Last name; or first and last name, city, state.

BRASCHLER, CRAIG W.
HC2 Box 498, Zalma, MO 63787, Phone: 573-495-2203
Specialties: Art knives, Bowies, utility hunters, slip joints, miniatures, engraving. **Technical:** Flat grinds. Does own selective heat treating. Does own engraving. **Prices:** Starting at $200. **Remarks:** Full-time maker since 2003. **Mark:** Braschler over Martin Oval stamped.

BRATCHER, BRETT
11816 County Rd 302, Plantersville, TX 77363, Phone: 936-894-3788, Fax: (936) 894-3790, brett_bratcher@msn.com
Specialties: Hunting and skinning knives. **Patterns:** Clip and drop point. Hand forged. **Technical:** Material 5160, D2, 1095 and Damascus. **Price:** $200 to $500. **Mark:** Bratcher.

BRAY JR., W LOWELL
6931 Manor Beach Rd, New Port Richey, FL 34652, Phone: 727-846-0830, brayknives@aol.com Web: www.brayknives.com
Specialties: Traditional working and using straight knives and collector pieces. **Patterns:** One of a kind pieces, hunters, fighters and utility knives. **Technical:** Grinds 440C and ATS-34; forges 52100 and Damascus. **Prices:** $125 to $800. **Remarks:** Spare-time maker; first knife sold in 1992. **Mark:** Lowell Bray Knives in shield or Bray Primative in shield.

BREED, KIM
733 Jace Dr, Clarksville, TN 37040, Phone: 931-980-4956, sfbreed@yahoo.com
Specialties: High end through working folders and straight knives. **Patterns:** Hunters, fighters, daggers, Bowies. His design or customers. Likes one-of-a-kind designs. **Technical:** Makes own Mosiac and regular Damascus, but will use stainless steels. Offers filework and sculpted material. **Prices:** $150 to $2000. **Remarks:** Full-time maker. First knife sold in 1990. **Mark:** Last name.

BREND, WALTER
4094 Columbia Hwy., Ridge Springs, SC 29129, Phone: 256-736-3520, walterbrend@ hotmail.com Web: www.brendknives.com
Specialties: Tactical-style knives, fighters, automatics. **Technical:** Grinds D-Z and 440C blade steels, 154CM steel. **Prices:** Micarta handles, titanium handles.

BRENNAN, JUDSON
PO Box 1165, Delta Junction, AK 99737, Phone: 907-895-5153, Fax: 907-895-5404
Specialties: Period pieces. **Patterns:** All kinds of Bowies, rifle knives, daggers. **Technical:** Forges miscellaneous steels. **Prices:** Upscale, good value. **Remarks:** Muzzle-loading gunsmith; first knife sold in 1978. **Mark:** Name.

BRESHEARS, CLINT
1261 Keats, Manhattan Beach, CA 90266, Phone: 310-372-0739, Fax: 310-372-0739, breshears1@verizon.net; Web: www.clintknives.com
Specialties: Working straight knives and folders. **Patterns:** Hunters, Bowies and survival knives. Folders are mostly hunters. **Technical:** Grinds 440C, 154CM and ATS-34; prefers mirror finishes. **Prices:** $125 to $750; some to $1800. **Remarks:** Part-time maker; first knife sold in 1978. **Mark:** First name.

BREUER, LONNIE
PO Box 877384, Wasilla, AK 99687-7384
Specialties: Fancy working straight knives. **Patterns:** Hunters, camp knives and axes, folders and Bowies. **Technical:** Grinds 440C, AEB-L and D2; likes wire inlay, scrimshaw, decorative filing. **Prices:** $60 to $150; some to $300. **Remarks:** Part-time maker; first knife sold in 1977. **Mark:** Signature.

BREWER, CRAIG
425 White Cedar, Killeen, TX 76542, Phone: 254-634-6934, craig6@embarqmail.com
Specialties: Folders; slip joints, some lock backs and an occasional liner lock. **Patterns:** I like the old traditional patterns. **Technical:** Grinds CPM steels most being CPM-154, 1095 for carbon and some Damascus. **Prices:** $450 and up. **Remarks:** Full-time maker; first knife sold in 2005. **Mark:** BREWER.

BRITTON, TIM
5645 Murray Rd., Winston-Salem, NC 27106, Phone: 336-923-2062, tim@timbritton.

com; Web: www.timbritton.com
Specialties: Small and simple working knives, sgian dubhs, slip joint folders and special tactical designs. **Technical:** Forges and grinds stainless steel. **Prices:** $165 to ???. **Remarks:** Veteran knifemaker. **Mark:** Etched signature.

BROADWELL, DAVID
PO Box 4314, Wichita Falls, TX 76308, Phone: 940-782-4442, david@broadwellstudios. com; Web: www.broadwellstudios.com
Specialties: Sculpted high-art straight and folding knives. **Patterns:** Daggers, sub-hilted fighters, folders, sculpted art knives and some Bowies. **Technical:** Grinds mostly Damascus; carves; prefers natural handle materials, including stone. Some embellishment. **Prices:** $500 to $4000; some higher. **Remarks:** Full-time maker since 1989; first knife sold in 1981. **Mark:** Stylized emblem bisecting "B"/with last name below.

BROCK, KENNETH L
PO Box 375, 207 N Skinner Rd, Allenspark, CO 80510, Phone: 303-747-2547, brockknives@nedernet.net
Specialties: Custom designs, full-tang working knives and button lock folders of his design. **Patterns:** Hunters, miniatures and minis. **Technical:** Flat-grinds D2 and 440C; makes own sheaths; heat-treats. **Prices:** $75 to $800. **Remarks:** Full-time maker; first knife sold in 1978. **Mark:** Last name, city, state and serial number.

BRODZIAK, DAVID
27 Stewart St, PO Box 1130, Albany, WA, AUSTRALIA 6331, Phone: 61 8 9841 3314, Fax: 61898115065, brodziak3@bigpond.com; Web: www.brodziakcustomknives.com

BROMLEY, PETER
BROMLEY KNIVES, 1408 S Bettman, Spokane, WA 99212, Phone: 509-534-4235 or 509-710-8365, Fax: 509-536-2666, bromleyknives@q.com
Specialties: Period Bowies, folder, hunting knives; all sizes and shapes. **Patterns:** Bowies, boot knives, hunters, utility, folder, working knives. **Technical:** High-carbon steel (1084, 1095 and 5160). Stock removal and forge. **Prices:** $85 to $750. **Remarks:** Almost full-time, first knife sold in 1987. A.B.S. Journeyman Smith. **Mark:** Bromley, Spokane, WA.

BROOKER, DENNIS
55858 260th Ave., Chariton, IA 50049, Phone: 641-862-3263, dbrooker@dbrooker. com Web: www.dbrooker.com
Specialties: Fancy straight knives and folders of his design. Obsidian and glass knives. **Patterns:** Hunters, folders and boots. **Technical:** Forges and grinds. Full-time engraver and designer; instruction available. **Prices:** Moderate to upscale. **Remarks:** Part-time maker. Takes no orders; sells only completed work. **Mark:** Name.

BROOKS, BUZZ
2345 Yosemite Dr, Los Angles, CA 90041, Phone: 323-256-2892

BROOKS, MICHAEL
2811 64th St, Lubbock, TX 79413, Phone: 806-438-3862, chiang@clearwire.net
Specialties: Working straight knives of his design or to customer specs. **Patterns:** Martial art, Bowies, hunters, and fighters. **Technical:** Grinds 440C, D2 and ATS-34; offers wide variety of handle materials. **Prices:** $75 & up. **Remarks:** Part-time maker; first knife sold in 1985. **Mark:** Initials.

BROOKS, STEVE R
1610 Dunn Ave, Walkerville, MT 59701, Phone: 406-782-5114, Fax: 406-782-5114, steve@brooksmoulds.com; Web: brooksmoulds.com
Specialties: Working straight knives and folders; period pieces. **Patterns:** Hunters, Bowies and camp knives; folding lockers; axes, tomahawks and buckskinner knives; swords and stilettos. **Technical:** Damascus and mosaic Damascus. Some knives come embellished. **Prices:** $400 to $2000. **Remarks:** Full-time maker; first knife sold in 1982. **Mark:** Lazy initials.

BROOME, THOMAS A
1212 E. Aliak Ave, Kenai, AK 99611-8205, Phone: 907-283-9128, tomlei@ptialaska. ent; Web: www.alaskanknives.com
Specialties: Working hunters and folders **Patterns:** Traditional and custom orders. **Technical:** Grinds ATS-34, BG-42, CPM-S30V. **Prices:** $175 to $350. **Remarks:** Full-time maker; first knife sold in 1979. Doing business as Thom's Custom Knives, Alaskan Man O; Steel Knives. **Mark:** Full name, city, state.

BROTHERS, DENNIS L.
2007 Kent Rd., Oneonta, AL 35121, Phone: 205-466-3276, blademan@brothersblades. com Web: www.brothersblades.com
Specialties: Fixed blade hunting/working knives of maker's deigns. Works with customer designed specifications. **Patterns:** Hunters, camp knives, kitchen/utility, bird, and trout. Standard patterns and customer designed. **Technical:** Stock removal. Works with stainless and tool steels. SS cryo-treatment. Hollow and flat grinds. **Prices:** $200 - $400. **Remarks:** Sole authorship knives and customer leather sheaths. Part-time maker. Find on facebook "Brothers Blades by D.L. Brothers" **Mark:** "D.L. Brothers, 4B, Oneonta, AL" on obverse side of blade.

BROTHERS, ROBERT L
989 Philpott Rd, Colville, WA 99114, Phone: 509-684-8922
Specialties: Traditional working and using straight knives and folders of his design and to customer specs. **Patterns:** Bowies, fighters and hunters. **Technical:** Grinds D2; forges Damascus. Makes own Damascus from saw steel wire rope and chain; part-time goldsmith and stone-setter. **Prices:** $100 to $400; some higher. **Remarks:** Part-time maker; first knife sold in 1986. **Mark:** Initials and year made.

BROUS, JASON
5940 Matthews St., Goleta, CA 93110, Phone: 805-717-7192, contact@brousblades.com Web: www.brousblades.com
Patterns: Mostly fixed blades. **Technical:** Stock removal method using D2, CPM 154, 440c, ATS-34 or 1095 steels. **Prices:** $100 - $400. **Remarks:** Started May 2010.

BROUWER, JERRY
Vennewaard 151, 1824 KD, Alkmaar, NETHERLANDS, Phone: 00-31-618-774146, brouwern1@hotmail.nl; Web: www.brouwerknives.com
Specialties: Tactical fixed blades with epoxy-soaked Japanese wrapped handles, tactical and outdoor knives with Micarta or G-10 handles, tactical frame-lock folders. Fine, embellished knives for the demanding VIP. **Patterns:** Fixed-blade tantos, drop points, either V-ground or chisel ground, hunting knives, outdoor knives, folders, desk knives, pocket tools. **Technical:** Stock removal, only premium powder metallurgy steels and fine stainless damascus. **Prices:** $100 to $1,000. **Remarks:** Part-time maker; first knife sold in 2010. **Mark:** Laser etched "Brouwer" with a jack-o-lantern logo.

BROWER, MAX
2016 Story St, Boone, IA 50036, Phone: 515-432-2938, mbrower@mchsi.com
Specialties: Hunters. Working/using straight knives. **Patterns:** Bowies, hunters and boots. **Technical:** Grinds 440C and ATS-34. **Prices:** $280 and up. **Remarks:** Spare-time maker; first knife sold in 1981. **Mark:** Last name.

BROWN, DENNIS G
1633 N 197th Pl, Shoreline, WA 98133, Phone: 206-542-3997, denjilbro@msn.com

BROWN, DOUGLAS
1500 Lincolnshire Way, Fort Worth, TX 76134, www.debrownphotography.com

BROWN, HAROLD E
3654 NW Hwy 72, Arcadia, FL 34266, Phone: 863-494-7514, brknives@strato.net
Specialties: Fancy and exotic working knives. **Patterns:** Folders, slip-lock, locking several kinds. **Technical:** Grinds D2 and ATS-34. Embellishment available. **Prices:** $175 to $1000. **Remarks:** Part-time maker; first knife sold in 1976. **Mark:** Name and city with logo.

BROWN, JIM
1097 Fernleigh Cove, Little Rock, AR 72210

BROWN, ROB E
PO Box 15107, Emerald Hill, Port Elizabeth, EC, SOUTH AFRICA 6011, Phone: 27-41-3661086, Fax: 27-41-4511731, rbknives@global.co.za
Specialties: Contemporary-designed straight knives and period pieces. **Patterns:** Utility knives, hunters, boots, fighters and daggers. **Technical:** Grinds 440C, D2, ATS-34 and commercial Damascus. Knives mostly mirror finished; African handle materials. **Prices:** $100 to $1500. **Remarks:** Full-time maker; first knife sold in 1985. **Mark:** Name and country.

BROWNE, RICK
980 West 13th St, Upland, CA 91786, Phone: 909-985-1728
Specialties: Sheffield pattern pocket knives. **Patterns:** Hunters, fighters and daggers. No heavy-duty knives. **Technical:** Grinds ATS-34. **Prices:** Start at $450. **Remarks:** Part-time maker; first knife sold in 1975. **Mark:** R.E. Browne, Upland, CA.

BROWNING, STEVEN W
3400 Harrison Rd, Benton, AR 72015, Phone: 501-316-2450

BRUCE, RICHARD L.
13174 Surcease Mine Road, Yankee Hill, CA 95965, Phone: 530-532-0880, richardkarenbruce@yahoo.com
Specialties: Working straight knives. Prefers natural handle material; stag bone and woods. Admires the classic straight knife look. **Patterns:** Hunters, Fighters, Fishing Knives. **Technical:** Uses 01, 1095, L6, W2 steel. Stock removal method, flat grind, heat treats and tempers own knives. Builds own sheaths; simple but sturdy. **Prices:** $150-$400. **Remarks:** Sold first knife in 2006; part-time maker. **Mark:** RL Bruce.

BRUNCKHORST, LYLE
COUNTRY VILLAGE, 23706 7th Ave SE Ste B, Bothell, WA 98021, Phone: 425-402-3484, bronks@bronksknifeworks.com; Web: www.bronksknifeworks.com
Specialties: Forges own Damascus with 1084 and 15N20, forges 5160, 52100. Grinds CPM 154 CM, ATS-34, S30V. Hosts Biannual Northwest School of Knifemaking and Northwest Hammer In. Offers online and in-house sharpening services and knife sharpeners. Maker of the Double L Hoofknife. Traditional working and using knives, the new patent pending Xross-Bar Lock folders, tomahawks and irridescent RR spike knives. **Patterns:** Damascus Bowies, hunters, locking folders and featuring the ultra strong locking tactical folding knives. **Prices:** $185 to $1500; some to $3750. **Remarks:** Full-time maker; first knife made in 1976. **Mark:** Bucking horse or bronk.

BRUNER, FRED JR.
BRUNER BLADES, E10910W Hilldale Dr, Fall Creek, WI 54742, Phone: 715-877-2496, brunerblades@meca.net
Specialties: Pipe tomahawks, swords, makes his own. **Patterns:** Drop point hunters. **Prices:** $65 to $1500. **Remarks:** Voting member of the Knifemakers Guild. **Mark:** Fred Bruner.

BUCHANAN, THAD
THAD BUCHANAN CUSTOM KNIVES, 16401 S.W. Ranchview Rd., Powell Butte, OR 97753, buchananblades@gmail.com; Web: www.buchananblades.com
Specialties: Fixed blades. **Patterns:** Various hunters, trout, bird, utility, boots & fighters, including most Loveless patterns. **Technical:** Stock removal, high polish, variety handle materials. **Prices:** $450 to $2000. **Remarks:** 2005 and 2008 Blade Magazine handmade award for hunter/utility. 2006 Blade West best fixed blade award; 2008 Blade West best hunter/utility. 2010 and 2011 Best Fixed Blade at Plaza Cutlery Show. **Mark:** Thad Buchanan - maker

BUCHANAN, ZAC
168 Chapel Dr., Eugene, OR 97404, Phone: 541-815-6706, zacbuchananknives@gmail.com; Web: www.zacbuchananknives.com
Specialties: R.W. Loveless-style fixed knifemaker. **Technical:** Stock-removal knifemaker using CPM-154 blade steel, 416 stainless steel fittings and pre-ban elephant ivory, mammoth ivory, buffalo horn, stag and Micarta handles. **Prices:** $500 to $2,000. **Remarks:** Full-time maker; first knife sold in 2009. **Mark:** Zac Buchanan Eugene, Oregon.

BUCHARSKY, EMIL
37 26321 SH627 Spruce Grove, Alberta, CANADA T7Y 1C7, ebuch@telus.net; Web: www.ebuchknives.com
Specialties: Fancy working utility hunters and art folders, usually carved with overlays or inlays of damascus, hidden frames and screws. **Patterns:** Folders, hunters, bowies of maker's own design. **Technical:** Forges own damascus using 1095, 1084, 15N20 and nickel, stock-removal steels from Crucible, CPM alloys and UHB Elmax, natural handle materials of pearl, ancient ivory, bone, stabilized woods and others such as carbon fiber, titanium, stainless steel, mokume gane and gemstones. **Prices:** $400 to $1,000; art knives $1,500 and up. **Remarks:** Full-time maker; first knife made in 1989. **Mark:** Name, city and province in oval on fixed blades. Hand-engraved first name, initial and last name with year, in lower case, on folders.

BUCHNER, BILL
PO Box 73, Idleyld Park, OR 97447, Phone: 541-498-2247, blazinhammer@earthlink.net; Web: www.home.earthlin.net/~blazinghammer
Specialties: Working straight knives, kitchen knives and high-art knives of his design. **Technical:** Uses W1, L6 and his own Damascus. Invented "spectrum metal" for letter openers, folder handles and jewelry. Likes sculpturing and carving in Damascus. **Prices:** $40 to $3000; some higher. **Remarks:** Full-time maker; first knife sold in 1978. **Mark:** Signature.

BUCKBEE, DONALD M
243 South Jackson Trail, Grayling, MI 49738, Phone: 517-348-1386
Specialties: Working straight knives, some fancy, in standard patterns; concentrating on kitchen knives. **Patterns:** Kitchen knives, hunters, Bowies. **Technical:** Grinds D2, 440C, ATS-34. Makes ultra-lights in hunter patterns. **Prices:** $100 to $250; some to $350. **Remarks:** Part-time maker; first knife sold in 1984. **Mark:** Antlered bee—a buck bee.

BUCKNER, JIMMIE H
PO Box 162, Putney, GA 31782, Phone: 229-436-4182
Specialties: Camp knives, Bowies (one-of-a-kind), liner-lock folders, tomahawks, camp axes, neck knives for law enforcement and hide-out knives for body guards and professional people. **Patterns:** Hunters, camp knives, Bowies. **Technical:** Forges 1084, 5160 and Damascus (own), own heat treats. **Prices:** $195 to $795 and up. **Remarks:** Full-time maker; first knife sold in 1980, ABS Master Smith. **Mark:** Name over spade.

BUDELL, MICHAEL
3733 Wieghat Ln., Brenham, TX 77833, Phone: 979-836-3148, mbbudell@att.net
Specialties: Slip Joint Folders. **Technical:** Grinds 01, 440C. File work springs, blades and liners. Natural material scales giraffe, mastadon ivory, elephant ivory, and jigged bone. **Prices:** $175 - $350. **Remarks:** Part-time maker; first knife sold 2006. **Mark:** XA

BUEBENDORF, ROBERT E
108 Lazybrooke Rd, Monroe, CT 06468, Phone: 203-452-1769
Specialties: Traditional and fancy straight knives of his design. **Patterns:** Hand-makes and embellishes belt buckle knives. **Technical:** Forges and grinds 440C, O1, W2, 1095, his own Damascus and 154CM. **Prices:** $200 to $500. **Remarks:** Full-time maker; first knife sold in 1978. **Mark:** First and middle initials, last name and MAKER.

BULLARD, BENONI
4416 Jackson 4, Bradford, AR 72020, Phone: 501-344-2672, benandbren@earthlink.net
Specialties: Bowies and hunters. **Patterns:** Camp knives, bowies, hunters, slip joints, folders, lock blades, miniatures, Hawks Tech. **Technical:** Makes own Damascus. Forges 5160, 1085, 15 N 20. Favorite is 5160. **Prices:** $150 - $1500. **Remarks:** Part-time maker. Sold first knife in 2006. **Mark:** Benoni with a star over the letter i.

BULLARD, RANDALL
7 Mesa Dr., Canyon, TX 79015, Phone: 806-655-0590
Specialties: Working/using straight knives and folders of his design or to customer specs. **Patterns:** Hunters, locking folders and slip-joint folders. **Technical:** Grinds 01, ATS-34 and 440C. Does file work. **Prices:** $125 to $300; some $500. **Remarks:** Part-time maker; first knife sold in 1993. Doing business as Bullard Custom Knives. **Mark:** First and middle initials, last name, maker, city and state.

BULLARD, TOM
117 MC 8068, Flippin, AR 72634, Phone: 870-656-3428, tbullard8@live.com
Specialties: Traditional folders and hunters. **Patterns:** Bowies, hunters, single and 2-blade trappers, lockback folders. **Technical:** Grinds 440C, A2, D2, ATS-34 and O1. **Prices:** $175 and up. **Remarks:** Offers filework and engraving by Norvell Foster and Terry Thies. Does not make screw-together knives. **Mark:** T Bullard.

BUMP, BRUCE D.
1103 Rex Ln, Walla Walla, WA 99362, Phone: 509-386-8879, brucebump1@gmail.com; Web: www.brucebumpknives.com
Specialties: "One-of-a-kind" folders to cut and shoots. **Patterns:** Damascus patterns including feather patterns. **Technical:** Dual threat weapons of his own design. **Prices:** Call for prices. **Remarks:** Full-time maker ABS mastersmith 2003. **Mark:** Bruce D. Bump "Custom", Bruce D. Bump "MS".

custom knifemakers

BURDEN—CAFFREY

BURDEN, JAMES
405 Kelly St, Burkburnett, TX 76354

BURGER, FRED
Box 436, Munster, KZN, SOUTH AFRICA 4278, Phone: 27 39 3192316, info@swordcane.com; Web: www.swordcane.com
Specialties: Sword canes, folders, and fixed blades. **Patterns:** 440C and carbon steel blades. **Technical:** Double hollow ground and Poniard-style blades. **Prices:** $300 to $3000. **Remarks:** Full-time maker with son, Barry, since 1987. Member South African Guild. **Mark:** Last name in oval pierced by a dagger.

BURGER, PON
12 Glenwood Ave, Woodlands, Bulawayo, ZIMBABWE 75514
Specialties: Collector's items. **Patterns:** Fighters, locking folders of traditional styles, buckles. **Technical:** Scrimshaws 440C blade. Uses polished buffalo horn with brass fittings. Cased in buffalo hide book. **Prices:** $450 to $1100. **Remarks:** Full-time maker; first knife sold in 1973. Doing business as Burger Products. **Mark:** Spirit of Africa.

BURGER, TIAAN
69 Annie Botha Ave, Riviera,, Pretoria, GT, SOUTH AFRICA, tiaan_burger@hotmail.com
Specialties: Sliplock and multi-blade folder. **Technical:** High carbon or stainless with African handle materials **Remarks:** Occasional fixed blade knives.

BURKE, BILL
20 Adams Ranch Rd., Boise, ID 83716, Phone: 208-336-3792, billburke@bladegallery.com
Specialties: Hand-forged working knives. **Patterns:** Fowler pronghorn, clip point and drop point hunters. **Technical:** Forges 52100 and 5160. Makes own Damascus from 15N20 and 1084. **Prices:** $450 and up. **Remarks:** Dedicated to fixed-blade high-performance knives. ABS Journeyman. Also makes "Ed Fowler" miniatures. **Mark:** Initials connected.

BURKE, DAN
29 Circular Rd., Springdale, NL, CANADA A0J 1T0, Phone: 708-867-2026, dansknives@eastlink.ca
Specialties: Slip joint folders. **Patterns:** Traditional folders. **Technical:** Grinds D2 and BG-42. Prefers natural handle materials; heat-treats. **Prices:** $440 to $1900. **Remarks:** Full-time maker; first knife sold in 1976. **Mark:** First initial and last name.

BURNLEY, LUCAS
1005 La Font Rd. SW, Albuquerque, NM 87105, Phone: 505-814-9964, burnleyknives@comcast.net; www.burnleyknives.com
Specialties: Contemporary tactical fixed blade, and folder designs, some art knives. **Patterns:** Hybrids, neo Japanese, defensive, utility and field knives. **Technical:** Grinds CPM154, A2, D2, BG42, Stainless Damascus as well as titanium and aerospace composites. **Prices:** Most models $225 to $1,500. Some specialty pieces higher. **Remarks:** Full-time maker, first knife sold in 2003. **Mark:** Last name or BRNLY.

BURNS, ROBERT
104 W. 6th St., Carver, MN 55315, Phone: 412-477-4677, wildernessironworks@gmail.com; www.wildernessironworks.org
Specialties Utility knives, fighters, axes, pattern-welded axes and Viking swords. **Technical:** Trained as a blacksmith in Colonial style, forges 1095, 1090, 1084, 15N20, 5160, W1, W2, D2, 440C and wrought iron. **Prices:** $85 to $1,500-plus. **Remarks:** Full-time maker; first knife made in 2005. **Mark:** A compass rose with all of the cardinal directions, and underneath, in cursive, "Wilderness Ironworks."

BURRIS, PATRICK R
1263 Cty. Rd. 750, Athens, TN 37303, Phone: 423-336-5715, burrispr@gmail.com
Specialties: Traditional straight knives and locking-liner folders. **Patterns:** Hunters, bowies, locking-liner folders. **Technical:** Flat grinds high-grade stainless and damascus. **Remarks:** Offers filework, embellishment, exotic materials and damascus **Mark:** Last name in script.

BURROWS, CHUCK
WILD ROSE TRADING CO, 289 La Posta Canyon Rd, Durango, CO 81303, Phone: 970-259-8396, chuck@wrtcleather.com; Web: www.wrtcleather.com
Specialties: Presentation knives, hawks, and sheaths based on the styles of the American frontier incorporating carving, beadwork, rawhide, braintan, and other period correct materials. Also makes other period style knives such as Scottish Dirks and Moorish jambiyahs. **Patterns:** Bowies, Dags, tomahawks, war clubs, and all other 18th and 19th century frontier style edged weapons and tools. **Technical:** Carbon steel only: 5160, 1080/1084, 1095, O1, Damascus-Our Frontier Shear Steel, plus other styles available on request. Forged knives, hawks, etc. are made in collaborations with bladesmiths. Gib Guignard (under the name of Cactus Rose) and Mark Williams (under the name UB Forged). Blades are usually forge finished and all items are given an aged period look. **Prices:** $500 plus. **Remarks:** Full-time maker, first knife sold in 1973. 40+ years experience working leather. **Mark:** A lazy eight or lazy eight with a capital T at the center. On leather either the lazy eight with T or a WRTC makers stamp.

BURROWS, STEPHEN R
1020 Osage St, Humboldt, KS 66748, Phone: 816-921-1573
Specialties: Fantasy straight knives of his design, to customer specs and in standard patterns; period pieces. **Patterns:** Fantasy, bird and trout knives, daggers, fighters and hunters. **Technical:** Forges 5160 and 1095 high-carbon steel, O1 and his Damascus. Offers lost wax casting in bronze or silver of cross guards and pommels. **Prices:** $65 to $600; some to $2000. **Remarks:** Full-time maker; first knife sold in 1983. Doing business as Gypsy Silk. **Mark:** Etched name.

BUSBIE, JEFF
John 316 Knife Works, 170 Towles Rd., Bloomingdale, GA 31302, Phone: 912-656-8238, jbusbie@comcast.net; Web: www.john316knifeworks.com
Specialties: Working full-tang and hidden-tang fixed blades, locking-liner folders and hard-use knives. **Patterns:** Bowies, skinners, fighters, neck knives, work knives, bird knives, swords, art knives and other creations. **Technical:** Stock-removal maker using Alabama Damascus, CPM stainless steels and D2. Handles from hardwoods, G-10, ivory, bone and exotic materials. **Prices:** $100 to $800 and up. **Remarks:** Part-time maker building 150 to 200 knives a year; first knife sold in 2008. **Mark:** john 316 knife works with a cross in the middle.

BUSCH, STEVE
1989 Old Town Loop, Oakland, OR 97462, Phone: 541-459-2833, steve@buschcustomknives.com; Web: wwwbuschcustomknives.blademakers.com
Specialties: D/A automatic right and left handed, folders, fixed blade working mainly in Damascus file work, functional art knives, nitrate bluing, heat bluing most all scale materials. **Prices:** $150 to $2000. **Remarks:** Trained under Vallotton family 3 1/2 years on own since 2002. **Mark:** Signature and date of completion on all knives.

BUSFIELD, JOHN
153 Devonshire Circle, Roanoke Rapids, NC 27870, Phone: 252-537-3949, Fax: 252-537-8704, busfield@charter.net; Web: www.busfieldknives.com
Specialties: Investor-grade folders; high-grade working straight knives. **Patterns:** Original price-style and trailing-point interframe and sculpted-frame folders, drop-point hunters and semi-skinners. **Technical:** Grinds 154CM and ATS-34. Offers interframes, gold frames and inlays; uses jade, agate and lapis. **Prices:** $275 to $2000. **Remarks:** Full-time maker; first knife sold in 1979. **Mark:** Last name and address.

BUSSE, JERRY
11651 Co Rd 12, Wauseon, OH 43567, Phone: 419-923-6471
Specialties: Working straight knives. **Patterns:** Heavy combat knives and camp knives. **Technical:** Grinds D2, A2, INFI. **Prices:** $1100 to $3500. **Remarks:** Full-time maker; first knife sold in 1983. **Mark:** Last name in logo.

BUTLER, BART
822 Seventh St, Ramona, CA 92065, Phone: 760-789-6431

BUTLER, JOHN
777 Tyre Rd, Havana, FL 32333, Phone: 850-539-5742
Specialties: Hunters, Bowies, period. **Technical:** Damascus, 52100, 5160, L6 steels. **Prices:** $80 and up. **Remarks:** Making knives since 1986. Journeyman (ABS). **Mark:** JB.

BUTLER, JOHN R
20162 6th Ave N E, Shoreline, WA 98155, Phone: 206-362-3847, rjjjrb@sprynet.com

BUXTON, BILL
155 Oak Bend Rd, Kaiser, MO 65047, Phone: 573-348-3577, camper@yhti.net; Web: www.billbuxtonknives.com
Specialties: Forged fancy and working straight knives and folders. Mostly one-of-a-kind pieces. **Patterns:** Fighters, daggers, Bowies, hunters, linerlock folders, axes and tomahawks. **Technical:** Forges 52100, 0-1, 1080. Makes own Damascus (mosaic and random patterns) from 1080, 1095, 15n20, and powdered metals 1084 and 4800a. Offers sterling silver inlay, n/s pin patterning and pewter pouring on axe and hawk handles. **Prices:** $300 to $2,500. **Remarks:** Full-time maker, sold first knife in 1998. **Mark:** First initial and last name.

BUZEK, STANLEY
PO Box 731, Waller, TX 77484, Phone: 936-372-1933, stan@sbuzekknives.com; Web: www.sbuzekknives.com
Specialties: Traditional slip-joint pocketknives, LinerLocks and frame-lock folders, and fixed-blade hunters and skinners. **Technical:** Grinds, heat treats and Rockwell tests CPM-154, and some traditional folders in O1 tool steel. Hand-rubbed finishes. Dyed jigged bone, mammoth ivory and fine stabilized woods. **Prices:** $250 and up. **Remarks:** Serious part-time maker; first knife sold in 2006. **Mark:** S. Buzek on riccasso.

BYBEE, BARRY J
795 Lock Rd. E, Cadiz, KY 42211-8615
Specialties: Working straight knives of his design. **Patterns:** Hunters, fighters, boot knives, tantos and Bowies. **Technical:** Grinds ATS-34, 440C. Likes stag and Micarta for handle materials. **Prices:** $125 to $200; some to $1000. **Remarks:** Part-time maker; first knife sold in 1968. **Mark:** Arrowhead logo with name, city and state.

BYRD, WESLEY L
189 Countryside Dr, Evensville, TN 37332, Phone: 423-775-3826, w.l.byrd@worldnet.att.net
Specialties: Hunters, fighters, Bowies, dirks, sgian dubh, utility, and camp knives. **Patterns:** Wire rope, random patterns. Twists, W's, Ladder, Kite Tail. **Technical:** Uses 52100, 1084, 5160, L6, and 15n20. **Prices:** Starting at $180. **Remarks:** Prefer to work with customer for their design preferences. ABS Journeyman Smith. **Mark:** BYRD, WB <X.

C

CABRERA, SERGIO B
24500 Broad Ave, Wilmington, CA 90744

CAFFREY, EDWARD J
2608 Central Ave West, Great Falls, MT 59404, Phone: 406-727-9102, caffreyknives@gmail.com; Web: www.caffreyknives.net
Specialties: One-of-a-kind using and collector quality pieces. Will accept some customer

designs. **Patterns:** Bowies, folders, hunters, fighters, camp/utility, tomahawks and hatchets. **Technical:** Forges all types of Damascus, specializing in Mosaic Damascus, 52100, 5160, 1080/1084 and most other commonly forged steels. **Prices:** Starting at $185; typical hunters start at $400; collector pieces can range into the thousands. **Remarks:** Offers one-on-one basic and advanced bladesmithing classes. ABS Mastersmith. Full-time maker. **Mark:** Stamped last name and MS on straight knives. Etched last name with MS on folders.

CALDWELL, BILL
255 Rebecca, West Monroe, LA 71292, Phone: 318-323-3025
Specialties: Straight knives and folders with machined bolsters and liners. **Patterns:** Fighters, Bowies, survival knives, tomahawks, razors and push knives. **Technical:** Owns and operates a very large, well-equipped blacksmith and bladesmith shop with six large forges and eight power hammers. **Prices:** $400 to $3500; some to $10,000. **Remarks:** Full-time maker and self-styled blacksmith; first knife sold in 1962. **Mark:** Wild Bill and Sons.

CALLAHAN, F TERRY
PO Box 880, Boerne, TX 78006, Phone: 210-260-2378, ftclaw@gvtc.com
Specialties: Custom hand-forged edged knives, collectible and functional. **Patterns:** Bowies, folders, daggers, hunters & camp knives . **Technical:** Forges damascus and 5160. Offers filework, silver inlay and handmade sheaths. **Prices:** $150 to $500. **Remarks:** First knife sold in 1990. ABS/Journeyman Bladesmith. **Mark:** Initial "F" inside a keystone.

CALVERT JR., ROBERT W (BOB)
911 Julia, Rayville, LA 71269, Phone: 318-348-4490, rcalvert1@gmail.com
Specialties: Using and hunting knives; your design or his. Since 1990. **Patterns:** Forges own Damascus; all patterns. **Technical:** 5160, D2, 52100, 1084. Prefers natural handle material. **Prices:** $250 and up. **Remarks:** TOMB Member, ABS. Journeyman Smith. ABS Board of directors **Mark:** Calvert (Block) J S.

CAMBRON, HENRY
169 Severn Way, Dallas, GA 30132-0317, Phone: 770-598-5721, worldclassknives@bellsouth.net; Web: www.worldclassknives.com
Specialties: Everyday carry, working and small neck knives. **Patterns:** Hunters, bowies, camp, utility and combat. **Technical:** Forge, stock removal, filework. Differential quench. Tuff-etched finish. Hand-sewn and Kydex sheaths. **Prices:** $65 to $650. **Remarks:** Full-time maker. **Mark:** First and last name over USA on blades. HC on sheaths.

CAMERER, CRAIG
3766 Rockbridge Rd, Chesterfield, IL 62630, Phone: 618-753-2147, craig@camererknives.com; Web: www.camererknives.com
Specialties: Everyday carry knives, hunters and Bowies. **Patterns:** D-guard, historical recreations and fighters. **Technical:** Most of his knives are forged to shape. **Prices:** $100 and up. **Remarks:** Member of the ABS and PKA. Journeymen Smith ABS.

CAMERON, RON G
PO Box 183, Logandale, NV 89021, Phone: 702-398-3356, rntcameron@mvdsl.com
Specialties: Fancy and embellished working/using straight knives and folders of his design. **Patterns:** Bowies, hunters and utility/camp knives. **Technical:** Grinds ATS-34, AEB-L and Devin Thomas Damascus or own Damascus from 1084 and 15N20. Does filework, fancy pins, mokume fittings. Uses exotic hardwoods, stag and Micarta for handles. Pearl & mammoth ivory. **Prices:** $175 to $850 some to $1000. **Remarks:** Part-time maker; first knife sold in 1994. Doing business as Cameron Handmade Knives. **Mark:** Last name, town, state or last name.

CAMPBELL, DICK
196 Graham Rd, Colville, WA 99114, Phone: 509-684-6080, dicksknives@aol.com
Specialties: Working straight knives, folders & period pieces. **Patterns:** Hunters, fighters, boots: 19th century Bowies, Japanese swords and daggers. **Technical:** Grinds 440C, 154CM. **Prices:** $200 to $2500. **Remarks:** Full-time maker. First knife sold in 1975. **Mark:** Name.

CAMPBELL, DOUG
46 W Boulder Rd., McLeod, MT 59052, Phone: 406-222-8153, dkcampbl@yahoo.com
Specialties: Sole authorship of most any fixed blade knife. **Patterns:** Capers, hunters, camp knives, bowies, fighters. **Technical:** Forged from 1084, 5160, 52100, and self forged pattern-welded Damascus. **Prices:** $150-$750. **Remarks:** Part-time knifesmith. Built first knife in 1987, tried to make every knife since better than the one before. ABS JourneymanSmith . **Mark:** Grizzly track surrounded by a C.

CAMPOS, IVAN
R.XI de Agosto 107, Tatui, SP, BRAZIL 18270-000, Phone: 00-55-15-2518092, Fax: 00-55-15-2594368, ivan@ivancampos.com; Web: www.ivancompos.com
Specialties: Brazilian handmade and antique knives.

CANDRELLA, JOE
1219 Barness Dr, Warminster, PA 18974, Phone: 215-675-0143
Specialties: Working straight knives, some fancy. **Patterns:** Daggers, boots, Bowies. **Technical:** Grinds 440C and 154CM. **Prices:** $100 to $200; some to $1000. **Remarks:** Part-time maker; first knife sold in 1985. Does business as Franjo. **Mark:** FRANJO with knife as J.

CANTER, RONALD E
96 Bon Air Circle, Jackson, TN 38305, Phone: 731-668-1780, canterr@charter.net
Specialties: Traditional working knives to customer specs. **Patterns:** Beavertail skinners, Bowies, hand axes and folding lockers. **Technical:** Grinds 440C, Micarta & deer antler. **Prices:** $75 and up. **Remarks:** Spare-time maker; first knife sold in 1973. **Mark:** Three last initials intertwined.

CANTRELL, KITTY D
19720 Hwy 78, Ramona, CA 92076, Phone: 760-788-8304

CAPDEPON, RANDY
553 Joli Rd, Carencro, LA 70520, Phone: 318-896-4113, Fax: 318-896-8753
Specialties: Straight knives and folders of his design. **Patterns:** Hunters and locking folders. **Technical:** Grinds ATS-34, 440C and D2. **Prices:** $200 to $600. **Remarks:** Part-time maker; first knife made in 1992. Doing business as Capdepon Knives. **Mark:** Last name.

CAPDEPON, ROBERT
829 Vatican Rd, Carencro, LA 70520, Phone: 337-896-8753, Fax: 318-896-8753
Specialties: Traditional straight knives and folders of his design. **Patterns:** Boots, hunters and locking folders. **Technical:** Grinds ATS-34, 440C and D2. Hand-rubbed finish on blades. Likes natural horn materials for handles, including ivory. Offers engraving. **Prices:** $250 to $750. **Remarks:** Full-time maker; first knife made in 1992. **Mark:** Last name.

CAREY, PETER
P.O. Box 4712, Lago Vista, TX 78645, Phone: 512-358-4839, Web: www.careyblade.com
Specialties: Tactical folders, Every Day Carry to presentation grade. Working straight knives, hunters, and tactical. **Patterns:** High-tech patterns of his own design, Linerlocks, Framelocks, Flippers. **Technical:** Hollow grinds CPM154, CPM S35VN, stainless Damascus, Stellite. Uses titanium, zirconium, carbon fiber, G10, and select natural handle materials. **Prices:** Starting at $450. **Remarks:** Full-time maker, first knife sold in 2002. **Mark:** Last name in diamond.

CARLISLE, JEFF
PO Box 282 12753 Hwy 200, Simms, MT 59477, Phone: 406-264-5693

CARPENTER, RONALD W
Rt. 4 Box 323, Jasper, TX 75951, Phone: 409-384-4087

CARR, JOSEPH E.
W183 N8974 Maryhill Drive, Menomonee Falls, WI 53051, Phone: 920-625-3607, carsmith1@SBCGlobal.net; Web: Hembrook3607@charter.net
Specialties: JC knives. **Patterns:** Hunters, Bowies, fighting knives, every day carries. **Technical:** Grinds ATS-34 and Damascus. **Prices:** $200 to $750. **Remarks:** Full-time maker for 2 years, being taught by Ron Hembrook.

CARR, TIM
3660 Pillon Rd, Muskegon, MI 49445, Phone: 231-766-3582, tim@blackbearforgemi.com Web:www.blackbearforgemi.com
Specialties: Hunters, camp knives. **Patterns:** His or yours. **Technical:** Hand forges 5160, 52100 and Damascus. **Prices:** $125 to $700. **Remarks:** Part-time maker. **Mark:** The letter combined from maker's initials TRC.

CARRILLO, DWAINE
C/O AIRKAT KNIVES, 1021 SW 15th St, Moore, OK 73160, Phone: 405-503-5879, Web: www.airkatknives.com

CARROLL, CHAD
12182 McClelland, Grant, MI 49327, Phone: 231-834-9183, CHAD724@msn.com
Specialties: Hunters, Bowies, folders, swords, tomahawks. **Patterns:** Fixed blades, folders. **Prices:** $100 to $2000. **Remarks:** ABS Journeyman May 2002. **Mark:** A backwards C next to a forward C, maker's initials.

CARSON, HAROLD J "KIT"
1076 Brizendine Lane, Vine Grove, KY 40175, Phone: 270 877-6300, Fax: 270 877 6338, KCKnives@bbtel.com; Web: www.kitcarsonknives.com/album
Specialties: Military fixed blades and folders; art pieces. **Patterns:** Fighters, D handles, daggers, combat folders and Crosslock-styles, tactical folders, tactical fixed blades. **Technical:** Grinds Stellite 6K, Talonite, CPM steels, Damascus. **Prices:** $400 to $750; some to $5000. **Remarks:** Full-time maker; first knife sold in 1973. BLADE Magazine Hall-Of-Fame Induction 2012. **Mark:** Name stamped or engraved.

CARTER, FRED
5219 Deer Creek Rd, Wichita Falls, TX 76302, Phone: 904-723-4020, fcarter40@live.com
Specialties: High-art investor-class straight knives; some working hunters and fighters. **Patterns:** Classic daggers, Bowies; interframe, stainless and blued steel folders with gold inlay. **Technical:** Grinds a variety of steels. Uses no glue or solder. Engraves and inlays. **Prices:** Generally upscale. **Remarks:** Full-time maker. **Mark:** Signature in oval logo.

CARTER, MIKE
2522 Frankfort Ave, Louisville, KY 40206, Phone: 502-387-4844, mike@cartercrafts.com Web: www.cartercrafts.com
Remarks: Voting Member Knifemakers Guild.

CARTER, MURRAY M
22097 NW West Union Rd, Hillsboro, OR 97124, Phone: 503-447-1029, murray@cartercutlery.com; Web: www.cartercutlery.com
Specialties: Traditional Japanese cutlery, utilizing San soh ko (three layer) or Kata-ha (two layer) blade construction. Laminated neck knives, traditional Japanese etc. **Patterns:** Works from over 200 standard Japanese and North American designs. **Technical:** Hot forges and cold forges Hitachi white steel #1, Hitachi blue super steel exclusively. **Prices:** $800 to $10,000. **Remarks:** Owns and operates North America's most exclusive traditional Japanese bladesmithing school; web site available at which viewers can subscribe to 10 free knife sharpening and maintenance reports. **Mark:** Name in cursive, often appearing with Japanese characters. **Other:** Very interestng and informative monthly newsletter.

custom knifemakers

CARTER, SHAYNE
5302 Rosewood Cir., Payson, UT 84651, Phone: 801-913-0181, shaynemcarter@hotmail.com
   Specialties: Fixed blades. **Patterns:** Hunters, bowies and fighters. **Technical:** Flat grinds, hand finishes, forges blade steel, including own damascus, some 1084, 52100 and 5160. **Remarks:** Part-time maker; first damascus made in 1984.

CASEY, KEVIN
10583 N. 42nd St., Hickory Corners, MI 49060, Phone: 269-719-7412, kevincasey@tds.net; Web: www.kevincaseycustomknives.com
   Specialties: Fixed blades and folders. **Patterns:** Liner lock folders and feather Damascus pattern, mammoth ivory. **Technical:** Forges Damascus and carbon steels. **Prices:** Starting at $500 - $2500. **Remarks:** Member ABS, Knifemakers Guild, Custom Knifemakers Collectors Association.

CASHEN, KEVIN R
Matherton Forge, 5615 Tyler St., Hubbardston, MI 48845, Phone: 989-981-6780, kevin@cashenblades.com; Web: www.cashenblades.com
   Specialties: User-oriented straight knives and medieval and renaissance period European swords and daggers. **Patterns:** Hunters and skinners, bowies and camp knives, swords and daggers. **Technical:** Hand forged blades of O1, L6 and maker's own O1-L6-and-O2 damascus, occasionally W2 or 1095, all heat-treated to exacting metallurgical standards. **Prices:** $200 for small hunters to $9,000+ for museum-quality swords, with an average range of $400-$2,000. **Remarks:** Full-time maker, instructor/speaker/consultant; first knife sold in 1985. **Mark:** Gothic "K.C." with master smith stamp. On period pieces, a crowned castle encircled with "Cashen."

CASTEEL, DIANNA
PO Box 63, Monteagle, TN 37356, Phone: 931-212-4341, ddcasteel@charter.net; Web: www.casteelcustomknives.com
   Specialties: Small, delicate daggers and miniatures; most knives one-of-a-kind. **Patterns:** Daggers, boot knives, fighters and miniatures. **Technical:** Grinds 440C. Offers stainless Damascus. **Prices:** Start at $350; miniatures start at $250. **Remarks:** Full-time maker. **Mark:** Di in script.

CASTEEL, DOUGLAS
PO Box 63, Monteagle, TN 37356, Phone: 931-212-4341, Fax: 931-723-1856, ddcasteel@charter.net; Web: www.casteelcustomknives.com
   Specialties: One-of-a-kind collector-class period pieces. **Patterns:** Daggers, Bowies, swords and folders. **Technical:** Grinds 440C. Offers gold and silver castings.Offers stainless Damascus **Prices:** Upscale. **Remarks:** Full-time maker; first knife sold in 1982. **Mark:** Last name.

CASTELLUCIO, RICH
220 Stairs Rd, Amsterdam, NY 12010, Phone: 518-843-5540, rcastellucio@nycap.rr.com
   Patterns: Bowies, push daggers, and fantasy knives. **Technical:** Uses ATS-34, 440C, 154CM. I use stabilized wood, bone for the handles. Guards are made of copper, brass, stainless, nickle, and mokume.

CASTON, DARRIEL
125 Ashcat Way, Folsom, CA 95630, Phone: 916-539-0744, darrielc@gmail.com

CASWELL, JOE
173 S Ventu Park Rd, Newbury, CA 91320, Phone: 805-499-0707, Web:www.caswellknives.com
   Specialties: Historic pattern welded knives and swords, hand forged. Also high precision folding and fixed blade "gentleman" and "tactical" knives of his design, period firearms. Inventor of the "In-Line" retractable pocket clip for folding knives. **Patterns:**Hunters, tactical/utility, fighters, bowies, daggers, pattern welded medieval swords, precision folders. **Technical:**Forges own Damascus especially historic forms. Sometimes uses modern stainless steels and Damascus of other makers. Makes some pieces entirely by hand, others using the latest CNC techniques and by hand. Makes sheaths too. **Prices:**$100-$5,500. **Remarks:**Full time makers since 1995. Making mostly historic recreations for exclusive clientele. Recently moving into folding knives and 'modern' designs. **Mark:**CASWELL or CASWELL USA Accompanied by a mounted knight logo.

CATOE, DAVID R
4024 Heutte Dr, Norfolk, VA 23518, Phone: 757-480-3191
   Technical: Does own forging, Damascus and heat treatments. **Price:** $200 to $500; some higher. **Remarks:** Part-time maker; trained by Dan Maragni 1985-1988; first knife sold 1989. **Mark:** Leaf of a camellia.

CECCHINI, GUSTAVO T.
R. XV Novembro 2841, Sao Jose Rio Preto, SPAIN 15015110, Phone: 55 1732224267, tomaki@terra.com.be Web: www.gtcknives.com
   Specialties: Tactical and HiTech folders. **Technical:** Stock removal. Stainless steel fixed blades. S30V, S35Vn, S90V, CowryX, Damasteel, Chad Nichols SS damascus, RWL 34, CPM 154 CM, BG 42. **Prices:** $500 - $1500. **Remarks:** Full-time since 2004. **Mark:** Tang Stamp "GTC"

CEPRANO, PETER J.
213 Townsend Brooke Rd., Auburn, ME 04210, Phone: 207-786-5322, bpknives@gmail.com
   Specialties: Traditional working/using straight knives; tactical/defense straight knives. Own designs or to a customer's specs. **Patterns:** Hunters, skinners, utility, Bowies, fighters, camp and survival, neck knives. **Technical:** Forges 1095, 5160, W2, 52100 and old files; grinds CPM154cm, ATS-34, 440C, D2, CPMs30v, Damascus from other makes and other tool steels. Hand-sewn and tooled leather and Kydex sheaths. **Prices:** Starting at $125. **Remarks:** Full-time maker, first knife sold in 2001. Doing business as Big Pete Knives. **Mark:** Bold BPK over small BigPeteKnivesUSA.

CHAFFEE, JEFF L
14314 N. Washington St, PO Box 1, Morris, IN 47033, Phone: 812-212-6188
   Specialties: Fancy working and utility folders and straight knives. **Patterns:** Fighters, dagger, hunter and locking folders. **Technical:** Grinds commercial Damascus, 440C, ATS-34, D2 and O1. Prefers natural handle materials. **Prices:** $350 to 2000. **Remarks:** Part-time maker; first knife sold in 1988. **Mark:** Last name.

CHAMBERLAIN, CHARLES R
PO Box 156, Barren Springs, VA 24313-0156, Phone: 703-381-5137

CHAMBERLAIN, JON A
15 S. Lombard, E. Wenatchee, WA 98802, Phone: 509-884-6591
   Specialties: Working and kitchen knives to customer specs; exotics on special order. **Patterns:** Over 100 patterns in stock. **Technical:** Prefers ATS-34, D2, L6 and Damascus. **Prices:** Start at $50. **Remarks:** First knife sold in 1986. Doing business as Johnny Custom Knifemakers. **Mark:** Name in oval with city and state enclosing.

CHAMBERLIN, JOHN A
11535 Our Rd., Anchorage, AK 99516, Phone: 907-346-1524, Fax: 907-562-4583
   Specialties: Art and working knives. **Patterns:** Daggers and hunters; some folders;. **Technical:** Grinds ATS-34, 440C, A2, D2 and Damascus. Uses Alaskan handle materials such as oosic, jade, whale jawbone, fossil ivory. **Prices:** Start at $200. **Remarks:** Favorite knives to make are double-edged. Does own heat treating and cryogenic deep freeze. Full-time maker; first knife sold in 1984. **Mark:** Name over English shield and dagger.

CHAMBERS, RONNY
1900 W. Mississippi St., Beebe, AR 72012, Phone: 501-288-1476, chambersronny@yahoo.com; Web: www.chamberscustomknives.net

CHAMBLIN, JOEL
960 New Hebron Church Rd, Concord, GA 30206, Phone: 678-588-6769, chamblinknives@yahoo.com Web: chamblinknives.com
   Specialties: Fancy and working folders. **Patterns:** Fancy locking folders, traditional, multi-blades and utility. **Technical:** Uses ATS-34, CPM 154, and commercial Damascus. Offers filework. **Prices:** Start at $400. **Remarks:** Full-time maker; first knife sold in 1989. **Mark:** Last name.

CHAMPION, ROBERT
7001 Red Rock Rd., Amarillo, TX 79118, Phone: 806-622-3970, rchampknives@gmail.com; www.rchampknives.com
   Specialties: Traditional working straight knives. **Patterns:** Hunters, skinners, camp knives, Bowies, daggers. **Technical:** Grinds 440C and D2. **Prices:** $100 to $800. **Remarks:** Part-time maker; first knife sold in 1979. Stream-line hunters. **Mark:** Last name with dagger logo, city and state.

CHAPO, WILLIAM G
45 Wildridge Rd, Wilton, CT 06897, Phone: 203-544-9424
   Specialties: Classic straight knives and folders of his design and to customer specs; period pieces. **Patterns:** Boots, Bowies and locking folders. **Technical:** Forges stainless Damascus. Offers filework. **Prices:** $750 and up. **Remarks:** Full-time maker; first knife sold in 1989. **Mark:** First and middle initials, last name, city, state.

CHARD, GORDON R
104 S. Holiday Lane, Iola, KS 66749, Phone: 620-365-2311, Fax: 620-365-2311, gchard@cox.net
   Specialties: High tech folding knives in one-of-a-kind styles. **Patterns:** Liner locking folders of own design. Also fixed blade Art Knives. **Technical:** Clean work with attention to fit and finish. Blade steel mostly ATS-34 and 154CM, some CPM440V Vaso Wear and Damascus. **Prices:** $150 to $2500. **Remarks:** First knife sold in 1983. **Mark:** Name, city and state surrounded by wheat on each side.

CHASE, ALEX
208 E. Pennsylvania Ave., DeLand, FL 32724, Phone: 386-734-9918, chase8578@bellsouth.net
   Specialties: Historical steels, classic and traditional straight knives of his design and to customer specs. **Patterns:** Art, fighters, hunters and Japanese style. **Technical:** Forges O1-L6 Damascus, meteoric Damascus, 52100, 5160; uses fossil walrus and mastodon ivory etc. **Prices:** $150 to $1000; some to $3500. **Remarks:** Full-time maker; Guild member since 1996. Doing business as Confederate Forge. **Mark:** Stylized initials-A.C.

CHASE, JOHN E
217 Walnut, Aledo, TX 76008, Phone: 817-441-8331, jchaseknives@sbcglobal.net
   Specialties: Straight working knives in standard patterns or to customer specs. **Patterns:** Hunters, fighters, daggers and Bowies. **Technical:** Grinds D2 and O1; offers mostly satin finishes. **Prices:** Start at $325. **Remarks:** Part-time maker; first knife sold in 1974. **Mark:** Last name in logo.

CHAUVIN, JOHN
200 Anna St, Scott, LA 70583, Phone: 337-237-6138, Fax: 337-230-7980
   Specialties: Traditional working and using straight knives of his design, to customer specs and in standard patterns. **Patterns:** Bowies, fighters, and hunters. **Technical:** Grinds ATS-34, 440C and O1 high-carbon. Paul Bos heat treating. Uses ivory, stag, oosic and stabilized Louisiana swamp maple for handle materials. Makes sheaths using alligator and ostrich. **Prices:** $200 and up. Bowies start at $500. **Remarks:** Part-time maker; first knife sold in 1995. **Mark:** Full name, city, state.

CHAVEZ, RAMON
314 N. 5th St., Belen, NM 87002, Phone: 505-453-6008, ramonchaveskknives@gmail.com; Web: www.chaveskknives.com
Specialties: Fixed blades and traditional everyday working knives, some custom. **Patterns:** Hunters, skinners, bushcraft, tactical, neck knives and utility. **Technical:** Grind/stock removal of CPM-D2 and D2. Handles are mostly canvas and linen phenolic resin, will use some stabilized woods. Thermal molding plastic for sheaths. **Prices:** Start at $175. **Remarks:** Part-time maker; first knife made in 1993, first knife sold in 2010. **Mark:** CHAVES USA with skeleton key.

CHEATHAM, BILL
PO Box 636, Laveen, AZ 85339, Phone: 602-237-2786, blademan76@aol.com
Specialties: Working straight knives and folders. **Patterns:** Hunters, fighters, boots and axes; locking folders. **Technical:** Grinds 440C. **Prices:** $150 to $350; exceptional knives to $600. **Remarks:** Full-time maker; first knife sold in 1976. **Mark:** Name, city, state.

CHERRY, FRANK J
3412 Tiley N.E., Albuquerque, NM 87110, Phone: 505-883-8643

CHEW, LARRY
3025 De leon Dr., Weatherford, TX 76087, Phone: 817-573-8035, chewman@swbell.net; Web: www.voodooinside.com
Specialties: High-tech folding knives. **Patterns:** Double action automatic and manual folding patterns of his design. **Technical:** CAD designed folders utilizing roller bearing pivot design known as "VooDoo." Double action automatic folders with a variety of obvious and disguised release mechanisms, some with lock-outs. **Prices:** Manual folders start at $475, double action autos start at $750. **Remarks:** Made and sold first knife in 1988, first folder in 1989. Full-time maker since 1997. **Mark:** Name and location etched in blade, Damascus autos marked on spring inside frame. Earliest knives stamped LC.

CHILDERS, DAVID
4106 Mossy Oaks, W. Spring, TX 77389, Phone: 281-353-4113, Web: www.davidchildersknives.com

CHINNOCK, DANIEL T.
380 River Ridge Dr., Union, MO 63084, Phone: 314-276-6936, Web: www.DanChinnock.com; email: Sueanddanc@cs.com
Specialties: One of a kind folders in Damascus and Mammoth Ivory. Performs intricate pearl inlays into snake wood and giraffe bone. Makes matchingt ivory pistol grips for colt 1911's and Colt SAA. **Patterns:** New folder designs each year, thin ground and delicate gentleman's folders, large "hunting" folders in stainless Damascus and CPM154. Several standard models carried by Internet dealers. **Prices:** $500-$1500 **Remarks:** Full-time maker in 2005 and a voting member of the Knifemakers Guild. Performs intricate file work on all areas of knife. **Mark:** Signature on inside of backbar, starting in 2009 blades are stamped with a large "C" and "Dan" buried inside the "C".

CHOATE, MILTON
1665 W. County 17-1/2, Somerton, AZ 85350, Phone: 928-627-7251, mccustom@juno.com
Specialties: Classic working and using straight knives of his design, to customer specs and in standard patterns. **Patterns:** Bowies, hunters and utility/camp knives. **Technical:** Grinds 440C; grinds and forges 1095 and 5160. Does filework on top and guards on request. **Prices:** $200 to $800. **Remarks:** Full-time maker, first knife made in 1990. All knives come with handmade sheaths by Judy Choate. **Mark:** Knives marked "Choate."

CHOMILIER, ALAIN AND JORIS
20 rue des Hauts de Chanturgue, Clermont-Ferrand, FRANCE 63100, Phone: + 33 4 73 25 64 47, jo_chomilier@yahoo.fr
Specialties: One-of-a-kind knives; exclusive designs; art knives in carved patinated bronze, mainly folders, some straight knives and art daggers. **Patterns:** Liner-lock, side-lock, button-lock, lockback folders. **Technical:** Grind carbon and stainless damascus; also carve and patinate bronze. **Prices:** $400 to $3000, some to $4000. **Remarks:** Spare-time makers; first knife sold in 1995; Use fossil stone and ivory, mother-of-pearl, (fossil) coral, meteorite, bronze, gemstones, high karat gold. **Mark:** A. J. Chomilier in italics.

CHRISTENSEN, JON P
516 Blue Grouse, Stevensville, MT 59870, Phone: 406-697-8377, jpcknives@gmail.com; Web: www.jonchristenseknives.com
Specialties: Hunting/utility knives, folders, art knives. **Patterns:** Mosaic damascus **Technical:** Sole authorship, forges 01, 1084, 52100, 5160, Damascus from 1084/15N20. **Prices:** $220 and up. **Remarks:** ABS Mastersmith, first knife sold in 1999. **Mark:** First and middle initial surrounded by last initial.

CHURCHMAN, T W (TIM)
475 Saddle Horn Drive, Bandera, TX 78003, Phone: 210-240-0317, tim.churchman@nustarenergy.com
Specialties: Fancy and traditional straight knives. Bird/trout knives of his design and to customer specs. **Patterns:** Bird/trout knives, Bowies, daggers, fighters, boot knives, some miniatures. **Technical:** Grinds 440C, D2 and 154CM. Offers stainless fittings, fancy filework, exotic and stabilized woods, elk and other antler, and hand sewed lined sheaths. Also flower pins as a style. **Prices:** $350 to $450; some to $2,250. **Remarks:** Part-time maker; first knife made in 1981 after reading "KNIVES '81." Doing business as "Custom Knives Churchman Made." **Mark:** "Churchman" over Texas outline, "Bandera" under.

CLAIBORNE, JEFF
1470 Roberts Rd, Franklin, IN 46131, Phone: 317-736-7443, jeff@claiborneknives.com; Web: www.claiborneknives.com
Specialties: Multi blade slip joint folders. All one-of-a-kind by hand, no jigs or fixtures,

swords, straight knives, period pieces, camp knives, hunters, fighters, ethnic swords all periods. Handle: uses stag, pearl, oosic, bone ivory, mastadon-mammoth, elephant or exotic woods. **Technical:** Forges high-carbon steel, makes Damascus, forges cable grinds, O1, 1095, 5160, 52100, L6. **Prices:** $250 and up. **Remarks:** Part-time maker; first knife sold in 1989. **Mark:** Stylized initials in an oval.

CLAIBORNE, RON
2918 Ellistown Rd, Knox, TN 37924, Phone: 615-524-2054, Bowie@icy.net
Specialties: Multi-blade slip joints, swords, straight knives. **Patterns:** Hunters, daggers, folders. **Technical:** Forges Damascus: mosaic, powder mosaic. Prefers bone and natural handle materials; some exotic woods. **Prices:** $125 to $2500. **Remarks:** Part-time maker; first knife sold in 1979. Doing business as Thunder Mountain Forge Claiborne Knives. **Mark:** Claiborne.

CLARK, D E (LUCKY)
413 Lyman Lane, Johnstown, PA 15909-1409
Specialties: Working straight knives and folders to customer specs. **Patterns:** Customer designs. **Technical:** Grinds D2, 440C, 154CM. **Prices:** $100 to $200; some higher. **Remarks:** Part-time maker; first knife sold in 1975. **Mark:** Name on one side; "Lucky" on other.

CLARK, HOWARD F
115 35th Pl, Runnells, IA 50237, Phone: 515-966-2126, howard@mvforge.com; Web: mvforge.com
Specialties: Currently Japanese-style swords. **Patterns:** Katana. **Technical:** Forges L6 and 1086. **Prices:** $1200 to 5000. **Remarks:** Full-time maker; first knife sold in 1979. Doing business as Morgan Valley Forge. **Prior Mark:** Block letters and serial number on folders; anvil/initials logo on straight knives. **Current Mark:** Two character kanji "Big Ear."

CLARK, NATE
604 Baird Dr, Yoncalla, OR 97499, nateclarkkives@hotmail.com; Web: www.nateclarkkives.com
Specialties: Automatics (push button and hidden release) ATS-34 mirror polish or satin finish, Damascus, pearl, ivory, abalone, woods, bone, Micarta, G-10, filework and carving and sheath knives. **Prices:** $100 to $2500. **Remarks:** Full-time knifemaker since 1996. **Mark:** Nate Clark on spring, spacer or blade.

CLARK, R W
R.W. CLARK CUSTOM KNIVES, 17602 W. Eugene Terrace, Surprise, AZ 85388-5047, Phone: 909-279-3494, info@rwclarkknives.com
Specialties: Military field knives and Asian hybrids. Hand carved leather sheaths. **Patterns:** Fixed blade hunters, field utility and military. Also presentation and collector grade knives. **Technical:** First maker to use liquid metals LM1 material in knives. Other materials include S30V, O1, stainless and carbon Damascus. **Prices:** $75 to $2000. Average price $300. **Remarks:** Started knifemaking in 1990, full-time in 2000. **Mark:** R.W. Clark, Custom, Corona, CA in standard football shape. Also uses three Japanese characters, spelling Clark, on Asian Hybrids.

CLAY, WAYNE
Box 125B, Pelham, TN 37366, Phone: 931-467-3472, Fax: 931-467-3076
Specialties: Working straight knives and folders in standard patterns. **Patterns:** Hunters and kitchen knives; gents and hunter patterns. **Technical:** Grinds ATS-34. **Prices:** $125 to $500; some to $1000. **Remarks:** Full-time maker; first knife sold in 1978. **Mark:** Name.

CLINCO, MARCUS
821 Appelby Street, Venice, CA 90291, Phone: 818-610-9640, marcus@clincoknives.com; Web: www.clincoknives.com
Specialties: I make mostly fixed blade knives with an emphasis on everyday working and tactical models. Most of my knives are stock removal with the exception of my sole authored damascus blades. I have several integral models including a one piece tactical model named the viper. **Technical:** Most working knife models in ATS 34. Integrals in O-1, D-2 and 440 C. Damascus in 1080 and 15 N 20. Large camp and Bowie models in 5160 and D-2. Handle materials used include micarta, stabilized wood, G-10 and occasionally stag and ivory. **Prices:** $200 - $600.

COATS, KEN
317 5th Ave, Stevens Point, WI 54481, Phone: 715-544-0115
Specialties: Does own jigged bone scales **Patterns:** Traditional slip joints - shadow patterns **Technical:** ATS-34 Blades and springs. Milled frames. Grinds ATS-34, 440C. Stainless blades and backsprings. Does all own heat treating and freeze cycle. Blades are drawn to 60RC. Nickel silver or brass bolsters on folders are soldered, neutralized and pinned. Handles are jigged bone, hardwoods antler, and Micarta. Cuts and jigs own bone, usually shades of brown or green. **Prices:** $300 and up

COCKERHAM, LLOYD
1717 Carolyn Ave, Denham Springs, IA 70726, Phone: 225-665-1565

COFFEE, JIM
2785 Rush Rd., Norton, OH 44203, Phone: 330-631-3355, jcoffee735@aol.com; Web: jcoffeecustomknives.com
Specialties: Stock Removal, hunters, skinners, fighters. **Technical:** Bowie handle material - stabilized wood, micarta, mammoth ivory, stag. Full tang and hidden tang. Steels - 0-1, d-2, 5160, damascus **Prices:** $150 to $500 and up. **Remarks:** Part-time maker since 2008. **Mark:** full name in a football etch.

COFFEY, BILL
68 Joshua Ave, Clovis, CA 93611, Phone: 559-299-4259
Specialties: Working and fancy straight knives and folders of his design. **Patterns:** Hunters, fighters, utility, LinerLock® folders and fantasy knives. **Technical:** Grinds 440C, ATS-34, A-Z and commercial Damascus. **Prices:** $250 to $1000; some to $2500. **Remarks:** Full-time maker. First knife sold in 1993. **Mark:** First and last name, city, state.

COFFMAN, DANNY
541 Angel Dr S, Jacksonville, AL 36265-5787, Phone: 256-435-1619
Specialties: Straight knives and folders of his design. Now making liner locks for $650 to $1200 with natural handles and contrasting Damascus blades and bolsters. **Patterns:** Hunters, locking and slip-joint folders. **Technical:** Grinds Damascus, 440C and D2. Offers filework and engraving. **Prices:** $100 to $400; some to $800. **Remarks:** Spare-time maker; first knife sold in 1992. Doing business as Customs by Coffman. **Mark:** Last name stamped or engraved.

COHEA, JOHN M
114 Rogers Dr., Nettleton, MS 38855, Phone: 662-322-5916, jhncohea@hotmail.com
Web: http://jmcknives.blademakers.com
Specialties: Frontier style knives, hawks, and leather. **Patterns:** Bowies, hunters, patch/ neck knives, tomahawks, and friction folders. **Technical:** Makes both forged and stock removal knives using high carbon steels and damascus. Uses natural handle materials that include antler, bone, ivory, horn, and figured hardwoods. Also makes rawhide covered sheaths that include fringe, tacks, antique trade beads, and other period correct materials. **Prices:** $100 - $1500, some higher. **Remarks:** Part-time maker, first knife sold in 1999. **Mark:** COHEA stamped on riccasso.

COHEN, N J (NORM)
2408 Sugarcone Rd, Baltimore, MD 21209, Phone: 410-484-3841, inquiry@njknives. com; Web:www.njcknives.com
Specialties: Working class knives. **Patterns:** Hunters, skinners, bird knives, push daggers, boots, kitchen and practical customer designs. **Technical:** Stock removal 440C, ATS-34. Uses Micarta, Corian. Some woods and stabilized woods in handles. **Prices:** $50 to $250. **Remarks:** Part-time maker; first knife sold in 1982. **Mark:** NJC engraved.

COLE, JAMES M
505 Stonewood Blvd, Bartonville, TX 76226, Phone: 817-430-0302, dogcole@swbell. net

COLE, WELBORN I
365 Crystal Ct, Athens, GA 30606, Phone: 404-261-3977
Specialties: Traditional straight knives of his design. **Patterns:** Hunters. **Technical:** Grinds 440C, ATS-34 and D2. Good wood scales. **Prices:** NA. **Remarks:** Full-time maker; first knife sold in 1983. **Mark:** Script initials.

COLEMAN, JOHN A
7325 Bonita Way, Citrus Heights, CA 95610-3003, Phone: 916-335-1568, slimsknifes@ yahoo.com
Specialties: Minis, hunters, bowies of his design or yours. **Patterns:** Plain to fancy file back working knives. **Technical:** Grinds 440C, ATS-34, 145CM, D2, 1095, 5160, 01. Some hand-forged blades. Exotic woods bone, antler and stone. **Prices:** $100 to $500. **Remarks:** Does some carving in handles. Part-time maker. First knife sold in 1989. OKCA 2010 Award winner for best mini of show. **Mark:** Cowboy setting on log whittling Slim's Custom Knives above cowboy and name and state under cowboy.

COLLINS, LYNN M
138 Berkley Dr, Elyria, OH 44035, Phone: 440-366-7101
Specialties: Working straight knives. **Patterns:** Field knives, boots and fighters. **Technical:** Grinds D2, 154CM and 440C. **Prices:** Start at $200. **Remarks:** Spare-time maker; first knife sold in 1980. **Mark:** Initials, asterisks.

COLTER, WADE
PO Box 2340, Colstrip, MT 59323, Phone: 406-748-4573; Shop: 406-748-2010, Fax: Cell: 406-740-1554
Specialties: Fancy and embellished straight knives, folders and swords of his design; historical and period pieces. **Patterns:** Bowies, swords and folders. **Technical:** Hand forges 52100 ball bearing steel and L6, 1090, cable and chain Damascus from 5N20 and 1084. Carves and makes sheaths. **Prices:** $250 to $3500. **Remarks:** SemiRetired; first knife sold in 1990. Doing business as "Colter's Hell" Forge. **Mark:** Initials on left side ricasso.

CONKLIN, GEORGE L
Box 902, Ft. Benton, MT 59442, Phone: 406-622-3268, Fax: 406-622-3410, 7bbgrus@3rivers.net
Specialties: Designer and manufacturer of the "Brisket Breaker." **Patterns:** Hunters, utility/camp knives and hatchets. **Technical:** Grinds 440C, ATS-34, D2, 1095, 154CM and 5160. Offers some forging and heat-treats for others. Offers some jewelling. **Prices:** $65 to $200; some to $1000. **Remarks:** Full-time maker. Doing business as Rocky Mountain Knives. **Mark:** Last name in script.

CONLEY, BOB
1013 Creasy Rd, Jonesboro, TN 37659, Phone: 423-753-3302
Specialties: Working straight knives and folders. **Patterns:** Lockers, two-blades, gents, hunters, traditional-styles, straight hunters. **Technical:** Grinds 440C, 154CM and ATS-34. Engraves. **Prices:** $250 to $450; some to $600. **Remarks:** Full-time maker; first knife sold in 1979. **Mark:** Full name, city, state.

CONN JR., C T
206 Highland Ave, Attalla, AL 35954, Phone: 205-538-7688
Specialties: Working folders, some fancy. **Patterns:** Full range of folding knives. **Technical:** Grinds O2, 440C and 154CM. **Prices:** $125 to $300; some to $600. **Remarks:** Part-time maker; first knife sold in 1982. **Mark:** Name.

CONNOLLY, JAMES
2486 Oro-Quincy Hwy, Oroville, CA 95966, Phone: 530-534-5363, rjconnolly@ sbcglobal.net
Specialties: Classic working and using knives of his design. **Patterns:** Boots, Bowies,

daggers and swords. **Technical:** Grinds ATS-34, BG42, A2, O1. **Prices:** $100 to $500; some to $1500. **Remarks:** Part-time maker; first knife sold in 1980. Doing business as Gold Rush Designs. **Mark:** First initial, last name, Handmade.

CONNOR, JOHN W
PO Box 12981, Odessa, TX 79768-2981, Phone: 915-362-6901

CONNOR, MICHAEL
Box 502, Winters, TX 79567, Phone: 915-754-5602
Specialties: Straight knives, period pieces, some folders. **Patterns:** Hunters to camp knives to traditional locking folders to Bowies. **Technical:** Forges 5160, O1, 1084 steels and his own Damascus. **Prices:** Moderate to upscale. **Remarks:** Spare-time maker; first knife sold in 1974. ABS Master Smith 1983. **Mark:** Last name, M.S.

CONTI, JEFFREY D
21104 75th St E, Bonney Lake, WA 98390, Phone: 253-447-4660, Fax: 253-512-8629
Specialties: Working straight knives. **Patterns:** Fighters and survival knives; hunters, camp knives and fishing knives. **Technical:** Grinds D2, 154CM and O1. Engraves. **Prices:** Start at $80. **Remarks:** Part-time maker; first knife sold in 1980. Does own heat treating. **Mark:** Initials, year, steel type, name and number of knife.

CONWAY, JOHN
13301 100th Place NE, Kirkland, WA 98034, Phone: 425-823-2821, jcknives@Frontier. com
Specialities: Folders; working and Damascus. Straight knives, camp, utility and fighting knives. **Patterns:** LinerLock® folders of own design. Hidden tang straight knives of own design. **Technical:** Flat grinds forged carbon steels and own Damascus steel, including mosaic. **Prices:** $300 to $850. **Remarks:** Part-time maker since 1999. **Mark:** Oval with stylized initials J C inset.

COOGAN, ROBERT
1560 Craft Center Dr, Smithville, TN 37166, Phone: 615-597-6801, http://iweb.tntech. edu/rcoogan/
Specialities: One-of-a-kind knives. **Patterns:** Unique items like ulu-style Appalachian herb knives. **Technical:** Forges; his Damascus is made from nickel steel and W1. **Prices:** Start at $100. **Remarks:** Part-time maker; first knife sold in 1979. **Mark:** Initials or last name in script.

COOK, JAMES R
455 Anderson Rd, Nashville, AR 71852, Phone: 870 845 5173, jr@jrcookknives.com; Web: www.jrcookknives.com
Specialties: Working straight knives and folders of his design or to customer specs. **Patterns:** Bowies, hunters and camp knives. **Technical:** Forges 1084 and high-carbon Damascus. **Prices:** $500 to $10000. **Remarks:** Full-time maker; first knife sold in 1986. **Mark:** First and middle initials, last name.

COOK, LOUISE
475 Robinson Ln, Ozark, IL 62972, Phone: 618-777-2932
Specialties: Working and using straight knives of her design and to customer specs; period pieces. **Patterns:** Bowies, hunters and utility/camp knives. **Technical:** Forges 5160. Filework; pin work; silver wire inlay. **Prices:** Start at $50/inch. **Remarks:** Part-time maker; first knife sold in 1990. Doing business as Panther Creek Forge. **Mark:** First name and Journeyman stamp on one side; panther head on the other.

COOK, MIKE
475 Robinson Ln, Ozark, IL 62972, Phone: 618-777-2932
Specialties: Traditional working and using straight knives of his design and to customer specs. **Patterns:** Bowies, hunters and utility/camp knives. **Technical:** Forges 5160. Filework; pin work. **Prices:** Start at $50/inch. **Remarks:** Spare-time maker; first knife sold in 1991. **Mark:** First initial, last name and Journeyman stamp on one side; panther head on the other.

COOK, MIKE A
10927 Shilton Rd, Portland, MI 48875, Phone: 517-242-1352, macook@hughes.net
Web: www.artofishi.com
Specialties: Fancy/embellished and period pieces of his design. **Patterns:** Daggers, fighters and hunters. **Technical:** Stone bladed knives in agate, obsidian and jasper. Scrimshaws; opal inlays. **Prices:** $60 to $300; some to $800. **Remarks:** Part-time maker; first knife sold in 1988. Doing business as Art of Ishi. **Mark:** Initials and year.

COOMBS JR., LAMONT
546 State Rt 46, Bucksport, ME 04416, Phone: 207-469-3057, Fax: 207-469-3057, theknifemaker@hotmail.com; Web: www.knivesby.com/coombs-knives.html
Specialties: Classic fancy and embellished straight knives; traditional working and using straight knives. Knives of his design and to customer specs. **Patterns:** Hunters, folders and utility/camp knives. **Technical:** Hollow- and flat-grinds ATS-34, 440C, A2, D2 and O1; grinds Damascus from other makers. **Prices:** $100 to $500; some to $3500. **Remarks:** Full-time maker; first knife sold in 1988. **Mark:** Last name on banner, handmade underneath.

COON, RAYMOND C
21135 S.E. Tillstrom Rd, Damascus, OR 97089, Phone: 503-658-2252, Raymond@ damascusknife.com; Web: Damascusknife.com
Specialties: Working straight knives in standard patterns. **Patterns:** Hunters, Bowies, daggers, boots and axes. **Technical:** Forges high-carbon steel and Damascus or 97089. **Prices:** Start at $235. **Remarks:** Full-time maker; does own leatherwork, makes own Damascus, daggers; first knife sold in 1995. **Mark:** First initial, last name.

COOPER, PAUL
9 Woods St., Woburn, MA 01801, Phone: 781-938-0519, byksm@yahoo.com
Specialties: Forged, embellished, hand finished fixed-blade knives. **Patterns:** One of a kind

designs, often inspired by traditional and historic pieces. **Technical:** Works in tool steel, damascus and natural materials. **Prices:** $500 - $2000. **Remarks:** Part-time maker, formally apprenticed under J.D. Smith. Sold first piece in 2006. **Mark:** Letter C inside bleeding heart.

COPELAND, THOM

171 Country Line Rd S, Nashville, AR 71852, tcope@cswnet.com
Specialties: Hand forged fixed blades; hunters, Bowies and camp knives. **Remarks:** Member of ABS and AKA (Arkansas Knifemakers Association). **Mark:** Copeland.

COPPINS, DANIEL

8651 B Georgetown Rd., Cambridge, OH 43725, Phone: 740-680-2438, Web: www.battlehorseknives.com or www.kickassknives.com
Specialties: Bushcraft knives, tacticals, hunting. **Technical:** Grinds 440C, D2. Antler handles. **Patterns:** Many. **Prices:** $40 to $600. **Remarks:** Sold first knife in 2002; formally Blind Horse Knives. **Mark:** Horse-Kicking Donkey.

CORBY, HAROLD

218 Brandonwood Dr, Johnson City, TN 37604, Phone: 423-926-9781
Specialties: Large fighters and Bowies; self-protection knives; art knives. Along with art knives and combat knives, Corby now has a all new automatic MO.PB1, also side lock MO LL-1 with titanium liners G-10 handles. **Patterns:** Sub-hilt fighters and hunters. **Technical:** Grinds 154CM, ATS-34 and 440C. **Prices:** $200 to $6000. **Remarks:** Full-time maker; first knife sold in 1969. Doing business as Knives by Corby. **Mark:** Last name.

CORDOVA, JOEY

1594 S. Hill Rd., Bernalillo, NM 87004, Phone: 505-410-3809, joeyscordova@gmail.com, www.joelouiknives.com
Patterns: High-carbon full-tang knives and hidden-tang bowies, as well as small neck knives. **Technical:** Differentially heat-treats blades producing hamons (temper lines). **Prices:** $120 and up. **Remarks:** Full-time knifemaker and part-time ring maker.

CORDOVA, JOSEPH G

1450 Lillie Dr, Bosque Farms, NM 87068, Phone: 505-869-3912, kcordova@rt66.com
Specialties: One-of-a-kind designs, some to customer specs. **Patterns:** Fighter called the 'Gladiator', hunters, boots and cutlery. **Technical:** Forges 1095, 5160; grinds ATS-34, 440C and 154CM. **Prices:** Moderate to upscale. **Remarks:** Full-time maker; first knife sold in 1953. Past chairman of American Bladesmith Society. **Mark:** Cordova made.

CORICH, VANCE

12012 W. Dumbarton Dr., Morrison, CO 80465, Phone: 303-999-1553, vancecorichcutlery@gmail.com; https://sites.google.com/site/vancesproject/
Specialties: Fixed blades, usually 2 to 7 inches, recurved blades, locking-liner folders and friction folders. **Technical:** Forges most fixed-blade knives; stock removal on folders and small utility pieces; mainly working in 1095, high-carbon damascus, D2 and AEB-L steels; flat grinds. Uses stabilized woods and phenolics for handles, but not limited to those materials. **Prices:** $150 to $1,000. **Remarks:** Part-time maker working on going full time.

CORKUM, STEVE

34 Basehoar School Rd, Littlestown, PA 17340, Phone: 717-359-9563, sco7129849@aol.com; Web: www.hawknives.com

CORNETT, BRIAN

1511 N. College St., McKinney, TX 75069, Phone: 972-310-7289, devildogdesign@tx.rr.com; www.d3devildogdesigns.com
Patterns: Tactical, hunting, neck knives and personal-defense tools. **Technical:** Stock removal of 1095, O1 tool steel, 52100, D2, CPM 154 and damascus. **Prices:** $50 to $300. **Remarks:** Full-time maker; first knife made in 2011. **Mark:** D3.

CORNWELL, JEFFREY

Treasure Art Blades, PO Box 244014, Anchorage, AK 99524, Phone: 907-887-1661, cornwellsjej@alaska.net
Specialties: Organic, sculptural shapes of original design from damascus steel and mokume gane. **Technical:** Blade creations from Robert Eggerling damascus and Mike Sakmar mokume. **Remarks:** Free-time maker. **Mark:** Stylized J inside a circle.

COSTA, SCOTT

409 Coventry Rd, Spicewood, TX 78669, Phone: 830-693-3431
Specialties: Working straight knives. **Patterns:** Hunters, skinners, axes, trophy sets, custom boxed steak sets, carving sets and bar sets. **Technical:** Grinds D2, ATS-34, 440 and Damascus. Heat-treats. **Prices:** $225 to $2000. **Remarks:** Full-time maker; first knife sold in 1985. **Mark:** Initials connected.

COTTRILL, JAMES I

1776 Ransburg Ave, Columbus, OH 43223, Phone: 614-274-0020
Specialties: Working straight knives of his design. **Patterns:** Caters to the boating and hunting crowd; cutlery. **Technical:** Grinds O1, D2 and 440C. Likes filework. **Prices:** $95 to $250; some to $500. **Remarks:** Full-time maker; first knife sold in 1977. **Mark:** Name, city, state, in oval logo.

COUSINO, GEORGE

7818 Norfolk, Onsted, MI 49265, Phone: 517-467-4911, cousinoknives@yahoo.com; Web: www.cousinoknives.com
Specialties: Hunters, Bowies using knives. **Patterns:** Hunters, Bowies, buckskinners, folders and daggers. **Technical:** Grinds 440C. **Prices:** $95 to $300. **Remarks:** Part-time maker; first knife sold in 1981. **Mark:** Last name.

COVER, JEFF

11355 Allen Rd, Potosi, MO 63664, Phone: 573-749-0008, jeffcovercustomknives@hotmail.com
Specialties: Folders and straight knives. **Patterns: Technical:** Various knife steels and handle materials. **Prices:** $70 to $500. **Mark:** Jeff Cover J.C. Custom Knives.

COVER, RAYMOND A

16235 State Hwy. U, Mineral Point, MO 63660, Phone: 573-749-3783
Specialties: High-tech working straight knives and folders in working patterns. **Patterns:** Slip joints, lockbacks, multi-blade folders. **Technical:** Various knife steels and handle materials. **Prices:** Swords from bare blades to complete high art $200 to $600. **Mark:** "R Cover"

COWLES, DON

1026 Lawndale Dr, Royal Oak, MI 48067, Phone: 248-541-4619, don@cowlesknives.com; Web: www.cowlesknives.com
Specialties: Straight, non-folding pocket knives of his design. **Patterns:** Gentlemen's pocket knives. **Technical:** Grinds CPM154, S30V, Damascus, Talonite. Engraves; pearl inlays in some handles. **Prices:** Start at $300. **Remarks:** Full-time maker; first knife sold in 1994. **Mark:** Full name with oak leaf.

COX, LARRY

701 W. 13th St, Murfreesboro, AR 71958, Phone: 870-258-2429, Fax: Cell: 870-557-8062
Patterns: Hunters, camp knives, Bowies, and skinners. **Technical:** Forges carbon steel 1084, 1080, 15N29, 5160 and Damascus. Forges own pattern welded Damascus as well as doing own heat treat. **Prices:** $150 and up. **Remarks:** Sole ownership; knives and sheaths. Part-time maker; first knife sold in 2007. Member ABS and Arkansas Knifemakers Association. **Mark:** COX.

COX, SAM

1756 Love Springs Rd, Gaffney, SC 29341, Phone: 864-489-1892, Web: www.coxworks.com
Remarks: Started making knives in 1981 for another maker. 1st knife sold under own name in 1983. Full-time maker 1985-2009. Retired in 2010. Now part time. **Mark:** Different logo each year.

COYE, BILL

PO Box 470684, Tulsa, OK 74147, Phone: 918-232-5721, info@coyeknives.com; Web: www.coyeknives.com
Specialties: Tactical and utility knives. **Patterns:** Fighters and utility. **Technical:** Grinds CPM154CM, 154CM, CTS-XHP and Elmax stainless steels. **Prices:** $210 to $320. **Remarks:** Part-time maker. First knife sold in 2009. **Mark:** COYE.

CRADDOCK, MIKE

300 Blythe Dr., Thomasville, NC 27360, Phone: 336-382-8461, ncbladesmith@gmail.com
Specialties: Fighters, bowies. **Patterns:** Hunters and working knives. **Technical:** Forges and grinds high-carbon steel, and does own damascus. **Prices:** $350 to $1,500. **Mark:** CRADDOCK.

CRAIG, ROGER L

2617 SW Seabrook Ave, Topeka, KS 66614, Phone: 785-249-4109
Specialties: Working and camp knives, some fantasy; all his design. **Patterns:** Fighters, hunter. **Technical:** Grinds 1095 and 5160. Most knives have file work. **Prices:** $50 to $250. **Remarks:** Part-time maker; first knife sold in 1991. Doing business as Craig Knives. **Mark:** Last name-Craig.

CRAIN, JACK W

PO Box 212, Granbury, TX 76048, jack@jackcrainknives.com Web: www.jackcrainknives.com
Specialties: Fantasy and period knives; combat and survival knives. **Patterns:** One-of-a-kind art or fantasy daggers, swords and Bowies; survival knives. **Technical:** Forges Damascus; grinds stainless steel. Carves. **Prices:** $350 to $2500; some to $20,000. **Remarks:** Full-time maker; first knife sold in 1969. Designer and maker of the knives seen in the films Dracula 2000, Executive Decision, Demolition Man, Predator I and II, Commando, Die Hard I and II, Road House, Ford Fairlane and Action Jackson, and television shows War of the Worlds, Air Wolf, Kung Fu: The Legend Cont. and Tales of the Crypt. **Mark:** Stylized crane.

CRAMER, BRENT

PO BOX 99, Wheatland, IN 47597, Phone: 812-881-9961, Bdcramer@juno.com Web: BDCramerKnives.com
Specialties: Traditional and custom working and using knives. **Patterns:** Traditional single blade slip-joint folders and standard fixed blades. **Technical:** Stock removal only. Pivot bushing construction on folders. Steel: D-2, 154 CM, ATS-34, CPM-D2, CPM-154CM, O-1, 52100, A-2. All steels heat treated in shop with LN Cryo. Handle Material: Stag, Bone, Wood, Ivory, and Micarta. **Prices:** $150 - $550. **Remarks:** Part-time maker. First fixed blade sold in 2003. First folder sold in 2007. **Mark:** BDC and B.D.Cramer.

CRAWFORD, PAT AND WES

205 N. Center, West Memphis, AR 72301, Phone: 870-732-2452, patcrawford1@earthlink.com; Web: www.crawfordknives.com
Specialties: Stainless steel Damascus. High-tech working self-defense and combat types and folders. **Patterns:** Tactical-more fancy knives now. **Technical:** Grinds S30V. **Prices:** $400 to $2000. **Remarks:** Full-time maker; first knife sold in 1973. **Mark:** Last name.

CRAWLEY, BRUCE R

16 Binbrook Dr, Croydon, VIC, AUSTRALIA 3136
Specialties: Folders. **Patterns:** Hunters, lockback folders and Bowies. **Technical:** Grinds 440C, ATS-34 and commercial Damascus. Offers filework and mirror polish. **Prices:** $160 to $3500. **Remarks:** Part-time maker; first knife sold in 1990. **Mark:** Initials.

CRENSHAW, AL

Rt 1 Box 717, Eufaula, OK 74432, Phone: 918-452-2128

custom knifemakers

CREWS—DAMASTEEL STAINLESS DAMASCUS

Specialties: Folders of his design and in standard patterns. **Patterns:** Hunters, locking folders, slip-joint folders, multi blade folders. **Technical:** Grinds 440C, D2 and ATS-34. Does filework on back springs and blades; offers scrimshaw on some handles. **Prices:** $150 to $300; some higher. **Remarks:** Full-time maker; first knife sold in 1981. Doing business as A. Crenshaw Knives. **Mark:** First initial, last name, Lake Eufaula, state stamped; first initial last name in rainbow; Lake Eufaula across bottom with Okla. in middle.

CREWS, RANDY
627 Cricket Trail Rd., Patriot, OH 45658, Phone: 740-379-2329, randy.crews@ sbcglobal.net
Specialties: Fixed blades, bowies and hunters. **Technical:** 440C, Alabama Damascus, 1095 with file work. Stock removal method. **Prices:** Start at $150. **Remarks:** Collected knives for 30 years. Part-time maker; first knife made in 2002. **Mark:** Crews Patriot OH.

CRIST, ZOE
2274 Deep Gap Rd., Flat Rock, NC 28731, Phone: 828-275-6689, zoe@zoecristknives. com Web: www.zoecristknives.com
Specialties: San mai and stainless steel. Custom damascus and traditional damascus working and art knives. Also makes Mokume. Works to customer specs. **Patterns:** All damascus hunters, bowies, fighters, neck, boot and high-end art knives. **Technical:** Makes all his own damascus steel from 1095, L6, 15n20. Forges all knives, heat treats, filework, differential heat treatment. **Prices:** $150 - $2500. **Remarks:** Full-time maker, has been making knives since 1988, went full-time 2009. Also makes own leather sheaths. **Mark:** Small "z" with long tail on left side of blade at ricasso.

CROCKFORD, JACK
1859 Harts Mill Rd, Chamblee, GA 30341, Phone: 770-457-4680
Specialties: Lockback folders. **Patterns:** Hunters, fishing and camp knives, traditional folders. **Technical:** Grinds A2, D2, ATS-34 and 440C. Engraves and scrimshaws. **Prices:** Start at $175. **Remarks:** Part-time maker; first knife sold in 1975. **Mark:** Name.

CROSS, KEVIN
5 Pear Orchard Rd., Portland, CT 06480, Phone: 860-894-2385, kevincross@comcast. net; Web: www.kevincrossknives.com
Specialties: Working/using and presentation grade fixed-blade knives and custom kitchen knives. **Patterns:** Hunters, skinners, fighters. Bowies, camp knives. **Technical:** Stock removal maker. Uses O1, 1095, 154 CPM as well as Damascus from Eggerling, Ealy, Donnelly, Nichols, Thomas and others. Most handles are natural materials such as burled and spalted woods, stag and ancient ivory. **Prices:** $200 - $1,200. **Remarks:** Part-time maker. First knife sold around 1997. **Mark:** Name.

CROSS, ROBERT
RMB 200B, Manilla Rd, Tamworth, NSW, AUSTRALIA 2340, Phone: 067-618385

CROTTS, DAN
PO Box 68, Elm Springs, AR 72728, Phone: 479-248-7116, dancrottsknives@yahoo. com Web: www.facebook.com/dancrottsknives
Specialties: User grade, hunting, tactical and folders. **Technical:** High-end tool steel. **Prices:** $2200. **Remarks:** Specializes in making performance blades. **Mark:** Crotts.

CROWDER, GARY L
461401 E. 1125 Rd., Sallisaw, OK 74955, Phone: 918-775-9009, gcrowder99@yahoo. com
Specialties: Folders, multi-blades. **Patterns:** Traditional with a few sheath knives. **Technical:** Flat grinds ATS-34, D2 and others, as well as Damascus via stock-removal. **Prices:** $150 to $600. **Remarks:** Retired, part-time maker. First knife sold in 1994.**Mark:** small acid-etched "Crowder" on blade.

CROWDER, ROBERT
Box 1374, Thompson Falls, MT 59873, Phone: 406-827-4754
Specialties: Traditional working knives to customer specs. **Patterns:** Hunters, Bowies, fighters and fillets. **Technical:** Grinds ATS-34, 154CM, 440C, Vascowear and commercial Damascus. **Prices:** $225 to $500; some to $2500. **Remarks:** Full-time maker; first knife sold in 1985. **Mark:** R Crowder signature & Montana.

CROWELL, JAMES L
676 Newnata Cutoff, Mtn. View, AR 72560, Phone: 870-746-4215, crowellknives@ yahoo.com; Web: www.crowellknives.com
Specialties: Bowie knives; fighters and working knives. **Patterns:** Hunters, fighters, Bowies, daggers and folders. Period pieces: War hammers, Japanese and European. **Technical:** Forges 10 series carbon steels as well as O1, L6 and his own Damascus. **Prices:** $425 to $4500; some to $7500. **Remarks:** Full-time maker; first knife sold in 1980. Earned ABS Master Bladesmith in 1986. 2011 Marked 25 years as an ABS Mastersmith. **Mark:** A shooting star.

CROWL, PETER
5786 County Road 10, Waterloo, IN 46793, Phone: 260-488-2532, pete@ petecrowlknives.com; Web: www.petecrowlknives.com
Specialties: Bowie, hunters. **Technical:** Forges 5160, 1080, W2, 52100. **Prices:** $200 and up. **Remarks:** ABS Journeyman smith. **Mark:** Last name in script.

CROWNER, JEFF
1565 Samuel Drive, Cottage Grove, OR 97424, Phone: 541-201-3182, Fax: 541-579-3762
Specialties: Custom knife maker. I make some of the following: wilderness survival blades, martial art weapons, hunting blades. **Technical:** I differentially heat treat every knife. I use various steels like 5160, L-6, Cable Damascus, 52100, 6150, and some stainless types. I use the following for handle materials: TeroTuf by Columbia Industrial products and exotic hardwoods and horn. I make my own custom sheaths as well with

either kydex or leather.

CROWTHERS, MARK F
PO Box 4641, Rolling Bay, WA 98061-0641, Phone: 206-842-7501

CUCCHIARA, MATT
387 W. Hagler, Fresno, CA 93711, Phone: 559-917-2328, matt@cucchiaraknives.com Web: www.cucchiaraknives.com
Specialties: I make large and small, plain or hand carved Ti handled Tactical framelock folders. All decoration and carving work done by maker. Also known for my hand carved Ti pocket clips. **Prices:** Start at around $400 and go as high as $1500 or so.

CULHANE, SEAN K.
8 Ranskroon Dr., Horizon, Roodepoort, 1740, SOUTH AFRICA, Phone: +27 82 453-1741, sculhane@wbs.co.za; www.culhaneknives.co.za
Specialties: Traditional working straight knives and folders in standard patterns and to customer specifications. **Patterns:** Fighters, hunters, kitchen cutlery, utility and Scottish dirks and sgian dubhs. **Technical:** Hollow grinding Sandvik 12C27 and commercial damascus. Full process, including heat treating and sheaths done by maker. **Prices:** From $180 up, depending on design and materials. **Remarks:** Part-time maker; first knife sold in 1988. **Mark:** First and surname in Gothic script curved over the word "Maker."

CULVER, STEVE
5682 94th St, Meriden, KS 66512, Phone: 785-484-0146, Web: www.culverart.com
Specialties: Edged tools and weapons, collectible and functional. **Patterns:** Bowies, daggers, swords, hunters, folders and edged tools. **Technical:** Forges carbon steels and his own pattern welded steels. **Prices:** $500 to $5,000. **Remarks:** Full-time maker; first knife sold in 1989. **Mark:** Last name, M. S.

CUMMING, BOB
CUMMING KNIVES, 35 Manana Dr, Cedar Crest, NM 87008, Phone: 505-286-0509, cumming@comcast.net; Web: www.cummingknives.com
Specialties: One-of-a-kind exhibition grade custom Bowie knives, exhibition grade and working hunters, bird & trout knives, salt and fresh water fillet knives. Low country oyster knives, custom tanto's plains Indian style sheaths & custom leather, all types of exotic handle materials, scrimshaw and engraving. Added folders in 2006. Custom oyster knives. **Prices:** $95 to $3500 and up. **Remarks:** Mentored by the late Jim Nolen, sold first knife in 1978 in Denmark. Retired U.S. Foreign Service Officer. Member NCCKG. **Mark:** Stylized CUMMING.

CURTISS, DAVID
Curtiss Knives, PO Box 902, Granger, IN 46530, Phone: 574-651-2158, david@ curtissknives.com; Web: www.curtissknives.com
Specialties: Specialize in custom tactical-style folders and flipper folders, with some of the best sellers being in the Nano and Cruze series. The Nano is now being produced by Boker Knives. Many new knife designs coming soon.

CURTISS, STEVE L
PO Box 448, Eureka, MT 59914, Phone: 406-889-5510, Fax: 406-889-5510, slc@ bladerigger.com; Web: http://www.bladerigger.com
Specialties: True custom and semi-custom production (SCP), specialized concealment blades; advanced sheaths and tailored body harnessing systems. **Patterns:** Tactical/personal defense fighters, swords, utility and custom patterns. **Technical:** Grinds A2 and Talonite®; heat-treats. Sheaths: Kydex or Kydex-lined leather laminated or Kydex-lined with Rigger Coat™. Exotic materials available. **Prices:** $50 to $10,000. **Remarks:** Full-time maker. Doing business as Blade Rigger L.L.C. Martial artist and unique defense industry tools and equipment. **Mark:** For true custom: Initials and for SCP: Blade Rigger.

D

DAILEY, G E
577 Lincoln St, Seekonk, MA 02771, Phone: 508-336-5088, gedailey@msn.com; Web: www.gedailey.com
Specialties: One-of-a-kind exotic designed edged weapons. **Patterns:** Folders, daggers and swords. **Technical:** Reforges and grinds Damascus; prefers hollow-grinding. Engraves, carves, offers filework and sets stones and uses exotic gems and gold. **Prices:** Start at $1100. **Remarks:** Full-time maker. First knife sold in 1982. **Mark:** Last name or stylized initialed logo.

DAKE, C M
19759 Chef Menteur Hwy, New Orleans, LA 70129-9602, Phone: 504-254-0357, Fax: 504-254-9501
Specialties: Fancy working folders. **Patterns:** Front-lock lockbacks, button-lock folders. **Technical:** Grinds ATS-34 and Damascus. **Prices:** $500 to $2500; some higher. **Remarks:** Full-time maker; first knife sold in 1988. Doing business as Bayou Custom Cutlery. **Mark:** Last name.

DAKE, MARY H
Rt 5 Box 287A, New Orleans, LA 70129, Phone: 504-254-0357

DALLYN, KELLY
124 Deerbrook Place S.E., Calgary, AB, CANADA T2J 6J5, Phone: 403-475-3056, info@dallyn-knives.com Web: dallyn-knives.com
Specialties: Kitchen, utility, and hunting knives

DAMASTEEL STAINLESS DAMASCUS
3052 Isim Rd., Norman, OK 73026, Phone: 888-804-0683; 405-321-3614, damascus@ newmex.com; Web: www.ssdamacus.com
Patterns: Rose, Odin's eye, 5, 20, 30 twists Hakkapelitta, TNT, and infinity, Big Rose, Mumin

DAMLOVAC, SAVA
10292 Bradbury Dr, Indianapolis, IN 46231, Phone: 317-839-4952
Specialties: Period pieces, fantasy, Viking, Moran type all Damascus daggers. **Patterns:** Bowies, fighters, daggers, Persian-style knives. **Technical:** Uses own Damascus, some stainless, mostly hand forges. **Prices:** $150 to $2500; some higher. **Remarks:** Full-time maker; first knife sold in 1993. Specialty, Bill Moran all Damascus dagger sets, in Moran-style wood case. **Mark:** "Sava" stamped in Damascus or etched in stainless.

D'ANDREA, JOHN
8517 N Linwood Loop, Citrus Springs, FL 34433-5045, Phone: 352-489-2803, shootist1@tampabay.rr.com
Specialties: Fancy working straight knives and folders with filework and distinctive leatherwork. **Patterns:** Hunters, fighters, daggers, folders and an occasional sword. **Technical:** Grinds ATS-34, 154CM, 440C and D2. **Prices:** $220 to $1000. **Remarks:** Part-time maker; first knife sold in 1986. **Mark:** First name, last initial imposed on samurai sword.

D'ANGELO, LAURENCE
14703 NE 17th Ave, Vancouver, WA 98686, Phone: 360-573-0546
Specialties: Straight knives of his design. **Patterns:** Bowies, hunters and locking folders. **Technical:** Grinds D2, ATS-34 and 440C. Hand makes all sheaths. **Prices:** $100 to $200. **Remarks:** Full-time maker; first knife sold in 1987. **Mark:** Football logo—first and middle initials, last name, city, state, Maker.

DANIEL, TRAVIS E
PO Box 1223, Thomaston, GA 30286, Phone: 252-362-1229, tedsknives@mail.com
Specialties: Traditional working straight knives of his design or to customer specs. **Patterns:** Hunters, fighters and utility/camp knives. **Technical:** Grinds ATS-34, 440-C, 154CM, forges his own Damascus. Stock removal. **Prices:** $90 to $1200. **Remarks:** Full-time maker; first knife sold in 1976. **Mark:** TED.

DANIELS, ALEX
1416 County Rd 415, Town Creek, AL 35672, Phone: 256-685-0943, akdknives@gmail.com; Web: http://alexdanielscustomknives.com
Specialties: Working and using straight knives and folders; period pieces, reproduction Bowies. **Patterns:** Mostly reproduction Bowies but offers full line of knives. **Technical:** BG-42, 440C, 1095, 52100 forged blades. **Prices:** $350 to $5500. **Remarks:** Full-time maker; first knife sold in 1963. **Mark:** First and middle initials, last name, city and state.

DANNEMANN, RANDY
RIM RANCH, 27752 P25 Rd, Hotchkiss, CO 81419, randann14@gmail.com
Specialties: Hunting knives. **Patterns:** Utility hunters, trout. **Technical:** 440C and D2.**Price:** $95 to $450. **Remarks:** First knife sold 1974. **Mark:** R. Dannemann Colorado or stamped Dannemann.

DARBY, DAVID T
30652 S 533 Rd, Cookson, OK 74427, Phone: 918-457-4868, knfmkr@fullnet.net
Specialties: Forged blades only, all styles. **Prices:** $350 and up. **Remarks:** ABS Journeyman Smith. **Mark:** Stylized quillion dagger incorporates last name (Darby).

DARBY, JED
7878 E Co Rd 50 N, Greensburg, IN 47240, Phone: 812-663-2696
Specialties: Traditional working/using straight knives of his design and to customer specs. **Patterns:** Bowies, hunters and utility/camp knives. **Technical:** Grinds 440C, ATS-34 and Damascus. **Prices:** $70 to $550; some to $1000. **Remarks:** Full-time maker; first knife sold in 1992. Doing business as Darby Knives. **Mark:** Last name and year.

DARBY, RICK
71 Nestingrock Ln, Levittown, PA 19054
Specialties: Working straight knives. **Patterns:** Boots, fighters and hunters with mirror finish. **Technical:** Grinds 440C and CPM440V. **Prices:** $125 to $300. **Remarks:** Part-time maker; first knife sold in 1974. **Mark:** First and middle initials, last name.

DARCEY, CHESTER L
1608 Dominik Dr, College Station, TX 77840, Phone: 979-696-1656, DarceyKnives@yahoo.com
Specialties: Lockback, LinerLock® and scale release folders. **Patterns:** Bowies, hunters and utilities. **Technical:** Stock removal on carbon and stainless steels, forge own Damascus. **Prices:** $200 to $1000. **Remarks:** Part-time maker, first knife sold in 1999. **Mark:** Last name in script.

DARK, ROBERT
2218 Huntington Court, Oxford, AL 36203, Phone: 256-831-4645, dark@darkknives.com; Web: www.darkknives.com
Specialties: Fixed blade working knives of maker's designs. Works with customer designed specifications. **Patterns:** Hunters, Bowies, camp knives, kitchen/utility, bird and trout. Standard patterns and customer designed. **Technical:** Forged and stock removal. Works with high carbon, stainless and Damascus steels. Hollow and flat grinds. **Prices:** $175 to $750. **Remarks:** Sole authorship knives and custom leather sheaths. Full-time maker. **Mark:** "R Dark" on left side of blade.

DARPINIAN, DAVE
PO Box 2643, Olathe, KS 66063, Phone: 913-244-7114, darpo1956@yahoo.com Web: www.kansasknives.org
Specialties: Hunters, fighters, utilities and slip-joint folders. **Patterns:** Full range of straight knives including art daggers. **Technical:** Art grinds damascus and 1095, clay-temper hammon, stock removal and forging. **Prices:** $300 to $1000. **Remarks:** First knife sold in 1986, part-time maker, member of Kansas Custom Knifemakers Association. **Mark:** Last name.

DAUGHTERY, TONY
18661 Daughtery Ln., Loxley, AL 36551, Phone: 251-964-5670 or 251-213-0461

DAVIDSON, EDMUND
3345 Virginia Ave, Goshen, VA 24439, Phone: 540-997-5651, davidson.edmund@gmail.com; Web: www.edmunddavidson.com
Specialties: High class art integrals. **Patterns:** Many hunters and art models. **Technical:** CPM 154-CM. **Prices:** $100 to infinity. **Remarks:** Full-time maker; first knife sold in 1986. **Mark:** Name in deer head or custom logos.

DAVIDSON, LARRY
14249 River Rd., New Braunfels, TX 78132, Phone: 830-214-5144, lazza@davidsonknives.com; Web: www.davidsonknives.com

DAVIDSON, SCOTT
SOLID ROCK KNIVES, 149 Pless Cir., Alto, GA 30510, Phone: 770-869-3173 or 770-869-0882, solidrockknives@bellsouth.net
Specialties: Tactical knives, some hunters, skinners, bird-and-trout and neck knives. **Technical:** Stock-removal method of blade making, using CPM S30V, 440C and ATS-34 steels, also O1 and 1095HC tool steels. **Prices:** $100 to $1,200, depending on materials used. **Remarks:** Part-time maker; first knife made in 1996. **Mark:** "Ichthys," the Christian fish, with maker's name and address in or around the fish.

DAVIS, BARRY L
4262 US 20, Castleton, NY 12033, Phone: 518-477-5036, daviscustomknives@yahoo.com
Specialties: Collector grade Damascus folders. Traditional designs with focus on turn-of-the-century techniques employed. Sole authorship. Forges own Damascus, does all carving, filework, gold work and piquet. Uses only natural handle material. Enjoys doing multi-blade as well as single blade folders and daggers. **Prices:** Prices range from $2000 to $7000. **Remarks:** First knife sold in 1980.

DAVIS, CHARLIE
ANZA KNIVES, PO Box 457, Lakeside, CA 92040-9998, Phone: 619-561-9445, Fax: 619-390-6283, sales@anzaknives.com; Web: www.anzaknives.com
Specialties: Fancy and embellished working straight knives of his design. **Patterns:** Hunters, camp and utility knives. **Technical:** Grinds high-carbon files. **Prices:** $20 to $185, custom depends. **Remarks:** Full-time maker; first knife sold in 1980. Now offers custom. **Mark:** ANZA U.S.A.

DAVIS, DON
8415 Coyote Run, Loveland, CO 80537-9665, Phone: 970-669-9016, Fax: 970-669-8072
Specialties: Working straight knives in standard patterns or to customer specs. **Patterns:** Hunters, utility knives, skinners and survival knives. **Technical:** Grinds 440C, ATS-34. **Prices:** $75 to $250. **Remarks:** Full-time maker; first knife sold in 1985. **Mark:** Signature, city and state.

DAVIS, JESSE W
3853 Peyton Rd., Coldwater, MS 38618, Phone: 901-849-7250, jandddvais1@earthlink.net
Specialties: Working straight knives and boots in standard patterns and to customer specs. **Patterns:** Boot knives, daggers, fighters, subhilts & Bowies. **Technical:** Grinds A2, D2, 440C and commercial Damascus. **Prices:** $125 to $1000. **Remarks:** Full-time maker; first knife sold in 1977. Former member Knifemakers Guild (in good standing). **Mark:** Name or initials.

DAVIS, JOEL
74538 165th, Albert Lea, MN 56007, Phone: 507-377-0808, joelknives@yahoo.com
Specialties: Complete sole authorship presentation grade highly complex pattern-welded mosaic Damascus blade and bolster stock. **Patterns:** To date Joel has executed over 900 different mosaic Damascus patterns in the past four years. Anything conceived by maker's imagination. **Technical:** Uses various heat colorable "high vibrancy" steels, nickel 200 and some powdered metal for bolster stock only. Uses 1095, 1075 and 15N20. High carbon steels for cutting edge blade stock only. **Prices:** 15 to $50 per square inch and up depending on complexity of pattern. **Remarks:** Full-time mosaic Damascus metal smith focusing strictly on never-before-seen mosaic patterns. Most of maker's work is used for art knives ranging between $1500 to $4500.

DAVIS, JOHN
235 Lampe Rd, Selah, WA 98942, Phone: 509-697-3845, 509-945-4570, jdwelds@charter.net
Specialties: Damascus and mosaic Damascus, working knives, working folders, art knives and art folders. **Technical:** Some ATS-34 and stainless Damascus. Embellishes with fancy stabilized wood, mammoth and walrus ivory. **Prices:** Start at $150. **Remarks:** Part-time maker; first knife sold in 1996. **Mark:** Name city and state on Damascus stamp initials; name inside back RFR.

DAVIS, STEVE
3370 Chatsworth Way, Powder Springs, GA 30127, Phone: 770-427-5740, bsdavis@bellsouth.net
Specialties: Gents and ladies folders. **Patterns:** Straight knives, slip-joint folders, locking-liner folders. **Technical:** Grinds ATS-34 forges own Damascus. Offers filework; prefers hand-rubbed finishes and natural handle materials. Uses pearl, ivory, stag and exotic woods. **Prices:** $250 to $800; some to $1500. **Remarks:** Full-time maker; first knife sold in 1988. Doing business as Custom Knives by Steve Davis. **Mark:** Name engraved on blade.

custom knifemakers

DAVIS—DEMPSEY

DAVIS, TERRY
Box 111, Sumpter, OR 97877, Phone: 541-894-2307
Specialties: Traditional and contemporary folders. **Patterns:** Multi-blade folders, whittlers and interframe multiblades; sunfish patterns. **Technical:** Flat-grinds ATS-34. **Prices:** $400 to $1000; some higher. **Remarks:** Full-time maker; first knife sold in 1985. **Mark:** Name in logo.

DAVIS, VERNON M
2020 Behrens Circle, Waco, TX 76705, Phone: 254-799-7671
Specialties: Presentation-grade straight knives. **Patterns:** Bowies, daggers, boots, fighters, hunters and utility knives. **Technical:** Hollow-grinds 440C, ATS-34 and D2. Grinds an aesthetic grind line near choil. **Prices:** $125 to $550; some to $5000. **Remarks:** Part-time maker; first knife sold in 1980. **Mark:** Last name and city inside outline of state.

DAVIS, W C
1955 S 1251 Rd, El Dorado Springs, MO 64744, Phone: 417-876-1259
Specialties: Fancy working straight knives and folders. **Patterns:** Folding lockers and slip-joints; straight hunters, fighters and Bowies. **Technical:** Grinds A2, ATS-34, 154, CPM T490V and CPM 530V. **Prices:** $100 to $300; some to $1000. **Remarks:** Full-time maker; first knife sold in 1972. **Mark:** Name.

DAVIS JR., JIM
5129 Ridge St, Zephyrhills, FL 33541, Phone: 813-779-9213 813-469-4241 Cell, jimdavisknives@aol.com
Specialties: Presentation-grade fixed blade knives w/composite hidden tang handles. Employs a variety of ancient and contemporary ivories. **Patterns:** One-of-a-kind gents, personal, and executive knives and hunters w/unique cam-lock pouch sheaths and display stands. **Technical:** Flat grinds ATS-34 and stainless Damascus w/most work by hand w/assorted files. **Prices:** $300 and up. **Remarks:** Full-time maker, first knives sold in 2000. **Mark:** Signature w/printed name over "HANDCRAFTED."

DAVISON, TODD A.
230 S. Wells St., Kosciusko, MS 39090, Phone: 620-894-0402, crazyknifeblade@yahoo.com; Web: www.tadscustomknives.com
Specialties: Making working/using and collector folders of his design. All knives are truly made one of a kind. Each knife has a serial number inside the liner. **Patterns:** Single and double blade traditional slip-joint pocket knives. **Technical:** Free hand hollow ground blades, hand finished. Using only the very best materials possible. Holding the highest standards to fit & finish and detail. Does his own heat treating. ATS34 and D2 steel. **Prices:** $450 to $900, some higher. **Remarks:** Full time maker, first knife sold in 1981. **Mark:** T.A. DAVISON USA.

DAWKINS, DUDLEY L
221 NW Broadmoor Ave., Topeka, KS 66606-1254, Phone: 785-817-9343, dawkind@reagan.com or dawkind@sbcglobal.net
Specialties: Stylized old or "Dawkins Forged" with anvil in center. New tang stamps. **Patterns:** Straight knives. **Technical:** Mostly carbon steel; some Damascus-all knives forged. **Prices:** Knives: $275 and up; Sheaths: $95 and up. **Remarks:** All knives supplied with wood-lined sheaths. ABS Member, sole authorship. **Mark:** Stylized "DLD or Dawkins Forged with anvil in center.

DAWSON, BARRY
7760 E Hwy 69, Prescott Valley, AZ 86314, Phone: 928-255-9830, dawsonknives@yahoo.com; Web: www.dawsonknives.com
Specialties: Samurai swords, combat knives, collector daggers, tactical, folding and hunting knives. **Patterns:** Offers over 60 different models. **Technical:** Grinds 440C, ATS-34, own heat-treatment. **Prices:** $75 to $1500; some to $5000. **Remarks:** Full-time maker; first knife sold in 1975. **Mark:** Last name, USA in print or last name in script.

DAWSON, LYNN
7760 E Hwy 69 #C-5 157, Prescott Valley, AZ 86314, Phone: 928-713-2812, lynnknives@yahoo.com; Web: www.lynnknives.com
Specialties: Swords, hunters, utility, and art pieces. **Patterns:** Over 25 patterns to choose from. **Technical:** Grinds 440C, ATS-34, own heat treating. **Prices:** $80 to $1000. **Remarks:** Custom work and her own designs. **Mark:** The name "Lynn" in print or script.

DE MARIA JR., ANGELO
12 Boronda Rd, Carmel Valley, CA 93924, Phone: 831-659-3381, Fax: 831-659-1315, angelodemaria1@mac.com
Specialties: Damascus, fixed and folders, sheaths. **Patterns:** Mosiac and random. **Technical:** Forging 5160, 1084 and 15N20. **Prices:** $200+. **Remarks:** Part-time maker. **Mark:** Angelo de Maria Carmel Valley, CA etch or AdM stamp.

DE MESA, JOHN
1565 W. Main St., STE. 208 #229, Lewisville, TX 75057, Phone: 972-310-3877, TogiArts@me.com; Web: http://togiarts.com/ and http://togiarts.com/CSC/index.html
Specialties: Japanese sword polishing. **Technical:** Traditional sword polishing of Japanese swords made by sword makers in Japan and U.S. **Prices:** Starting at $75 per inch. **Remarks:** Custom Swords Collaborations IN collaboration with Jose De Braga, we can mount Japanese style sword with custom carved handles, sword fittings and scabbards to customer specs.

DE WET, KOBUS
2601 River Road, Yakima, WA 98902, Phone: 509-728-3736, kobus@moderndamascus.com, Web: www.moderndamascus.com
Specialties: Working and art knives **Patterns:** Every knife is unique. Fixed blades and folders. Hunting, Bowie, Tactical and Utility knives. **Technical:** I enjoy forging my own damascus steel, mainly from 15N20 and 1084. I also use stock removal and stainless steels. **Prices:** Starting at $200 **Remarks:** Part time maker, started in 2007 **Mark:** Circled "K" / Modern Damascus - Kobus de Wet

DEAN, HARVEY J
3266 CR 232, Rockdale, TX 76567, Phone: 512-446-3111, Fax: 512-446-5060, dean@tex1.net; Web: www.harveydean.com
Specialties: Collectible, functional knives. **Patterns:** Bowies, hunters, folders, daggers, swords, battle axes, camp and combat knives. **Technical:** Forges 1095, O1 and his Damascus. **Prices:** $350 to $10,000. **Remarks:** Full-time maker; first knife sold in 1981. **Mark:** Last name and MS.

DEBAUD, JAKE
2403 Springvale Lane, Dallas, TX 75234, Phone: 214-916-1891, jake.debaud@gmail.com Web: www.debaudknives.com
Specialties: Custom damascus art knives, hunting knives and tactical knives. **Technical:** A2, D2, O1, 1095 and some stainless if requested ATS-34 or 154CM and S30V. **Remarks:** Full-time maker. Have been making knives for three years.

DEBRAGA, JOSE C.
1341 9e Rue, Trois Rivieres, QC, CANADA G8Y 2Z2, Phone: 418-948-5864, josecdebraga@cgocable.ca
Specialties: Art knives, fantasy pieces and working knives of his design or to customer specs. **Patterns:** Knives with sculptured or carved handles, from miniatures to full-size working knives. **Technical:** Grinds and hand-files 440C and ATS-34. A variety of steels and handle materials available. Offers lost wax casting. **Prices:** Start at $300. **Remarks:** Full-time maker; wax modeler, sculptor and knifemaker; first knife sold in 1984. **Mark:** Initials in stylized script and serial number.

DEBRAGA, JOVAN
141 Notre Dame des Victoir, Quebec, CANADA G2G 1J3, Phone: 418-997-0819/418-877-1915, jovancdebraga@msn.com
Specialties: Art knives, fantasy pieces and working knives of his design or to customer specs. **Patterns:** Knives with sculptured or carved handles, from miniatures to full-sized working knives. **Technical:** Grinds and hand-files 440C, and ATS-34. A variety of steels and handle materials available. **Prices:** Start at $300. **Remarks:** Full time maker. Sculptor and knifemaker. First knife sold in 2003. **Mark:** Initials in stylized script and serial number.

DEL RASO, PETER
28 Mayfield Dr, Mt. Waverly, VIC, AUSTRALIA 3149, Phone: 613 98060644, delraso@optusnet.com.au
Specialties: Fixed blades, some folders, art knives. **Patterns:** Daggers, Bowies, tactical, boot, personal and working knives. **Technical:** Grinds ATS-34, commercial Damascus and any other type of steel on request. **Prices:** $100 to $1500. **Remarks:** Part-time maker, first show in 1993. **Mark:** Maker's surname stamped.

DELAROSA, JIM
2116 N Pontiac Dr, Janesville, WI 53545, Phone: 262-422-8604, D-knife@hotmail.com
Specialties: Working straight knives and folders of his design or customer specs. **Patterns:** Hunters, skinners, fillets, utility and locking folders. **Technical:** Grinds ATS-34, 440-C, D2, O1 and commercial Damascus. **Prices:** $100 to $500; some higher. **Remarks:** Part-time maker. **Mark:** First and last name.

DELL, WOLFGANG
Am Alten Berg 9, Owen-Teck, GERMANY D-73277, Phone: 49-7021-81802, wolfgang@dell-knives.de; Web: www.dell-knives.de
Specialties: Fancy high-art straight of his design and to customer specs. **Patterns:** Fighters, hunters, Bowies and utility/camp knives. **Technical:** Grinds ATS-34, RWL-34, Elmax, Damascus (Fritz Schneider). Offers high gloss finish and engraving. **Prices:** $500 to $1000; some to $1600. **Remarks:** Full-time maker; first knife sold in 1992. **Mark:** Hopi hand of peace.

DELLANA
STARLANI INT'L INC, 1135 Terminal Way Ste #209, Reno, NV 89502, Phone: 304-727-5512; 702-569-7827, 1dellana@gmail.com; Web: www.dellana.cc
Specialties: Collector grade fancy/embellished high art folders and art daggers. **Patterns:** Locking folders and art daggers. **Technical:** Forges her own Damascus and W-2. Engraves, does stone setting, filework, carving and gold/platinum fabrication. Prefers exotic, high karat gold, platinum, silver, gemstone and mother-of-pearl handle materials. **Price:** Upscale. **Remarks:** Sole authorship, full-time maker, first knife sold in 1994. Also does one high art collaboration a year with Van Barnett. Member: Art Knife Invitational and ABS. **Mark:** First name.

DELONG, DICK
PO Box 1024, Centerville, TX 75833-1024, Phone: 903-536-1454
Specialties: Fancy working knives and fantasy pieces. **Patterns:** Hunters and small skinners. **Technical:** Grinds and files O1, D2, 440C and Damascus. Offers cocobolo and Osage orange for handles. **Prices:** Start at $50. **Remarks:** Part-time maker. Member of Art Knife Invitational. Voting member of Knifemakers Guild. Member of ABS. **Mark:** Last name; some unmarked.

DEMENT, LARRY
PO Box 1807, Prince Fredrick, MD 20678, Phone: 410-586-9011
Specialties: Fixed blades. **Technical:** Forged and stock removal. **Prices:** $75 to $200. **Remarks:** Affordable, good feelin', quality knives. Part-time maker.

DEMPSEY, GORDON S
PO Box 7497, N. Kenai, AK 99635, Phone: 907-394-0894, dempseygordon@aol.com
Specialties: Working straight knives. **Patterns:** Small hunters. **Technical:** Pattern-welded damascus and carbon steel. **Prices:** On request. **Remarks:** Part-time maker; first knife sold in 1974. **Mark:** Name.

DENNEHY, JOHN D
2959 Zachary Drive, Loveland, CO 80537, Phone: 970-218-7128, www.thewildirishrose.com
Specialties: Working straight knives, throwers, and leatherworker's knives. **Technical:** 440C, & O1, heat treats own blades, part-time maker, first knife sold in 1989. **Patterns:** Small hunting to presentation Bowies, leatherworks round and head knives. **Prices:** $200 and up. **Remarks:** Custom sheath maker, sheath making seminars at the Blade Show.

DENNING, GENO
CAVEMAN ENGINEERING, 135 Allenvalley Rd, Gaston, SC 29053, Phone: 803-794-6067, cden101656@aol.com; Web: www.cavemanengineering.com
Specialties: Mirror finish. **Patterns:** Hunters, fighters, folders. **Technical:** ATS-34, 440V, S-30-V D2. **Prices:** $100 and up. **Remarks:** Full-time maker since 1996. Sole income since 1999. Instructor at Montgomery Community College (Grinding Blades). A director of SCAK: South Carolina Association of Knifemakers. **Mark:** Troy NC.

DERESPINA, RICHARD
info@derespinaknives.com; Web: www.derespinaknives.com
Specialties: Custom fixed blades and folders, Kris and Karambit. **Technical:** I use the stock removal method. Steels I use are S30V, 154CM, D2, 440C, BG42. Handles made of G10 particularly Micarta, etc. **Prices:** $150 to $550 depending on model. **Remarks:** Full-time maker. My etched logos are two, my last name and Brooklyn NY mark as well as the Star/Yin Yang logo. The star being both representative of various angles of attack common in combat as well as being three triangles, each points to levels of metaphysical understanding. The Yin and Yang have my company initials on each side D & K. Yin and Yang shows the ever present physics of life.

DERINGER, CHRISTOPH
625 Chemin Lower, Cookshire, QC, CANADA J0B 1M0, Phone: 819-345-4260, cdsab@sympatico.ca
Specialties: Traditional working/using straight knives and folders of his design and to customer specs. **Patterns:** Boots, hunters, folders, art knives, kitchen knives and utility/camp knives. **Technical:** Forges 5160, O1 and Damascus. Offers a variety of filework. **Prices:** Start at $250. **Remarks:** Full-time maker; first knife sold in 1989. **Mark:** Last name stamped/engraved.

DERR, HERBERT
413 Woodland Dr, St. Albans, WV 25177, Phone: 304-727-3866
Specialties: Damascus one-of-a-kind knives, carbon steels also. **Patterns:** Birdseye, ladder back, mosaics. **Technical:** All styles functional as well as artistically pleasing. **Prices:** $90 to $175 carbon, Damascus $250 to $800. **Remarks:** All Damascus made by maker. **Mark:** H.K. Derr.

DESAULNIERS, ALAIN
100 Pope Street, Cookshire, QC, CANADA J0B 1M0, pinklaperez@sympatico.ca Web: www.desoknives.com
Specialties: Mostly Loveless style knives. **Patterns:** Double grind fighters, hunters, daggers, etc. **Technical:** Stock removal, ATS-34, CPM. High-polished blades, tapered tangs, high-quality handles. **Remarks:** Full-time. Collaboration with John Young. **Prices:** $425 and up. **Mark:** Name and city in logo.

DESROSIERS, ADAM
PO Box 1954, Petersburg, AK 99833, Phone: 907-518-4570, adam@alaskablades.com Web: www.alaskablades.com
Specialties: High performance, forged, carbon steel and damascus camp choppers, and hunting knives. Hidden tang, full tang, and full integral construction. High performance heat treating. Knife designs inspired by life in Alaskan bush. **Technical:** Hand forges tool steels and damascus. Sole authorship. Full range of handle materials, micarta to Ivory. Preferred steels: W-2, O-1, L-6, 15n20, 1095. **Prices:** $200 - $3000. **Remarks:** ABS member. Has trained with Masters around the world. **Mark:** DrsRosiers over Alaska, underlined with a rose.

DESROSIERS, HALEY
PO Box 1954, Petersburg, AK 99833, Phone: 907-518-1416, haley@alaskablades.com Web: www.alaskablades.com
Specialties: Hunting knives, integrals and a few choppers, high performance. **Technical:** Hand forged blades designed for hard use, exotic wood, antler and ivory handles. **Prices:** $300 - $1500. **Remarks:** Forged first knife in 2001. Part-time bladesmith all year except for commercial fishing season. **Mark:** Capital HD.

DETMER, PHILLIP
14140 Bluff Rd, Breese, IL 62230, Phone: 618-526-4834, jpdetmer@att.net
Specialties: Working knives. **Patterns:** Bowies, daggers and hunters. **Technical:** Grinds ATS-34 and D2. **Prices:** $60 to $400. **Remarks:** Part-time maker; first knife sold in 1977. **Mark:** Last name with dagger.

DEUBEL, CHESTER J.
6211 N. Van Ark Rd., Tucson, AZ 85743, Phone: 520-440-7255, cjdeubel@yahoo.com; Web: www.cjdeubel.com
Specialties: Fancy working straight knives and folders of his or customer design, with intricate file work. **Patterns:** Fighters, Bowies, daggers, hunters, camp knives, and cowboy. **Technical:** Flat guard, hollow grind, antiqued, all types Damascus, 154cpm Stainsteel, high carbon steel, 440c Stainsteel. **Prices:** From $250 to $3500. **Remarks:** Started making part-time in 1980; went to full-time in 2000. Don Patch is my engraver. **Mark:** C.J. Deubel.

DEVERAUX, BUTCH
PO Box 1356, Riverton, WY 82501, Phone: 307-851-0601, bdeveraux@wyoming.com;

Web: www.deverauxknives.com
Specialties: High-performance working straight knives. **Patterns:** Hunters, fighters, EDC's, miniatures and camp knives. **Technical:** Forged 52100 blade steel, brass guards, sheep-horn handles, as well as stag, cocobolo, she-oak and ironwood. **Prices:** $400 to $3,000. **Remarks:** Part-time maker; first knife sold in 2005. **Mark:** Deveraux on circled "R" on ricasso.

DEYONG, CLARENCE
302 Greenfield Cir., Geneva, IL 60134, Phone: 630-208-1595; or cell: 630-853-6340, cmdeyong@yahoo.com
Patterns: Mainly creates full-tang hunters, skinners and fighters. **Technical:** Stock removal with some forging, using rasps and files for blade stock with an emphasis on natural handle materials. **Prices:** $150 to $300 with custom sheaths. **Remarks:** Making knives since 1981. **Mark:** DeYong and blade # engraved on the blade.

DIAZ, JOSE
409 W. 12th Ave, Ellensburg, WA 98926, jose@diaztools.com Web: www.diaztools.com
Specialties: Affordable custom user-grade utility and camp knives. Also makes competition cutting knives. **Patterns:** Mas. **Technical:** Blade materials range from high carbon steels and Damascus to high performance tool and stainless steels. Uses both forge and stock removal methods in shaping the steel. Handle materials include Tero Tuf, Black Butyl Burl, Micarta, natural woods and G10. **Prices:** $65-$700. **Remarks:** Part-time knife maker; made first knife in 2008. **Mark:** Reclining tree frog with a smile, and "Diaz Tools."

DICK, DAN
P.O. Box 2303, Hutchinson, KS 67504-2303, Phone: 620-669-6805, Dan@DanDickKnives.com; Web: www.dandickknives.com
Specialties: Traditional working/using fixed bladed knives of maker's design. **Patterns:** Hunters, skinners and utility knives. **Technical:** Stock removal maker using CTS-XHP and D2. Prefers such materials as exotic and fancy burl woods. Makes his own sheaths, all leather with tooling. **Prices:** $135 and up. **Remarks:** Part-time maker since 2006. **Marks:** Name in outline border of Kansas.

DICKERSON, GAVIN
PO Box 7672, Petit, GT, SOUTH AFRICA 1512, Phone: +27 011-965-0988, Fax: +27 011-965-0988
Specialties: Straight knives of his design or to customer specs. **Patterns:** Hunters, skinners, fighters and Bowies. **Technical:** Hollow-grinds D2, 440C, ATS-34, 12C27 and Damascus upon request. Prefers natural handle materials; offers synthetic handle materials. **Prices:** $190 to $2500. **Remarks:** Part-time maker; first knife sold in 1982. **Mark:** Name in full.

DICKISON, SCOTT S
179 Taylor Rd, Portsmouth, RI 02871, Phone: 401-847-7398, squared22@cox .net; Web: http://sqauredknives.com
Specialties: Straight knives, locking folders and slip joints of his design. **Patterns:** Sgain dubh, bird and trout knives. **Technical:** Forges and grinds commercial Damascus, D2, O1 and sandvik stainless. **Prices:** $400 to $1000; some higher. **Remarks:** Part-time maker; first knife sold in 1989. **Mark:** Stylized initials.

DICRISTOFANO, ANTHONY P
10519 Nevada Ave., Melrose Park, IL 60164, Phone: 847-845-9598, sukemitsu@sbcglobal.net Web: www.namahagesword.com or www.sukemitsu.com
Specialties: Japanese-style swords. **Patterns:** Katana, Wakizashi, Otanto, Kozuka. **Technical:** Tradition and some modern steels. All clay tempered and traditionally hand polished using Japanese wet stones. **Remarks:** Part-time maker. **Prices:** Varied, available on request. **Mark:** Blade tang signed in "SUKEMITSU."

DIETZ, HOWARD
421 Range Rd, New Braunfels, TX 78132, Phone: 830-885-4662
Specialties: Lock-back folders, working straight knives. **Patterns:** Folding hunters, high-grade pocket knives. ATS-34, 440C, CPM 440V, D2 and stainless Damascus. **Prices:** $300 to $1000. **Remarks:** Full-time gun and knifemaker; first knife sold in 1995. **Mark:** Name, city, and state.

DIETZEL, BILL
PO Box 1613, Middleburg, FL 32068, Phone: 904-282-1091
Specialties: Forged straight knives and folders. **Patterns:** His interpretations. **Technical:** Forges his Damascus and other steels. **Prices:** Middle ranges. **Remarks:** Likes natural materials; uses titanium in folder liners. Master Smith (1997). **Mark:** Name.

DIGANGI, JOSEPH M
PO Box 257, Los Ojos, NM 87551, Phone: 505-929-2987, Fax: 505-753-8144, Web: www.digangidesigns.com
Specialties: Kitchen and table cutlery. **Patterns:** French chef's knives, carving sets, steak knife sets, some camp knives and hunters. Holds patents and trademarks for "System II" kitchen cutlery set. **Technical:** Grinds ATS-34. **Prices:** $150 to $595; some to $1200. **Remarks:** Full-time maker; first knife sold in 1983. **Mark:** DiGangi Designs.

DILL, DAVE
7404 NW 30th St, Bethany, OK 73008, Phone: 405-789-0750
Specialties: Folders of his design. **Patterns:** Various patterns. **Technical:** Hand-grinds 440C, ATS-34. Offers engraving and filework on all folders. **Prices:** Starting at $450. **Remarks:** Full-time maker; first knife sold in 1987. **Mark:** First initial, last name.

DILL, ROBERT
1812 Van Buren, Loveland, CO 80538, Phone: 970-667-5144, Fax: 970-667-5144, dillcustomknives@msn.com
Specialties: Fancy and working knives of his design. **Patterns:** Hunters, Bowies and

fighters. **Technical:** Grinds 440C and D2. **Prices:** $100 to $800. **Remarks:** Full-time maker; first knife sold in 1984. **Mark:** Logo stamped into blade.

DILLUVIO, FRANK J
311 Whitetail Dr., Prudenville, MI 48651, Phone: 989-202-4051, fjdknives@hotmail.com; Web: www.fdilluviocustomknives.com
Specialties: Folders, fixed blades. **Patterns:** Many. **Technical:** Grinds 440-c, D-2. Precision fits. **Prices:** $225 and up. **Remarks:** Full-time maker; first knife sold in 1984. **Mark:** Name and state.

DINTRUFF, CHUCK
1708 E. Martin Luther King Blvd., Seffner, FL 33584, Phone: 813-381-6916, DINTRUFFKNIVES@aol.com; Web: dintruffknives.com and spinwellfab.com

DION, GREG
3032 S Jackson St, Oxnard, CA 93033, Phone: 519-981-1033
Specialties: Working straight knives, some fancy. Welcomes special orders. **Patterns:** Hunters, fighters, camp knives, Bowies and tantos. **Technical:** Grinds ATS-34, 154CM and 440C. **Prices:** $85 to $300; some to $600. **Remarks:** Part-time maker; first knife sold in 1985. **Mark:** Name.

DIOTTE, JEFF
DIOTTE KNIVES, 159 Laurier Dr, LaSalle, ON, CANADA N9J 1L4, Phone: 519-978-2764

DIPPOLD, AL
90 Damascus Ln, Perryville, MO 63775, Phone: 573-547-1119, adippold@midwest.net
Specialties: Fancy one-of-a-kind locking folders. **Patterns:** Locking folders. **Technical:** Forges and grinds mosaic and pattern welded Damascus. Offers filework on all folders. **Prices:** $500 to $3500; some higher. **Remarks:** Full-time maker; first knife sold in 1980. **Mark:** Last name in logo inside of liner.

DISKIN, MATT
PO Box 653, Freeland, WA 98249, Phone: 360-730-0451, info@volcanknives.com; Web: www.volcanknives.com
Specialties: Damascus autos. **Patterns:** Dirks and daggers. **Technical:** Forges mosaic Damascus using 15N20, 1084, 02, 06, L6; pure nickel. **Prices:** Start at $500. **Remarks:** Full-time maker. **Mark:** Last name.

DIXON JR., IRA E
PO Box 26, O'Brien, OR 97534, irasknives@yahoo.com
Specialties: Straight knives of his design. **Patterns:** All patterns include art knives. **Technical:** Grinds CPM materials, Damascus and some tool steels. **Prices:** $275 to $2000. **Remarks:** Full-time maker; first knife sold in 1993. **Mark:** First name, Handmade.

DOBRATZ, ERIC
25371 Hillary Lane, Laguna Hills, CA 92653, Phone: 949-233-5170, knifesmith@gmail.com
Specialties: Differentially quenched blades with Hamon of his design or with customer input. **Patterns:** Hunting, camp, kitchen, fighters, bowies, traditional tanto, and unique fixed blade designs. **Technical:** Hand-forged high carbon and damascus. Prefers natural material for handles; rare/exotic woods and stag, but also uses micarta and homemade synthetic materials. **Prices:** $150 - $1500. **Remarks:** Part-time maker; first knife made in 1995. **Mark:** Stylized Scarab beetle.

DODD, ROBERT F
4340 E Canyon Dr, Camp Verde, AZ 86322, Phone: 928-567-3333, rfdknives@commspeed.net; Web: www.rfdoddknives.com
Specialties: Folders, fixed blade hunter/skinners, Bowies, daggers. **Patterns:** Drop point. **Technical:** ATS-34 and Damascus. **Prices:** $250 and up. **Remarks:** Hand tooled leather sheaths. **Mark:** R. F. Dodd, Camp Verde AZ.

DOGGETT, BOB
1310 Vinetree Rd, Brandon, FL 33510, Phone: 813-205-5503, dogman@tampabay.rr.com; Web: www.doggettcustomknives.com
Specialties: Clean, functional working knives. **Patterns:** Classic-styled hunter, fighter and utility fixed blades; liner locking folders. **Technical:** Uses stainless steel and commercial Damascus, 416 stainless for bolsters and hardware, hand-rubbed satin finish, top quality handle materials and titanium liners on folders. **Prices:** Start at $175. **Remarks:** Part-time maker. **Mark:** Last name.

DOIRON, DONALD
6 Chemin Petit Lac des Ced, Messines, QC, CANADA J0X-2J0, Phone: 819-465-2489

DOMINY, CHUCK
PO Box 593, Colleyville, TX 76034, Phone: 817-498-4527
Specialties: Titanium LinerLock® folders. **Patterns:** Hunters, utility/camp knives and LinerLock® folders. **Technical:** Grinds 440C and ATS-34. **Prices:** $250 to $3000. **Remarks:** Full-time maker; first knife sold in 1976. **Mark:** Last name.

DOOLITTLE, MIKE
13 Denise Ct, Novato, CA 94947, Phone: 415-897-3246
Specialties: Working straight knives in standard patterns. **Patterns:** Hunters and fishing knives. **Technical:** Grinds 440C, 154CM and ATS-34. **Prices:** $125 to $200; some to $750. **Remarks:** Part-time maker; first knife sold in 1981. **Mark:** Name, city and state.

DORNELES, LUCIANO OLIVEIRIA
Rua 15 De Novembro 2222, Nova Petropolis, RS, BRAZIL 95150-000, Phone: 011-55-54-303-303-90, tchebufalo@hotmail.com
Specialties: Traditional "true" Brazilian-style working knives and to customer specs. **Patterns:** Brazilian hunters, utility and camp knives, Bowies, Dirk. A master at the making of the true "Faca Campeira Gaucha," the true camp knife of the famous Brazilian

Gauchos. A Dorneles knife is 100 percent hand-forged with sledge hammers only. Can make spectacular Damascus hunters/daggers. **Technical:** Forges only 52100 and his own Damascus, can put silver wire inlay on customer design handles on special orders; uses only natural handle materials. **Prices:** $250 to $1000. **Mark:** Symbol with L. Dorneles.

DOTSON, TRACY
1280 Hwy C-4A, Baker, FL 32531, Phone: 850-537-2407
Specialties: Folding fighters and small folders. **Patterns:** LinerLock® and lockback folders. **Technical:** Hollow-grinds ATS-34 and commercial Damascus. **Prices:** Start at $250. **Remarks:** Part-time maker; first knife sold in 1995. **Mark:** Last name.

DOUCETTE, R
CUSTOM KNIVES, 19 Evelyn St., Brantford, ON, CANADA N3R 3G8, Phone: 519-756-9040, randy@randydoucetteknives.com; Web: www.randydoucetteknives.com
Specialties: High-end tactical folders with filework and multiple grinds. **Patterns:** Tactical folders. **Technical:** All knives are handmade. The only outsourcing is heat treatment. **Prices:** $900 to $2,500. **Remarks:** Full-time knifemaker; 2-year waiting list. Maker is proud to produce original knife designs every year!Im **Mark:** R. Doucette

DOURSIN, GERARD
Chemin des Croutoules, Pernes les Fontaines, FRANCE 84210
Specialties: Period pieces. **Patterns:** Liner locks and daggers. **Technical:** Forges mosaic Damascus. **Prices:** $600 to $4000. **Remarks:** First knife sold in 1983. **Mark:** First initial, last name and I stop the lion.

DOUSSOT, LAURENT
1008 Montarville, St. Bruno, QC, CANADA J3V 3T1, Phone: 450-441-3298, doussot@skalja.com; Web: www.skalja.com, www.doussot-knives.com
Specialties: Fancy and embellished folders and fantasy knives. **Patterns:** Fighters and locking folders. **Technical:** Grinds ATS-34 and commercial Damascus. Scale carvings on all knives; most bolsters are carved titanium. **Prices:** $350 to $3000. **Remarks:** Part-time maker; first knife was sold in 1992. **Mark:** Stylized initials inside circle.

DOWNIE, JAMES T
1295 Sandy Ln., Apt. 1208, Sarnia, Ontario, CANADA N7V 4K5, Phone: 519-491-8234
Specialties: Serviceable straight knives and folders; period pieces. **Patterns:** Hunters, Bowies, camp knives, fillet and miniatures. **Technical:** Grinds D2, 440C and ATS-34, Damasteel, stainless steel Damascus. **Prices:** $195 and up. **Remarks:** Full-time maker; first knife sold in 1978. **Mark:** Signature of first and middle initials, last name.

DOWNING, LARRY
12268 State Route 181 N, Bremen, KY 42325, Phone: 270-525-3523, larrydowning@bellsouth.net; Web: www.downingknives.com
Specialties: Working straight knives and folders. **Patterns:** From mini-knives to daggers, folding lockers to interframes. **Technical:** Forges and grinds 154CM, ATS-34 and his own Damascus. **Prices:** $195 to $950; some higher. **Remarks:** Part-time maker; first knife sold in 1979. **Mark:** Name in arrowhead.

DOWNING, TOM
2675 12th St, Cuyahoga Falls, OH 44223, Phone: 330-923-7464
Specialties: Working straight knives; period pieces. **Patterns:** Hunters, fighters and tantos. **Technical:** Grinds 440C, ATs-34 and CPM-T-440V. Prefers natural handle materials. **Prices:** $150 to $900, some to $1500. **Remarks:** Part-time maker; first knife sold in 1979. **Mark:** First and middle initials, last name.

DOWNS, JAMES F
2247 Summit View Rd, Powell, OH 43065, Phone: 614-766-5350, jfdowns1@yahoo.com
Specialties: Working straight knives of his design or to customer specs. **Patterns:** Folders, Bowies, boot, hunters, utility. **Technical:** Grinds 440C and other steels. Prefers mastodon ivory, all pearls, stabilized wood and elephant ivory. **Prices:** $75 to $1200. **Remarks:** Full-time maker; first knife sold in 1980. **Mark:** Last name.

DOX, JAN
Zwanebloemlaan 27, Schoten, BELGIUM B 2900, Phone: 32 3 658 77 43, jan.dox@scarlet.be; Web: doxblades.weebly.com
Specialties: Working/using knives, from kitchen to battlefield. **Patterns:** Own designs, some based on traditional ethnic patterns (Scots, Celtic, Scandinavian and Japanese) or to customer specs. **Technical:** Grinds D2/A2 and stainless, forges carbon steels, convex edges. Handles: Wrapped in modern or traditional patterns, resin impregnated if desired. Natural or synthetic materials, some carved. **Prices:** $50 and up. **Remarks:** Spare-time maker, first knife sold 2001. **Mark:** Name or stylized initials.

DOYLE, JOHN
4779 W. M-61, Gladwin, MI 48624, Phone: 989-802-9470, jdoyleknives@gmail.com
Specialties. Hunters, camp knives and bowies. **Technical:** Forges 1075, 1080, 1084, 1095 and 5160. Will practice stock-removal method of blademaking on small knives at times. **Remarks:** Full-time maker; first knife made in 2009. **Mark:** J. Doyle in "Invitation" style print font

DOZIER, BOB
PO Box 1941, Springdale, AR 72765, Phone: 888-823-0023/479-756-0023, Fax: 479-756-9139, info@dozierknives.com; Web www.dozierknives.com
Specialties: Using knives (fixed blades and folders). **Patterns:** Some fine collector-grade knives. **Technical:** Uses D2. Prefers Micarta handle material. **Prices:** Using knives: $195 to $700. **Remarks:** Full-time maker; first knife sold in 1965. No longer doing semi-handmade line. **Mark:** State, made, last name in a circle (for fixed blades); Last name with arrow through 'D' and year over name (for folders).

DRAPER, AUDRA
#10 Creek Dr, Riverton, WY 82501, Phone: 307-856-6807 or 307-851-0426 cell, adraper@wyoming.com; Web: www.draperknives.com
Specialties: One-of-a-kind straight and folding knives. Also pendants, earring and bracelets of Damascus. **Patterns:** Design custom knives, using, Bowies, and minis. **Technical:** Forge Damascus; heat-treats all knives. **Prices:** Vary depending on item. **Remarks:** Full-time maker; master bladesmith in the ABS. Member of the PKA; first knife sold in 1995. **Mark:** Audra.

DRAPER, MIKE
#10 Creek Dr, Riverton, WY 82501, Phone: 307-856-6807, adraper@wyoming.com
Specialties: Mainly folding knives in tactical fashion, occasonal fixed blade. **Patterns:** Hunters, Bowies and camp knives, tactical survival. **Technical:** Grinds S30V stainless steel. **Prices:** Starting at $250+. **Remarks:** Full-time maker; first knife sold in 1996. **Mark:** Initials M.J.D. or name, city and state.

DREW, GERALD
213 Hawk Ridge Dr, Mill Spring, NC 28756, Phone: 828-713-4762
Specialties: Blade ATS-34 blades. Straight knives. **Patterns:** Hunters, camp knives, some Bowies and tactical. **Technical:** ATS-34 preferred. **Price:** $65 to $400. **Mark:** GL DREW.

DRISCOLL, MARK
4115 Avoyer Pl, La Mesa, CA 91941, Phone: 619-670-0695, markdriscoll91941@yahoo.com
Specialties: High-art, period pieces and working/using knives of his design or to customer specs; some fancy. **Patterns:** Swords, Bowies, fighters, daggers, hunters and primitive (mountain man-styles). **Technical:** Forges 52100, 5160, O1, L6, 1095, 15n20, W-2 steel and makes his own Damascus and mokume; also does multiple quench heat treating. Uses exotic hardwoods, ivory and horn, offers fancy file work, carving, scrimshaws. **Prices:** $150 to $550; some to $1500. **Remarks:** Part-time maker; first knife sold in 1986. Doing business as Mountain Man Knives. **Mark:** Double "M."

DROST, JASON D
Rt 2 Box 49, French Creek, WV 26218, Phone: 304-472-7901
Specialties: Working/using straight knives and folders of all designs. **Patterns:** Hunters and utility/camp knives. **Technical:** Grinds 154CM and D2. **Prices:** $125 to $5000. **Remarks:** Spare-time maker; first knife sold in 1995. **Mark:** First and middle initials, last name, maker, city and state.

DROST, MICHAEL B
Rt 2 Box 49, French Creek, WV 26218, Phone: 304-472-7901
Specialties: Working/using straight knives and folders of all designs. **Patterns:** Hunters, locking folders and utility/camp knives. **Technical:** Grinds ATS-34, D2 and CPM-T-440V. Offers dove-tailed bolsters and spacers, filework and scrimshaw. **Prices:** $125 to $400; some to $740. **Remarks:** Full-time maker; first knife sold in 1990. Doing business as Drost Custom Knives. **Mark:** Name, city and state.

DRUMM, ARMIN
Lichtensteinstrasse 33, Dornstadt, GERMANY 89160, Phone: 49-163-632-2842, armin@drumm-knives.de; Web: www.drumm-knives.de
Specialties: One-of-a-kind forged and Damascus fixed blade knives and folders. **Patterns:** Classic Bowie knives, daggers, fighters, hunters, folders, swords. **Technical:** Forges own Damascus and carbon steels, filework, carved handles. **Prices:** $250 to $800, some higher. **Remarks:** First knife sold in 2001, member of the German Knifemakers Guild. **Mark:** First initial, last name.

DUCKER, BRIAN
Lamorna Cottage, Common End, Colkirk, ENGLAND NR21 7JD, Phone: 01-328-856-183, admin@grommitbaileyknives.com; Web: www.grommitbaileyknives.com
Specialties: Hunters, utility pieces, bowies, camp knives, fighters and folders. **Technical:** Stock removal and forged 1095, 1075 and 80CrV2. Forging own damascus, using exotic and native hardwoods, stag, leather, Micarta and other synthetic materials, with brass and 301 stainless steel fittings. Own leatherwork and heat treating. **Remarks:** Part-time maker since 2009, full time Dec. 2013. All knives and sheaths are sole authorship. **Mark:** GROMMIT UK MAKER & BAILEY GROMMIT MAKERS.

DUFF, BILL
2801 Ash St, Poteau, OK 74953, Phone: 918-647-4458
Specialties: Straight knives and folders, some fancy. **Patterns:** Hunters, folders and miniatures. **Technical:** Grinds 440-C and commercial Damascus. **Prices:** $250 and up. **Remarks:** First knife sold in 1976. **Mark:** Bill Duff.

DUFOUR, ARTHUR J
8120 De Armoun Rd, Anchorage, AK 99516, Phone: 907-345-1701
Specialties: Working straight knives from standard patterns. **Patterns:** Hunters, Bowies, camp and fishing knives—grinded thin and pointed. **Technical:** Grinds 440C, ATS-34, AEB-L. Tempers 57-58R; hollow-grinds. **Prices:** $135; some to $250. **Remarks:** Part-time maker; first knife sold in 1970. **Mark:** Prospector logo.

DUGDALE, DANIEL J.
11 Eleanor Road, Walpole, MA 02081, Phone: 508-668-3528, dlpdugdale@comcast.net
Specialties: Button-lock and straight knives of his design. **Patterns:** Utilities, hunters, skinners, and tactical. **Technical:** Falt grinds D-2 and 440C, aluminum handles with anodized finishes. **Prices:** $150 to $500. **Remarks:** Part-time maker since 1977. **Mark:** Deer track with last name, town and state.

DUNCAN, RON
5090 N. Hwy. 63, Cairo, MO 65239, Phone: 660-263-8949, www.duncanmadeknives.com
Remarks: Duncan Made Knives

DUNKERLEY, RICK
PO Box 601, Lincoln, MT 59639, Phone: 406-210-4101, dunkerleyknives@gmail.com Web: www.dunkerleyknives.com
Specialties: Mosaic Damascus folders and carbon steel utility knives. **Patterns:** One-of-a-kind folders, standard hunters and utility designs. **Technical:** Forges 52100, Damascus and mosaic Damascus. Prefers natural handle materials. **Prices:** $200 and up. **Remarks:** Full-time maker; first knife sold in 1984, ABS Master Smith. Doing business as Dunkerley Custom Knives. Dunkerley handmade knives, sole authorship. **Mark:** Dunkerley, MS.

DUNLAP, JIM
800 E. Badger Lee Rd., Sallisaw, OK 74955, Phone: 918-774-2700, dunlapknives@gmail.com
Specialties: Traditional slip-joint folders. **Patterns:** Single- and multi-blade traditional slip joints. **Technical:** Grinds ATS-34, CPM-154 and damascus. **Prices:** $250 and up. **Remarks:** Part-time maker; first knife sold in 2009. **Mark:** Dunlap.

DUNN, CHARLES K
17740 GA Hwy 116, Shiloh, GA 31826, Phone: 706-846-2666
Specialties: Fancy and working straight knives and folders of his design and to customer specs. **Patterns:** Bowies, hunters and locking folders. **Technical:** Grinds 440C and ATS-34. Engraves; filework offered. **Prices:** $75 to $300. **Remarks:** Part-time maker; first knife sold in 1988. **Mark:** First initial, last name, city, state.

DUNN, STEVE
376 Biggerstaff Rd, Smiths Grove, KY 42171, Phone: 270-563-9830, dunnknives@windstream.net; Web: www.stevedunnknives.com
Specialties: Working and using straight knives of his design; period pieces. Offers engraving and gold inlay. **Patterns:** Hunters, skinners, Bowies, fighters, camp knives, folders, swords and battle axes. **Technical:** Forges own Damascus, 1075, 15N20, 52100, 1084, L6. **Prices:** Moderate to upscale. **Remarks:** Full-time maker; first knife sold in 1990. **Mark:** Last name and MS.

DURAN, JERRY T
PO Box 9753, Albuquerque, NM 87119, Phone: 505-873-4676, jtdknives@hotmail.com; Web: http://www.google.com/profiles/jtdknivesLLC
Specialties: Tactical folders, Bowies, fighters, liner locks, autopsy and hunters. **Patterns:** Folders, Bowies, hunters and tactical knives. **Technical:** Forges own Damascus and forges carbon steel. **Prices:** Moderate to upscale. **Remarks:** Full-time maker; first knife sold in 1978. **Mark:** Initials in elk rack logo.

DURHAM, KENNETH
BUZZARD ROOST FORGE, 10495 White Pike, Cherokee, AL 35616, Phone: 256-359-4287, www.home.hiwaay.net/~jamesd/
Specialties: Bowies, dirks, hunters. **Patterns:** Traditional patterns. **Technical:** Forges 1095, 5160, 52100 and makes own Damascus. **Prices:** $85 to $1600. **Remarks:** Began making knives about 1995. Received Journeyman stamp 1999. Got Master Smith stamp in 2004. **Mark:** Bull's head with Ken Durham above and Cherokee AL below.

DURIO, FRED
144 Gulino St, Opelousas, LA 70570, Phone: 337-948-4831/cell 337-351-2652, fdurio@yahoo.com
Specialties: Folders. **Patterns:** Liner locks; plain and fancy. **Technical:** Makes own Damascus. **Prices:** Moderate to upscale. **Remarks:** Full-time maker. **Mark:** Last name-Durio.

DUVALL, FRED
10715 Hwy 190, Benton, AR 72015, Phone: 501-778-9360
Specialties: Working straight knives and folders. **Patterns:** Locking folders, slip joints, hunters, fighters and Bowies. **Technical:** Grinds D2 and CPM440V; forges 5160. **Prices:** $100 to $400; some to $800. **Remarks:** Part-time maker; first knife sold in 1973. **Mark:** Last name.

DWYER, DUANE
120 N. Pacific St., L7, San Marcos, CA 92069, Phone: 760-471-8275, striderknives@aol.com Web: www.striderknives.com
Specialties: Primarily tactical. **Patterns:** Fixed and folders. **Technical:** Primarily stock removal specializing in highly technical materials. **Prices:** $100 and up, based on the obvious variables. **Remarks:** Full-time maker since 1996.

DYER, DAVID
4531 Hunters Glen, Granbury, TX 76048, Phone: 817-573-1198
Specialties: Working skinners and early period knives. **Patterns:** Customer designs, his own patterns. **Technical:** Coal forged blades; 5160 and 52100 steels. Grinds D2, 1095, L6. **Prices:** $150 for neck knives and small (3" to 3-1/2"). To $600 for large blades and specialty blades. **Mark:** Last name DYER electro etched.

DYESS, EDDIE
1005 Hamilton, Roswell, NM 88201, Phone: 505-623-5599, eddyess@msn.com
Specialties: Working and using straight knives in standard patterns. **Patterns:** Hunters and fighters. **Technical:** Grinds 440C, 154CM and D2 on request. **Prices:** $150 to $300, some higher. **Remarks:** Spare-time maker; first knife sold in 1980. **Mark:** Last name.

E

EAKER, ALLEN L
416 Clinton Ave Dept KI, Paris, IL 61944, Phone: 217-466-5160
Specialties: Traditional straight knives and folders of his design. **Patterns:** Hunters, locking folders and slip-joint folders. **Technical:** Grinds 440C; inlays. **Prices:** $200 to $500. **Remarks:** Spare-time maker; first knife sold in 1994. **Mark:** Initials in tankard logo stamped on tang, serial number and surname on back.

EALY, DELBERT
PO Box 121, Indian River, MI 49749, Phone: 231-238-4705

EATON, FRANK L JR
5365 W. Meyer Rd., Farmington, MO 63640, Phone: 703-314-8708, eatontactical@me.com; Web: www.frankeatonknives.com
Specialties: Full tang/hidden tang fixed working and art knives of his own design. **Patterns:** Hunters, skinners, fighters, Bowies, tacticals and daggers. **Technical:** Stock removal maker, prefer using natural materials. **Prices:** $175 to $400. **Remarks:** Part-time maker - Active Duty Airborn Ranger-Making 4 years. **Mark:** Name over 75th Ranger Regimental Crest.

EATON, RICK
313 Dailey Rd, Broadview, MT 59015, Phone: 406-667-2405, rick@eatonknives.com; Web: www.eatonknives.com
Specialties: Interframe folders and one-hand-opening side locks. **Patterns:** Bowies, daggers, fighters and folders. **Technical:** Grinds 154CM, ATS-34, 440C and other maker's Damascus. Makes own mosaic Damascus. Offers high-quality hand engraving, Bulino and gold inlay. **Prices:** Upscale. **Remarks:** Full-time maker; first knife sold in 1982. **Mark:** Full name or full name and address.

EBISU, HIDESAKU
3-39-7 Koi Osako, Nishi Ku, Hiroshima, JAPAN 733 0816

ECHOLS, RODGER
2853 Highway 371 W, Nashville, AR 71852-7577, Phone: 870-845-9173 or 870-845-0400, blademanechols@aol.com; Web: www.echolsknives.com
Specialties: Liner locks, auto-scale release, lock backs. **Patterns:** His or yours. **Technical:** Autos. **Prices:** $500 to $1700. **Remarks:** Likes to use pearl, ivory and Damascus the most. Made first knife in 1984. Part-time maker; tool and die maker by trade. **Mark:** Name.

EDDY, HUGH E
211 E Oak St, Caldwell, ID 83605, Phone: 208-459-0536

EDGE, TOMMY
1244 County Road 157, Cash, AR 72421, Phone: 870-897-6150, tedge@tex.net
Specialties: Fancy/embellished working knives of his design. **Patterns:** Bowies, hunters and utility/camping knives. **Technical:** Grinds 440C, ATS-34 and D2. Makes own cable Damascus; offers filework. **Prices:** $70 to $250; some to $1500. **Remarks:** Part-time maker; first knife sold in 1973. **Mark:** Stamped first initial, last name and stenciled name, city and state in oval shape.

EDMONDS, WARRICK
, Adelaide Hills, SOUTH AUSTRALIA, Phone: 61-8-83900339, warrick@riflebirdknives.com Web: www.riflebirdknives.com
Specialties: Fixed blade knives with select and highly figured exotic or unique Australian wood handles. Themed collectors knives to individually designed working knives from Damascus, RWL34, 440C or high carbon steels. **Patterns:** Hunters, utilities and workshop knives, cooks knives with a Deco to Modern flavour. Hand sewn individual leather sheaths. **Technical:** Stock removal using only steel from well known and reliable sources. **Prices:** $250Aust to $1000Aust. **Remarks:** Part-time maker since 2004. **Mark:** Name stamped into sheath.

EDWARDS, MITCH
303 New Salem Rd, Glasgow, KY 42141, Phone: 270-404-0758 / 270-404-0758, medwards@glasgow-ky.com; Web: www.traditionalknives.com
Specialties: Period pieces. **Patterns:** Neck knives, camp, rifleman and Bowie knives. **Technical:** All hand forged, forges own Damascus O1, 1084, 1095, L6, 15N20. **Prices:** $200 to $1000. **Remarks:** Journeyman Smith. **Mark:** Broken heart.

EHRENBERGER, DANIEL ROBERT
1213 S Washington St, Mexico, MO 65265, Phone: 573-633-2010
Specialties: Affordable working/using straight knives of his design and to custom specs. Patterns: 10" western Bowie, fighters, hunting and skinning knives. **Technical:** Forges 1085, 1095, his own Damascus and cable Damascus. **Prices:** $80 to $500. **Remarks:** Full-time maker, first knife sold 1994. **Mark:** Ehrenberger JS.

EKLUND, MAIHKEL
Fone Stam V9, Farila, SWEDEN 82041, info@art-knives.com; Web: www.art-knives.com
Specialties: Collector-grade working straight knives. **Patterns:** Hunters, Bowies and fighters. **Technical:** Grinds ATS-34, Uddeholm and Dama steel. Engraves and scrimshaws. **Prices:** $200 to $2000. **Remarks:** Full-time maker; first knife sold in 1983. **Mark:** Initials or name.

ELDRIDGE, ALLAN
7731 Four Winds Dr, Ft. Worth, TX 76133, Phone: 817-370-7778; Cell: 817-296-3528
Specialties: Fancy classic straight knives in standard patterns. **Patterns:** Hunters, Bowies, fighters, folders and miniatures. **Technical:** Grinds O1 and Damascus. Engraves silver-wire inlays, pearl inlays, scrimshaws and offers filework. **Prices:** $50 to $500; some to $1200. **Remarks:** Spare-time maker; first knife sold in 1965. **Mark:** Initials.

ELISHEWITZ, ALLEN
875 Hwy. 321 N, Ste. 600, #212, Lenoir City, TN 37771, Phone: 865-816-3309, allen@elishewitzknives.com; Web: elishewitzknives.com
Specialties: Collectible high-tech working straight knives and folders of his design. **Patterns:** Working, utility and tactical knives. **Technical:** Designs and uses innovative locking mechanisms. All designs drafted and field-tested. **Prices:** $600 to $1000. **Remarks:** Full-time maker; first knife sold in 1989. **Mark:** Gold medallion inlaid in blade.

ELLEFSON, JOEL
PO Box 1016, 310 S 1st St, Manhattan, MT 59741, Phone: 406-284-3111
Specialties: Working straight knives, fancy daggers and one-of-a-kinds. **Patterns:** Hunters, daggers and some folders. **Technical:** Grinds A2, 440C and ATS-34. Makes own mokume in bronze, brass, silver and shibuishi; makes brass/steel blades. **Prices:** $100 to $500; some to $2000. **Remarks:** Part-time maker; first knife sold in 1978. **Mark:** Stylized last initial.

ELLERBE, W B
3871 Osceola Rd, Geneva, FL 32732, Phone: 407-349-5818
Specialties: Period and primitive knives and sheaths. **Patterns:** Bowies to patch knives, some tomahawks. **Technical:** Grinds Sheffield O1 and files. **Prices:** Start at $35. **Remarks:** Full-time maker; first knife sold in 1971. Doing business as Cypress Bend Custom Knives. **Mark:** Last name or initials.

ELLIOTT, JERRY
4507 Kanawha Ave, Charleston, WV 25304, Phone: 304-925-5045, elliottknives@verizon.net
Specialties: Classic and traditional straight knives and folders of his design and to customer specs. **Patterns:** Hunters, locking folders and Bowies. **Technical:** Grinds ATS-34, 154CM, O1, D2 and T-440-V. All guards silver-soldered; bolsters are pinned on straight knives, spot-welded on folders. **Prices:** $80 to $265; some to $1000. **Remarks:** Full-time maker; first knife sold in 1972. **Mark:** First and middle initials, last name, knife maker, city, state.

ELLIS, WILLIAM DEAN
2767 Edgar Ave, Sanger, CA 93657, Phone: 559-314-4459, urleebird@comcast.net; Web: www.billysblades.com
Specialties: Classic and fancy knives of his design. **Patterns:** Boots, fighters and utility knives. **Technical:** Grinds ATS-34, D2 and Damascus. Offers tapered tangs and six patterns of filework; tooled multi-colored sheaths. **Prices:** $250 to $1500. **Remarks:** Part-time maker; first knife sold in 1991. Doing business as Billy's Blades. Also make shave-ready straight razors for actual use. **Mark:** "B" in a five-point star next to "Billy," city and state within a rounded-corner rectangle.

ELLIS, WILLY B
1025 Hamilton Ave., Tarpon Springs, FL 34689, Phone: 727-942-6420, Web: www.willyb.com
Specialties: One-of-a-kind high art and fantasy knives of his design. Occasional customs full size and miniatures. **Patterns:** Bowies, fighters, hunters and others. **Technical:** Grinds 440C, ATS-34, 1095, carbon Damascus, ivory bone, stone and metal carving. **Prices:** $175 to $15,000. **Remarks:** Full-time maker, first knife made in 1973. Member Knifemakers Guild and FEGA. Jewel setting inlays. **Mark:** Willy B. or WB'S C etched or carved.

ELROD, ROGER R
58 Dale Ave, Enterprise, AL 36330, Phone: 334-347-1863

EMBRETSEN, KAJ
FALUVAGEN 67, Edsbyn, SWEDEN 82830, Phone: 46-271-21057, Fax: 46-271-22961, kay.embretsen@telia.com Web:www.embretsenknives.com
Specialties: Damascus folding knives. **Patterns:** Uses mammoth ivory and some pearl. **Technical:** Uses own Damascus steel. **Remarks:** Full time since 1983. **Prices:** $2500 to $8000. **Mark:** Name inside the folder.

EMERSON, ERNEST R
1234 W. 254th, Harbor City, CA 90710, Phone: 310-539-5633, info@emersonknives.com; Web: www.emersonknives.com
Specialties: High-tech folders and combat fighters. **Patterns:** Fighters, LinerLock® combat folders and SPECWAR combat knives. **Technical:** Grinds 154CM and Damascus. Makes folders with titanium fittings, liners and locks. Chisel grind specialist. **Prices:** $550 to $850; some to $10,000. **Remarks:** Full-time maker; first knife sold in 1983. **Mark:** Last name and Specwar knives.

EMMERLING, JOHN
1368 Pacific Way, Gearheart, OR 97138, Phone: 800-738-5434, ironwerks@linet.com

ENCE, JIM
145 S 200 East, Richfield, UT 84701, Phone: 435-896-6206
Specialties: High-art period pieces (spec in California knives) art knives. **Patterns:** Art, boot knives, fighters, Bowies and occasional folders. **Technical:** Grinds 440C for polish and beauty boys; makes own Damascus. **Prices:** Upscale. **Remarks:** Full-time maker; first knife sold in 1977. Does own engraving, gold work and stone work. Guild member since 1977. Founding member of the AKI. **Mark:** Ence, usually engraved.

ENGLAND, VIRGIL
1340 Birchwood St, Anchorage, AK 99508, Phone: 907-274-9494, WEB:www.virgilengland.com
Specialties: Edged weapons and equipage, one-of-a-kind only. **Patterns:** Axes, swords, lances and body armor. **Technical:** Forges and grinds as pieces dictate. Offers stainless and Damascus. **Prices:** Upscale. **Remarks:** A veteran knifemaker. No commissions. **Mark:** Stylized initials.

ENGLE, WILLIAM
16608 Oak Ridge Rd, Boonville, MO 65233, Phone: 816-882-6277
Specialties: Traditional working and using straight knives of his design. **Patterns:** Hunters, Bowies and fighters. **Technical:** Grinds 440C, ATS-34 and 154 CM. **Prices:** $250 to $500; some higher. **Remarks:** Part-time maker; first knife sold in 1982. All knives come with certificate of authenticity. **Mark:** Last name in block lettering.

ENGLISH, JIM
14586 Olive Vista Dr, Jamul, CA 91935, Phone: 619-669-0833
Specialties: Traditional working straight knives to customer specs. **Patterns:** Hunters, bowies, fighters, tantos, daggers, boot and utility/camp knives. **Technical:** Grinds 440C, ATS-34, commercial Damascus and customer choice. **Prices:** $130 to $350. **Remarks:** Part-time maker; first knife sold in 1985. In addition to custom line, also does business as Mountain Home Knives. **Mark:** Double "A," Double "J" logo.

ENNIS, RAY
1220S 775E, Ogden, UT 84404, Phone: 800-410-7603, Fax: 501-621-2683, nifmakr@hotmail.com; Web:www.ennis-entrekusa.com

ENOS III, THOMAS M
12302 State Rd 535, Orlando, FL 32836, Phone: 407-239-6205, tmenos3@att.net
Specialties: Heavy-duty working straight knives; unusual designs. **Patterns:** Swords, machetes, daggers, skinners, filleting, period pieces. **Technical:** Grinds 440C. **Prices:** $75 to $1500. **Remarks:** Full-time maker; first knife sold in 1972. No longer accepting custom requests. Will be making his own designs. Send SASE for listing of items for sale. **Mark:** Name in knife logo and year, type of steel and serial number.

ENTIN, ROBERT
127 Pembroke St 1, Boston, MA 02118

EPTING, RICHARD
4021 Cody Dr, College Station, TX 77845, Phone: 979-690-6496, rgeknives@hotmail.com; Web: www.eptingknives.com
Specialties: Folders and working straight knives. **Patterns:** Hunters, Bowies, and locking folders. **Technical:** Forges high-carbon steel and his own Damascus. **Prices:** $200 to $800; some to $1800. **Remarks:** Part-time maker, first knife sold 1996. **Mark:** Name in arch logo.

ERICKSON, DANIEL
Ring Of Fire Forge, 20011 Welch Rd., Snohomish, WA 98296, Phone: 206-355-1793, Web: www.ringoffireforge.com
Specialties: Likes to fuse traditional and functional with creative concepts. **Patterns:** Hunters, fighters, bowies, folders, slip joints, art knives, the Phalanx. **Technical:** Forges own pattern-welded damascus blades (1080/15N20), 5160, CruForgeV, 52100 and W2. Uses figured burls, stabilized woods, fossil ivories and natural and unique materials for handles. Custom stands and sheaths. **Prices:** $250 to $1,500. **Remarks:** Sole authorship, designer and inventor. Started making in 2003; first knife sold in 2004. ABS journeyman smith. **Mark:** "Ring of Fire" with Erickson moving through it.

ERICKSON, L.M.
1379 Black Mountain Cir, Ogden, UT 84404, Phone: 801-737-1930
Specialties: Straight knives; period pieces. **Patterns:** Bowies, fighters, boots and hunters. **Technical:** Grinds 440C, 154CM and commercial Damascus. **Prices:** $200 to $900; some to $5000. **Remarks:** Part-time maker; first knife sold in 1981. **Mark:** Name, city, state.

ERICKSON, WALTER E.
22280 Shelton Tr, Atlanta, MI 49709, Phone: 989-785-5262, wberic@racc2000.com
Specialties: Unusual survival knives and high-tech working knives. **Patterns:** Butterflies, hunters, tantos. **Technical:** Grinds ATS-34 or customer choice. **Prices:** $150 to $500; some to $1500. **Remarks:** Full-time maker; first knife sold in 1981. **Mark:** Using pantograph with assorted fonts (no longer stamping).

ERIKSEN, JAMES THORLIEF
dba VIKING KNIVES, 3830 Dividend Dr, Garland, TX 75042, Phone: 972-494-3667, Fax: 972-235-4932, VikingKnives@aol.com
Specialties: Heavy-duty working and using straight knives and folders utilizing traditional, Viking original and customer specification patterns. Some high-tech and fancy/embellished knives available. **Patterns:** Bowies, hunters, skinners, boot and belt knives, utility/camp knives, fighters, daggers, locking folders, slip-joint folders and kitchen knives. **Technical:** Hollow-grinds 440C, D2, ASP-23, ATS-34, 154CM, Vascowear. **Prices:** $150 to $300; some to $600. **Remarks:** Full-time maker; first knife sold in 1985. Doing business as Viking Knives. For a color catalog showing 50 different models, mail $5 to above address. **Mark:** VIKING or VIKING USA for export.

ERNEST, PHIL (PJ)
PO Box 5240, Whittier, CA 90607-5240, Phone: 562-556-2324, hugger883562@yahoo.com; Web:www.ernestcustomknives.com
Specialties: Fixed blades. **Patterns:** Wide range. Many original as well as hunters, camp, fighters, daggers, bowies and tactical. Specialzin in Wharncliff's of all sizes. **Technical:** Grinds commercial Damascus, Mosaid Damascus. ATS-34, and 440C. Full Tangs with bolsters. Handle material includes all types of exotic hardwood, abalone, peal mammoth tooth, mammoth ivory, Damascus steel and Mosaic Damascus. **Remarks:** Full time maker. First knife sold in 1999. **Prices:** $200 to $1800. Some to $2500. **Mark:** Owl logo with PJ Ernest Whittier CA or PJ Ernest.

ESPOSITO, EMMANUEL
Via Reano 70, Buttigliera Alta TO, ITALY 10090, Phone: 39-011932-16-21, www.emmanuelmaker.it
Specialties: Folding knife with his patent system lock mechanism with mosaic inlay.

ESSEGIAN, RICHARD
7387 E Tulare St, Fresno, CA 93727, Phone: 309-255-5950
Specialties: Fancy working knives of his design; art knives. **Patterns:** Bowies and some small hunters. **Technical:** Grinds A2, D2, 440C and 154CM. Engraves and inlays. **Prices:** Start at $600. **Remarks:** Part-time maker; first knife sold in 1986. **Mark:** Last name, city and state.

ESTABROOK, ROBBIE
1014 Madge Ct., Conway, SC 29526, Phone: 803-917-3786, robbieestabrook@gmail.com

ETZLER, JOHN
11200 N Island, Grafton, OH 44044, Phone: 440-748-2460, jetzler@bright.net; Web: members.tripod.com/~etzlerknives/
Specialties: High-art and fantasy straight knives and folders of his design and to customer specs. **Patterns:** Folders, daggers, fighters, utility knives. **Technical:** Forges and grinds nickel Damascus and tool steel; grinds stainless steels. Prefers exotic, natural materials. **Prices:** $250 to $1200; some $6500. **Remarks:** Full-time maker; first knife sold in 1992. **Mark:** Name or initials.

EVANS, BRUCE A
409 CR 1371, Booneville, MS 38829, Phone: 662-720-0193, beknives@avsia.com; Web: www.bruceevans.homestead.com/open.html
Specialties: Forges blades. **Patterns:** Hunters, Bowies, or will work with customer. **Technical:** 5160, cable Damascus, pattern welded Damascus. **Prices:** $200 and up. **Mark:** Bruce A. Evans Same with JS on reverse of blade.

EVANS, CARLTON
PO Box 46, Gainesville, TX 76241, Phone: 817-886-9231, carlton@carltonevans.com; Web: www.carltonevans.com
Specialties: High end folders and fixed blades. **Technical:** Uses the stock removal methods. The materials used are of the highest quality. **Remarks:** Full-time knifemaker, voting member of Knifemakers Guild, member of the Texas Knifemakers and Collectors Association.

EVANS, PHIL
594 SE 40th, Columbus, KS 66725, Phone: 620-249-0639, phil@glenviewforge.com Web: www.glenviewforge.com
Specialties: Working knives, hunters, skinners, also enjoys making Bowies and fighters, high carbon or Damascus. **Technical:** Forges own blades and makes own Damascus. Uses all kinds of ancient Ivory and bone. Stabilizes own native hardwoods. **Prices:** $150 - $1,500. **Remarks:** Part-time maker. Made first knife in 1995. **Mark:** EVANS.

EVANS, RONALD B
209 Hoffer St, Middleton, PA 17057-2723, Phone: 717-944-5464

EVANS, VINCENT K AND GRACE
HC 1 Box 5275, Keaau, HI 96749-9517, Phone: 808-966-8978, evansvk@gmail.com Web: www.picturetrail.com/vevans
Specialties: Period pieces; swords. **Patterns:** Scottish, Viking, central Asian. **Technical:** Forges 5160 and his own Damascus. **Prices:** $700 to $4000; some to $8000. **Remarks:** Full-time maker; first knife sold in 1983. **Mark:** Last initial with fish logo.

EWING, JOHN H
3276 Dutch Valley Rd, Clinton, TN 37716, Phone: 865-457-5757, johnja@comcast.net
Specialties: Working straight knives, hunters, camp knives. **Patterns:** Hunters. **Technical:** Grinds 440-D2. Forges 5160, 1095 prefers forging. **Prices:** $150 and up. **Remarks:** Part-time maker; first knife sold in 1985. **Mark:** First initial, last name, some embellishing done on knives.

F

FAIRLY, DANIEL
2209 Bear Creek Canyon Rd, Bayfield, CO 81122, danielfairlyknives@gmail.com; Web: www.danielfairlyknives.com
Specialties: "Craftsmanship without compromise. **Patterns:** Ultralight titanium utilities, everyday carry, folders, kitchen knives, Japanese-influenced design. **Technical:** Grinds mostly tool steel and carbidized titanium in .050" to .360" thick material. Uses heavy duty handle materials and flared test tube fasteners or epoxy soaked wrapped handles. Most grinds are chisel; flat convex and hollow grinds used. **Prices:** $85 to $1,850. **Remarks:** Full-time maker since first knife sold in Feb. 2011. **Mark:** Fairly written in all capitals with larger F.

FANT JR., GEORGE
1983 CR 3214, Atlanta, TX 75551-6515, Phone: (903) 846-2938

FARID, MEHR R
8 Sidney Close, Tunbridge Wells, Kent, ENGLAND TN2 5QQ, Phone: 011-44-1892 520345, farid@faridknives.com; Web: www.faridknives.com
Specialties: Hollow handle survival knives. High tech folders. **Patterns:** Flat grind blades & chisel ground LinerLock® folders. **Technical:** Grinds 440C, CPMT-440V, CPM-420V, CPM-15V, CPM5125V, and T-1 high speed steel. **Prices:** $550 to $5000. **Remarks:** Full-time maker; first knife sold in 1991. **Mark:** First name stamped.

FARR, DAN
285 Glen Ellyn Way, Rochester, NY 14618, Phone: 585-721-1388
Specialties: Hunting, camping, fighting and utility. **Patterns:** Fixed blades. **Technical:** Forged or stock removal. **Prices:** $150 to $750.

FASSIO, MELVIN G
420 Tyler Way, Lolo, MT 59847, Phone: 406-544-1391, fassiocustomknives@gmail.com; Web: www.fassiocustomknives.com
Specialties: Working folders to customer specs. **Patterns:** Locking folders, hunters and traditional-style knives. **Technical:** Grinds 440C. **Prices:** $125 to $350. **Remarks:** Part-time maker; first knife sold in 1975. **Mark:** Name and city, dove logo.

custom knifemakers

FAUCHEAUX—FLYNT

FAUCHEAUX, HOWARD J

PO Box 206, Loreauville, LA 70552, Phone: 318-229-6467

Specialties: Working straight knives and folders; period pieces. Also a hatchet with capping knife in the handle. **Patterns:** Traditional locking folders, hunters, fighters and Bowies. **Technical:** Forges W2, 1095 and his own Damascus; stock removal D2. **Prices:** Start at $200. **Remarks:** Full-time maker; first knife sold in 1969. **Mark:** Last name.

FAUST, DICK

624 Kings Hwy N, Rochester, NY 14617, Phone: 585-544-1948, dickfaustknives@mac.com

Specialties: High-performance working straight knives. **Patterns:** Hunters and utility/camp knives. **Technical:** Hollow grinds 154CM full tang. Exotic woods, stag and Micarta handles. Provides a custom leather sheath with each knife. **Prices:** From $200 to $600, some higher. **Remarks:** Full-time maker. **Mark:** Signature.

FAUST, JOACHIM

Kirchgasse 10, Goldkronach, GERMANY 95497

FELIX, ALEXANDER

PO Box 4036, Torrance, CA 90510, Phone: 310-320-1836, sgiandubh@dslextreme.com

Specialties: Straight working knives, fancy ethnic designs. **Patterns:** Hunters, Bowies, daggers, period pieces. **Technical:** Forges carbon steel and Damascus; forged stainless and titanium jewelry, gold and silver casting. **Prices:** $110 and up. **Remarks:** Jeweler, ABS Journeyman Smith. **Mark:** Last name.

FELLOWS, MIKE

P.O. Box 184, Riversdale 6670, SOUTH AFRICA, Phone: 27 82 960 3868, karatshin@gmail.com

Specialties: Miniatures, art knives and folders with occasional hunters and skinners. **Patterns:** Own designs. **Technical:** Uses own damascus. **Prices:** Upon request. **Remarks:** Uses only indigenous materials. Exotic hardwoods, horn and ivory. Does all own embellishments. **Mark:** "SHIN" letter from Hebrew alphabet over Hebrew word "Karat." **Other:** Member of Knifemakers Guild of South Africa.

FERGUSON, JIM

3543 Shadyhill Dr, San Angelo, TX 76904, Phone: 325-655-1061

Specialties: Straight working knives and folders. **Patterns:** Working belt knives, hunters, Bowies and some folders. **Technical:** Grinds ATS-34, D2 and Vascowear. Flat-grinds hunting knives. **Prices:** $200 to $600; some to $1000. **Remarks:** Full-time maker; first knife sold in 1987. **Mark:** First and middle initials, last name.

FERGUSON, JIM

4652 Hackett St., Lakewood, CA 90713, Phone: 562-342-4890, jim@twistednickel.com; Web: www.twistednickel.com, www.howtomakeaknife.net

Specialties: Bowies and push blades. **Patterns:** All styles. **Technical:** Flat and hollow grinds. Sells in U.S. and Canada. **Prices:** $100 to $1,200. **Mark:** Push blade with "Ferguson-USA." Also makes swords, battle axes and utilities.

FERGUSON, LEE

1993 Madison 7580, Hindsville, AR 72738, Phone: 479-443-0084, info@fergusonknives.com; Web: www.fergusonknives.com

Specialties: Straight working knives and folders, some fancy. **Patterns:** Hunters, daggers, swords, locking folders and slip-joints. **Technical:** Grinds D2, 440C and ATS-34; heat-treats. **Prices:** $50 to $600; some to $4000. **Remarks:** Full-time maker; first knife sold in 1977. **Mark:** Full name.

FERRARA, THOMAS

122 Madison Dr, Naples, FL 33942, Phone: 813-597-3363, Fax: 813-597-3363

Specialties: High-art, traditional and working straight knives and folders of all designs. **Patterns:** Boots, Bowies, daggers, fighters and hunters. **Technical:** Grinds 440C, D2 and ATS-34; heat-treats. **Prices:** $100 to $700; some to $1300. **Remarks:** Part-time maker; first knife sold in 1983. **Mark:** Last name.

FERRIER, GREGORY K

3119 Simpson Dr, Rapid City, SD 57702, Phone: 605-342-9280

FERRY, TOM

16005 SE 322nd St, Auburn, WA 98092, Phone: 253-939-4468, tomferryknives@Q.com; Web: tomferryknives.com

Specialties: Presentation grade knives. **Patterns:** Folders and fixed blades. **Technical:** Specialize in Damascus and engraving. **Prices:** $500 and up. **Remarks:** DBA: Soos Creek Ironworks. ABS Master Smith. **Mark:** Combined T and F in a circle and/or last name.

FILIPPOU, IOANNIS-MINAS

23 Vryouron Str, Nea Smyrni 17122, Athens, GREECE 17122, Phone: (1) 935-2093, knifemaker_gr@yahoo.gr

FINCH, RICKY D

1179 Hwy 844, West Liberty, KY 41472, Phone: 606-743-7151, finchknives@mrtc.com; Web: www.finchknives.com

Specialties: Traditional working/using straight knives of his design or to customer spec. **Patterns:** Hunters, skinners and utility/camp knives. LinerLock® of his design. **Technical:** Grinds 440C, ATS-34 and CPM154, hand rubbed stain finish, use Micarta, stabilized wood, natural and exotic. **Prices:** $85 to $225. **Remarks:** Part-time maker, first knife made 1994. Doing business as Finch Knives. **Mark:** Last name inside outline of state of Kentucky.

FIORINI, BILL

703 W. North St., Grayville, IL 62844, Phone: 618-375-7191, smallflowerlonchura@yahoo.com

Specialties: Fancy working knives. **Patterns:** Hunters, boots, Japanese-style knives and kitchen/utility knives and folders. **Technical:** Forges own Damascus, mosaic and mokune-gane. **Prices:** Full range. **Remarks:** Full-time metal smith researching pattern materials. **Mark:** Orchid crest with name KOKA in Japanese.

FISHER, JAY

1405 Edwards, Clovis, NM 88101, jayfisher@jayfisher.com Web: www.JayFisher.com

Specialties: High-art, working and collector's knives of his design and client's designs. Military working and commemoratives. Gemstone handles. Locking combat sheaths. **Patterns:** Hunters, daggers, folding knives, museum pieces and high-art sculptures. **Technical:** 440C, ATS-34, CPMS30V, D2, O1, CPM154CM, CPMS35VN. Prolific maker of stone-handled knives and swords. **Prices:** $850 to $150,000. **Remarks:** Full-time maker; first knife sold in 1980. High resolution etching, computer and manual engraving. **Mark:** Signature "JaFisher"

FISHER, JOSH

JN Fisher Knives, 8419 CR 3615, Murchison, TX 75778, Phone: 903-203-2130, fisherknives@aol.com; Web: www.jnfisherknives.com

Specialties: Frame-handle fighters. **Technical:** Forge 5160 and 1084 blade steels. **Prices:** $125 to $1,000. **Remarks:** Part-time maker; first knife made in 2007. ABS journeyman smith. **Mark:** Josh Fisher etched. "JS" also etched on the reverse.

FISHER, LANCE

9 Woodlawn Ave., Pompton Lakes, NJ 07442, Phone: 973-248-8447, lance.fisher@sandvik.com

Specialties: Wedding cake knives and servers, forks, etc. Including velvet lined wood display cases. **Patterns:** Drop points, upswept skinners, Bowies, daggers, fantasy, medieval, San Francisco style, chef or kitchen cutlery. **Technical:** Stock removal method only. Steels include but are not limited to CPM 154, D2, CPM S35VN, CPM S90V and Sandvik 13C26. Handle materials include stag, sheep horn, exotic woods, micarta, and G10 as well as reconstituted stone. **Prices:** $350 - $2000. **Remarks:** Part-time maker, will become full-time on retirement. Made and sold first knife in 1981 and has never looked back. **Mark:** Tang stamp.

FISK, JERRY

10095 Hwy 278 W, Nashville, AR 71852, Phone: 870-845-4456, jerry@jerryfisk.com; Web: www.jerryfisk.com or Facebook: Jerry Fisk, MS Custom Knives

Specialties: Edged weapons, collectible and functional. **Patterns:** Bowies, daggers, swords, hunters, camp knives and others. **Technical:** Forges carbon steels and his own pattern welded steels. **Prices:** $1100 to $20,000. **Remarks:** National living treasure. **Mark:** Name, MS.

FISTER, JIM

PO Box 307, Simpsonville, KY 40067

Specialties: One-of-a-kind collectibles and period pieces. **Patterns:** Bowies, camp knives, hunters, buckskinners, and daggers. **Technical:** Forges, 1085, 5160, 52100, his own Damascus, pattern and turkish. **Prices:** $150 to $2500. **Remarks:** Part-time maker; first knife sold in 1982. **Mark:** Name and MS.

FITCH, JOHN S

45 Halbrook Rd, Clinton, AR 72031-8910, Phone: 501-893-2020

FITZGERALD, DENNIS M

4219 Alverado Dr, Fort Wayne, IN 46816-2847, Phone: 219-447-1081

Specialties: One-of-a-kind collectibles and period pieces. **Patterns:** Skinners, fighters, camp and utility knives; period pieces. **Technical:** Forges 1085, 1095, L6, 5160, 52100, his own pattern and Turkish Damascus. **Prices:** $100 to $500. **Remarks:** Part-time maker; first knife sold in 1985. Doing business as The Ringing Circle. **Mark:** Name and circle logo.

FLINT, ROBERT

2902 Aspen, Anchorage, AK 99517, Phone: 907-243-6706

Specialties: Working straight knives and folders. **Patterns:** Utility, hunters, fighters and gents. **Technical:** Grinds ATS-34, BG-42, D2 and Damascus. **Prices:** $150 and up. **Remarks:** Part-time maker, first knife sold in 1998. **Mark:** Last name; stylized initials.

FLOURNOY, JOE

5750 Lisbon Rd, El Dorado, AR 71730, Phone: 870-863-7208, flournoy@ipa.net

Specialties: Working straight knives and folders. **Patterns:** Hunters, Bowies, camp knives, folders and daggers. **Technical:** Forges only high-carbon steel, steel cable and his own Damascus. **Prices:** $350 Plus. **Remarks:** First knife sold in 1977. **Mark:** Last name and MS in script.

FLYNT, ROBERT G

15173 Christy Lane, Gulfport, MS 39503, Phone: 228-832-3378 or cell: 228-265-0410, robertflynt@cableone.net; Web: www.flyntstoneknifeworks.com

Specialties: All types of fixed blades: drop point, clip point, trailing point, bull-nose hunters, tactical, fighters and bowies. LinerLock, slip-joint and lockback folders. **Technical:** Using 154CM, CPM-154, ATS-34, 440C, CPM-3V and 52100 steels. Most blades made by stock removal, hollow and flat grind methods. Forges some cable damascus and uses numerous types of damascus purchased in billets from various makers. All filework and bluing done by the maker. Various wood handles, bone and horn materials, including some with wire inlay and other embellishments. Most knives sold with custom-fit leather sheaths, most include exotic skin inlay when appropriate. **Prices:** $150 and up, depending on embellishments on blade and sheath. **Remarks:** Full-time maker; first knife made in 1966. Knifemakers' Guild member. **Mark:** Last name in cursive letters or a knife striking a flint stone.

FOGARIZZU, BOITEDDU

via Crispi 6, Pattada, ITALY 07016

Specialties: Traditional Italian straight knives and folders. **Patterns:** Collectible folders. **Technical:** forges and grinds 12C27, ATS-34 and his Damascus. **Prices:** $200 to $3000. **Remarks:** Full-time maker; first knife sold in 1958. **Mark:** Full name and registered logo.

FONTENOT, GERALD J

901 Maple Ave, Mamou, LA 70554, Phone: 318-468-3180

FORREST, BRIAN

FORREST KNIVES, PO Box 611, Descanso, CA 91916, Phone: 619-445-6343, forrestforge@gmail.com; Web: www.forrestforge.biz

Specialties: Forged tomahawks, working knives, big Bowies. **Patterns:** Traditional and extra large Bowies. **Technical:** Hollow grinds: 440C, 1095, S160 Damascus. **Prices:**"$125 and up. **Remarks:** Member of California Knifemakers Association. Full-time maker. First knife sold in 1971. **Mark:** Forrest USA/Tomahawks marked FF (Forrest Forge).

FORTHOFER, PETE

5535 Hwy 93S, Whitefish, MT 59937, Phone: 406-862-2674

Specialties: Interframes with checkered wood inlays; working straight knives. **Patterns:** Interframe folders and traditional-style knives; hunters, fighters and Bowies. **Technical:** Grinds D2, 440C, 154CM and ATS-34. **Prices:** $350 to $2500; some to $1500. **Remarks:** Part-time maker; full-time gunsmith. First knife sold in 1979. **Mark:** Name and logo.

FOSTER, AL

118 Woodway Dr, Magnolia, TX 77355, Phone: 936-372-9297

Specialties: Straight knives and folders. **Patterns:** Hunting, fishing, folders and Bowies. **Technical:** Grinds 440-C, ATS-34 and D2. **Prices:** $100 to $1000. **Remarks:** Full-time maker; first knife sold in 1981. **Mark:** Scorpion logo and name.

FOSTER, BURT

23697 Archery Range Rd, Bristol, VA 24202, Phone: 276-669-0121, burt@burtfoster.com; Web:www.burtfoster.com

Specialties: Working straight knives, laminated blades, and some art knives of his design. **Patterns:** Bowies, hunters, daggers. **Technical:** Forges 52100, W-2 and makes own Damascus. Does own heat treating. **Remarks:** ABS MasterSmith. Full-time maker, believes in sole authorship. **Mark:** Signed "BF" initials.

FOSTER, NORVELL C

7945 Youngsford Rd, Marion, TX 78124-1713, Phone: 830-914-2078

Specialties: Engraving; ivory handle carving. **Patterns:** American-large and small scroll-oak leaf and acorns. **Prices:** $25 to $400. **Remarks:** Have been engraving since 1957. **Mark:** N.C. Foster - Marion - Tex and current year.

FOSTER, RONNIE E

95 Riverview Rd., Morrilton, AR 72110, Phone: 501-354-5389

Specialties: Working, using knives, some period pieces, work with customer specs. **Patterns:** Hunters, fighters, Bowies, liner-lock folders, camp knives. **Technical:** Forge-5160, 1084, O1, 15N20-makes own Damascus. **Prices:** $200 (start). **Remarks:** Part-time maker. First knife sold 1994. **Mark:** Ronnie Foster MS.

FOSTER, TIMOTHY L

723 Sweet Gum Acres Rd, El Dorado, AR 71730, Phone: 870-863-6188

FOWLER, CHARLES R

226 National Forest Rd 48, Ft McCoy, FL 32134-9624, Phone: 904-467-3215

FOWLER, ED A.

Willow Bow Ranch, PO Box 1519, Riverton, WY 82501, Phone: 307-856-9815

Specialties: High-performance working and using straight knives. **Patterns:** Hunter, camp, bird, and trout knives and Bowies. New model, the gentleman's Pronghorn. **Technical:** Low temperature forged 52100 from virgin 5-1/2 round bars, multiple quench heat treating, engraves all knives, all handles domestic sheep horn processed and aged at least 5 years. Makes heavy duty hand-stitched waxed harness leather pouch type sheaths. **Prices:** $800 to $7000. **Remarks:** Full-time maker. First knife sold in 1962. **Mark:** Initials connected.

FOWLER, JERRY

610 FM 1660 N, Hutto, TX 78634, Phone: 512-846-2860, fowler@inetport.com

Specialties: Using straight knives of his design. **Patterns:** A variety of hunting and camp knives, combat knives. Custom designs considered. **Technical:** Forges 5160, his own Damascus and cable Damascus. Makes sheaths. Prefers natural handle materials. **Prices:** Start at $150. **Remarks:** Part-time maker; first knife sold in 1986. Doing business as Fowler Forge Knife Works. **Mark:** First initial, last name, date and J.S.

FOWLER, STEPHAN

1965 Stilesboro Dr., Kennesaw, GA 30152, stephan@fowlerblades.com

Specialties: Bowies. **Patterns:** Bowies, hunters, chef's knives (American and Japanese style). **Technical:** Primarily W2 blade steel, also 52100, 1084, 1095 and various damascus patterns. **Prices:** $200 and up. **Remarks:** Part-time maker since 2004. **Mark:** Fowler.

FRALEY, D B

1355 Fairbanks Ct, Dixon, CA 95620, Phone: 707-678-0393, dbtfnives@sbcglobal.net; Web:www.dbfraleyknives.com

Specialties: Usable gentleman's fixed blades and folders. **Patterns:** Four locking-liner and frame-lock folders in four different sizes. **Technical:** Grinds CPM S30V, 154CM and 6K Stellite. **Prices:** $250 and up. **Remarks:** Part-time maker. First knife sold in 1990. **Mark:** First and middle initials, last name over a buffalo.

FRAMSKI, WALTER P

24 Rek Ln, Prospect, CT 06712, Phone: 203-758-5634

FRANCE, DAN

Box 218, Cawood, KY 40815, Phone: 606-573-6104

Specialties: Traditional working and using straight knives of his design. **Patterns:** Hunters, Bowies and utility/camp knives. **Technical:** Forges and grinds O1, 5160 and L6. **Prices:** $35 to $125; some to $350. **Remarks:** Spare-time maker; first knife sold in 1985. **Mark:** First name.

FRANCIS, JOHN D

FRANCIS KNIVES, 18 Miami St., Ft. Loramie, OH 45845, Phone: 937-295-3941, jdfrancis72@gmail.com

Specialties: Utility and hunting-style fixed bladed knives of 440 C and ATS-34 steel; Micarta, exotic woods, and other types of handle materials. **Prices:** $90 to $150 range. **Remarks:** Exceptional quality and value at factory prices. **Mark:** Francis-Ft. Loramie, OH stamped on tang.

FRANK, HEINRICH H

1147 SW Bryson St, Dallas, OR 97338, Phone: 503-831-1489, Fax: 503-831-1489

Specialties: High-art investor-class folders, handmade and engraved. **Patterns:** Folding daggers, hunter-size folders and gents. **Technical:** Grinds 07 and O1. **Prices:** $4800 to $16,000. **Remarks:** Full-time maker; first knife sold in 1965. Doing business as H.H. Frank Knives. **Mark:** Name, address and date.

FRANKLIN, MIKE

9878 Big Run Rd, Aberdeen, OH 45101, Phone: 937-549-2598, Web: www.mikefranklinknives.com, hawgcustomknives.com

Specialties: High-tech tactical folders. **Patterns:** Tactical folders. **Technical:** Grinds CPM-T-440V, 440-C, ATS-34; titanium liners and bolsters; carbon fiber scales. Uses radical grinds and severe serrations. **Prices:** $100 to $1000. **Remarks:** Full-time maker; first knife sold in 1969. All knives made one at a time, 100% by the maker. **Mark:** Stylized boar with HAWG.

FRAPS, JOHN R

3810 Wyandotte Tr, Indianapolis, IN 46240-3422, Phone: 317-849-9419, jfraps@att.net; Web: www.frapsknives.com

Specialties: Working and collector grade LinerLock® and slip joint folders. **Patterns:** One-of-a kind linerlocks and traditional slip joints. **Technical:** Flat and hollow grinds ATS-34, Damascus, Talonite, CPM S30V, 154Cm, Stellite 6K; hand rubbed or mirror finish. **Prices:** $200 to $1500, some higher. **Remarks:** Voting member of the Knifemaker's Guild; Full-time maker; first knife sold in 1997. **Mark:** Cougar Creek Knives and/or name.

FRAZIER, JIM

6315 Wagener Rd., Wagener, SC 29164, Phone: 803-564-6467, jbfrazierknives@gmail.com; Web: www.jbfrazierknives.com

Specialties: Hunters, semi skinners, oyster roast knives, bird and trout, folders, many patterns of own design with George Herron/Geno Denning influence. **Technical:** Stock removal maker using CPM-154, ATS-34, CPM-S30V and D2. Hollow grind, mainly mirror finish, some satin finish. Prefer to use natural handle material such as stag, horn, mammoth ivory, highly figured woods, some Micarta, others on request. Makes own leather sheaths on 1958 straight needle stitcher. **Prices:** $125 to $600. **Remarks:** Part-time maker since 1989. **Mark:** JB Frazier in arch with Knives under it. Stamp on sheath is outline of state of SC, JB Frazier Knives Wagener SC inside outline.

FRED, REED WYLE

3149 X S, Sacramento, CA 95817, Phone: 916-739-0237

Specialties: Working using straight knives of his design. **Patterns:** Hunting and camp knives. **Technical:** Forges any 10 series, old files and carbon steels. Offers initialing upon request; prefers natural handle materials. **Prices:** $30 to $300. **Remarks:** Part-time maker; first knife sold in 1994. Doing business as R.W. Fred Knifemaker. **Mark:** Engraved first and last initials.

FREDEEN, GRAHAM

5121 Finadene Ct., Colorado Springs, CO 80916, Phone: 719-331-5665, fredeenblades@hotmail.com Web: www.fredeenblades.com

Specialties: Working class knives to high-end custom knives. Traditional pattern welding and mosaic Damascus blades.**Patterns:** All types: Bowies, fighters, hunters, skinners, bird and trout, camp knives, utility knives, daggers, etc. Occasionally swords, both European and Asian.**Technical:** Differential heat treatment and Hamon. Damascus steel rings and jewelry. Hand forged blades and Damascus steel. High carbon blade steels: 1050, 1075/1080, 1084, 1095, 5160, 52100, W1, W2, O1, 15n20 **Prices:** $100 - $2,000. **Remarks:** Sole authorship. Part-time maker. First blade produced in 2005. Member of American Bladesmith Society and Professional Knifemaker's Association **Mark:** "Fredeen" etched on the ricasso or on/along the spine of the blade.

FREDERICK, AARON

459 Brooks Ln, West Liberty, KY 41472-8961, Phone: 606-7432015, aaronf@mrtc.com; Web: www.frederickknives.com

Specialties: Makes most types of knives, but as for now specializes in the Damascus folder. Does all own Damascus and forging of the steel. Also prefers natural handle material such as ivory and pearl. Prefers 14k gold screws in most of the knives he do. Also offer several types of file work on blades, spacers, and liners. Has just recently started doing carving and can do a limited amount of engraving.

FREEMAN, MATT

5767 N. Channing Way, Fresno, CA 93711, Phone: 559-375-4408, kathur420@yahoo.com; Web: www.youtube.com/FTWCM

Specialties: Fixed blades and butterfly knives. **Technical:** Using mostly 1084, 154CM, D2 and file steel, works in any requested materials via stock removal. Also does knife modifications and leather/Kydex work. Three months or less waiting list. **Prices:** $75+. **Mark:** "FTW," "FTWCM" or "FTW 3-13."

FREER, RALPH
114 12th St, Seal Beach, CA 90740, Phone: 562-493-4925, Fax: same, ralphfreer@adelphia.net

Specialties: Exotic folders, liner locks, folding daggers, fixed blades. **Patters:** All original. **Technical:** Lots of Damascus, ivory, pearl, jeweled, thumb studs, carving ATS-34, 420V, 530V. **Prices:** $400 to $2500 and up. **Mark:** Freer in German-style text, also Freer shield.

FREY JR., W FREDERICK
305 Walnut St, Milton, PA 17847, Phone: 570-742-9576, wffrey@ptd.net

Specialties: Working straight knives and folders, some fancy. **Patterns:** Wide range miniatures, boot knives and lock back folders. **Technical:** Grinds A2, O1 and D2; vaseo wear, cru-wear and CPM S90V. **Prices:** $100 to $250; some to $1200. **Remarks:** Spare-time maker; first knife sold in 1983. All knives include quality hand stitched leather sheaths. **Mark:** Last name in script.

FRIEDLY, DENNIS E
12 Cottontail Lane E, Cody, WY 82414, Phone: 307-527-6811, friedlyknives@hotmail.com Web: www.friedlyknives.com

Specialties: Fancy working straight knives and daggers, lock back folders and liner locks. Also embellished bowies. **Patterns:** Hunters, fighters, short swords, minis and miniatures; new line of full-tang hunters/boots. **Technical:** Grinds 440C, commercial Damascus, mosaic Damascus and ATS-34 blades; prefers hidden tangs and full tangs. Both flat and hollow grinds. **Prices:** $350 to $2500. Some to $10,000. **Remarks:** Full-time maker; first knife sold in 1972. **Mark:** D.E. Friedly-Cody, WY. Friedly Knives

FRIGAULT, RICK
1189 Royal Pines Rd, Golden Lake, ON, CANADA K0J 1X0, Phone: 613-401-2869, Web: www.rfrigaultknives.ca

Specialties: Fixed blades. **Patterns:** Hunting, tactical and large Bowies. **Technical:** Grinds ATS-34, 440-C, D-2, CPMS30V, CPMS60V, CPMS90V, BG42 and Damascus. Use G-10, Micarta, ivory, antler, ironwood and other stabilized woods for carbon fiber handle material. Makes leather sheaths by hand. Tactical blades include a Concealex sheath made by "On Scene Tactical." **Remarks:** Sold first knife in 1997. Member of Canadian Knifemakers Guild. **Mark:** RFRIGAULT.

FRITZ, ERIK L
837 River St Box 1203, Forsyth, MT 59327, Phone: 406-351-1101, tacmedic45@yahoo.com

Specialties: Forges carbon steel 1084, 5160, 52100 and Damascus. **Patterns:** Hunters, camp knives, bowies and folders as well as forged tactical. **Technical:** Forges own Mosaic and pattern welded Damascus as well as doing own heat treat. **Prices:** A$200 and up. **Remarks:** Sole authorship knives and sheaths. Part time maker first knife sold in 2004. ABS member. **Mark:** E. Fritz in arc on left side ricasso.

FRITZ, JESSE
900 S. 13th St, Slaton, TX 79364, Phone: 806-828-5083

Specialties: Working and using straight knives in standard patterns. **Patterns:** Hunters, utility/camp knives and skinners with gut hook, Bowie knives, kitchen carving sets by request. **Technical:** Grinds 440C, O1 and 1095. Uses 1095 steel. Fline-napped steel design, blued blades, filework and machine jewelling. Inlays handles with turquoise, coral and mother-of-pearl. Makes sheaths. **Prices:** $85 to $275; some to $500. **Mark:** Last name only (FRITZ).

FRIZZELL, TED
14056 Low Gap Rd, West Fork, AR 72774, Phone: 501-839-2516, mmhwaxes@aol.com Web: www.mineralmountain.com

Specialties: Swords, axes and self-defense weapons. **Patterns:** Small skeleton knives to large swords. **Technical:** Grinds 5160 almost exclusively—1/4" to 1/2"— bars some O1 and A2 on request. All knives come with Kydex sheaths. **Prices:** $45 to $1200. **Remarks:** Full-time maker; first knife sold in 1984. Doing business as Mineral Mountain Hatchet Works. Wholesale orders welcome. **Mark:** A circle with line in the middle; MM and HW within the circle.

FRIZZI, LEONARDO
Via Kyoto 31, Firenze, ITALY 50126, Phone: 335-344750, postmaster@frizzi-knives.com; Web: www.frizzi-knives.com

Specialties: Fancy handmade one-of-a kind folders of his own design, some fixed blade and dagger. **Patterns:** Folders liner loch and back locks. **Technical:** Grinds rwl 34, cpm 154, cpm s30v, stainless damascus and the best craft damascus, own heat treating. I usually prefer satin finish the flat of the blade and mirror polish the hollow grind; special 18k gold, filework. **Prices:** $600 to $4,000. **Remarks:** Part-time maker, first knife sold in 2003. **Mark:** Full name, city, country, or initial, last name and city, or initial in square logo.

FRONEFIELD, DANIEL
20270 Warriors Path, Peyton, CO 80831, Phone: 719-749-0226, dfronfld@hiwaay.com

Specialties: Fixed and folding knives featuring meteorites and other exotic materials. **Patterns:** San-mai Damascus, custom Damascus. **Prices:** $500 to $3000.

FROST, DEWAYNE
1016 Van Buren Rd, Barnesville, GA 30204, Phone: 770-358-1426, lbrtyhill@aol.com

Specialties: Working straight knives and period knives. **Patterns:** Hunters, Bowies and utility knives. **Technical:** Forges own Damascus, cable, etc. as well as stock removal. **Prices:** $150 to $500. **Remarks:** Part-time maker ABS Journeyman Smith. **Mark:** Liberty Hill Forge Dewayne Frost w/liberty bell.

FRUHMANN, LUDWIG
Stegerwaldstr 8, Burghausen, GERMANY 84489

Specialties: High-tech and working straight knives of his design. **Patterns:** Hunters, fighters and boots. **Technical:** Grinds ATS-34, CPM-T-440V and Schneider Damascus. Prefers natural handle materials. **Prices:** $200 to $1500. **Remarks:** Spare-time maker; first knife sold in 1990. **Mark:** First initial and last name.

FRY, JASON
1701 North Willis, Abilene, TX 79603, Phone: 325-669-4805, frycustomknives@gmail.com; Web: www.frycustomknives.com

Specialties: Prefers drop points, both with or without bolsters. Prefers native Texas woods and often does contrasting wood bolsters. Also does own leather work. **Patterns:** Primarily EDC and hunting/skinning knives under 8 inches. Also slip-joint folders, primarily single-blade trappers and jacks. **Technical:** 1080 carbon steel, D2 tool steel, and 154CM stainless. Makes knives by stock removal and does own heat treating in a digitally controlled kiln. **Prices:** $150 to $500. **Remarks:** Part-time maker since July 2008, and 2013 probationary member of the Knifemakers' Guild. **Mark:** Jason Fry over Abilene, TX.

FUEGEN, LARRY
617 N Coulter Circle, Prescott, AZ 86303, Phone: 928-776-8777, fuegen@cableone.net; Web: www.larryfuegen.com

Specialties: High-art folders and classic and working straight knives. **Patterns:** Forged scroll folders, lockback folders and classic straight knives. **Technical:** Forges 5160, 1095 and his own Damascus. Works in exotic leather; offers elaborate filework and carving; likes natural handle materials, now offers own engraving. **Prices:** $600 to $12,000. **Remarks:** Full-time maker; first knife sold in 1975. Sole authorship on all knives. ABS Mastersmith. **Mark:** Initials connected.

FUJIKAWA, SHUN
Sawa 1157, Kaizuka, Osaka, JAPAN 597 0062, Phone: 81-724-23-4032, Fax: 81-726-23-9229

Specialties: Folders of his design and to customer specs. **Patterns:** Locking folders. **Technical:** Grinds his own steel. **Prices:** $450 to $2500; some to $3000. **Remarks:** Part-time maker.

FUKUTA, TAK
38-Umeagae-cho, Seki-City, Gifu, JAPAN, Phone: 0575-22-0264

Specialties: Bench-made fancy straight knives and folders. **Patterns:** Sheffield-type folders, Bowies and fighters. **Technical:** Grinds commercial Damascus. **Prices:** Start at $300. **Remarks:** Full-time maker. **Mark:** Name in knife logo.

FULLER, BRUCE A
3366 Ranch Rd. 32, Blanco, TX 78606, Phone: 832-262-0529, fullcoforg@aol.com

Specialties: One-of-a-kind working/using straight knives and folders of his designs. **Patterns:** Bowies, hunters, folders, and utility/camp knives. **Technical:** Forges high-carbon steel and his own Damascus. Prefers El Solo Mesquite and natural materials. Offers filework. **Prices:** $200 to $500; some to $1800. **Remarks:** Spare-time maker; first knife sold in 1991. Doing business as Fullco Forge. **Mark:** Fullco, M.S.

FULLER, JACK A
7103 Stretch Ct, New Market, MD 21774, Phone: 301-798-0119

Specialties: Straight working knives of his design and to customer specs. **Patterns:** Fighters, camp knives, hunters, tomahawks and art knives. **Technical:** Forges 5160, O1, W2 and his own Damascus. Does silver wire inlay and own leather work, wood lined sheaths for big camp knives. **Prices:** $400 and up. **Remarks:** Part-time maker. Master Smith in ABS; first knife sold in 1979. **Mark:** Fuller's Forge, MS.

FULTON, MICKEY
406 S Shasta St, Willows, CA 95988, Phone: 530-934-5780

Specialties: Working straight knives and folders of his design. **Patterns:** Hunters, Bowies, lockback folders and steak knife sets. **Technical:** Hand-filed, sanded, buffed ATS-34, 440C and A2. **Prices:** $65 to $600; some to $1200. **Remarks:** Full-time maker; first knife sold in 1979. **Mark:** Signature.

G

GADBERRY, EMMET
82 Purple Plum Dr, Hattieville, AR 72063, Phone: 501-354-4842

GADDY, GARY LEE
205 Ridgewood Lane, Washington, NC 27889, Phone: 252-946-4359

Specialties: Working/using straight knives of his design; period pieces. **Patterns:** Bowies, hunters, utility/camp knives, oyster knives. **Technical:** Grinds ATS-34, O1; forges 1095. **Prices:** $175+ **Remarks:** Spare-time maker; first knife sold in 1991. No longer accepts orders. **Mark:** Quarter moon stamp.

GAETA, ANGELO
R. Saldanha Marinho 1295, Centro Jau, SP, BRAZIL 17201-310, Phone: 0146-224543, Fax: 0146-224543

Specialties: Straight using knives to customer specs. **Patterns:** Hunters, fighting, daggers, belt push dagger. **Technical:** Grinds D6, ATS-34 and 440C stainless. Titanium nitride golden finish upon request. **Prices:** $60 to $300. **Remarks:** Full-time maker; first knife sold in 1992. **Mark:** First initial, last name.

GAINES, BUDDY
GAINES KNIVES, 155 Red Hill Rd., Commerce, GA 30530, Web: www.gainesknives.com

Specialties: Collectible and working folders and straight knives. **Patterns:** Folders, hunters, Bowies, tactical knives. **Technical:** Forges own Damascus, grinds ATS-34, D2, commercial Damascus. Prefers mother-of-pearl and stag. **Prices:** Start at $200. **Remarks:** Part-time maker, sold first knife in 1985. **Mark:** Last name.

GAINEY, HAL
904 Bucklevel Rd, Greenwood, SC 29649, Phone: 864-223-0225, Web: www.scak.org
Specialties: Traditional working and using straight knives and folders. **Patterns:** Hunters, slip-joint folders and utility/camp knives. **Technical:** Hollow-grinds ATS-34 and D2; makes sheaths. **Prices:** $95 to $145; some to $500. **Remarks:** Full-time maker; first knife sold in 1975. **Mark:** Eagle head and last name.

GALLAGHER, BARRY
135 Park St, Lewistown, MT 59457, Phone: 406-538-7056, Web: www.gallagherknives.com
Specialties: One-of-a-kind Damascus folders. **Patterns:** Folders, utility to high art, some straight knives, hunter, Bowies, and art pieces. **Technical:** Forges own mosaic Damascus and carbon steel, some stainless. **Prices:** $400 to $5000+. **Remarks:** Full-time maker; first knife sold in 1993. Doing business as Gallagher Custom Knives. **Mark:** Last name.

GAMBLE, FRANK
4676 Commercial St SE #26, Salem, OR 97302, Phone: 503-581-7993, gamble6831@comcast.net
Specialties: Fantasy and high-art straight knives and folders of his design. **Patterns:** Daggers, fighters, hunters and special locking folders. **Technical:** Grinds 440C and ATS-34; forges Damascus. Inlays; offers jewelling. Prices $150 to $10,000. **Remarks:** Full-time maker; first knife sold in 1976. **Mark:** First initial, last name.

GAMBLE, ROGER
18515 N.W. 28th Pl., Newberry, FL 32669, ROGERLGAMBLE@COX.NET
Specialties: Traditional working/using straight knives and folders of his design. **Patterns:** Liner locks and hunters. **Technical:** Grinds ATS-34 and Damascus. **Prices:** $150 to $2000. **Remarks:** Part-time maker; first knife sold in 1982. Doing business as Gamble Knives. **Mark:** First name in a fan of cards over last name.

GANN, TOMMY
2876 State Hwy. 198, Canton, TX 75103, Phone: 903-848-9375
Specialties: Art and working straight knives of my design or customer preferences/design. **Patterns:** Bowie, fighters, hunters, daggers. **Technical:** Forges Damascus 52100 and grinds ATS-34 and D2. **Prices:** $200 to $2500. **Remarks:** Full-time knifemaker, first knife sold in 2002. ABS journey bladesmith. **Mark:** TGANN.

GANSHORN, CAL
123 Rogers Rd., Regina, SK, CANADA S4S 6T7, Phone: 306-584-0524
Specialties: Working and fancy fixed blade knives. **Patterns:** Bowies, hunters, daggers, and filleting. **Technical:** Makes own forged Damascus billets, ATS, salt heat treating, and custom forges and burners. **Prices:** $250 to $1500. **Remarks:** Part-time maker. **Mark:** Last name etched in ricasso area.

GARAU, MARCELLO
Via Alagon 42, Oristano, ITALY 09170, Phone: 00393479073454, marcellogarau@libero.it Web: www.knifecreator.com
Specialties: Mostly lock back folders with interframe. **Technical:** Forges own damascus for both blades and frames. **Prices:** 200 - 2,700 Euros. **Remarks:** Full-time maker; first knife made in 1995. Attends Milano Knife Show and ECCKSHOW yearly. **Mark:** M.Garau inside handle.

GARCIA, MARIO EIRAS
Rua Edmundo Scannapieco 300, Caxingui, SP, BRAZIL 05516-070, Phone: 011-37218304, Fax: 011-37214528
Specialties: Fantasy knives of his design; one-of-a-kind only. **Patterns:** Fighters, daggers, boots and two-bladed knives. **Technical:** Forges car leaf springs. Uses only natural handle material. **Prices:** $100 to $200. **Remarks:** Part-time maker; first knife sold in 1976. **Mark:** Two "B"s, one opposite the other.

GARDNER, ROBERT
13462 78th Pl. N, West Palm Beach, FL 33412
Specialties: Straight blades, forged and clay hardened or differentially heat treated. Kydex and leather sheath maker. **Patterns:** Working/using knives, some to customer specs, and high-end knives, daggers, bowies, ethnic knives, and Steelhead and Lil' Chub woodland survival/bushcraft knife set with an elaborate, versatile sheath system. Affordable hard-use production line of everyday carry belt knives, and less-expensive forged knives, neck knives and "wrench" knives. **Technical:** Grinds, forges and heat treats high-carbon 1084, 1095, 1075, W1, W2, 5160 and 52100 steels, some natural handle materials and Micarta for full-tang knives. **Prices:** $60 and up; sheaths $30 and up. **Remarks:** Full-time maker since 2010; first knife sold in 1986. **Mark:** Initials in angular script, stamped, engraved or etched.

GARNER, GEORGE
7527 Calhoun Dr. NE, Albuquerque, NM 87109, Phone: 505-797-9317, razorbackblades@msn.com Web: www.razorbackblades.com
Specialties: High art locking liner folders and Daggers of his own design. Working and high art straight knives. **Patterns:** Bowies, daggers, fighters and locking liner folders. **Technical:** Grinds 440C, CPM-154, ATS34 and others. Damascus, Mosaic Damascus and Mokume. Makes own custom leather sheaths. **Prices:** $150 - $2,500. **Remarks:** Part-time maker since 1993. Full-time maker as of 2011. Company name is Razorback Blades. **Mark:** GEORGE GARNER.

GARNER, LARRY W
13069 FM 14, Tyler, TX 75706, Phone: 903-597-6045, lwgarner@classicnet.net

Specialties: Fixed blade hunters and Bowies. **Patterns:** His designs or yours. **Technical:** Hand forges 5160. **Prices:** $200 to $500. **Remarks:** Apprentice bladesmith. **Mark:** Last name.

GARVOCK, MARK W
RR 1, Balderson, ON, CANADA K1G 1A0, Phone: 613-833-2545, Fax: 613-833-2208, garvock@travel-net.com
Specialties: Hunters, Bowies, Japanese, daggers and swords. **Patterns:** Cable Damascus, random pattern welded or to suit. **Technical:** Forged blades; hi-carbon. **Prices:** $250 to $900. **Remarks:** CKG member and ABS member. Shipping and taxes extra. **Mark:** Big G with M in middle.

GATLIN, STEVE
103 Marian Ct., Leesburg, GA 31763, Phone: 229-328-5074, stevegatlinknives@hotmail.com; Web: www.stevegatlinknives.com
Specialties: Loveless-style knives, double-ground fighters and traditional hunters. Some tactical models of maker's design. Fixed blades only. **Technical:** Grinds CPM-154, ATS-34 and 154CM. **Prices:** $450 to $1,500 on base models. **Remarks:** Voting member of Knifemakers' Guild since 2009; first knife sold in 2008. **Mark:** Typical football shape with name on top and city below.

GEDRAITIS, CHARLES J
GEDRAITIS HAND CRAFTED KNIVES, 444 Shrewsbury St, Holden, MA 01520, Phone: 508-963-1861, gedraitisknives@yahoo.com; Web: www.gedraitisknives.com
Specialties: One-of-a-kind folders & automatics of his own design. **Patterns:** One-of-a-kind. **Technical:** Forges to shape mostly stock removal. **Prices:** $300 to $2500. **Remarks:** Full-time maker. **Mark:** 3 scallop shells with an initial inside each one: CJG.

GENOVESE, RICK
PO Box 226, 182 Purtill Tr., Tonto Basin, AZ 85553, Phone: 928-274-7739, genoveseknives@hotmail.com; Web: www.rickgenoveseknives.com
Specialties Interframe-style folders. **Patterns:** Sleek folders in gentleman's designs. Also folding dirks and daggers. **Technical:** Main blade material is CPM 154. Also uses damascus by Devin Thomas and Jerry Rados. Inlays gemstones such as lapis lazuli, jade, opal, dinosaur bone, tiger eye, jasper, agate, malachite, petrified wood, as well as various pearls. **Prices:** $1,500-$10,000. **Remarks:** Full-time maker; first knife sold in 1975. **Mark:** Genovese in stylized letters.

GEORGE, HARRY
3137 Old Camp Long Rd, Aiken, SC 29805, Phone: 803-649-1963, hdkk-george@scescape.net
Specialties: Working straight knives of his design or to customer specs. **Patterns:** Hunters, skinners and utility knives. **Technical:** Grinds ATS-34. Prefers natural handle materials, hollow-grinds and mirror finishes. **Prices:** Start at $70. **Remarks:** Part-time maker; first knife sold in 1985. Trained under George Herron. Member SCAK. Member Knifemakers Guild. **Mark:** Name, city, state.

GEORGE, LES
6521 Fenwick Dr., Corpus Christi, TX 78414, Phone: 361-288-9777, les@georgeknives.com; Web: www.georgeknives.com
Specialties: Tactical frame locks and fixed blades. **Patterns:** Folders, balisongs, and fixed blades. **Technical:** CPM154, S30V, Chad Nichols Damascus. **Prices:** $200 to $800. **Remarks:** Full-time maker, first knife sold in 1992. Doing business as www.georgeknives.com. **Mark:** Last name over logo.

GEORGE, TOM
550 Aldbury Dr, Henderson, NV 89014, tagmaker@aol.com
Specialties: Working straight knives, display knives, custom meat cleavers, and folders of his design. **Patterns:** Hunters, Bowies, daggers, buckskinners, swords and folders. **Technical:** Uses D2, 440C, ATS-34 and 154CM. **Prices:** $500 to $13,500. **Remarks:** Custom orders not accepted "at this time". Full-time maker. First knife1982; first 350 knives were numbered; after that no numbers. Almost all his knives today are Bowies and swords. Creator and maker of the "Past Glories" series of knives. **Mark:** Tom George maker.

GEPNER, DON
2615 E Tecumseh, Norman, OK 73071, Phone: 405-364-2750
Specialties: Traditional working and using straight knives of his design. **Patterns:** Bowies and daggers. **Technical:** Forges his Damascus, 1095 and 5160. **Prices:** $100 to $400; some to $1000. **Remarks:** Spare-time maker; first knife sold in 1991. Has been forging since 1954; first edged weapon made at 9 years old. **Mark:** Last initial.

GERNER, THOMAS
PO Box 301, Walpole, WA, AUSTRALIA 6398, gerner@bordernet.com.au; Web: www.deepriverforge.com
Specialties: Forged working knives; plain steel and pattern welded. **Patterns:** Tries most patterns heard or read about. **Technical:** 5160, L6, O1, 52100 steels; Australian hardwood handles. **Prices:** $220 and up. **Remarks:** Achieved ABS Master Smith rating in 2001. **Mark:** Like a standing arrow and a leaning cross, T.G. in the Runic (Viking) alphabet.

GHIO, PAOLO
4330 Costa Mesa, Pensacola, FL 32504-7849, Phone: 850-393-0135, paologhio@hotmail.com
Specialties: Folders, fillet knives and skinners. **Patterns:** Maker's own design, or will work from a customer's pattern. **Technical:** Stock removal, all work in house, including heat treat. **Prices:** $200 to $500. **Mark:** PKG.

custom knifemakers

GIAGU—GOODPASTURE

GIAGU, SALVATORE AND DEROMA MARIA ROSARIA
Via V Emanuele 64, Pattada (SS), ITALY 07016, Phone: 079-755918, Fax: 079-755918, coltelligiagupattada@tiscali.it Web: www.culterpattada.it
 Specialties: Using and collecting traditional and new folders from Sardegna. **Patterns:** Folding, hunting, utility, skinners and kitchen knives. **Technical:** Forges ATS-34, 440, D2 and Damascus. **Prices:** $200 to $2000; some higher. **Mark:** First initial, last name and name of town and muflon's head.

GIBERT, PEDRO
Los Alamos 410, San Martin de los Andes, Neuquen, ARGENTINA 8370, Phone: 054-2972-410868, rosademayo@infovia.com.ar
 Specialties: Hand forges: Stock removal and integral. High quality artistic knives of his design and to customer specifications. **Patterns:** Country (Argentine gaucho-style), knives, folders, Bowies, daggers, hunters. Others upon request. **Technical:** Blade: Bohler k110 Austrian steel (high resistance to waste). Handles: (Natural materials) ivory elephant, killer whale, hippo, walrus tooth, deer antler, goat, ram, buffalo horn, bone, rhea, sheep, cow, exotic woods (South America native woods) hand carved and engraved guards and blades. Stainless steel guards, finely polished: semi-matte or shiny finish. Sheaths: Raw or tanned leather, hand-stitched; rawhide or cotton yarn embroidered. Box: One wood piece, hand carved. Wooden hinges and locks. **Prices:** $600 and up. **Remarks:** Full-time maker. Made first knife in 1987. **Mark:** Only a rose logo. Buyers initials upon request.

GIBO, GEORGE
PO Box 4304, Hilo, HI 96720, Phone: 808-987-7002, geogibo@hilo808.net
 Specialties: Straight knives and folders. **Patterns:** Hunters, bird and trout, utility, gentlemen and tactical folders. **Technical:** Grinds ATS-34, BG-42, Talonite, Stainless Steel Damascus. **Prices:** $250 to $1000. **Remarks:** Spare-time maker; first knife sold in 1995. **Mark:** Name, city and state around Hawaiian "Shaka" sign.

GILBERT, CHANTAL
291 Rue Christophe-Colomb est #105, Quebec City, QC, CANADA G1K 3T1, Phone: 418-525-6961, Fax: 418-525-4666, gilbertc@medion.qc.ca; Web:www.chantalgilbert.com
 Specialties: Straight art knives that may resemble creatures, often with wings, shells and antennae, always with a beak of some sort, fixed blades in a feminine style. **Technical:** ATS-34 and Damascus. Handle materials usually silver that she forms to shape via special molds and a press; ebony and fossil ivory. **Prices:** Range from $500 to $4000. **Remarks:** Often embellishes her art knives with rubies, meteorite, 18k gold and similar elements.

GILBREATH, RANDALL
55 Crauswell Rd, Dora, AL 35062, Phone: 205-648-3902
 Specialties: Damascus folders and fighters. **Patterns:** Folders and fixed blades. **Technical:** Forges Damascus and high-carbon; stock removal stainless steel. **Prices:** $300 to $1500. **Remarks:** Full-time maker; first knife sold in 1979. **Mark:** Name in ribbon.

GILJEVIC, BRANKO
35 Hayley Crescent, Queanbeyan 2620, New South Wales, AUSTRALIA 0262977613
 Specialties: Classic working straight knives and folders of his design. **Patterns:** Hunters, Bowies, skinners and locking folders. **Technical:** Grinds 440C. Offers acid etching, scrimshaw and leather carving. **Prices:** $150 to $1500. **Remarks:** Part-time maker; first knife sold in 1987. Doing business as Sambar Custom Knives. **Mark:** Company name in logo.

GINGRICH, JUSTIN
5329 Anna Belle Ln., Wade, NC 28395, Phone: 507-230-0398, justin@gingrichtactical.com Web: www.gingrichtactical.com
 Specialties: Anything from bushcraft to tactical, heavy on the tactical. **Patterns:** Fixed blades and folders. **Technical:** Uses all types of steel and handle material, method is stock-removal. **Prices:** $30 - $1000. **Remarks:** Full-time maker. **Mark:** Tang stamp is the old Ranger Knives logo.

GIRTNER, JOE
409 Catalpa Ave, Brea, CA 92821, Phone: 714-529-2388, conceptsinknives@aol.com
 Specialties: Art knives and miniatures. **Patterns:** Mainly Damascus (some carved). **Technical:** Many techniques and materials combined. Wood carving knives and tools, hunters, custom orders. **Prices:** $55 to $3000. **Mark:** Name.

GITTINGER, RAYMOND
6940 S Rt 100, Tiffin, OH 44883, Phone: 419-397-2517

GLOVER, RON
100 West Church St., Mason, OH 45040, Phone: 513-404-7107, r.glover@zoomtown.com
 Specialties: High-tech working straight knives and folders. **Patterns:** Hunters to Bowies; some interchangeable blade models; unique locking mechanisms. **Technical:** Grinds 440C, 154CM; buys Damascus. **Prices:** $70 to $500; some to $800. **Remarks:** Part-time maker; first knife sold in 1981. **Mark:** Name in script.

GLOVER, WARREN D
dba BUBBA KNIVES, PO Box 475, Cleveland, GA 30528, Phone: 706-865-3998, Fax: 706-348-7176, warren@bubbaknives.net; Web: www.bubbaknives.net
 Specialties: Traditional and custom working and using straight knives of his design and to customer request. **Patterns:** Hunters, skinners, bird and fish, utility and kitchen knives. **Technical:** Grinds 440, ATS-34 and stainless steel Damascus. **Prices:** $75 to $400 and up. **Remarks:** Full-time maker; sold first knife in 1995. **Mark:** Bubba, year, name, state.

GODDARD, WAYNE
473 Durham Ave, Eugene, OR 97404, Phone: 541-689-8098, wgoddard44@comcast.net

Specialties: Working/using straight knives and folders. **Patterns:** Hunters and folders. **Technical:** Works exclusively with wire Damascus and his own-pattern welded material. **Prices:** $250 to $4000. **Remarks:** Full-time maker; first knife sold in 1963. **Mark:** Blocked initials on forged blades; regular capital initials on stock removal.

GODLESKY, BRUCE F.
1002 School Rd., Apollo, PA 15613, Phone: 724-840-5786, brucegodlesky@yahoo.com; Web: www.birdforge.com
 Specialties: Working/using straight knives and tomahawks, mostly forged. **Patterns:** Hunters, birds and trout, fighters and tomahawks. **Technical:** Most forged, some stock removal. Carbon steel only. 5160, O-1, W2, 10xx series. Makes own Damascus and welded cable. **Prices:** Starting at $75. **Mark:** BIRDOG FORGE.

GOERS, BRUCE
3423 Royal Ct S, Lakeland, FL 33813, Phone: 941-646-0984
 Specialties: Fancy working and using straight knives of his design and to customer specs. **Patterns:** Hunters, fighters, Bowies and fantasy knives. **Technical:** Grinds ATS-34, some Damascus. **Prices:** $195 to $600; some to $1300. **Remarks:** Part-time maker; first knife sold in 1990. Doing business as Vulture Cutlery. **Mark:** Buzzard with initials.

GOLDBERG, DAVID
321 Morris Rd, Ft Washington, PA 19034, Phone: 215-654-7117, david@goldmountainforge.com; Web: www.goldmountainforge.com
 Specialties: Japanese-style designs, will work with special themes in Japanese genre. **Patterns:** Kozuka, Tanto, Wakazashi, Katana, Tachi, Sword canes, Yari and Naginata. **Technical:** Forges his own Damascus and makes his own handmade tamehagane steel from straw ash, iron, carbon and clay. Uses traditional materials, carves fittings handles and cases. Hardens all blades in traditional Japanese clay differential technique. **Remarks:** Full-time maker; first knife sold in 1987. Japanese swordsmanship teacher (jaido) and Japanese self-defense teach (aikido). **Mark:** Name (kinzan) in Japanese Kanji on Tang under handle.

GOLDEN, RANDY
6492 Eastwood Glen Dr, Montgomery, AL 36117, Phone: 334-271-6429, rgolden1@mindspring.com
 Specialties: Collectable quality hand rubbed finish, hunter, camp, Bowie straight knives, custom leather sheaths with exotic skin inlays and tooling. **Technical:** Stock removal ATS-34, CPM154, S30V and BG-42. Natural handle materials primarily stag and ivory. **Prices:** $500 to $1500. **Remarks:** Full-time maker, member Knifemakers Guild, first knife sold in 2000. **Mark:** R. R. Golden Montgomery, AL.

GONZALEZ, LEONARDO WILLIAMS
Ituzaingo 473, Maldonado, URUGUAY 20000, Phone: 598 4222 1617, Fax: 598 4222 1617, willyknives@hotmail.com; Web: www.willyknives.com
 Specialties: Classic high-art and fantasy straight knives; traditional working and using knives of his design, in standard patterns or to customer specs. **Patterns:** Hunters, Bowies, daggers, fighters, boots, swords and utility/camp knives. **Technical:** Forges and grinds high-carbon and stainless Bohler steels. **Prices:** $100 to $2500. **Remarks:** Full-time maker; first knife sold in 1985. **Mark:** Willy, whale, R.O.U.

GOO, TAI
5920 W Windy Lou Ln, Tucson, AZ 85742, Phone: 520-744-9777, taigoo@msn.com; Web: www.taigoo.com
 Specialties: High art, neo-tribal, bush and fantasy. **Technical:** Hand forges, does own heat treating, makes own Damascus. **Prices:** $150 to $500 some to $10,000. **Remarks:** Full-time maker; first knife sold in 1978. **Mark:** Chiseled signature.

GOOD, D.R.
D.R. Good Custom Knives and Weaponry, 6125 W. 100 S., Tipton, IN 46072, Phone: 765-963-6971, drntammigood@bluemarble.net
 Specialties: Working knives, own design, Scagel style, "critter" knives, carved handles. **Patterns:** Bowies, large and small, neck knives and miniatures. Offers carved handles, snake heads, eagles, wolves, bear, skulls. **Technical:** Damascus, some stelite, 6K, pearl, ivory, moose. **Prices:** $150 - $1500. **Remarks:** Full-time maker. First knife was Bowie made from a 2-1/2 truck bumper in military. **Mark:** D.R. Good in oval and for minis, DR with a buffalo skull.

GOODE, BEAR
PO Box 6474, Navajo Dam, NM 87419, Phone: 505-632-8184
 Specialties: Working/using straight knives of his design and in standard patterns. **Patterns:** Bowies, hunters and utility/camp knives. **Technical:** Grinds 440C, ATS-34, 154-CM; forges and grinds 1095, 5160 and other steels on request; uses Damascus. **Prices:** $60 to $225; some to $500 and up. **Remarks:** Part-time maker; first knife sold in 1993. Doing business as Bear Knives. **Mark:** First and last name with a three-toed paw print.

GOODE, BRIAN
203 Gordon Ave, Shelby, NC 28152, Phone: 704-434-6496, web:www.bgoodeknives.com
 Specialties: Flat ground working knives with etched/antique or brushed finish. **Patterns:** Field, camp, hunters, skinners, survival, kitchen, maker's design or yours. Currently full tang only with supplied leather sheath. **Technical:** O-1, D2 and other ground flat stock. Stock removal and differential heat treat preferred. Etched antique/etched satin working finish preferred. Micarta and hardwoods for strength. **Prices:** $150 to $700. **Remarks:** Part-time maker and full-time knife lover. First knife sold in 2004. **Mark:** B. Goode with NC separated by a feather.

GOODPASTURE, TOM
13432 Farrington Road, Ashland, VA 23005, Phone: 804-752-8363, rtg007@aol.com;

web: goodpastureknives.com

Specialties: Working/using straight knives of his own design, or customer specs. File knives and primative reproductions. **Patterns:** Hunters, bowies, small double-edge daggers, kitchen, custom miniatures and camp/utility. **Technical:** Stock removal, D-2, 0-1, 12C27, 420 HC, 52100. Forged blades of W-2, 1084, and 1095. Flat grinds only. **Prices:** $60 - $300. **Remarks:** Part-time maker, first knife sold at Blade Show 2005. Lifetime guarantee and sharpening. **Mark:** Early mark were initials RTG, current mark: Goodpasture.

GORDON, LARRY B
23555 Newell Cir W, Farmington Hills, MI 48336, Phone: 248-477-5483, lbgordon1@aol.com

Specialties: Folders, small fixed blades. New design rotating scale release automatic. **Patterns:** Rotating handle locker. Ambidextrous fire (R&L) **Prices:** $450 minimum. **Remarks:** High line materials preferred. **Mark:** Gordon.

GORENFLO, JAMES T (JT)
9145 Sullivan Rd, Baton Rouge, LA 70818, Phone: 225-261-5868

Specialties: Traditional working and using straight knives of his design. **Patterns:** Bowies, hunters and utility/camp knives. **Technical:** Forges 5160, 1095, 52100 and his own Damascus. **Prices:** Start at $200. **Remarks:** Part-time maker; first knife sold in 1992. **Mark:** Last name or initials, J.S. on reverse.

GOSHOVSKYY, VASYL
BL.4, C. San Jaime 65, Torreblanca 12596, Castellon de la Plana, SPAIN, Phone: +34-664-838-882, baz_knife@mail.ru; Web: www.goshovskyy-knives.com

Specialties: Presentation and working fixed-blade knives. **Patterns:** R.W. Loveless-pattern knives, primarily hunters and skinners. **Technical:** Stock-removal method. Prefers natural materials for handle scales. Uses primarily RWL-34, CPM-154, N690 or similar blade steel. **Remarks:** Full-time maker.

GOSSMAN, SCOTT
PO Box 41, Whiteford, MD 21160, Phone: 443-617-2444, scogos@peoplepc.com; Web:www.gossmanknives.com

Specialties: Heavy duty knives for big-game hunting and survival. **Patterns:** Modified clip-point/spear-point blades, bowies, hunters and bushcraft. **Technical:** Grinds A2, O1, CPM-154, CPM-3V, S7, flat/convex grinds and convex micro-bevel edges. **Price:** $65 to $500. **Remarks:** Full-time maker doing business as Gossman Knives. **Mark:** Gossman and steel type.

GOTTAGE, DANTE
43227 Brooks Dr, Clinton Twp., MI 48038-5323, Phone: 810-286-7275

Specialties: Working knives of his design or to customer specs. **Patterns:** Large and small skinners, fighters, Bowies and fillet knives. **Technical:** Grinds O1, 440C and 154CM and ATS-34. **Prices:** $150 to $600. **Remarks:** Part-time maker; first knife sold in 1975. **Mark:** Full name in script letters.

GOTTAGE, JUDY
43227 Brooks Dr, Clinton Twp., MI 48038-5323, Phone: 586-286-7275, jgottage@remaxmetropolitan.com

Specialties: Custom folders of her design or to customer specs. **Patterns:** Interframes or integral. **Technical:** Stock removal. **Prices:** $300 to $3000. **Remarks:** Full-time maker; first knife sold in 1980. **Mark:** Full name, maker in script.

GOTTSCHALK, GREGORY J
12 First St. (Ft. Pitt), Carnegie, PA 15106, Phone: 412-279-6692

Specialties: Fancy working straight knives and folders to customer specs. **Patterns:** Hunters to tantos, locking folders to minis. **Technical:** Grinds 440C, 154CM, ATS-34. Now making own Damascus. Most knives have mirror finishes. **Prices:** Start at $150. **Remarks:** Part-time maker; first knife sold in 1977. **Mark:** Full name in crescent.

GOUKER, GARY B
PO Box 955, Sitka, AK 99835, Phone: 907-747-3476

Specialties: Hunting knives for hard use. **Patterns:** Skinners, semi-skinners, and such. **Technical:** Likes natural materials, inlays, stainless steel. **Prices:** Moderate. **Remarks:** New Alaskan maker. **Mark:** Name.

GRAHAM, GORDON
3145 CR 4008, New Boston, TX 75570, Phone: 903-293-2610, Web: www.grahamknives.com

Prices: $325 to $850. **Mark:** Graham.

GRAHAM, LEVI
6608 W. 3rd St. #66, Greeley, CO 80634, Phone: 970-371-0477, lgknives@hotmail.com; Web: www.levigrahamknives.com

Specialties: Forged frontier/period/Western knives. **Patterns:** Hunters, patch knives, skinners, camp, belt and bowies, sometimes kitchen cutlery. **Technical:** Forges high-carbon steels and some stock removal in 1095, 1084, 5160, L6, 80CRV2 and 52100. Handle materials include antler, bone, ivory, horn, hardwoods, Micarta and G-10. Rawhide-covered, vegetable-tanned sheaths decorated with deer fringe, quill work for a band or medicine wheel, beads, cones, horse hair, etc. Custom orders welcome. **Prices:** $300 and up. **Remarks:** Member of ABS and PKA. **Mark:** "lg" stamped in lower case letters.

GRANGER, PAUL J
704 13th Ct. SW, Largo, FL 33770-4471, Phone: 727-953-3249, grangerknives@live.com Web: http://palehorsefighters.blogspot.com

Specialties: Working straight knives of his own design and a few folders. **Patterns:** 2.75" to 4" work knives, tactical knives and Bowies from 5"-9." **Technical:** Grinds CPM154-

CM, ATS-34 and forges 52100 and 1084. Offers filework. **Prices:** $95 to $500. **Remarks:** Part-time maker since 1997. Sold first knife in 1997. Doing business as Granger Knives and Pale Horse Fighters. Member of ABS and Florida Knifemakers Association. **Mark:** "Granger" or "Palehorse Fighters."

GRAVELINE, PASCAL AND ISABELLE
38 Rue de Kerbrezillic, Moelan-sur-Mer, FRANCE 29350, Phone: 33 2 98 39 73 33, atelier.graveline@wanadoo.fr; Web: www.graveline-couteliers.com

Specialties: French replicas from the 17th, 18th and 19th centuries. **Patterns:** Traditional folders and multi-blade pocket knives; traveling knives, fruit knives and fork sets; puzzle knives and friend's knives; rivet less knives. **Technical:** Grind 12C27, ATS-34, Damascus and carbon steel. **Prices:** $500 to $5000. **Remarks:** Full-time makers; first knife sold in 1992. **Mark:** Last name over head of ram.

GRAVES, DAN
4887 Dixie Garden Loop, Shreveport, LA 71105, Phone: 318-865-8166, Web: wwwtheknifemaker.com

Specialties: Traditional forged blades and Damascus. **Patterns:** Bowies (D guard also), fighters, hunters, large and small daggers. **Remarks:** Full-time maker. **Mark:** Initials with circle around them.

GRAY, BOB
8206 N Lucia Court, Spokane, WA 99208, Phone: 509-468-3924

Specialties: Straight working knives of his own design or to customer specs. **Patterns:** Hunter, fillet and carving knives. **Technical:** Forges 5160, L6 and some 52100; grinds 440C. **Prices:** $100 to $600. **Remarks:** Part-time knifemaker; first knife sold in 1991. Doing business as Hi-Land Knives. **Mark:** HI-L.

GRAY, DANIEL
GRAY KNIVES, 686 Main Rd., Brownville, ME 04414, Phone: 207-965-2191, mail@grayknives.com; Web: www.grayknives.com

Specialties: Straight knives, fantasy, folders, automatics and traditional of his own design. **Patterns:** Automatics, fighters, hunters. **Technical:** Grinds O1, 154CM and D2. **Prices:** From $155 to $750. **Remarks:** Full-time maker; first knife sold in 1974. **Mark:** Gray Knives.

GRAY, ROBB
6026 46th Ave. SW, Seattle, WA 98136, Phone: 206-280-7622, robb.gray@graycloud-designs.com; Web: www.graycloud-designs.com

Specialties: Hunting, fishing and leather-workers' knives, along with daggers and utility ranch knives. **Technical:** Stock-removal maker using 440C, CPM-S30V, CPM-154, CPM-12C27, CPM-13C26 and CPM-19C27 stainless steels. Also engraves knives in Sheridan, single point and Western bright cut styles. Owner of "Resinwood," a certified wood fiber product sold to knifemaker supply companies for handle material. **Remarks:** Full-time artist/maker; first knife made in 2009. **Mark:** A rain cloud with name "Graycloud" next to it, surrounded by an oval.

GREBE, GORDON S
PO Box 296, Anchor Point, AK 99556-0296, Phone: 907-235-8242

Specialties: Working straight knives and folders, some fancy. **Patterns:** Tantos, Bowies, boot fighter sets, locking folders. **Technical:** Grinds stainless steels; likes 1/4" inch stock and glass-bead finishes. **Prices:** $75 to $250; some to $2000. **Remarks:** Full-time maker; first knife sold in 1968. **Mark:** Initials in lightning logo.

GRECO, JOHN
100 Mattie Jones Rd, Greensburg, KY 42743, Phone: 270-932-3335, johngreco@grecoknives.com; Web: www.grecoknives.com

Specialties: Folders. **Patterns:** Tactical, fighters, camp knives, short swords. **Technical:** Stock removal carbon steel. **Prices:** Affordable. **Remarks:** Full-time maker since 1979. First knife sold in 1979. **Mark:** GRECO

GREEN, BILL
6621 Eastview Dr, Sachse, TX 75048, Phone: 972-463-3147

Specialties: High-art and working straight knives and folders of his design and to customer specs. **Patterns:** Bowies, hunters, kitchen knives and locking folders. **Technical:** Grinds ATS-34, D2 and 440V. Hand-tooled custom sheaths. **Prices:** $70 to $350; some to $750. **Remarks:** Part-time maker; first knife sold in 1990. **Mark:** Last name.

GREEN, WILLIAM (BILL)
46 Warren Rd, View Bank, VIC, AUSTRALIA 3084, Fax: 03-9459-1529

Specialties: Traditional high-tech straight knives and folders. **Patterns:** Japanese-influenced designs, hunters, Bowies, folders and miniatures. **Technical:** Forges O1, D2 and his own Damascus. Offers lost wax castings for bolsters and pommels. Likes natural handle materials, gems, silver and gold. **Prices:** $400 to $750; some to $1200. **Remarks:** Full-time maker. **Mark:** Initials.

GREENAWAY, DON
3325 Dinsmore Tr, Fayetteville, AR 72704, Phone: 501-521-0323

Specialties: Liner locks and bowies. **Prices:** $150 to $1500. **Remarks:** 20 years experience. **Mark:** Greenaway over Fayetteville, Ark.

GREENE, CHRIS
707 Cherry Lane, Shelby, NC 28150, Phone: 704-434-5620

GREENE, DAVID
570 Malcom Rd, Covington, GA 30209, Phone: 770-784-0657

Specialties: Straight working using knives. **Patterns:** Hunters. **Technical:** Forges mosaic and twist Damascus. Prefers stag and desert ironwood for handle material.

GREENE, STEVE
DUNN KNIVES INC, PO Box 307 1449 Nocatee St., Intercession City, FL 33848, Phone: 800-245-6483, s.greene@earthlink.net; Web: www.dunnknives.com
Specialties: Skinning & fillet knives. **Patterns:** Skinners, drop points, clip points and fillets. **Technical:** CPM-S30V powdered metal steel manufactured by Niagara Specialty Metals. **Prices:** $100 to $350. **Mark:** Dunn by Greene and year. **Remarks:** Full-time knifemaker. First knife sold in 1972. Each knife is handcrafted and includes holster-grade leather sheath.

GREENFIELD, G O
2605 15th St #310, Everett, WA 98201, Phone: 425-244-2902, garyg1946@yahoo.com
Specialties: High-tech and working straight knives and folders of his design. **Patterns:** Boots, daggers, hunters and one-of-a-kinds. **Technical:** Grinds ATS-34, D2, 440C and T-440V. Makes sheaths for each knife. **Prices:** $100 to $800; some to $10,000. **Remarks:** Part-time maker; first knife sold in 1978. **Mark:** Springfield®, serial number.

GREGORY, MATTHEW M.
74 Tarn Tr., Glenwood, NY 14069, Phone: 716-863-1215, mgregoryknives@yahoo.com; Web: www.mgregoryknives.com
Patterns: Wide variation of styles, as I make what I like to make. Bowies, fighters, Neo-American/Japanese-inspired blades, occasionally kitchen knives. **Technical:** Forging and stock removal, using forging steels such as 1084, 1095, W2 and CruForgeV, as well as high-alloy steels like CPM-3V and CPM-S110V. Hamon (blade temper line) development and polishing. **Prices:** $350 and up. **Remarks:** Part-time maker since 2005. **Mark:** M. Gregory.

GREGORY, MICHAEL
211 Calhoun Rd, Belton, SC 29627, Phone: 864-338-8898, gregom.123@charter.net
Specialties: Interframe folding knives, working hunters and period pieces. Hand rubbed finish, engraving by maker. **Patterns:** Hunters, bowies, daggers and folding knives. **Technical:** Grinds ATS-34 and other makers' damascus. **Prices:** $200 and up. **Remarks:** Full-time maker; first knife sold in 1980. **Mark:** Name, city in logo.

GREINER, RICHARD
1073 E County Rd 32, Green Springs, OH 44836, Phone: 419-483-4613, rgreiner7295@yahoo.com
Specialties: High-carbon steels, edge hardened. **Patterns:** Most. **Technical:** Hand forged. **Prices:** $125 and up. **Remarks:** Have made knives for 30 years. **Mark:** Maple leaf.

GREISS, JOCKL
Herrenwald 15, Schenkenzell, GERMANY 77773, Phone: +49 7836 95 71 69 or +49 7836 95 55 76, www.jocklgreiss@yahoo.com
Specialties: Classic and working using straight knives of his design. **Patterns:** Bowies, daggers and hunters. **Technical:** Uses only Jerry Rados Damascus. All knives are one-of-a-kind made by hand; no machines are used. **Prices:** $700 to $2000; some to $3000. **Remarks:** Full-time maker; first knife sold in 1984. **Mark:** An "X" with a long vertical line through it.

GREY, PIET
PO Box 363, Naboomspruit, LP, SOUTH AFRICA 0560, Phone: 014-743-3613
Specialties: Fancy working and using straight knives of his design. **Patterns:** Fighters, hunters and utility/camp knives. **Technical:** Grinds ATS-34 and AEB-L; forges and grinds Damascus. Solder less fitting of guards. Engraves and scrimshaws. **Prices:** $125 to $750; some to $1500. **Remarks:** Part-time maker; first knife sold in 1970. **Mark:** Last name.

GRIFFIN, RENDON, MARK AND JOHN
9706 Cedardale, Houston, TX 77055, Phone: 713-468-0436, rendon@griffinknives.com
Specialties: Working folders, fixed blades and automatics of their designs. **Patterns:** Standard lockers, fixed blades and slip joints. **Technical:** Most blade steels; stock removal. **Prices:** Start at $450. **Remarks:** Rendon's first knife sold in 1966; Mark's in 1974. **Mark:** Last name logo.

GRIFFIN JR., HOWARD A
14299 SW 31st Ct, Davie, FL 33330, Phone: 954-474-5406, mgriffin18@aol.com
Specialties: Working straight knives and folders. **Patterns:** Hunters, Bowies, locking folders with his own push-button lock design. **Technical:** Grinds 440C. **Prices:** $100 to $200; some to $500. **Remarks:** Part-time maker; first knife sold in 1983. **Mark:** Initials.

GRIMES, MARK
PO BOX 1293, Bedford, TX 76095, Phone: 817-320-7274, ticktock107@gmail.com
Specialties: Qs. **Patterns:** Hunters, fighters, bowies. **Technical:** Custom hand forged 1084 steel blades full and hidden tang, heat treating, sheathes. **Prices:** $150-$400. **Remarks:** Part-time maker, first knife sold in 2009. **Mark:** Last name.

GRIZZARD, JIM
3626 Gunnels Ln., Oxford, AL 36203, Phone: 256-403-1232, grizzardforgiven@aol.com
Specialties: Hand carved art knives inspired by sole authorship. **Patterns:** Fixedblades, folders, and swords. **Technical:** Carving handles, artgrinding, forged and stock removal. **Prices:** Vary. **Remarks:** Uses knives mostly as a ministry to bless others. **Mark:** FOR HIS GLORY CUSTOM KNIVES OR j grizzard in a grizzly bear.

GROSPITCH, ERNIE
18440 Amityville Dr, Orlando, FL 32820, Phone: 407-568-5438, shrpknife@aol.com; Web: www.erniesknives.com
Specialties: Bowies, hunting, fishing, kitchen, lockback folders, leather craft and knifemaker logo stenciling/blue lightning stencil. **Patterns:** My design or customer's.

Technical: Stock removal using most available steels. **Prices:** Vary. **Remarks:** Full-time maker, sold first knife in 1990. **Mark:** Etched name over Thunderbird image.

GROSS, W W
109 Dylan Scott Dr, Archdale, NC 27263-3858
Specialties: Working knives. **Patterns:** Hunters, boots, fighters. **Technical:** Grinds. **Prices:** Moderate. **Remarks:** Full-time maker. **Mark:** Name.

GROSSMAN, STEWART
24 Water St #419, Clinton, MA 01510, Phone: 508-365-2291; 800-mysword
Specialties: Miniatures and full-size knives and swords. **Patterns:** One-of-a-kind miniatures—jewelry, replicas—and wire-wrapped figures. Full-size art, fantasy and combat knives, daggers and modular systems. **Technical:** Forges and grinds most metals and Damascus. Uses gems, crystals, electronics and motorized mechanisms. **Prices:** $20 to $300; some to $4500 and higher. **Remarks:** Full-time maker; first knife sold in 1985. **Mark:** G1.

GRUSSENMEYER, PAUL G
310 Kresson Rd, Cherry Hill, NJ 08034, Phone: 856-428-1088, pgrussentne@comcast.net; Web: www.pgcarvings.com
Specialties: Assembling fancy and fantasy straight knives with his own carved handles. **Patterns:** Bowies, daggers, folders, swords, hunters and miniatures. **Technical:** Uses forged steel and Damascus, stock removal and knapped obsidian blades. **Prices:** $250 to $4000. **Remarks:** Spare-time maker; first knife sold in 1991. **Mark:** First and last initial hooked together on handle.

GUARNERA, ANTHONY R
42034 Quail Creek Dr, Quartzhill, CA 93536, Phone: 661-722-4032
Patterns: Hunters, camp, Bowies, kitchen, fighter knives. **Technical:** Forged and stock removal. **Prices:** $100 and up.

GUINN, TERRY
13026 Hwy 6 South, Eastland, TX 76448, Phone: 254-629-8603, Web: www.terryguinn.com
Specialties: Working fixed blades and balisongs. **Patterns:** Almost all types of folding and fixed blades, from patterns and "one of a kind". **Technical:** Stock removal all types of blade steel with preference for air hardening steel. Does own heat treating, all knives Rockwell tested in shop. **Prices:** $200 to $2,000. **Remarks:** Part time maker since 1982, sold first knife 1990. **Mark:** Full name with cross in the middle.

GUNTER, BRAD
13 Imnaha Rd., Tijeras, NM 87059, Phone: 505-281-8080

GUNTHER, EDDIE
11 Nedlands Pl Burswood, Auckland, NEW ZEALAND 2013, Phone: 006492722373, eddit.gunther49@gmail.com
Specialties: Drop point hunters, boot, Bowies. All mirror finished. **Technical:** Grinds D2, 440C, 12c27. **Prices:** $250 to $800. **Remarks:** Part-time maker, first knife sold in 1986. **Mark:** Name, city, country.

H

HAAS, RANDY
HHH Knives, 6518 Chard St., Marlette, MI 48453, Phone: 989-635-7059, Web: www.hhhcustomknives.com
Specialties: Handmade custom kitchen and culinary knives, hunters, fighters, folders and art knives. **Technical:** Damascus maker and sales. **Remarks:** Full-time maker for 10 years. **Mark:** Three H's with a knife behind the HHH.

HACKNEY, DANA A.
33 Washington St., Monument, CO 80132, Phone: 719-481-3940; Cell: 719-651-5634, danahackneyknives@gmail.com and dshackney@Q.com; Web: www.hackneycustomknives.com
Specialties: Hunters, bowies and everyday carry knives, and some kitchen cutlery. **Technical:** ABS journeyman smith who forges 1080 series, 5160, 52100, 01, W2 and his own damascus. Uses CPM-154 mostly for stainless knives. **Prices:** $150 and up. **Remarks:** Sole ownership knives and sheaths. Full-time maker as of July 2012. Sold first knife in 2005. ABS, MKA and PKA member. **Mark:** Last name, HACKNEY on left-side ricasso.

HAGEN, DOC
PO Box 58, 41780 Kansas Point Ln, Pelican Rapids, MN 56572, Phone: 218-863-8503, dochagen@gmail.com; Web: www.dochagencustomknives.com
Specialties: Folders. Autos:bolster release-dual action. Slipjoint folders**Patterns:** Defense-related straight knives; wide variety of folders. **Technical:** Dual action release, bolster release autos. **Prices:** $300 to $800; some to $3000. **Remarks:** Full-time maker; first knife sold in 1975. Makes his own Damascus. **Mark:** DOC HAGEN in shield, knife, banner logo; or DOC.

HAGGERTY, GEORGE S
PO Box 88, Jacksonville, VT 05342, Phone: 802-368-7437, swewater@sover.net
Specialties: Working straight knives and folders. **Patterns:** Hunters, claws, camp and fishing knives, locking folders and backpackers. **Technical:** Forges and grinds W2, 440C and 154CM. **Prices:** $85 to $300. **Remarks:** Part-time maker; first knife sold in 1981. **Mark:** Initials or last name.

HAGUE, GEOFF
Unit 5, Project Workshops, Lains Farm, Quarley, Hampshire, UNITED KINGDOM SP11 8PX, Phone: (+44) 01672-870212, Fax: (+44) 01672 870212, geoff@hagueknives.com; Web: www.hagueknives.com

Specialties: Fixed blade and folding knives. **Patterns:** Back lock, locking liner, slip joint, and friction folders. **Technical:** Grinds D2, RWL-34 and damascus. Mainly natural handle materials. **Prices:** $500 to $2,000. **Remarks:** Full-time maker. **Mark:** Last name.

HAINES, JEFF
Haines Custom Knives, W3678 Bay View Rd., Mayville, WI 53050, Phone: 920-387-0212, knifeguy95@gmail.com; Web: www.hainescustom.com
Patterns: Hunters, skinners, camp knives, customer designs welcome. **Technical:** Forges 1095, 5160, and Damascus, grinds A2. **Prices:** $75 and up. **Remarks:** Part-time maker since 1995. **Mark:** Last name.

HALE, LLOYD
7593 Beech Hill Rd., Pulaski, TN 38478, Phone: 931-424-5846, lloydahale@gmail.com
Specialties: Museum-grade, one-of-a-kind daggers, folders and sub-hilt fighting knives. **Remarks:** Full-time maker for 44+ years. Spent 20+ years creating a one-of-a-kind knife collection for Owsley Brown Frazier of Louisville, KY. I don't accept orders anymore.

HALFRICH, JERRY
340 Briarwood, San Marcos, TX 78666, Phone: 512-353-2582, jerryhalfrich@grandecom.net; Web: www.halfrichknives.com
Specialties: Working straight and specialty utility knives for the professional and serious hunter. Uses proven designs in both straight and folding knives. Pays close attention to fit and finish. Art knives on special request. **Patterns:** Hunters, skinners, and lockback, LinerLock and slip-joint folders. **Technical:** Grinds both flat and hollow D2, Damasteel and CPM 154, makes high precision folders. **Prices:** $450 to $1,500. **Remarks:** Full-time maker since 2000. DBA Halfrich Custom Knives. **Mark:** HALFRICH.

HALL, JEFF
179 Niblick Rd, # 180, Paso Robles, CA 93446, Phone: 562-594-4740, info@nemesis-knives.com; Web: nemisis-knives.com
Specialties: Collectible and working folders and fixed blades of his design. **Technical:** Grinds CPM-S35VN, CPM-154, and various makers' damascus. **Patterns:** Fighters, gentleman's, hunters and utility knives. **Prices:** $100 and up. **Remarks:** Full-time maker. First knife sold 1998. **Mark:** Last name.

HALL, KEN
606 Stevenson Cove Rd., Waynesville, NC 28785, Phone: 828-627-2135, khall@hallenergyconsulting.com; Web: http://www.hallenergyconsulting.com/KHKindex.html
Specialties: Standard and one-of-a-kind fixed-blade knives with leather sheaths. **Patterns:** Hunters, bowies, fighters, chef's knives and tantos. **Technical:** Forges high-carbon steel, flat grinds. **Prices:** $150 to $700+. **Remarks:** Part-time maker; first knives sold in 2010. **Mark:** Etched "Ken Hall" or "KHall JS."

HALL, SCOTT M.
5 Hickory Hts., Geneseo, IL 61254, Phone: 309-945-2184, smhall@theinter.com; www.hallcustomknives.com
Specialties: Fixed-blade, hollow-ground working knives of his own design and to customer specs. **Patterns:** Designs catering to soldiers and outdoorsmen, including variations of hunters, bowies, fighters and occasionally fillet and kitchen knives. **Technical:** Usually grinds CPM S30V and 154CM, but uses other steels upon request. Handle materials include G-10, Micarta, stag, horn and exotic woods. Most knives are offered with hand-tooled and stitched leather sheaths or Spec Ops sheaths. **Prices:** $150 to $350+. **Remarks:** Part-time maker; first knife sold in 2000. **Mark:** Last name.

HALLIGAN, ED
3434 Sun Lit Grove, San Antonio, TX 78247, Phone: 210-912-8167, beano101010@yahoo.com
Specialties: Working straight knives and folders, some fancy. **Patterns:** Liner locks, hunters, skinners, boots, fighters and swords. **Technical:** Grinds ATS-34; forges 5160; makes cable and pattern Damascus. **Prices:** $160 to $2500. **Remarks:** Full-time maker; first knife sold in 1985. Doing business as Halligan Knives. **Mark:** Last name, city, state and USA.

HAMLET JR., JOHNNY
300 Billington, Clute, TX 77531, Phone: 979-265-6929, nifeman@swbell.net; Web: www.hamlets-handmade-knives.com
Specialties: Working straight knives and folders. **Patterns:** Hunters, fighters, fillet and kitchen knives, locking folders. Likes upswept knives and trailing-points. **Technical:** Grinds 440C, D2, ATS-34. Makes sheaths. **Prices:** $125 and up. **Remarks:** Full-time maker; sold first knife in 1988. **Mark:** Hamlet's Handmade in script.

HAMMOND, HANK
189 Springlake Dr, Leesburg, GA 31763, Phone: 229-434-1295, godogs57@bellsouth.net
Specialties: Traditional hunting and utility knives of his design. Will also design and produce knives to customer's specifications. **Patterns:** Straight or sheath knives, hunters skinners as well as Bowies and fighters. **Technical:** Grinds (hollow and flat grinds) CPM 154CM, ATS-34. Also uses Damascus and forges 52100. Offers filework on blades. Handle materials include all exotic woods, red stag, sambar stag, deer, elk, oosic, bone, fossil ivory, Micarta, etc. All knives come with sheath handmade for that individual knife. **Prices:** $100 up to $500. **Remarks:** Part-time maker. Sold first knife in 1981. Doing business as Double H Knives. **Mark:** "HH" inside 8 point deer rack.

HAMMOND, JIM
PO Box 486, Arab, AL 35016, Phone: 256-586-4151, hammondj@otelco.net; Web: www.jimhammondknives.com
Specialties: High-tech fighters and folders. **Patterns:** Proven-design fighters. **Technical:**

Grinds 440C, 440V, S30V and other specialty steels. **Prices:** $385 to $1200; some to $9200. **Remarks:** Full-time maker; first knife sold in 1977. Designer for Columbia River Knife and Tool. **Mark:** Full name, city, state in shield logo.

HAMMOND, RAY
POB 963, Buford, GA 30515, Phone: 678-300-2883, rayhammond01@yahoo.com; Web: www.biggamehuntingblades.com
Specialties: Fixed blades, primarily hunting knives, utility knives and bowies. **Technical:** Stock removal and forged blades, including 5160, 1095, CPM-154 and damascus blade steels. **Prices:** Start at $300. **Remarks:** Part-time maker; first knife built in 2008. **Mark:** Capital letters RH surrounded by a broken circle, pierced by a knife silhouette, atop the circle is my name, and below the circle the words "custom knives." Will soon alter this to simply my last name.

HANCOCK, TIM
29125 N. 153rd St., Scottsdale, AZ 85262, Phone: 480-998-8849, westernbladesmith@gmail.com
Specialties: High-art and working straight knives and folders of his design and to customer preferences. **Patterns:** Bowies, fighters, daggers, tantos, swords, folders. **Technical:** Forges damascus and 52100; grinds ATS-34. Makes damascus. Silver-wire inlays; offers carved fittings and file work. **Prices:** $500 to $20,000. **Remarks:** Full-time maker; first knife sold in 1988. ABS master smith. **Mark:** Last name or heart.

HAND, BILL
PO Box 717, 1103 W. 7th St., Spearman, TX 79081, Phone: 806-659-2967, Fax: 806-659-5139, klinker43@yahoo.com
Specialties: Traditional working and using straight knives and folders of his design or to customer specs. **Patterns:** Hunters, Bowies, folders and fighters. **Technical:** Forges 5160, 52100 and Damascus. **Prices:** Start at $150. **Remarks:** Part-time maker; Journeyman Smith. Current delivery time 12 to 16 months. **Mark:** Stylized initials.

HANKALA, JUKKA
Tuhkurintie 225, 39580 Riitiala, FINLAND, Phone: +358-400-684-625, jukka@hankala.com; www.hankala.com
Specialties: Traditional puukkos and maker's own knife models. **Patterns:** Maker's own puukko models, hunters, folders and ART-knives. **Technical:** Forges Silversteel, Bohler K510, Damasteel stainless damascus and RWL-34 blade steels, as well as his own 15N20-and-1.2842 damascus, mosaic damascus and color damascus. **Prices:** Start at $300. **Remarks:** Full-time maker since 1985. **Mark:** J. Hankala.

HANSEN, LONNIE
PO Box 4956, Spanaway, WA 98387, Phone: 253-847-4632, lonniehansen@msn.com; Web: lchansen.com
Specialties: Working straight knives of his design. **Patterns:** Tomahawks, tantos, hunters, fillet. **Technical:** Forges 1086, 52100, grinds 440V, BG-42. **Prices:** Starting at $300. **Remarks:** Part-time maker since 1989. **Mark:** First initial and last name. Also first and last initial.

HANSEN, ROBERT W
35701 University Ave NE, Cambridge, MN 55008, Phone: 763-689-3242
Specialties: Working straight knives, folders and integrals. **Patterns:** From hunters to minis, camp knives to miniatures; folding lockers and slip-joints in original styles. **Technical:** Grinds O1, 440C and 154CM; likes filework. **Prices:** $100 to $450; some to $600. **Remarks:** Part-time maker; first knife sold in 1983. **Mark:** Fish w/h inside surrounded by Bob Hansen maker.

HANSON III, DON L.
PO Box 13, Success, MO 65570-0013, Phone: 573-674-3045, Web: www.sunfishforge.com; Web: www.donhansonknives.com
Specialties: One-of-a-kind damascus folders, slip joints and forged fixed blades. **Patterns:** Small, fancy pocket knives, large folding fighters and Bowies. **Technical:** Forges own pattern welded Damascus, file work and carving also carbon steel blades with hamons. **Prices:** $800 and up. **Remarks:** Full-time maker, first knife sold in 1984. ABS mastersmith. **Mark:** Sunfish.

HARA, KOJI
292-2 Osugi, Seki-City, Gifu, JAPAN 501-3922, Phone: 0575-24-7569, Fax: 0575-24-7569, info@knifehousehara.com; Web: www.knifehousehara.com
Specialties: High-tech and working straight knives of his design; some folders. **Patterns:** Hunters, locking folders and utility/camp knives. **Technical:** Grinds Cowry X, Cowry Y and ATS-34. Prefers high mirror polish; pearl handle inlay. **Prices:** $400 to $2500. **Remarks:** Full-time maker; first knife sold in 1980. Doing business as Knife House "Hara." **Mark:** First initial, last name in fish.

HARDING, CHAD
12365 Richland Ln, Solsberry, IN 47459, hardingknives@yahoo.com; www.hardingknives.net
Specialties: Hunters and camp knives, occasional fighters or bowies. No folders. **Technical:** Hand forge 90% of work. Prefer 10XX steels and tool steels. Makes own damascus and cable and chainsaw chain damascus. 100% sole authorship on knives and sheaths. Mostly natural handle material, prefer wood and stag. **Prices:** $150 to $1,000. **Remarks:** Part-time maker, member of ABS. First knife sold in 2005. **Mark:** Last name.

HARDY, DOUGLAS E
114 Cypress Rd, Franklin, GA 30217, Phone: 706-675-6305

HARDY, SCOTT
639 Myrtle Ave, Placerville, CA 95667, Phone: 530-622-5780, Web: www.innercite.com/~shardy

Specialties: Traditional working and using straight knives of his design. **Patterns:** Most anything with an edge. **Technical:** Forges carbon steels. Japanese stone polish. Offers mirror finish; differentially tempers. **Prices:** $100 to $1000. **Remarks:** Part-time maker; first knife sold in 1982. **Mark:** First initial, last name and Handmade with bird logo.

HARKINS, J A
PO Box 218, Conner, MT 59827, Phone: 406-821-1060, kutter@customknives.net; Web: customknives.net

Specialties: OTFs. **Patterns:** OTFs, Automatics, Folders. **Technical:** Grinds ATS-34. Engraves; offers gem work. **Prices:** $1500 and up. **Remarks:** Celebrating 20th year as full-time maker . **Mark:** First and middle initials, last name.

HARLEY, LARRY W
348 Deerfield Dr, Bristol, TN 37620, Phone: 423-878-5368 (shop); cell: 423-530-1133, Web: www.lonesomepineknives.com

Specialties: One-of-a-kind Persian in one-of-a-kind Damascus. Working knives, period pieces. **Technical:** Forges and grinds ATS-34, 440c, L6, 15, 20, 1084, and 52100. **Patterns:** Full range of straight knives, tomahawks, razors, buck skinners and hog spears. **Prices:** $200 and up. **Mark:** Pine tree.

HARLEY, RICHARD
348 Deerfield Dr, Bristol, TN 37620, Phone: 423-878-5368; cell: 423-408-5720

Specialties: Hunting knives, Bowies, friction folders, one-of-a-kind. **Technical:** Forges 1084, S160, 52100, Lg. **Prices:** $150 to $1000. **Mark:** Pine tree with name.

HARM, PAUL W
818 Young Rd, Attica, MI 48412, Phone: 810-724-5582, harm@blclinks.net

Specialties: Early American working knives. **Patterns:** Hunters, skinners, patch knives, fighters, folders. **Technical:** Forges and grinds 1084, O1, 52100 and own Damascus. **Prices:** $75 to $1000. **Remarks:** First knife sold in 1990. **Mark:** Connected initials.

HARNER III, "BUTCH" LLOYD R.
745 Kindig Rd., Littlestown, PA 17340, butch@harnerknives.com; Web: www.harnerknives.com

Specialties: Kitchen knives and straight razors. **Technical:** CPM-3V, CPM-154 and various Carpenter powdered steel alloys. **Remarks:** Full-time maker since 2007. **Mark:** L.R. Harner (2005-Sept. 2012) and Harner III (after Oct. 2012)

HARRINGTON, ROGER
P.O. Box 157, Battle, East Sussex, ENGLAND TN 33 3 DD, Phone: 0854-838-7062, info@bisonbushcraft.co.uk; Web: www.bisonbushcraft.co.uk

Specialties: Working straight knives to his or customer's designs, flat saber Scandinavia-style grinds on full tang knives, also hollow and convex grinds. **Technical:** Grinds O1, D2, Damascus. **Prices:** $200 to $800. **Remarks:** First knife made by hand in 1997 whilst traveling around the world. **Mark:** Bison with bison written under.

HARRIS, CASS
19855 Fraiser Hill Ln, Bluemont, VA 20135, Phone: 540-554-8774, Web: www.tdogforge.com

Prices: $160 to $500.

HARRIS, JAY
991 Johnson St, Redwood City, CA 94061, Phone: 415-366-6077

Specialties: Traditional high-tech straight knives and folders of his design. **Patterns:** Daggers, fighters and locking folders. **Technical:** Uses 440C, ATS-34 and CPM. **Prices:** $250 to $850. **Remarks:** Spare-time maker; first knife sold in 1980.

HARRIS, JOHN
14131 Calle Vista, Riverside, CA 92508, Phone: 951-653-2755, johnharrisknives@yahoo.com

Specialties: Hunters, daggers, Bowies, bird and trout, period pieces, Damascus and carbon steel knives, forged and stock removal. **Prices:** $200 to $1000.

HARRIS, RALPH DEWEY
2607 Bell Shoals Rd, Brandon, FL 33511, Phone: 813-681-5293, Fax: 813-654-8175

Specialties: Collector quality interframe folders. **Patterns:** High tech locking folders of his own design with various mechanisms. **Technical:** Grinds 440C, ATS-34 and commercial Damascus. Offers various frame materials including 416ss, and titanium; file worked frames and his own engraving. **Prices:** $400 to $3000. **Remarks:** Full-time maker; first knife sold in 1978. **Mark:** Last name, or name and city.

HARRISON, BRIAN
BFH KNIVES, 2359 E Swede Rd, Cedarville, MI 49719, Phone: 906-430-0720, bfh_knives@yahoo.com

Specialties: High grade fixed blade knives. **Patterns:** Many sizes & variety of patterns from small pocket carries to large combat and camp knives. Mirror and bead blast finishes. All handles of high grade materials from ivory to highly figured stabilized woods to stag, deer & moose horn and Micarta. Hand sewn fancy sheaths for pocket or belt. **Technical:** Flat & hollow grinds usually ATS-34 but some O1, L6 and stellite 6K. **Prices:** $150 to $1200. **Remarks:** Full-time maker, sole authorship. Made first knife in 1980, sold first knife in 1999. Received much knowledge from the following makers: George Young, Eric Erickson, Webster Wood, Ed Kalfayan who are all generous men. **Mark:** Engraved blade outline w/BFH Knives over the top edge, signature across middle & Cedarville, MI underneath.

HARRISON, JIM (SEAMUS)
721 Fairington View Dr, St. Louis, MO 63129, Phone: 314-894-2525, jrh@seamusknives.com; Web: www.seamusknives.com

Specialties: "Crossover" folders, liner-locks and frame-locks. **Patterns:** Uber, Author, Skyy Folders, Grant Survivor, Fixed blade. **Technical:** Use CPM S30V and 154, Stellite 6k

and S.S. Damascus by Norris, Thomas and Damasteel. **Prices:** Folders $375 to $1,000. **Remarks:** Full-time maker since 2008, Maker since 1999. **Mark:** Seamus

HARSEY, WILLIAM H
82710 N. Howe Ln, Creswell, OR 97426, Phone: 541-510-8707, billharsey@gmail.com

Specialties: High-tech kitchen and outdoor knives. **Patterns:** Folding hunters, trout and bird folders; straight hunters, camp knives and axes. **Technical:** Grinds; etches. **Prices:** $125 to $300; some to $1500. Folders start at $350. **Remarks:** Full-time maker; first knife sold in 1979. **Mark:** Full name, state, U.S.A.

HART, BILL
647 Cedar Dr, Pasadena, MD 21122, Phone: 410-255-4981

Specialties: Fur-trade era working straight knives and folders. **Patterns:** Springback folders, skinners, Bowies and patch knives. **Technical:** Forges and stock removes 1095 and 5160 wire Damascus. **Prices:** $100 to $600. **Remarks:** Part-time maker; first knife sold in 1986. **Mark:** Name.

HARTMAN, ARLAN (LANNY)
6102 S Hamlin Cir, Baldwin, MI 49304, Phone: 231-745-4029

Specialties: Working straight knives and folders. **Patterns:** Drop-point hunters, coil spring lockers, slip-joints. **Technical:** Flat-grinds D2, 440C and ATS-34. **Prices:** $300 to $2000. **Remarks:** Part-time maker; first knife sold in 1982. **Mark:** Last name.

HARTMAN, TIM
3812 Pedroncelli Rd NW, Albuquerque, NM 87107, Phone: 505-385-6924, tbonz1@comcast.net

Specialties: Exotic wood scales, sambar stag, filework, hunters. **Patterns:** Fixed blade hunters, skinners, utility and hiking. **Technical:** 154CM, Ats-34 and D2. Mirror finish and contoured scales. **Prices:** Start at $200-$450. **Remarks:** Started making knives in 2004. **Mark:** 3 lines Ti Hartman, Maker, Albuquerque NM

HARVEY, HEATHER
HEAVIN FORGE, PO Box 768, Belfast, MP, SOUTH AFRICA 1100, Phone: 27-13-253-0914, heather@heavinforge.co.za; Web: www.heavinforge.co.za

Specialties: Integral hand forged knives, traditional African weapons, primitive folders and by-gone forged-styles. **Patterns:** All forged knives, war axes, spears, arrows, forks, spoons, and swords. **Technical:** Own carbon Damascus and mokume. Also forges stainless, brass, copper and titanium. Traditional forging and heat-treatment methods used. **Prices:** $300 to $5000, average $1000. **Remarks:** Full-time maker and knifemaking instructor. Master bladesmith with ABS. First Damascus sold in 1995, first knife sold in 1998. Often collaborate with husband, Kevin (ABS MS) using the logo "Heavin." **Mark:** First name and sur name, oval shape with "M S" in middle.

HARVEY, KEVIN
HEAVIN FORGE, PO Box 768, Belfast, LP, SOUTH AFRICA 1100, Phone: 27-13-253-0914, info@heavinforge.co.za Web: www.heavinforge.co.za

Specialties: Large knives of presentation quality and creative art knives. **Patterns:** Fixed blades of Bowie, dagger and fighter-styles, occasionally folders and swords. **Technical:** Stock removal of stainless and forging of carbon steel and own Damascus. Indigenous African handle materials preferred. Own engraving Often collaborate with wife, Heather (ABS MS) under the logo "Heavin." **Prices:** $500 to $5000 average $1500. **Remarks:** Full-time maker and knifemaking instructor. Master bladesmith with ABS. First knife sold in 1984. **Mark:** First name and surnname, oval with "M S" in the middle.

HARVEY, MAX
6 Winchester Way, Leeming, Perth, Western Australia 6149, AUSTRALIA, Phone: 61 (8) 93101103 or 61-478-633-356, mcharveyknives@outlook.com; http://mcharveycustomknives.com/wordpress/?page_id=84

Specialties: Fixed-blade knives of all styles. **Patterns:** Camp knives, skinners, bowies, daggers and high-end art knives. **Technical:** Stock-removal using ATS-34, 154CM, 440C and damascus. Do all my own faceting of gem stones in the high-end knives. **Prices:** $250 to $5,000. **Remarks:** Full-time maker; first knife sold in 1981, and founding member of the Australian Knife Makers Guild. **Mark:** First and middle initials, and surname (M C Harvey).

HARVEY, MEL
P.O. Box 176, Nenana, AK 99760, Phone: 907-832-5660, tinker1@nenana.net

Specialties: Fixed blade knives for hunting and fishing. **Patterns:** Hunters, skinners. **Technical:** Stock removal on ATS-34, 440C, 01, 1095; Damascus blades using 1095 and 15N20. **Prices:** Starting at $350. **Remarks:** ABS member, attended Bill Moran School; 50+ knives sold since 2007. **Mark:** Mel Harvey over serial number over Nenana, AK.

HASLINGER, THOMAS
6460 Woodland Dr., British Columbia V1B 3G7, CANADA, Phone: 250-558-9962, Web: www.haslinger-knives.com; www.haslinger-culinary.com

Specialties: One-of-a-kind using, working and art knives HCK signature sweeping grind lines. Maker of New Generation and Evolution Chef series. Differential heat treated stainless steel. **Patterns:** Likes to work with customers on design. **Technical:** Grinds various specialty alloys, including Damascus, High end satin finish. Prefers natural handle materials e.g. ancient ivory stag, pearl, abalone, stone and exotic woods. Does inlay work with stone, some sterling silver, niobium and gold wire work. Custom sheaths using matching woods or hand stitched with unique leather. Offers engraving. **Prices:** $300 and up. **Remarks:** Full-time maker; first knife sold in 1994. Doing business as Haslinger Custom Knives. **Mark:** Two marks used, high end work uses stylized initials, other uses elk antler with Thomas Haslinger, Canada, handcrafted above.

HAWES, CHUCK
HAWES FORGE, PO Box 176, Weldon, IL 61882, Phone: 217-736-2479

Specialties: 95 percent of all work in own Damascus. **Patterns:** Slip-joints liner locks, hunters, Bowie's, swords, anything in between. **Technical:** Forges everything, uses all high-carbon steels, no stainless. **Prices:** $150 to $4000. **Remarks:** Like to do custom orders, his style or yours. Sells Damascus. Full-time maker since 1995. **Mark:** Small football shape. Chuck Hawes maker Weldon, IL.

HAWK, GRANT AND GAVIN
Box 401, Idaho City, ID 83631, Phone: 208-392-4911, blademaker25@msn.com; www.hawkknifedesigns.com
Specialties: Large folders with unique locking systems, D.O.G. lock, toad lock. **Technical:** Grinds ATS-34, titanium folder parts. **Prices:** $450 and up. **Remarks:** Full-time maker. **Mark:** First initials and last names.

HAWKINS, BUDDY
PO Box 5969, Texarkana, TX 75505-5969, Phone: 903-838-7917, buddyhawkins@cableone.net

HAWKINS, RADE
110 Buckeye Rd, Fayetteville, GA 30214, Phone: 770-964-1177, radeh@bellsouth.net; Web: wwwhawkinscustomknives.com
Specialties: All styles. **Patterns:** All styles. **Technical:** Grinds and forges. Makes own Damascus **Prices:** Start at $190. **Remarks:** Full-time maker; first knife sold in 1972. Member knifemakers guild, ABS Journeyman Smith. **Mark:** Rade Hawkins Custom Knives.

HAWKINS JR., CHARLES R.
2764 Eunice, San Angelo, TX 76901, Phone: 325-947-7875, chawk12354@aol.com; Web: www.hawkcustomknives.com
Specialties: Custom knives, fixed blades, railroad spike knives and rasp file knives. **Technical:** Stock removal and some forging, using 1095 and 440C steel. **Prices:** $135 and up. **Remarks:** Part-time maker; first knife sold in 2008. **Mark:** Full name, city and state.

HAYES, WALLY
9960, 9th Concession, RR#1, Essex, ON, CANADA N8M-2X5, Phone: 519-776-1284, Web: www.hayesknives.com
Specialties: Classic and fancy straight knives and folders. **Patterns:** Daggers, Bowies, fighters, tantos. **Technical:** Forges own Damascus and O1; engraves. **Prices:** $150 to $14,000. **Mark:** Last name, M.S. and serial number.

HAYNES, JERRY
260 Forest Meadow Dr, Gunter, TX 75058, Phone: 903-433-1424, jhaynes@arrow-head.com; Web: http://www.arrow-head.com
Specialties: Working straight knives and folders of his design, also historical blades. **Patterns:** Hunters, skinners, carving knives, fighters, renaissance daggers, locking folders and kitchen knives. **Technical:** Grinds ATS-34, CPM, Stellite 6K, D2 and acquired Damascus. Prefers exotic handle materials. Has B.A. in design. Studied with R. Buckminster Fuller. **Prices:** $200 to $1200. **Remarks:** Part-time maker. First knife sold in 1953. **Mark:** Arrowhead and last name.

HAYS, MARK
HAYS HANDMADE KNIVES, 1008 Kavanagh Dr., Austin, TX 78748, Phone: 512-292-4410, markhays@austin.rr.com
Specialties: Working straight knives and folders. Patterns inspired by Randall and Stone. **Patterns:** Bowies, hunters and slip-joint folders. **Technical:** 440C stock removal. Repairs and restores Stone knives. **Prices:** Start at $200. **Remarks:** Part-time maker, brochure available, with Stone knives 1974-1983, 1990-1991. **Mark:** First initial, last name, state and serial number.

HEADRICK, GARY
122 Wilson Blvd, Juan Les Pins, FRANCE 06160, Phone: 033 610282885, headrickgary@wanadoo.fr; Web: couteaux-scrimshaw.com
Specialties: Hi-tech folders with natural furnishings. Back lock & back spring. **Patterns:** Damascus and mokumes. **Technical:** Self made Damascus all steel (no nickel). All chassis titanium. **Prices:** $500 to $2000. **Remarks:** Full-time maker for last 7 years. German Guild-French Federation. 10 years active. **Mark:** HEADRICK on ricosso is new marking.

HEANEY, JOHN D
9 Lefe Court, Haines City, FL 33844, Phone: 863-422-5823, jdh199@msn.com; Web: www.heaneyknives.com
Specialties: Forged 5160, O1 and Damascus. Prefers using natural handle material such as bone, stag and oosic. Plans on using some of the various ivories on future knives. **Prices:** $250 and up.**Remarks:** ABS member. Received journeyman smith stamp in June. **Mark:** Heaney JS.

HEARD, TOM
Turning Point Knives, 2240 Westwood Dr., Waldorf, MD 20601, Phone: 301-843-8626; cell: 301-752-1944, turningpointknives@comcast.net
Specialties: Gent's working/using LinerLock folders of his design. Standard handle materials, as well as mammoth ivory, bone and stabilized wood. **Patterns:** Fixed blades of varying styles, folders and neck knives. **Technical:** Flat grinds 1095, O1, damascus and 154CM. Offers acid-etched blade embellishments, scrimshaw and hand-tooled custom leather sheaths. Does own heat-treating. **Prices:** $100 to $600. **Remarks:** Full-time maker since retiring; first knife sold in 2012. **Mark:** TH over last name.

HEASMAN, H G
28 St Mary's Rd, Llandudno, N. Wales, UNITED KINGDOM LL302UB, Phone: (UK)0492-876351
Specialties: Miniatures only. **Patterns:** Bowies, daggers and swords. **Technical:** Files

from stock high-carbon and stainless steel. **Prices:** $400 to $600. **Remarks:** Part-time maker; first knife sold in 1975. Doing business as Reduced Reality. **Mark:** NA.

HEATH, WILLIAM
PO Box 131, Bondville, IL 61815, Phone: 217-863-2576
Specialties: Classic and working straight knives, folders. **Patterns:** Hunters and Bowies LinerLock® folders. **Technical:** Grinds ATS-34, 440C, 154CM, Damascus, handle materials Micarta, woods to exotic materials snake skins cobra, rattle snake, African flower snake. Does own heat treating. **Prices:** $75 to $300 some $1000. **Remarks:** Full-time maker. First knife sold in 1979. **Mark:** W. D. HEATH.

HEBEISEN, JEFF
310 19th Ave N, Hopkins, MN 55343, Phone: 952-935-4506, jhebeisen@peoplepc.com
Specialties: One of a kind fixed blade of any size up to 16". **Patterns:** Miniature, Hunters, Skinners, Daggers, Bowies, Fighters and Neck knives. **Technical:** Stock removal using CPM-154, D2, 440C. Handle mterial varies depending on intended use, mostly natural materials such as bone, horn, antler, and wood. Filework on many. Heavy duty sheaths made to fit. **Prices:** From $100 to $750. **Remarks:** Full-time maker. First knife sold in 2007. **Mark:** Started new mark in 2012: J. Hebeisen, Hopkins, MN. Older mark: arched name over buffalo skull.

HEDGES, DEE
192 Carradine Rd., Bedfordale, WA, AUSTRALIA 6112, dark_woods_forge@yahoo.com.au; Web: www.darkwoodsforge.com
Patterns: Makes any and all patterns and style of blades from working blades to swords to Japanese inspired. Favors exotic and artistic variations and unique one-off pieces. **Technical:** Forges all blades from a range of steels, favoring 1084, W2, 52100, 5160 and Damascus steels she makes from a 1084/15n20 mix. **Prices:** Start at $200. **Remarks:** Full-time bladesmith and jeweller. Started making blades professionally in 1999, earning my Journeyman Smith rating in 2010. **Mark:** "Dark Woods" atop an ivy leaf, with "Forge" underneath.

HEDLUND, ANDERS
Samstad 400, Brastad, SWEDEN 45491, Phone: 46-523-139 48, anderskniv@passagen.se; Web: http://hem.passagen.se/anderskniv
Specialties: Fancy high-end collectible folders, high-end collectible Nordic hunters with leather carvings on the sheath. Carvings combine traditional designs with own designs. **Patterns:** Own designs. **Technical:** Grinds most steels, but prefers mosaic Damascus and RWL-34. Prefers mother-of-pearl, mammoth, and mosaic steel for folders. Prefers desert ironwood, mammoth, stabilized arctic birch, willow burl, and Damascus steel or RWL-34 for stick tang knives. **Prices:** Starting at $750 for stick tang knives and staring at $1500 for folders. **Remarks:** Part-time maker, first knife sold in 1988. Nordic champion (five countries) several times and Swedish champion 20 times in different classes. **Mark:** Stylized initials or last name.

HEDRICK, DON
131 Beechwood Hills, Newport News, VA 23608, Phone: 757-877-8100, donaldhedrick@cox.net; Web: www.donhedrickknives.com
Specialties: Working straight knives; period pieces and fantasy knives. **Patterns:** Hunters, boots, Bowies and miniatures. **Technical:** Grinds 440C and commercial Damascus. Also makes micro-mini Randall replicas. **Prices:** $150 to $550; some $1200. **Remarks:** Part-time maker; first knife sold in 1982. **Mark:** First initial, last name in oval logo.

HEFLIN, CHRISTOPHER M
6013 Jocely Hollow Rd, Nashville, TN 37205, Phone: 615-352-3909, blix@bellsouth.net

HEGE, JOHN B.
P.O. Box 316, Danbury, NC 27106, Phone: 336-593-8324, jbhege@embarqmail.com; www.jbhegecustomknives.com
Specialties: Period-style knives and traditional bowies, utility hunters and fancy pieces. **Technical:** Forges larger pieces and often uses stock removal for knives 6 inches and smaller. **Remarks:** ABS journeyman smith since 2013.

HEGWALD, J L
1106 Charles, Humboldt, KS 66748, Phone: 316-473-3523
Specialties: Working straight knives, some fancy. **Patterns:** Makes Bowies, miniatures. **Technical:** Forges or grinds O1, L6, 440C; mixes materials in handles. **Prices:** $35 to $200; some higher. **Remarks:** Part-time maker; first knife sold in 1983. **Mark:** First and middle initials.

HEHN, RICHARD KARL
Lehnmuehler Str 1, Dorrebach, GERMANY 55444, Phone: 06724 3152
Specialties: High-tech, full integral working knives. **Patterns:** Hunters, fighters and daggers. **Technical:** Grinds CPM T-440V, CPM T-420V, forges his own stainless Damascus. **Prices:** $1000 to $10,000. **Remarks:** Full-time maker; first knife sold in 1963. **Mark:** Runic last initial in logo.

HEIMDALE, J E
7749 E 28 CT, Tulsa, OK 74129, Phone: 918-640-0784, heimdale@sbcglobal.net
Specialties: Art knives **Patterns:** Bowies, daggers **Technical:** Makes allcomponents and handles - exotic woods and sheaths. Uses Damascus blades by other Blademakers, notably R.W. Wilson. **Prices:** $300 and up. **Remarks:** Part-time maker. First knife sold in 1999. **Marks:** JEHCO

HEINZ, JOHN
611 Cafferty Rd, Upper Black Eddy, PA 18972, Phone: 610-847-8535, Web: www.herugrim.com

Specialties: Historical pieces / copies. **Technical:** Makes his own steel. **Prices:** $150 to $800. **Mark:** "H."

HEITLER, HENRY
8106 N Albany, Tampa, FL 33604, Phone: 813-933-1645
Specialties: Traditional working and using straight knives of his design and to customer specs. **Patterns:** Fighters, hunters, utility/camp knives and fillet knives. **Technical:** Flat-grinds ATS-34; offers tapered tangs. **Prices:** $135 to $450; some to $600. **Remarks:** Part-time maker; first knife sold in 1990. **Mark:** First initial, last name, city, state circling double H's.

HELSCHER, JOHN W
2645 Highway 1, Washington, IA 52353, Phone: 319-653-7310

HELTON, ROY
HELTON KNIVES, 2941 Comstock St., San Diego, CA 92111, Phone: 858-277-5024

HEMPERLEY, GLEN
13322 Country Run Rd, Willis, TX 77318, Phone: 936-228-5048, hemperley.com
Specialties: Specializes in hunting knives, does fixed and folding knives.

HENDRICKS, SAMUEL J
2162 Van Buren Rd, Maurertown, VA 22644, Phone: 703-436-3305
Specialties: Integral hunters and skinners of thin design. **Patterns:** Boots, hunters and locking folders. **Technical:** Grinds ATS-34, 440C and D2. Integral liners and bolsters of N-S and 7075 T6 aircraft aluminum. Does leatherwork. **Prices:** $50 to $250; some to $500. **Remarks:** Full-time maker; first knife sold in 1992. **Mark:** First and middle initials, last name, city and state in football-style logo.

HENDRICKSON, E JAY
4204 Ballenger Creek Pike, Frederick, MD 21703, Phone: 301-663-6923, Fax: 301-663-6923, ejayhendrickson@comcast.net
Specialties: Specializes in silver wire inlay. **Patterns:** Bowies, Kukri's, camp, hunters, and fighters. **Technical:** Forges 06, 1084, 5160, 52100, D2, L6 and W2; makes Damascus. Moran-styles on order. **Prices:** $400 to $8,000. **Remarks:** Full-time maker; first knife made in 1972; first knife sold in 1974. **Mark:** Last name, M.S.

HENDRICKSON, SHAWN
2327 Kaetzel Rd, Knoxville, MD 21758, Phone: 301-432-4306
Specialties: Hunting knives. **Patterns:** Clip points, drop points and trailing point hunters. **Technical:** Forges 5160, 1084 and L6. **Prices:** $175 to $400.

HENDRIX, JERRY
HENDRIX CUSTOM KNIVES, 175 Skyland Dr. Ext., Clinton, SC 29325, Phone: 864-833-2659, jhendrix@backroads.net
Specialties: Traditional working straight knives of all designs. **Patterns:** Hunters, utility, boot, bird and fishing. **Technical:** Grinds ATS-34 and 440C. **Prices:** $85 to $275. **Remarks:** Full-time maker. Hand stitched, waxed leather sheaths. **Mark:** Full name in shape of knife.

HENDRIX, WAYNE
9636 Burton's Ferry Hwy, Allendale, SC 29810, Phone: 803-584-3825, Fax: 803-584-3825, whendrixknives@gmail.com Web: www.hendrixknives.com
Specialties: Working/using knives of his design. **Patterns:** Hunters and fillet knives. **Technical:** Grinds ATS-34, D2 and 440C. **Prices:** $100 and up. **Remarks:** Full-time maker; first knife sold in 1985. **Mark:** Last name.

HENNINGSSON, MICHAEL
Tralasvagen 1, 426 68 Vastra Frolunda (Gothenburg), SWEDEN, Phone: 46 31-471073; Cell: 46702555745, michael.henningsson@gmail.com; Web: henningssonknives.wordpress.com
Specialties: Handmade folding knives, mostly tactical linerlocks and framelocks. **Patterns:** Own design in both engravings and knife models. **Technical:** All kinds of stee; such as Damascus, but prefer clean RWL-43. Tweaking a lot with hand engraving and therefore likes clean steel mostly. Work a lot with inlays of various materials. **Prices:** Starting at $1200 and up, depending on decoration and engravings. **Remarks:** Part-time maker, first knife sold in 2010. **Mark:** Hand engraved name or a Viking sail with initials in runes

HENSLEY, WAYNE
PO Box 904, Conyers, GA 30012, Phone: 770-483-8938
Specialties: Period pieces and fancy working knives. **Patterns:** Boots to Bowies, locking folders to miniatures. Large variety of straight knives. **Technical:** Grinds ATS-34, 440C, D2 and commercial Damascus. **Prices:** $85 and up. **Remarks:** Full-time maker; first knife sold in 1974. **Mark:** Last name.

HERBST, GAWIE
PO Box 59158, Karenpark, Akasia, GT, SOUTH AFRICA 0118, Phone: +27 72 060 3687, Fax: +27 12 549 1876, gawie@herbst.co.za Web: www.herbst.co.za
Specialties: Hunters, Utility knives, Art knives and Liner lock folders.

HERBST, PETER
Komotauer Strasse 26, Lauf a.d. Pegn., GERMANY 91207, Phone: 09123-13315, Fax: 09123-13379
Specialties: Working/using knives and folders of his design. **Patterns:** Hunters, fighters and daggers; interframe and integral. **Technical:** Grinds CPM-T-440V, UHB-Elmax, ATS-34 and stainless Damascus. **Prices:** $300 to $3000; some to $8000. **Remarks:** Full-time maker; first knife sold in 1981. **Mark:** First initial, last name.

HERBST, THINUS
PO Box 59158, Karenpark, Akasia, GT, SOUTH AFRICA 0118, Phone: +27 82 254 8016, thinus@herbst.co.za; Web: www.herbst.co.za
Specialties: Plain and fancy working straight knives of own design and liner lock folders. **Patterns:** Hunters, utility knives, art knives, and liner lock folders. **Technical:** Prefer exotic materials for handles. Most knives embellished with file work, carving and scrimshaw. **Prices:** $200 to $2000. **Remarks:** Full-time maker, member of the Knifemakers Guild of South Africa.

HERMAN, TIM
517 E. 126 Terrace, Olathe, KS 66061-2731, Phone: 913-839-1924, HermanKnives@comcast.net
Specialties: Investment-grade folders of his design; interframes and bolster frames. **Patterns:** Interframes and new designs in carved stainless. **Technical:** Grinds ATS-34 and damasteel Damascus. Engraves and gold inlays with pearl, jade, lapis and Australian opal. **Prices:** $1500 to $20,000 and up. **Remarks:** Full-time maker; first knife sold in 1978. Inventor of full-color bulino engraving since 1993. **Mark:** Etched signature.

HERNDON, WM R "BILL"
32520 Michigan St, Acton, CA 93510, Phone: 661-269-5860, bherndons1@roadrunner.com
Specialties: Straight knives, plain and fancy. **Technical:** Carbon steel (white and blued), Damascus, stainless steels. **Prices:** Start at $175. **Remarks:** Full-time maker; first knife sold in 1976. American Bladesmith Society journeyman smith. **Mark:** Signature and/or helm logo.

HERRING, MORRIS
Box 85 721 W Line St, Dyer, AR 72935, Phone: 501-997-8861, morrish@ipa.com

HETHCOAT, DON
Box 1764, Clovis, NM 88101, Phone: 575-762-5721, dhethcoat@plateautel.net; Web: www.donhethcoat.com
Specialties: Liner locks, lock backs and multi-blade folder patterns. **Patterns:** Hunters, Bowies. **Technical:** Grinds stainless; forges Damascus. **Prices:** Moderate to upscale. **Remarks:** Full-time maker; first knife sold in 1969. **Mark:** Last name on all.

HEWITT, RONALD "COTTON"
P.O. Box 326, Adel, GA 31620, Phone: 229-896-6366 or 229-237-4378, gobbler12@msn.com; www.hewittknives.com
Specialties: LinerLock folders with occasional fixed blade. **Technical:** Grinds 440C. **Prices:** $300 and up. **Remarks:** Full-time maker; first knife sold in 1975. **Mark:** Last name.

HIBBEN, DARYL
PO Box 172, LaGrange, KY 40031-0172, Phone: 502-222-0983, dhibben1@bellsouth.net
Specialties: Working straight knives, some fancy to customer specs. **Patterns:** Hunters, fighters, Bowies, short sword, art and fantasy. **Technical:** Grinds 440C, ATS-34, 154CM, Damascus; prefers hollow-grinds. **Prices:** $275 and up. **Remarks:** Full-time maker; first knife sold in 1979. **Mark:** Etched full name in script.

HIBBEN, GIL
PO Box 13, LaGrange, KY 40031, Phone: 502-222-1397, Fax: 502-222-2676, gil@hibbenknives.com Web: www.hibbenknives.com
Specialties: Working knives and fantasy pieces to customer specs. **Patterns:** Full range of straight knives, including swords, axes and miniatures; some locking folders. **Technical:** Grinds ATS-34, 440C and D2. **Prices:** $300 to $2000; some to $10,000. **Remarks:** Full-time maker; first knife sold in 1957. Maker and designer of Rambo III knife; made swords for movie Marked for Death and throwing knife for movie Under Seige; made belt buckle knife and knives for movie Perfect Weapon; made knives featured in movie Star Trek the Next Generation , Star Trek Nemesis. 1990 inductee Cutlery Hall of Fame; designer for United Cutlery. Official klingon armourer for Star Trek. Knives also for movies of the Expendables and the Expendables sequel. Over 37 movies and TV productions. President of the Knifemakers Guild. Celebrating 55 years since first knife sold. **Mark:** Hibben Knives. City and state, or signature.

HIBBEN, JOLEEN
PO Box 172, LaGrange, KY 40031, Phone: 502-222-0983, dhibben1@bellsouth.net
Specialties: Miniature straight knives of her design; period pieces. **Patterns:** Hunters, axes and fantasy knives. **Technical:** Grinds Damascus, 1095 tool steel and stainless 440C or ATS-34. Uses wood, ivory, bone, feathers and claws on/for handles. **Prices:** $60 to $600. **Remarks:** Spare-time maker; first knife sold in 1991. Design knives, make & tool leather sheathes. Produced first inlaid handle in 2005, used by Daryl on a dagger. **Mark:** Initials or first name.

HIBBEN, WESTLEY G
14101 Sunview Dr, Anchorage, AK 99515
Specialties: Working straight knives of his design or to customer specs. **Patterns:** Hunters, fighters, daggers, combat knives and some fantasy pieces. **Technical:** Grinds 440C mostly. Filework available. **Prices:** $200 to $400; some to $3000. **Remarks:** Part-time maker; first knife sold in 1988. **Mark:** Signature.

HICKS, GARY
341 CR 275, Tuscola, TX 79562, Phone: 325-554-9762

HIELSCHER, GUY
PO Box 992, 6550 Otoe Rd., Alliance, NE 69301, Phone: 308-762-4318, g-hielsc@bbcwb.net Web: www.ghknives.com
Specialties: Working Damascus fixed blade knives. **Patterns:** Hunters, fighters, capers, skinners, bowie, drop point. **Technical:** Forges own Damascus using 1018 and 0-1 tool steels. **Prices:** $285 and up. **Remarks:** Member of PKA. Part-time maker; sold first knife

in 1988. **Mark:** Arrowhead with GH inside.

HIGH, TOM
5474 S 1128 Rd, Alamosa, CO 81101, Phone: 719-589-2108, www.rockymountainscrimshaw.com
Specialties: Hunters, some fancy. **Patterns:** Drop-points in several shapes; some semi-skinners. Knives designed by and for top outfitters and guides. **Technical:** Grinds ATS-34; likes hollow-grinds, mirror finishes; prefers scrimable handles. **Prices:** $300 to $8000.. **Remarks:** Full-time maker; first knife sold in 1965. Limited edition wildlife series knives. **Mark:** Initials connected; arrow through last name.

HILL, HOWARD E
41785 Mission Lane, Polson, MT 59860, Phone: 406-883-3405, Fax: 406-883-3486, knifeman@bigsky.net
Specialties: Autos, complete new design, legal in Montana (with permit). **Patterns:** Bowies, daggers, skinners and lockback folders. **Technical:** Grinds 440C; uses micro and satin finish. **Prices:** $150 to $1000. **Remarks:** Full-time maker; first knife sold in 1981. **Mark:** Persuader.

HILL, RICK
20 Nassau, Maryville, IL 62062-5618, Phone: 618-288-4370
Specialties: Working knives and period pieces to customer specs. **Patterns:** Hunters, locking folders, fighters and daggers. **Technical:** Grinds D2, 440C and 154CM; forges his own Damascus. **Prices:** $75 to $500; some to $3000. **Remarks:** Part-time maker; first knife sold in 1983. **Mark:** Full name in hill shape logo.

HILL, STEVE E
217 Twin Lake Tr., Spring Branch, TX 78070, Phone: 830-624-6258 (cell) or 830-885-6108 (home), kingpirateboy2@juno.com or kingpirateboy2@gvtc.com; Web: www.stevehillknives.com
Specialties: Fancy manual and automatic LinerLock® folders, small fixed blades and classic Bowie knives. **Patterns:** Classic to cool folding and fixed blade designs. **Technical:** Grinds Damascus and occasional 440C, D2. Prefers natural handle materials; offers elaborate filework, carving, and inlays. **Prices:** $400 to $6000, some higher. **Remarks:** Full-time maker; first knife sold in 1978. Google search: Steve Hill custom knives. **Mark:** First initial, last name and handmade. (4400, D2). Damascus folders; mark inside handle.

HILLMAN, CHARLES
225 Waldoboro Rd, Friendship, ME 04547, Phone: 207-832-4634
Specialties: Working knives of his own or custom design. Heavy Scagel influence. **Patterns:** Hunters, fishing, camp and general utility. Occasional folders. **Technical:** Grinds D2 and 440C. File work, blade and handle carving, engraving. Natural handle materials-antler, bone, leather, wood, horn. Sheaths made to order. **Prices:** $60 to $500. **Remarks:** Part-time maker; first knife sold 1986. **Mark:** Last name in oak leaf.

HINDERER, RICK
5373 Columbus Rd., Shreve, OH 44676, Phone: 330-263-0962, Fax: 330-263-0962, rhind64@earthlink.net; Web: www.rickhindererknives.com
Specialties: Working tactical knives, and some one-of-a kind. **Patterns:** Makes his own. **Technical:** Grinds Duratech 20 CV and CPM S30V. **Prices:** $150 to $4000. **Remarks:** Full-time maker doing business as Rick Hinderer Knives, first knife sold in 1988. **Mark:** R. Hinderer.

HINDMARCH, GARTH
PO Box 135, Carlyle, SK, CANADA S0C 0R0, Phone: 306-453-2568
Specialties: Working and fancy straight knives, Bowies. **Patterns:** Hunters, skinners, Bowies. **Technical:** Grind 440C, ATS-34, some Damascus. **Prices:** $175 - $700. **Remarks:** Part-time maker; first knife sold 1994. All knives satin finish. Does file work, offers engraving, stabilized wood, Giraffe bone, some Micarta. **Mark:** First initial last name, city, province.

HINK III, LES
1599 Aptos Lane, Stockton, CA 95206, Phone: 209-547-1292
Specialties: Working straight knives and traditional folders in standard patterns or to customer specs. **Patterns:** Hunting and utility/camp knives; others on request. **Technical:** Grinds carbon and stainless steels. **Prices:** $80 to $200; some higher. **Remarks:** Part-time maker; first knife sold in 1980. **Mark:** Last name, or last name 3.

HINMAN, THEODORE
186 Petty Plain Road, Greenfield, MA 01301, Phone: 413-773-0448, armenemargosian@verizon.net
Specialties: Tomahawks and axes. Offers classes in bladesmithing and toolmaking.

HINSON AND SON, R
2419 Edgewood Rd, Columbus, GA 31906, Phone: 706-327-6801
Specialties: Working straight knives and folders. **Patterns:** Locking folders, liner locks, combat knives and swords. **Technical:** Grinds 440C and commercial Damascus. **Prices:** $200 to $450; some to $1500. **Remarks:** Part-time maker; first knife sold in 1983. Son Bob is co-worker. **Mark:** HINSON, city and state.

HINTZ, GERALD M
5402 Sahara Ct, Helena, MT 59602, Phone: 406-458-5412
Specialties: Fancy, high-art, working/using knives of his design. **Patterns:** Bowies, hunters, daggers, fish fillet and utility/camp knives. **Technical:** Forges ATS-34, 440C and D2. Animal art in horn handles or in the blade. **Prices:** $75 to $400; some to $1000. **Remarks:** Part-time maker; first knife sold in 1980. Doing business as Big Joe's Custom Knives. Will take custom orders. **Mark:** F.S. or W.S. with first and middle initials and last name.

HIRAYAMA, HARUMI
4-5-13 Kitamachi, Warabi City, Saitama, JAPAN 335-0001, Phone: 048-443-2248, Fax: 048-443-2248, swanbird3@gmail.com; Web: www.ne.jp/asahi/harumi/knives
Specialties: High-tech working knives of her design. **Patterns:** Locking folders, interframes, straight gents and slip-joints. **Technical:** Grinds 440C or equivalent; uses natural handle materials and gold. **Prices:** Start at $2500. **Remarks:** Part-time maker; first knife sold in 1985. **Mark:** First initial, last name.

HIROTO, FUJIHARA
2-34-7 Koioosako, Nishi-ku, Hiroshima, JAPAN, Phone: 082-271-8389, fjhr8363@crest.ocn.ne.jp

HITCHMOUGH, HOWARD
95 Old Street Rd, Peterborough, NH 03458-1637, Phone: 603-924-9646, Fax: 603-924-9595, hhrlm@comcast.net; Web: www.hitchmoughknives.com
Specialties: High class folding knives. **Patterns:** Lockback folders, liner locks, pocket knives. **Technical:** Uses ATS-34, stainless Damascus, titanium, gold and gemstones. Prefers hand-rubbed finishes and natural handle materials. **Prices:** $2500 - $7500. **Remarks:** Full-time maker; first knife sold in 1967. **Mark:** Last name.

HOBART, GENE
100 Shedd Rd, Windsor, NY 13865, Phone: 607-655-1345

HOCKENSMITH, DAN
104 North Country Rd 23, Berthoud, CO 80513, Phone: 970-231-6506, blademan@skybeam.com; Web: www.dhockensmithknives.com
Specialties: Traditional working and using straight knives of his design. **Patterns:** Hunters, Bowies, folders and utility/camp knives. **Technical:** Uses his Damascus, 5160, carbon steel, 52100 steel and 1084 steel. Hand forged. **Prices:** $250 to $1500. **Remarks:** Part-time maker; first knife sold in 1987. **Mark:** Last name or stylized "D" with H inside.

HODGE III, JOHN
422 S 15th St, Palatka, FL 32177, Phone: 904-328-3897
Specialties: Fancy straight knives and folders. **Patterns:** Various. **Technical:** Pattern-welded Damascus—"Southern-style." **Prices:** To $1000. **Remarks:** Part-time maker; first knife sold in 1981. **Mark:** JH3 logo.

HOEL, STEVE
PO Box 283, Pine, AZ 85544-0283, Phone: 928-476-6523
Specialties: Investor-class folders, straight knives and period pieces of his design. **Patterns:** Folding interframes lockers and slip-joints; straight Bowies, boots and daggers. **Technical:** Grinds 154CM, ATS-34 and commercial Damascus. **Prices:** $600 to $1200; some to $7500. **Remarks:** Full-time maker. **Mark:** Initial logo with name and address.

HOFER, LOUIS
BOX 125, Rose Prairie, BC, CANADA V0C 2H0, Phone: 250-827-3999, anvil_needles@hotmail.cq; www.anvilandneedles.com
Specialties: Damascus knives, working knives, fixed blade bowies, daggers. **Patterns:** Hunting, skinning, custom. **Technical:** Wild damascus, random damascus. **Prices:** $450 and up. **Remarks:** Part-time maker since 1995. **Mark:** Logo of initials.

HOFFMAN, JAY
Hoffman Haus + Heraldic Device, 911 W Superior St., Munising, MI 49862, Phone: 906-387-3440, hoffmanhaus1@yahoo.com; Web: www.hoffmanhausknives.com
Technical: Scrimshaw, metal carving, own casting of hilts and pommels, etc. Most if not all leather work for sheaths. **Remarks:** Has been making knives for 50 + years. Professionally since 1991. **Mark:** Early knives marked "Hoffman Haus" and year. Now marks "Hoffman Haus Knives" on the blades. Starting in 2010 uses heraldic device. Will build to your specs. Lag time 1-2 months.

HOFFMAN, KEVIN L
28 Hopeland Dr, Savannah, GA 31419, Phone: 912-920-3579, Fax: 912-920-3579, kevh052475@aol.com; Web: www.KLHoffman.com
Specialties: Distinctive folders and fixed blades. **Patterns:** Titanium frame lock folders. **Technical:** Sculpted guards and fittings cast in sterling silver and 14k gold. Grinds ATS-34, CPM S30V damascus. Makes kydex sheaths for his fixed blade working knives. **Prices:** $400 and up. **Remarks:** Full-time maker since 1981. **Mark:** KLH.

HOGAN, THOMAS R
2802 S. Heritage Ave, Boise, ID 83709, Phone: 208-362-7848

HOGSTROM, ANDERS T
Halmstadsvagen 36, Johanneshov, SWEDEN 12153, Phone: 46 702 674 574, andershogstrom@hotmail.com or info@andershogstrom.com; Web: www.andershogstrom.com
Specialties: Short and long daggers, fighters and swords For select pieces makes wooden display stands. **Patterns:** Daggers, fighters, short knives and swords and an occasional sword. **Technical:** Grinds 1050 High Carbon, Damascus and stainless, forges own Damasus on occasion, fossil ivories. Does clay tempering and uses exotic hardwoods. **Prices:** Start at $850. **Marks:** Last name in maker's own signature.

HOKE, THOMAS M
3103 Smith Ln, LaGrange, KY 40031, Phone: 502-222-0350
Specialties: Working/using knives, straight knives. Own designs and customer specs. **Patterns:** Daggers, Bowies, hunters, fighters, short swords. **Technical:** Grind 440C, Damascus and ATS-34. Filework on all knives. Tooling on sheaths (custom fit on all knives). Any handle material, mostly exotic. **Prices:** $100 to $700; some to $1500. **Remarks:** Full-time maker, first knife sold in 1986. **Mark:** Dragon on banner which says T.M. Hoke.

HOLBROOK, H L

PO Box 483, Sandy Hook, KY 41171, Phone: Cell: 606-794-1497, hhknives@mrtc.com
Specialties: Traditional working using straight knives of his design, to customer specs and in standard patterns. Stabilized wood. **Patterns:** Hunters, mild tacticals and neck knives with kydex sheaths. **Technical:** Grinds CPM154CM, 154CM. Blades have hand-rubbed satin finish. Uses exotic woods, stag and Micarta. Hand-sewn sheath with each straight knife. **Prices:** $125 - $400. **Remarks:** Part-time maker; first knife sold in 1983. Doing business as Holbrook Knives. **Mark:** Name, city, state.

HOLDER, D'ALTON

18910 McNeil Rd., Wickenburg, AZ 85390, Phone: 928-684-2025, Fax: 623-878-3964, dholderknives@commspeed.net; Web: dholder.com
Specialties: Deluxe working knives and high-art hunters. **Patterns:** Drop-point hunters, fighters, Bowies. **Technical:** Grinds ATS-34; uses amber and other materials in combination on stick tangs. **Prices:** $400 to $1000; some to $2000. **Remarks:** Full-time maker; first knife sold in 1966. **Mark:** D'HOLDER, city and state.

HOLLOWAY, PAUL

714 Burksdale Rd, Norfolk, VA 23518, Phone: 757-547-6025, houdini969@yahoo.com
Specialties: Working straight knives and folders to customer specs. **Patterns:** Lockers, fighters and boots, push knives, from swords to miniatures. **Technical:** Grinds A2, D2, 154CM, 440C and ATS-34. **Prices:** $210 to $1,200; some to $1,500, higher. **Remarks:** Part-time maker; retired; first knife sold in 1981. USN 28 years, deputy sheriff 16 years. **Mark:** Name and city in logo.

HOOK, BOB

3247 Wyatt Rd, North Pole, AK 99705, Phone: 907-488-8886, grayling@alaska.net; Web: www.alaskaknifeandforge.com
Specialties: Forged carbon steel. Damascus blades. **Patterns:** Pronghorns, bowies, drop point hunters and knives for the kitchen. **Technical:** 5160, 52100, carbon steel and 1084 and 15N20 pattern welded steel blades are hand forged. Heat treated and ground by maker. Handles are natural materials from Alaska. I favor sole authorship of each piece. **Prices:** $300-$1000. **Remarks:** Journeyman smith with ABS. I have attended the Bill Moran School of Bladesmithing. Knife maker since 2000. **Mark:** Hook.

HORN, DES

PO Box 322, Onrusrivier, WC, SOUTH AFRICA 7201, Phone: 27283161795, Fax: +27866280824, deshorn@usa.net
Specialties: Folding knives. **Patterns:** Ball release side lock mechanism and interframe automatics. **Technical:** Prefers working in totally stainless materials. **Prices:** $800 to $7500. **Remarks:** Full-time maker. Enjoys working in gold, titanium, meteorite, pearl and mammoth. **Mark:** Des Horn.

HORN, JESS

2526 Lansdown Rd, Eugene, OR 97404, Phone: 541-463-1510, jandahorn@earthlink.net
Specialties: Investor-class working folders; period pieces; collectibles. **Patterns:** High-tech design and finish in folders; liner locks, traditional slip-joints and featherweight models. **Technical:** Grinds ATS-34, 154CM. **Prices:** Start at $1000. **Remarks:** Full-time maker; first knife sold in 1968. **Mark:** Full name or last name.

HORNE, GRACE

The Old Public Convenience, 469 Fulwood Road, Sheffield, UNITED KINGDOM S10 3QA, gracehorne@hotmail.co.uk Web: www.gracehorn.co.uk
Specialties: Knives of own design, mainly slip-joint folders. **Technical:** Grinds RWL34, Damasteel and own Damascus for blades. Scale materials vary from traditional (coral, wood, precious metals, etc) to unusual (wool, fabric, felt, etc), **Prices:** $500 - $1500**Remarks:** Part-time maker. **Mark:** 'gH' and 'Sheffield'.

HORRIGAN, JOHN

433 C.R. 200 D, Burnet, TX 78611, Phone: 512-756-7545 or 512-636-6562, jhorrigan@yahoo.com Web: www.eliteknives.com
Specialties: High-end custom knives. **Prices:** $200 - $6500. **Remarks:** Part-time maker. Obtained Mastersmith stamp 2005. First knife made in 1982. **Mark:** Horrigan M.S.

HORTON, SCOT

PO Box 451, Buhl, ID 83316, Phone: 208-543-4222
Specialties: Traditional working stiff knives and folders. **Patterns:** Hunters, skinners, utility, hatchets and show knives. **Technical:** Grinds ATS-34 and D-2 tool steel. **Prices:** $400 to $2500. **Remarks:** First knife sold in 1990. **Mark:** Full name in arch underlined with arrow, city, state.

HOSSOM, JERRY

3585 Schilling Ridge, Duluth, GA 30096, Phone: 770-449-7809, jerry@hossom.com; Web: www.hossom.com
Specialties: Working straight knives of his own design. **Patterns:** Fighters, combat knives, modern Bowies and daggers, modern swords, concealment knives for military and LE uses. **Technical:** Grinds 154CM, S30V, CPM-3V, CPM-154 and stainless Damascus. Uses natural and synthetic handle materials. **Prices:** $350-1500, some higher. **Remarks:** Full-time maker since 1997. First knife sold in 1983. **Mark:** First initial and last name, includes city and state since 2002.

HOSTETLER, LARRY

10626 Pine Needle Dr., Fort Pierce, FL 34945, Phone: 772-465-8352, hossknives@bellsouth.net Web: www.hoss-knives.com
Specialties: EDC working knives and custom collector knives. Utilizing own designs and customer designed creations. Maker uses a wide variety of exotic materials. **Patterns:** Bowies, hunters and folders. **Technical:** Stock removal, grinds ATS-34, carbon and stainless Damascus, embellishes most pieces with file work. **Prices:** $200 - $1500. Some custom orders higher. **Remarks:** Motto: "EDC doesn't have to be ugly." First knife made in 2001, part-time maker, voting member in the Knife Maker's Guild. Doing business as "Hoss Knives." **Mark:** "Hoss" etched into blade with a turn of the century fused bomb in place of the "O" in Hoss.

HOSTETTER, WALLY

P.O. Box 404, San Mateo, FL 32187, Phone: 386-649-0731, shiningmoon_13@yahoo.com; www.shiningmoon13.com
Specialties: Japanese swords and pole arms, and all their mountings from different time periods, other sword styles. **Technical:** Hand forges 1075 on up to 1095 steels, some with vanadium alloys. **Prices:** $1,200 to $6,500. **Remarks:** Full-time maker; first sword was a katana in 1999. **Mark:** Signature on tang in Japanese kanji is Wally San.

HOUSE, CAMERON

2001 Delaney Rd Se, Salem, OR 97306, Phone: 503-585-3286, chouse357@aol.com
Specialties: Working straight knives. **Patterns:** Hunters, Bowies, fighters. **Technical:** Grinds ATS-34, 530V, 154CM. **Remarks:** Part-time maker, first knife sold in 1993. **Prices:** $150 and up. **Mark:** HOUSE.

HOUSE, GARY

2851 Pierce Rd, Ephrata, WA 98823, Phone: 509-754-3272, spindry101@aol.com
Specialties: Bowies, hunters, daggers and some swords. **Patterns:** Unlimited, SW Indian designs, geometric patterns, bowies, hunters and daggers. **Technical:** Mosaic damascus bar stock, forged blades, using 1084, 15N20 and some nickel. Forged company logos and customer designs in mosaic damascus. **Prices:** $500 & up. **Remarks:** Some of the finest and most unique patterns available. ABS master smith. **Marks:** Initials GTH, G hanging T, H.

HOWARD, DURVYN M.

4220 McLain St S, Hokes Bluff, AL 35903, Phone: 256-504-1853
Specialties: Collectible upscale folders; one-of-a-kind, gentlemen's folders. Unique mechanisms and multiple patents. **Patterns:** Conceptual designs; each unique and different. **Technical:** Uses natural and exotic materials and precious metals. **Prices:** $7,500 to $35,000. **Remarks:** Full-time maker; 52 years experience. **Mark:** Howard.

HOWE, TORI

30020 N Stampede Rd, Athol, ID 83801, Phone: 208-449-1509, wapiti@knifescales.com; Web:www.knifescales.com
Specialties: Custom knives, knife scales & Damascus blades. **Remarks:** Carry James Luman polymer clay knife scales.

HOWELL, JASON G

1112 Sycamore, Lake Jackson, TX 77566, Phone: 979-297-9454, tinyknives@yahoo.com; Web:www.howellbladesmith.com
Specialties: Fixed blades and LinerLock® folders. Makes own Damascus. **Patterns:** Clip and drop point. **Prices:** $150 to $750. **Remarks:** Likes making Mosaic Damascus out of the ordinary stuff. Member of TX Knifemakers and Collectors Association; apprentice in ABS; working towards Journeyman Stamp. **Mark:** Name, city, state.

HOWELL, KEITH A.

67 Hidden Oaks Dr., Oxford, AL 36203, Phone: 256-283-3269, keith@howellcutlery.com; Web: www.howellcutlery.com
Specialties: Working straight knives and folders of his design or to customer specs. **Patterns:** Hunters, utility pieces, neck knives, everyday carry knives and friction folders. **Technical:** Grinds damascus, 1095 and 154CM. **Prices:** $100 to $250. **Remarks:** Part-time maker; first knife sold in 2007. **Mark:** Last name.

HOWELL, LEN

550 Lee Rd 169, Opelika, AL 36804, Phone: 334-749-1942
Specialties: Traditional and working knives of his design and to customer specs. **Patterns:** Buckskinner, hunters and utility/camp knives. **Technical:** Forges cable Damascus, 1085 and 5160; makes own Damascus. **Mark:** Engraved last name.

HOWELL, TED

1294 Wilson Rd, Wetumpka, AL 36092, Phone: 205-569-2281, Fax: 205-569-1764
Specialties: Working/using straight knives and folders of his design; period pieces. **Patterns:** Bowies, fighters, hunters. **Technical:** Forges 5160, 1085 and cable. Offers light engraving and scrimshaw; filework. **Prices:** $75 to $250; some to $450. **Remarks:** Part-time maker; first knife sold in 1991. Doing business as Howell Co. **Mark:** Last name, Slapout AL.

HOY, KEN

54744 Pinchot Dr, North Fork, CA 93643, Phone: 209-877-7805

HRISOULAS, JIM

SALAMANDER ARMOURY, 284-C Lake Mead Pkwy #157, Henderson, NV 89105, Phone: 702-566-8551, www.atar.com
Specialties: Working straight knives; period pieces. **Patterns:** Swords, daggers and sgian dubhs. **Technical:** Double-edged differential heat treating. **Prices:** $85 to $175; some to $600 and higher. **Remarks:** Full-time maker; first knife sold in 1973. Author of The Complete Bladesmith, The Pattern Welded Blade and The Master Bladesmith. Doing business as Salamander Armory. **Mark:** 8R logo and sword and salamander.

HUCKABEE, DALE

254 Hwy 260, Maylene, AL 35114, Phone: 205-664-2544, huckabeeknives@hotmail.com; Web: http://dalehuckabeeknives.weebly.com
Specialties: Fixed blade hunter and Bowies of his design. **Technical:** Steel used: 5160, 1084, and Damascus. **Prices:** $225 and up, depending on materials used. **Remarks:** Hand forged. Journeyman Smith. Part-time maker. **Mark:** Stamped Huckabee J.S.

HUCKS, JERRY

KNIVES BY HUCKS, 1807 Perch Road, Moncks Corner, SC 29461, Phone: 843-761-6481, Fax: Cell: 843-708-1649

Specialties: Drop points, bowies and oyster knives. **Patterns:** To customer specs or maker's own design. **Technical:** CPM-154, ATS-34, 5160, 15N20, D2 and 1095 mostly for damascus billets. **Prices:** $200 and up. **Remarks:** Full-time maker, retired as a machinist in 1990. Makes sheaths sewn by hand with some carving. Will custom make to order or by sketch. **Mark:** Robin Hood hat with Moncks Corner under.

HUDSON, C ROBBIN

497 Groton Hollow Rd, Rummney, NH 03266, Phone: 603-786-9944, bladesmith8@gmail.com

Specialties: High-art working knives. **Patterns:** Hunters, Bowies, fighters and kitchen knives. **Technical:** Forges W2, nickel steel, pure nickel steel, composite and mosaic Damascus; makes knives one-at-a-time. **Prices:** 500 to $1200; some to $5000. **Remarks:** Full-time maker; first knife sold in 1970. **Mark:** Last name and MS.

HUDSON, ROB

340 Roush Rd, Northumberland, PA 17857, Phone: 570-473-9588, robscustknives@aol.com Web:www.robscustomknives.com

Specialties: Presentation hunters and Bowies. **Technical:** Hollow grinds CPM-154 stainless and stainless Damascus. **Prices:** $400 to $2000. **Remarks:** Full-time maker. Does business as Rob's Custom Knives. **Mark:** Capital R, Capital H in script.

HUDSON, ROBERT

3802 Black Cricket Ct, Humble, TX 77396, Phone: 713-454-7207

Specialties: Working straight knives of his design. **Patterns:** Bowies, hunters, skinners, fighters and utility knives. **Technical:** Grinds D2, 440C, 154CM and commercial Damascus. **Prices:** $85 to $350; some to $1500. **Remarks:** Part-time maker; first knife sold in 1980. **Mark:** Full name, handmade, city and state.

HUGHES, DAN

301 Grandview Bluff Rd, Spencer, TN 38585, Phone: 931-946-3044

Specialties: Working straight knives to customer specs. **Patterns:** Hunters, fighters, fillet knives. **Technical:** Grinds 440C and ATS-34. **Prices:** $55 to $175; some to $300. **Remarks:** Part-time maker; first knife sold in 1984. **Mark:** Initials.

HUGHES, DARYLE

10979 Leonard, Nunica, MI 49448, Phone: 616-837-6623, hughes.builders@verizon.net

Specialties: Working knives. **Patterns:** Buckskinners, hunters, camp knives, kitchen and fishing knives. **Technical:** Forges and grinds 52100 and Damascus. **Prices:** $125 to $1000. **Remarks:** Part-time maker; first knife sold in 1979. **Mark:** Name and city in logo.

HUGHES, ED

280 1/2 Holly Lane, Grand Junction, CO 81503, Phone: 970-243-8547, edhughes26@msn.com

Specialties: Working and art folders. **Patterns:** Buys Damascus. **Technical:** Grinds stainless steels. Engraves. **Prices:** $300 and up. **Remarks:** Full-time maker; first knife sold in 1978. **Mark:** Name or initials.

HUGHES, LAWRENCE

207 W Crestway, Plainview, TX 79072, Phone: 806-293-5406

Specialties: Working and display knives. **Patterns:** Bowies, daggers, hunters, buckskinners. **Technical:** Grinds D2, 440C and 154CM. **Prices:** $125 to $300; some to $2000. **Remarks:** Full-time maker; first knife sold in 1979. **Mark:** Name with buffalo skull in center.

HUGHES, TONY

Tony Hughes Forged Blades, 7536 Trail North Dr., Littleton, CO 80125, Phone: 303-941-1092, tonhug@msn.com

Specialties: Fixed blades, bowies/fighters and hunters of maker's own damascus steel. **Technical:** Forges damascus and mosaic-damascus blades. Fittings are 416 stainless steel, 1095-and-nickel damascus, 1080-and-15N20 damascus or silicon bronze. Prefers ivory, desert ironwood, blackwood, ebony and other burls. **Prices:** $450 and up. **Remarks:** Full-time ABS journeyman smith forging knives for 20 years. **Mark:** Tony Hughes and JS on the other side.

HULETT, STEVE

115 Yellowstone Ave, West Yellowstone, MT 59758-0131, Phone: 406-646-4116, Web: www.seldomseenknives.com

Specialties: Classic, working/using, straight knives, folders. Your design, custom specs. **Patterns:** Utility/camp knives, hunters, and LinerLock folders, lock back pocket knives. **Technical:** Grinds 440C stainless steel, O1 Carbon, 1095. Shop is retail and knife shop; people watch their knives being made. We do everything in house: "all but smelt the ore, or tan the hide." **Prices:** Strarting $250 to $7000. **Remarks:** Full-time maker; first knife sold in 1994. **Mark:** Seldom seen knives/West Yellowstone Montana.

HULSEY, HOYT

379 Shiloh, Attalla, AL 35954, Phone: 256-538-6765

Specialties: Traditional working straight knives and folders of his design. **Patterns:** Hunters and utility/camp knives. **Technical:** Grinds 440C, ATS-34, O1 and A2. **Prices:** $75 to $250. **Remarks:** Part-time maker; first knife sold in 1989. **Mark:** Hoyt Hulsey Attalla AL.

HUME, DON

2731 Tramway Circle NE, Albuquerque, NM 87122, Phone: 505-796-9451

HUMENICK, ROY

PO Box 55, Rescue, CA 95672, rhknives@gmail.com; Web: www.humenick.com

Specialties: Traditional multiblades and tactical slipjoints. **Patterns:** Original folder and fixed blade designs, also traditional patterns. **Technical:** Grinds premium steels and Damascus. **Prices:** $350 and up; some to $1500. **Remarks:** First knife sold in 1984. **Mark:** Last name in ARC.

HUMPHREY, LON

4 Western Ave., Newark, OH 43055, Phone: 740-644-1137, lonhumphrey@gmail.com

Specialties: Hunters, tacticals, and bowie knives. **Prices:** I make knives that start in the $150 range and go up to $1000 for a large bowie. **Remarks:** Has been blacksmithing since age 13 and progressed to the forged blade.

HUMPHREYS, JOEL

90 Boots Rd, Lake Placid, FL 33852, Phone: 863-773-0439

Specialties: Traditional working/using straight knives and folders of his design and in standard patterns. **Patterns:** Hunters, folders and utility/camp knives. **Technical:** Grinds ATS-34, D2, 440C. All knives have tapered tangs, mitered bolster/handle joints, handles of horn or bone fitted sheaths. **Prices:** $135 to $225; some to $350. **Remarks:** Part-time maker; first knife sold in 1990. Doing business as Sovereign Knives. **Mark:** First name or "H" pierced by arrow.

HUNT, MAURICE

10510 N CR 650 E, Brownsburg, IN 46112, Phone: 317-892-2982, mdhuntknives@juno.com

Patterns: Bowies, hunters, fighters. **Prices:** $200 to $800. **Remarks:** Part-time maker. Journeyman Smith.

HUNTER, HYRUM

285 N 300 W, PO Box 179, Aurora, UT 84620, Phone: 435-529-7244

Specialties: Working straight knives of his design or to customer specs. **Patterns:** Drop and clip, fighters dagger, some folders. **Technical:** Forged from two-piece Damascus. **Prices:** Prices are adjusted according to size, complexity and material used. **Remarks:** Will consider any design you have. Part-time maker; first knife sold in 1990. **Mark:** Initials encircled with first initial and last name and city, then state. Some patterns are numbered.

HUNTER, RICHARD D

7230 NW 200th Ter, Alachua, FL 32615, Phone: 386-462-3150

Specialties: Traditional working/using knives of his design or customer suggestions; filework. **Patterns:** Folders of various types, Bowies, hunters, daggers. **Technical:** Traditional blacksmith; hand forges high-carbon steel (5160, 1084, 52100) and makes own Damascus; grinds 440C and ATS-34. **Prices:** $200 and up. **Remarks:** Part-time maker; first knife sold in 1992. **Mark:** Last name in capital letters.

HURST, JEFF

PO Box 247, Rutledge, TN 37861, Phone: 865-828-5729, jhurst@esper.com

Specialties: Working straight knives and folders of his design. **Patterns:** Tomahawks, hunters, boots, folders and fighters. **Technical:** Forges W2, O1 and his own Damascus. Makes mokume. **Prices:** $250 to $600. **Remarks:** Full-time maker; first knife sold in 1984. Doing business as Buzzard's Knob Forge. **Mark:** Last name; partnered knives are marked with Newman L. Smith, handle artisan, and SH in script.

HUSIAK, MYRON

PO Box 238, Altona, VIC, AUSTRALIA 3018, Phone: 03-315-6752

Specialties: Straight knives and folders of his design or to customer specs. **Patterns:** Hunters, fighters, lock-back folders, skinners and boots. **Technical:** Forges and grinds his own Damascus, 440C and ATS-34. **Prices:** $200 to $900. **Remarks:** Part-time maker; first knife sold in 1974. **Mark:** First initial, last name in logo and serial number.

HUTCHESON, JOHN

SURSUM KNIFE WORKS, 1237 Brown's Ferry Rd., Chattanooga, TN 37419, Phone: 423-667-6193, sursum5071@aol.com; Web: www.sursumknife.com

Specialties: Straight working knives, hunters. **Patterns:** Customer designs, hunting, speciality working knives. **Technical:** Grinds D2, S7, O1 and 5160, ATS-34 on request. **Prices:** $100 to $300, some to $600. **Remarks:** First knife sold 1985, also produces a mid-tech line. Doing business as Sursum Knife Works. **Mark:** Family crest boar's head over 3 arrows.

HUTCHINSON, ALAN

315 Scenic Hill Road, Conway, AR 72034, Phone: 501-470-9653, hutchinsonblades@yahoo.com

Specialties: Hunters, bowies, fighters, combat/survival knives. **Patterns:** Traditional edged weapons and tomahawks, custom patterns. **Technical:** Forges 10 series, 5160, L6, O1, CruForge V, damascus and his own patterns. **Prices:** $200 and up. **Remarks:** Prefers natural handle materials, part-time maker. **Mark:** Last name.

HYTOVICK, JOE "HY"

14872 SW 111th St, Dunnellon, FL 34432, Phone: 800-749-5339, Fax: 352-489-3732, hyclassknives@aol.com

Specialties: Straight, folder and miniature. **Technical:** Blades from Wootz, Damascus and Alloy steel. **Prices:** To $5000. **Mark:** HY.

I

IKOMA, FLAVIO

R Manoel Rainho Teixeira 108, Presidente Prudente, SP, BRAZIL 19031-220, Phone: 0182-22-0115, fikoma@itelesonica.com.br

Specialties: Tactical fixed blade knives, LinerLock® folders and balisongs. **Patterns:** Utility and defense tactical knives built with hi-tech materials. **Technical:** Grinds S30V

custom knifemakers

and Damasteel. **Prices:** $500 to $1000. **Mark:** Ikoma hand made beside Samurai

IMBODEN II, HOWARD L.
620 Deauville Dr, Dayton, OH 45429, Phone: 513-439-1536
Specialties: One-of-a-kind hunting, flint, steel and art knives. **Technical:** Forges and grinds stainless, high-carbon and Damascus. Uses obsidian, cast sterling silver, 14K and 18K gold guards. Carves ivory animals and more. **Prices:** $65 to $25,000. **Remarks:** Full-time maker; first knife sold in 1986. Doing business as Hill Originals. **Mark:** First and last initials, II.

IMEL, BILLY MACE
1616 Bundy Ave, New Castle, IN 47362, Phone: 765-529-1651
Specialties: High-art working knives, period pieces and personal cutlery. **Patterns:** Daggers, fighters, hunters; locking folders and slip-joints with interframes. **Technical:** Grinds D2, 440C and 154CM. **Prices:** $300 to $2000; some to $6000. **Remarks:** Part-time maker; first knife sold in 1973. **Mark:** Name in monogram.

IRIE, MICHAEL L
MIKE IRIE HANDCRAFT, 1606 Auburn Dr., Colorado Springs, CO 80909, Phone: 719-572-5330, mikeirie@aol.com
Specialties: Working fixed blade knives and handcrafted blades for the do-it-yourselfer. **Patterns:** Twenty standard designs along with custom. **Technical:** Blades are ATS-34, BG-43, 440C with some outside Damascus. **Prices:** Fixed blades $95 and up, blade work $45 and up. **Remarks:** Formerly dba Wood, Irie and Co. with Barry Wood. Full-time maker since 1991. **Mark:** Name.

ISAO, OHBUCHI
702-1 Nouso, Yame-City, Fukuoka, JAPAN, Phone: 0943-23-4439, www.5d.biglobe.ne.jp/~ohisao/

ISHIHARA, HANK
86-18 Motomachi, Sakura City, Chiba, JAPAN, Phone: 043-485-3208, Fax: 043-485-3208
Specialties: Fantasy working straight knives and folders of his design. **Patterns:** Boots, Bowies, daggers, fighters, hunters, fishing, locking folders and utility camp knives. **Technical:** Grinds ATS-34, 440C, D2, 440V, CV-134, COS25 and Damascus. Engraves. **Prices:** $250 to $1000; some to $10,000. **Remarks:** Full-time maker; first knife sold in 1987. **Mark:** HANK.

J

JACKS, JIM
344 S. Hollenbeck Ave, Covina, CA 91723-2513, Phone: 626-331-5665
Specialties: Working straight knives in standard patterns. **Patterns:** Bowies, hunters, fighters, fishing and camp knives, miniatures. **Technical:** Grinds Stellite 6K, 440C and ATS-34. **Prices:** Start at $100. **Remarks:** Spare-time maker; first knife sold in 1980. **Mark:** Initials in diamond logo.

JACKSON, CHARLTON R
6811 Leyland Dr, San Antonio, TX 78239, Phone: 210-601-5112

JACKSON, DAVID
214 Oleander Ave, Lemoore, CA 93245, Phone: 559-925-8547, jnbcrea@lemoorenet.com
Specialties: Forged steel. **Patterns:** Hunters, camp knives, Bowies. **Prices:** $150 and up. **Mark:** G.D. Jackson - Maker - Lemoore CA.

JACKSON, LARAMIE
POB 442, Claysprings, AZ 85923, Phone: 480-747-3804, ljacksonknives@yahoo.com
Specialties: Traditional hunting and working knives and folders, chef's knives. **Patterns:** Bowies, fighters, hunters, daggers and skinners. **Technical:** Grinds 440C, CPM D2, CPM S30V, W2, O1, 52100, 5160, L6, 1095, damascus and whatever customer wants. Offers sheaths. **Prices:** $100-$450+. **Remarks:** Full-time maker; first knife sold in 2010. **Mark:** First initial and last name.

JACQUES, ALEX
10 Exchange St., Apt 1, East Greenwich, RI 02818, Phone: 617-771-4441, customrazors@gmail.com Web: www.customrazors.com
Specialties: One-of-a-kind, heirloom quality straight razors … functional art. **Technical:** Damascus, O1, CPM154, and various other high-carbon and stainless steels. **Prices:** $450 and up. **Remarks:** First knife sold in 2008. **Mark:** Jack-O-Lantern logo with "A. Jacques" underneath.

JAKSIK JR., MICHAEL
427 Marschall Creek Rd, Fredericksburg, TX 78624, Phone: 830-997-1119
Mark: MJ or M. Jaksik.

JANGTANONG, SUCHAT
10901 W. Cave Blvd., Dripping Springs, TX 78620, Phone: 512-264-1501, shakeallpoints@yahoo.com; Web: www.mrdamascusknives.com
Specialties: One-of-a-kind handmade art knives, carving pearl and titanium. **Patterns:** Folders (lock back and LinerLock), some fixed blades and butterfly knives. **Technical:** Grinds ATS-34 and damascus steels. **Prices:** $500 to $3,000. **Remarks:** Third-generation, began making knives in 1982; full-time maker who lives in Uthai Thani Province of Thailand. **Mark:** Name (Suchat) on blade.

JANSEN VAN VUUREN, LUDWIG
311 Brighton Rd., Waldronville 9018, Dunedin, NEW ZEALAND, Phone: 64-3-7421012, ludwig@nzhandmadeknives.co.nz; Web: www.nzhandmadeknives.co.nz
Specialties: Fixed-blade knives of his design or custom specifications. **Patterns:** Hunting, fishing, bird-and-trout and chef's knives. **Technical:** Stock-removal maker, Sandvik 12C27, D2, O1, Damasteel, damascus and other blade steels on request. Handle material includes Micarta, antler and a wide selection of woods. **Prices:** Starting at $200 and up. **Remarks:** Part-time maker since 2008. **Mark:** L J van Vuuren.

JARVIS, PAUL M
30 Chalk St, Cambridge, MA 02139, Phone: 617-547-4355 or 617-661-3015
Specialties: High-art knives and period pieces of his design. **Patterns:** Japanese and Mid-Eastern knives. **Technical:** Grinds Myer Damascus, ATS-34, D2 and O1. Specializes in height-relief Japanese-style carving. Works with silver, gold and gems. **Prices:** $200 to $17,000. **Remarks:** Part-time maker; first knife sold in 1978.

JEAN, GERRY
25B Cliffside Dr, Manchester, CT 06040, Phone: 860-649-6449
Specialties: Historic replicas. **Patterns:** Survival and camp knives. **Technical:** Grinds A2, 440C and 154CM. Handle slabs applied in unique tongue-and-groove method. **Prices:** $125 to $250; some to $1000. **Remarks:** Spare-time maker; first knife sold in 1973. **Mark:** Initials and serial number.

JEFFRIES, ROBERT W
Route 2 Box 227, Red House, WV 25168, Phone: 304-586-9780, wvknifeman@hotmail.com; Web: www.jeffriesknceswv.tripod.com
Specialties: Hunters, Bowies, daggers, lockback folders and LinerLock push buttons. **Patterns:** Skinning types, drop points, typical working hunters, folders one-of-a-kind. **Technical:** Grinds all types of steel. Makes his own Damascus. **Prices:** $125 to $600. Private collector pieces to $3000. **Remarks:** Starting engraving. Custom folders of his design. Part-time maker since 1988. **Mark:** Name etched or on plate pinned to blade.

JENKINS, MITCH
194 East 500 South, Manti, Utah 84642, Phone: 435-813-2532, mitch.jenkins@gmail.com Web: MitchJenkinsKnives.com
Specialties: Hunters, working knives. **Patterns:** Johnson and Loveless Style. Drop points, skinners and semi-skinners, Capers and utilities. **Technical:** 154CM and ATS-34. Experimenting with S30V and love working with Damascus on occasion. **Prices:** $150 and up. **Remarks:** Slowly transitioning to full-time maker; first knife made in 2008. **Mark:** Jenkins Manti, Utah and M. Jenkins, Utah.

JENSEN, JOHN LEWIS
JENSEN KNIVES, 437 S. Orange Grove Blvd. #3, Pasadena, CA 91105, Phone: 323-559-7454, Fax: 626-449-1148, john@jensenknives.com; Web: www.jensenknives.com
Specialties: Designer and fabricator of modern, original one-of-a-kind, hand crafted, custom ornamental edged weaponry. Combines skill, precision, distinction and the finest materials, geared toward the discriminating art collector. **Patterns:** Folding knives and fixed blades, daggers, fighters and swords. **Technical:** High embellishment, BFA 96 Rhode Island School of Design: jewelry and metalsmithing. Grinds 440C, ATS-34, Damascus. Works with custom made Damascus to his specs. Uses gold, silver, gemstones, pearl, titanium, fossil mastodon and walrus ivories. Carving, file work, soldering, deep etches Damascus, engraving, layers, bevels, blood grooves. Also forges his own Damascus. **Prices:** Start at $10,000. **Remarks:** Available on a first come basis and via commission based on his designs. Knifemakers Guild voting member and ABS apprenticesmith and member of the Society of North American Goldsmiths. **Mark:** Maltese cross/butterfly shield.

JERNIGAN, STEVE
3082 Tunnel Rd., Milton, FL 32571, Phone: 850-994-0802, Fax: 850-994-0802, jerniganknives@mchsi.com
Specialties: Investor-class folders and various theme pieces. **Patterns:** Array of models and sizes in side plate locking interframes and conventional liner construction, including tactical and automatics. **Technical:** Grinds ATS-34, CPM-T-440V and damascus. Inlays mokume (and minerals) in blades and sculpts marble cases. **Prices:** $650 to $1,800; some to $6,000. **Remarks:** Full-time maker, first knife sold in 1982. **Mark:** Last name.

JOBIN, JACQUES
46 St Dominique, Levis, QC, CANADA G6V 2M7, Phone: 418-833-0283, Fax: 418-833-8378
Specialties: Fancy and working straight knives and folders; miniatures. **Patterns:** Minis, fantasy knives, fighters and some hunters. **Technical:** ATS-34, some Damascus and titanium. Likes native snake wood. Heat-treats. **Prices:** Start at $250. **Remarks:** Full-time maker; first knife sold in 1986. **Mark:** Signature on blade.

JOEHNK, BERND
Posadowskystrasse 22, Kiel, GERMANY 24148, Phone: 0431-7297705, Fax: 0431-7297705
Specialties: One-of-a-kind fancy/embellished and traditional straight knives of his design and from customer drawing. **Patterns:** Daggers, fighters, hunters and letter openers. **Technical:** Grinds and file 440C, ATS-34, powder metal orgical, commercial Damascus and various stainless and corrosion-resistant steels. **Prices:** Upscale. **Remarks:** Likes filework. Leather sheaths. Offers engraving. Part-time maker; first knife sold in1990. Doing business as metal design kiel. All knives made by hand. **Mark:** From 2005 full name and city, with certificate.

JOHANNING CUSTOM KNIVES, TOM
1735 Apex Rd, Sarasota, FL 34240 9386, Phone: 941-371-2104, Fax: 941-378-9427, Web: www.survivalknives.com
Specialties: Survival knives. **Prices:** $375 to $775.

JOHANSSON, ANDERS
Konstvartarevagen 9, Grangesberg, SWEDEN 77240, Phone: 46 240 23204, Fax: +46

21 358778, www.scrimart.u.se

Specialties: Scandinavian traditional and modern straight knives. **Patterns:** Hunters, fighters and fantasy knives. **Technical:** Grinds stainless steel and makes own Damascus. Prefers water buffalo and mammoth for handle material. **Prices:** Start at $100. **Remarks:** Spare-time maker; first knife sold in 1994. Works together with scrimshander Viveca Sahlin. **Mark:** Stylized initials.

JOHNS, ROB

1423 S. Second, Enid, OK 73701, Phone: 405-242-2707

Specialties: Classic and fantasy straight knives of his design or to customer specs; fighters for use at Medieval fairs. **Patterns:** Bowies, daggers and swords. **Technical:** Forges and grinds 440C, D2 and 5160. Handles of nylon, walnut or wire-wrap. **Prices:** $150 to $350; some to $2500. **Remarks:** Full-time maker; first knife sold in 1980. **Mark:** Medieval Customs, initials.

JOHNSON, C E GENE

1240 Coan Street, Chesterton, IN 46304, Phone: 219-787-8324, ddjlady55@aol.com

Specialties: Lock-back folders and springers of his design to customer specs. **Patterns:** Hunters, Bowies, survival lock-back folders. **Technical:** Grinds D2, 440C, A18, O1, Damascus; likes filework. **Prices:** $100 to $2000. **Remarks:** Full-time maker; first knife sold in 1975. **Mark:** Gene.

JOHNSON, DAVID A

1791 Defeated Creek Rd, Pleasant Shade, TN 37145, Phone: 615-774-3596, artsmith@mwsi.net

JOHNSON, GORDON A.

981 New Hope Rd, Choudrant, LA 71227, Phone: 318-768-2613

Specialties: Using straight knives and folders of my design, or customers. Offering filework and hand stitched sheaths. **Patterns:** Hunters, bowies, folders and miniatures. **Technical:** Forges 5160, 1084, 52100 and my own Damascus. Some stock removal on working knives and miniatures. **Prices:** Mid range. **Remarks:** First knife sold in 1990. ABS apprentice smith. **Mark:** Interlocking initials G.J. or G. A. J.

JOHNSON, JERRY

PO Box 491, Spring City, Utah 84662, Phone: 435-851-3604 or 435-462-3688, Web: sanpetesilver.com

Specialties: Hunter, fighters, camp. **Patterns:** Multiple. **Prices:** $225 - $3000. **Mark:** Jerry E. Johnson Spring City, UT in several fonts.

JOHNSON, JERRY L

29847 260th St, Worthington, MN 56187, Phone: 507-376-9253; Cell: 507-370-3523, Web: jljknives.com

Specialties: Straight knives, hunters, bowies, and fighting knives. **Patterns:** Drop points, trailing points, bowies, and some favorite Loveless patterns. **Technical:** Grinds ATS 34, 440C, S30V, forges own damascus, mirror finish, satin finish, file work and engraving done by self. **Prices:** $250 to $1500. **Remarks:** Part-time maker since 1991, member of knifemakers guild since 2009. **Mark:** Name over a sheep head or elk head with custom knives under the head.

JOHNSON, JOHN R

5535 Bob Smith Ave, Plant City, FL 33565, Phone: 813-986-4478, rottyjohn@msn.com

Specialties: Hand forged and stock removal. **Technical:** High tech. Folders. **Mark:** J.R. Johnson Plant City, FL.

JOHNSON, JOHN R

PO Box 246, New Buffalo, PA 17069, Phone: 717-834-6265, jrj@jrjknives.com; Web: www.jrjknives.com

Specialties: Working hunting and tactical fixed blade sheath knives. **Patterns:** Hunters, tacticals, Bowies, daggers, neck knives and primitives. **Technical:** Flat, convex and hollow grinds. ATS-34, CPM154CM, L6, O1, D2, 5160, 1095 and Damascus. **Prices:** $60 to $700. **Remarks:** Full-time maker; first knife sold in 1996. Doing business as JRJ Knives. Custom sheath made by maker for every knife, **Mark:** Initials connected.

JOHNSON, KEITH R.

9179 Beltrami Line Rd. SW, Bemidji, MN 56601, Phone: 218-368-7482, keith@greatriverforge.com; www.greatriverforge.com

Specialties: Slip-joint and lockback folders. **Patterns:** Mostly traditional patterns but with customer preferences, some of maker's own patterns. **Technical:** Mainly uses CPM 154, sometimes other high-quality stainless steels, Damasteel. Variety of handle materials, including bone, mammoth ivory, Micarta, G-10 and carbon fiber. **Remarks:** Full-time maker; first knife sold in 1986. **Mark:** KRJohnson in script.

JOHNSON, MIKE

38200 Main Rd, Orient, NY 11957, Phone: 631-323-3509, mjohnsoncustomknives@hotmail.com

Specialties: Large Bowie knives and cutters, fighters and working knives to customer specs. **Technical:** Forges 5160, O1. **Prices:** $325 to $1200. **Remarks:** Full-time bladesmith. **Mark:** Johnson.

JOHNSON, R B

Box 11, Clearwater, MN 55320, Phone: 320-558-6128, Fax: 320-558-6128, rb@rbjohnsonknives.com; Web: rbjohnsonknives.com

Specialties: Liner locks with titanium, mosaic Damascus. **Patterns:** LinerLock® folders, skeleton hunters, frontier Bowies. **Technical:** Damascus, mosaic Damascus, A-2, O1, 1095. **Prices:** $200 and up. **Remarks:** Full-time maker since 1973. Not accepting orders. **Mark:** R B Johnson (signature).

JOHNSON, RANDY

2575 E Canal Dr, Turlock, CA 95380, Phone: 209-632-5401

Specialties: Folders. **Patterns:** Locking folders. **Technical:** Grinds Damascus. **Prices:** $200 to $400. **Remarks:** Spare-time maker; first knife sold in 1989. Doing business as Puedo Knifeworks. **Mark:** PUEDO.

JOHNSON, RICHARD

W165 N10196 Wagon Trail, Germantown, WI 53022, Phone: 262-251-5772, rlj@execpc.com; Web: http://www.execpc.com/~rlj/index.html

Specialties: Custom knives and knife repair.

JOHNSON, RUFFIN

215 LaFonda Dr, Houston, TX 77060, Phone: 281-448-4407

Specialties: Working straight knives and folders. **Patterns:** Hunters, fighters and locking folders. **Technical:** Grinds 440C and 154CM; hidden tangs and fancy handles. **Prices:** $450 to $650; some to $1350. **Remarks:** Full-time maker; first knife sold in 1972. **Mark:** Wolf head logo and signature.

JOHNSON, RYAN M

3103 Excelsior Ave., Signal Mountain, TN 37377, Phone: 866-779-6922, rmjtactical@gmail.com Web: www.rmjforge.com www.rmjtactical.com

Specialties: Historical and Tactical Tomahawks. Some period knives and folders. **Technical:** Forges a variety of steels including own Damascus. **Prices:** $500 - $1200 **Remarks:** Full-time maker began forging in 1986. **Mark:** Sledge-hammer with halo.

JOHNSON, STEVEN R

202 E 200 N, PO Box 5, Manti, UT 84642, Phone: 435-835-7941, srj@mail.manti.com; Web: www.srjknives.com

Specialties: Investor-class working knives. **Patterns:** Hunters, fighters, boots. **Technical:** Grinds CPM-154CM and CTS-XHP. **Prices:** $1,500 to $20,000. **Remarks:** Full-time maker; first knife sold in 1972. Also see SR Johnson forum on www.knifenetwork.com. **Mark:** Registered trademark, including name, city, state, and optional signature mark.

JOHNSON, TOMMY

144 Poole Rd., Troy, NC 27371, Phone: 910-975-1817, tommy@tjohnsonknives.com Web: www.tjohnsonknives.com

Specialties: Straight knives for hunting, fishing, utility, and linerlock and slip joint folders since 1982.

JOHNSON, WM. C. "BILL"

225 Fairfield Pike, Enon, OH 45323, Phone: 937-864-7802, wjohnson64@woh.RR.com

Patterns: From hunters to art knives as well as custom canes, some with blades. **Technical:** Stock removal method utilizing 440C, ATS34, 154CPM, and custom Damascus. **Prices:** $175 to over $2500, depending on design, materials, and embellishments. **Remarks:** Full-time maker. First knife made in 1978. Member of the Knifemakers Guild since 1982. **Mark:** Crescent shaped WM. C. "BILL" JOHNSON, ENON OHIO. Also uses an engraved or electro signature on some art knives and on Damascus blades.

JOHNSTON, DR. ROBT

PO Box 9887 1 Lomb Mem Dr, Rochester, NY 14623

JOKERST, CHARLES

9312 Spaulding, Omaha, NE 68134, Phone: 402-571-2536

Specialties: Working knives in standard patterns. **Patterns:** Hunters, fighters and pocketknives. **Technical:** Grinds 440C, ATS-34. **Prices:** $90 to $170. **Remarks:** Spare-time maker; first knife sold in 1984. **Mark:** Early work marked RCJ; current work marked with last name and city.

JONAS, ZACHARY

204 Village Rd., Wilmot, NH 03287, Phone: 603-877-0128, zack@jonasblade.com; www.jonasblade.com

Specialties: Custom high-carbon damascus, sporting knives, kitchen knives and art knives. Always interested in adding to the repertoire. **Patterns:** Kitchen and bowie knives, hunters, daggers, push daggers, tantos, boot knives, all custom. **Technical:** Forges all damascus blades, works with high-carbon steels to suit the client's individual tastes and needs. **Remarks:** Full-time maker, ABS journeyman smith trained by ABS master smith J.D. Smith, juried member of League of New Hampshire Craftsmen. **Mark:**Sytlized "Z" symbol on one side, "JS" on other, either stamped, engraved or etched.

JONES, BARRY M AND PHILLIP G

221 North Ave, Danville, VA 24540, Phone: 804-793-5282

Specialties: Working and using straight knives and folders of their design and to customer specs; combat and self-defense knives. **Patterns:** Bowies, fighters, daggers, swords, hunters and LinerLock® folders. **Technical:** Grinds 440C, ATS-34 and D2; flat-grinds only. All blades hand polished. **Prices:** $100 to $1000, some higher. **Remarks:** Part-time maker; first knife sold in 1989. **Mark:** Jones Knives, city, state.

JONES, ENOCH

7278 Moss Ln, Warrenton, VA 20187, Phone: 540-341-0292

Specialties: Fancy working straight knives. **Patterns:** Hunters, fighters, boots and Bowies. **Technical:** Forges and grinds O1, W2, 440C and Damascus. **Prices:** $100 to $350; some to $1000. **Remarks:** Part-time maker; first knife sold in 1982. **Mark:** First name.

JONES, JACK P.

17670 Hwy. 2 East, Ripley, MS 38663, Phone: 662-837-3882, jacjones@ripleycable.net

Specialties: Working knives in classic design. **Patterns:** Hunters, fighters, and Bowies.

Technical: Grinds D2, A2, CPM-154, CTS-XHP and ATS-34. **Prices:** $200 and up. **Remarks:** Full-time maker since retirement in 2005, first knife sold in 1976. **Mark:** J.P. Jones, Ripley, MS.

JONES, JOHN A
779 SW 131 Hwy, Holden, MO 64040, Phone: 816-682-0238
Specialties: Working, using knives. Hunters, skinners and fighters. **Technical:** Grinds D2, O1, 440C, 1095. Prefers forging; creates own Damascus. File working on most blades. **Prices:** $50 to $500. **Remarks:** Part-time maker; first knife sold in 1996. Doing business as Old John Knives. **Mark:** OLD JOHN and serial number.

JONES, ROGER MUDBONE
GREENMAN WORKSHOP, 320 Prussia Rd, Waverly, OH 45690, Phone: 740-739-4562, greenmanworkshop@yahoo.com
Specialties: Working in cutlery to suit working woodsman and fine collector. **Patterns:** Bowies, hunters, folders, hatchets in both period and modern style, scale miniatures a specialty. **Technical:** All cutlery hand forged to shape with traditional methods; multiple quench and draws, limited Damascus production hand carves wildlife and historic themes in stag/antler/ivory, full line of functional and high art leather. All work sole authorship. **Prices:** $50 to $5000 **Remarks:** Full-time maker/first knife sold in 1979. **Mark:** Stamped R. Jones hand made or hand engraved sig. W/Bowie knife mark.

JORGENSEN, CARSON
1805 W Hwy 116, Mt Pleasant, UT 84647, tcjorgensenknife@gmail.com; Web: tcjknives.com
Specialties: Stock removal, Loveless Johnson and young styles. **Prices:** Most $100 to $800.

K

K B S, KNIVES
RSD 181, North Castlemaine, VIC, AUSTRALIA 3450, Phone: 0011 61 3 54 705864
Specialties: Historical pieces, fixed and folding. **Patterns:** Bowies, daggers, hunters and folders. **Technical:** Flat and hollow grinds, filework. **Prices:** $500 and up. **Remarks:** First knife sold in 1983, foundation member of Australian Knife Guild. **Mark:** Initials and address within Southern cross.

KACZOR, TOM
375 Wharncliffe Rd N, Upper London, ON, CANADA N6G 1E4, Phone: 519-645-7640

KAGAWA, KOICHI
1556 Horiyamashita, Hatano-Shi, Kanagawa, JAPAN
Specialties: Fancy high-tech straight knives and folders to customer specs. **Patterns:** Hunters, locking folders and slip-joints. **Technical:** Uses 440C and ATS-34. **Prices:** $500 to $2000; some to $20,000. **Remarks:** Part-time maker; first knife sold in 1986. **Mark:** First initial, last name-YOKOHAMA.

KAIN, CHARLES
KAIN DESIGNS, 1736 E. Maynard Dr., Indianapolis, IN 46227, Phone: 317-781-9549, Fax: 317-781-8521, charles@kaincustomknives.com; Web: www.kaincustomknives.com
Specialties: Unique Damascus art folders. **Patterns:** Any. **Technical:** Specialized & patented mechanisms. **Remarks:** Unique knife & knife mechanism design. **Mark:** Kain and Signet stamp for unique pieces.

KAJIN, AL
PO Box 1047, 342 South 6th Ave, Forsyth, MT 59327, Phone: 406-346-2442, kajinknives@cablemt.net
Specialties: Utility/working knives, hunters, kitchen cutlery. Produces own Damascus steel from 15N20 and 1084 and cable. Forges 52100, 5160, 1084, 15N20 and O1. Stock removal ATS-34, D2, O1, and L6. Patterns: All types, especially like to work with customer on their designs. Technical: Maker since 1989. ABS member since 1995. Does own differential heat treating, cryogenic soaking when appropriate. Does all leather work. Prices: Stock removal starts at $250. Forged blades and Damascus starts at $300. Kitchen cutlery starts at $100. Remarks: Likes to use exotic woods. Mark: Interlocked AK on forged blades, etched stylized Kajin in outline of Montana on stock removal knives.

KANKI, IWAO
691-2 Tenjincho, Ono-City, Hyogo, JAPAN 675-1316, Phone: 07948-3-2555, Web: www.chiyozurusadahide.jp
Specialties: Plane, knife. **Prices:** Not determined yet. **Remarks:**Masters of traditional crafts designated by the Minister of International Trade and Industry (Japan). **Mark:** Chiyozuru Sadahide.

KANSEI, MATSUNO
109-8 Uenomachi, Nishikaiden, Gifu, JAPAN 501-1168, Phone: 81-58-234-8643
Specialties: Folders of original design. **Patterns:** LinerLock® folder. **Technical:** Grinds VG-10, Damascus. **Prices:** $350 to $2000. **Remarks:** Full-time maker. First knife sold in 1993. **Mark:** Name.

KANTER, MICHAEL
ADAM MICHAEL KNIVES, 14550 West Honey Ln., New Berlin, WI 53151, Phone: 262-860-1136, mike@adammichaelknives.com; Web: www.adammichaelknives.com
Specialties: Fixed blades and folders. **Patterns:** Drop point hunters, Bowies and fighters. **Technical:** Jerry Rados Damascus, BG42, CPM, S60V and S30V. **Prices:** $375 and up. **Remarks:** Ivory, mammoth ivory, stabilized woods, and pearl handles. **Mark:** Engraved Adam Michael.

KARP, BOB
PO Box 47304, Phoenix, AZ 85068, Phone: 602 870-1234

602 870-1234, Fax: 602-331-0283
Remarks: Bob Karp "Master of the Blade."

KATO, SHINICHI
Rainbow Amalke 402, Moriyama-ku Nagoya, Aichi, JAPAN 463-0002, Phone: 81-52-736-6032, skato-402@u0l.gate01.com
Specialties: Flat grind and hand finish. **Patterns:** Bowie, fighter. Hunting and folding knives. **Technical:** Hand forged,flat grind. **Prices:** $100 to $2000. **Remarks:** Part-time maker. **Mark:** Name.

KATSUMARO, SHISHIDO
2-6-11 Kamiseno, Aki-ku, Hiroshima, JAPAN, Phone: 090-3634-9054, Fax: 082-227-4438, shishido@d8.dion.ne.jp

KAUFFMAN, DAVE
4 Clark Creek Loop, Montana City, MT 59634, Phone: 406-442-9328
Specialties: Field grade and exhibition grade hunting knives and ultra light folders. **Patterns:** Fighters, Bowies and drop-point hunters. **Technical:** S30V and SS Damascus. **Prices:** $155 to $1200. **Remarks:** Full-time maker; first knife sold in 1989. On the cover of Knives '94. **Mark:** First and last name, city and state.

KAY, J WALLACE
332 Slab Bridge Rd, Liberty, SC 29657

KAZSUK, DAVID
PO Box 390190, Anza, CA 92539-0190, Phone: 951-238-7460, ddkaz@hotmail.com
Specialties: Hand forged. **Prices:** $150+. **Mark:** Last name.

KEARNEY, JAROD
1505 Parkersburg Turnpike, Swoope, VA 24479, jarodkearney@gmail.com Web: www.jarodkearney
Patterns: Bowies, skinners, hunters, Japanese blades, Sgian Dubhs

KEESLAR, JOSEPH F
391 Radio Rd, Almo, KY 42020, Phone: 270-753-7919, Fax: 270-753-7919, sjkees@apex.net
Specialties: Classic and contemporary Bowies, combat, hunters, daggers and folders. **Patterns:** Decorative filework, engraving and custom leather sheaths available. **Technical:** Forges 5160, 52100 and his own Damascus steel. **Prices:** $300 to $3000. **Remarks:** Full-time maker; first knife sold in 1976. ABS Master Smith, and 50 years as a bladesmith (1962-2012). **Mark:** First and middle initials, last name in hammer, knife and anvil logo, M.S.

KEESLAR, STEVEN C
115 Lane 216 Hamilton Lake, Hamilton, IN 46742, Phone: 260-488-3161, sskeeslar@hotmail.com
Specialties: Traditional working/using straight knives of his design and to customer specs. **Patterns:** Bowies, hunters, utility/camp knives. **Technical:** Forges 5160, files 52100 Damascus. **Prices:** $100 to $600; some to $1500. **Remarks:** Part-time maker; first knife sold in 1976. ABS member. **Mark:** Fox head in flames over Steven C. Keeslar.

KEETON, WILLIAM L
6095 Rehobeth Rd SE, Laconia, IN 47135-9550, Phone: 812-969-2836, wlkeeton@hughes.net; Web: www.keetoncustomknives.com
Specialties: Plain and fancy working knives. **Patterns:** Hunters and fighters; locking folders and slip-joints. Names patterns after Kentucky Derby winners. **Technical:** Grinds any of the popular alloy steels. **Prices:** $185 to $8000. **Remarks:** Full-time maker; first knife sold in 1971. **Mark:** Logo of key.

KEHIAYAN, ALFREDO
Cuzco 1455 Ing., Maschwitz, Buenos Aires, ARGENTINA B1623GXU, Phone: 540-348-4442212, Fax: 54-077-75-4493-5359, alfredo@kehiayan.com.ar; Web: www.kehiayan.com.ar
Specialties: Functional straight knives. **Patterns:** Utility knives, skinners, hunters and boots. **Technical:** Forges and grinds SAE 52.100, SAE 6180, SAE 9260, SAE 5160, 440C and ATS-34, titanium with nitride. All blades mirror-polished; makes leather sheath and wood cases. **Prices:** From $350 up. **Remarks:** Full-time maker; first knife sold in 1983. Some knives are satin finish (utility knives). **Mark:** Name.

KEISUKE, GOTOH
105 Cosumo-City Otozu 202, Oita-city, Oita, JAPAN, Phone: 097-523-0750, k-u-an@ki.rim.or.jp

KELLER, BILL
12211 Las Nubes, San Antonio, TX 78233, Phone: 210-653-6609
Specialties: Primarily folders, some fixed blades. **Patterns:** Autos, liner locks and hunters. **Technical:** Grinds stainless and Damascus. **Prices:** $400 to $1000, some to $4000. **Remarks:** Part-time maker, first knife sold 1995. **Mark:** Last name inside outline of Alamo.

KELLEY, GARY
17485 SW Pheasant Lane, Aloha, OR 97006, Phone: 503-649-7867, garykelley@theblademaker.com; Web: wwwtheblademaker.com
Specialties: Primitive knives and blades. **Patterns:** Fur trade era rifleman's knives, tomahawks, and hunting knives. **Technical:** Hand-forges and precision investment casts. **Prices:** $35 to $125. **Remarks:** Family business. Doing business as The Blademaker. **Mark:** Fir tree logo.

KELLY, DAVE
865 S. Shenandoah St., Los Angeles, CA 90035, Phone: 310-657-7121, dakcon@sbcglobal.net

Specialties: Collector and user one-of-a-kind (his design) fixed blades, liner lock folders, and leather sheaths. **Patterns:** Utility and hunting fixed blade knives with hand-sewn leather sheaths, Gentleman liner lock folders. **Technical:** Grinds carbon steels, hollow, convex, and flat. Offers clay differentially hardened blades, etched and polished. Uses Sambar stag, mammoth ivory, and high-grade burl woods. Hand-sewn leather sheaths for fixed blades and leather pouch sheaths for folders. **Prices:** $250 to $750, some higher. **Remarks:** Full-time maker, first knife made in 2003. **Mark:** First initial, last name with large K.

KELLY, STEVEN

11407 Spotted Fawn Ln., Bigfork, MT 59911, Phone: 406-837-1489, www.skknives. com

Technical: Damascus from 1084 or 1080 and 15n20. 52100.

KELSEY, NATE

5901 Arctic Blvd., Unit M, Anchorage, AK 99518, Phone: 907-360-4469, edgealaska@ mac.com; Web: www.edgealaska.com

Specialties: Forges high-performance 52100, stock removal on 154CM for Extreme Duty Worldwide. **Patterns:** Hunters, fighters and bowies. **Prices:** Material dependent, $175 to $3,000. **Remarks:** Maker since 1990, member ABS. **Mark:** EDGE ALASKA.

KELSO, JIM

577 Collar Hill Rd, Worcester, VT 05682, Phone: 802-229-4254, Fax: 802-229-0595, kelsomaker@gmail.com; Web:www.jimkelso.com

Specialties: Fancy high-art straight knives and folders that mix Eastern and Western influences. Only uses own designs. **Patterns:** Daggers, swords and locking folders. **Technical:** Works with top bladesmiths. **Prices:** $6,000 to $50,000 . **Remarks:** Full-time maker; first knife sold in 1980. **Mark:** Stylized initials.

KEMP, LAWRENCE

8503 Water Tower Rd, Ooltewah, TN 37363, Phone: 423-344-2357, larry@kempknives. com Web: www.kempknives.com

Specialties: Bowies, hunters and working knives. **Patterns:** Bowies, camp knives, hunters and skinners. **Technical:** Forges carbon steel, and his own Damascus. **Prices:** $250 to $1500. **Remarks:** Part-time maker, first knife sold in 1991. ABS Journeyman Smith since 2006. **Mark:** L.A. Kemp.

KENNEDY JR., BILL

PO Box 850431, Yukon, OK 73085, Phone: 405-354-9150, bkfish1@gmail.com; www. billkennedyjrknives.com

Specialties: Working straight knives and folders. **Patterns:** Hunters, minis, fishing, and pocket knives. **Technical:** Grinds D2, 440C, ATS-34, BG42. **Prices:** $110 and up. **Remarks:** Part-time maker; first knife sold in 1980. **Mark:** Last name and year made.

KERANEN, PAUL

4122 S. E. Shiloh Ct., Tacumseh, KS 66542, Phone: 785-220-2141, pk6269@yahoo. com

Specialties: Specializes in Japanese style knives and swords. Most clay tempered with hamon. **Patterns:** Does bowies, fighters and hunters. **Technical:** Forges and grinds carbons steel only. Make my own Damascus. **Prices:** $75 to $800. **Mark:** Keranen arched over anvil.

KERN, R W

20824 Texas Trail W, San Antonio, TX 78257-1602, Phone: 210-698-2549, rkern@ ev1.net

Specialties: Damascus, straight and folders. **Patterns:** Hunters, Bowies and folders. **Technical:** Grinds ATS-34, 440C and BG42. Forges own Damascus. **Prices:** $200 and up. **Remarks:** First knives 1980; retired; work as time permits. Member ABS, Texas Knifemaker and Collectors Association. **Mark:** Outline of Alamo with kern over outline.

KEYES, DAN

6688 King St, Chino, CA 91710, Phone: 909-628-8329

KEYES, GEOFF P.

13027 Odell Rd NE, Duvall, WA 98019, Phone: 425-844-0758, 5ef@polarisfarm.com; Web: www5elementsforge.com

Specialties: Working grade fixed blades, 19th century style gents knives. **Patterns:** Fixed blades, your design or mine. **Technical:** Hnad-forged 5160, 1084, and own Damascus. **Prices:** $200 and up. **Remarks:** Geoff Keyes DBA 5 Elements Forge, ABS Journeyman Smith. **Mark:** Early mark KEYES etched in script. New mark as of 2009: pressed GPKeyes.

KHALSA, JOT SINGH

368 Village St, Millis, MA 02054, Phone: 508-376-8162, Fax: 508-532-0517, jotkhalsa@comcast.net; Web: www.khalsakirpans.com, www.lifeknives.com, and www.thekhalsaraj.com

Specialties: Liner locks, one-of-a-kind daggers, swords, and kirpans (Sikh daggers) all original designs. **Technical:** Forges own Damascus, uses others high quality Damascus including stainless, and grinds stainless steels. Uses natural handle materials frequently unusual minerals. Pieces are frequently engraved and more recently carved. **Prices:** Start at $700.

KHARLAMOV, YURI

Oboronnay 46, Tula, RUSSIA 300007

Specialties: Classic, fancy and traditional knives of his design. **Patterns:** Daggers and hunters. **Technical:** Forges only Damascus with nickel. Uses natural handle materials; engraves on metal, carves on nut-tree; silver and pearl inlays. **Prices:** $600 to $2380; some to $4000. **Remarks:** Full-time maker; first knife sold in 1988. **Mark:** Initials.

KI, SHIVA

5222 Ritterman Ave, Baton Rouge, LA 70805, Phone: 225-356-7274, shivakicustomknives@netzero.net; Web: www.shivakicustomknives.com

Specialties: Working straight knives and folders. **Patterns:** Emphasis on personal defense knives, martial arts weapons. **Technical:** Forges and grinds; makes own Damascus; prefers natural handle materials. **Prices:** $550 to $10,000.**Remarks:** Full-time maker; first knife sold in 1981. **Mark:** Name with logo.

KIEFER, TONY

112 Chateaugay Dr, Pataskala, OH 43062, Phone: 740-927-6910

Specialties: Traditional working and using straight knives in standard patterns. **Patterns:** Bowies, fighters and hunters. **Technical:** Grinds 440C and D2; forges D2. Flat-grinds Bowies; hollow-grinds drop-point and trailing-point hunters. **Prices:** $110 to $300; some to $200. **Remarks:** Spare-time maker; first knife sold in 1988. **Mark:** Last name.

KILBY, KEITH

1902 29th St, Cody, WY 82414, Phone: 307-587-2732

Specialties: Works with all designs. **Patterns:** Mostly Bowies, camp knives and hunters of his design. **Technical:** Forges 52100, 5160, 1095, Damascus and mosaic Damascus. **Prices:** $250 to $3500. **Remarks:** Part-time maker; first knife sold in 1974. Doing business as Foxwood Forge. **Mark:** Name.

KILEY, MIKE AND JANDY

ROCKING K KNIVES, 1325 Florida, Chino Valley, AZ 86323, Phone: 928-910-2647

Specialties: Period knives for cowboy action shooters and mountain men. **Patterns:** Bowies, drop-point hunters, skinners, sheepsfoot blades and spear points. **Technical:** Steels are 1095, 0-1, Damascus and others upon request. Handles include all types of wood, with cocobolo, ironwood, rosewood, maple and bacote being favorites as well as buffalo horn, stag, elk antler, mammoth ivory, giraffe boon, sheep horn and camel bone. **Prices:** $100 to $500 depending on style and materials. Hand-tooled leather sheaths by Jan and Mike. **Mark:** Stylized K on one side; Kiley on the other.

KILPATRICK, CHRISTIAN A

6925 Mitchell Ct, Citrus Hieghts, CA 95610, Phone: 916-729-0733, crimsonkil@gmail. com; Web:www.crimsonknives.com

Specialties: All forged weapons (no firearms) from ancient to modern. All blades produced are first and foremost useable tools, and secondly but no less importantly, artistic expressions. **Patterns:** Hunters, bowies, daggers, swords, axes, spears, boot knives, bird knives, ethnic blades and historical reproductions. Customer designs welcome. **Technical:** Forges and grinds, makes own Damascus. Does file work. **Prices:** $125 to $3200. **Remarks:** 26 year part time maker. First knife sold in 2002.

KIMBERLEY, RICHARD L.

86-B Arroyo Hondo Rd, Santa Fe, NM 87508, Phone: 505-820-2727

Specialties: Fixed-blade and period knives. **Technical:** 01, 52100, 9260 steels. **Remarks:** Member ABS. Marketed under "Kimberleys of Santa Fe." **Mark:** "By D. KIMBERLEY SANTA FE NM."

KIMSEY, KEVIN

198 Cass White Rd. NW, Cartersville, GA 30121, Phone: 770-387-0779 and 770-655-8879

Specialties: Tactical fixed blades and folders. **Patterns:** Fighters, folders, hunters and utility knives. **Technical:** Grinds 440C, ATS-34 and D2 carbon. **Prices:** $100 to $400; some to $600. **Remarks:** Three-time Blade magazine award winner, knifemaker since 1983. **Mark:** Rafter and stylized KK.

KING, BILL

14830 Shaw Rd, Tampa, FL 33625, Phone: 813-961-3455, billkingknives@yahoo.com

Specialties: Folders, lockbacks, liner locks, automatics and stud openers. **Patterns:** Wide varieties; folders. **Technical:** ATS-34 and some Damascus; single and double grinds. Offers filework and jewel embellishment; nickel-silver Damascus and mokume bolsters. **Prices:** $150 to $475; some to $850. **Remarks:** Full-time maker; first knife sold in 1976. All titanium fitting on liner-locks; screw or rivet construction on lock-backs. **Mark:** Last name in crown.

KING, FRED

430 Grassdale Rd, Cartersville, GA 30120, Phone: 770-382-8478, Web: http://www. fking83264@aol.com

Specialties: Fancy and embellished working straight knives and folders. **Patterns:** Hunters, Bowies and fighters. **Technical:** Grinds ATS-34 and D2: forges 5160 and Damascus. Offers filework. **Prices:** $100 to $3500. **Remarks:** Spare-time maker; first knife sold in 1984. **Mark:** Kings Edge.

KING JR., HARVEY G

32170 Hwy K4, Alta Vista, KS 66834, Phone: 785-499-5207, Web: www. harveykingknives.com

Specialties: Traditional working and using straight knives of his design and to customer specs. **Patterns:** Hunters, Bowies and fillet knives. **Technical:** Grinds O1, A2 and D2. Prefers natural handle materials; offers leatherwork. **Prices:** Start at $150. **Remarks:** Full-time maker; first knife sold in 1988. **Mark:** Name, city, state, and serial number.

KINKER, MIKE

8755 E County Rd 50 N, Greensburg, IN 47240, Phone: 812-663-5277, kinkercustomknives@gmail.com

Specialties: Working/using knives, straight knives. Starting to make folders. Your design. **Patterns:** Boots, daggers, hunters, skinners, hatchets. **Technical:** Grind 440C and ATS-34, others if required. Damascus, dovetail bolsters, jeweled blade. **Prices:** $125 to 375; some to $1000. **Remarks:** Part-time maker; first knife sold in 1991. Doing business as Kinker Custom Knives. **Mark:** Kinker

KINNIKIN, TODD
EUREKA FORGE, 7 Capper Dr., Pacific, MO 63069-3603, Phone: 314-938-6248
Specialties: Mosaic Damascus. **Patterns:** Hunters, fighters, folders and automatics. **Technical:** Forges own mosaic Damascus with tool steel Damascus edge. Prefers natural, fossil and artifact handle materials. **Prices:** $1200 to $2400. **Remarks:** Full-time maker; first knife sold in 1994. **Mark:** Initials connected.

KIOUS, JOE
1015 Ridge Pointe Rd, Kerrville, TX 78028, Phone: 830-367-2277, kious@hctc.net
Specialties: Investment-quality interframe and bolstered folders. **Patterns:** Folder specialist, all types. **Technical:** Both stainless and non-stainless Damascus. Also uses CPM 154CM, M4, and CPM D2. **Prices:** $1300 to $5000; some to $10,000. **Remarks:** Full-time maker; first knife sold in 1969. **Mark:** Last name, city and state or last name only.

KIRK, RAY
PO Box 1445, Tahlequah, OK 74465, Phone: 918-207-8076, ray@rakerknives.com; Web: www.rakerknives.com
Specialties: Folders, skinners fighters, and Bowies. **Patterns:** Neck knives and small hunters and skinners. Full and hidden-tang integrals from 52100 round bar. **Technical:** Forges all knives from 52100 and own damascus. **Prices:** $65 to $3000. **Remarks:** Started forging in 1989; makes own Damascus. **Mark:** Stamped "Raker" on blade.

KIRKES, BILL
235 Oaklawn Cir., Little Rock, AR 72206, Phone: 501-551-0135, bill@kirkesknives.com; Web: www.kirkesknives.com
Specialties: Handforged fixed blades. **Technical:** High-carbon 5160 and 1084 blade steels. Will build to customer's specs, prefers to use natural handle material. **Remarks:** ABS Journeyman smith. **Mark:** Kirkes.

KITSMILLER, JERRY
67277 Las Vegas Dr, Montrose, CO 81401, Phone: 970-249-4290
Specialties: Working straight knives in standard patterns. **Patterns:** Hunters, boots. **Technical:** Grinds ATS-34 and 440C only. **Prices:** $75 to $200; some to $300. **Remarks:** Spare-time maker; first knife sold in 1984. **Mark:** JandS Knives.

KLAASEE, TINUS
PO Box 10221, George, WC, SOUTH AFRICA 6530
Specialties: Hunters, skinners and utility knives. **Patterns:** Uses own designs and client specs. **Technical:** N690 stainless steel 440C Damascus. **Prices:** $700 and up. **Remarks:** Use only indigenous materials. Hardwood, horns and ivory. Makes his own sheaths and boxes. **Mark:** Initials and sur name over warthog.

KLEIN, KEVIN
129 Cedar St., Apt. 2, Boston, MA 02119, Phone: 609-937-8949, kevin.a.klein779@gmail.com
Specialties: Forged damascus blades using 15N20 and 1084. **Remarks:** Full-time maker; first knife made in 2012. Apprentice to J.D. Smith starting in 2012. **Mark:** KAK? or ?, depending on piece.

KNAPP, MARK
Mark Knapp Custom Knives, 1971 Fox Ave, Fairbanks, AK 99701, Phone: 907-452-7477, info@markknappcustomknives.com; Web: www.markknappcustomknives.com
Specialties: Mosaic handles of exotic natural materials from Alaska and around the world. Folders, fixed blades, full and hidden tangs. **Patterns:** Folders, hunters, skinners, and camp knives. **Technical:** Forges own Damascus, uses both forging and stock removal with ATS-34, 154CM, stainless Damascus, carbon steel and carbon Damascus. **Prices:** $800-$3000. **Remarks:** Full time maker, sold first knife in 2000. **Mark:** Mark Knapp Custom Knives Fairbanks, AK.

KNAPTON, CHRIS C.
76 Summerland Dr., Henderson, Aukland, NEW ZEALAND, Phone: 09-835-3598, knaptch76@gmail.com; Web: www.knappoknives.com
Specialties: Working and fancy straight and folding knives of his own design. **Patterns:** Tactical, utility, hunting fixed and folding knives. **Technical:** Predominate knife steels are Elmax, CPM-154 and D2. All blades made via the stock removal method. **Prices:** $120 - $500. **Remarks:** Part-time maker. **Mark:** Stylized letter K, country name and Haast eagle.

KNICKMEYER, HANK
6300 Crosscreek, Cedar Hill, MO 63016, Phone: 636-285-3210
Specialties: Complex mosaic Damascus constructions. **Patterns:** Fixed blades, swords, folders and automatics. **Technical:** Mosaic Damascus with all tool steel Damascus edges. **Prices:** $500 to $2000; some $3000 and higher. **Remarks:** Part-time maker; first knife sold in 1989. Doing business as Dutch Creek Forge and Foundry. **Mark:** Initials connected.

KNICKMEYER, KURT
6344 Crosscreek, Cedar Hill, MO 63016, Phone: 314-274-0481

KNIGHT, JASON
110 Paradise Pond Ln, Harleyville, SC 29448, Phone: 843-452-1163, jasonknightknives.com
Specialties: Bowies. **Patterns:** Bowies and anything from history or his own design. **Technical:** 1084, 5160, O1, 52102, Damascus/forged blades. **Prices:** $200 and up. **Remarks:** Bladesmith. **Mark:** KNIGHT.

KNIPSCHIELD, TERRY
808 12th Ave NE, Rochester, MN 55906, Phone: 507-288-7829, terry@knipknives.com; Web: www.knipknives.com

Specialties: Folders and fixed blades and leather working knives. **Patterns:** Variations of traditional patterns and his own new designs. **Technical:** Stock removal. Grinds CPM-154CM, ATS-34, stainless Damascus, 01.**Prices:** $60 to $1200 and higher for upscale folders. **Remarks:** Etchd logo on blade, KNIP with shield image.

KNOTT, STEVE
KNOTT KNIVES, 203 Wild Rose, Guyton, GA 31312, Phone: 912-536-7651, knottknives@yahoo.com; FaceBook: Knott Knives/Steve Knott
Technical: Uses ATS-34/440C and some commercial Damascus, single and double grinds with mirror or satin finishes. **Patterns:** Hunters, boot knives, bowies, and tantos, slip joint, LinerLock and lock-back folders. Uses a wide variety of handle materials to include ironwood, coca-bola and colored stabilized wood, also horn, bone and ivory upon customer request. **Remarks:** First knife sold in 1991. Part-time maker.

KNOWLES, SHAWN
750 Townsbury Rd, Great Meadows, NJ 07838, Phone: 973-670-3307, skcustomknives@gmail.com Web: shawnknowlescustomknives.com

KNUTH, JOSEPH E
3307 Lookout Dr, Rockford, IL 61109, Phone: 815-874-9597
Specialties: High-art working straight knives of his design or to customer specs. **Patterns:** Daggers, fighters and swords. **Technical:** Grinds 440C, ATS-34 and D2. **Prices:** $150 to $1500; some to $15,000. **Remarks:** Full-time maker; first knife sold in 1989. **Mark:** Initials on bolster face.

KOHLS, JERRY
N4725 Oak Rd, Princeton, WI 54968, Phone: 920-295-3648
Specialties: Working knives and period pieces. **Patterns:** Hunters-boots and Bowies, your designs or his. **Technical:** Grinds, ATS-34 440c 154CM and 1095 and commercial Damascus. **Remarks:** Part-time maker. **Mark:** Last name.

KOJETIN, W
20 Bapaume Rd Delville, Germiston, GT, SOUTH AFRICA 1401, Phone: 27118733305/mobile 27836256208
Specialties: High-art and working straight knives of all designs. **Patterns:** Daggers, hunters and his own Man hunter Bowie. **Technical:** Grinds D2 and ATS-34; forges and grinds 440B/C. Offers "wrap-around" pava and abalone handles, scrolled wood or ivory, stacked filework and setting of faceted semi-precious stones. **Prices:** $185 to $600; some to $11,000. **Remarks:** Spare-time maker; first knife sold in 1962. **Mark:** Billy K.

KOLITZ, ROBERT
W9342 Canary Rd, Beaver Dam, WI 53916, Phone: 920-887-1287
Specialties: Working straight knives to customer specs. **Patterns:** Bowies, hunters, bird and trout knives, boots. **Technical:** Grinds O1, 440C; commercial Damascus. **Prices:** $50 to $100; some to $500. **Remarks:** Spare-time maker; first knife sold in 1979. **Mark:** Last initial.

KOMMER, RUSS
4609 35th Ave N, Fargo, ND 58102, Phone: 701-281-1826, russkommer@yahoo.com Web: www.russkommerknives.com
Specialties: Working straight knives with the outdoorsman in mind. **Patterns:** Hunters, semi-skinners, fighters, folders and utility knives, art knives. **Technical:** Hollow-grinds ATS-34, 440C and 440V. **Prices:** $125 to $850; some to $3000. **Remarks:** Full-time maker; first knife sold in 1995. **Mark:** Bear paw—full name, city and state or full name and state.

KOPP, TODD M
PO Box 3474, Apache Jct., AZ 85217, Phone: 480-983-6143, tmkopp@msn.com
Specialties: Classic and traditional straight knives. Fluted handled daggers. **Patterns:** Bowies, boots, daggers, fighters, hunters, swords and folders. **Technical:** Grinds 5160, 440C, ATS-34. All Damascus steels, or customers choice. Some engraving and filework. **Prices:** $200 to $1200; some to $4000. **Remarks:** Part-time maker; first knife sold in 1989. **Mark:** Last name in Old English, some others name, city and state.

KOSTER, DANIEL
KOSTER KNIVES, 1711 Beverly Ct., Bentonville, AR 72712, Phone: 479-366-7794, dan@kosterknives.com; www.kosterknives.com
Patterns: Bushcraft, survival, outdoor and utility knives. **Technical:** Stock-removal method of blade making, using CPM 3V steel. **Prices:** $150 to $300. **Remarks:** Full-time knifemaker in business since 2005. **Mark:** "K" in a circle, negative shape.

KOSTER, STEVEN C
16261 Gentry Ln, Huntington Beach, CA 92647, Phone: 714-907-7250, kosterknives@verizon.net Web: www.kosterhandforgedknives.com
Specialties: Walking sticks, hand axes, tomahawks, Damascus.**Patterns:** Ladder, twists, round horn. **Technical:** Use 5160, 52100, 1084, 1095 steels. Ladder, twists, **Prices:** $200 to $1000. **Remarks:** Wood and leather sheaths with silver furniture. ABS Journeyman 2003. California knifemakers member. **Mark:** Koster squeezed between lines.

KOVACIK, ROBERT
Lavadska 722, 98556 Tomasovce, SLOVAKIA, Phone: Mobil:00427907644800, kovacikart@gmail.com Web: www.robertkovacik.com
Specialties: Engraved hunting knives, guns engraved; Knifemakers. **Technical:** Fixed blades, folder knives, miniatures. **Prices:** $350 to $10,000 U.S. **Mark:** R.

KOVAR, EUGENE
2626 W 98th St., Evergreen Park, IL 60642, Phone: 708-636-3724/708-790-4115, baldemaster333@aol.com
Specialties: One-of-a-kind miniature knives only. **Patterns:** Fancy to fantasy miniature knives; knife pendants and tie tacks. **Technical:** Files and grinds nails, nickel-silver and

sterling silver. **Prices:** $5 to $35; some to $100. **Mark:** GK.

KOYAMA, CAPTAIN BUNSHICHI
3-23 Shirako-cho, Nakamura-ku, Nagoya, Aichi, JAPAN City 453-0817, Phone: 052-461-7070, Fax: 052-461-7070
Specialties: Innovative folding knife. **Patterns:** General purpose one hand. **Technical:** Grinds ATS-34 and Damascus. **Prices:** $400 to $900; some to $1500. **Remarks:** Part-time maker; first knife sold in 1994. **Mark:** Captain B. Koyama and the shoulder straps of CAPTAIN.

KRAFT, STEVE
408 NE 11th St, Abilene, KS 67410, Phone: 785-263-1411
Specialties: Folders, lockbacks, scale release auto, push button auto. **Patterns:** Hunters, boot knives and fighters. **Technical:** Grinds ATS-34, Damascus; uses titanium, pearl, ivory etc. **Prices:** $500 to $2500. **Remarks:** Part-time maker; first knife sold in 1984. **Mark:** Kraft.

KRAPP, DENNY
1826 Windsor Oak Dr, Apopka, FL 32703, Phone: 407-880-7115
Specialties: Fantasy and working straight knives of his design. **Patterns:** Hunters, fighters and utility/camp knives. **Technical:** Grinds ATS-34 and 440C. **Prices:** $85 to $300; some to $800. **Remarks:** Spare-time maker; first knife sold in 1988. **Mark:** Last name.

KRAUSE, JIM
3272 Hwy H, Farmington, MO 63640, Phone: 573-756-7388, james_krause@sbcglobal.net
Specialties: Folders, fixed blades, neck knives. **Patterns:** Stock removal. **Technical:** K390, CPM-S35VN, CPM-S30V, most CPM steel, 1095, stainless and high-carbon damascus from the best makers. **Remarks:** Full-time maker; first knife made in 2000. **Mark:** Krause Handmade with Christian fish.

KRAUSE, ROY W
22412 Corteville, St. Clair Shores, MI 48081, Phone: 810-296-3995, Fax: 810-296-2663
Specialties: Military and law enforcement/Japanese-style knives and swords. **Patterns:** Combat and back-up, Bowies, fighters, boot knives, daggers, tantos, wakazashis and katanas. **Technical:** Grinds ATS-34, A2, D2, 1045, O1 and commercial Damascus; differentially hardened Japanese-style blades. **Prices:** Moderate to upscale. **Remarks:** Full-time maker. **Mark:** Last name on traditional knives; initials in Japanese characters on Japanese-style knives.

KREGER, THOMAS
1996 Dry Branch Rd., Lugoff, SC 29078, Phone: 803-438-4221, tdkreger@bellsouth.net
Specialties: South Carolina/George Herron style working/using knives. Customer designs considered. **Patterns:** Hunters, skinners, fillet, liner lock folders, kitchen, and camp knives. **Technical:** Hollow and flat grinds of ATS-34, CPM154CM, and 5160. **Prices:** $100 and up. **Remarks:** Full-time maker. President of the South Carolina Association of Knifemakers 2002-2006, and current president since 2013. **Mark:** TDKreger.

KREH, LEFTY
210 Wichersham Way, "Cockeysville", MD 21030

KREIBICH, DONALD L.
1638 Commonwealth Circle, Reno, NV 89503, Phone: 775-746-0533, dmkreno@sbcglobal.net
Specialties: Working straight knives in standard patterns. **Patterns:** Bowies, boots and daggers; camp and fishing knives. **Technical:** Grinds 440C, 154CM and ATS-34; likes integrals. **Prices:** $100 to $200; some to $500. **Remarks:** Part-time maker; first knife sold in 1980. **Mark:** First and middle initials, last name.

KREIN, TOM
P.O. Box 994, 337 E. Main St., Gentry, AR 72734, Phone: 479-233-0508, kreinknives@gmail.com; www.kreinknives.net
Specialties: LinerLock folders and fixed blades designed to be carried and used. **Technical:** Stock removal using D2, A2, CPM 3V, CPM 154, CPM M4, Stellite 6K and damascus, and makes his own sheaths. **Prices:** $250 to $500 and up. **Remarks:** Full-time maker; first knife made in 1993. **Mark:** Last name and the year the knife was made in the shape of a circle, with a bulldog in the middle.

KRESSLER, D F
Mittelweg 31 i, D-28832 Achim, GERMANY 28832, Phone: +49 (0) 42 02/76-5742, Fax: +49 (0) 42 02/7657 41, info@kresslerknives.com; Web: www.kresslerknives.com
Specialties: High-tech integral and interframe knives. **Patterns:** Hunters, fighters, daggers. **Technical:** Grinds new state-of-the-art steels; prefers natural handle materials. **Prices:** Upscale. **Mark:** Name in logo.

KUBASEK, JOHN A
74 Northhampton St, Easthampton, MA 01027, Phone: 413-527-7917, jaknife01@yahoo.com
Specialties: Left- and right-handed LinerLock® folders of his design or to customer specs. Also new knives made with Ripcord patent. **Patterns:** Fighters, tantos, drop points, survival knives, neck knives and belt buckle knives. **Technical:** Grinds 154CM, S30 and Damascus. **Prices:** $395 to $1500. **Remarks:** Part-time maker; first knife sold in 1985. **Mark:** Name and address etched.

KUKULKA, WOLFGANG
Golf Tower 2, Apt. 107, Greens, PO BOX 126229, Dubai, UNITED ARAB EMIRATES,
Phone: 00971-50-2201047, wolfgang.kukulka@hotmail.com
Specialties: Fully handmade from various steels: Damascus Steel, Japanese Steel, 1.2842, 1.2379, K110, K360, M390 microclean **Patterns:** Handles made from stabilized wood, different hard woods, horn and various materials **Technical:** Hardness of blades: 58-67 HRC.

L

LADD, JIM S
1120 Helen, Deer Park, TX 77536, Phone: 713-479-7286
Specialties: Working knives and period pieces. **Patterns:** Hunters, boots and Bowies plus other straight knives. **Technical:** Grinds D2, 440C and 154CM. **Prices:** $125 to $225; some to $550. **Remarks:** Part-time maker; first knife sold in 1965. Doing business as The Tinker. **Mark:** First and middle initials, last name.

LADD, JIMMIE LEE
1120 Helen, Deer Park, TX 77536, Phone: 713-479-7186
Specialties: Working straight knives. **Patterns:** Hunters, skinners and utility knives. **Technical:** Grinds 440C and D2. **Prices:** $75 to $225. **Remarks:** First knife sold in 1979. **Mark:** First and middle initials, last name.

LAINSON, TONY
114 Park Ave, Council Bluffs, IA 51503, Phone: 712-322-5222
Specialties: Working straight knives, liner locking folders. **Technical:** Grinds 154CM, ATS-34, 440C buys Damascus. Handle materials include Micarta, carbon fiber G-10 ivory pearl and bone. **Prices:** $95 to $600. **Remarks:** Part-time maker; first knife sold in 1987. **Mark:** Name and state.

LAIRSON SR., JERRY
H C 68 Box 970, Ringold, OK 74754, Phone: 580-876-3426, bladesmt@brightok.net; Web: www.lairson-custom-knives.net
Specialties: Damascus collector grade knives & high performance field grade hunters & cutting competition knives. **Patterns:** Damascus, random, raindrop, ladder, twist and others. **Technical:** All knives hammer forged. Mar Tempering**Prices:** Field grade knives $300. Collector grade $400 & up. **Mark:** Lairson. **Remarks:** Makes any style knife but prefer fighters and hunters. ABS Mastersmith, AKA member, KGA member. Cutting competition competitor.

LAKE, RON
3360 Bendix Ave, Eugene, OR 97401, Phone: 541-484-2683
Specialties: High-tech working knives; inventor of the modern interframe folder. **Patterns:** Hunters, boots, etc.; locking folders. **Technical:** Grinds 154CM and ATS-34. Patented interframe with special lock release tab. **Prices:** $2200 to $3000; some higher. **Remarks:** Full-time maker; first knife sold in 1966. **Mark:** Last name.

LALA, PAULO RICARDO P AND LALA, ROBERTO P.
R Daniel Martins 636, Presidente Prudente, SP, BRAZIL 19031-260, Phone: 0182-210125, korthknives@terra.com.br; Web: www.ikbsknifetech.com
Specialties: Straight knives and folders of all designs to customer specs. **Patterns:** Bowies, daggers fighters, hunters and utility knives. **Technical:** Grinds and forges D6, 440C, high-carbon steels and Damascus. **Prices:** $60 to $400; some higher. **Remarks:** Full-time makers; first knife sold in 1991. All stainless steel blades are ultra sub-zero quenched. **Mark:** Sword carved on top of anvil under KORTH.

LAMB, CURTIS J
3336 Louisiana Ter, Ottawa, KS 66067-8996, Phone: 785-242-6657

LAMBERT, JARRELL D
2321 FM 2982, Granado, TX 77962, Phone: 512-771-3744
Specialties: Traditional working and using straight knives of his design and to customer specs. **Patterns:** Bowies, hunters, tantos and utility/camp knives. **Technical:** Grinds ATS-34; forges W2 and his own Damascus. Makes own sheaths. **Prices:** $80 to $600; some to $1000. **Remarks:** Part-time maker; first knife sold in 1982. **Mark:** Etched first and middle initials, last name; or stamped last name.

LAMBERT, KIRBY
2131 Edgar St, Regina, SK, CANADA S4N 3K8, kirby@lambertknives.com; Web: www.lambertknives.com
Specialties: Tactical/utility folders. Tactical/utility Japanese style fixed blades. **Prices:** $200 to $1500 U.S. **Remarks:** Full-time maker since 2002. **Mark:** Black widow spider and last name Lambert.

LAMEY, ROBERT M
15800 Lamey Dr, Biloxi, MS 39532, Phone: 228-396-9066, Fax: 228-396-9022, rmlamey@ametro.net; Web: www.lameyknives.com
Specialties: Bowies, fighters, hard use knives. **Patterns:** Bowies, fighters, hunters and camp knives. **Technical:** Forged and stock removal. **Prices:** $125 to $350. **Remarks:** Lifetime reconditioning; will build to customer designs, specializing in hard use, affordable knives. **Mark:** LAMEY.

LAMPSON, FRANK G
1407 Bannon Cir., Chino Valley, AZ 86323, Phone: 916-549-3241, fglampson@yahoo.com
Specialties: Working folders; one-of-a-kinds. **Patterns:** Folders, hunters, utility knives, fillet knives and Bowies. **Technical:** Grinds ATS-34, 440C and 154CM. **Prices:** $100 to $750; some to $3500. **Remarks:** Full-time maker; first knife sold in 1971. **Mark:** Name in fish logo.

LANCASTER, C G
No 2 Schoonwinkel St, Parys, Free State, SOUTH AFRICA, Phone: 0568112090

custom knifemakers

Specialties: High-tech working and using knives of his design and to customer specs. Patterns: Hunters, locking folders and utility/camp knives. Technical: Grinds Sandvik 12C27, 440C and D2. Offers anodized titanium bolsters. Prices: $450 to $750; some to $1500. Remarks: Part-time maker; first knife sold in 1990. Mark: Etched logo.

LANCE, BILL
PO Box 4427, Eagle River, AK 99577, Phone: 907-694-1487
Specialties: Ulu sets and working straight knives; limited issue sets. Patterns: Several ulu patterns, drop-point skinners. Technical: Uses ATS-34 and AEBL; ivory, horn and high-class wood handles. Prices: $145 to $500; art sets to $7,500. Remarks: First knife sold in 1981. Mark: Last name over a lance.

LANCE, LUCAS
3600 N. Charley, Wasilla, AK 99654, Phone: 907-357-0349, lucas@lanceknives.com; Web: www.lanceknives.com
Specialties: Working with materials native to Alaska such as fossilized ivory, bone, musk ox bone, sheep horn, moose antler, all combined with exotic materials from around the world. Patterns: Fully functional knives of my own design. Technical: Mainly stock removal, flat grinds in ATS-34, 440C, 5160 and various makes of American-made damascus. Prices: $165 to $850. Remarks: Second-generation knifemaker who grew up and trained in father, Bill Lance's, shop. First knife designed and made in 1994. Mark: Last name over a lance.

LANDERS, JOHN
758 Welcome Rd, Newnan, GA 30263, Phone: 404-253-5719
Specialties: High-art working straight knives and folders of his design. Patterns: Hunters, fighters and slip-joint folders. Technical: Grinds 440C, ATS-34, 154CM and commercial Damascus. Prices: $85 to $250; some to $500. Remarks: Part-time maker; first knife sold in 1989. Mark: Last name.

LANG, DAVID
6153 Cumulus Circle, Kearns, UT 84118, Phone: 801-809-1241, dknifeguy@msn.com
Specialties: Hunters, Fighters, Push Daggers, Upscale Art Knives, Folders. Technical: Flat grind, hollow grind, hand carving, casting. Remarks: Will work from my designs or to your specifications. I have been making knives 10 years and have gleaned help from Jerry Johnson, Steven Rapp, Earl Black, Steven Johnson, and many others. Prices: $225 - $3000. Mark: Dland over UTAH.

LANGLEY, GENE H
1022 N. Price Rd, Florence, SC 29506, Phone: 843-669-3150
Specialties: Working knives in standard patterns. Patterns: Hunters, boots, fighters, locking folders and slip-joints. Technical: Grinds 440C, 154CM and ATS-34. Prices: $125 to $450; some to $1000. Remarks: Part-time maker; first knife sold in 1979. Mark: Name.

LANGLEY, MICK
1015 Centre Crescent, Qualicum Beach, BC, CANADA V9K 2G6, Phone: 250-752-4261
Specialties: Period pieces and working knives. Patterns: Bowies, push daggers, fighters, boots. Some folding lockers. Technical: Forges 5160, 1084, W2 and his own Damascus. Prices: $250 to $2500; some to $4500. Remarks: Full-time maker, first knife sold in 1977. Mark: Langley with M.S. (for ABS Master Smith)

LANKTON, SCOTT
8065 Jackson Rd. R-11, Ann Arbor, MI 48103, Phone: 313-426-3735
Specialties: Pattern welded swords, krisses and Viking period pieces. Patterns: One-of-a-kind. Technical: Forges W2, L6 nickel and other steels. Prices: $600 to $12,000. Remarks: Part-time bladesmith, full-time smith; first knife sold in 1976. Mark: Last name logo.

LAPEN, CHARLES
Box 529, W. Brookfield, MA 01585
Specialties: Chef's knives for the culinary artist. Patterns: Camp knives, Japanese-style swords and wood working tools, hunters. Technical: Forges 1075, car spring and his own Damascus. Favors narrow and Japanese tangs. Prices: $200 to $400; some to $2000. Remarks: Part-time maker; first knife sold in 1972. Mark: Last name.

LAPLANTE, BRETT
4545 CR412, McKinney, TX 75071, Phone: 972-838-9191, blap007@aol.com
Specialties: Working straight knives and folders to customer specs. Patterns: Survival knives, Bowies, skinners, hunters. Technical: Grinds D2 and 440C. Heat-treats. Prices: $200 to $800. Remarks: Part-time maker; first knife sold in 1987. Mark: Last name in Canadian maple leaf logo.

LARGIN, KEN
KELGIN Knifemakers Co-Op, 2001 S. State Rd. 1, Connersville, IN 47331, Phone: 765-969-5012, kelginfinecutlery@gmail.com; Web: www.kelgin.com
Specialties: Retired from general knifemaking. Only take limited orders in meteorite damascus or solid meteorite blades. Patterns: Any. Technical: Stock removal or forged. Prices: $500 & up. Remarks: Travels the U.S. full time teaching hands-on "History Of Cutting Tools" to Scouts and any interested group. Participants flint knap, forge and keep three tools they make! Mark: K.C. Largin (Kelgin mark retired in 2004).

LARK, DAVID
6641 Schneider Rd., Kingsley, MI 49649, Phone: 231-342-1076, dblark58@yahoo.com
Specialties: Traditional straight knives, art knives, folders. Patterns: All types. Technical: Grinds all types of knife making steel and makes damascus. Prices: $600 and up. Remarks: Full-time maker, custom riflemaker, and engraver. Mark: Lark in script and DBL on engraving.

LARSON, RICHARD
549 E Hawkeye Ave, Turlock, CA 95380, Phone: 209-668-1615, lebatardknives@aol.com
Specialties: Sound working knives, lightweight folders, practical tactical knives. Patterns: Hunters, trout and bird knives, fish fillet knives, Bowies, tactical sheath knives, one- and two-blade folders. Technical: Grinds ATS-34, A2, D2, CPM 3V and commercial Damascus; forges and grinds 52100, 01 and 1095. Machines folder frames from aircraft aluminum. Prices: $40 to $650. Remarks: Full-time maker. First knife made in 1974. Offers knife repair, restoration and sharpening. All knives are serial numbered and registered in the name of original purchaser. Mark: Stamped last name or etched logo of last name, city, and state.

LARY, ED
1016 19th St., Mosinee, WI 54455, laryblades@hotmail.com
Specialties: Upscale hunters and art knives with display presentations. Patterns: Hunters, period pieces. Technical: Grinds all steels, heat treats, fancy file work and engraving. Prices: Upscale. Remarks: Full-time maker since 1974. Mark: Hand engraved "Ed Lary" in script.

LAURENT, KERMIT
1812 Acadia Dr, LaPlace, LA 70068, Phone: 504-652-5629
Specialties: Traditional and working straight knives and folders of his design. Patterns: Bowies, hunters, utilities and folders. Technical: Forges own Damascus, plus uses most tool steels and stainless. Specializes in altering cable patterns. Uses stabilized handle materials, especially select exotic woods. Prices: $100 to $2500; some to $50,000. Remarks: Full-time maker; first knife sold in 1982. Doing business as Kermit's Knife Works. Favorite material is meteorite Damascus. Mark: First name.

LAWRENCE, ALTON
201 W Stillwell, De Queen, AR 71832, Phone: 870-642-7643, Fax: 870-642-4023, uncle21@riversidemachine.net; Web: riversidemachine.net
Specialties: Classic straight knives and folders to customer specs. Patterns: Bowies, hunters, folders and utility/camp knives. Technical: Forges 5160, 1095, 1084, Damascus and railroad spikes. Prices: Start at $100. Remarks: Part-time maker; first knife sold in 1988. Mark: Last name inside fish symbol.

LAY, L J
602 Mimosa Dr, Burkburnett, TX 76354, Phone: 940-569-1329
Specialties: Working straight knives in standard patterns; some period pieces. Patterns: Drop-point hunters, Bowies and fighters. Technical: Grinds ATS-34 to mirror finish; likes Micarta handles. Prices: Moderate. Remarks: Full-time maker; first knife sold in 1985. Mark: Name or name with ram head and city or stamp L J Lay.

LAY, R J (BOB)
Box 1225, Logan Lake, BC, CANADA V0K 1W0, Phone: 250-523-9923, rjlay@telus.net
Specialties: Traditional-styled, fancy straight knifes of his design. Specializing in hunters. Patterns: Bowies, fighters and hunters. Technical: Grinds high-performance stainless and tool steels. Uses exotic handle and spacer material. File cut, prefers narrow tang. Sheaths available. Price: $200 to $500, some to $5000. Remarks: Full-time maker, first knife sold in 1976. Doing business as Lay's Custom Knives. Mark: Signature acid etched.

LEAVITT JR., EARL F
Pleasant Cove Rd Box 306, E. Boothbay, ME 04544, Phone: 207-633-3210
Specialties: 1500-1870 working straight knives and fighters; pole arms. Patterns: Historically significant knives, classic/modern custom designs. Technical: Flat-grinds 01; heat-treats. Filework available. Prices: $90 to $350; some to $1000. Remarks: Full-time maker; first knife sold in 1981. Doing business as Old Colony Manufactory. Mark: Initials in oval.

LEBATARD, PAUL M
14700 Old River Rd, Vancleave, MS 39565, Phone: 228-826-4137, Fax: Cell phone: 228-238-7461, lebatardknives@aol.com
Specialties: Sound working hunting and fillet knives, folding knives, practical tactical knives. Patterns: Hunters, trout and bird knives, fish fillet knives, kitchen knives, Bowies, tactical sheath knives,one- and two-blade folders. Technical: Grinds ATS-34, D-2, CPM 3-V, CPM-154CM, and commercial Damascus; forges and grinds 1095, 01, and 52100. Prices: $75 to $650; some to $1200. Remarks: Full-time maker, first knife made in 1974. Charter member Gulf Coast Custom Knifemakers; Voting member Knifemaker's Guild. Mark: Stamped last name, or etched logo of last name, city, and state. Other: All knives are serial numbered and registered in the name of the original purchaser.

LEBER, HEINZ
Box 446, Hudson's Hope, BC, CANADA V0C 1V0, Phone: 250-783-5304
Specialties: Working straight knives of his design. Patterns: 20 models, from capers to Bowies. Technical: Hollow-grinds D2 and M2 steel; mirror-finishes and full tang only. Likes moose, elk, stone sheep for handles. Prices: $175 to $1000. Remarks: Full-time maker; first knife sold in 1975. Mark: Initials connected.

LEBLANC, GARY E
1403 Fairview Ln., Little Falls, MN 56345, Phone: 320-232-0245, butternutcove@hotmail.com
Specialties: Hunting and fishing, some kitchen knives and the Air Assault tactical knife. Does own leather and Kydex work. Patterns: Stock removal. Technical: Mostly ATS34 for spec knives--orders, whatever the customer desires. Prices: Full range: $85 for parring knife, up $4000 plus fro collector grade hunter and fillet set. Remarks: First knife made in 1998. Mark: Circular with star in center and LEBLANC on upper curve and KNIFEWORKS on lower curve.

LECK, DAL
Box 1054, Hayden, CO 81639, Phone: 970-276-3663
Specialties: Classic, traditional and working knives of his design and in standard patterns; period pieces. **Patterns:** Boots, daggers, fighters, hunters and push daggers. **Technical:** Forges O1 and 5160; makes his own Damascus. **Prices:** $175 to $700; some to $1500. **Remarks:** Part-time maker; first knife sold in 1990. Doing business as The Moonlight Smithy. **Mark:** Stamped: hammer and anvil with initials.

LEE, ETHAN
17200 N. Tucker School Rd., Sturgeon, MO 65284, Phone: 573-682-4364, Facebook page: ELEE Knives
Specialties: Practical using knives with an elegant touch of quality craftsmanship. **Technical:** Primarily uses damascus and hand-forged high-carbon steels, along with 440C or 154CM stainless. **Prices:** $200-$500. **Remarks:** Part-time maker; first knife made in 2007. **Mark:** ELEE.

LEE, RANDY
PO Box 1873, St. Johns, AZ 85936, Phone: 928-337-2594, Fax: 928-337-5002, randylee.knives@yahoo.com; Web: www.randyleeknives.com
Specialties: Traditional working and using straight knives of his design. **Patterns:** Bowies, fighters, hunters, daggers. **Technical:** Grinds ATS-34, 440C Damascus, and 154CPM. Offers sheaths. **Prices:** $325 to $2500. **Remarks:** Full-time maker; first knife sold in 1979. **Mark:** Full name, city, state.

LELAND, STEVE
2300 Sir Francis Drake Blvd, Fairfax, CA 94930-1118, Phone: 415-457-0318, Fax: 415-457-0995, Web: www.stephenleland@comcast.net
Specialties: Traditional and working straight knives and folders of his design. **Patterns:** Hunters, fighters, Bowies, chefs. **Technical:** Grinds O1, ATS-34 and 440C. Does own heat treat. Makes nickel silver sheaths. **Prices:** $150 to $750; some to $1500. **Remarks:** Part-time maker; first knife sold in 1987. Doing business as Leland Handmade Knives. **Mark:** Last name.

LEMAIRE, RYAN M.
14045 Leon Rd., Abbeville, LA 70510, Phone: 337-893-1937, ryanlemaire@yahoo.com
Specialties: All styles. Enjoys early American and frontier styles. Also, office desk sets for hunters and fishermen. **Patterns:** Hunters, camp knives, miniatures and period styles. **Technical:** Stock removal, carbon steel, stainless steel and damascus. Some forging of guards. Leather and wooden sheaths. **Prices:** Vary. **Remarks:** Member of American Bladesmith Society and Louisiana Craft Guild. **Mark:** First name, city and state in oval.

LEMCKE, JIM L
10649 Haddington Ste 180, Houston, TX 77043, Phone: 888-461-8632, Fax: 713-461-8221, jimll@hal-pc.org; Web: www.texasknife.com
Specialties: Large supply of custom ground and factory finished blades; knife kits; leather sheaths; in-house heat treating and cryogenic tempering; exotic handle material (wood, ivory, oosik, horn, stabilized woods); machines and supplies for knifemaking; polishing and finishing supplies; heat treat ovens; etching equipment; bar, sheet and rod material (brass, stainless steel, nickel silver); titanium sheet material. Catalog. $4.

LEMELIN, STEPHANIE
3495 Olivier St., Brossard, CANADA J4Y 2J9, Phone: 514-462-1322, stephlemelin@hotmail.com
Specialties: Art knives, mostly ornate. **Patterns:** Knives with sculptured or carved handles. Straight knives and folders. **Technical:** Grinds 440C, CPM 154 and ATS-34, all knives hand filed and flat ground. **Remarks:** Part-time maker, jeweler and knifemaker; first knife sold in 2013. **Mark:** Lemelin.

LEMOINE, DAVID C
1037 S College St, Mountain Home, AR 72653, Phone: 870-656-4730, dlemoine@davidlemoineknives.com; Web: davidlemoineknives.com
Specialties: Superior edge geometry on high performance custom classic and tactical straight blades and liner lock folders. **Patterns:** Hunters, skinners, bird and trout, fillet, camp, tactical, and military knives. Some miniatures. **Technical:** Flat and hollow grinds, CPMS90V, CPMS35V, CPMS30V, D2, A2, O1, 440C, ATS34, 154cm,Damasteel, Chad Nichols, Devin Thomas, and Robert Eggerling Damascus. Hidden and full tapered tangs, ultra-smooth folding mechanisms. File work, will use most all handle materials, does own professional in-house heat treatment and Rockwell testing. Hot blueing. **Prices:** $250 and up. **Remarks:** Part-time maker, giving and selling knives since 1986. Each patron receives a NIV Sportsman's Field Bible. **Mark:** Name, city and state in full oval with cross in the center. Reverse image on other side. The cross never changes.

LENNON, DALE
459 County Rd 1554, Alba, TX 75410, Phone: 903-765-2392, devildaddy1@netzero.net
Specialties: Working / using knives. **Patterns:** Hunters, fighters and Bowies. **Technical:** Grinds high carbon steels, ATS-34, forges some. **Prices:** Starts at $120. **Remarks:** Part-time maker, first knife sold in 2000. **Mark:** Last name.

LEONARD, RANDY JOE
188 Newton Rd, Sarepta, LA 71071, Phone: 318-994-2712

LEONE, NICK
9 Georgetown Dr, Pontoon Beach, IL 62040, Phone: 618-792-0734, nickleone@sbcglobal.net
Specialties: 18th century period straight knives. **Patterns:** Fighters, daggers, bowies. Besides period pieces makes modern designs. **Technical:** Forges 5160, W2, O1, 1098, 52100 and his own Damascus. **Prices:** $100 to $1000; some to $3500. **Remarks:** Full-time maker; first knife sold in 1987. Doing business as Anvil Head Forge. **Mark:** AHF, Leone, NL

LERCH, MATTHEW
N88 W23462 North Lisbon Rd, Sussex, WI 53089, Phone: 262-246-6362, Web: www.lerchcustomknives.com
Specialties: Folders and folders with special mechanisms. **Patterns:** Interframe and integral folders; lock backs, assisted openers, side locks, button locks and liner locks. **Technical:** Grinds ATS-34, 1095, 440 and Damascus. Offers filework and embellished bolsters. **Prices:** $900 and up. **Remarks:** Full-time maker; first knife made in 1986. **Mark:** Last name.

LESSWING, KEVIN
29A East 34th St, Bayonne, NJ 07002, Phone: 551-221-1841, klesswing@excite.com
Specialties: Traditonal working and using straight knives of his design or to customer specs. A few folders. Makes own leather sheaths. **Patterns:** Hunters, daggers, bowies, bird and trout. **Technical:** Forges high carbon and tool steels, makes own Damascus, grinds CPM154CM, Damasteel, and other stainless steels. Does own heat treating. **Remarks:** Voting member of Knifemakers Guild, part-time maker. **Mark:** KL on early knives, LESSWING on Current knives.

LEU, POHAN
PO BOX 15423, Rio Rancho, NM 87174, Phone: 949-300-6412, pohanleu@hotmail.com Web: www.leucustom.com
Specialties: Japanese influenced fixed blades made to your custom specifications. Knives and swords. A2 tool steel, Stock Removal. **Prices:** $180 and up. **Remarks:** Full-time; first knife sold in 2003. **Mark:** LEU or PL.

LEVENGOOD, BILL
15011 Otto Rd, Tampa, FL 33624, Phone: 813-961-5688, bill.levengood@verison.net; Web: www.levengoodknives.com
Specialties: Working straight knives and folders. **Patterns:** Hunters, Bowies, folders and collector pieces. **Technical:** Grinds ATS-34, S-30V, CPM-154 and Damascus. **Prices:** $175 to $1500. **Remarks:** Full time maker; first knife sold in 1983. **Mark:** Last name, city, state.

LEVIN, JACK
201 Brighton 1st Road, Suite 3R, Brooklyn, NY 11235, Phone: 718-415-7911, jacklevin1@yahoo.com
Specialties: Folders with mechanisms.

LEVINE, BOB
101 Westwood Dr, Tullahoma, TN 37388, Phone: 931-454-9943, levineknives@msn.com
Specialties: Working left- and right-handed LinerLock® folders. **Patterns:** Hunters and folders. **Technical:** Grinds ATS-34, 440C, D2, O1 and some Damascus; hollow and some flat grinds. Uses fossil ivory, Micarta and exotic woods. Provides custom leather sheath with each fixed knife. **Prices:** Starting at $135. **Remarks:** Full-time maker; first knife sold in 1984. Voting member Knifemakers Guild, German Messermaher Guild. **Mark:** Name and logo.

LEWIS, BILL
PO Box 63, Riverside, IA 52327, Phone: 319-461-1609, wildbill37@geticonnect.com
Specialties: Folders of all kinds including those made from one-piece of white tail antler with or without the crown. **Patterns:** Hunters, folding hunters, fillet, Bowies, push daggers, etc. **Prices:** $20 to $200. **Remarks:** Part-time maker; first knife sold in 1978. **Mark:** W.E.L.

LEWIS, MIKE
21 Pleasant Hill Dr, DeBary, FL 32713, Phone: 386-753-0936, dragonsteel@prodigy.net
Specialties: Traditional straight knives. **Patterns:** Swords and daggers. **Technical:** Grinds 440C, ATS-34 and 5160. Frequently uses cast bronze and cast nickel guards and pommels. **Prices:** $100 to $750. **Remarks:** Part-time maker; first knife sold in 1988. **Mark:** Dragon Steel and serial number.

LEWIS, TOM R
1613 Standpipe Rd, Carlsbad, NM 88220, Phone: 575-885-3616, lewisknives@carlsbadnm.com
Specialties: Traditional working straight knives. **Patterns:** Outdoor knives, hunting knives and Bowies. **Technical:** Grinds ATS-34 and CPM-154, forges 5168, W2, 1084 and O1. Makes wire, pattern welded and chainsaw Damascus. **Prices:** $140 to $1500. **Remarks:** Full-time maker; first knife sold in 1980. Doing business as TR Lewis Handmade Knives. **Mark:** Lewis family crest.

LICATA, STEVEN
LICATA CUSTOM KNIVES, 146 Wilson St. 1st Floor, Boonton, NJ 07005, Phone: 973-588-4909, kniveslicata@aol.com; Web: www.licataknives.com
Specialties: Fantasy swords and knives. One-of-a-kind sculptures in steel. **Prices:** $200 to $25,000.

LIEBENBERG, ANDRE
8 Hilma Rd, Bordeaux, Randburg, GT, SOUTH AFRICA 2196, Phone: 011-787-2303
Specialties: High-art straight knives of his design. **Patterns:** Daggers, fighters and swords. **Technical:** Grinds 440C and 12C27. **Prices:** $250 to $500; some $4000 and higher. Giraffe bone handles with semi-precious stones. **Remarks:** Spare-time maker; first knife sold in 1990. **Mark:** Initials.

LIEGEY, KENNETH R
288 Carney Dr, Millwood, WV 25262, Phone: 304-273-9545
Specialties: Traditional working/using straight knives of his design and to customer specs. **Patterns:** Hunters, utility/camp knives, miniatures. **Technical:** Grinds 440C. **Prices:** $125 and up. **Remarks:** Spare-time maker; first knife sold in 1977. **Mark:** First and middle initials, last name.

LIGHTFOOT, GREG
RR #2, Kitscoty, AB, CANADA T0B 2P0, Phone: 780-846-2812; 780-800-1061, Pitbull@lightfootknives.com; Web: www.lightfootknives.com
Specialties: Stainless steel and Damascus. **Patterns:** Boots, fighters and locking folders. **Technical:** Grinds BG-42, 440C, D2, CPM steels, Stellite 6K. Offers engraving. **Prices:** $500 to $2000. **Remarks:** Full-time maker; first knife sold in 1988. Doing business as Lightfoot Knives. **Mark:** Shark with Lightfoot Knives below.

LIN, MARCUS
4616 Rollando Dr., Rolling Hills Estates, CA 90274, Phone: 808-636-0977, marcuslin7@gmail.com; Web: www.linknives.com
Specialties: Working knives in the Loveless tradition. **Patterns:** Original patterns direct from the Loveless Shop, designed by R.W. Loveless and, on special request, maker's own patterns. **Technical:** Main blade material is Hitachi's ATS-34; other steels available. Please inquire. **Prices:** $550 to $1,750. **Remarks:** Part-time maker since 2004. Mentored by R.W. Loveless and Jim Merritt. Sole authorship work: knives and sheaths, except for heat treat (which goes to Paul Bos Heat Treat). **Mark:** Main logo is "Marcus Lin, maker, Loveless Design."

LINKLATER, STEVE
8 Cossar Dr, Aurora, ON, CANADA L4G 3N8, Phone: 905-727-8929, knifman@sympatico.ca
Specialties: Traditional working/using straight knives and folders of his design. **Patterns:** Fighters, hunters and locking folders. **Technical:** Grinds ATS-34, 440V and D2. **Prices:** $125 to $350; some to $600. **Remarks:** Part-time maker; first knife sold in 1987. Doing business as Links Knives. **Mark:** LINKS.

LISCH, DAVID K
9239 8th Ave. SW, Seattle, WA 98106, Phone: 206-919-5431, Web: www.davidlisch.com
Specialties: One-of-a-kind collectibles, straight knives and custom kitchen knives of own design and to customer specs. **Patterns:** Hunters, skinners, Bowies, and fighters. **Technical:** Forges all his own Damascus under 360-pound air hammer. Forges and chisels wrought iron, pure iron, and bronze butt caps. **Prices:** Starting at $800. **Remarks:** Full-time blacksmith, part-time bladesmith. **Mark:** D. Lisch J.S.

LISTER JR., WELDON E
116 Juniper Ln, Boerne, TX 78006, Phone: 210-269-0102, wlister@grtc.com; Web: www.weldonlister.com
Specialties: One-of-a-kind fancy and embellished folders. **Patterns:** Locking and slip-joint folders. **Technical:** Commercial Damascus and O1. All knives embellished. Engraves, inlays, carves and scrimshaws. **Prices:** Upscale. **Remarks:** Spare-time maker; first knife sold in 1991. **Mark:** Last name.

LITTLE, GARY M
94716 Conklin Meadows Ln, PO Box 156, Broadbent, OR 97414, Phone: 503-572-2656
Specialties: Fancy working knives. **Patterns:** Hunters, tantos, Bowies, axes and buckskinners; locking folders and interframes. **Technical:** Forges and grinds O1, L6m, 1095, and 15N20; makes his own Damascus; bronze fittings. **Prices:** $120 to $1500. **Remarks:** Full-time maker; first knife sold in 1979. Doing business as Conklin Meadows Forge. **Mark:** Name, city and state.

LITTLE, LARRY
1A Cranberry Ln, Spencer, MA 01562, Phone: 508-885-2301, littcran@aol.com
Specialties: Working straight knives of his design or to customer specs. Likes Scagel-style. **Patterns:** Hunters, fighters, Bowies, folders. **Technical:** Grinds and forges L6, O1, 5160, 1095, 1080. Prefers natural handle material especially antler. Uses nickel silver. Makes own heavy duty leather sheath. **Prices:** Start at $125. **Remarks:** Part-time maker. First knife sold in 1985. Offers knife repairs. **Mark:** Little on one side, LL brand on the other.

LIVESAY, NEWT
3306 S. Dogwood St, Siloam Springs, AR 72761, Phone: 479-549-3356, Fax: 479-549-3357, newt@newtlivesay.com; Web:www.newtlivesay.com
Specialties: Combat utility knives, hunting knives, titanium knives, swords, axes, KYDWX sheaths for knives and pistols, custom orders.

LIVINGSTON, ROBERT C
PO Box 6, Murphy, NC 28906, Phone: 704-837-4155
Specialties: Art letter openers to working straight knives. **Patterns:** Minis to machetes. **Technical:** Forges and grinds most steels. **Prices:** Start at $20. **Remarks:** Full-time maker; first knife sold in 1988. Doing business as Mystik Knifeworks. **Mark:** MYSTIK.

LOCKETT, LOWELL C.
344 Spring Hill Dr., Canton, GA 30115, Phone: 770-846-8114, lcl1932@gmail.com or spur1932@windstream.net
Technical: Forges 5160, 1095 and other blade steels, and uses desert ironwood, ivory and other handle materials. **Prices:** $150 to $1,500. **Remarks:** ABS journeyman smith.

LOCKETT, STERLING
527 E Amherst Dr, Burbank, CA 91504, Phone: 818-846-5799

Specialties: Working straight knives and folders to customer specs. **Patterns:** Hunters and fighters. **Technical:** Grinds. **Prices:** Moderate. **Remarks:** Spare-time maker. **Mark:** Name, city with hearts.

LOERCHNER, WOLFGANG
WOLFE FINE KNIVES, PO Box 255, Bayfield, ON, CANADA N0M 1G0, Phone: 519-565-2196
Specialties: Traditional straight knives, mostly ornate. **Patterns:** Small swords, daggers and stilettos; locking folders and miniatures. **Technical:** Grinds D2, 440C and 154CM; all knives hand-filed and flat-ground. **Prices:** Vary. **Remarks:** Full-time maker; first knife sold in 1983. Doing business as Wolfe Fine Knives. **Mark:** WOLFE.

LOGAN, IRON JOHN
4260 Covert, Leslie, MI 49251, ironjohnlogan@gmail.com; www.ironjohnlogan.com
Patterns: Hunting, camping, outdoor sheath knives, folding knives, axes, tomahawks, historical knives. swords, working chef's knives, and woodwork and leather work knives. **Technical:** Forges low-alloy steels, wrought iron, bloom and hearth materials, or high-alloy steel as the job insists. Makes own damascus and San Mai seel, modern materials and stainlesses. Vegetable-tanned leather sheaths, and American hardwood handles like hickory, walnut and cherry. **Prices:** $200 to $2,000. **Remarks:** Full-time bladesmith; first knife made in 1998. **Mark:** Two horizontal lines crossed by one vertical line and an angle off the bottom to crea a "J."

LONEWOLF, J AGUIRRE
481 Hwy 105, Demorest, GA 30535, Phone: 706-754-4660, Fax: 706-754-8470, lonewolfandsons@windstream.net, Web: www.knivesbylonewolf.com www.eagleswinggallery.com
Specialties: High-art working and using straight knives of his design. **Patterns:** Bowies, hunters, utility/camp knives and fine steel blades. **Technical:** Forges Damascus and high-carbon steel. Most knives have hand-carved moose antler handles. **Prices:** $55 to $500; some to $2000. **Remarks:** Full-time maker; first knife sold in 1980. Doing business as Lonewolf and Sons LLC. **Mark:** Stamp.

LONG, GLENN A
10090 SW 186th Ave, Dunnellon, FL 34432, Phone: 352-489-4272, galong99@att.net
Specialties: Classic working and using straight knives of his design and to customer specs. **Patterns:** Hunters, Bowies, utility. **Technical:** Grinds 440C D2 and 440V. **Prices:** $85 to $300; some to $800. **Remarks:** Part-time maker; first knife sold in 1990. **Mark:** Last name inside diamond.

LONGWORTH, DAVE
1200 Red Oak Ridge, Felicity, OH 45120, Phone: 513-876-2372
Specialties: High-tech working knives. **Patterns:** Locking folders, hunters, fighters and elaborate daggers. **Technical:** Grinds O1, ATS-34, 440C; buys Damascus. **Prices:** $125 to $600; some higher. **Remarks:** Part-time maker; first knife sold in 1980. **Mark:** Last name.

LOOS, HENRY C
210 Ingraham, New Hyde Park, NY 11040, Phone: 516-354-1943, hcloos@optonline.net
Specialties: Miniature fancy knives and period pieces of his design. **Patterns:** Bowies, daggers and swords. **Technical:** Grinds O1 and 440C. Uses sterling, 18K, rubies and emeralds. All knives come with handmade hardwood cases. **Prices:** $90 to $195; some to $250. **Remarks:** Spare-time maker; first knife sold in 1990. **Mark:** Script last initial.

LOUKIDES, DAVID E
76 Crescent Circle, Cheshire, CT 06410, Phone: 203-271-3023, Loussharp1@sbcglobal.net; Web: www.prayerknives.com
Specialties: Hand forged working blades and collectible pieces. **Patterns:** Chef knives, bowies, and hunting knives. . **Technical:** Uses 1084, 1095, 5160, W2, O1 and 1084-and-15N20 damascus. **Prices:** Normally $200 to $1,000. **Remarks:** part-time maker, Journeyman Bladesmith, Full-time Journeyman Toolmaker. **Mark:** Loukides JS.

LOVE, ED
19443 Mill Oak, San Antonio, TX 78258, Phone: 210-497-1021, Fax: 210-497-1021, annaedlove@sbcglobal.net
Specialties: Hunting, working knives and some art pieces. **Technical:** Grinds ATS-34, and 440C. **Prices:** $150 and up. **Remarks:** Part-time maker. First knife sold in 1980. **Mark:** Name in a weeping heart.

LOVESTRAND, SCHUYLER
1136 19th St SW, Vero Beach, FL 32962, Phone: 772-778-0282, Fax: 772-466-1126, lovestranded@aol.com
Specialties: Fancy working straight knives of his design and to customer specs; unusual fossil ivories. **Patterns:** Hunters, fighters, Bowies and fishing knives. **Technical:** Grinds stainless steel. **Prices:** $550 to $2,500. **Remarks:** Part-time maker; first knife sold in 1982. **Mark:** Name in logo.

LOVETT, MICHAEL
PO Box 121, Mound, TX 76558, Phone: 254-865-9956, michaellovett@embarqmail.com
Specialties: The Loveless Connection Knives as per R.W. Loveless-Jim Merritt. **Patterns:** All Loveless Patterns and Original Lovett Patterns. **Technical:** Complicated double grinds and premium fit and finish. **Prices:** $1000 and up. **Remarks:** High degree of fit and finish - Authorized collection by R. W. Loveless **Mark:** Loveless Authorized football or double nude.

LOZIER, DON
5394 SE 168th Ave, Ocklawaha, FL 32179, Phone: 352-625-3576
Specialties: Fancy and working straight knives of his design and in standard patterns.

Patterns: Daggers, fighters, boot knives, and hunters. **Technical:** Grinds ATS-34, 440C and Damascus. Most pieces are highly embellished by notable artisans. Taking limited number of orders per annum. **Prices:** Start at $250; most are $1250 to $3000; some to $12,000. **Remarks:** Full-time maker. **Mark:** Name.

LUCHAK, BOB
15705 Woodforest Blvd, Channelview, TX 77530, Phone: 281-452-1779
Specialties: Presentation knives; start of The Survivor series. **Patterns:** Skinners, Bowies, camp axes, steak knife sets and fillet knives. **Technical:** Grinds 440C. Offers electronic etching; filework. **Prices:** $50 to $1500. **Remarks:** Full-time maker; first knife sold in 1983. Doing business as Teddybear Knives. **Mark:** Full name, city and state with Teddybear logo.

LUCHINI, BOB
1220 Dana Ave, Palo Alto, CA 94301, Phone: 650-321-8095, rwluchin@bechtel.com

LUCIE, JAMES R
4191 E. Fruitport Rd., Fruitport, MI 49415, Phone: 231-865-6390, scagel@netonecom. net
Specialties: Hand-forges William Scagel-style knives. **Patterns:** Authentic scagel-style knives and miniatures. **Technical:** Forges 5160, 52100 and 1084 and forges his own pattern welded Damascus steel. **Prices:** Start at $1,250. **Remarks:** Full-time maker; first knife sold in 1975. Believes in sole authorship of his work. ABS Journeyman Smith. **Mark:** Scagel Kris with maker's name and address.

LUCKETT, BILL
108 Amantes Ln, Weatherford, TX 76088, Phone: 817-320-1568, luckettknives@gmail.com Web: www.billluckettcustomknives.com
Specialties: Uniquely patterned robust straight knives. **Patterns:** Fighters, Bowies, hunters. **Technical:** 154CM stainless. **Prices:** $550 to $1500. **Remarks:** Part-time maker; first knife sold in 1975. Knifemakers Guild Member. **Mark:** Last name over Bowie logo.

LUDWIG, RICHARD O
57-63 65 St, Maspeth, NY 11378, Phone: 718-497-5969
Specialties: Traditional working/using knives. **Patterns:** Boots, hunters and utility/camp knives folders. **Technical:** Grinds 440C, ATS-34 and BG42. File work on guards and handles; silver spacers. Offers scrimshaw. **Prices:** $325 to $400; some to $2000. **Remarks:** Full-time maker. **Mark:** Stamped first initial, last name, state.

LUI, RONALD M
4042 Harding Ave, Honolulu, HI 96816, Phone: 808-734-7746
Specialties: Working straight knives and folders in standard patterns. **Patterns:** Hunters, boots and liner locks. **Technical:** Grinds 440C and ATS-34. **Prices:** $100 to $700. **Remarks:** Spare-time maker; first knife sold in 1988. **Mark:** Initials connected.

LUMAN, JAMES R
Clear Creek Trail, Anaconda, MT 59711, Phone: 406-560-1461
Specialties: San Mai and composite end patterns. **Patterns:** Pool and eye Spirograph southwest composite patterns. **Technical:** All patterns with blued steel; all made by him. **Prices:** $200 to $800. **Mark:** Stock blade removal. Pattern welded steel. Bottom ricasso JRL.

LUNDSTROM, JAN-AKE
Mastmostigen 8, Dals-Langed, SWEDEN 66010, Phone: 0531-40270
Specialties: Viking swords, axes and knives in cooperation with handle makers. **Patterns:** All traditional-styles, especially swords and inlaid blades. **Technical:** Forges his own Damascus and laminated steel. **Prices:** $200 to $1000. **Remarks:** Full-time maker; first knife sold in 1985; collaborates with museums. **Mark:** Runic.

LUNDSTROM, TORBJORN (TOBBE)
Norrskenet 4, Are, SWEDEN 83013, 9lundstrm@telia.com Web: http://tobbeiare.se/site/
Specialties: Hunters and collectible knives. **Patterns:** Nordic-style hunters and art knives with unique materials such as mammoth and fossil walrus ivory. **Technical:** Uses forged blades by other makers, particularly Mattias Styrefors who mostly uses 15N20 and 20C steels and is a mosaic blacksmith. **Remarks:** First knife made in 1986.

LUNN, GAIL
434 CR 1422, Mountain Home, AR 72653, Phone: 870-424-2662, gail@lunnknives. com; Web: www.lunnknives.com
Specialties: Fancy folders and double action autos, some straight blades. **Patterns:** One-of-a-kind, all types. **Technical:** Stock removal, hand made. **Prices:** $300 and up. **Remarks:** Fancy file work, exotic materials, inlays, stone etc. **Mark:** Name in script.

LUNN, LARRY A
434 CR 1422, Mountain Home, AR 72653, Phone: 870-424-2662, larry@lunnknives. com; Web: www.lunnknives.com
Specialties: Fancy folders and double action autos; some straight blades. **Patterns:** All types; his own designs. **Technical:** Stock removal; commercial Damascus. **Prices:** $125 and up. **Remarks:** File work inlays and exotic materials. **Mark:** Name in script.

LUPOLE, JAMIE G
KUMA KNIVES, 285 Main St., Kirkwood, NY 13795, Phone: 607-775-9368, jlupole@stny.rr.com
Specialties: Working and collector grade fixed blades, ethnic-styled blades. **Patterns:** Fighters, Bowies, tacticals, hunters, camp, utility, personal carry knives, some swords. **Technical:** Forges and grinds 10XX series and other high-carbon steels, grinds ATS-34 and 440C, will use just about every handle material available. **Prices:** $80 to $500 and up. **Remarks:** Part-time maker since 1999. **Marks:** "KUMA" hot stamped, name, city and state-etched, or "Daiguma saku" in kanji.

LUTZ, GREG
127 Crescent Rd, Greenwood, SC 29646, Phone: 864-229-7340
Specialties: Working and using knives and period pieces of his design and to customer specs. **Patterns:** Fighters, hunters and swords. **Technical:** Forges 1095 and O1; grinds ATS-34. Differentially heat-treats forged blades; uses cryogenic treatment on ATS-34. **Prices:** $50 to $350; some to $1200. **Remarks:** Part-time maker; first knife sold in 1986. Doing business as Scorpion Forge. **Mark:** First initial, last name.

LYLE III, ERNEST L
LYLE KNIVES, PO Box 1755, Chiefland, FL 32644, Phone: 352-490-6693, ernestlyle@msn.com
Specialties: Fancy period pieces; one-of-a-kind and limited editions. **Patterns:** Arabian/Persian influenced fighters, military knives, Bowies and Roman short swords; several styles of hunters. **Technical:** Grinds 440C, D2 and 154 CM. Engraves. **Prices:** $200 - $7500. **Remarks:** Full-time maker; first knife sold in 1972. **Mark:** Lyle Knives over Chiefland, Fla.

LYNCH, TAD
140 Timberline Dr., Beebe, AR 72012, Phone: 501-626-1647, lynchknives@yahoo. com Web: lynchknives.com
Specialties: Forged fixed blades. **Patterns:** Bowies, choppers, fighters, hunters. **Technical:** Hand-forged W-2, 1084, 1095 clay quenched 52100, 5160. **Prices:** Starting at $250. **Remarks:** Part-time maker, also offers custom leather work via wife Amy Lynch. **Mark:** T.D. Lynch over anvil.

LYNN, ARTHUR
29 Camino San Cristobal, Galisteo, NM 87540, Phone: 505-466-3541, lynnknives@aol.com
Specialties: Handforged Damascus knives. **Patterns:** Folders, hunters, Bowies, fighters, kitchen. **Technical:** Forges own Damascus. **Prices:** Moderate.

LYTTLE, BRIAN
Box 5697, High River, AB, CANADA T1V 1M7, Phone: 403-558-3638, brian@lyttleknives.com; Web: www.lyttleknives.com
Specialties: Fancy working straight knives and folders; art knives. **Patterns:** Bowies, daggers, dirks, sgian dubhs, folders, dress knives, tantos, short swords. **Technical:** Forges Damascus steel; engraving; scrimshaw; heat-treating; classes. **Prices:** $450 to $15,000. **Remarks:** Full-time maker; first knife sold in 1983. **Mark:** Last name, country.

M

MACCAUGHTRY, SCOTT F.
Fullerton Forge, 1824 Sorrel St, Camarillo, CA 93010, Phone: 805-750-2137, smack308@hotmail.com
Specialties: Fixed blades and folders. **Technical:** Forges 5160, 52100, W2 and his own damascus using 1084 and 15N20 steels. **Prices:** $275 and up. **Remarks:** ABS journeyman smith. **Mark:** S. MacCaughtry in script, and J.S. on the back side.

MACDONALD, DAVID
2824 Hwy 47, Los Lunas, NM 87031, Phone: 505-866-5866

MACDONALD, JOHN
310 Rte 27, Apt 18, Raymond, NH 03077, Phone: 603-244-2988
Specialties: Working/using straight knives of his design and to customer specs. **Patterns:** Japanese cutlery, Bowies, hunters and working knives. **Technical:** Grinds O1, L6 and ATS-34. Swords have matching handles and scabbards with Japanese flair. **Prices:** $70 to $250; some to $500. **Remarks:** Part-time maker; first knife sold in 1988. Custom knife cases made from pine and exotic hardwoods for table display or wall hanging. Doing business as Mac the Knife. **Mark:** Initials.

MACKIE, JOHN
13653 Lanning, Whittier, CA 90605, Phone: 562-945-6104
Specialties: Forged. **Patterns:** Bowie and camp knives. **Technical:** Attended ABS Bladesmith School. **Prices:** $75 to $500. **Mark:** JSM in a triangle.

MACKRILL, STEPHEN
PO Box 1580, Pinegowrie, Johannesburg, GT, SOUTH AFRICA 2123, Phone: 27-11-474-7139, Fax: 27-11-474-7139, info@mackrill.co.za; Web: www.mackrill.net
Specialties: Art fancy, historical, collectors and corporate gifts cutlery. **Patterns:** Fighters, hunters, camp, custom lock back and LinerLock® folders. **Technical:** N690, 12C27, ATS-34, silver and gold inlay on handles; wooden and silver sheaths. **Prices:** $330 and upwards. **Remarks:** First knife sold in 1978. **Mark:** Mackrill fish with country of origin.

MADRULLI, MME JOELLE
Residence Ste Catherine B1, Salon De Provence, FRANCE 13330

MAE, TAKAO
1-119 1-4 Uenohigashi, Toyonaka, Osaka, JAPAN 560-0013, Phone: 81-6-6852-2758, Fax: 81-6-6481-1649, takamae@nifty.com
Remarks: Distinction stylish in art-forged blades, with lacquered ergonomic handles.

MAESTRI, PETER A
S11251 Fairview Rd, Spring Green, WI 53588, Phone: 608-546-4481
Specialties: Working straight knives in standard patterns. **Patterns:** Camp and fishing knives, utility green-river-styled. **Technical:** Grinds 440C, 154CM and 440A. **Prices:** $15 to $45; some to $150. **Remarks:** Full-time maker; first knife sold in 1981. Provides professional cutler service to professional cutters. **Mark:** CARISOLO, MAESTRI BROS., or signature.

MAGEE, JIM
741 S. Ohio St., Salina, KS 67401, Phone: 785-820-6928, jimmagee@cox.net
Specialties: Working and fancy folding knives. **Patterns:** Liner locking folders, favorite is his Persian. **Technical:** Grinds ATS-34, Devin Thomas & Eggerling Damascus, titanium. Liners Prefer mother-of-pearl handles. **Prices:** Start at $225 to $1200. **Remarks:** Part-time maker, first knife sold in 2001. Purveyor since 1982. Past president of the Professional Knifemakers Association **Mark:** Last name.

MAGRUDER, JASON
460 Arnos Rd, Unit 66, Talent, OR 97540, Phone: 719-210-1579, belstain@hotmail.com; jason@magruderknives.com; web: MagruderKnives.com
Specialties: Unique and innovative designs combining the latest modern materials with traditional hand craftsmanship. **Patterns:** Fancy neck knives. Tactical gents folders. Working straight knives. **Technical:** Flats grinds CPM3v, CPM154, ATS34, 1080, and his own forged damascus. Hand carves carbon fiber, titanium, wood, ivory, and pearl handles. Filework and carving on blades. **Prices:** $150 and up. **Remarks:** Part-time maker; first knife sold in 2000. **Mark:** Last name.

MAHOMEDY, A R
PO Box 76280, Marble Ray, KZN, SOUTH AFRICA 4035, Phone: +27 31 577 1451, arm-koknives@mweb.co.za; Web: www.arm-koknives.co.za
Specialties: Daggers and elegant folders of own design finished with finest exotic materials currently available. **Technical:** Via stock removal, grinds Damasteel, Damascus and the famous hardenable stainless steels. **Prices:** U.S. $650 and up. **Remarks:** Part-time maker. First knife sold in 1995. Voting member knifemakers guild of SA, FEGA member starting out Engraving. **Mark:** Initials A R M crowned with a "Minaret."

MAHOMEDY, HUMAYD A.R.
PO BOX 76280, Marble Ray, KZN, SOUTH AFRICA 4035, Phone: +27 31 577 1451, arm-koknives@mweb.co.za
Specialties: Tactical folding and fixed blade knives. **Patterns:** Fighters, utilities, tacticals, folders and fixed blades, daggers, modern interpretation of Bowies. **Technical:** Stock-removal knives of Bohler N690, Bohler K110, Bohler K460, Sandvik 12C27, Sandvik RWL 34. Handle materials used are G10, Micarta, Cape Buffalo horn, Water Buffalo horn, Kudu horn, Gemsbok horn, Giraffe bone, Elephant ivory, Mammoth ivory, Arizona desert ironwood, stabilised and burl burls. **Prices:** $250 - $1000. **Remarks:** First knife sold in 2002. Full-time knifemaker since 2002. First person of color making knives full-time in South Africa. Doing business as HARM EDGED TOOLS. **Mark:** HARM and arrow over EDGED TOOLS.

MAIENKNECHT, STANLEY
38648 S R 800, Sardis, OH 43946

MAINES, JAY
SUNRISE RIVER CUSTOM KNIVES, 5584 266th St., Wyoming, MN 55092, Phone: 651-462-5301, jaymaines@fronternet.net; Web: http://www.sunrisecustomknives.com
Specialties: Heavy duty working, classic and traditional fixed blades. Some high-tech and fancy embellished knives available. **Patterns:** Hunters, skinners, fillet, bowies tantos, boot daggers etc. etc. **Technical:** Hollow ground, stock removal blades of 440C, ATS-34 and CPM S-90V. Prefers natural handle materials, exotic hard woods, and stag, rams and buffalo horns. Offers dovetailed bolsters in brass, stainless steel and nickel silver. Custom sheaths from matching wood or hand-stitched from heavy duty water buffalo hide. **Prices:** Moderate to up-scale. **Remarks:** Part-time maker; first knife sold in 1992. Doing business as Sunrise River Custom Knives. Offers fixed blade knives repair and handle conversions. **Mark:** Full name under a Rising Sun logo.

MAISEY, ALAN
PO Box 197, Vincentia, NSW, AUSTRALIA 2540, Phone: 2-4443 7829, tosanaji@excite.com
Specialties: Daggers, especially krisses; period pieces. **Technical:** Offers knives and finished blades in Damascus and nickel Damascus. **Prices:** $75 to $2000; some higher. **Remarks:** Part-time maker; provides complete restoration service for krisses. Trained by a Japanese Kris smith. **Mark:** None, triangle in a box, or three peaks.

MAJORS, CHARLIE
1911 King Richards Ct, Montgomery, TX 77316, Phone: 713-826-3135, charliemajors@sbcglobal.net
Specialties: Fixed-blade hunters and slip-joint and lock-back folders. **Technical:** Practices stock removal method, preferring CPM154 steel and natural handle materials such as ironwood, stag, and mammoth ivory. Also takes customer requests. Does own heat treating and cryogenic quenching. **Remarks:** First knife made in 1980.

MAKOTO, KUNITOMO
3-3-18 Imazu-cho, Fukuyama-city, Hiroshima, JAPAN, Phone: 084-933-5874, kunitomo@po.iijnet.or.jp

MALABY, RAYMOND J
835 Calhoun Ave, Juneau, AK 99801, Phone: 907-586-6981, Fax: 907-523-8031, malaby@gci.net
Specialties: Straight working knives. **Patterns:** Hunters, skiners, Bowies, and camp knives. **Technical:** Hand forged 1084, 5160, O1 and grinds ATS-34 stainless. **Prices:** $195 to $400. **Remarks:** First knife sold in 1994. **Mark:** First initial, last name, city, and state.

MALLOY, JOE
1039 Schwabe St, Freeland, PA 18224, Phone: 570-436-6416, jdmalloy@msn.com
Specialties: Working straight knives and lock back folders—plain and fancy—of his

design. **Patterns:** Hunters, utility, folders, tactical designs. **Technical:** 154CM, ATS-34, 440C, D2 and A2, damascus, other exotic steel on request. **Prices:** $100 to $1800. **Remarks:** Part-time maker; first knife sold in 1982. **Mark:** First and middle initials, last name, city and state.

MANARO, SAL
10 Peri Ave., Holbrook, NY 11741, Phone: 631-737-1180, maker@manaroknives.com
Specialties: Tactical folders, bolstered titanium LinerLocks, handmade folders, and fixed blades with hand-checkered components. **Technical:** Compound grinds, hidden fasteners and welded components, with blade steels including CPM-154, damascus, Stellite, D2, S30V and O-1 by the stock-removal method of blade making. **Prices:** $500 and up. **Remarks:** Part-time maker, made first knife in 2001. **Mark:** Last name with arrowhead underline.

MANDT, JOE
3735 Overlook Dr. NE, St. Petersburg, FL 33703, Phone: 813-244-3816, jmforge@mac.com
Specialties: Forged Bowies, camp knives, hunters, skinners, fighters, boot knives, military style field knives. **Technical:** Forges plain carbon steel and high carbon tool steels, including W2, 1084, 5160, O1, 9260, 15N20, cable Damascus, pattern welded Damascus, flat and convex grinds. Prefers natural handle materials, hand-rubbed finishes, and stainless low carbon steel, Damascus and wright iron fittings. Does own heat treat. **Prices:** $150 to $750. **Remarks:** Part-time maker, first knife sold in 206. **Mark:** "MANDT".

MANEKER, KENNETH
RR 2, Galiano Island, BC, CANADA V0N 1P0, Phone: 604-539-2084
Specialties: Working straight knives; period pieces. **Patterns:** Camp knives and hunters; French chef knives. **Technical:** Grinds 440C, 154CM and Vascowear. **Prices:** $50 to $200; some to $300. **Remarks:** Part-time maker; first knife sold in 1981. Doing business as Water Mountain Knives. **Mark:** Japanese Kanji of initials, plus glyph.

MANLEY, DAVID W
3270 Six Mile Hwy, Central, SC 29630, Phone: 864-654-1125, dmanleyknives@bellsouth.net
Specialties: Working straight knives of his design or to custom specs. **Patterns:** Hunters, boot and fighters. **Technical:** Grinds 440C and ATS-34. **Prices:** $80 to $400. **Remarks:** Part-time maker; first knife sold in 1994. **Mark:** First initial, last name, year and serial number.

MANN, MICHAEL L
IDAHO KNIFE WORKS, PO Box 144, Spirit Lake, ID 83869, Phone: 509 994-9394, Web: www.idahoknifeworks.com
Specialties: Good working blades-historical reproduction, modern or custom design. **Patterns:** Cowboy Bowies, Mountain Man period blades, old-style folders, designer and maker of "The Cliff Knife", hunter knives, hand ax and fish fillet. **Technical:** High-carbon steel blades-hand forged 5160. Stock removed 15N20 steel. Also Damascus. **Prices:** $130 to $670+. **Remarks:** Made first knife in 1965. Full-time making knives as Idaho Knife Works since 1986. Functional as well as collectible. Each knife truly unique! **Mark:** Four mountain peaks are his initials MM.

MANN, TIM
BLADEWORKS, PO Box 1196, Honokaa, HI 96727, Phone: 808-775-0949, Fax: 808-775-0949, birdman@shaka.com
Specialties: Hand-forged knives and swords. **Patterns:** Bowies, tantos, pesh kabz, daggers. **Technical:** Use 5160, 1050, 1075, 1095 and ATS-34 steels, cable Damascus. **Prices:** $200 to $800. **Remarks:** Just learning to forge Damascus. **Mark:** None yet.

MARAGNI, DAN
RD 1 Box 106, Georgetown, NY 13072, Phone: 315-662-7490
Specialties: Heavy-duty working knives, some investor class. **Patterns:** Hunters, fighters and camp knives, some Scottish types. **Technical:** Forges W2 and his own Damascus; toughness and edge-holding a high priority. **Prices:** $125 to $500; some to $1000. **Remarks:** Full-time maker; first knife sold in 1975. **Mark:** Celtic initials in circle.

MARCHAND, RICK
Wildertools, 824 Main St., POB 402, Mahone Bay, NS, CANADA B0J 2E0, Phone: 226-783-8771, rickmarchand@wildertools.com; Web: www.wildertools.net
Specialties: Specializing in multicultural, period stylized blades and accoutrements. **Technical:** Hand forged from 1070/84 and 5160 steel. **Prices:** $175 - $900. **Remarks:** 3 years full-time maker. ABS Apprentice Smith. **Mark:** Tang stamp: "MARCHAND" along with two Japanese-style characters resembling "W" and "M."

MARINGER, TOM
2692 Powell St., Springdale, AR 72764, maringer@arkansas.net; Web: shirepost.com/cutlery.
Specialties: Working straight and curved blades with stainless steel furniture and wire-wrapped handles. **Patterns:** Subhilts, daggers, boots, swords. **Technical:** Grinds D-2, A-2, ATS-34. May be safely disassembled by the owner via pommel screw or pegged construction. **Prices:** $2000 to $3000, some to $20,000. **Remarks:** Former full-time maker, now part-time. First knife sold in 1975. **Mark:** Full name, year, and serial number etched on tang under handle.

MARKLEY, KEN
7651 Cabin Creek Lane, Sparta, IL 62286, Phone: 618-443-5284
Specialties: Traditional working and using knives of his design and to customer specs. **Patterns:** Fighters, hunters and utility/camp knives. **Technical:** Forges 5160, 1095 and L6; makes his own Damascus; does file work. **Prices:** $150 to $800; some to $2000.

Remarks: Part-time maker; first knife sold in 1991. Doing business as Cabin Creek Forge. **Mark:** Last name, JS.

MARLOWE, CHARLES

10822 Poppleton Ave, Omaha, NE 68144, Phone: 402-933-5065, cmarlowe1@cox.net; Web: www.marloweknives.com

Specialties: Folding knives and balisong. **Patterns:** Tactical pattern folders. **Technical:** Grind ATS-34, S30V, CPM154, 154CM, Damasteel, others on request. Forges/grinds 1095 on occasion. **Prices:** Start at $450. **Remarks:** First knife sold in 1993. Full-time since 1999. **Mark:** Turtle logo with Marlowe above, year below.

MARLOWE, DONALD

2554 Oakland Rd, Dover, PA 17315, Phone: 717-764-6055

Specialties: Working straight knives in standard patterns. **Patterns:** Bowies, fighters, boots and utility knives. **Technical:** Grinds D2 and 440C. Integral design hunter models. **Prices:** $130 to $850. **Remarks:** Spare-time maker; first knife sold in 1977. **Mark:** Last name.

MARSH, JEREMY

6169 3 Mile NE, Ada, MI 49301, Phone: 616-889-1945, steelbean@hotmail.com; Web: www.marshcustomknives.com

Specialties: Locking liner folders, dressed-up gents knives, tactical knives, and dress tacticals. **Technical:** CPM S30V stainless and Damascus blade steels using the stock-removal method of bladesmithing. **Prices:** $450 to $1500. **Remarks:** Self-taught, part-time knifemaker; first knife sold in 2004. **Mark:** Maker's last name and large, stylized M.

MARSHALL, REX

1115 State Rte. 380, Wilmington, OH 45177, Phone: 937-604-8430, rexmarshall@hotmail.com; www.rexmarshallcustomknives.com

Specialties Hunters, skinners and bowies, plain to fancy. **Technical:** Forges and stock removal, using ATS-34 and 5160 steels. Will custom build to customer's specifications. **Prices:** $125 and up. **Remarks:** First knife made in 2011. **Mark:** Rex Marshall over eagle.

MARSHALL, STEPHEN R

975 Harkreader Rd, Mt. Juliet, TN 37122

MARTIN, BRUCE E

Rt. 6, Box 164-B, Prescott, AR 71857, Phone: 501-887-2023

Specialties: Fancy working straight knives of his design. **Patterns:** Bowies, camp knives, skinners and fighters. **Technical:** Forges 5160, 1095 and his own Damascus. Uses natural handle materials; filework available. **Prices:** $75 to $350; some to $500. **Remarks:** Part-time maker; first knife sold in 1979. **Mark:** Name in arch.

MARTIN, GENE

PO Box 396, Williams, OR 97544, Phone: 541-846-6755, bladesmith@customknife.com

Specialties: Straight knives and folders. **Patterns:** Fighters, hunters, skinners, boot knives, spring back and lock back folders. **Technical:** Grinds ATS-34, 440C, Damascus and 154CM. Forges; makes own Damascus; scrimshaws. **Prices:** $150 to $2500. **Remarks:** Full-time maker; first knife sold in 1993. Doing business as Provision Forge. **Mark:** Name and/or crossed staff and sword.

MARTIN, HAL W

781 Hwy 95, Morrilton, AR 72110, Phone: 501-354-1682, hal.martin@sbcglobal.net

Specialties: Hunters, Bowies and fighters. **Prices:** $250 and up. **Mark:** MARTIN.

MARTIN, HERB

2500 Starwood Dr, Richmond, VA 23229, Phone: 804-747-1675, hamjlm@hotmail.com

Specialties: Working straight knives. **Patterns:** Skinners, hunters and utility. **Technical:** Hollow grinds ATS-34, and Micarta handles. **Prices:** $85 to $125. **Remarks:** Part-time Maker. First knife sold in 2001. **Mark:** HA MARTIN.

MARTIN, MICHAEL W

Box 572, Jefferson St, Beckville, TX 75631, Phone: 903-678-2161

Specialties: Classic working/using straight knives of his design and in standard patterns. **Patterns:** Hunters. **Technical:** Grinds ATS-34, 440C, O1 and A2. Bead blasted, Parkerized, high polish and satin finishes. Sheaths are handmade. Also hand forges cable Damascus. **Prices:** $185 to $280 some higher. **Remarks:** Part-time maker; first knife sold in 1995. Doing business as Michael W. Martin Knives. **Mark:** Name and city, state in arch.

MARTIN, PETER

28220 N. Lake Dr, Waterford, WI 53185, Phone: 262-706-3076, Web: www.petermartinknives.com

Specialties: Fancy, fantasy and working straight knives and folders of his design and in standard patterns. **Patterns:** Bowies, fighters, hunters, locking folders and liner locks. **Technical:** Forges own Mosaic Damascus, powdered steel and his own Damascus. Prefers natural handle material; offers file work and carved handles. **Prices:** Moderate. **Remarks:** Full-time maker; first knife sold in 1988. Doing business as Martin Custom Products. **Mark:** Martin Knives.

MARTIN, RANDALL J

51 Bramblewood St, Bridgewater, MA 02324, Phone: 508-279-0682

Specialties: High tech folding and fixed blade tactical knives employing the latest blade steels and exotic materials. Employs a unique combination of 3d-CNC machining and hand work on both blades and handles. All knives are designed for hard use. Clean, radical grinds and ergonomic handles are hallmarks of RJ's work, as is his reputation for producing "Scary Sharp" knives. **Technical:** Grinds CPM30V, CPM 3V, CPM154CM, A2 and stainless Damascus. Other CPM alloys used on request. Performs all heat treating and cryogenic processing in-house. **Remarks:** Full-time maker since 2001 and materials

engineer. Former helicopter designer. First knife sold in 1976.

MARTIN, TONY

PO Box 10, Arcadia, MO 63621, Phone: 573-546-2254, arcadian@charter.net; Web: www.arcadianforge.com

Specialties: Specializes in historical designs, esp. puukko, skean dhu. **Remarks:** Premium quality blades, exotic wood handles, unmatched fit and finish. **Mark:** AF.

MARTIN, WALTER E

570 Cedar Flat Rd, Williams, OR 97544, Phone: 541-846-6755

MARTIN

MARTIN, JOHN ALEXANDER

821 N Grand Ave, Okmulgee, OK 74447, Phone: 918-758-1099, jam@jamblades.com; Web: www.jamblades.com

Specialties: Inlaid and engraved handles. **Patterns:** Bowies, fighters, hunters and traditional patterns. Swords, fixed blade knives, folders and axes. **Technical:** Forges 5160, 1084, 10XX, O1, L6 and his own Damascus. **Prices:** Start at $300. **Remarks:** Part-time maker. **Mark:** Two initials with last name and MS or 5 pointed star.

MARZITELLI, PETER

19929 35A Ave, Langley, BC, CANADA V3A 2R1, Phone: 604-532-8899, marzitelli@shaw.ca

Specialties: Specializes in unique functional knife shapes and designs using natural and synthetic handle materials. **Patterns:** Mostly folders, some daggers and art knives. **Technical:** Grinds ATS-34, S/S Damascus and others. **Prices:** $220 to $1000 (average $375). **Remarks:** Full-time maker; first knife sold in 1984. **Mark:** Stylized logo reads "Marz."

MASON, BILL

9306 S.E. Venns St., Hobe Sound, FL 33455, Phone: 772-545-3649

Specialties: Combat knives; some folders. **Patterns:** Fighters to match knife types in book Cold Steel. **Technical:** Grinds O1, 440C and ATS-34. **Prices:** $115 to $250; some to $350. **Remarks:** Spare-time maker; first knife sold in 1979. **Mark:** Initials connected.

MASSEY, AL

Box 14 Site 15 RR#2, Mount Uniacke, NS, CANADA B0N 1Z0, Phone: 902-866-4754, armjan@eastlink.ca

Specialties: Working knives and period pieces. **Patterns:** Swords and daggers of Celtic to medieval design, Bowies. **Technical:** Forges 5160, 1084 and 1095. Makes own Damascus. **Prices:** $200 to $500, damascus $300-$1000. **Remarks:** Part-time maker, first blade sold in 1988. **Mark:** Initials and JS on Ricasso.

MASSEY, ROGER

4928 Union Rd, Texarkana, AR 71854, Phone: 870-779-1018, rmassey668@aol.com

Specialties: Traditional and working straight knives and folders of his design and to customer specs. **Patterns:** Bowies, hunters, daggers and utility knives. **Technical:** Forges 1084 and 52100, makes his own Damascus. Offers filework and silver wire inlay in handles. **Prices:** $200 to $1500; some to $2500. **Remarks:** Part-time maker; first knife sold in 1991. **Mark:** Last name, M.S.

MASSEY, RON

61638 El Reposo St., Joshua Tree, CA 92252, Phone: 760-366-9239 after 5 p.m., Fax: 763-366-4620

Specialties: Classic, traditional, fancy/embellished, high art, period pieces, working/using knives, straight knives, folders, and automatics. Your design, customer specs, about 175 standard patterns. **Patterns:** Automatics, hunters and fighters. All folders are side-locking folders. Unless requested as lock books slip joint he specializes or custom designs. **Technical:** ATS-34, 440C, D-2 upon request. Engraving, filework, scrimshaw, most of the exotic handle materials. All aspects are performed by him: inlay work in pearls or stone, handmade Pem' work. **Prices:** $110 to $2500; some to $6000. **Remarks:** Part-time maker; first knife sold in 1976.

MATA, LEONARD

3583 Arruza St, San Diego, CA 92154, Phone: 619-690-6935

MATHEWS, CHARLIE AND HARRY

TWIN BLADES, 121 Mt Pisgah Church Rd., Statesboro, GA 30458, Phone: 912-865-9098, twinblades@bulloch.net; Web: www.twinxblades.com

Specialties: Working straight knives, carved stag handles. **Patterns:** Hunters, fighters, Bowies and period pieces. **Technical:** Grinds D2, CPMS30V, CPM3V, ATS-34 and commercial Damascus; handmade sheaths some with exotic leather, file work. Forges 1095, 1084, and 5160. **Prices:** Starting at $125. **Remarks:** Twin brothers making knives full-time under the label of Twin Blades. Charter members Georgia Custom Knifemakers Guild. Members of The Knifemakers Guild. **Mark:** Twin Blades over crossed knives, reverse side steel type.

MATSUNO, KANSEI

109-8 Uenomachi, Nishikaiden, Gifu-City, JAPAN 501-1168, Phone: 81 58 234 8643

MATSUOKA, SCOT

94-415 Ukalialii Place, Mililani, HI 96789, Phone: 808-625-6658, Fax: 808-625-6658, scottym@hawaii.rr.com; Web: www.matsuokaknives.com

Specialties: Folders, fixed blades with custom hand-stitched sheaths. **Patterns:** Gentleman's knives, hunters, tactical folders. **Technical:** CPM 154CM, 440C, 154, BG42, bolsters, file work, and engraving. **Prices:** Starting price $350. **Remarks:** Part-time maker, first knife sold in 2002. **Mark:** Logo, name and state.

MATSUSAKI, TAKESHI

MATSUSAKI KNIVES, 151 Ono-Cho, Sasebo-shi, Nagasaki, JAPAN, Phone: 0956-47-

2938, Fax: 0956-47-2938
Specialties: Working and collector grade front look and slip joint. **Patterns:** Sheffierd type folders. **Technical:** Grinds ATS-34 k-120. **Price:** $250 to $1000, some to $8000. **Remarks:** Part-time maker, first knife sold in 1990. **Mark:** Name and initials.

MAXEN, MICK
2 Huggins Welham Green, Hatfield, Herts, UNITED KINGDOM AL97LR, Phone: 01707 261213, mmaxen@aol.com
Specialties: Damascus and Mosaic. **Patterns:** Medieval-style daggers and Bowies. **Technical:** Forges CS75 and 15N20 / nickel Damascus. **Mark:** Last name with axe above.

MAXFIELD, LYNN
382 Colonial Ave, Layton, UT 84041, Phone: 801-544-4176, lcmaxfield@msn.com
Specialties: Sporting knives, some fancy. **Patterns:** Hunters, fishing, fillet, special purpose: some locking folders. **Technical:** Grinds 440-C, 154-CM, CPM154, D2, CPM S30V, and Damascus. **Prices:** $125 to $400; some to $900. **Remarks:** Part-time maker; first knife sold in 1979. **Mark:** Name, city and state.

MAXWELL, DON
1484 Celeste Ave, Clovis, CA 93611, Phone: 559-299-2197, maxwellknives@aol.com; Web: maxwellknives.com
Specialties: Fancy folding knives and fixed blades of his design. **Patterns:** Hunters, fighters, utility/camp knives, LinerLock® folders, flippers and fantasy knives. **Technical:** Grinds 440C, ATS-34, D2, CPM 154, and commercial Damascus. **Prices:** $250 to $1000; some to $2500. **Remarks:** Full-time maker; first knife sold in 1987. **Mark:** Last name only or Maxwell MAX-TAC.

MAY, CHARLES
10024 McDonald Rd., Aberdeen, MS 39730, Phone: 662-369-0404, charlesmayknives@yahoo.com; Web: charlesmayknives.blademakers.com
Specialties: Fixed-blade sheath knives. **Patterns:** Hunters and fillet knives. **Technical:** Scandinavian-ground D2 and S30V blades, black micarta and wood handles, nickel steel pins with maker's own pocket carry or belt-loop pouches. **Prices:** $215 to $495. **Mark:** "Charles May Knives" and a knife in a circle.

MAYNARD, LARRY JOE
PO Box 493, Crab Orchard, WV 25827
Specialties: Fancy and fantasy straight knives. **Patterns:** Big knives; a Bowie with a full false edge; fighting knives. **Technical:** Grinds standard steels. **Prices:** $350 to $500; some to $1000. **Remarks:** Full-time maker; first knife sold in 1986. **Mark:** Middle and last initials.

MAYNARD, WILLIAM N.
2677 John Smith Rd, Fayetteville, NC 28306, Phone: 910-425-1615
Specialties: Traditional and working straight knives of all designs. **Patterns:** Combat, Bowies, fighters, hunters and utility knives. **Technical:** Grinds 440C, ATS-34 and commercial Damascus. Offers fancy filework; handmade sheaths. **Prices:** $100 to $300; some to $750. **Remarks:** Full-time maker; first knife sold in 1988. **Mark:** Last name.

MAYO JR., HOMER
18036 Three Rivers Rd., Biloxi, MS 39532, Phone: 228-326-8298
Specialties: Traditional working straight knives, folders and tactical. **Patterns:** Hunters, fighters, tactical, bird, Bowies, fish fillet knives and lightweight folders. **Technical:** Grinds 440C, ATS-34, D-2, Damascus, forges and grinds 52100 and custom makes sheaths. **Prices:** $100 to $1000. **Remarks:** Part-time maker **Mark:** All knives are serial number and registered in the name of the original purchaser, stamped last name or etched.

MAYO JR., TOM
67 412 Alahaka St, Waialua, HI 96791, Phone: 808-637-6560, mayot001@hawaii.rr.com; Web: www.mayoknives.com
Specialties: Framelocks/tactical knives. **Patterns:** Combat knives, hunters, Bowies and folders. **Technical:** Titanium/stellite/S30V. **Prices:** $500 to $1000. **Remarks:** Full-time maker; first knife sold in 1982. **Mark:** Volcano logo with name and state.

MAYVILLE, OSCAR L
2130 E. County Rd 910S, Marengo, IN 47140, Phone: 812-338-4159
Specialties: Working straight knives; period pieces. **Patterns:** Kitchen cutlery, Bowies, camp knives and hunters. **Technical:** Grinds A2, O1 and 440C. **Prices:** $50 to $350; some to $500. **Remarks:** Full-time maker; first knife sold in 1984. **Mark:** Initials over knife logo.

MCABEE, WILLIAM
27275 Norton Grade, Colfax, CA 95713, Phone: 530-389-8163
Specialties: Working/using knives. **Patterns:** Fighters, Bowies, Hunters. **Technical:** Grinds ATS-34. **Prices:** $75 to $200; some to $350. **Remarks:** Part-time maker; first knife sold in 1990. **Mark:** Stylized WM stamped.

MCCALLEN JR., HOWARD H
110 Anchor Dr, So Seaside Park, NJ 08752

MCCARLEY, JOHN
4165 Harney Rd, Taneytown, MD 21787
Specialties: Working straight knives; period pieces. **Patterns:** Hunters, Bowies, camp knives, miniatures, throwing knives. **Technical:** Forges W2, O1 and his own Damascus. **Prices:** $150 to $300; some to $1000. **Remarks:** Part-time maker; first knife sold in 1977. **Mark:** Initials in script.

MCCARTY, HARRY
1479 Indian Ridge Rd, Blaine, TN 37709, harry@indianridgeforge.com; Web: www.indianridgeforge.com
Specialties: Period pieces. **Patterns:** Trade knives, Bowies, 18th and 19th century folders and hunting swords. **Technical:** Forges and grinds high-carbon steel. **Prices:** $75 to $1300. **Remarks:** Full-time maker; first knife sold in 1977. Doing business as Indian Ridge Forge.**Mark:** Stylized initials inside a shamrock.

MCCLURE, JERRY
3052 Isim Rd, Norman, OK 73026, Phone: 405-321-3614, jerry@jmcclureknives.net; Web: www.jmcclureknives.net
Specialties: Gentleman's folder, linerlock with my jeweled pivot system of eight rubies, forged one-of-a-kind Damascus Bowies, and a line of hunting/camp knives. **Patterns:** Folders, Bowie, and hunting/camp **Technical** Forges own Damascus, also uses Damasteel and does own heat treating. **Prices** $500 to $3,000 and up **Remarks** Full-time maker, made first knife in 1965. **Mark** J.MCCLURE

MCCLURE, MICHAEL
803 17th Ave, Menlo Park, CA 94025, Phone: 650-323-2596, mikesknives@att.net; Web: www.customknivesbymike.com
Specialties: Working/using straight knives of his design and to customer specs. **Patterns:** Bowies, hunters, skinners, utility/camp, tantos, fillets and boot knives. **Technical:** Forges high-carbon and Damascus; also grinds stainless, all grades. **Prices:** Start at $300. **Remarks:** Part-time maker; first knife sold in 1991. ABS Journeyman Smith. **Mark:** Mike McClure.

MCCONNELL JR., LOYD A
309 County Road 144-B, Marble Falls, TX 78654, Phone: 830-798-8087, ccknives@ccknives.com; Web: www.ccknives.com
Specialties: Working straight knives and folders, some fancy. **Patterns:** Hunters, boots, Bowies, locking folders and slip-joints. **Technical:** Grinds CPM Steels, ATS-34 and BG-42 and commercial Damascus. **Prices:** $450 to $10,000. **Remarks:** Full-time maker; first knife sold in 1975. Doing business as Cactus Custom Knives. Markets product knives under name: Lone Star Knives. **Mark:** Name, city and state in cactus logo.

MCCORNOCK, CRAIG
MCC MTN OUTFITTERS, 4775 Rt. 212/PO 162, Willow, NY 12495, Phone: 845-679-9758, Mccmtn@aol.com; Web: www.mccmtn.com
Specialties: Carry, utility, hunters, defense type knives and functional swords. **Patterns:** Drop points, hawkbills, tantos, waklzashis, katanas **Technical:** Stock removal, forged and Damascus, (yes, he still flints knap). **Prices:** $200 to $2000. **Mark:** McM.

MCCOUN, MARK
14212 Pine Dr, DeWitt, VA 23840, Phone: 804-469-7631, mccounandsons@live.com
Specialties: Working/using straight knives of his design and in standard patterns; custom miniatures. **Patterns:** Locking liners, integrals. **Technical:** Grinds Damascus, ATS-34 and 440C. **Prices:** $150 to $500. **Remarks:** Part-time maker; first knife sold in 1989. **Mark:** Name, city and state.

MCCRACKIN, KEVIN
3720 Hess Rd, House Spings, MO 63051, Phone: 636-677-6066

MCCRACKIN AND SON, V J
3720 Hess Rd, House Springs, MO 63051, Phone: 636-677-6066
Specialties: Working straight knives in standard patterns. **Patterns:** Hunters, Bowies and camp knives. **Technical:** Forges L6, 5160, his own Damascus, cable Damascus. **Prices:** $125 to $700; some to $1500. **Remarks:** Part-time maker; first knife sold in 1983. Son Kevin helps make the knives. **Mark:** Last name, M.S.

MCCULLOUGH, JERRY
274 West Pettibone Rd, Georgiana, AL 36033, Phone: 334-382-7644, ke4er@alaweb.com
Specialties: Standard patterns or custom designs. **Technical:** Forge and grind scrap-tool and Damascus steels. Use natural handle materials and turquoise trim on some. Filework on others. **Prices:** $65 to $250 and up. **Remarks:** Part-time maker. **Mark:** Initials (JM) combined.

MCDONALD, RICH
5010 Carmel Rd., Hillboro, OH 45133, Phone: 937-466-2071, rmclongknives@aol.com; Web: www.longknivesandleather.com
Specialties: Traditional working/using and art knives of his design. **Patterns:** Bowies, hunters, folders, primitives and tomahawks. **Technical:** Forges 5160, 1084, 1095, 52100 and his own Damascus. Fancy filework. **Prices:** $200 to $1500. **Remarks:** Full-time maker; first knife sold in 1994. **Mark:** First and last initials connected.

MCDONALD, ROBERT J
14730 61 Court N, Loxahatchee, FL 33470, Phone: 561-790-1470
Specialties: Traditional working straight knives to customer specs. **Patterns:** Fighters, swords and folders. **Technical:** Grinds 440C, ATS-34 and forges own Damascus. **Prices:** $150 to $1000. **Remarks:** Part-time maker; first knife sold in 1988. **Mark:** Electro-etched name.

MCDONALD, W.J. "JERRY"
7173 Wickshire Cove E, Germantown, TN 38138, Phone: 901-756-9924, wjmcdonaldknives@msn.com; Web: www.mcdonaldknives.com
Specialties: Classic and working/using straight knives of his design and in standard patterns. **Patterns:** Bowies, hunters kitchen and traditional spring back pocket knives. **Technical:** Grinds ATS-34, 154CM, D2, 440V, BG42 and 440C. **Prices:** $125 to $1000. **Remarks:** Full-time maker; first knife sold in 1989. **Mark:** First and middle initials, last name, maker, city and state. Some of his knives are stamped McDonald in script.

MCFALL, KEN
PO Box 458, Lakeside, AZ 85929, Phone: 928-537-2026, Fax: 928-537-8066, knives@citlink.net

Specialties: Fancy working straight knives and some folders. **Patterns:** Daggers, boots, tantos, Bowies; some miniatures. **Technical:** Grinds D2, ATS-34 and 440C. Forges his own Damascus. **Prices:** $200 to $1200. **Remarks:** Part-time maker; first knife sold in 1984. **Mark:** Name, city and state.

MCFARLIN, ERIC E
PO Box 2188, Kodiak, AK 99615, Phone: 907-486-4799
Specialties: Working knives of his design. **Patterns:** Bowies, skinners, camp knives and hunters. **Technical:** Flat and convex grinds 440C, A2 and AEB-L. **Prices:** Start at $200. **Remarks:** Part-time maker; first knife sold in 1989. **Mark:** Name and city in rectangular logo.

MCFARLIN, J W
3331 Pocohantas Dr, Lake Havasu City, AZ 86404, Phone: 928-453-7612, Fax: 928-453-7612, aztheedge@NPGcable.com
Technical: Flat grinds, D2, ATS-34, 440C, Thomas and Peterson Damascus. **Remarks:** From working knives to investment. Customer designs always welcome. 100 percent handmade. Made first knife in 1972. **Prices:** $150 to $3000. **Mark:** Hand written in the blade.

MCGHEE, E. SCOTT
7136 Lisbon Rd., Clarkton, NC 28433, Phone: 910-448-2224, guineahogforge@gmail.com; Web: www.guineahogforge.com
Specialties: Hunting knives, kitchen blades, presentation blades, tactical knives and sword canes. **Technical:** Forge and stock removal, all flat-ground blades, including 1080-and-15N20 damascus, 1084, O1 and W2. **Prices:** $200 to $3,500. **Remarks:** Planning to be full time in 2014; first knife sold in 2009. Currently an ABS journeyman smith. **Mark:** E. Scott McGhee (large print) above Guinea Hog Forge (small print).

MCGILL, JOHN
PO Box 302, Blairsville, GA 30512, Phone: 404-745-4686
Specialties: Working knives. **Patterns:** Traditional patterns; camp knives. **Technical:** Forges L6 and 9260; makes Damascus. **Prices:** $50 to $250; some to $500. **Remarks:** Full-time maker; first knife sold in 1982. **Mark:** XYLO.

MCGOWAN, FRANK E
12629 Howard Lodge Rd., Sykesville, MD 21784, Phone: 443-745-2611, fmcgowan11@verizon.net
Specialties: Fancy working knives and folders to customer specs. **Patterns:** Survivor knives, fighters, fishing knives, folders and hunters. **Technical:** Grinds and forges O1, 440C, 5160, ATS-34, 52100, or customer choice. **Prices:** $100 to $1000; some more. **Remarks:** Full-time maker; first knife sold in 1986. **Mark:** Last name.

MCGRATH, PATRICK T
8343 Kenyon Ave, Westchester, CA 90045, Phone: 310-338-8764, hidinginLA@excite.com

MCGRODER, PATRICK J
5725 Chapin Rd, Madison, OH 44057, Phone: 216-298-3405, Fax: 216-298-3405
Specialties: Traditional working/using knives of his design. **Patterns:** Bowies, hunters and utility/camp knives. **Technical:** Grinds ATS-34, D2 and customer requests. Does reverse etching; heat-treats; prefers natural handle materials; custom made sheath with each knife. **Prices:** $125 to $250. **Remarks:** Part-time maker. **Mark:** First and middle initials, last name, maker, city and state.

MCGUANE IV, THOMAS F
410 South 3rd Ave, Bozeman, MT 59715, Phone: 406-586-0248, Web: http://www.thomasmcguane.com
Specialties: Multi metal inlaid knives of handmade steel. **Patterns:** Lock back and LinerLock® folders, fancy straight knives. **Technical:** 1084/1SN20 Damascus and Mosaic steel by maker. **Prices:** $1000 and up. **Mark:** Surname or name and city, state.

MCHENRY, WILLIAM JAMES
Box 67, Wyoming, RI 02898, Phone: 401-539-8353
Specialties: Fancy high-tech folders of his design. **Patterns:** Locking folders with various mechanisms. **Technical:** One-of-a-kind only, no duplicates. Inventor of the Axis Lock. Most pieces disassemble and feature top-shelf materials including gold, silver and gems. **Prices:** Upscale. **Remarks:** Full-time maker; first knife sold in 1988. Former goldsmith. **Mark:** Last name or first and last initials.

MCINTYRE, SHAWN
71 Leura Grove, Hawthornm, E VIC, AUSTRALIA 3123, Phone: 61 3 9813 2049/Cell 61 412 041 062, macpower@netspace.net.au; Web: www.mcintyreknives.com
Specialties: Damascus & CS fixed blades and art knives. **Patterns:** Bowies, hunters, fighters, kukris, integrals. **Technical:** Forges, makes own Damascus including pattern weld, mosaic, and composite multi-bars form O1 & 15N20 Also uses 1084, W2, and 52100. **Prices:** $275 to $2000. **Remarks:** Full-time maker since 1999. **Mark:** Mcintyre in script.

MCKEE, NEIL
674 Porter Hill Rd., Stevensville, MT 59870, Phone: 406-777-3507, mckeenh@wildblue.net
Specialties: Early American. **Patterns:** Nessmuk, DeWeese, French folders, art pieces. **Technical:** Engraver. **Prices:** $150 to $1000. **Mark:** Oval with initials.

MCKENZIE, DAVID BRIAN
2311 B Ida Rd, Campbell River, BC, CANADA V9W-4V7

MCKIERNAN, STAN
11751 300th St, Lamoni, IA 50140, Phone: 641-784-6873/641-781-0368, slmck@hotmailc.om
Specialties: Self-sheathed knives and miniatures. **Patterns:** Daggers, ethnic designs and individual styles. **Technical:** Grinds Damascus and 440C. **Prices:** $200 to $500, some to $1500. **Mark:** "River's Bend" inside two concentric circles.

MCLUIN, TOM
36 Fourth St, Dracut, MA 01826, Phone: 978-957-4899, tmcluin@comcast.net; Web: www.mcluinknives.com
Specialties: Working straight knives and folders of his design. **Patterns:** Boots, hunters and folders. **Technical:** Grinds ATS-34, 440C, O1 and Damascus; makes his own mokume. **Prices:** $100 to $400; some to $700. **Remarks:** Part-time maker; first knife sold in 1991. **Mark:** Last name.

MCLURKIN, ANDREW
2112 Windy Woods Dr, Raleigh, NC 27607, Phone: 919-834-4693, mclurkincustomknives.com
Specialties: Collector grade folders, working folders, fixed blades, and miniatures. Knives made to order and to his design. **Patterns:** Locking liner and lock back folders, hunter, working and tactical designs. **Technical:** Using patterned Damascus, Mosaic Damascus, ATS-34, BG-42, and CPM steels. Prefers natural handle materials such as pearl, ancient ivory and stabilized wood. Also using synthetic materials such as carbon fiber, titanium, and G10. **Prices:** $250 and up. **Mark:** Last name. Mark is often on inside of folders.

MCNABB, TOMMY
CAROLINA CUSTOM KNIVES, PO Box 327, Bethania, NC 27010, Phone: 336-924-6053, tommy@tmcnabb.com; Web: carolinaknives.com
Specialties: Classic and working knives of his own design or to customer's specs. **Patterns:** Traditional bowies. Tomahawks, hunters and customer designs. **Technical:** Forges his own Damascus steel, hand forges or grinds ATS-34 and other hi-tech steels. Prefers mirror finish or satin finish on working knives. Uses exotic or natural handle material and stabilized woods. **Price:** $300-$3500. **Remarks:** Full time maker. Made first knife in 1982. **Mark:**"Carolina Custom Knives" on stock removal blades "T. McNabb" on custom orders and Damascus knives.

MCNEES, JONATHAN
15203 Starboard Pl, Northport, AL 35475, Phone: 205-391-8383, jmackusmc@yahoo.com; Web: www.mcneescustomknives.com
Specialties: Tactical, outdoors, utility. **Technical:** Stock removal method utilizing carbon and stainless steels to include 1095, cpm154, A2, cpms35v. **Remarks:** Part-time maker, first knife made in 2007. **Mark:** Jmcnees

MCRAE, J MICHAEL
6100 Lake Rd, Mint Hill, NC 28227, Phone: 704-545-2929, scotia@carolina.rr.com; Web: www.scotiametalwork.com
Specialties: Scottish dirks, sgian dubhs, broadswords. **Patterns:** Traditional blade styles with traditional and slightly non-traditional handle treatments. **Technical:** Forges 5160 and his own Damascus. Prefers stag and exotic hardwoods for handles, many intricately carved. **Prices:** Starting at $125, some to $3500. **Remarks:** Journeyman Smith in ABS, member of ABANA. Full-time maker, first knife sold in 1982. Doing business as Scotia Metalwork. **Mark:** Last name underlined with a claymore.

MCWILLIAMS, SEAN
PO Box 1685, Carbondale, CO 81623, Phone: 970-963-7489, info@seanmcwilliamsforge.com; Web: www.seanmcwilliamsforge.com
Specialties: Tactical, survival and working knives in Kydex-and-nylon sheaths. **Patterns:** Fighters, bowies, hunters and sports knives, period pieces, swords, martial arts blades and some folders. **Technical:** Forges only, including ATS-34, BG-42, CPM-T440V, CPM-T420V, CTS-1375P, CTS-204P. **Prices:** $165 to $2,500. **Remarks:** Full-time maker; first knife sold in 1972. **Mark:** Stylized bear paw.

MEERDINK, KURT
248 Yulan Barryville Rd., Barryville, NY 12719-5305, Phone: 845-557-0783
Specialties: Working straight knives. **Patterns:** Hunters, Bowies, tactical and neck knives. **Technical:** Grinds ATS-34, 440C, D2, Damascus. **Prices:** $95 to $1100. **Remarks:** Full-time maker, first knife sold in 1994. **Mark:** Meerdink Maker, Rio NY.

MEERS, ANDREW
1100 S Normal Ave., Allyn Bldg MC 4301, Carbondale, IL 62901, Phone: 774-217-3574, namsuechool@gmail.com
Specialties: Pattern welded blades, in the New England style. **Patterns:** Can do open or closed welding and fancies middle eastern style blades. **Technical:** 1095, 1084, 15n20, 5160, w1, w2 steels **Remarks:** Part-time maker attending graduate school at SIUC; looking to become full-time in the future as well as earn ABS Journeyman status. **Mark:** Korean character for south.

MEIER, DARYL
75 Forge Rd, Carbondale, IL 62903, Phone: 618-549-3234, Web: www.meiersteel.com
Specialties: One-of-a-kind knives and swords. **Patterns:** Collaborates on blades. **Technical:** Forges his own Damascus, W1 and A203E, 440C, 431, nickel 200 and clad steel. **Prices:** $500 and up. **Remarks:** Full-time smith and researcher since 1974; first knife sold in 1974. **Mark:** Name.

MELIN, GORDON C
14207 Coolbank Dr, La Mirada, CA 90638, Phone: 562-946-5753

MELOY, SEAN
7148 Rosemary Lane, Lemon Grove, CA 91945-2105, Phone: 619-465-7173
Specialties: Traditional working straight knives of his design. **Patterns:** Bowies, fighters and utility/camp knives. **Technical:** Grinds 440C, ATS-34 and D2. **Prices:** $125 to $300.

MENEFEE, RICKY BOB
2440 County Road 1322, Blawchard, OK 73010, rmenefee@pldi.net
Specialties: Working straight knives and pocket knives. **Patterns:** Hunters, fighters, minis & Bowies. **Technical:** Grinds ATS-34, 440C, D2, BG42 and S30V. **Price:** $130 to $1000. **Remarks:** Part-time maker, first knife sold in 2001. Member of KGA of Oklahoma, also Knifemakers Guild. **Mark:** Menefee made or Menefee stamped in blade.

MENSCH, LARRY C
Larry's Knife Shop, 578 Madison Ave, Milton, PA 17847, Phone: 570-742-9554
Specialties: Custom orders. **Patterns:** Bowies, daggers, hunters, tantos, short swords and miniatures. **Technical:** Grinds ATS-34, stainless steel Damascus; blade grinds hollow, flat and slack. Filework; bending guards and fluting handles with finger grooves. **Prices:** $200 and up. **Remarks:** Full-time maker; first knife sold in 1993. Doing business as Larry's Knife Shop. **Mark:** Connected capital "L" and small "m" in script.

MERCER, MIKE
149 N. Waynesville Rd, Lebanon, OH 45036, Phone: 513-932-2837, mmercer08445@roadrunner.com
Specialties: Miniatures and autos. **Patterns:** All folder patterns. **Technical:** Diamonds and gold, one-of-a-kind, Damascus, O1, stainless steel blades. **Prices:** $500 to $5000. **Remarks:** Carved wax - lost wax casting. **Mark:** Stamp - Mercer.

MERCHANT, TED
7 Old Garrett Ct, White Hall, MD 21161, Phone: 410-343-0380
Specialties: Traditional and classic working knives. **Patterns:** Bowies, hunters, camp knives, fighters, daggers and skinners. **Technical:** Forges W2 and 5160; makes own Damascus. Makes handles with wood, stag, horn, silver and gem stone inlay; fancy filework. **Prices:** $125 to $600; some to $1500. **Remarks:** Full-time maker; first knife sold in 1985. **Mark:** Last name.

MERZ III, ROBERT L
1447 Winding Canyon, Katy, TX 77493, Phone: 281-391-2897, bobmerz@consolidated.net; Web: www.merzknives.com
Specialties: Folders. **Prices:** $350 to $1,400. **Remarks:** Full time maker; first knife sold in 1974. **Mark:** MERZ.

MESENBOURG, NICK
2545 Upper 64th Ct. E, Inver Grove Heights, MN 55076, Phone: 651-457-2753 or 651-775-7505, mesenbourg_nicholas@hotmail.com; www.ndmknives.com
Specialties Working straight knives of his design or to customer specs, also sport-themed knives. **Patterns:** Hunters, skinners, bowies, fighters, utility and fillet knives. **Technical:** Grinds 440C stainless steel and commercial damascus. **Prices:** $175-$450, special knives higher. **Remarks:** Part-time maker; first knife sold in 2008. **Mark:** Encircled N D M capital letters.

MESHEJIAN, MARDI
5 Bisbee Court 109 PMB 230, Santa Fe, NM 87508, Phone: 505-310-7441, toothandnail13@yahoo.com
Specialties: One-of-a-kind fantasy and high art straight knives & folders. **Patterns:** Swords, daggers, folders and other weapons. **Technical:** Forged steel Damascus and titanium Damascus. **Prices:** $300 to $5000 some to $7000. **Mark:** Stamped stylized "M."

MESSER, DAVID T
134 S Torrence St, Dayton, OH 45403-2044, Phone: 513-228-6561
Specialties: Fantasy period pieces, straight and folding, of his design. **Patterns:** Bowies, daggers and swords. **Technical:** Grinds 440C, O1, 06 and commercial Damascus. Likes fancy guards and exotic handle materials. **Prices:** $100 to $225; some to $375. **Remarks:** Spare-time maker; first knife sold in 1991. **Mark:** Name stamp.

METHENY, H A "WHITEY"
7750 Waterford Dr, Spotsylvania, VA 22551, Phone: 540842-1440, Fax: 540-582-3095, hametheny@aol.com; Web: www.methenyknives.com
Specialties: Working and using straight knives of his design and to customer specs. **Patterns:** Hunters and kitchen knives. **Technical:** Grinds 440C and ATS-34. Offers filework; tooled custom sheaths. **Prices:** $350 to $450. **Remarks:** Spare-time maker; first knife sold in 1990. **Mark:** Initials/full name football logo.

METSALA, ANTHONY
30557 103rd St. NW, Princeton, MN 55371, Phone: 763-389-2628, acmetsala@izoom.net; Web: www.metsalacustomknives.com
Specialties: Sole authorship one-off mosaic Damascus liner locking folders, sales of makers finished one-off mosaic Damascus blades. **Patterns:** Except for a couple EDC folding knives, maker does not use patterns. **Technical:** Forges own mosaic Damascus carbon blade and bolster material. All stainless steel blades are heat treated by Paul Bos. **Prices:** $250 to $1500. **Remarks:** Full-time knifemaker and Damascus steel maker, first knife sold in 2005. **Mark:** A.C. Metsala or Metsala.

METZ, GREG T
c/o Yellow Pine Bar HC 83, BOX 8080, Cascade, ID 83611, Phone: 208-382-4336, metzenterprise@yahoo.com
Specialties: Hunting and utility knives. **Prices:** $350 and up. **Remarks:** Natural handle materials; hand forged blades; 1084 and 1095. **Mark:** METZ (last name).

MEYER, CHRISTOPHER J
737 Shenipsit Lake Rd, Tolland, CT 06084, Phone: 860-875-1826, shenipsitforge.cjm@gmail.com
Specialties: Handforged tool steels. **Technical:** Forges tool steels, grinds stainless. **Remarks:** Spare-time maker; sold first knife in 2003. **Mark:** Name and/or "Shenipsit Forge."

MICHINAKA, TOSHIAKI
I-679 Koyamacho-nishi, Tottori-shi, Tottori, JAPAN 680-0947, Phone: 0857-28-5911
Specialties: Art miniature knives. **Patterns:** Bowies, hunters, fishing, camp knives & miniatures. **Technical:** Grinds ATS-34 and 440C. **Prices:** $300 to $900 some higher. **Remarks:** Part-time maker. First knife sold in 1982. **Mark:** First initial, last name.

MICKLEY, TRACY
42112 Kerns Dr, North Mankato, MN 56003, Phone: 507-947-3760, tracy@mickleyknives.com; Web: www.mickleyknives.com
Specialties: Working and collectable straight knives using mammoth ivory or burl woods, LinerLock® folders. **Patterns:** Custom and classic hunters, utility, fighters and Bowies. **Technical:** Grinding 154-CM, BG-42 forging O1 and 52100. **Prices:** Starting at $325 **Remarks:** Part-time since 1999. **Mark:** Last name.

MIDGLEY, BEN
PO Box 577, Wister, OK 74966, Phone: 918-655-6701, mauricemidgley@windstream.net
Specialties: Multi-blade folders, slip-joints, some lock-backs and hunters. File work, engraving and scrimshaw. **Patterns:** Reproduce old patterns, trappers, muskrats, stockman, whittlers, lockbacks an hunters. **Technical:** Grinds ATS-34, 440C, 12-C-27, CPM-154, some carbon steel, and commercial Damascus. **Prices:** $385 to $1875. **Remarks:** Full-time maker, first knife sold in 2002. **Mark:** Name, city, and state stamped on blade.

MIKOLAJCZYK, GLEN
4650 W. 7 Mile Rd., Caledonia, WI 53108, Phone: 414-791-0424, Fax: 262-835-9697, glenmikol@aol.com Web: www.customtomahawk.com
Specialties: Pipe hawks, fancy folders, bowies, long blades, hunting knives, all of his own design. **Technical:** Sole-author, forges own Damascus and powdered steel. Works with ivory, bone, tortoise, horn and antlers, tiger maple, pearl for handle materials. Designs and does intricate file work and custom sheaths. Enjoys exotic handle materials. **Prices:** Moderate. **Remarks:** Founded Weg Von Wennig Forge in 2003, first knife sold in 2004. Also, designs and builds mini-forges. Will build upon request. International sales accepted. **Mark:** Tomahawk and name.

MILES JR., C R "IRON DOCTOR"
1541 Porter Crossroad, Lugoff, SC 29078, Phone: 803-600-9397
Specialties: Traditional working straight knives of his design or made to custom specs. **Patterns:** Hunters, fighters, utility camp knives and hatches. **Technical:** Grinds O1, D2, ATS-34, 440C, 1095, and 154 CPM. Forges 18th century style cutlery of high carbon steels. Also forges and grinds old files and farrier's rasps to make knives. Custom leather sheaths. **Prices:** $100 and up. **Remarks:** Part-time maker, first knife sold in 1997. **Mark:** Iron doctor plus name and serial number.

MILITANO, TOM
CUSTOM KNIVES, 77 Jason Rd., Jacksonville, AL 36265-6655, Phone: 256-435-7132, jeffkin57@aol.com
Specialties: Fixed blade, one-of-a-kind knives. **Patterns:** Bowies, fighters, hunters and tactical knives. **Technical:** Grinds 440C, CPM 154CM, A2, and Damascus. Hollow grinds, flat grinds, and decorative filework. **Prices:** $150 plus. **Remarks:** Part-time maker. Sold first knives in the mid to late 1980s. Memberships: Founding member of New England Custom Knife Association. **Mark:** Name engraved in ricasso area - type of steel on reverse side.

MILLARD, FRED G
27627 Kopezyk Ln, Richland Center, WI 53581, Phone: 608-647-5376
Specialties: Working/using straight knives of his design or to customer specs. **Patterns:** Bowies, hunters, utility/camp knives, kitchen/steak knives. **Technical:** Grinds ATS-34, O1, D2 and 440C. Makes sheaths. **Prices:** $110 to $300. **Remarks:** Full-time maker; first knife sold in 1993. Doing business as Millard Knives. **Mark:** Mallard duck in flight with serial number.

MILLER, HANFORD J
Box 97, Cowdrey, CO 80434, Phone: 970-723-4708
Specialties: Working knives in Moran styles, Bowie, period pieces, Cinquedea. **Patterns:** Daggers, Bowies, working knives. **Technical:** All work forged: W2, 1095, 5160 and Damascus. ABS methods; offers fine silver repousse, scabboard mountings and wire inlay, oak presentation cases. **Prices:** $400 to $1000; some to $3000 and up. **Remarks:** Full-time maker; first knife sold in 1968. **Mark:** Initials or name within Bowie logo.

MILLER, JAMES P
9024 Goeller Rd, RR 2, Box 28, Fairbank, IA 50629, Phone: 319-635-2294, Web: www.damascusknives.biz
Specialties: All tool steel Damascus; working knives and period pieces. **Patterns:** Hunters, Bowies, camp knives and daggers. **Technical:** Forges and grinds 1095, 52100, 440C and his own Damascus. **Prices:** $175 to $500; some to $1500. **Remarks:** Full-time maker; first knife sold in 1970. **Mark:** First and middle initials, last name with knife logo.

MILLER, M A
11625 Community Center Dr, Unit #1531, Northglenn, CO 80233, Phone: 303-280-3816
Specialties: Using knives for hunting. 3-1/2"-4" Loveless drop-point. Made to customer specs. **Patterns:** Skinners and camp knives. **Technical:** Grinds 440C, D2, O1 and ATS-34 Damascus miniatures. **Prices:** $225 to $350; miniatures $75 to $150. **Remarks:** Part-time maker; first knife sold in 1988. **Mark:** Last name stamped in block letters or first and middle initials, last name, maker, city and state with triangles on either side etched.

MILLER, MICHAEL
3030 E Calle Cedral, Kingman, AZ 86401, Phone: 928-757-1359, mike@mmilleroriginals.com
Specialties: Hunters, Bowies, and skinners with exotic burl wood, stag, ivory and gemstone handles. **Patterns:** High carbon steel knives. **Technical:** High carbon and nickel alloy Damascus and high carbon and meteorite Damascus. Also mosaic Damascus. **Prices:** $235 to $4500. **Remarks:** Full-time maker since 2002, first knife sold 2000; doing business as M Miller Originals. **Mark:** First initial and last name with 'handmade' underneath.

MILLER, MICHAEL E
910146 S. 3500 Rd., Chandler, OK 74834, Phone: 918-377-2411, mimiller1@brightok.net
Specialties: Traditional working/using knives of his design. **Patterns:** Bowies, hunters and kitchen knives. **Technical:** Grinds ATS-34, CPM 440V; forges Damascus and cable Damascus and 52100. Prefers scrimshaw, fancy pins, basket weave and embellished sheaths. **Prices:** $80 to $300; some to $500. **Remarks:** Part-time maker; first knife sold in 1984. Doing business as Miller Custom Knives. Member of KGA of Oklahoma and Salt Fork Blacksmith Association. **Mark:** First and middle initials, last name, maker.

MILLER, NATE
Sportsman's Edge, 1075 Old Steese Hwy N, Fairbanks, AK 99712, Phone: 907-479-4774, sportsmansedge@gci.net Web: www.alaskasportsmansedge.com
Specialties: Fixed blade knives for hunting, fishing, kitchen and collector pieces. **Patterns:** Hunters, skinners, utility, tactical, fishing, camp knives-your pattern or mine. **Technical:** Stock removal maker, ATS-34, 154CM, 440C, D2, 1095, other steels on request. Handle material includes micarta, horn, antler, fossilized ivory and bone, wide selection of woods. **Prices:** $225-$800. **Remarks:** Full time maker since 2002. **Mark:** Nate Miller, Fairbanks, AK.

MILLER, RICK
516 Kanaul Rd, Rockwood, PA 15557, Phone: 814-926-2059
Specialties: Working/using straight knives of his design and in standard patterns. **Patterns:** Bowies, daggers, hunters and friction folders. **Technical:** Grinds L6. Forges 5160, L6 and Damascus. Patterns for Damascus are random, twist, rose or ladder. **Prices:** $75 to $250; some to $400. **Remarks:** Part-time maker; first knife sold in 1982. **Mark:** Script stamp "R.D.M."

MILLER, RONALD T
12922 127th Ave N, Largo, FL 34644, Phone: 813-595-0378 (after 5 p.m.)
Specialties: Working straight knives in standard patterns. **Patterns:** Combat knives, camp knives, kitchen cutlery, fillet knives, locking folders and butterflies. **Technical:** Grinds D2, 440C and ATS-34; offers brass inlays and scrimshaw. **Prices:** $45 to $325; some to $750. **Remarks:** Part-time maker; first knife sold in 1984. **Mark:** Name, city and state in palm tree logo.

MILLER, STEVE
1376 Pine St., Clearwater, FL 33756, Phone: 727-461-4180, millknives@aol.com; Web: www.millerknives.com
Patterns: Bowies, hunters, skinners, folders. **Technical:** 440-C, ATS-34, Sandvic Stainless, CPM-S30-V, Damascus. Exotic hardwoods, bone, horn, antler, ivory, synthetics. All leather work and sheaths made by me and handstitched. **Remarks:** Have been making custom knives for sale since 1990. Part-time maker, hope to go full time in about five and a half years (after retirement from full-time job). **Mark:** Last name inside a pentagram.

MILLER, TERRY
P.O. Box 262, Healy, AK 99743, Phone: 907-683-1239, terry@denalidomehome.com
Specialties: Alaskan ulus with wood or horn. **Remarks:** New to knifemaking (5 years).

MILLS, LOUIS G
9450 Waters Rd, Ann Arbor, MI 48103, Phone: 734-668-1839
Specialties: High-art Japanese-style period pieces. **Patterns:** Traditional tantos, daggers and swords. **Technical:** Makes steel from iron; makes his own Damascus by traditional Japanese techniques. **Prices:** $900 to $2000; some to $8000. **Remarks:** Spare-time maker. **Mark:** Yasutomo in Japanese Kanji.

MILLS, MICHAEL
151 Blackwell Rd, Colonial Beach, VA 22443-5054, Phone: 804-224-0265
Specialties: Working knives, hunters, skinners, utility and Bowies. **Technical:** Forge 5160 differential heat-treats. **Prices:** $300 and up. **Remarks:** Part-time maker, ABS Journeyman. **Mark:** Last name in script.

MINCHEW, RYAN
3310 Cimmaron Ave., Midland, TX 79707-5802, Phone: 806-752-0223, ryan@minchewknives.com Web: www.minchewknives.com
Specialties: Hunters and folders. **Patterns:** Standard hunters and bird-and-trout knives. **Prices:** $150 to $500. **Mark:** Minchew.

MINNICK, JIM & JOYCE
144 North 7th St, Middletown, IN 47356, Phone: 765-354-4108, jmjknives@aol.com; Web: www.minnickknives@aol.com
Specialties: Lever-lock folding art knives, liner-locks. **Patterns:** Stilettos, Persian and one-of-a-kind folders. **Technical:** Grinds and carves Damascus, stainless, and high-carbon. **Prices:** $950 to $7000. **Remarks:** Part-time maker; first knife sold in 1976. Husband and wife team. **Mark:** Minnick and JMJ.

MIRABILE, DAVID
PO BOX 20417, Juneau, AK 99802, Phone: 907-321-1103, dmirabile02@gmail.com; Web: www.mirabileknives.com
Specialties: Elegant edged weapons and hard use Alaskan knives. **Patterns:** Fighters, personal carry knives, special studies of the Tlinget dagger. **Technical:** Uses W-2, 1080, 15n20, 1095, 5160, and his own Damascus, and stainless/high carbon San Mai.

MITCHELL, JAMES A
PO Box 4646, Columbus, GA 31904, Phone: 404-322-8582
Specialties: Fancy working knives. **Patterns:** Hunters, fighters, Bowies and locking folders. **Technical:** Grinds D2, 440C and commercial Damascus. **Prices:** $100 to $400; some to $900. **Remarks:** Part-time maker; first knife sold in 1976. Sells knives in sets. **Mark:** Signature and city.

MITCHELL, MAX DEAN AND BEN
3803 VFW Rd, Leesville, LA 71440, Phone: 318-239-6416
Specialties: Hatchet and knife sets with folder and belt and holster all match. **Patterns:** Hunters, 200 L6 steel. **Technical:** L6 steel; soft back, hand edge. **Prices:** $300 to $500. **Remarks:** Part-time makers; first knife sold in 1965. Custom orders only; no stock. **Mark:** First names.

MITCHELL, WM DEAN
PO Box 2, Warren, TX 77664, Phone: 409-547-2213
Specialties: Functional and collectable cutlery. **Patterns:** Personal and collector's designs. **Technical:** Forges own Damascus and carbon steels. **Prices:** Determined by the buyer. **Remarks:** Gentleman knifemaker. ABS Master Smith 1994. **Mark:** Full name with anvil and MS or WDM and MS.

MITSUYUKI, ROSS
PO Box 29577, Honolulu, HI 96820, Phone: 808-671-3335, Fax: 808-671-3335, rossman@hawaiiantel.net; Web: www.picturetrail.com/homepage/mrbing
Specialties: Working straight knives and folders/engraving titanium & 416 S.S. **Patterns:** Hunting, fighters, utility knives and boot knives. **Technical:** 440C, BG42, ATS-34, S30V, CPM154, and Damascus. **Prices:** $100 and up. **Remarks:** Spare-time maker, first knife sold in 1998. **Mark:** (Honu) Hawaiian sea turtle.

MIVILLE-DESCHENES, ALAIN
1952 Charles A Parent, Quebec, CANADA G2B 4B2, Phone: 418-845-0950, Fax: 418-845-0950, amd@miville-deschenes.com; Web: www.miville-deschenes.com
Specialties: Working knives of his design or to customer specs and art knives. **Patterns:** Bowies, skinner, hunter, utility, camp knives, fighters, art knives. **Technical:** Grinds ATS-34, CPMS30V, 0-1, D2, and sometime forge carbon steel. **Prices:** $250 to $700; some higher. **Remarks:** Part-time maker; first knife sold in 2001. **Mark:** Logo (small hand) and initials (AMD).

MOELLER, HARALD
#17-493 Pioneer Crescent, Parksville, BC, CANADA V9P 1V2, Phone: 250-248-0391, moeknif@shaw.ca; Web: www.collectiblecustomknives.com
Specialties: Collector grade San Fransisco Dagger; small fighters, Fantasy Axes, Bowies, Survival Knives. Special design award winning liner lock folders; Viper throwing knives. **Technical:** Steels - 440-C, ATS34, damascus, etc. **Materials:** mammoth, Abalone, MOP, Black Water Buffalo, 14K Gold, rubies, diamonds, etc. **Prices: Throwing knives - $80 to $350; Fighters - $400 to $600; Axe - $3200; Folders - $600 to $3400; Dagger - Up to $9,000** **Remarks:** Now part time maker, first knife sold in 1979. member Southern California Blades; Member Oregon Knife Collectors Assoc. **Mark:** Moeller

MOEN, JERRY
4478 Spring Valley Rd., Dallas, TX 75244, Phone: 972-839-1609, jmoen@moencustomknives.com Web: moencustomknives.com
Specialties: Hunting, pocket knives, fighters tactical, and exotic. **Prices:** $500 to $5,000.

MOIZIS, STAN
8213 109B St., Delta, British Columbia (BC), CANADA V4C 4G9, Phone: 604-597-8929, moizis@telus.net
Specialties: Automatic and spring-assist folding knives and soon to come out-the-fronts. **Patterns:** Well-made carry knives with some upper-end materials available for steel and handles. All patterns are freehand, and thus each knife is unique. **Marks:** "SM" on blade with date and place of manufacture on inside of spacer. On knives with professionally out-of-house machined parts, mark is "BRNO BORN."

MOJZIS, JULIUS
B S Timravy 6, 98511 Halic, SLOVAKIA, julius.mojzis@gmail.com; Web: www.juliusmojzis.com
Specialties: Art Knives. **Prices:** USD $2000. **Mark:** MOJZIS.

MONCUS, MICHAEL STEVEN
1803 US 19 N, Smithville, GA 31787, Phone: 912-846-2408

MONTANO, GUS A
11217 Westonhill Dr, San Diego, CA 92126-1447, Phone: 619-273-5357
Specialties: Traditional working/using straight knives of his design. **Patterns:** Boots, Bowies and fighters. **Technical:** Grinds 1095 and 5160; grinds and forges cable. Double or triple hardened and triple drawn; hand-rubbed finish. Prefers natural handle materials. **Prices:** $200 to $400; some to $600. **Remarks:** Spare-time maker; first knife sold in 1997. **Mark:** First initial and last name.

MONTEIRO, VICTOR
31 Rue D'Opprebais, Maleves Ste Marie, BELGIUM 1360, Phone: 010 88 0441, victor.monteiro@skynet.be
Specialties: Working and fancy straight knives, folders and integrals of his design. **Patterns:** Fighters, hunters and kitchen knives. **Technical:** Grinds ATS-34, 440C, D2, Damasteel and other commercial Damascus, embellishment, filework and domed pins. **Prices:** $300 to $1000, some higher. **Remarks:** Part-time maker; first knife sold in 1989.

Mark: Logo with initials connected.

MONTELL, TY
PO BOX 1312, Thatcher, AZ 85552, Phone: 928-792-4509, Fax: Cell: 575-313-4373, montellfamily@aol.com
Specialties: Automatics, slip-joint folders, hunting and miniatures.**Technical:** Stock removal. Steel of choice is CPM-154, Devin Thomas Damascus. **Prices:** $250 and up. **Remarks:** First knife made in 1980. **Mark:** Tang stamp - Montell.

MOONEY, MIKE
19432 E. Cloud Rd., Queen Creek, AZ 85142, Phone: 480-244-7768, mike@moonblades.com; Web: www.moonblades.com
Specialties: Hand-crafted high-performing straight knives of his or customer's design. **Patterns:** Bowies, fighters, hunting, camp and kitchen users or collectible. **Technical:** Flat-grind, hand-rubbed finish, S30V, CMP-154, Damascus, any steel. **Prices:** $300 to $3000. **Remarks:** Doing business as moonblades.com. Commissions are welcome. **Mark:** M. Mooney followed by crescent moon.

MOORE, DAVY
Moyriesk, Quin, Co Clare, IRELAND, Phone: 353 (0)65 6825975, davy@mooreireland.com; Web: http://www.mooreireland.com
Specialties: Traditional and Celtic outdoor hunting and utility knives. **Patterns:** Traditional hunters and skinners, Celtic pattern hunting knives, Bushcrafting, fishing, utility/camp knives. **Technical:** Stock removal knives O1, D2, RWL 34, ATS 34, CPM 154, Damasteel (various).**Prices:** 250-1700 Euros.**Remarks:** Full-time maker, first knife sold in 2004. **Mark:** Three stars over rampant lion / MOORE over Ireland.

MOORE, JAMES B
1707 N Gillis, Ft. Stockton, TX 79735, Phone: 915-336-2113
Specialties: Classic working straight knives and folders of his design. **Patterns:** Hunters, Bowies, daggers, fighters, boots, utility/camp knives, locking folders and slip-joint folders. **Technical:** Grinds 440C, ATS-34, D2, L6, CPM and commercial Damascus. **Prices:** $85 to $700; exceptional knives to $1500. **Remarks:** Full-time maker; first knife sold in 1972. **Mark:** Name, city and state.

MOORE, JON P
304 South N Rd, Aurora, NE 68818, Phone: 402-849-2616, Web: www.sharpdecisionknives.com
Specialties: Working and fancy straight knives using antler, exotic bone, wood and Micarta. Will use customers' antlers on request. **Patterns:** Hunters, skinners, camp and bowies. **Technical:** Hand-forged high carbon steel. Makes his own damascus. **Prices:** Start at $125. **Remarks:** Full-time maker, sold first knife in 2003. Does on-location knife forging demonstrations. **Mark:** Sword through anvil with name.

MOORE, MARVE
HC 89 Box 393, Willow, AK 99688, Phone: 907-232-0478, marvemoore@aol.com
Specialties: Fixed blades forged and stock removal. **Patterns:** Hunter, skinners, fighter, short swords. **Technical:** 100 percent of his work is done by hand. **Prices:** $100 to $500. **Remarks:** Also makes his own sheaths. **Mark:** -MM-.

MOORE, MICHAEL ROBERT
70 Beaulieu Rd, Lowell, MA 01850, Phone: 978-479-0589, Fax: 978-441-1819

MOORE, TED
340 E Willow St, Elizabethtown, PA 17022, Phone: 717-367-3939, tedmoore@tedmooreknives.com; Web: www.tedmooreknives.com
Specialties: Damascus folders, cigar cutters, high art. **Patterns:** Slip joints, linerlock, cigar cutters. **Technical:** Grinds Damascus and stainless steels. **Prices:** $250 and up. **Remarks:** Part-time maker; first knife sold 1993. **Mark:** Moore U.S.A.

MORETT, DONALD
116 Woodcrest Dr, Lancaster, PA 17602-1300, Phone: 717-746-4888

MORGAN, JEFF
9200 Arnaz Way, Santee, CA 92071, Phone: 619-448-8430
Specialties: Early American style knives. **Patterns:** Hunters, bowies, etc. **Technical:** Carbon steel and carbon steel damascus. **Prices:** $60 to $400.

MORGAN, TOM
14689 Ellett Rd, Beloit, OH 44609, Phone: 330-537-2023
Specialties: Working straight knives and period pieces. **Patterns:** Hunters, boots and presentation tomahawks. **Technical:** Grinds O1, 440C and 154CM. **Prices:** Knives, $65 to $200; tomahawks, $100 to $325. **Remarks:** Full-time maker; first knife sold in 1977. **Mark:** Last name and type of steel used.

MORRIS, C H
1590 Old Salem Rd, Frisco City, AL 36445, Phone: 334-575-7425
Specialties: LinerLock® folders. **Patterns:** Interframe liner locks. **Technical:** Grinds 440C and ATS-34. **Prices:** Start at $350. **Remarks:** Full-time maker; first knife sold in 1973. Doing business as Custom Knives. **Mark:** First and middle initials, last name.

MORRIS, ERIC
306 Ewart Ave, Beckley, WV 25801, Phone: 304-255-3951

MORRIS, MICHAEL S.
609 S. Main St., Yale, MI 48097, Phone: 810-887-7817, michaelmorrisknives@gmail.com
Specialties: Hunting and Tactical fixed blade knives of his design made from files. **Technical:** All knives hollow ground on 16" wheel. Hand stitches his own sheaths also. **Prices:** From $60 to $350 with most in the $90 to $125 range. **Remarks:** Machinist since 1980, made his first knife in 1984, sold his first knife in 2004. Now full-time maker. **Mark:**

Last name with date of manufacture.

MOSES, STEVEN
1610 W Hemlock Way, Santa Ana, CA 92704

MOSIER, DAVID
1725 Millburn Ave., Independence, MO 64056, Phone: 816-796-3479, dmknives@aol.com Web: www.dmknives.com
Specialties: Tactical folders and fixed blades. **Patterns:** Fighters and concealment blades. **Technical:** Uses S35VN, CPM 154, S30V, 154CM, ATS-34, 440C, A2, D2, Stainless damascus, and Damasteel. Fixed blades come with Kydex sheaths made by maker. **Prices:** $150 to $1000. **Remarks:** Full-time maker, business name is DM Knives. **Mark:** David Mosier Knives encircling sun.

MOSIER, JOSHUA J
SPRING CREEK KNIFE WORKS, PO Box 476/608 7th St, Deshler, NE 68340, Phone: 402-365-4386, joshmoiser50@gmail.com; Web:www.sc-kw.com
Specialties: Working straight and folding knives of his designs with customer specs. **Patterns:** Hunter/utility LinerLock® folders. **Technical:** Forges random pattern Damascus, 01, and 5160. **Prices:** $85 and up. **Remarks:** Part-time maker, sold first knife in 1986. **Mark:** SCKW.

MOULTON, DUSTY
135 Hillview Lane, Loudon, TN 37774, Phone: 865-408-9779, Web: www.moultonknives.com
Specialties: Fancy and working straight knives. **Patterns:** Hunters, fighters, fantasy and miniatures. **Technical:** Grinds ATS-34 and Damascus. **Prices:** $300 to $2000. **Remarks:** Full-time maker; first knife sold in 1991. Now doing engraving on own knives as well as other makers. **Mark:** Last name.

MOYER, RUSS
1266 RD 425 So, Havre, MT 59501, Phone: 406-395-4423
Specialties: Working knives to customer specs. **Patterns:** Hunters, Bowies and survival knives. **Technical:** Forges W2 & 5160. **Prices:** $150 to $350. **Remarks:** Part-time maker; first knife sold in 1976. **Mark:** Initials in logo.

MULKEY, GARY
533 Breckenridge Rd, Branson, MO 65616, Phone: 417-335-0123, gary@mulkeyknives.com; Web: www.mulkeyknives.com
Specialties: Sole authorship damascus and high-carbon steel hunters, bowies and fighters. **Patterns:** Fixed blades (hunters, bowies, and fighters). **Prices:** $450 and up. **Remarks:** Full-time maker since 1997. **Mark:** MUL above skeleton key.

MULLER, JODY
3359 S. 225th Rd., Goodson, MO 65663, Phone: 417-752-3260, mullerforge2@hotmail.com; Web: www.mullerforge.com
Specialties: Hand engraving, carving and inlays, fancy folders and oriental styles. **Patterns:** One-of-a-kind fixed blades and folders in all styles. **Technical:** Forges own Damascus and high carbon steel. **Prices:** $300 and up. **Remarks:** Full-time knifemaker, does hand engraving, carving and inlay. All work done by maker. **Mark:** Muller

MUNJAS, BOB
600 Beebe Rd., Waterford, OH 45786, Phone: 740-336-5538, Web: hairofthebear.com
Specialties: Damascus and carbon steel sheath knives. **Patterns:** Hunters and neck knives. **Technical:** My own Damascus, 5160, 1095, 1984, L6, and W2. Forge and stock removal. Does own heat treating and makes own sheaths. **Prices:** $100 to $500. **Remarks:** Part-time maker. **Mark:** Moon Munjas.

MURSKI, RAY
12129 Captiva Ct, Reston, VA 22091-1204, Phone: 703-264-1102, rmurski@gmail.com
Specialties: Fancy working/using folders of his design. **Patterns:** Hunters, slip-joint folders and utility/camp knives. **Technical:** Grinds CPM-3V **Prices:** $125 to $500. **Remarks:** Spare-time maker; first knife sold in 1996. **Mark:** Engraved name with serial number under name.

MUTZ, JEFF
8210 Rancheria Dr. Unit 7, Rancho Cucamonga, CA 91730, Phone: 909-559-7129, jmutzknives@hotmail.com; Web: www.jmutzknives.com
Specialties: Traditional working/using fixed blade and slip-jointed knives of own design and customer specs. **Patterns:** Hunters, skinners, and folders. **Technical:** Forges and grinds all steels Offers scrimshaw. **Prices:** $225 to $800. **Remarks:** Full-time maker, first knife sold in 1998. **Mark:** First initial, last name over "maker."

MYERS, PAUL
644 Maurice St, Wood River, IL 62095, Phone: 618-258-1707
Specialties: Fancy working straight knives and folders. **Patterns:** Full range of folders, straight hunters and Bowies; tie tacks; knife and fork sets. **Technical:** Grinds D2, 440C, ATS-34 and 154CM. **Prices:** $100 to $350; some to $3000. **Remarks:** Full-time maker; first knife sold in 1974. **Mark:** Initials with setting sun on front; name and number on back.

MYERS, STEVE
1429 Carolina Ave., Springfield, IL 62702, Phone: 217-416-0800, myersknives@ymail.com
Specialties: Working straight knives and integrals. **Patterns:** Camp knives, hunters, skinners, Bowies, and boot knives.**Technical:** Forges own Damascus and high carbon steels. **Prices:** $250 to $1,000. **Remarks:** Full-time maker, first knife sold in 1985. **Mark:** Last name in logo.

N

NADEAU, BRIAN
SHARPBYDESIGN LLC, 8 Sand Hill Rd., Stanhope, NJ 07874, Phone: 862-258-0792, nadeau@sharpbydesign.com; Web: www.sharpbydesign.com
Specialties: High-quality tactical fixed blades and folders, collector and working blades. All blades and sheaths of maker's own design. Designs, writes programs and machines all components on CNC equipment, nothing water jet, everything hand finished. **Technical:** Works with new CPM steels, but loves to get an order for a W2 blade with a nice hamon or temper line. **Prices:** $100 and up. **Remarks:** Part-time maker. **Mark:** Name in script, or initials "BN" skewed on top of one another.

NARASADA, MAMORU
9115-8 Nakaminowa, Minowa-machi, Kamiina-gun, NAGANO, JAPAN 399-4601, Phone: 81-265-79-3960, Fax: 81-265-79-3960
Specialties: Utility working straight knife. **Patterns:** Hunting, fishing, and camping knife. **Technical:** Grind and forges / ATS34, VG10, 440C, CRM07. **Prices:** $150 to $500, some higher. **Remarks:** First knife sold in 2003. **Mark:** M.NARASADA with initial logo.

NATEN, GREG
1804 Shamrock Way, Bakersfield, CA 93304-3921
Specialties: Fancy and working/using folders of his design. **Patterns:** Fighters, hunters and locking folders. **Technical:** Grinds 440C, ATS-34 and CPM440V. Heat-treats; prefers desert ironwood, stag and mother-of-pearl. Designs and sews leather sheaths for straight knives. **Prices:** $175 to $600; some to $950. **Remarks:** Spare-time maker; first knife sold in 1992. **Mark:** Last name above battle-ax, handmade.

NAUDE, LOUIS
15 Auction St, Dalsig, Malmesbury, WC, SOUTH AFRICA 7560, Phone: +264 (0)81-38-36-285, info@louisnaude.co.za Web: www.louisnaude.co.za
Specialties: Folders, Hunters, Custom.. Patterns: See Website. **Technical:** Stock removal, African materials. **Prices:** See website. **Remarks:** Still the tool! **Mark:** Louis Naude Knives with family crest.

NEALY, BUD
125 Raccoon Way, Stroudsburg, PA 18360, Phone: 570-402-1018, Fax: 570-402-1018, bnealy@ptd.net; Web: www.budnealyknifemaker.com
Specialties: Original design concealment knives with designer multi-concealment sheath system. **Patterns:** Fixed Blades and Folders **Technical:** Grinds CPM 154, XHP, and Damascus. **Prices:** $200 to $2500. **Remarks:** Full-time maker; first knife sold in 1980. **Mark:** Name, city, state or signature.

NEASE, WILLIAM
2336 Front Rd., LaSalle, ON, CANADA Canada N9J 2C4, wnease@hotmail.com Web: www.unsubtleblades.com
Specialties: Hatchets, choppers, and Japanese-influenced designs. **Technical:** Stock removal. Works A-2, D-2, S-7, O-1, powder stainless alloys, composite laminate blades with steel edges. **Prices:** $125 to $2200. **Remarks:** Part-time maker since 1994. **Mark:** Initials W.M.N. engraved in cursive on exposed tangs or on the spine of blades.

NEDVED, DAN
206 Park Dr, Kalispell, MT 59901, bushido2222@yahoo.com
Specialties: Slip joint folders, liner locks, straight knives. **Patterns:** Mostly traditional or modern blend with traditional lines. **Technical:** Grinds ATS-34, 440C, 1095 and uses other makers Damascus. **Prices:** $95 and up. Mostly in the $150 to $200 range. **Remarks:** Part-time maker, averages 2 a month. **Mark:** Dan Nedved or Nedved with serial # on opposite side.

NEELY, GREG
5419 Pine St, Bellaire, TX 77401, Phone: 713-991-2677, gtneely64@comcast.net
Specialties: Traditional patterns and his own patterns for work and/or collecting. **Patterns:** Hunters, Bowies and utility/camp knives. **Technical:** Forges own Damascus, 1084, 5160 and some tool steels. Differentially tempers. **Prices:** $225 to $5000. **Remarks:** Part-time maker; first knife sold in 1987. **Mark:** Last name or interlocked initials, MS.

NEILSON, J
291 Scouten Rd., Wyalusing, PA 18853, Phone: 570-721-0470, mountainhollow@epix.net; Web: www.mountainhollow.net
Specialties: Working and collectable fixed blade knives. **Patterns:** Hunter/fighters, Bowies, neck knives and daggers. **Technical:** 1084, 1095, 5160, W-2, 52100, maker's own Damascus. **Prices:** $175 to $2500. **Remarks:** ABS Master Smith, full-time maker, first knife sold in 2000, doing business as Neilson's Mountain Hollow. Each knife comes with a sheath. **Mark:** J. Neilson MS.

NELL, CHAD
2491 S. 2110E Cir., St. George, UT 84790, Phone: 435-229-6442, chad@nellknives.com; Web: www.nellknives.com
Specialties: Fixed blade working knives. **Patterns:** hunters, fighters, daggers. **Technical:** Grinds CPM-154, ATS-34. **Prices:** Starting at $300. **Remarks:** Full-time maker since Sep 2011, First knife made in May 2010. **Mark:** Nell Knives, Nell Knives Kona, Hi, C. Nell Kona, Hawaii and C. Nell Utah, USA.

NELSON, KEN
2712 17th St., Racine, WI 53405, Phone: 262-456-7519 or 262-664-5293, ken@ironwolfonline.com Web: www.ironwolfonline.com
Specialties: Working straight knives, period pieces. **Patterns:** Utility, hunters, dirks, daggers, throwers, hawks, axes, swords, pole arms and blade blanks as well. **Technical:** Forges 5160, 52100, W2, 10xx, L6, carbon steels and own Damascus. Does his own heat treating. **Prices:** $50 to $350, some to $3000. **Remarks:** Part-time maker. First knife sold in 1995. Doing business as Iron Wolf Forge. **Mark:** Stylized wolf paw print.

NETO JR.,, NELSON AND DE CARVALHO, HENRIQUE M.
R. Joao Margarido No 20-V, Braganca Paulista, SP, BRAZIL 12900-000, Phone: 011-7843-6889, Fax: 011-7843-6889
Specialties: Straight knives and folders. **Patterns:** Bowies, katanas, jambyias and others. **Technical:** Forges high-carbon steels. **Prices:** $70 to $3000. **Remarks:** Full-time makers; first knife sold in 1990. **Mark:** HandN.

NEVLING, MARK
BURR OAK KNIVES, 3567 N. M52, Owosso, MI 48867, Phone: 989-472-3167, burroakknives@aol.com; Web: www.burroakknives.com
Specialties: Tactical folders using stainless over high-carbon San Mai. **Patterns:** Hunters, fighters, bowies, folders and small executive knives. **Technical:** Convex grinds, forges, uses only high-carbon and damascus. **Prices:** $200 to $4,000. **Remarks:** Full-time maker, first knife sold 1988. Apprentice damascus smith to George Werth and Doug Ponzio.

NEWBERRY, ALLEN
PO BOX 301, Lowell, AR 72745, Phone: 479-530-6439, newberry@newberryknives.com Web: www.newberryknives.com
Specialties: Fixed blade knives both forged and stock removal. **Patterns:** Traditional patterns as well as newer designs inspired by historical and international blades. **Technical:** Uses 1095, W2, 5160, 154-CM, other steels by request. **Prices:** $150 to $450+. **Remarks:** Many of the knives feature hamons. **Mark:** Newberry with a capital N for forged pieces and newberry with a lower case n for stock removal pieces.

NEWCOMB, CORBIN
628 Woodland Ave, Moberly, MO 65270, Phone: 660-263-4639
Specialties: Working straight knives and folders; period pieces. **Patterns:** Hunters, axes, Bowies, folders, buckskinned blades and boots. **Technical:** Hollow-grinds D2, 440C and 154CM; prefers natural handle materials. Makes own Damascus; offers cable Damascus. **Prices:** $100 to $500. **Remarks:** Full-time maker; first knife sold in 1982. Doing business as Corbin Knives. **Mark:** First name and serial number.

NEWHALL, TOM
3602 E 42nd Stravenue, Tucson, AZ 85713, Phone: 520-721-0562, gggaz@aol.com

NEWTON, LARRY
1758 Pronghorn Ct, Jacksonville, FL 32225, Phone: 904-537-2066, lnewton1@comcast.net; Web: larrynewtonknives.com
Specialties: Traditional and slender high-grade gentlemen's automatic folders, locking liner type tactical, and working straight knives. **Patterns:** Front release locking folders, interframes, hunters and skinners. **Technical:** Grinds Damascus, ATS-34, 440C and D2. **Prices:** Folders start at $350, straights start at $150. **Remarks:** Retired teacher. Full-time maker. First knife sold in 1989. Won Best Folder for 2008 - Blade Magazine. **Mark:** Last name.

NEWTON, RON
223 Ridge Ln, London, AR 72847, Phone: 479-293-3001, rnewton@centurylink.net
Specialties: All types of folders and fixed blades. Blackpowder gun knife combos. **Patterns:** Traditional slip joint, multi-blade patterns, antique bowie repros. **Technical:** Forges traditional and mosaid damascus. Performs engraving and gold inlay. **Prices:** $500 and up. **Remarks:** Creates hidden mechanisms in assisted opening folders. **Mark:** NEWTON M.S. in a western invitation font."

NICHOLS, CALVIN
710 Colleton Rd., Raleigh, NC 27610, Phone: 919-523-4841, calvin.nichols@nicholsknives.com; Web: http://nicholsknives.com
Specialties: Flame-colored high carbon damascus. **Patterns:** Fixed blades or folders, bowies and daggers. **Technical:** Stock removal. **Prices:** Start at $200. **Remarks:** Full-time maker, 22 years experience, own heat treating, 2012 Best Custom and High Art winner, National and North Carolina Knifemakers Guild member. **Mark:** First, last name--city, state.

NICHOLS, CHAD
1125 Cr 185, Blue Springs, MS 38828, Phone: 662-538-5966, chadn28@hotmail.com Web: chadnicholsdamascus.com
Specialties: Gents folders and everyday tactical/utility style knives and fixed hunters. **Technical:** Makes own stainless damascus, mosaic damascus, and high carbon damascus. **Prices:** $450 - $1000. **Mark:** Name and Blue Springs.

NICHOLSON, R. KENT
PO Box 204, Phoenix, MD 21131, Phone: 410-323-6925
Specialties: Large using knives. **Patterns:** Bowies and camp knives in the Moran-style. **Technical:** Forges W2, 9260, 5160; makes Damascus. **Prices:** $150 to $995. **Remarks:** Part-time maker; first knife sold in 1984. **Mark:** Name.

NIELSON, JEFF V
1060 S Jones Rd, Monroe, UT 84754, Phone: 435-527-4242, jvn1u205@hotmail.com
Specialties: Classic knives of his design and to customer specs. **Patterns:** Fighters, hunters; miniatures. **Technical:** Grinds 440C stainless and Damascus. **Prices:** $100 to $1200. **Remarks:** Part-time maker; first knife sold in 1991. **Mark:** Name, location.

NIEMUTH, TROY
3143 North Ave, Sheboygan, WI 53083, Phone: 414-452-2927
Specialties: Period pieces and working/using straight knives of his design and to customer specs. **Patterns:** Hunters and utility/camp knives. **Technical:** Grinds 440C, 1095 and A2. **Prices:** $85 to $350; some to $500. **Remarks:** Full-time maker; first knife

sold in 1995. **Mark:** Etched last name.

NILSSON, JONNY WALKER
Akkavare 16, 93391 Arvidsjaur, SWEDEN, Phone: +46 702144207, 0960.13048@telia.com; Web: www.jwnknives.com
Specialties: High-end collectible Nordic hunters, engraved reindeer antler. World class freehand engravings. Matching engraved sheaths in leather, bone and Arctic wood with inlays. Combines traditional techniques and design with his own innovations. Master Bladesmith who specializes in forging mosaic Damascus. Sells unique mosaic Damascus bar stock to folder makers. **Patterns:** Own designs and traditional Sami designs. **Technical:** Mosaic Damascus of UHB 20 C 15N20 with pure nickel, hardness HRC 58-60. **Prices:** $1500 to $6000. **Remarks:** Full-time maker since 1988. Nordic Champion (5 countries) numerous times, 50 first prizes in Scandinavian shows. Yearly award in his name in Nordic Championship. Knives inspired by 10,000 year old indigenous Sami culture. **Mark:** JN on sheath, handle, custom wood box. JWN on blade.

NIRO, FRANK
1948 Gloaming Dr, Kamloops, B.C., CANADA V1S1P8, Phone: 250-372-8332, niro@telus.net
Specialties: Liner locking folding knives in his designs in what might be called standard patterns. **Technical:** Enjoys grinding mosaic Damascus with pure nickel of the make up for blades that are often double ground; as well as meteorite for bolsters which are then etched and heat colored. Uses 416 stainless for spacers with inlays of natural materials, gem stones with also file work. Liners are made from titanium are most often fully file worked and anodized. Only uses natural materials particularly mammoth ivory for scales. **Prices:** $500 to $1500 **Remarks:** Full time maker. Has been selling knives for over thirty years. **Mark:** Last name on the inside of the spacer.

NISHIUCHI, MELVIN S
6121 Forest Park Dr, Las Vegas, NV 89156, Phone: 702-501-3724, msnknives@yahoo.com
Specialties: Collectable quality using/working knives. **Patterns:** Locking liner folders, fighters, hunters and fancy personal knives. **Technical:** Grinds ATS-34 and Devin Thomas Damascus; prefers semi-precious stone and exotic natural handle materials. **Prices:** $375 to $2000. **Remarks:** Part-time maker; first knife sold in 1985. **Mark:** Circle with a line above it.

NOLEN, STEVE
2069 Palomino Tr, Keller, TX 76248-3102, Phone: 903-786-2454, nolen_tx@netzero.net; Web: www.nolenknives.com
Specialties: Working knives; display pieces. **Patterns:** Wide variety of straight knives, butterflies and buckles. **Technical:** Grind D2, 440C and 154CM. Offer filework; make exotic handles. **Prices:** $150 to $800; some higher. **Remarks:** Full-time maker; Steve is third generation maker. **Mark:** NK in oval logo.

NOLTE, BARBIE
10801 Gram B Cir., Lowell, AR 72745, Phone: 479-283-2095, barbie.b@gmail.com
Specialties: Collector-grade high art knives. **Technical:** Hollow grinds high-carbon, mosaic-damascus blades. Limited supply. **Prices:** Start at $600. All prices include handmade exotic leather sheaths. **Mark:** B Bell and B Nolte.

NOLTE, STEVE
10801 Gram B Cir., Lowell, AR 72745, Phone: 479-629-1676, snolte@alertalarmsys.com; Web: www.snolteknives.com
Specialties: Fancy hunters and skinners, a few fighters, some collector-grade, high-art knives. One-of-a-kind mosaic handle creations including exotic stone work. **Technical:** Mostly high-carbon damascus, some stainless damascus with very few straight stainless blades. Hollow grinds. **Prices:** Start at $400. All prices include handmade sheaths, mostly exotic leathers. **Mark:** S.Nolte.

NORDELL, INGEMAR
SkarpŒvegen 5, FŠrila, SWEDEN 82041, Phone: 0651-23347, ingi@ingemarnordell.se; Web: www.ingemarnordell.se
Specialties: Classic working and using straight knives. **Patterns:** Hunters, Bowies and fighters. **Technical:** Forges and grinds ATS-34, D2 and Sandvik. **Prices:** $300 to $3,000. **Remarks:** Part-time maker; first knife sold in 1985. **Mark:** Initials or name.

NOREN, DOUGLAS E
14676 Boom Rd, Springlake, MI 49456, Phone: 616-842-4247, gnoren@icsdata.com
Specialties: Hand forged blades, custom built and made to order. Hand file work, carving and casting. Stag and stacked handles. Replicas of Scagel and Joseph Rogers. Hand tooled custom made sheaths. **Technical:** Master smith, 5160, 52100 and 1084 steel. **Prices:** Start at $250. **Remarks:** Sole authorship, works in all mediums, ABS Mastersmith, all knives come with a custom hand-tooled sheath. Also makes anvils. Enjoys the challenge and meeting people.

NORFLEET, ROSS W
4110 N Courthouse Rd, Providence Forge, VA 23140-3420, Phone: 804-966-2596, rossknife@aol.com
Specialties: Classic, traditional and working/using knives of his design or in standard patterns. **Patterns:** Hunters and folders. **Technical:** Hollow-grinds 440C and ATS-34. **Prices:** $150 to $550. **Remarks:** Part-time maker; first knife sold in 1992. **Mark:** Last name.

NORTON, DON
95N Wilkison Ave, Port Townsend, WA 98368-2534, Phone: 306-385-1978
Specialties: Fancy and plain straight knives. **Patterns:** Hunters, small Bowies, tantos, boot knives, fillets. **Technical:** Prefers 440C, Micarta, exotic woods and other natural

handle materials. Hollow-grinds all knives except fillet knives. **Prices:** $185 to $2800; average is $200. **Remarks:** Full-time maker; first knife sold in 1980. **Mark:** Full name, Hsi Shuai, city, state.

NOWACKI, STEPHEN R.
167 King Georges Ave, Regents Park, Southampton, Hampshire, ENGLAND SO154LD, Phone: 023 81 785 630 or 079 29 737 872, stephen.nowacki@hotmail.co.uk Web: www.whitetigerknives.com
Specialties: Hand-forged, bowies, daggers, tactical blades, hunters and mountain-man style folders. **Technical:** Hitachi white paper steel and stainless carbon San Mai. Heat treats and uses natural handle materials. **Prices:** $200 - $1500. **Remarks:** Part-time maker. First knife sold in 2000. Doing business as White Tiger Knives. **Mark:** Stylized W T.

NOWLAND, RICK
3677 E Bonnie Rd, Waltonville, IL 62894, Phone: 618-279-3170, ricknowland@frontiernet.net
Specialties: Slip joint folders in traditional patterns. **Patterns:** Trapper, whittler, sowbelly, toothpick and copperhead. **Technical:** Uses ATS-34, bolsters and liners have integral construction. **Prices:** $225 to $1000. **Remarks:** Part-time maker. **Mark:** Last name.

NUCKELS, STEPHEN J
1105 Potomac Ave, Hagerstown, MD 21742, Phone: 301-739-1287, sgnucks@myactv.net
Specialties: Traditional using/working/everyday carry knives and small neck knives. **Patterns:** Hunters, bowies, Drop and trailing point knives, frontier styles. **Technical:** Hammer forges carbon steels, stock removal. Modest silver wire inlay and file work. Sheath work. **Remarks:** Spare-time maker forging under Potomac Forge, first knife made in 2008. Member W.F. Moran Jr. Foundation, American Bladesmith Society. **Mark:** Initials.

NUNN, GREGORY
HC64 Box 2107, Castle Valley, UT 84532, Phone: 435-259-8607
Specialties: High-art working and using knives of his design; new edition knife with handle made from anatomized dinosaur bone, first ever made. **Patterns:** Flaked stone knives. **Technical:** Uses gem-quality agates, jaspers and obsidians for blades. **Prices:** $250 to $2300. **Remarks:** Full-time maker; first knife sold in 1989. **Mark:** Name, knife and edition numbers, year made.

O

OATES, LEE
PO BOX 1391, La Porte, TX 77572, Phone: 281-471-6060, bearoates@att.net Web: www.bearclawknives.com
Specialties: Friction folders, period correct replicas, traditional, working and primitive knives of my design or to customer specs. **Patterns:** Bowies, teflon-coated fighters, daggers, hunters, fillet and kitchen cutlery. **Technical:** Heat treating service for other makers. Teaches blacksmithing/bladesmithing classes. Forges carbon, 440C, D2, and makes own Damascus, stock removal on SS and kitchen cutlery, Teflon coatings available on custom hunters/fighters, makes own sheaths. **Prices:** $150 to $2500. **Remarks:** Full-time maker and heat treater since 1996. First knife sold in 1988. **Mark:** Harmony (yin/yang) symbol with two bear tracks inside all forged blades; etched "Commanche Cutlery" on SS kitchen cutlery.

O'BRIEN, MIKE J.
3807 War Bow, San Antonio, TX 78238, Phone: 210-256-0673, obrien8700@att.net
Specialties: Quality straight knives of his design. **Patterns:** Mostly daggers (safe queens), some hunters. **Technical:** Grinds 440c, ATS-34, and CPM-154. Emphasis on clean workmanship and solid design. Likes hand-rubbed blades and fittings, exotic woods. **Prices:** $300 to $700 and up. **Remarks:** Part-time maker, made first knife in 1988. **Mark:** O'BRIEN in semi-circle.

OCHS, CHARLES F
124 Emerald Lane, Largo, FL 33771, Phone: 727-536-3827, Fax: 727-536-3827, charlesox@oxforge.com; Web: www.oxforge.com
Specialties: Working knives; period pieces. **Patterns:** Hunters, fighters, Bowies, buck skinners and folders. **Technical:** Forges 52100, 5160 and his own Damascus. **Prices:** $150 to $1800; some to $2500. **Remarks:** Full-time maker; first knife sold in 1978. **Mark:** OX Forge.

OCHS, ERIC
PO BOX 1311, Sherwood, OR 97140, Phone: 503-925-9790, Fax: 503-925-9790, eric@ochs.com Web: www.ochssherworx.com
Specialties: Tactical folders and flippers, as well as fixed blades for tactical, hunting, camping and chopping uses. **Patterns:** Tactical liner- and frame-lock folders with texture in various synthetic and natural materials. **Technical:** Focus on powder metals, including CPM-S30V, Elmax, CPM-154, CPM-3V and CPM-S35VN, as well as damascus steels. Flat, hollow and compound convex grinds. **Prices:** $200 - $1,500. **Remarks:** Full-time maker; made first knife in 2008 and started selling knives in mid-2009. **Mark:** The words "Ochs Sherworx" separated by an eight point compass insignia.

ODOM JR., VICTOR L.
PO Box 572, North, SC 29112, Phone: 803-247-2749, cell 803-608-0829, vlodom3@tds.net Web: www.knifemakercentral.com
Specialties: Forged knives and tomahawks; stock removal knives. **Patterns:** Hunters, Bowies, George Herron patterns, and folders. **Technical:** Use 1095, 5160, 52100 high carbon and alloy steels, ATS-34, and 154 CM. **Prices:** Straight knives $60 and up. Folders $250 and up. **Remarks:** Student of Mr. George Henron. SCAK.ORG. Secretary of the Couth Carolina Association of Knifemakers. **Mark:** Steel stamp "ODOM" and etched "Odom Forge North, SC" plus a serial number.

OELOFSE, TINUS

P.O. Box 33879, Glenstantia, Pretoria, SOUTH AFRICA 0100, Phone: +27-82-3225090, tinusoelofseknives@gmail.com

Specialties Top-class folders, mainly LinerLocks, and practical fixed blades. **Technical:** Using damascus, mostly Damasteel, and blade billets. Mammoth ivory, mammoth tooth, mother-of-pearl, gold and black-lip-pearl handles for folders. Giraffe bone, warthog ivory, horn and African hardwoods for hunters. Deep relief engraving, mostly leaf and scroll, and daughter Mariscke's scrimshaw. Likes to work on themed knives and special projects. Hand-stitched sheaths by Kitty. **Prices:** $350 to $1,500. **Mark:** Tinus Oelofse in an oval logo with a dagger outline used for the "T."

OGDEN, BILL

OGDEN KNIVES, PO Box 52, Avis

AVIS, PA 17721, Phone: 570-974-9114

Specialties: One-of-a-kind, liner-lock folders, hunters, skinners, minis. **Technical:** Grinds ATS-34, 440-C, D2, 52100, Damascus, natural and unnatural handle materials, hand-stitched custom sheaths. **Prices:** $50 and up. **Remarks:** Part-time maker since 1992. **Marks:** Last name or "OK" stamp (Ogden Knives).

OGLETREE JR., BEN R

2815 Israel Rd, Livingston, TX 77351, Phone: 409-327-8315

Specialties: Working/using straight knives of his design. **Patterns:** Hunters, kitchen and utility/camp knives. **Technical:** Grinds ATS-34, W1 and 1075; heat-treats. **Prices:** $200 to $400. **Remarks:** Part-time maker; first knife sold in 1955. **Mark:** Last name, city and state in oval with a tree on either side.

O'HARE, SEAN

1831 Rte. 776, Grand Manan, NB, CANADA E5G 2H9, Phone: 506-662-8524, sean@ohareknives.com; Web: www.ohareknives.com

Specialties: Fixed blade hunters and folders. **Patterns:** Small to large hunters and daily carry folders. **Technical:** Stock removal, flat ground. **Prices:** $220 USD to $1200 USD. **Remarks:** Strives to balance aesthetics, functionality and durability. **Mark:** 1st line - "OHARE KNIVES", 2nd line - "CANADA."

OLIVE, MICHAEL E

6388 Angora Mt Rd, Leslie, AR 72645, Phone: 870-363-4668

Specialties: Fixed blades. **Patterns:** Bowies, camp knives, fighters and hunters. **Technical:** Forged blades of 1084, W2, 5160, Damascus of 1084, and1572. **Prices:** $250 and up. **Remarks:** Received J.S. stamp in 2005. **Mark:** Olive.

OLIVER, TODD D

719 Artesian Rd. #63, Cheyenne, WY 82007, Phone: 812-821-5928, tdblues7@aol.com

Specialties: Damascus hunters and daggers. High-carbon as well. **Patterns:** Ladder, twist random. **Technical:** Sole author of all his blades. **Prices:** $350 and up. **Remarks:** Learned bladesmithing from Jim Batson at the ABS school and Damascus from Billy Merritt in Indiana. **Mark:** T.D. Oliver Spencer IN. Two crossed swords and a battle ax.

OLSON, DARROLD E

PO Box 1182, McMinnville, OR 97128, Phone: 541-285-1412

Specialties: Straight knives and folders of his design and to customer specs. **Patterns:** Hunters, liner locks and slip joints. **Technical:** Grinds ATS-34, 154CM and 440C. Uses anodized titanium; sheaths wet-molded. **Prices:** $125 to $550 and up. **Remarks:** Part-time maker; first knife sold in 1989. **Mark:** Name, type of steel and year.

OLSON, JOE

210 W. Simson Ave, Geyser, MT 59447, Phone: 406-735-4404, joekeri@3rivers.net Web: www.olsonhandmade.com

Specialties: Theme based art knives specializing in mosaic Damascus autos, folders, and straight knives, all sole authorship. **Patterns:** Mas. **Technical:** Foix. **Prices:** $300 to $5000 with most in the $3500 range. **Remarks:** Full-time maker for 15 years. **Mark:** Folders marked OLSON relief carved into back bar. Carbon steel straight knives stamped OLSON, forged hunters also stamped JS on reverse side.

OLSON, ROD

Box 373, Nanton, AB, CANADA T0L 1R0, Phone: 403-646-5838, rod.olson@hotmail.com

Patterns: Button lock folders. **Technical:** Grinds RWL 34 blade steel, titanium frames. **Prices:** Mid range. **Remarks:** Part-time maker; first knife sold in 1979. **Mark:** Last name.

OLSZEWSKI, STEPHEN

1820 Harkney Hill Rd, Coventry, RI 02816, Phone: 401-397-4774, blade5377@yahoo.com; Web: www.olszewskiknives.com

Specialties: Lock back, liner locks, automatics (art knives). **Patterns:** One-of-a-kind art knives specializing in figurals. **Technical:** Damascus steel, titanium file worked liners, fossil ivory and pearl. Double actions. **Prices:** $400 to $20,000. **Remarks:** Will custom build to your specifications. Quality work with guarantee. **Mark:** SCO inside fish symbol. Also "Olszewski."

O'MACHEARLEY, MICHAEL

129 Lawnview Dr., Wilmington, OH 45177, Phone: 937-728-2818, omachearleycustomknives@yahoo.com

Specialties: Forged and Stock removal; hunters, skinners, bowies, plain to fancy. **Technical:** ATS-34 and 5160, forges own Damascus. **Prices:** $180-$1000 and up. **Remarks:** Full-time maker, first knife made in 1999. **Mark:** Last name and shamrock.

O'MALLEY, DANIEL

4338 Evanston Ave N, Seattle, WA 98103, Phone: 206-527-0315

Specialties: Custom chef's knives. **Remarks:** Making knives since 1997.

ONION, KENNETH J

47-501 Hui Kelu St, Kaneohe, HI 96744, Phone: 808-239-1300, shopjunky@aol.com; Web: www.kenonionknives.com

Specialties: Folders featuring speed safe as well as other invention gadgets. **Patterns:** Hybrid, art, fighter, utility. **Technical:** S30V, CPM 154V, Cowry Y, SQ-2 and Damascus. **Prices:** $500 to $20,000. **Remarks:** Full-time maker; designer and inventor. First knife sold in 1991. **Mark:** Name and state.

O'QUINN, W. LEE

2654 Watson St., Elgin, SC 29045, Phone: 803-438-8322, wleeoquinn@bellsouth.net; Web: www.creativeknifeworks.com

Specialties: Hunters, utility, working, tactical and neck knives. **Technical:** Grinds ATS-34, CPM-154, 5160, D2, 1095 and damascus steels. **Prices:** Start at $100. **Remarks:** Member of South Carolina Association of Knifemakers. **Mark:** O'Quinn.

ORFORD, BEN

Nethergreen Farm, Ridgeway Cross, Malvern, Worcestershire, ENGLAND WR13 5JS, Phone: 44 01886 880410, web@benorford.com

Specialties: Working knives for woodcraft and the outdoorsman, made to his own designs. **Patterns:** Mostly flat Scandinavian grinds, full and partial tang. Also makes specialist woodcraft tools and hook knives. Custom leather sheaths by Lois, his wife. **Technical:** Grinds and forges 01, EN9, EN43, EN45 plus recycled steels. Heat treats. **Prices:** $25 - $650. **Remarks:** Full-time maker; first knife made in 1997. **Mark:** Celtic knot with name underneath.

ORTON, RICH

739 W. Palm Dr., Covina, CA 91722, Phone: 626-332-3441, rorton2@ca.rr.com

Specialties: Straight knives only. **Patterns:** Fighters, hunters, skinners. **Technical:** Grinds ATS-34. Heat treats by Paul Bos. **Prices:** $100 to $1000. **Remarks:** Full-time maker; first knife sold in 1992. Doing business as Orton Knife Works. **Mark:** Last name, city state (maker)

OSBORNE, DONALD H

5840 N McCall, Clovis, CA 93611, Phone: 559-299-9483, Fax: 559-298-1751, oforge@sbcglobal.net

Specialties: Traditional working using straight knives and folder of his design. **Patterns:** Working straight knives, Bowies, hunters, camp knives and folders. **Technical:** Forges carbon steels and makes Damascus. Grinds ATS-34, 154CM, and 440C. **Prices:** $150 and up. **Remarks:** Part-time maker. **Mark:** Last name logo and J.S.

OSBORNE, WARREN

#2-412 Alysa Ln, Waxahachie, TX 75167, Phone: 972-935-0899, Fax: 972-937-9004, ossie6@mac.com Web: www.osborneknives.com

Specialties: Investment grade collectible, interframes, one-of-a-kinds; unique locking mechanisms and cutting competition knives. **Patterns:** Folders; bolstered and interframes; conventional lockers, front lockers and back lockers; some slip-joints; some high-art pieces. **Technical:** Grinds CPM M4, BG42, CPM S30V, Damascus - some forged and stock removed cutting competition knives. **Prices:** $1200 to $3500; some to $5000. Interframes $1250 to $3000. **Remarks:** Full-time maker; first knife sold in 1980. **Mark:** Last name in boomerang logo.

OTT, FRED

1257 Rancho Durango Rd, Durango, CO 81303, Phone: 970-375-9669, fredsknives@wildblue.net

Patterns: Bowies, hunters tantos and daggers. **Technical:** Forges 1086M, W2 and Damascus. **Prices:** $250 to $2,000. **Remarks:** Full-time maker. **Mark:** Last name.

OTT, TED

154 Elgin Woods Ln., Elgin, TX 78621, Phone: 512-413-2243, tedottknives@aol.com

Specialties: Fixed blades, chef knives, butcher knives, bowies, fillet and hunting knives. **Technical:** Use mainly CPM powder steel, also ATS-34 and D-2. B>**Prices:** $250 - $1000, depending on embellishments, including scrimshaw and engraving. **Remarks:** Part-time maker; sold first knife in 1993. Won world cutting competition title in 2010 and 2012, along with the Bladesports championship. **Mark:** Ott Knives Elgin Texas.

OUYE, KEITH

PO Box 25307, Honolulu, HI 96825, Phone: 808-395-7000, keith@keithouyeknives.com; Web: www.keithouyeknives.com

Specialties: Folders with 1/8 blades and titanium handles. **Patterns:** Tactical design with liner lock and flipper. **Technical:** Blades are stainless steel ATS 34, CPM154 and S30V. Titanium liners (.071) and scales 3/16 pivots and stop pin, titanium pocket clip. Heat treat by Paul Bos. **Prices:** $495 to $995, with engraved knives starting at $1,200. **Remarks:** Engraving done by C.J. Cal, Bruce Shaw, Lisa Tomlin and Tom Ferry. Retired, so basically a full time knifemaker. Sold first fixed blade in 2004 and first folder in 2005. **Mark:** Ouye/Hawaii with steel type on back side **Other:** Selected by Blade Magazine (March 2006 issue) as one of five makers to watch in 2006.

OVEREYNDER, T R

1800 S. Davis Dr, Arlington, TX 76013, Phone: 817-277-4812, Fax: 817-277-4812, trovereynder@gmail.com or tom@overeynderknives.com; Web: www.overeynderknives.com

Specialties: Highly finished collector-grade knives. Multi-blades. **Patterns:** Fighters, Bowies, daggers, locking folders, 70 percent collector-grade multi blade slip joints, 25 percent interframe, 5 percent fixed blade **Technical:** Grinds CPM-D2, CPM-S60V, CPM-S30V, CPM-154, CPM-M4, BG-42, CTS-XHP, PSF27, RWL-34 and vendor supplied damascus. Has been making titanium-frame folders since 1977. **Prices:** $750 to $2000, some to $7000. **Remarks:** Full-time maker; first knife sold in 1977. Doing business as

OWEN—PARRISH

TRO Knives. **Mark:** T.R. OVEREYNDER KNIVES, city and state.

OWEN, DAVID J.A.
30 New Forest Rd., Forest Town, Johannesburg, SOUTH AFRICA, Phone: +27-11-486-1086; cell: +27-82-990-7178, djaowen25@gmail.com
Specialties: Steak knife sets, carving sets, bird-and-trout knives, top-end hunting knives, LinerLock folders. **Patterns:** Variety of knives and techniques. **Technical:** Stock-removal method, freehand hollow and flat grinds, exotic handle materials such as African hardwoods, giraffe bone, hippo tooth and warthog tusk. **Prices:** $150 and up. **Remarks:** Full-time maker since 1993. **Mark:** Two knives back-to-back with words "Owen" and "original" acid etched above and below the knives.

OWENS, DONALD
2274 Lucille Ln, Melbourne, FL 32935, Phone: 321-254-9765

OWENS, JOHN
14500 CR 270, Nathrop, CO 81236, Phone: 719-207-0067
Specialties: Hunters. **Prices:** $225 to $425 some to $700. **Remarks:** Spare-time maker. **Mark:** Last name.

OWNBY, JOHN C
708 Morningside Tr., Murphy, TX 75094-4365, Phone: 972-442-7352, john@johnownby.com; Web: www.johnownby.com
Specialties: Hunters, utility/camp knives. **Patterns:** Hunters, locking folders and utility/camp knives. **Technical:** 440C, D2 and ATS-34. All blades are flat ground. Prefers natural materials for handles—exotic woods, horn and antler. **Prices:** $150 to $350; some to $500. **Remarks:** Part-time maker; first knife sold in 1993. Doing business as John C. Ownby Handmade Knives. **Mark:** Name, city, state.

OYSTER, LOWELL R
543 Grant Rd, Corinth, ME 04427, Phone: 207-884-8663
Specialties: Traditional and original designed multi-blade slip-joint folders. **Patterns:** Hunters, minis, camp and fishing knives. **Technical:** Grinds O1; heat-treats. **Prices:** $55 to $450; some to $750. **Remarks:** Full-time maker; first knife sold in 1981. **Mark:** A scallop shell.

P

PACKARD, RONNIE
301 White St., Bonham, TX 75418, Phone: 903-227-3131, packardknives@gmail.com; Web: www.packardknives.com
Specialties: Bowies, folders (lockback, slip joint, frame lock, Hobo knives) and hunters of all sizes. **Technical:** Grinds 440C, ATS-34, D2 and stainless damascus. Makes own sheaths, does heat treating and sub-zero quenching in shop. **Prices:** $160 to $2,000. **Remarks:** Part-time maker; first knife sold in 1975. **Mark:** Last name over year.

PADILLA, GARY
PO Box 5706, Bellingham, WA 98227, Phone: 360-756-7573, gkpadilla@yahoo.com
Specialties: Unique knives of all designs and uses. **Patterns:** Hunters, kitchen knives, utility/camp knives and obsidian ceremonial knives. **Technical:** Grinds 440C, ATS-34, O1 and Damascus. **Prices:** Generally $100 to $200. **Remarks:** Part-time maker; first knife sold in 1977. **Mark:** Stylized name.

PAGE, LARRY
1200 Mackey Scott Rd, Aiken, SC 29801-7620, Phone: 803-648-0001
Specialties: Working knives of his design. **Patterns:** Hunters, boots and fighters. **Technical:** Grinds ATS-34. **Prices:** Start at $85. **Remarks:** Part-time maker; first knife sold in 1983. **Mark:** Name, city and state in oval.

PAGE, REGINALD
6587 Groveland Hill Rd, Groveland, NY 14462, Phone: 716-243-1643
Specialties: High-art straight knives and one-of-a-kind folders of his design. **Patterns:** Hunters, locking folders and slip-joint folders. **Technical:** Forges O1, 5160 and his own Damascus. Prefers natural handle materials but will work with Micarta. **Remarks:** Spare-time maker; first knife sold in 1985. **Mark:** First initial, last name.

PAINTER, TONY
87 Fireweed Dr, Whitehorse, YT, CANADA Y1A 5T8, Phone: 867-633-3323, yukonjimmies@gmail.com; Web: www.tonypainterdesigns.com
Specialties: One-of-a-kind using knives, some fancy, fixed and folders. **Patterns:** No fixed patterns. **Technical:** Grinds ATS-34, D2, O1, S30V, Damascus satin finish. Prefers to use exotic woods and other natural materials. Micarta and G10 on working knives. **Prices:** Starting at $200. **Remarks:** Full-time knifemaker and carver. First knife sold in 1996. **Mark:** Two stamps used: initials TP in a circle and painter.

PALIKKO, J-T
B30 B1, Suomenlinna, 00190 Helsinki, FINLAND, Phone: +358-400-699687, jt@kp-art.fi; Web: www.art-helsinki.com
Specialties: One-of-a-kind knives and swords. **Patterns:** Own puukko models, hunters, integral & semi-integral knives, swords & other historical weapons and friction folders. **Technical:** Forges 52100 & other carbon steels, Damasteel stainless damascus & RWL-34, makes own damascus steel, makes carvings on walrus ivory and antler. **Prices:** Starting at $250. **Remarks:** Full-time maker; first knife sold in 1989. **Mark:** JT

PALM, RIK
10901 Scripps Ranch Blvd, San Diego, CA 92131, Phone: 858-530-0407, rikpalm@knifesmith.com; Web: www.knifesmith.com
Specialties: Sole authorship of one-of-a-kind unique art pieces, working/using knives and sheaths. **Patterns:** Carved nature themed knives, camp, hunters, friction folders, tomahawks, and small special pocket knives. **Technical:** Makes own Damascus, forges

5160H, 1084, 1095, W2, O1. Does his own heat treating including clay hardening. **Prices:** $80 and up. **Remarks:** American Bladesmith Society Journeyman Smith. First blade sold in 2000. **Mark:** Stamped, hand signed, etched last name signature.

PALMER, TAYLOR
TAYLOR-MADE SCENIC KNIVES INC., Box 97, Blanding, UT 84511, Phone: 435-678-2523, taylormadewoodeu@citlink.net
Specialties: Bronze carvings inside of blade area. **Prices:** $250 and up. **Mark:** Taylor Palmer Utah.

PANAK, PAUL S
6103 Leon Rd., Andover, OH 44003, Phone: 330-442-2724, burn@burnknives.com; Web: www.burnknives.com
Specialties: Italian-styled knives. DA OTF's, Italian style stilettos. **Patterns:** Vintage-styled Italians, fighting folders and high art gothic-styles all with various mechanisms. **Technical:** Grinds ATS-34, 154 CM, 440C and Damascus. **Prices:** $800 to $3000. **Remarks:** Full-time maker, first knife sold in 1998. **Mark:** "Burn."

PANCHENKO, SERGE
5927 El Sol Way, Citrus Heights, CA 95621, Phone: 916-588-8821, serge@sergeknives.com Web: www.sergeknives.com
Specialties: Unique art knives using natural materials, copper and carbon steel for a rustic look. **Patterns:** Art knives, tactical folders, Japanese- and relic-style knives. **Technical:** Forges carbon steel, grinds carbon and stainless steels. **Prices:** $100 to $800. **Remarks:** Part-time maker, first knife sold in 2008. **Mark:** SERGE

PARDUE, JOE
PO Box 569, Hillister, TX 77624, Phone: 409-429-7074, Fax: 409-429-5657, joepardue@hughes.net; Web: www.melpardueknives.com/Joeparadueknives/index.htm

PARDUE, MELVIN M
4461 Jerkins Rd., Repton, AL 36475, Phone: 251-248-2686, mpardue@frontiernet.net; Web: www.pardueknives.com
Specialties: Folders, collectable, combat, utility and tactical. **Patterns:** Lockback, liner lock, push button; all blade and handle patterns. **Technical:** Grinds 154CM, 440C, 12C27. Forges mokume and Damascus. Uses titanium. **Prices:** $400 to $1600. **Remarks:** Full-time maker, Guild member, ABS member, AFC member. First knife made in 1957; first knife sold professionally in 1974. **Mark:** Mel Pardue.

PARKER, CLIFF
6350 Tulip Dr, Zephyrhills, FL 33544, Phone: 813-973-1682, cooldamascus@aol.com Web: cliffparkerknives.com
Specialties: Damascus gent knives. **Patterns:** Locking liners, some straight knives. **Technical:** Mostly use 1095, 1084, 15N20, 203E and powdered steel. **Prices:** $700 to $2100. **Remarks:** Making own Damascus and specializing in mosaics; first knife sold in 1996. Full-time beginning in 2000. **Mark:** CP.

PARKER, J E
11 Domenica Cir, Clarion, PA 16214, Phone: 814-226-4837, jimparkerknives@hotmail.com Web:www.jimparkerknives.com
Specialties: Fancy/embellished, traditional and working straight knives of his design and to customer specs. Engraving and scrimshaw by the best in the business. **Patterns:** Bowies, hunters and LinerLock® folders. **Technical:** Grinds 440C, 440V, ATS-34 and nickel Damascus. Prefers mastodon, oosik, amber and malachite handle material. **Prices:** $75 to $5200. **Remarks:** Full-time maker; first knife sold in 1991. Doing business as Custom Knife. **Mark:** J E Parker and Clarion PA stamped or etched in blade.

PARKER, ROBERT NELSON
1527 E Fourth St, Royal Oak, MI 48067, Phone: 248-545-8211, rnparkerknives@gmail.com or rnparkerknives@wowway.com; Web: www.classicknifedesign.com
Specialties: Traditional working and using straight knives of his design. **Patterns:** Chutes, subhilts, hunters, and fighters. **Technical:** Grinds CPM-154, CPM-D2, BG-42 and ATS-34, no forging, hollow and flat grinds, full and hidden tangs. Hand-stitched leather sheaths. **Prices:** $400 to $2,000, some to $3,000. **Remarks:** Full-time maker; first knife sold in 1986. I do forge sometimes. **Mark:** Full name.

PARKS, BLANE C
15908 Crest Dr, Woodbridge, VA 22191, Phone: 703-221-4680
Specialties: Knives of his design. **Patterns:** Boots, Bowies, daggers, fighters, hunters, kitchen knives, locking and slip-joint folders, utility/camp knives, letter openers and friction folders. **Technical:** Grinds ATS-34, 440C, D2 and other carbon steels. Offers filework, silver wire inlay and wooden sheaths. **Prices:** Start at $250 to $650; some to $1000. **Remarks:** Part-time maker; first knife sold in 1993. Doing business as B.C. Parks Knives. **Mark:** First and middle initials, last name.

PARKS, JOHN
3539 Galilee Church Rd, Jefferson, GA 30549, Phone: 706-367-4916
Specialties: Traditional working and using straight knives of his design. **Patterns:** Hunters, integral bolsters, and personal knives. **Technical:** Forges 1095 and 5168. **Prices:** $275 to $600; some to $800. **Remarks:** Part-time maker; first knife sold in 1989. **Mark:** Initials.

PARLER, THOMAS O
11 Franklin St, Charleston, SC 29401, Phone: 803-723-9433

PARRISH, ROBERT
271 Allman Hill Rd, Weaverville, NC 28787, Phone: 828-645-2864
Specialties: Heavy-duty working knives of his design or to customer specs. **Patterns:**

Survival and duty knives; hunters and fighters. **Technical:** Grinds 440C, D2, O1 and commercial Damascus. **Prices:** $200 to $300; some to $6000. **Remarks:** Part-time maker; first knife sold in 1970. **Mark:** Initials connected, sometimes with city and state.

PARRISH III, GORDON A
940 Lakloey Dr, North Pole, AK 99705, Phone: 907-488-0357, ga-parrish@gci.net
Specialties: Classic and high-art straight knives of his design and to customer specs; working and using knives. **Patterns:** Bowies and hunters. **Technical:** Grinds tool steel and ATS-34. Uses mostly Alaskan handle materials. **Prices:** Starting at $300. **Remarks:** Spare-time maker; first knife sold in 1980. **Mark:** Last name, FBKS. ALASKA

PARSONS, LARRY
1038 W Kyle Way, Mustang, OK 73064, Phone: 405-376-9408, Fax: 405-376-9408, l.j.parsons@sbcglobal.net
Specialties: Variety of sheaths from plain leather, geometric stamped, also inlays of various types. **Prices:** Starting at $35 and up

PARSONS, PETE
5905 High Country Dr., Helena, MT 59602, Phone: 406-202-0181, Parsons14@MT.net; Web: www.ParsonsMontanaKnives.com
Specialties: Forged utility blades in straight steel or Damascus (will grind stainless on customer request). Folding knives of my own design. **Patterns:** Hunters, fighters, Bowies, hikers, camp knives, everyday carry folders, tactical folders, gentleman's folders. Some customer designed patterns. **Technical:** Forges carbon steel, grinds carbon steel and some stainless. Forges own Damascus. **Mark:** Left side of blade PARSONS stamp or Parsons Helena, MT etch.

PARTRIDGE, JERRY D.
P.O. Box 977, DeFuniak Springs, FL 32435, Phone: 850-520-4873, jerry@partridgeknives.com; Web: www.partridgeknives.com
Specialties: Fancy and working straight knives and straight razors of his designs. **Patterns:** Hunters, skinners, fighters, chef's knives, straight razors, neck knives, and miniatures. **Technical:** Grinds 440C, ATS-34, carbon Damascus, and stainless Damascus. **Prices:** $250 and up, depending on materials used. **Remarks:** Part-time maker, first knife sold in 2007. **Mark:** Partridge Knives logo on the blade; Partridge or Partridge Knives engraved in script.

PASSMORE, JIMMY D
316 SE Elm, Hoxie, AR 72433, Phone: 870-886-1922

PATRICK, BOB
12642 24A Ave, S. Surrey, BC, CANADA V4A 8H9, Phone: 604-538-6214, Fax: 604-888-2683, bob@knivesonnet.com; Web: www.knivesonnet.com
Specialties: Maker's designs only, No orders. **Patterns:** Bowies, hunters, daggers, throwing knives. **Technical:** D2, 5160, Damascus. **Prices:** Good value. **Remarks:** Full-time maker; first knife sold in 1987. Doing business as Crescent Knife Works. **Mark:** Logo with name and province or Crescent Knife Works.

PATRICK, CHUCK
4650 Pine Log Rd., Brasstown, NC 28902, Phone: 828-837-7627, chuckandpeggypatrick@gmail.com Web: www.chuckandpeggypatrick.com
Specialties: Period pieces. **Patterns:** Hunters, daggers, tomahawks, pre-Civil War folders. **Technical:** Forges hardware, his own cable and Damascus, available in fancy pattern and mosaic. **Prices:** $150 to $1000; some higher. **Remarks:** Full-time maker. **Mark:** Hand-engraved name or flying owl.

PATRICK, PEGGY
4650 Pine Log Rd., Brasstown, NC 28902, Phone: 828-837-7627, chuckandpeggypatrick@gmail.com Web: www.chuckandpeggypatrick.com
Specialties: Authentic period and Indian sheaths, braintan, rawhide, beads and quill work. **Technical:** Does own braintan, rawhide; uses only natural dyes for quills, old color beads.

PATRICK, WILLARD C
PO Box 5716, Helena, MT 59604, Phone: 406-458-6552, wilamar@mt.net
Specialties: Working straight knives and one-of-a-kind art knives of his design or to customer specs. **Patterns:** Hunters, Bowies, fish, patch and kitchen knives. **Technical:** Grinds ATS-34, 1095, O1, A2 and Damascus. **Prices:** $100 to $2000. **Remarks:** Full-time maker; first knife sold in 1989. Doing business as Wil-A-Mar Cutlery. **Mark:** Shield with last name and a dagger.

PATTAY, RUDY
8739 N. Zurich Way, Citrus Springs, FL 34434, Phone: 516-318-4538, dolphin51@att.net; Web: www.pattayknives.com
Specialties: Fancy and working straight knives of his design. **Patterns:** Bowies, hunters, utility/camp knives, drop point, skinners. **Technical:** Hollow-grinds ATS-34, 440C, O1. Offers commercial Damascus, stainless steel soldered guards; fabricates guard and butt cap on lathe and milling machine. Heat-treats. Prefers synthetic handle materials. Offers hand-sewn sheaths. **Prices:** $100 to $350; some to $500. **Remarks:** Full-time maker; first knife sold in 1990. **Mark:** First initial, last name in sorcerer logo.

PATTERSON, PAT
Box 246, Barksdale, TX 78828, Phone: 830-234-3586, pat@pattersonknives.com
Specialties: Traditional fixed blades and LinerLock folders. **Patterns:** Hunters and folders. **Technical:** Grinds 440C, ATS-34, D2, O1 and Damascus. **Prices:** $250 to $1000. **Remarks:** Full-time maker. First knife sold in 1991. **Mark:** Name and city.

PATTON, DICK AND ROB
6803 View Ln, Nampa, ID 83687, Phone: 208-468-4123, grpatton@pattonknives.com; Web: www.pattonknives.com
Specialties: Custom Damascus, hand forged, fighting knives, Bowie and tactical. **Patterns:** Mini Bowie, Merlin Fighter, Mandrita Fighting Bowie. **Prices:** $100 to $2000.

PATTON, PHILLIP
PO BOX 113, Yoder, IN 46798, phillip@pattonblades.com Web: www.pattonblades.com
Specialties: Tactical fixed blades, including fighting, camp, and general utility blades. Also makes Bowies and daggers. Known for leaf and recurve blade shapes. **Technical:** Forges carbon, stainless, and high alloy tool steels. Makes own damascus using 1084/15n20 or O1/L6. Makes own carbon/stainless laminated blades. For handle materials, prefers high end woods and synthetics. Uses 416 ss and bronze for fittings. **Prices:** $175 - $1000 for knives; $750 and up for swords. **Remarks:** Full-time maker since 2005. Two-year backlog. ABS member. **Mark:** "Phillip Patton" with Phillip above Patton.

PAULO, FERNANDES R
Raposo Tavares No 213, Lencois Paulista, SP, BRAZIL 18680, Phone: 014-263-4281
Specialties: An apprentice of Jose Alberto Paschoarelli, his designs are heavily based on the later designs. **Technical:** Grinds tool steels and stainless steels. Part-time knifemaker. **Prices:** Start from $100. **Mark:** P.R.F.

PAWLOWSKI, JOHN R
19380 High Bluff Ln., Barhamsville, VA 23011, Phone: 757-870-4284, Fax: 757-223-5935, www.bigjohnknives.com
Specialties: Traditional working and using straight knives and folders. **Patterns:** Hunters, Bowies, fighters and camp knives. **Technical:** Stock removal, grinds 440C, ATS-34, 154CM and buys Damascus. **Prices:** $250 and up. **Remarks:** Part-time maker, first knife sold in 1983, Knifemaker Guild Member. **Mark:** Name with attacking eagle.

PEAGLER, RUSS
PO Box 1314, Moncks Corner, SC 29461, Phone: 803-761-1008
Specialties: Traditional working straight knives of his design and to customer specs. **Patterns:** Hunters, fighters, boots. **Technical:** Hollow-grinds 440C, ATS-34 and O1; uses Damascus steel. Prefers bone handles. **Prices:** $85 to $300; some to $500. **Remarks:** Spare-time maker; first knife sold in 1983. **Mark:** Initials.

PEARCE, LOGAN
1013 Dogtown Rd, De Queen, AR 71832, Phone: 580-212-0995, night_everclear@hotmail.com; Web: www.pearceknives.com
Specialties: Edged weapons, art knives, stright working knives. **Patterns:** Bowie, hunters, tomahawks, fantasy, utility, daggers, and slip-joint. **Technical:** Fprges 1080, L6, 5160, 440C, steel cable, and his own Damascus. **Prices:** $35 to $500. **Remarks:** Full-time maker, first knife sold in 1992. Doing business as Pearce Knives **Mark:** Name

PEASE, W D
657 Cassidy Pike, Ewing, KY 41039, Phone: 606-845-0387, Web: www.wdpeaseknives.com
Specialties: Display-quality working folders. **Patterns:** Fighters, tantos and boots; locking folders and interframes. **Technical:** Grinds ATS-34 and commercial Damascus; has own side-release lock system. **Prices:** $500 to $1000; some to $3000. **Remarks:** Full-time maker; first knife sold in 1970. **Mark:** First and middle initials, last name and state. W. D. Pease Kentucky.

PEDERSEN, OLE
23404 W. Lake Kayak Dr., Monroe, WA 98272, Phone: 425-931-5750, ole@pedersenknives.com; www.pedersenknives.com
Specialties Fixed blades of own design. **Patterns:** Hunters, working and utility knives. **Technical:** Stock removal, hollow grinds CPM 154 and stainless steel, 416 stainless fittings, makes own custom sheaths. Handles are mostly stabilized burl wood, some G-10. Heat treats and tempers own knives. **Prices:** $275 to $500. **Remarks:** Full-time maker; sold first knife in 2012. **Mark:** Ole Pedersen - Maker.

PEELE, BRYAN
219 Ferry St, PO Box 1363, Thompson Falls, MT 59873, Phone: 406-827-4633, banana_peele@yahoo.com
Specialties: Fancy working and using knives of his design. **Patterns:** Hunters, Bowies and fighters. **Technical:** Grinds 440C, ATS-34, D2, O1 and commercial Damascus. **Prices:** $110 to $300; some to $900. **Remarks:** Part-time maker; first knife sold in 1985. **Mark:** The Elk Rack, full name, city, state.

PELLEGRIN, MIKE
MP3 Knives, 107 White St., Troy, IL 62294-1126, Phone: 618-667-6777, Web: MP3knives.com
Specialties: Lockback folders with stone inlays, and one-of-a-kind art knives with stainless steel or damascus handles. **Technical:** Stock-removal method of blade making using 440C, Damasteel or high-carbon damascus blades. **Prices:** $800 and up. **Remarks:** Making knives since 2000. **Mark:** MP (combined) 3.

PENDLETON, LLOYD
24581 Shake Ridge Rd, Volcano, CA 95689, Phone: 209-296-3353, Fax: 209-296-3353
Specialties: Contemporary working knives in standard patterns. **Patterns:** Hunters, fighters and boots. **Technical:** Grinds and ATS-34; mirror finishes. **Prices:** $400 to $900 **Remarks:** Full-time maker; first knife sold in 1973. **Mark:** First initial, last name logo, city and state.

PENDRAY, ALFRED H
13950 NE 20th St, Williston, FL 32696, Phone: 352-528-6124
Specialties: Working straight knives and folders; period pieces. **Patterns:** Fighters and hunters, axes, camp knives and tomahawks. **Technical:** Forges Wootz steel; makes his

custom knifemakers

PENFOLD—PIERGALLINI

own Damascus; makes traditional knives from old files and rasps. **Prices:** $125 to $1000; some to $3500. **Remarks:** Part-time maker; first knife sold in 1954. **Mark:** Last initial in horseshoe logo.

PENFOLD, MICK

PENFOLD KNIVES, 5 Highview Close, Tremar, Cornwall, ENGLAND PL14 5SJ, Phone: 01579-345783, mickpenfold@btinternet.com

Specialties: Hunters, fighters, Bowies. **Technical:** Grinds 440C, ATS-34, Damasteel, and Damascus. **Prices:** $200 to $1800. **Remarks:** Part-time maker. First knives sold in 1999. **Mark:** Last name.

PENNINGTON, C A

163 Kainga Rd, Kainga Christchurch, NEW ZEALAND 8009, Phone: 03-3237292, capennington@xtra.co.nz

Specialties: Classic working and collectors knives. Folders a specialty. **Patterns:** Classical styling for hunters and collectors. **Technical:** Forges his own all tool steel Damascus. Grinds D2 when requested. **Prices:** $240 to $2000. **Remarks:** Full-time maker; first knife sold in 1988. Color brochure $3. **Mark:** Name, country.

PEPIOT, STEPHAN

73 Cornwall Blvd, Winnipeg, MB, CANADA R3J-1E9, Phone: 204-888-1499

Specialties: Working straight knives in standard patterns. **Patterns:** Hunters and camp knives. **Technical:** Grinds 440C and industrial hack-saw blades. **Prices:** $75 to $125. **Remarks:** Spare-time maker; first knife sold in 1982. Not currently taking orders. **Mark:** PEP.

PERRY, CHRIS

1654 W. Birch, Fresno, CA 93711, Phone: 559-246-7446, chris.perry4@comcast.net

Specialties: Traditional working/using straight knives of his design. **Patterns:** Boots, hunters and utility/camp knives. **Technical:** Grinds ATS-34, Damascus, 416ss fittings, silver and gold fittings, hand-rubbed finishes. **Prices:** Starting at $250. **Remarks:** Part-time maker, first knife sold in 1995. **Mark:** Name above city and state.

PERRY, JIM

Hope Star PO Box 648, Hope, AR 71801, jenn@comfabinc.com

PERRY, JOHN

9 South Harrell Rd, Mayflower, AR 72106, Phone: 501-470-3043, jpknives@cyberback.com

Specialties: Investment grade and working folders; Antique Bowies and slip joints. **Patterns:** Front and rear lock folders, liner locks, hunters and Bowies. **Technical:** Grinds CPM440V, D2 and making own Damascus. Offers filework. **Prices:** $375 to $1200; some to $3500. **Remarks:** Part-time maker; first knife sold in 1991. Doing business as Perry Custom Knives. **Mark:** Initials or last name in high relief set in a diamond shape.

PERRY, JOHNNY

PO Box 35, Inman, SC 29349, Phone: 864-431-6390, perr3838@bellsouth.net

Mark: High Ridge Forge.

PERSSON, CONNY

PL 588, Loos, SWEDEN 82050, Phone: +46 657 10305, Fax: +46 657 413 435, connyknives@swipnet.se; Web: www.connyknives.com

Specialties: Mosaic Damascus. **Patterns:** Mosaic Damascus. **Technical:** Straight knives and folders. **Prices:** $1000 and up. **Mark:** C. Persson.

PETEAN, FRANCISCO AND MAURICIO

R. Dr. Carlos de Carvalho Rosa 52, Birigui, SP, BRAZIL 16200-000, Phone: 0186-424786

Specialties: Classic knives to customer specs. **Patterns:** Bowies, boots, fighters, hunters and utility knives. **Technical:** Grinds D6, 440C and high-carbon steels. Prefers natural handle material. **Prices:** $70 to $500. **Remarks:** Full-time maker; first knife sold in 1985. **Mark:** Last name, hand made.

PETERS, DANIEL

5589 Poydasheff Ct., Columbus, GA 31907, Phone: 360-451-9386, dan@danpeterscustomknives.com; www.danpeterscustomknives.com

Specialties: Hunters, skinners, tactical and combat knives. **Patterns:** Drop points, daggers, folders, hunters, skinners, Kukri style and fillet knives, often to customer's specs. **Technical:** CPM S35VN, CPM 3V, CPM 154 and a few other high-end specialty steels. **Prices:** $75 for bottle openers, and $150 and up on all others. **Remarks:** Part-time maker, full-time military. **Mark:** PETERS USA etched.

PETERSEN, DAN L

10610 SW 81st, Auburn, KS 66402, Phone: 785-220-8043, dan@petersenknives.com; Web: www.petersenknives.com

Specialties: Period pieces and forged integral hilts on hunters and fighters. **Patterns:** Texas-style Bowies, boots and hunters in high-carbon and Damascus steel. **Technical:** Precision heat treatments. Bainite blades with mantensite cores. **Prices:** $800 to $10,000. **Remarks:** First knife sold in 1978. ABS Master Smith. **Mark:** Stylized initials.

PETERSON, CHRIS

Box 143, 2175 W Rockyford, Salina, UT 84654, Phone: 435-529-7194

Specialties: Working straight knives of his design. **Patterns:** Large fighters, boots, hunters and some display pieces. **Technical:** Forges 01 and meteor. Makes and sells his own Damascus. Engraves, scrimshaws and inlays. **Prices:** $150 to $600; some to $1500. **Remarks:** Full-time maker; first knife sold in 1986. **Mark:** A drop in a circle with a line through it.

PETERSON, ELDON G

368 Antelope Trl, Whitefish, MT 59937, Phone: 406-862-2204, draino@digisys.net;

Web: http://www.kmg.org/egpeterson

Specialties: Fancy and working folders, any size. **Patterns:** Lockback interframes, integral bolster folders, liner locks, and two-blades. **Technical:** Grinds 440C and ATS-34. Offers gold inlay work, gem stone inlays and engraving. **Prices:** $285 to $5000. **Remarks:** Full-time maker; first knife sold in 1974. **Mark:** Name, city and state.

PETERSON, LLOYD (PETE) C

64 Halbrook Rd, Clinton, AR 72031, Phone: 501-893-0000, wmblade@cyberback.com

Specialties: Miniatures and mosaic folders. **Prices:** $250 and up. **Remarks:** Lead time is 6-8 months. **Mark:** Pete.

PFANENSTIEL, DAN

1824 Lafayette Ave, Modesto, CA 95355, Phone: 209-575-5937, dpfan@sbcglobal.net

Specialties: Japanese tanto, swords. One-of-a-kind knives. **Technical:** Forges simple carbon steels, some Damascus. **Prices:** $200 to $1000. **Mark:** Circle with wave inside.

PHILIPPE, D A

PO Box 306, Cornish, NH 03746, Phone: 603-543-0662

Specialties: Traditional working straight knives. **Patterns:** Hunters, trout and bird, camp knives etc. **Technical:** Grinds ATS-34, 440C, A-2, Damascus, flat and hollow ground. Exotic woods and antler handles. Brass, nickel silver and stainless components. **Prices:** $125 to $800. **Remarks:** Full-time maker, first knife sold in 1984. **Mark:** First initial, last name.

PHILLIPS, ALISTAIR

, Amaroo, ACT, AUSTRALIA 2914, alistair.phillips@knives.mutantdiscovery.com; Web: http://knives.mutantdiscovery.com

Specialties: Slipjoint folders, forged or stock removal fixed blades. **Patterns:** Single blade slipjoints, smaller neck knives, and hunters. **Technical:** Flat grnds O1, ATS-34, and forged 1055. **Prices:** $80 to $400. **Remarks:** Part-time maker, first knife made in 2005. **Mark:** Stamped signature.

PHILLIPS, DENNIS

16411 West Bennet Rd, Independence, LA 70443, Phone: 985-878-8275

Specialties: Specializes in fixed blade military combat tacticals.

PHILLIPS, DONAVON

905 Line Prairie Rd., Morton, MS 39117, Phone: 662-907-0322, bigdknives@gmail.com

Specialties: Flat ground, tapered tang working/using knives. **Patterns:** Hunters, Capers, Fillet, EDC, Field/Camp/Survival, Competition Cutters. Will work with customers on custom designs or changes to own designs. **Technical:** Stock removal maker using CPM-M4, CPM-154, and other air-hardening steels. Will use 5160 or 52100 on larger knives. G-10 or rubber standard, will use natural material if requested including armadillo. Kydex sheath is standard, outsourced leather available.†Heat treat is done by maker. **Prices:** $100 - $1000 **Remarks:** Part-time/hobbyist maker. First knife made in 2004; first sold 2007. **Mark:** Mark is etched, first and last name forming apex of triangle, city and state at the base, D in center.

PICKENS, SELBERT

2295 Roxalana Rd, Dunbar, WV 25064, Phone: 304-744-4048

Specialties: Using knives. **Patterns:** Standard sporting knives. **Technical:** Stainless steels; stock removal method. **Prices:** Moderate. **Remarks:** Part-time maker. **Mark:** Name.

PICKETT, TERRELL

66 Pickett Ln, Lumberton, MS 39455, Phone: 601-794-6125, pickettfence66@bellsouth.net

Specialties: Fix blades, camp knives, Bowies, hunters, & skinners. Forge and stock removal and some firework. **Technical:** 5160, 1095, 52100, 440C and ATS-34. **Prices:** Range from $150 to $550. **Mark:** Logo on stock removal T.W. Pickett and on forged knives Terrell Pickett's Forge.

PIENAAR, CONRAD

19A Milner Rd, Bloemfontein, Free State, SOUTH AFRICA 9300, Phone: 027 514364180, Fax: 027 514364180

Specialties: Fancy working and using straight knives and folders of his design, to customer specs and in standard patterns. **Patterns:** Hunters, locking folders, cleavers, kitchen and utility/camp knives. **Technical:** Grinds 12C27, D2 and ATS-34. Uses some Damascus. Embellishments; scrimshaws; inlays gold. Knives come with wooden box and custom-made leather sheath. **Prices:** $300 to $1000. **Remarks:** Part-time maker; first knife sold in 1981. Doing business as C.P. Knifemaker. Makes slip joint folders and liner locking folders. **Mark:** Initials and serial number.

PIERCE, HAROLD L

106 Lyndon Lane, Louisville, KY 40222, Phone: 502-429-5136

Specialties: Working straight knives, some fancy. **Patterns:** Big fighters and Bowies. **Technical:** Grinds D2, 440C, 154CM; likes sub-hilts. **Prices:** $150 to $450; some to $1200. **Remarks:** Full-time maker; first knife sold in 1982. **Mark:** Last name with knife through the last initial.

PIERCE, RANDALL

903 Wyndam, Arlington, TX 76017, Phone: 817-468-0138

PIERGALLINI, DANIEL E

4011 N. Forbes Rd, Plant City, FL 33565, Phone: 813-754-3908 or 813-967-1471, coolnifedad@wildblue.net

Specialties: Traditional and fancy straight knives and folders of his design or to customer's specs. **Patterns:** Hunters, fighters, skinners, working and camp knives. **Technical:** Grinds 440C, O1, D2, ATS-34, some Damascus; forges his own mokume.

Uses natural handle material. **Prices:** $450 to $800; some to $1800. **Remarks:** Full-time maker; sold first knife in 1994. **Mark:** Last name, city, state or last name in script.

PIESNER, DEAN

1786 Sawmill Rd, Conestogo, ON, CANADA N0B 1N0, Phone: 519-664-3648, dean47@rogers.com

Specialties: Classic and period pieces of his design and to customer specs. **Patterns:** Bowies, skinners, fighters and swords. **Technical:** Forges 5160, 52100, steel Damascus and nickel-steel Damascus. Makes own mokume gane with copper, brass and nickel silver. Silver wire inlays in wood. **Prices:** Start at $150. **Remarks:** Full-time maker; first knife sold in 1990. **Mark:** First initial, last name, JS.

PITMAN, DAVID

PO Drawer 2566, Williston, ND 58802, Phone: 701-572-3325

PITT, DAVID F

6812 Digger Pine Ln, Anderson, CA 96007, Phone: 530-357-2393, handcannons@tds. net or bearpawcustoms@dtds.net; Web: http://bearpawcustoms.blademakers.com

Specialties: Fixed blade, hunters and hatchets. Flat ground mirror finish. **Patterns:** Hatchets with gut hook, small gut hooks, guards, bolsters or guard less. **Technical:** Grinds A2, 440C, 154CM, ATS-34, D2. **Prices:** $150 to $1,000. **Remarks:** All work done in-house including heat treat. **Mark:** Bear paw with David F. Pitt Maker.

PLOPPERT, TOM

1407 2nd Ave. SW, Cullman, AL 35055, Phone: 256-962-4251, tomploppert3@ bellsouth.net

Specialties: Highly finished single- to multiple-blade slip-joint folders in standard and traditional patterns, some lockbacks. **Technical:** Hollow grinds CPM-154, 440V, damascus and other steels upon customer request. Uses elephant ivory, mammoth ivory, bone and pearl. **Mark:** Last name stamped on main blade.

PLUNKETT, RICHARD

29 Kirk Rd, West Cornwall, CT 06796, Phone: 860-672-3419; Toll free: 888-KNIVES-8

Specialties: Traditional, fancy folders and straight knives of his design. **Patterns:** Slip-joint folders and small straight knives. **Technical:** Grinds O1 and stainless steel. Offers many different file patterns. **Prices:** $150 to $450. **Remarks:** Full-time maker; first knife sold in 1994. **Mark:** Signature and date under handle scales.

PODMAJERSKY, DIETRICH

9219 15th Ave NE, Seattle, WA 98115, Phone: 206-552-0763, podforge@gmail.com; Web: podforge.com

Specialties: Kitchen, utility and art knives, blending functionality with pleasing lines. **Technical:** Stainless and carbon steel, utilizing stock removal or forging where appropriate. All heat traeting is done in house, including cryogenic as needed. **Prices:** $150 and up.

POIRIER, RICK

1149 Sheridan Rd., McKees Mills, New Brunswick E4V 2W7, CANADA, Phone: 506-525-2818, ripknives@gmail.com; Web: www.ripcustomknives.com

Specialties: Working straight knives of his design or to customer specs, hunters, fighters, bowies, utility, camp, tantos and short swords. **Technical:** Forges own damascus and cable damascus using 1084, 15N20, O1 and mild steel. Varied handle materials inlcude G-10, Micarta, wood, bone, horn and Japanese cord wrap. **Prices:** $200 and up. **Remarks:** Full-time maker, apprenticed under ABS master smith Wally Hayes; first knife sold in 1998. **Marks:** R P (pre. 2007), RIP (2007 on), also etches gravestone RIP.

POLK, CLIFTON

4625 Webber Creek Rd, Van Buren, AR 72956, Phone: 479-474-3828, cliffpolkknives1@ aol.com; Web: www.polkknives.com

Specialties: Fancy working folders. **Patterns:** One blades spring backs in five sizes, LinerLock®, automatics, double blades spring back folder with standard drop & clip blade or bird knife with drop and vent hook or cowboy's knives with drop and hoof pick and straight knives. **Technical:** Uses D2 & ATS-34. Makes all own Damascus using 1084, 1095, O1, 15N20, 5160. Using all kinds of exotic woods. Stag, pearls, ivory, mastodon ivory and other bone and horns. **Prices:** $200 to $3000. **Remarks:** Retired fire fighter, made knives since 1974. **Mark:** Polk.

POLK, RUSTY

5900 Wildwood Dr, Van Buren, AR 72956, Phone: 870-688-3009, polkknives@yahoo. com; Web: www.facebook.com/polkknives

Specialties: Skinners, hunters, Bowies, fighters and forging working knives fancy Damascus, daggers, boot knives, survival knives, and folders. **Patterns:** Drop point, and forge to shape. **Technical:** ATS-34, 440C, Damascus, D2, 51/60, 1084, 15N20, does all his forging. **Prices:** $200 to $2000. **Mark:** R. Polk

POLLOCK, WALLACE J

806 Russet Valley Dr., Cedar Park, TX 78613, Phone: 512-918-0528, jarlsdad@gmail. com; Web: www.pollackknives.com

Specialties: Using knives, skinner, hunter, fighting, camp knives. **Patterns:** Use his own patterns or yours. Traditional hunters, daggers, fighters, camp knives. **Technical:** Grinds ATS-34, D-2, BG-42, makes own Damascus, D-2, 0-1, ATS-34, prefer D-2, handles exotic wood, horn, bone, ivory. **Remarks:** Full-time maker, sold first knife 1973. **Prices:** $250 to $2500. **Mark:** Last name, maker, city/state.

POLZIEN, DON

1912 Inler Suite-L, Lubbock, TX 79407, Phone: 806-791-0766, blindinglightknives.net

Specialties: Traditional Japanese-style blades; restores antique Japanese swords, scabbards and fittings. **Patterns:** Hunters, fighters, one-of-a-kind art knives. **Technical:**

1045-1050 carbon steels, 440C, D2, ATS-34, standard and cable Damascus. **Prices:** $150 to $2500. **Remarks:** Full-time maker. First knife sold in 1990. **Mark:** Oriental characters inside square border.

PONZIO, DOUG

10219 W State Rd 81, Beloit, WI 53511, Phone: 608-313-3223, prfgdoug@hughes. net; Web: www.ponziodamascus.com

Specialties: Mosaic Damascus, stainless Damascus. **Mark:** P.F.

POOLE, MARVIN O

PO Box 552, Commerce, GA 30529, Phone: 803-225-5970

Specialties: Traditional working/using straight knives and folders of his design and in standard patterns. **Patterns:** Bowies, fighters, hunters, locking folders, bird and trout knives. **Technical:** Grinds 440C, D2, ATS-34. **Prices:** $50 to $150; some to $750. **Remarks:** Part-time maker; first knife sold in 1980. **Mark:** First initial, last name, year, serial number.

POTIER, TIMOTHY F

PO Box 711, Oberlin, LA 70655, Phone: 337-639-2229, tpotier@hotmail.com

Specialties: Classic working and using straight knives to customer specs; some collectible. **Patterns:** Hunters, Bowies, utility/camp knives and belt axes. **Technical:** Forges carbon steel and his own Damascus; offers filework. **Prices:** $300 to $1800; some to $4000. **Remarks:** Part-time maker; first knife sold in 1981. **Mark:** Last name, MS.

POTTER, BILLY

6323 Hyland Dr., Dublin, OH 43017, Phone: 614-589-8324, potterknives@yahoo.com; Web: www.potterknives.com

Specialties: Working straight knives; his design or to customers patterns. **Patterns:** Bowie, fighters, utilities, skinners, hunters, folding lock blade, miniatures and tomahawks. **Technical:** Grinds and forges, carbon steel, L6, 0-1, 1095, 5160, 1084 and 52000. Grinds 440C stainless. Forges own Damascus. Handles: prefers exotic hardwood, curly and birdseye maples. Bone, ivory, antler, pearl and horn. Some scrimshaw. **Prices:** Start at $100 up to $800. **Remarks:** Part-time maker; first knife sold 1996. **Mark:** First and last name (maker).

POWELL, ROBERT CLARK

PO Box 321, 93 Gose Rd., Smarr, GA 31086, Phone: 478-994-5418

Specialties: Composite bar Damascus blades. **Patterns:** Art knives, hunters, combat, tomahawks. **Patterns:** Hand forges all blades. **Prices:** $300 and up. **Remarks:** ABS Journeyman Smith. **Mark:** Powell.

POWERS, WALTER R.

PO BOX 82, Lolita, TX 77971, Phone: 361-874-4230, carlyn@laward.net Web: waltscustomknives.blademakers.com

Specialties: Skinners and hunters. Technical: Uses mainly CPMD2, CPM154 and CPMS35VN, but will occasionally use 3V. Stock removal. **Prices:** $140 - $200. **Remarks:** Part-time maker; first knife made in 2002. **Mark:** WP

PRATER, MIKE

PRATER AND COMPANY, 81 Sanford Ln., Flintstone, GA 30725, Phone: 706-820-7300, cmprater@aol.com; Web: www.pratercustoms.com

Specialties: Customizing factory knives. **Patterns:** Buck knives, case knives, hen and rooster knives. **Technical:** Manufacture of mica pearl. **Prices:** Varied. **Remarks:** First knife sold in 1980. **Mark:** Mica pearl.

PRESSBURGER, RAMON

59 Driftway Rd, Howell, NJ 07731, Phone: 732-363-0816

Specialties: BG-42. Only knifemaker in U.S.A. that has complete line of affordable hunting knives made from BG-42. **Technical:** Uses all steels; main steels are D-2 and BG-42. **Prices:** $75 to $500. **Remarks:** Full-time maker; has been making hunting knives for 30 years. Makes knives to your patterning. **Mark:** NA.

PRESTI, MATT

5280 Middleburg Rd, Union Bridge, MD 21791, Phone: 410-775-1520; Cell: 240-357-3592

Specialties: Hunters and chef's knives, fighters, bowies, and period pieces. **Technical:** Forges 5160, 52100, 1095, 1080, W2, and O1 steels as well as his own Damascus. Does own heat treating and makes sheaths. Prefers natural handle materials, particularly antler and curly maple. **Prices:** $150 and up. **Remarks:** Part-time knifemaker who made his first knife in 2001. **Mark:** MCP.

PRICE, DARRELL MORRIS

92 Union, Plymouth, Devon, ENGLAND PL1 3EZ, Phone: 0752 223546

Specialties: Traditional Japanese knives, Bowies and high-art knives. **Technical:** Nickel Damascus and mokume. **Prices:** $1000 to $4000. **Remarks:** Part-time maker; first knife sold in 1990. **Mark:** Initials and Japanese name—Kuni Shigae.

PRICE, TIMMY

PO Box 906, Blairsville, GA 30514, Phone: 706-745-5111

PRIDGEN JR., LARRY

PO BOX 707, Fitzgerald, GA 31750, Phone: 229-591-0013, pridgencustomknives@ gmail.com Web: www.pridgencustomknives.com

Specialties: Bowie and Liner Lock Folders. **Patterns:** Bowie, fighter, skinner, trout, liner lock, and custom orders. **Technical:** I do stock removal and use carbon and stainless Damascus and stainless steel. **Prices:** $250 and up. **Remarks:** Each knife comes with a hand-crafted custom sheath and life-time guarantee. **Mark:** Distinctive logo that looks like a brand with LP and a circle around it.

custom knifemakers

PRIMOS, TERRY

932 Francis Dr, Shreveport, LA 71118, Phone: 318-686-6625, tprimos@sport.rr.com or terry@primosknives.com; Web: www.primosknives.com
Specialties: Traditional forged straight knives. **Patterns:** Hunters, Bowies, camp knives, and fighters. **Technical:** Forges primarily 1084 and 5160; also forges Damascus. **Prices:** $250 to $600. **Remarks:** Full-time maker; first knife sold in 1993. **Mark:** Last name.

PRINSLOO, THEUNS

PO Box 2263, Bethlehem, Free State, SOUTH AFRICA 9700, Phone: 27824663885, theunsmes@yahoo.com; Web: www.theunsprinsloo.co.za
Specialties: Handmade folders and fixed blades. **Technical:** Own Damascus and mokume. I try to avoid CNC work, laser cutting and machining as much as possible. **Prices:** $650 and up. **Mark:** Handwritten name with bushman rock art and mountain scene.

PRITCHARD, RON

613 Crawford Ave, Dixon, IL 61021, Phone: 815-284-6005
Specialties: Plain and fancy working knives. **Patterns:** Variety of straight knives, locking folders, interframes and miniatures. **Technical:** Grinds 440C, 154CM and commercial Damascus. **Prices:** $100 to $200; some to $1500. **Remarks:** Part-time maker; first knife sold in 1979. **Mark:** Name and city.

PROVENZANO, JOSEPH D

39043 Dutch Lane, Ponchatoula, LA 70454, Phone: 225-615-4846, gespro61@gmail.com
Specialties: Working straight knives and folders in standard patterns. **Patterns:** Hunters, Bowies, folders, camp and fishing knives. **Technical:** Grinds ATS-34, 440C, 154CM, CPM-S60V, CPM-S90V, CPM-3V and damascus. Hollow-grinds hunters. **Prices:** $125 to $300; some to $1,000. **Remarks:** Part-time maker; first knife sold in 1980. **Mark:** Joe-Pro.

PROVOST, J.C.

1634 Lakeview Dr., Laurel, MS 39440, Phone: 601-498-1143, jcprovost2@gmail.com; Web: www.jcprovost.com
Specialties: Classic working straight knives and folders. **Patterns:** Hunters, skinners, bowies, daggers, fighters, fillet knives, chef's and steak knives, folders and customs. **Technical:** Grinds 440C, CPM-154 and commercial damascus. **Prices:** $175 and up. **Remarks:** Part-time maker; first knife made in 1979. Taught by R.W. Wilson. **Mark:** Name, city and state.

PRUYN, PETER

Brothersville Custom Knives, 110 Reel La., Grants Pass, OR 97527, Phone: 631-793-9052, Fax: 541-479-1889, brothersvilleknife@gmail.com Web: brothersvilleknife.com
Specialties: Chef knives and fighters in damascus and san mai, as well as stainless steels. **Patterns:** Fixed-blade knives of all styles, some folding models. **Technical:** Damascus, high-carbon and stainless steels; does own heat treating. **Prices:** $200 to $1,000, with a discount to active and retired military personnel. **Remarks:** Full-time maker, first knife sold in 2009. **Mark:** Anvil with "Brothersville" crested above.

PULIS, VLADIMIR

CSA 230-95, 96701 Kremnica, SLOVAKIA, Phone: 00421 903 340076, vpulis@gmail.com; Web: www.vpulis.host.sk
Specialties: Fancy and high-art straight knives of his design. **Patterns:** Daggers and hunters. **Technical:** Forges Damascus steel. All work done by hand. **Prices:** $250 to $3000; some to $10,000. **Remarks:** Full-time maker; first knife sold in 1990. **Mark:** Initials in sixtagon.

PURSLEY, AARON

8885 Coal Mine Rd, Big Sandy, MT 59520, Phone: 406-378-3200
Specialties: Fancy working knives. **Patterns:** Locking folders, straight hunters and daggers, personal wedding knives and letter openers. **Technical:** Grinds O1 and 440C; engraves. **Prices:** $900 to $2500. **Remarks:** Full-time maker; first knife sold in 1975. **Mark:** Initials connected with year.

PURVIS, BOB AND ELLEN

2416 N Loretta Dr, Tucson, AZ 85716, Phone: 520-795-8290, repknives2@cox.net
Specialties: Hunter, skinners, Bowies, using knives, gentlemen folders and collectible knives. **Technical:** Grinds ATS-34, 440C, Damascus, Dama steel, heat-treats and cryogenically quenches. We do gold-plating, salt bluing, scrimshawing, filework and fashion handmade leather sheaths. Materials used for handles include exotic woods, mammoth ivory, mother-of-pearl, G-10 and Micarta. **Prices:** $165 to $800. **Remarks:** Knifemaker since retirement in 1984. Selling them since 1993. **Mark:** Script or print R.E. Purvis ~ Tucson, AZ or last name only.

PUTNAM, DONALD S

590 Wolcott Hill Rd, Wethersfield, CT 06109, Phone: 860-563-9718, Fax: 860-563-9718, dpknives@cox.net
Specialties: Working knives for the hunter and fisherman. **Patterns:** His design or to customer specs. **Technical:** Uses stock removal method, O1, W2, D2, ATS-34, 154CM, 440C and CPM REX 20; stainless steel Damascus on request. **Prices:** $250 and up. **Remarks:** Full-time maker; first knife sold in 1985. **Mark:** Last name with a knife outline.

Q

QUAKENBUSH, THOMAS C

2426 Butler Rd, Ft Wayne, IN 46808, Phone: 219-483-0749

QUARTON, BARR

PO Box 4335, McCall, ID 83638, Phone: 208-634-3641
Specialties: Plain and fancy working knives; period pieces. **Patterns:** Hunters, tantos and swords. **Technical:** Forges and grinds 154CM, ATS-34 and his own Damascus. **Prices:** $180 to $450; some to $4500. **Remarks:** Part-time maker; first knife sold in 1978. Doing business as Barr Custom Knives. **Mark:** First name with bear logo.

QUATTLEBAUM, CRAIG

912 Scooty Dr., Beebe, AR 72012-3454, mustang376@gci.net
Specialties: Traditional straight knives and one-of-a-kind knives of his design; period pieces. **Patterns:** Bowies and fighters. **Technical:** Forges 5168, 1095 and own Damascus. **Prices:** $300 to $2000. **Remarks:** Part-time maker; first knife sold in 1988. **Mark:** Stylized initials.

QUESENBERRY, MIKE

110 Evergreen Cricle, Blairsden, CA 96103, Phone: 775-233-1527, quesenberry@psln.com; Web: www.quesenberryknives.com
Specialties: Hunters, daggers, Bowies, and integrals. **Technical:** Forges 52100, 1095, 1084, 5160. Makes own Damascus. Will use stainless on customer requests. Does own heat-treating and own leather work. **Prices:** Starting at $300. **Remarks:** Parttime maker. ABS member since 2006. Journeyman Bladesmith **Mark:** Last name.

R

RABUCK, JASON

W3080 Hay Lake Road, Springbrook, WI 54875, Phone: 715-766-8220, sales@rabuckhandmadeknives.com; web: www.rabuckhandmadeknives.com
Patterns: Hunters, skinners, camp knives, fighters, survival/tactical, neck knives, kitchen knives. Include whitetail antler, maple, walnut, as well as stabilized woods and micarta. **Technical:** Flat grinds 1095, 5160, and 0-1 carbon steels. Blades are finished with a hand-rubbed satin blade finish. Hand stitched leather sheaths specifically fit to each knife. Boot clips, swivel sheaths, and leg ties include some of the available sheath options. **Prices:** $140 - $560. **Remarks:** Also knife restoration (handle replacement, etc.) Custom and replacement sheath work available for any knife. **Mark:** "RABUCK" over a horseshoe

RACHLIN, LESLIE S

412 Rustic Ave., Elmira, NY 14905, Phone: 607-733-6889, lrachlin@stry.rr.com
Specialties: Classic and working kitchen knives, carving sets and outdoors knives. **Technical:** Grinds 440C or cryogenically heat-treated A2. **Prices:** $65 to $1,400. **Remarks:** Spare-time maker; first knife sold in 1989. Doing business as Tinkermade Knives. **Mark:** LSR

RADER, MICHAEL

23706 7th Ave. SE, Ste. D, Bothell, WA 98021, michael@raderblade.com; Web: www.raderblade.com
Specialties: Swords, kitchen knives, integrals. **Patterns:** Non traditional designs. Inspired by various cultures. **Technical:** Damascus is made with 1084 and 15N-20, forged blades in 52100, W2 and 1084. **Prices:** $350 - $5,000 **Remarks:** ABS Journeyman Smith **Mark:** ABS Mastersmith Mark "Rader" on one side, "M.S." on other

RADOS, JERRY F

134 Willie Nell Rd., Columbia, KY 42728, Phone: 606-303-3334, jerry@radosknives.com Web: www.radosknives.com
Specialties: Deluxe period pieces. **Patterns:** Hunters, fighters, locking folders, daggers and camp knives. **Technical:** Forges and grinds his own Damascus which he sells commercially; makes pattern-welded Turkish Damascus. **Prices:** Start at $900. **Remarks:** Full-time maker; first knife sold in 1981. **Mark:** Last name.

RAFN, DAN C.

Smedebakken 24, Hadsten, DENMARK 8370, contact@dcrknives.com Web: www.dcrknives.com
Specialties: One of a kind collector art knives of own design. **Patterns:** Mostly fantasy style fighters and daggers. But also swords, hunters, and folders. **Technical:** Grinds RWL-34, sleipner steel, damasteel, and hand forges Damascus. **Prices:** Start at $500. **Remarks:** Part-time maker since 2003. **Mark:** Rafn. or DCR. or logo.

RAGSDALE, JAMES D

160 Clear Creek Valley Tr., Ellijay, GA 30536, Phone: 706-636-3180, jimmarrags@etcmail.com
Specialties: Fancy and embellished working knives of his design or to customer specs. **Patterns:** Hunters, folders and fighters. **Technical:** Grinds 440C, ATS-34 and A2. Uses some Damascus **Prices:** $150 and up. **Remarks:** Full-time maker; first knife sold in 1984. **Mark:** Fish symbol with name above, town below.

RAINVILLE, RICHARD

126 Cockle Hill Rd, Salem, CT 06420, Phone: 860-859-2776, w1jo@comcast.net
Specialties: Traditional working straight knives. **Patterns:** Outdoor knives, including fishing knives. **Technical:** L6, 400C, ATS-34. **Prices:** $100 to $800. **Remarks:** Full-time maker; first knife sold in 1982. **Mark:** Name, city, state in oval logo.

RALEY, R. WAYNE

825 Poplar Acres Rd, Collierville, TN 38017, Phone: 901-853-2026

RALPH, DARREL

BRIAR KNIVES, 12034 S. Profit Row, Forney, TX 75126, Phone: 469-728-7242, dralph@earthlink.net; Web: www.darrelralph.com
Specialties: Tactical and tactical dress folders and fixed blades. **Patterns:** Daggers, fighters and swords. **Technical:** High tech. Forges his own damascus, nickel and high-carbon. Uses mokume and damascus, mosaics and special patterns. Engraves and heat treats. Prefers pearl, ivory and abalone handle material; uses stones and jewels. **Prices:** $600 to $30,000. **Remarks:** Full-time maker; first knife sold in 1987. Doing business as

Briar Knives. **Mark:** DDR.

RAMONDETTI, SERGIO
VIA MARCONI N 24, CHIUSA DI PESIO (CN), ITALY 12013, Phone: 0171 734490, Fax: 0171 734490, info@ramon-knives.com Web: www.ramon-knives.com
Specialties: Folders and straight knives of his design. **Patterns:** Utility, hunters and skinners. **Technical:** Grinds RWL-34 and Damascus. **Prices:** $500 to $2000. **Remarks:** Part-time maker; first knife sold in 1999. **Mark:** Logo (S.Ramon) with last name.

RAMSEY, RICHARD A
8525 Trout Farm Rd, Neosho, MO 64850, Phone: 417-451-1493, rams@direcway.com; Web: www.ramseyknives.com
Specialties: Drop point hunters. **Patterns:** Various Damascus. **Prices:** $125 to $1500. **Mark:** RR double R also last name-RAMSEY.

RANDALL, PATRICK
Patrick Knives, 1160 Mesa Ave., Newbury Park, CA 91320, Phone: 805-390-5501, pat@patrickknives.com; Web: www.patrickknives.com
Specialties: Chef's and kitchen knives, bowies, hunters and utility folding knives. **Technical:** Preferred materials include 440C, 154CM, CPM-3V, 1084, 1095 and ATS-34. Handle materials include stabilized wood, Micarta, stag and jigged bone. **Prices:** $125 to $225. **Remarks:** Part-time maker since 2005.

RANDALL, STEVE
3438 Oak Ridge Cir., Lincolnton, NC 28092, Phone: 704-732-2498, steve@ksrblades.com; Web: www.ksrblades.com
Specialties: Mostly working straight knives and one-of-a-kind pieces, some fancy fixed blades. **Patterns:** Bowies, hunters, choppers, camp and utility knives. **Technical:** Forged high-carbon-steel blades; 5160, 52100, W2, CruForgeV, high-carbon simple steels like 1075, 1084 and 1095. **Prices:** $275 and up. **Remarks:** Part-time maker, first knife sold in 2009. Earned journeyman smith rating in 2012. Doing business as Knives By Steve Randall or KSR Blades. **Mark:** KS Randall on left side, JS on right side.

RANDALL JR., JAMES W
11606 Keith Hall Rd, Keithville, LA 71047, Phone: 318-925-6480, Fax: 318-925-1709, jw@jwrandall.com; Web: www.jwrandall.com
Specialties: Collectible and functional knives. **Patterns:** Bowies, hunters, daggers, swords, folders and combat knives. **Technical:** Forges 5160, 1084, O1 and his Damascus. **Prices:** $400 to $8000. **Remarks:** Part-time. First knife sold in 1998. **Mark:** JW Randall, MS.

RANDALL MADE KNIVES
4857 South Orange Blossom Trail, Orlando, FL 32839, Phone: 407-855-8075, Fax: 407-855-9054, Web: http://www.randallknives.com
Specialties: Working straight knives. **Patterns:** Hunters, fighters and Bowies. **Technical:** Forges and grinds O1 and 440B. **Prices:** $170 to $550; some to $450. **Remarks:** Full-time maker; first knife sold in 1937. **Mark:** Randall made, city and state in scimitar logo.

RANDOW, RALPH
7 E. Chateau Estates Dr., Greenbrier, AR 72058, Phone: 318-729-3368, randow3368@gmail.com

RANKL, CHRISTIAN
Possenhofenerstr 33, Munchen, GERMANY 81476, Phone: 0049 01 71 3 66 26 79, Fax: 0049 8975967265, Web: http://www.german-knife.com/german-knifemakers-guild.html
Specialties: Tail-lock knives. **Patterns:** Fighters, hunters and locking folders. **Technical:** Grinds ATS-34, D2, CPM1440V, RWL 34 also stainless Damascus. **Prices:** $450 to $950; some to $2000. **Remarks:** Part-time maker; first knife sold in 1989. **Mark:** Electrochemical etching on blade.

RAPP, STEVEN J
8033 US Hwy 25-70, Marshall, NC 28753, Phone: 828-649-1092
Specialties: Gold quartz; mosaic handles. **Patterns:** Daggers, Bowies, fighters and San Francisco knives. **Technical:** Hollow- and flat-grinds 440C and Damascus. **Prices:** Start at $500. **Remarks:** Full-time maker; first knife sold in 1981. **Mark:** Name and state.

RAPPAZZO, RICHARD
142 Dunsbach Ferry Rd, Cohoes, NY 12047, Phone: 518-783-6843
Specialties: Damascus locking folders and straight knives. **Patterns:** Folders, dirks, fighters and tantos in original and traditional designs. **Technical:** Hand-forges all blades; specializes in Damascus; uses only natural handle materials. **Prices:** $400 to $1500. **Remarks:** Part-time maker; first knife sold in 1985. **Mark:** Name, date, serial number.

RARDON, A D
1589 SE Price Dr, Polo, MO 64671, Phone: 660-354-2330
Specialties: Folders, miniatures. **Patterns:** Hunters, buck skinners, Bowies, miniatures and daggers. **Technical:** Grinds O1, D2, 440C and ATS-34. **Prices:** $150 to $2000; some higher. **Remarks:** Full-time maker; first knife sold in 1954. **Mark:** Fox logo.

RARDON, ARCHIE F
1589 SE Price Dr, Polo, MO 64671, Phone: 660-354-2330
Specialties: Working knives. **Patterns:** Hunters, Bowies and miniatures. **Technical:** Grinds O1, D2, 440C, ATS-34, cable and Damascus. **Prices:** $50 to $500. **Remarks:** Part-time maker. **Mark:** Boar hog.

RASSENTI, PETER
218 Tasse, St-Eustache, Quebec J7P 4C2, CANADA, Phone: 450-598-6250, guireandgimble@hotmail.com
Specialties: Tactical mono-frame folding knives.

RAY, ALAN W
1287 FM 1280 E, Lovelady, TX 75851, awray@rayzblades.com; Web: www.rayzblades.com
Specialties: Working straight knives of his design. **Patterns:** Hunters. **Technical:** Forges O1, L6 and 5160 for straight knives. **Prices:** $200 to $1000. **Remarks:** Full-time maker; first knife sold in 1979. **Mark:** Stylized initials.

REBELLO, INDIAN GEORGE
358 Elm St, New Bedford, MA 02740-3837, Phone: 508-951-2719, indgeo@juno.com; Web: www.indiangeorgesknives.com
Specialties: One-of-a-kind fighters and Bowies. **Patterns:** To customer's specs, hunters and utilities. **Technical:** Forges his own Damascus, 5160, 52100, 1084, 1095, cable and O1. Grinds S30V, ATS-34, 154CM, 440C, D2 and A2. **Prices:** Starting at $250. **Remarks:** Full-time maker, first knife sold in 1991. Doing business as Indian George's Knives. Founding father and President of the Southern New England Knife-Makers Guild. Member of the N.C.C.A. **Mark:** Indian George's Knives.

RED, VERNON
2020 Benton Cove, Conway, AR 72034, Phone: 501-450-7284, knivesvr@conwaycorp.net
Specialties: Custom design straight knives or folders of own design or customer's. **Patterns:** Hunters, fighters, Bowies, folders. **Technical:** Hollow grind, flat grind, stock removal and forged blades. Uses 440C, D-2, ATS-34, 1084, 1095, and Damascus. **Prices:** $150 and up. **Remarks:** Made first knife in 1982, first folder in 1992. Member of (AKA) Arkansas Knives Association. Doing business as Custom Made Knives by Vernon Red. **Mark:** Last name.

REDD, BILL
2647 West 133rd Circle, Broomfield, Colorado 80020, Phone: 303-469-9803, unlimited_design@msn.com
Prices: Contact maker. **Remarks:** Full-time custom maker, member of PKA and RMBC (Rocky Mountain Blade Collectors). **Mark:** Redd Knives, Bill Redd.

REDDIEX, BILL
27 Galway Ave, Palmerston North, NEW ZEALAND, Phone: 06-357-0383, Fax: 06-358-2910
Specialties: Collector-grade working straight knives. **Patterns:** Traditional-style Bowies and drop-point hunters. **Technical:** Grinds 440C, D2 and O1; offers variety of grinds and finishes. **Prices:** $130 to $750. **Remarks:** Full-time maker; first knife sold in 1980. **Mark:** Last name around kiwi bird logo.

REED, JOHN M
3937 Sunset Cove Dr., Port Orange, FL 32129, Phone: 386-310-4569
Specialties: Hunter, utility, some survival knives. **Patterns:** Trailing Point, and drop point sheath knives. **Technical:** ATS-34, Rockwell 60 exotic wood or natural material handles. **Prices:** $135 to $450. Depending on handle material. **Remarks:** Likes the stock removal method. "Old Fashioned trainling point blades." Handmade and sewn leather sheaths. **Mark:** "Reed" acid etched on left side of blade.

REEVE, CHRIS
2949 Victory View Way, Boise, ID 83709-2946, Phone: 208-375-0367, Fax: 208-375-0368, crkinfo@chrisreeve.com; Web: www.chrisreeve.com
Specialties: Originator and designer of the One Piece range of fixed blade utility knives and of the Sebenza Integral Lock folding knives made by Chris Reeve Knives. Currently not making or taking custom orders. **Patterns:** Art folders and fixed blades; one-of-a-kind. **Technical:** Grinds specialty stainless steels, damascus and other materials to his own design. **Prices:** $1,000 and up. **Remarks:** Full-time in knife business; first knife sold in 1982. **Mark:** Signature and date.

REEVES, J.R.
5181 South State Line, Texarkana, AR 71854, Phone: 870-773-5777, jos123@netscape.com
Specialties: Working straight knives of my design or customer design if a good flow. **Patterns:** Hunters, fighters, bowies, camp, bird, and trout knives. **Technical:** Forges and grinds 5160, 1084, 15n20, L6, 52100 and some damascus. Also some stock removal 440C, 01, D2, and 154 CM steels. I offer flat or hollow grinds. Natural handle material to include Sambar stag, desert Ironwood, sheep horn, other stabilized exotic woods and ivory. Custom filework offered. **Prices:** $200 - $1500. **Remarks:** Full-time maker, first knife sold in 1985. **Mark:** JR Reeves.

REGEL, JEAN-LOUIS
les ichards, Saint Leger de Fougeret, FRANCE 58120, Phone: 0033-66-621-6185, jregel2@hotmail.com
Specialties: Bowies, camp knives, swords and folders. **Technical:** Forges own Wootz steel by hand, and damascus and high-carbon blade steels. **Remarks:** American Bladesmith Society journeyman smith. **Mark:** Jean-louis on right side of blade.

REGGIO JR., SIDNEY J
PO Box 851, Sun, LA 70463, Phone: 504-886-5886
Specialties: Miniature classic and fancy straight knives of his design or in standard patterns. **Patterns:** Fighters, hunters and utility/camp knives. **Technical:** Grinds 440C, ATS-34 and commercial Damascus. Engraves; scrimshaws; offers filework. Hollow grinds most blades. Prefers natural handle material. Offers handmade sheaths. **Prices:** $85 to $250; some to $500. **Remarks:** Part-time maker; first knife sold in 1988. Doing business as Sterling Workshop. **Mark:** Initials.

REID, JIM
6425 Cranbrook St. NE, Albuquerque, NM 87111, jhrabq7@Q.com

Specialties: Fixed-blade knives. **Patterns:** Hunting, neck, and cowboy bowies. **Technical:** A2, D2, and damascus, stock removal. **Prices:** $125 to $300. **Mark:** Jim Reid over New Mexico zia sign.

RENNER, TERRY
TR Blades, Inc., 707 13th Ave. Cir. W, Palmetto, FL 34221, Phone: 941-729-3226; 941-545-6320, terrylmusic@gmail.com Web: www.trblades.com
Specialties: High art folders and straight-blades, specialty locking mechanisms. Designer of the Neckolas knife by CRKT. Deep-relief carving. **Technical:** Prefer CPM154, S30V, 1095 carbon, damascus by Rob Thomas, Delbert Ealey, Bertie Reitveld, Todd Fischer, Joel Davis. Does own heat treating. **Remarks:** Full-time maker as of 2005. Formerly in bicylce manufacturing business, with patents for tooling and fixtures. President of the Florida Knifemaker's Association since 2009. **Mark:** TR* stylized

REPKE, MIKE
4191 N. Euclid Ave., Bay City, MI 48706, Phone: 517-684-3111
Specialties: Traditional working and using straight knives of his design or to customer specs; classic knives; display knives. **Patterns:** Hunters, Bowies, skinners, fighters boots, axes and swords. **Technical:** Grind 440C. Offer variety of handle materials. **Prices:** $99 to $1500. **Remarks:** Full-time makers. Doing business as Black Forest Blades. **Mark:** Knife logo.

REVERDY, NICOLE AND PIERRE
5 Rue de L'egalite', Romans, FRANCE 26100, Phone: 334 75 05 10 15, Web: http://www.reverdy.com
Specialties: Art knives; legend pieces. Pierre and Nicole, his wife, are creating knives of art with combination of enamel on pure silver (Nicole) and poetic Damascus (Pierre) such as the "La dague a la licorne." **Patterns:** Daggers, folding knives Damascus and enamel, Bowies, hunters and other large patterns. **Technical:** Forges his Damascus and "poetic Damascus"; where animals such as unicorns, stags, dragons or star crystals appear, works with his own EDM machine to create any kind of pattern inside the steel with his own touch. **Prices:** $2000 and up. **Remarks:** Full-time maker since 1989; first knife sold in 1986. Nicole (wife) collaborates with enamels. **Mark:** Reverdy.

REVISHVILI, ZAZA
2102 Linden Ave, Madison, WI 53704, Phone: 608-243-7927
Specialties: Fancy/embellished and high-art straight knives and folders of his design. **Patterns:** Daggers, swords and locking folders. **Technical:** Uses Damascus; silver filigree, silver inlay in wood; enameling. **Prices:** $1000 to $9000; some to $15,000. **Remarks:** Full-time maker; first knife sold in 1987. **Mark:** Initials, city.

REXFORD, TODD
518 Park Dr., Woodland Park, CO 80863, Phone: 719-650-6799, todd@rexfordknives.com; Web: www.rexfordknives.com
Specialties: Dress tactical and tactical folders and fixed blades. **Technical:** I work in stainless steels, stainless damascus, titanium, Stellite and other high performance alloys. All machining and part engineering is done in house.

REXROAT, KIRK
527 Sweetwater Circle Box 224, Wright, WY 82732, Phone: 307-464-0166, rexknives@vcn.com; Web: www.rexroatknives.com
Specialties: Using and collectible straight knives and folders of his design or to customer specs. **Patterns:** Bowies, hunters, folders. **Technical:** Forges Damascus patterns, mosaic and 52100. **Prices:** $400 and up. **Remarks:** Part-time maker, Master Smith in the ABS; first knife sold in 1984. Doing business as Rexroat Knives. **Mark:** Last name.

REYNOLDS, DAVE
1404 Indian Creek, Harrisville, WV 26362, Phone: 304-643-2889, wvreynolds@zoomintevnet.net
Specialties: Working straight knives of his design. **Patterns:** Bowies, kitchen and utility knives. **Technical:** Grinds and forges L6, 1095 and 440C. Heat-treats. **Prices:** $50 to $85; some to $175. **Remarks:** Full-time maker; first knife sold in 1980. Doing business as Terra-Gladius Knives. **Mark:** Mark on special orders only; serial number on all knives.

REYNOLDS, JOHN C
#2 Andover HC77, Gillette, WY 82716, Phone: 307-682-6076
Specialties: Working knives, some fancy. **Patterns:** Hunters, Bowies, tomahawks and buck skinners; some folders. **Technical:** Grinds D2, ATS-34, 440C and forges own Damascus and knives. Scrimshaws. **Prices:** $200 to $3000. **Remarks:** Spare-time maker; first knife sold in 1969. **Mark:** On ground blades JC Reynolds Gillette, WY, on forged blades, initials make the mark-JCR.

RHEA, LIN
413 Grant 291020, Prattsville, AR 72129, Phone: 870-942-6419, lwrhea@rheaknives.com; Web: www.rheaknives.com
Specialties: Traditional and early American styled Bowies in high carbon steel or Damascus. **Patterns:** Bowies, hunters and fighters. **Technical:** Filework wire inlay. Sole authorship of construction, Damascus and embellishment. **Prices:** $280 to $1500. **Remarks:** Serious part-time maker and rated as a Master Smith in the ABS.

RHO, NESTOR LORENZO
Prinera Junta 589, Junin, Buenos Aires, ARGENTINA CP 6000, Phone: +54-236-154670686, info@cuchillosrho.com.ar; Web: www.cuchillosrho.com.ar
Specialties: Classic and fancy knives of his design. **Patterns:** Bowies, fighters and hunters. **Technical:** Grinds 420C, 440C, 1084, 5160, 52100, L6 and W1. Offers semi-precious stones on handles, acid etching on blades and blade engraving. **Prices:** $90 to $500, some to $1500. **Remarks:** Full-time maker; first knife sold in 1975. **Mark:** Name.

RIBONI, CLAUDIO
Via L Da Vinci, Truccazzano (MI), ITALY, Phone: 02 95309010, Web: www.riboni-knives.com

RICARDO ROMANO, BERNARDES
Ruai Coronel Rennò 1261, Itajuba MG, BRAZIL 37500, Phone: 0055-2135-622-5896
Specialties: Hunters, fighters, Bowies. **Technical:** Grinds blades of stainless and tools steels. **Patterns:** Hunters. **Prices:** $100 to $700. **Mark:** Romano.

RICHARD, RAYMOND
31047 SE Jackson Rd., Gresham, OR 97080, Phone: 503-663-1219, rayskee13@hotmail.com; Web: www.hawknknives.com
Specialties: Hand-forged knives, tomahawks, axes, and spearheads, all one-of-a-kind. **Prices:** $200 and up, some to $3000. **Remarks:** Full-time maker since 1994. **Mark:** Name on spine of blades.

RICHARDS, CHUCK
7243 Maple Tree Lane SE, Salem, OR 97317, Phone: 503-569-5549, woodchuckforge@gmail.com; Web: www.acrichardscustomknives.com
Specialties: Fixed blade Damascus. One-of-a-kind. **Patterns:** Hunters, fighters. **Prices:** $300 to $1,500+ **Remarks:** Likes to work with customers on a truly custom knife. **Mark:** A.C. Richards J.S. or ACR J.S.

RICHARDS, RALPH (BUD)
6413 Beech St, Bauxite, AR 72011, Phone: 501-602-5367, DoubleR042@aol.com; Web: www.ralphrichardscustomknives.com
Specialties: Forges 55160, 1084, and 15N20 for Damascus. S30V, 440C, and others. Wood, mammoth, giraffe and mother of pearl handles.

RICHARDSON JR., PERCY
1400 SM Tucker Rd., Pollok, TX 75969, Phone: 936-288-1690, Percy@Richardsonhandmadeknives.com; Web: www.Richardsonhandmadeknives.com
Specialties: Working straight knives and folders. **Patterns:** Hunters, skinners, bowies, fighters and folders. **Technical:** Mostly grinds CPM-154. **Prices:** $175 - $750 some bowies to $1200. **Remarks:** Full-time maker, first knife sold in 1990. Doing business as Richardsons Handmade Knives. **Mark:** Texas star with last name across it.

RICHERSON, RON
P.O. Box 51, Greenburg, KY 42743, Phone: 270-405-0491, Fax: 270-932-5601, RRicherson1@windstream.net
Specialties: Collectible and functional fixed blades, locking liners, and autos of his design. **Technical:** Grinds ATS-34, S30V, S60V, CPM-154, D2, 440, high carbon steel, and his and others' Damascus. Prefers natural materials for handles and does both stock removal and forged work, some with embellishments. **Prices:** $250 to $850, some higher. **Remarks:** Full-time maker. Member American Bladesmith Society. Made first knife in September 2006, sold first knife in December 2006. **Mark:** Name in oval with city and state. Also name in center of oval Green River Custom Knives.

RICKE, DAVE
1209 Adams St, West Bend, WI 53090, Phone: 262-334-5739, R.L5710@sbcglobal.net
Specialties: Working knives; period pieces. **Patterns:** Hunters, boots, Bowies; locking folders and slip joints. **Technical:** Grinds ATS-34, A2, 440C and 154CM. **Prices:** $145 and up. **Remarks:** Full-time maker; first knife sold in 1976. **Mark:** Last name.

RICKS, KURT J.
Darkhammer Forge, 29 N. Center, Trenton, UT 84338, Phone: 435-563-3471, kopsh@hotmail.com; http://darkhammerworks.tripod.com
Specialties: Fixed blade working knives of all designs and to customer specs. **Patterns:** Fighters, daggers, hunters, swords, axes, and spears. **Technical:** Uses a coal fired forge. Forges high carbon, tool and spring steels. Does own heat treat on forge. Prefers natural handle materials. Leather sheaths available. **Prices:** Start at $50 plus shipping. **Remarks:** A knife should be functional first and pretty second. Part-time maker; first knife sold in 1994. **Mark:** Initials.

RIDER, DAVID M
PO Box 5946, Eugene, OR 97405-0911, Phone: 541-343-8747

RIDGE, TIM
SWAMP FOX KNIVES, 1282 W. Creston Rd., Crossville, TN 38571, Phone: 931-484-0216, swampfoxknives@frontiernet.net; www.swampfoxknives.com
Specialties Handforged historical American knives circa 1700 to 1865, colonial through Civil War eras. **Technical:** Forges 1095, 5160, 1084 and 1075 high-carbon steels. **Prices:** $135 to $2,000, depending on style and size of knife. **Remarks:** Full-time maker for 17 years. **Mark:** Patented running fox with TR in the body.

RIDLEY, ROB
RR1, Sundre, AB, CANADA T0M 1X0, Phone: 405-556-1113, rob@rangeroriginal.com; www.rangeroriginal.com, www.knifemaker.ca
Specialties: The knives I make are mainly fixed blades, though I'm exploring the complex world of folders. **Technical:** I favour high-end stainless alloys and exotic handle materials because a knife should provide both cutting ability and bragging rights. **Remarks:** I made my first knife in 1998 and still use that blade today. I've gone from full time, to part time, to hobby maker, but I still treasure time in the shop or spent with other enthusiasts. Operates Canadian Knifemakers Supply

RIEPE, RICHARD A
17604 E 296 St, Harrisonville, MO 64701

RIETVELD, BERTIE
PO Box 53, Magaliesburg, GT, SOUTH AFRICA 1791, Phone: 2783 232 8766, bertie@rietveldknives.com; Web: www.rietveldknives.com
Specialties: Art daggers, Bolster lock folders, Persian designs, embraces elegant designs. **Patterns:** Mostly one-of-a-kind. **Technical:** Sole authorship, work only in own Damascus, gold inlay, blued stainless fittings. **Prices:** $500 - $8,000 **Remarks:** First knife made in 1979. Annual shows attended: ECCKS, Blade Show, Milan Show, South African Guild Show. **Marks:** Logo is elephant in half circle with name, enclosed in Stanhope lens

RIGNEY JR., WILLIE
191 Colson Dr, Bronston, KY 42518, Phone: 606-679-4227
Specialties: High-tech period pieces and fancy working knives. **Patterns:** Fighters, boots, daggers and push knives. **Technical:** Grinds 440C and 154CM; buys Damascus. Most knives are embellished. **Prices:** $150 to $1500; some to $10,000. **Remarks:** Full-time maker; first knife sold in 1978. **Mark:** First initial, last name.

RINKES, SIEGFRIED
Am Sportpl 2, Markterlbach, GERMANY 91459

RITCHIE, ADAM
Koi Knifeworks, 10925 Sheridan Ave. S, Bloomington, MN 55431, Phone: 651-503-2818, adamkara2@earthlink.net
Specialties: Japanese-influenced fixed blades. **Patterns:** Small utility knives to larger hunter/tactical pieces, Kwaikens, tantos and Kiridashis. **Technical:** Flat and convex grinds O1 tool steel and 1095, differentially heat treated to 58-60 Rockwell hardness. **Prices:** $150-$1,000. **Remarks:** Part-time maker, full-time firefighter/EMT/FEO. **Mark:** Koi Knifeworks in circle around Kanji or Koi.

RIZZI, RUSSELL J
37 March Rd, Ashfield, MA 01330, Phone: 413-625-2842
Specialties: Fancy working and using straight knives and folders of his design or to customer specs. **Patterns:** Hunters, locking folders and fighters. **Technical:** Grinds 440C, D2 and commercial Damascus. **Prices:** $150 to $750; some to $2500. **Remarks:** Part-time maker; first knife sold in 1990. **Mark:** Last name, Ashfield, MA.

ROBBINS, BILL
2160 E. Fry Blvd., Ste. C5, Sierra Vista, AZ 85635-2794, billrknifemaker@aol.com
Specialties: Plain and fancy working straight knives. Makes to his designs and most anything you can draw. **Patterns:** Hunting knives, utility knives, and Bowies. **Technical:** Grinds ATS-34, 440C, tool steel, high carbon, buys Damascus. **Prices:** $70 to $450. **Remarks:** Part-time maker, first knife sold in 2001. **Mark:** Last name or desert scene with name.

ROBBINS, HOWARD P
1310 E. 310th Rd., Flemington, MO 65650, Phone: 417-282-5055, ARobb1407@aol.com
Specialties: High-tech working knives with clean designs, some fancy. **Patterns:** Folders, hunters and camp knives. **Technical:** Grinds 440C. Heat-treats; likes mirror finishes. Offers leatherwork. **Prices:** $100 to $500; some to $1000. **Remarks:** Full-time maker; first knife sold in 1982. **Mark:** Name, city and state.

ROBBINS, LANDON
2370 State Hwy. U, Crane, MO 65633, Phone: 417-207-4290, lwrobbins71@gmail.com
Specialties: Fixed blades using high-carbon damascus. **Patterns:** Hunters, bowies and fighters. **Technical:** Hand-forged, flat-ground 1084, 1074, 5160, 52100 and maker's own damascus. **Prices:** $300 and up. **Remarks:** Part-time maker, ABS journeyman smith. **Mark:** Robbins with an arrow under name.

ROBERTS, CHUCK
PO Box 7174, Golden, CO 80403, Phone: 303-642-2388, chuck@crobertsart.com; Web: www.crobertsart.com
Specialties: Price daggers, large Bowies, hand-rubbed satin finish. **Patterns:** Bowies and California knives. **Technical:** Grinds 440C, 5160 and ATS-34. Handles made of stag, ivory or mother-of-pearl. **Prices:** $1250. **Remarks:** Full-time maker. Company name is C. Roberts - Art that emulates the past. **Mark:** Last initial or last name.

ROBERTS, GEORGE A
PO Box 31228, 211 Main St., Whitehorse, YT, CANADA Y1A 5P7, Phone: 867-667-7099, Fax: 867-667-7099, gr1898@northwestel.net; Web: www.yuk-biz.com/bandit blades
Specialties: Mastadon ivory, fossil walrus ivory handled knives, scrimshawed or carved. **Patterns:** Side lockers, fancy bird and trout knives, hunters, fillet blades. **Technical:** Grinds stainless Damascus, all surgical steels. **Prices:** Up to $3500 U.S. **Remarks:** Full-time maker; first knives sold in 1986. Doing business as Bandit Blades. Most recent works have gold nuggets in fossilized Mastodon ivory. Something new using mosaic pins in mokume bolster and in mosaic Damascus, it creates a new look. **Mark:** Bandit Yukon with pick and shovel crossed.

ROBERTS, JACK
10811 Sagebluff Dr, Houston, TX 77089, Phone: 281-481-1784, jroberts59@houston.rr.com
Specialties: Hunting knives and folders, offers scrimshaw by wife Barbara. **Patterns:** Drop point hunters and LinerLock® folders. **Technical:** Grinds 440-C, offers file work, texturing, natural handle materials and Micarta. **Prices:** $200 to $800 some higher. **Remarks:** Part-time maker, sold first knife in 1965. **Mark:** Name, city, state.

ROBERTS, MICHAEL
601 Oakwood Dr, Clinton, MS 39056, Phone: 601-540-6222, Fax: 601-213-4891
Specialties: Working and using knives in standard patterns and to customer specs. **Patterns:** Hunters, Bowies, tomahawks and fighters. **Technical:** Forges 5160, O1, 1095 and his own Damascus. Uses only natural handle materials. **Prices:** $145 to $500; some to $1100. **Remarks:** Part-time maker; first knife sold in 1988. **Mark:** Last name or first and last name in Celtic script.

ROBERTS, T. C. (TERRY)
142131 Lake Forest Heights Rd., Siloam Springs, AR 72761, Phone: 479-373-6502, carolcroberts@cox.net
Specialties: Working straight knives and folders of the maker's original design. **Patterns:** Bowies, daggers, fighters, locking folders, slip joints to include multiblades and whittlers. **Technical:** Grinds all types of carbon and stainless steels and commercially available Damascus. Works in stone and casts in bronze and silver. Some inlays and engraving. **Prices:** $250 - $3500. **Remarks:** Full-time maker; sold first knife in 1983. **Mark:** Stamp is oval with initials inside.

ROBERTSON, LEO D
3728 Pleasant Lake Dr, Indianapolis, IN 46227, Phone: 317-882-9899, ldr52@juno.com
Specialties: Hunting and folders. **Patterns:** Hunting, fillet, Bowie, utility, folders and tantos. **Technical:** Uses ATS-34, 154CM, 440C, 1095, D2 and Damascus steels. **Prices:** Fixed knives $75 to $350, folders $350 to $600. **Remarks:** Handles made with stag, wildwoods, laminates, mother-of-pearl. Made first knife in 1990. Member of American Bladesmith Society. **Mark:** Logo with full name in oval around logo.

ROBINSON, CALVIN
5501 Twin Creek Circle, Pace, FL 32571, Phone: 850 572 1504, calvinshandmadeknives@yahoo.com; Web: www.CalvinRobinsonKnives.com
Specialties: Working knives of my own design. **Patterns:** Hunters, fishing, folding and kitchen and purse knives. **Technical:** Now using 14C28N stainless blade steel, as well as 12C27, 13C26 and D2. **Prices:** $180 to $2500. **Remarks:** Full-time maker. Probationary member and voting member of the Knifemaker's Guild. **Mark:** Calvin Robinson Pace, Florida.

ROBINSON, CHARLES (DICKIE)
PO Box 221, Vega, TX 79092, Phone: 806-676-6428, dickie@amaonline.com; Web: www.robinsonknives.com
Specialties: Classic and working/using knives. Does his own engraving. **Patterns:** Bowies, daggers, fighters, hunters and camp knives. **Technical:** Forges O1, 5160, 52100 and his own Damascus. **Prices:** $350 to $850; some to $5000. **Remarks:** Part-time maker; first knife sold in 1988. Doing business as Robinson Knives. ABS Master Smith. **Mark:** Robinson MS.

ROBINSON, CHUCK
SEA ROBIN FORGE, 1423 Third Ave., Picayune, MS 39466, Phone: 601-798-0060, robi5515@bellsouth.net
Specialties: Deluxe period pieces and working / using knives of his design and to customer specs. **Patterns:** Bowies, fighters, hunters, utility knives and original designs. **Technical:** Forges own damascus, 52100, O1, W2, L6 and 1070 thru 1095. **Prices:** Start at $225. **Remarks:** First knife 1958. **Mark:** Fish logo, anchor and initials C.R.

ROBINSON III, REX R
10531 Poe St, Leesburg, FL 34788, Phone: 352-787-4587
Specialties: One-of-a-kind high-art automatics of his design. **Patterns:** Automatics, liner locks and lock back folders. **Technical:** Uses tool steel and stainless Damascus and mokume; flat grinds. Hand carves folders. **Prices:** $1800 to $7500. **Remarks:** First knife sold in 1988. **Mark:** First name inside oval.

ROCHFORD, MICHAEL R
PO Box 577, Dresser, WI 54009, Phone: 715-755-3520, mrrochford@centurytel.net
Specialties: Working straight knives and folders. Classic Bowies and Moran traditional. **Patterns:** Bowies, fighters, hunters: slip-joint, locking and liner locking folders. **Technical:** Grinds ATS-34, 440C, 154CM and D-2; forges W2, 5160, and his own Damascus. Offers metal and metal and leather sheaths. Filework and wire inlay. **Prices:** $150 to $1000; some to $2000. **Remarks:** Part-time maker; first knife sold in 1984. **Mark:** Name.

RODDY, ROY "TIM"
7640 Hub-Bedford Rd., Hubbard, OH 44425, Phone: 330-770-5921, pfr2rtr@hotmail.com
Specialties: Any type of knife a customer wants, large knives, small knives and anything in between. **Patterns:** Hunters, fighters, martial arts knives, hide-outs, neck knives, throwing darts and locking-liner folders. Leather or Kydex sheaths with exotic-skin inlays. **Technical:** 440C, D2, ATS-34 or damascus blade steels. **Remarks:** Started making knives 25 years ago. **Mark:** Railroad sign (circle with an X inside and an R on either side of the X).

RODEBAUGH, JAMES L
P.O. Box 404, Carpenter, WY 82054, Phone: 307-649-2394

RODEWALD, GARY
447 Grouse Ct, Hamilton, MT 59840, Phone: 406-363-2192
Specialties: Bowies of his design as inspired from historical pieces. **Patterns:** Hunters, Bowies and camp/combat. Forges 5160 1084 and his own Damascus of 1084, 15N20, field grade hunters AT-34-440C, 440V, and BG42. **Prices:** $200 to $1500. **Remarks:** Sole author on knives, sheaths done by saddle maker. **Mark:** Rodewald.

RODKEY, DAN
18336 Ozark Dr, Hudson, FL 34667, Phone: 727-863-8264
Specialties: Traditional straight knives of his design and in standard patterns. **Patterns:**

Boots, fighters and hunters. **Technical:** Grinds 440C, D2 and ATS-34. **Prices:** Start at $200. **Remarks:** Full-time maker; first knife sold in 1985. Doing business as Rodkey Knives. **Mark:** Etched logo on blade.

ROE JR., FRED D

4005 Granada Dr, Huntsville, AL 35802, Phone: 205-881-6847

Specialties: Highly finished working knives of his design; period pieces. **Patterns:** Hunters, fighters and survival knives; locking folders; specialty designs like diver's knives. **Technical:** Grinds 154CM, ATS-34 and Damascus. Field-tests all blades. **Prices:** $125 to $250; some to $2000. **Remarks:** Part-time maker; first knife sold in 1980. **Mark:** Last name.

ROEDER, DAVID

426 E. 9th Pl., Kennewick, WA 99336, d.roeder1980@yahoo.com

Specialties: Fixed blade field and exposition grade knives. **Patterns:** Favorite styles are Bowie and hunter. **Technical:** Forges primarily 5160 and 52100. Makes own Damascus. **Prices:** Start at $150. **Remarks:** Made first knife in September, 1996. **Mark:** Maker's mark is a D and R with the R resting at a 45-degree angle to the lower right of the D.

ROGERS, RAY

PO Box 126, Wauconda, WA 98859, Phone: 509-486-8069, knives @rayrogers.com; Web: www.rayrogers.com

Specialties: LinerLock® folders. Asian and European professional chef's knives. **Patterns:** Rayzor folders, chef's knives and cleavers of his own and traditional designs, drop point hunters and fillet knives. **Technical:** Stock removal S30V, 440, 1095, O1 Damascus and other steels. Does all own heat treating, clay tempering, some forging G-10, Micarta, carbon fiber on folders, stabilized burl woods on fixed blades. **Prices:** $200 to $450. **Remarks:** Knives are made one-at-a-time to the customer's order. Happy to consider customizing knife designs to suit your preferences and sometimes create entirely new knives when necessary. As a full-time knifemaker is willing to spend as much time as it takes (usually through email) discussing the options and refining details of a knife's design to insure that you get the knife you really want.

ROGERS, RICHARD

PO Box 769, Magdalena, NM 87825, Phone: 575-838-7237, r.s.rogers@hotmail.com; Web: www.richardrogersknives.com

Specialties: Traditional and modern folders. **Patterns:** Folders: various traditional patterns. One-of-a-kind fixed blades: Bowies, daggers, hunters, utility knives. **Prices:** $300 and up. **Mark:** Last name.

ROGHMANS, MARK

607 Virginia Ave, LaGrange, GA 30240, Phone: 706-885-1273

Specialties: Classic and traditional knives of his design. **Patterns:** Bowies, daggers and fighters. **Technical:** Grinds ATS-34, D2 and 440C. **Prices:** $250 to $500. **Remarks:** Part-time maker; first knife sold in 1984. Doing business as LaGrange Knife. **Mark:** Last name and/or LaGrange Knife.

ROHN, FRED

7675 W Happy Hill Rd, Coeur d'Alene, ID 83814, Phone: 208-667-0774

Specialties: Hunters, boot knives, custom patterns. **Patterns:** Drop points, double edge, etc. **Technical:** Grinds 440 or 154CM. **Prices:** $85 and up. **Remarks:** Part-time maker. **Mark:** Logo on blade; serial numbered.

ROLLERT, STEVE

PO Box 65, Keenesburg, CO 80643-0065, Phone: 303-732-4858, steve@doveknives. com; Web: www.doveknives.com

Specialties: Highly finished working knives. **Patterns:** Variety of straight knives; locking folders and slip-joints. **Technical:** Forges and grinds W2, 1095, ATS-34 and his pattern-welded, cable Damascus and nickel Damascus. **Prices:** $300 to $1000; some to $3000. **Remarks:** Full-time maker; first knife sold in 1980. Doing business as Dove Knives. **Mark:** Last name in script.

ROMEIS, GORDON

1521 Coconut Dr., Fort Myers, FL 33901, Phone: 239-940-5060, gordonromeis@ gmail.com Web: Romeisknives.com

Specialties: Smaller using knives. **Patterns:** I have a number of standard designs that include both full tapered tangs and narrow tang knives. Custom designs are welcome. Many different types. No folders. **Technical:** Standard steel is 440C. Also uses Alabama Damascus steel. **Prices:** Start at $165. **Remarks:** I am a part-time maker however I do try to keep waiting times to a minimum. **Mark:** Either my name, city, and state or simply ROMEIS depending on the knife.

RONZIO, N. JACK

PO Box 248, Fruita, CO 81521, Phone: 970-858-0921

ROOSEVELT, RUSSELL

398 County Rd. 450 E, Albion, IL 62806-4753, Phone: 618-445-3226 or 618-302-7272, rroosevelt02@gmail.com

Specialties: Using straight knives of his design and to customers' specs. **Patterns:** Hunters, utility and camp knives. **Technical:** Forges 1084 and high-carbon damascus. **Prices:** $250 to $1,200. **Remarks:** Part-time maker, first knife sold in 1999. **Mark:** Full name left side, ABS JS stamp right side.

ROOT, GARY

644 East 14th St, Erie, PA 16503, Phone: 814-459-0196

Specialties: Damascus Bowies with hand carved eagles, hawks and snakes for handles. Few folders made. **Patterns:** Daggers, fighters, hunter/field knives. **Technical:** Using handforged Damascus from Ray Bybar Jr (M.S.) and Robert Eggerling. Grinds D2, 440C, 1095 and 5160. Some 5160 is hand forged. **Prices:** $80 to $300 some to $1000.

Remarks: Full time maker, first knife sold in 1976. **Mark:** Name over Erie, PA.

ROSE, BOB

PO BOX 126, Wagontown, PA 19376, Phone: 484-883-3925, bobmedit8@comcast.net Web: www.bobroseknives.com

Patterns: Bowies, fighters, drop point hunters, daggers, bird and trout, camp, and other fixed blade styles. **Technical:** Mostly using 1095 and damascus steel, desert ironwood and other top-of-the-line exotic woods as well as mammoth tooth. **Prices:** $49 - $300. **Remarks:** Been making and selling knives since 2004. "Knife Making is a meditation technique for me."

ROSE, DEREK W

14 Willow Wood Rd, Gallipolis, OH 45631, Phone: 740-446-4627

ROSE II, DOUN T.

Ltc US Special Operations Command (ret.), 1795/96 W Sharon Rd SW, Fife Lake, MI 49633, Phone: 231-645-1369, rosecutlery@gmail.com; Web: www.rosecutlery.com

Specialties: Straight working, collector and presentation knives to a high level of fit and finish. Design in collaboration with customer. **Patterns:** Field knives, Scagel, bowies, tactical, period pieces, axes and tomahawks, fishing and hunting spears and fine kitchen cutlery. **Technical:** Forged and billet ground, high carbon and stainless steel appropriate to end use. Steel from leading industry sources. Some period pieces from recovered stock. Makes own damascus (to include multi-bar and mosaic) and mokume gane. **Remarks:** Full-time maker, ABS since 2000, William Scagel Memorial Scholarship 2002, Bill Moran School of Blade Smithing 2003, apprentice under Master Blacksmith Dan Nickels at Black Rock Forge current. Working at Crooked Pine Forge. **Mark:** Last name ROSE in block letters with five petal "wild rose" in place of O. Doing business as Rose Cutlery.

ROSENBAUGH, RON

2806 Stonegate Dr, Crystal Lake, IL 60012, Phone: 815-477-9233 or 815-345-1633, ron@rosenbaughknives.com; Web: www.rosenbaughknives.com

Specialties: Fancy and plain working knives using own designs, collaborations, and traditional patterns. **Patterns:** Bird, trout, boots, hunters, fighters, some Bowies. **Technical:** Grinds high alloy stainless, tool steels, and Damascus; forges 1084,5160, 52100, carbon and spring steels. **Prices:** $150 to $1000. **Remarks:** Part-time maker, first knife sold in 2004. **Mark:** Last name, logo, city.

ROSENFELD, BOB

955 Freeman Johnson Rd, Hoschton, GA 30548, Phone: 770-867-2647, www.1bladesmith@msn.com

Specialties: Fancy and embellished working/using straight knives of his design and in standard patterns. **Patterns:** Daggers, hunters and utility/camp knives. **Technical:** Forges 52100, A203E, 1095 and L6 Damascus. Offers engraving. **Prices:** $125 to $650; some to $1000. **Remarks:** Full-time maker; first knife sold in 1984. Also makes folders; ABS Journeyman. **Mark:** Last name or full name, Knifemaker.

ROSS, D L

27 Kinsman St, Dunedin, NEW ZEALAND, Phone: 64 3 464 0239, Fax: 64 3 464 0239

Specialties: Working straight knives of his design. **Patterns:** Hunters, various others. **Technical:** Grinds 440C. **Prices:** $100 to $450; some to $700 NZ (not U.S. $). **Remarks:** Part-time maker; first knife sold in 1988. **Mark:** Dave Ross, Maker, city and country.

ROSS, STEPHEN

534 Remington Dr, Evanston, WY 82930, Phone: 307-789-7104

Specialties: One-of-a-kind collector-grade classic and contemporary straight knives and folders of his design and to customer specs; some fantasy pieces. **Patterns:** Combat and survival knives, hunters, boots and folders. **Technical:** Grinds stainless and tool steels. Engraves, scrimshaws. Makes leather sheaths. **Prices:** $160 to $3000. **Remarks:** Part-time maker; first knife sold in 1971. **Mark:** Last name in modified Roman; sometimes in script.

ROSS, TIM

3239 Oliver Rd, Thunder Bay, ON, CANADA P7G 1S9, Phone: 807-935-2667, Fax: 807-935-3179, rosscustomknives@gmail.com

Specialties: Fixed blades, natural handle material. **Patterns:** Hunting, fishing, Bowies, fighters. **Technical:** 440C, D2, 52100, Cable, 5160, 1084, L6, W2. **Prices:** $150 to $750 some higher. **Remarks:** Forges and stock removal. **Mark:** Ross Custom Knives.

ROSSDEUTSCHER, ROBERT N

133 S Vail Ave, Arlington Heights, IL 60005, Phone: 847-577-0404, Web: www. rnrknives.com

Specialties: Frontier-style and historically inspired knives. **Patterns:** Trade knives, Bowies, camp knives and hunting knives, tomahawks and lances. **Technical:** Most knives are hand forged, a few are stock removal. **Prices:** $135 to $1500. **Remarks:** Journeyman Smith of the American Bladesmith Society. **Mark:** Back-to-back "R's", one upside down and backwards, one right side up and forward in an oval. Sometimes with name, town and state; depending on knife style.

ROTELLA, RICHARD A

643 75th St., Niagara Falls, NY 14304, richarpo@roadrunner.com

Specialties: Highly finished working knives of his own design, as well as some Loveless-style designs. **Patterns:** Hunters, fishing, small game, utility, fighters and boot knives. **Technical:** Grinds ATS-34, 154CM, CPM 154 and 440C. **Prices:** $150 to $600. **Remarks:** Part-time maker; first knife sold in 1977. Sells completed knives only and does not take orders; makes about 70 knives a year. **Mark:** Name and city.

ROULIN, CHARLES

113 B Rt. de Soral, Geneva, SWITZERLAND 1233, Phone: 022-757-4479, Fax: 079-

218-9754, charles.roulin@bluewin.ch; Web: www.coutelier-roulin.com
Specialties: Fancy high-art straight knives and folders of his design. **Patterns:** Bowies, locking folders, slip-joint folders and miniatures. **Technical:** Grinds 440C, ATS-34 and D2. Engraves; carves nature scenes and detailed animals in steel, ivory, on handles and blades. **Prices:** $500 to $3000; some to Euro: 14,600. **Remarks:** Full-time maker; first knife sold in 1988. **Mark:** Symbol of fish with name or name engraved.

ROUSH, SCOTT
Big Rock Forge, 31920 Maki Rd, Washburn, WI 54891, Phone: 715-373-2334, scott@bigrockforge.com; Web: bigrockforge.com
Specialties: Forged blades representing a diversity of styles from trasditional hunters, fighters, camp knives, and EDC's to artistic pieces of cultural and historical inspiration with an emphasis in unique materials. **Technical:** Forges Aldo 1084, W2, low MN 1075, stainless/high carbon san mai, wrought iron/high carbon san mai, damascus. **Prices:** $85 to $1000 **Remarks:** Full-time maker; first knife sold in 2010.**Mark:** Stamped initials (SAR) set in a diamond.

ROWE, FRED
BETHEL RIDGE FORGE, 3199 Roberts Rd, Amesville, OH 45711, Phone: 866-325-2164, fred.rowe@bethelridgeforge.com; Web: www.bethelridgeforge.com
Specialties: Damascus and carbon steel sheath knives. **Patterns:** Bowies, hunters, fillet small kokris. **Technical:** His own Damascus, 52100, O1, L6, 1095 carbon steels, mosaics. **Prices:** $200 to $2000. **Remarks:** All blades are clay hardened. **Mark:** Bethel Ridge Forge.

ROYER, KYLE
1962 State Route W, Mountain View, MO 65548, Phone: 417-934-6394; cell: 417-247-5572, royerknifeworks@live.com; Web: www.kyleroyerknives.com
Specialties: Folders and fixed-blade knives. **Technical:** Mosaic damascus and engraving. **Prices:** $350 to $7,500. **Remarks:** ABS master smith. **Mark:** K~ROYER~MS.

ROZAS, CLARK D
1436 W "G" St, Wilmington, CA 90744, Phone: 310-518-0488
Specialties: Hand forged blades. **Patterns:** Pig stickers, toad stabbers, whackers, choppers. **Technical:** Damascus, 52100, 1095, 1084, 5160. **Prices:** $200 to $600. **Remarks:** A.B.S. member; part-time maker since 1995. **Mark:** Name over dagger.

RUA, GARY
400 Snell St., Apt. 2, Fall River, MA 02721, Phone: 508-677-2664
Specialties: Working straight knives of his design. 1800 to 1900 century standard patterns. **Patterns:** Bowies, hunters, fighters, and patch knives. **Technical:** Forges and grinds. Damascus, 5160, 1095, old files. Uses only natural handle material. **Prices:** $350 - $2000. **Remarks:** Part-time maker. (Harvest Moon Forge) **Mark:** Last name.

RUANA KNIFE WORKS
Box 520, Bonner, MT 59823, Phone: 406-258-5368, Fax: 406-258-2895, info@ruanaknives.com; Web: www.ruanaknives.com
Specialties: Working knives and period pieces. **Patterns:** Variety of straight knives. **Technical:** Forges 5160 chrome alloy for Bowies and 1095. **Prices:** $200 and up. **Remarks:** Full-time maker; first knife sold in 1938. Brand new non catalog knives available on ebay under seller name ruanaknives. For free catalog email regular mailing address to info@ruanaknives.com **Mark:** Name.

RUCKER, THOMAS
30222 Mesa Valley Dr., Spring, TX 77386, Phone: 832-216-8122, admin@knivesbythomas.com Web: www.knivesbythomas.com
Specialties: Personal design and custom design. Hunting, tactical, folding knives, and cutlery. **Technical:** Design and grind ATS34, D2, O1, Damascus, and VG10. **Prices:** $150 - $5,000. **Remarks:** Full-time maker and custom scrimshaw and engraving done by wife, Debi Rucker. First knife done in 1969; first design sold in 1975 **Mark:** Etched logo and signature.

RUPERT, BOB
301 Harshaville Rd, Clinton, PA 15026, Phone: 724-573-4569, rbrupert@aol.com
Specialties: Wrought period pieces with natural elements. **Patterns:** Elegant straight blades, friction folders. **Technical:** Forges colonial 7; 1095; 5160; diffuse mokume-gane and Damascus. **Prices:** $150 to $1500; some higher. **Remarks:** Part-time maker; first knife sold in 1980. Evening hours studio since 1980. Likes simplicity that disassembles. **Mark:** R etched in Old English.

RUPLE, WILLIAM H
201 Brian Dr., Pleasanton, TX 78064, Phone: 830-569-0007, bknives@devtex.net
Specialties: Multi-blade folders, slip joints, some lock backs. **Patterns:** Like to reproduce old patterns. Offers filework and engraving. **Technical:** Grinds CPM-154 and other carbon and stainless steel and commercial Damascus. **Prices:** $950 to $2500. **Remarks:** Full-time maker; first knife sold in 1988. **Mark:** Ruple.

RUSS, RON
5351 NE 160th Ave, Williston, FL 32696, Phone: 352-528-2603, RussRs@aol.com
Specialties: Damascus and mokume. **Patterns:** Ladder, rain drop and butterfly. **Technical:** Most knives, including Damascus, are forged from 52100-E. **Prices:** $65 to $2500. **Mark:** Russ.

RUSSELL, MICK
4 Rossini Rd, Pari Park, Port Elizabeth, EC, SOUTH AFRICA 6070
Specialties: Art knives. **Patterns:** Working and collectible bird, trout and hunting knives, defense knives and folders. **Technical:** Grinds D2, 440C, ATS-34 and Damascus. Offers mirror or satin finishes. **Prices:** Start at $100. **Remarks:** Full-time maker; first knife sold in 1986. **Mark:** Stylized rhino incorporating initials.

RUSSELL, TOM
6500 New Liberty Rd, Jacksonville, AL 36265, Phone: 205-492-7866
Specialties: Straight working knives of his design or to customer specs. **Patterns:** Hunters, folders, fighters, skinners, Bowies and utility knives. **Technical:** Grinds D2, 440C and ATS-34; offers filework. **Prices:** $75 to $225. **Remarks:** Part-time maker; first knife sold in 1987. Full-time tool and die maker. **Mark:** Last name with tulip stamp.

RUTH, MICHAEL G
3101 New Boston Rd, Texarkana, TX 75501, Phone: 903-832-7166/cell:903-277-3663, Fax: 903-832-4710, mike@ruthknives.com; Web: www.ruthknives.com
Specialties: Hunters, bowies & fighters. Damascus & carbon steel. **Prices:** $375 & up. **Mark:** Last name.

RUTH, JR., MICHAEL
5716 Wilshire Dr., Texarkana, TX 75503, Phone: 903-293-2663, michael@ruthlesscustomknives.com; Web: www.ruthlesscustomknives.com
Specialties: Custom hand-forged blades, utilizing high carbon and Damascus steels. **Patterns:** Bowies, hunters and fighters ranging from field to presentation-grade pieces. **Technical:** Steels include 5160, 1084, 15n20, W-2, 1095, and O-1. Handle materials include a variety of premium hardwoods, stag, assorted ivories and micarta.**Mark:** 8-pointed star with capital "R" in center.

RUUSUVUORI, ANSSI
Verkkotie 38, Piikkio, FINLAND 21500, Phone: 358-50-520 8057, anssi.ruusuvuori@akukon.fi; Web: www.mmkhorasani.com/razmafzar/smiths
Specialties: Traditional and modern puukko knives and hunters. Sole author except for Damascus steel.**Technical:** Forges mostly 1080 steel and grinds RWL-34. **Prices:** $200 to $500; some to $1200. **Remarks:** Part-time maker.**Mark:** A inside a circle (stamped)

RYBAR JR., RAYMOND B
2328 S. Sunset Dr., Camp Verde, AZ 86322, Phone: 928-567-6372, ray.rybar@gmail.com; Web: www.rybarknives.com
Specialties: Straight knives or folders with customers name, logo, etc. in mosaic pattern. **Patterns:** Common patterns plus mosaics of all types. **Technical:** Forges own Damascus. Primary forging of self smelted steel - smelting classes. **Prices:** $200 to $1200; Bible blades to $10,000. **Remarks:** Master Smith (A.B.S.) Primary focus toward Biblicaly themed blades **Mark:** Rybar or stone church forge or Rev. 1:3 or R.B.R. between diamonds.

RYDBOM, JEFF
PO Box 548, Annandale, MN 55302, Phone: 320-274-9639, jry1890@hotmail.com
Specialties: Ring knives. **Patterns:** Hunters, fighters, Bowie and camp knives. **Technical:** Straight grinds O1, A2, 1566 and 5150 steels. **Prices:** $150 to $1000. **Remarks:** No pinning of guards or pommels. All silver brazed. **Mark:** Capital "C" with J R inside.

RYUICHI, KUKI
504-7 Tokorozawa-Shinmachi, Tokorozawa-city, Saitama, JAPAN, Phone: 042-943-3451

RZEWNICKI, GERALD
8833 S Massbach Rd, Elizabeth, IL 61028-9714, Phone: 815-598-3239

S

SAINDON, R BILL
233 Rand Pond Rd, Goshen, NH 03752, Phone: 603-863-1874, dayskier71@aol.com
Specialties: Collector-quality folders of his design or to customer specs. **Patterns:** Latch release, LinerLock® and lockback folders. **Technical:** Offers limited amount of own Damascus; also uses Damas makers steel. Prefers natural handle material, gold and gems. **Prices:** $500 to $4000. **Remarks:** Full-time maker; first knife sold in 1981. Doing business as Daynia Forge. **Mark:** Sun logo or engraved surname.

SAKAKIBARA, MASAKI
20-8 Sakuragaoka 2-Chome, Setagaya-ku, Tokyo, JAPAN 156-0054, Phone: 81-3-3420-0375

SAKMAR, MIKE
903 S. Latson Rd. #257, Howell, MI 48843, Phone: 517-546-6388, Fax: 517-546-6399, sakmarent@yahoo.com; Web: www.sakmarenterprises.com
Specialties: Mokume in various patterns and alloy combinations. **Patterns:** Bowies, fighters, hunters and integrals. **Technical:** Grinds ATS-34, Damascus and high-carbon tool steels. Uses mostly natural handle materials—elephant ivory, walrus ivory, stag, wildwood, oosic, etc. Makes mokume for resale. **Prices:** $250 to $2500; some to $4000. **Remarks:** Part-time maker; first knife sold in 1990. Supplier of mokume. **Mark:** Last name.

SALLEY, JOHN D
3965 Frederick-Ginghamsburg Rd., Tipp City, OH 45371, Phone: 937-698-4588, Fax: 937-698-4131
Specialties: Fancy working knives and art pieces. **Patterns:** Hunters, fighters, daggers and some swords. **Technical:** Grinds ATS-34, 12C27 and W2; buys Damascus. **Prices:** $85 to $1000; some to $6000. **Remarks:** Part-time maker; first knife sold in 1979. **Mark:** First initial, last name.

SALTER, GREGG
Salter Fine Cutlery, POB 384571, Waikoloa, HI 96738-4571, Phone: 808-883-0128, saltent@aol.com; Web: www.salterfinecutlery.com
Specialties: Custom, made-to-order cutlery, chopping boards and boxes, including kitchen knife sets, steak knife sets, carving sets, chef's knives and collectible knives and

custom knifemakers

SAMPSON—SCHLUETER

swords. Work in collaboration with several individual bladesmiths who create blades to our specifications. **Technical:** Variety of steels available, including VG-10, Aogami Super, SG2, OU-31, YSS White Paper Shirogami, YSS Aogami Blue Paper and Tamahagane (swords). Damascus patterns and, in the case of swords, hand-etched scenes available. **Prices:** Range widely, from approximately $250 to over $1 million in the case of one spectacular collectible. Average price for chef's knives in the $500-$750 range. **Remarks:** Full-time business making a range of products based around knives. **Mark:** Hawaiian koa tree with crossed chef's knives and the outline of a crown between them.

SAMPSON, LYNN
381 Deakins Rd, Jonesborough, TN 37659, Phone: 423-348-8373
    Specialties: Highly finished working knives, mostly folders. **Patterns:** Locking folders, slip-joints, interframes and two-blades. **Technical:** Grinds D2, 440C and ATS-34; offers extensive filework. **Prices:** Start at $300. **Remarks:** Full-time maker; first knife sold in 1982. **Mark:** Name and city in logo.

SANDBERG, RONALD B
24784 Shadowwood Ln, Brownstown, MI 48134-9560, Phone: 734-671-6866, msc2009@comcast.net
    Specialties: Good looking and functional hunting knives, filework, mixing of handle materials. **Patterns:** Hunters, skinners and Bowies. **Prices:** $120 and up. **Remarks:** Full lifetime workmanship guarantee. **Mark:** R.B. SANDBERG

SANDERS, BILL
335 Bauer Ave, PO Box 957, Mancos, CO 81328, Phone: 970-533-7223, Fax: 970-533-7390, billsand@frontier.net; Web: www.billsandershandmadeknives.com
    Specialties: Survival knives, working straight knives, some fancy and some fantasy, of his design. **Patterns:** Hunters, boots, utility knives, using belt knives. **Technical:** Grinds 440C, ATS-34 and commercial Damascus. Provides wide variety of handle materials. **Prices:** $170 to $800. **Remarks:** Full-time maker. Formerly of Timberline Knives. **Mark:** Name, city and state.

SANDERS, MICHAEL M
PO Box 1106, Ponchatoula, LA 70454, Phone: 225-294-3601, sanders@bellsouth.net
    Specialties: Working straight knives and folders, some deluxe. **Patterns:** Hunters, fighters, Bowies, daggers, large folders and deluxe Damascus miniatures. **Technical:** Grinds O1, D2, 440C, ATS-34 and Damascus. **Prices:** $75 to $650; some higher. **Remarks:** Full-time maker; first knife sold in 1967. **Mark:** Name and state.

SANDOW, BRENT EDWARD
50 O'Halloran Road, Howick, Auckland, NEW ZEALAND 2014, Phone: 64 9 537 4166, knifebug@vodafone.co.nz; Web: www.brentsandowknives.com
    Specialties: Tactical fixed blades, hunting, camp, Bowie. **Technical:** All blades made by stock removal method. **Prices:** From US $200 upward. **Mark:** Name etched or engraved.

SANDOW, NORMAN E
61 O'Halloran Rd., Howick, Manukau 2014, Auckland, NEW ZEALAND, Phone: 0064-9-5328912, sanknife@xtra.co.nz
    Specialties: Quality LinerLock® folders. Working and fancy straight knives. Some one-of-a-kind. Embellishments available. **Patterns:** Most patterns, hunters, boot, bird and trout, etc., and to customer's specs. **Technical:** Predominate knife steel ATS-34. Also in use 12C27, D2 and Damascus. High class handle material used on both folders and straight knives. All blades made via the stock removal method. **Prices:** $350 to $4000. **Remarks:** Full-time maker. **Mark:** Norman E Sandow in semi-circular design.

SANDS, SCOTT
2 Lindis Ln, New Brighton, Christchurch 9, NEW ZEALAND
    Specialties: Classic working and fantasy swords. **Patterns:** Fantasy, medieval, celtic, viking, katana, some daggers. **Technical:** Forges own Damascus; 1080 and L6; 5160 and L6; O1 and L6. All hand-polished, does own heat-treating, forges non-Damascus on request. **Prices:** $1500 to $15,000+. **Remarks:** Full-time maker; first blade sold in 1996. **Mark:** Stylized Moon.

SANFORD, DICK
9 Satsop Court, Montesano, WA 98563, Phone: 360-249-5776, richardsanfo364@centurytel.net
    Remarks: Ten years experience hand forging knives

SANTA, LADISLAV "LASKY"
Stara Voda 264/10, 97637 Hrochot, SLOVAKIA, Phone: +421-907-825-2-77, lasky@lasky.sk; Web: www.lasky.sk
    Specialties: Damascus hunters, daggers and swords. **Patterns:** Various damascus patterns. **Prices:** $300 to $6,000 U.S. **Mark:** L or Lasky.

SANTIAGO, ABUD
Av Gaona 3676 PB, Buenos Aires, ARGENTINA 1416, Phone: 5411 4612 8396, info@phi-sabud.com; Web: www.phi-sabud.com/blades.html

SANTINI, TOM
101 Clayside Dr, Pikeville, NC 27863, Phone: 586-354-0245, tomsantiniknives@hotmail.com; Web: www.tomsantiniknives.com
    Specialties: working/using straight knives, tactical, and some slipjoints **Technical:** Grinds ATS-34, S-90-V, D2, and damascus. I handstitch my leather sheaths. **Prices:** $150 - $500. **Remarks:** Full-time maker, first knife sold in 2004. **Mark:** Full name.

SARGANIS, PAUL
2215 Upper Applegate Rd, Jacksonville, OR 97530, Phone: 541-899-2831, paulsarganis@hotmail.com; Web: www.sarganis.50megs.com
    Specialties: Hunters, folders, Bowies. **Technical:** Forges 5160, 1084. Grinds ATS-34 and

440C. **Prices:** $120 to $500. **Remarks:** Spare-time maker, first knife sold in 1987. **Mark:** Last name.

SASS, GARY N
2048 Buckeye Dr, Sharpsville, PA 16150, Phone: 724-866-6165, gnsass@yahoo.com
    Specialties: Working straight knives of his design or to customer specifications. **Patterns:** Hunters, fighters, utility knives, push daggers. **Technical:** Grinds 440C, ATS-34 and Damascus. Uses exotic wood, buffalo horn, warthog tusk and semi-precious stones. **Prices:** $50 to $250, some higher. **Remarks:** Part-time maker. First knife sold in 2003. **Mark:** Initials G.S. formed into a diamond shape or last name.

SAVIANO, JAMES
124 Wallis St., Douglas, MA 01516, Phone: 508-476-7644, jimsaviano@gmail.com
    Specialties: Straight knives. **Patterns:** Hunters, bowies, fighters, daggers, short swords. **Technical:** Hand-forged high-carbon and my own damascus steel. **Prices:** Starting at $300. **Remarks:** ABS mastersmith, maker since 2000, sole authorship. **Mark:** Last name or stylized JPS initials.

SAWBY, SCOTT
480 Snowberry Ln, Sandpoint, ID 83864, Phone: 208-263-4253, scotmar3@gmail.com; Web: www.sawbycustomknives.com
    Specialties: Folders, working and fancy. **Patterns:** Locking folders, patent locking systems and interframes. **Technical:** Grinds D2, 440C, CPM154, ATS-34, S30V, and Damascus. **Prices:** $700 to $3000. **Remarks:** Full-time maker; first knife sold in 1974. Engraving by wife Marian. **Mark:** Last name, city and state.

SCARROW, WIL
c/o LandW Mail Service, PO Box 1036, Gold Hill, OR 97525, Phone: 541-855-1236, willsknife@earthlink.net
    Specialties: Carving knives, also working straight knives in standard patterns or to customer specs. **Patterns:** Carving, fishing, hunting, skinning, utility, swords and Bowies. **Technical:** Forges and grinds: A2, L6, W1, D2, 5160, 1095, 440C, AEB-L, ATS-34 and others on request. Offers some filework. **Prices:** $105 to $850; some higher. Prices include sheath (carver's $40 and up). **Remarks:** Spare-time maker; first knife sold in 1983. Two to eight month construction time on custom orders. Doing business as Scarrow's Custom Stuff and Gold Hill Knife works (in Oregon). Carving knives available at Raven Dog Enterprises. Contact at Ravedog@aol.com. **Mark:** SC with arrow and year made.

SCHALLER, ANTHONY BRETT
5609 Flint Ct. NW, Albuquerque, NM 87120, Phone: 505-899-0155, brett@schallerknives.com; Web: www.schallerknives.com
    Specialties: Straight knives and locking-liner folders of his design and in standard patterns. **Patterns:** Boots, fighters, utility knives and folders. **Technical:** Grinds CPM154, S30V, and stainless Damascus. Offers filework, hand-rubbed finishes and full and narrow tangs. Prefers exotic woods or Micarta for handle materials, G-10 and carbon fiber to handle materials. **Prices:** $100 to $350; some to $500. **Remarks:** Part-time maker; first knife sold in 1990. **Mark:** A.B. Schaller - Albuquerque NM - handmade.

SCHEID, MAGGIE
124 Van Stallen St, Rochester, NY 14621-3557
    Specialties: Simple working straight knives. **Patterns:** Kitchen and utility knives; some miniatures. **Technical:** Forges 5160 high-carbon steel. **Prices:** $100 to $200. **Remarks:** Part-time maker; first knife sold in 1986. **Mark:** Full name.

SCHEMPP, ED
PO Box 1181, Ephrata, WA 98823, Phone: 509-754-2963, Fax: 509-754-3212, edschempp@yahoo.com
    Specialties: Mosaic Damascus and unique folder designs. **Patterns:** Primarily folders. **Technical:** Grinds CPM440V; forges many patterns of mosaic using powdered steel. **Prices:** $100 to $400; some to $2000. **Remarks:** Part-time maker; first knife sold in 1991. Doing business as Ed Schempp Knives. **Mark:** Ed Schempp Knives over five heads of wheat, city and state.

SCHEMPP, MARTIN
PO Box 1181, 5430 Baird Springs Rd NW, Ephrata, WA 98823, Phone: 509-754-2963, Fax: 509-754-3212
    Specialties: Fantasy and traditional straight knives of his design, to customer specs and in standard patterns; Paleolithic-styles. **Patterns:** Fighters and Paleolithic designs. **Technical:** Uses opal, Mexican rainbow and obsidian. Offers scrimshaw. **Prices:** $15 to $100; some to $250. **Remarks:** Spare-time maker; first knife sold in 1995. **Mark:** Initials and date.

SCHEURER, ALFREDO E FAES
Av Rincon de los Arcos 104, Col Bosque Res del Sur, Distrito Federal, MEXICO 16010, Phone: 5676 47 63
    Specialties: Fancy and fantasy knives of his design. **Patterns:** Daggers. **Technical:** Grinds stainless steel; casts and grinds silver. Sets stones in silver. **Prices:** $2000 to $3000. **Remarks:** Spare-time maker; first knife sold in 1989. **Mark:** Symbol.

SCHIPPNICK, JIM
PO Box 326, Sanborn, NY 14132, Phone: 716-731-3715, ragnar@ragweedforge.com; Web: www.ragweedforge.com
    Specialties: Nordic, early American, rustic. **Mark:** Runic R. **Remarks:** Also imports Nordic knives from Norway, Sweden and Finland.

SCHLUETER, DAVID
2136 Cedar Gate Rd., Madison Heights, VA 24572, Phone: 434-384-8642, drschlueter@hotmail.com

Specialties: Japanese-style swords. **Patterns:** Larger blades. O-tanto to Tachi, with focus on less common shapes. **Technical:** Forges and grinds carbon steels, heat-treats and polishes own blades, makes all fittings, does own mounting and finishing. **Prices:** Start at $3000. **Remarks:** Sells fully mounted pieces only, doing business as Odd Frog Forge. **Mark:** Full name and date.

SCHMITZ, RAYMOND E
PO Box 1787, Valley Center, CA 92082, Phone: 760-749-4318

SCHNEIDER, CRAIG M
5380 N Amity Rd, Claremont, IL 62421, Phone: 217-377-5715, raephtownslam@att.blackberry.net
Specialties: Straight knives of his own design. **Patterns:** Bowies, hunters, tactical, bird & trout. **Technical:** Forged high-carbon steel and Damascus. Flat grind and differential heat treatment use a wide selection of handle, guard and bolster material, also offers leather sheaths. **Prices:** $150 to $3000. **Remarks:** Part-time maker; first knife sold in 1985. **Mark:** Stylized initials.

SCHNEIDER, HERMAN J.
14084 Apple Valley Rd, Apple Valley, CA 92307, Phone: 760-946-9096
Specialties: Presentation pieces, Fighters, Hunters. **Prices:** Starting at $900. **Mark:** H.J. Schneider-Maker or maker's last name.

SCHOEMAN, CORRIE
Box 28596, Danhof, Free State, SOUTH AFRICA 9310, Phone: 027 51 4363528 Cell: 027 82-3750789, corries@intekom.co.za
Specialties: High-tech folders of his design or to customer's specs. **Patterns:** Linerlock folders and automatics. **Technical:** ATS-34, Damascus or stainless Damascus with titanium frames; prefers exotic materials for handles. **Prices:** $650 to $2000. **Remarks:** Full-time maker; first knife sold in 1984. All folders come with filed liners and back and jeweled inserts. **Mark:** Logo in knife shape engraved on inside of back bar.

SCHOENFELD, MATTHEW A
RR #1, Galiano Island, BC, CANADA V0N 1P0, Phone: 250-539-2806
Specialties: Working knives of his design. **Patterns:** Kitchen cutlery, camp knives, hunters. **Technical:** Grinds 440C. **Prices:** $85 to $500. **Remarks:** Part-time maker; first knife sold in 1978. **Mark:** Signature, Galiano Is. B.C., and date.

SCHOENINGH, MIKE
49850 Miller Rd, North Powder, OR 97867, Phone: 541-856-3239

SCHOLL, TIM
1389 Langdon Rd, Angier, NC 27501, Phone: 910-897-2051, tschollknives@live.com
Specialties: Fancy and working/using straight knives and folders of his design and to customer specs. **Patterns:** Bowies, hunters, tomahawks, daggers & fantasy knives. **Technical:** Forges high carbon and tool steel makes Damascus, grinds ATS-34 and D2 on request. **Prices:** $150 to $6000. **Remarks:** Part-time maker; first knife sold in 1990. Doing business as Tim Scholl Custom Knives. President North Carolina Custom Knifemakers Guild. American Bladesmith Society journeyman smith. **Mark:** S pierced by arrow.

SCHRADER, ROBERT
55532 Gross De, Bend, OR 97707, Phone: 541-598-7301
Specialties: Hunting, utility, Bowie. **Patterns:** Fixed blade. **Prices:** $150 to $600.

SCHRAP, ROBERT G
CUSTOM LEATHER KNIFE SHEATH CO., 7024 W Wells St, Wauwatosa, WI 53213-3717, Phone: 414-771-6472 or 414-379-6819, Fax: 414-479-9765, knifesheaths@aol.com; Web: www.customsheaths.com
Specialties: Leatherwork. **Prices:** $35 to $100. **Mark:** Schrap in oval.

SCHROEN, KARL
4042 Bones Rd, Sebastopol, CA 95472, Phone: 707-823-4057, Fax: 707-823-2914, Web: http://users.ap.net/~schroen
Specialties: Using knives made to fit. **Patterns:** Sgian dubhs, carving sets, wood-carving knives, fishing knives, kitchen knives and new cleaver design. **Technical:** Forges A2, ATS-34, D2 and L6 cruwear S30V S90V. **Prices:** $150 to $6000. **Remarks:** Full-time maker; first knife sold in 1968. Author of The Hand Forged Knife. **Mark:** Last name.

SCHUCHMANN, RICK
3975 Hamblen Dr, Cincinnati, OH 45255, Phone: 513-553-4316
Specialties: Replicas of antique and out-of-production Scagels and Randalls, primarily miniatures. **Patterns:** All sheath knives, mostly miniatures, hunting and fighting knives, some daggers and hatchets. **Technical:** Stock removal, 440C and O1 steel. Most knives are flat ground, some convex. **Prices:** $175 to $600 and custom to $4000. **Remarks:** Part-time maker, sold first knife in 1997. Knives on display in the Randall Museum. Sheaths are made exclusively at Sullivan's Holster Shop, Tampa, FL **Mark:** SCAR.

SCHUTTE, NEILL
01 Moffet St., Fichardt Park, Bloemfontein, SOUTH AFRICA 9301, Phone: +27(0) 82 787 3429, neill@schutteknives.co.za, www.schutteknives.co.za
Specialties: Bob Loveless-style knives, George Herron fighters, custom designs and designs/requests from clients. **Technical:** Mainly stock removal of Bohler N690, RWL-34 and ATS-34, if available, blade steels. Uses the materials clients request. **Prices:** $450 to $1,250. **Remarks:** Full-time maker; first knife made at 10 years old, seriously started knifemaking in 2008. **Mark:** Kneeling archer/bowman (maker's surname, Schutte, directly translates to archer or bowman.)

SCHWARZER, LORA SUE
119 Shoreside Trail, Crescent City, FL 32112, Phone: 386-698-2840, auntielora57@yahoo.com
Specialties: Scagel style knives. **Patterns:** Hunters and miniatures **Technical:** Forges 1084 and Damascus. **Prices:** Start at $400. **Remarks:** Part-time maker; first knife sold in 1997. Journeyman Bladesmith, American Bladesmith Society. Now working with Steve Schwarzer on some projects.**Mark:** Full name - JS on reverse side.

SCHWARZER, STEPHEN
119 Shoreside Trail, Crescent City, FL 32112, Phone: 386-698-2840, Fax: 386-698-2840, schwarzeranvil@gmail.com; Web: www.steveschwarzer.com
Specialties: Mosaic Damascus and picture mosaic in folding knives. All Japanese blades are finished working with Wally Hostetter considered the top Japanese lacquer specialist in the U.S.A. Also produces a line of carbon steel skinning knives at $300. **Patterns:** Folders, axes and buckskinner knives. **Technical:** Specializes in picture mosaic Damascus and powder metal mosaic work. Sole authorship; all work including carving done in-house. Most knives have file work and carving. Hand carved steel and precious metal guards. **Prices:** $1500 to $5000, some higher; carbon steel and primitive knives much less. **Remarks:** Full-time maker; first knife sold in 1976, considered by many to be one of the top mosaic Damascus specialists in the world. Mosaic Master level work. I am now working with Lora Schwarzer on some projects. **Mark:** Schwarzer + anvil.

SCIMIO, BILL
4554 Creek Side Ln., Spruce Creek, PA 16683, Phone: 814-632-3751, sprucecreekforge@gmail.com Web: www.sprucecreekforge.com
Specialties: Hand-forged primitive-style knives with curly maple, antler, bone and osage handles.

SCORDIA, PAOLO
Via Terralba 144, Torrimpietra, Roma, ITALY 00050, Phone: 06-61697231, paolo.scordia@uni.net; Web: www.scordia-knives.com
Specialties: Working, fantasy knives, Italian traditional folders and fixed blades of own design. **Patterns:** Any. **Technical:** Forge mosaic Damascus, forge blades, welds own mokume and grinds ATS-34, etc. use hardwoods and Micarta for handles, brass and nickel-silver for fittings. Makes sheaths. **Prices:** $200 to $2000, some to $4000. **Remarks:** Part-time maker; first knife sold in 1988. **Mark:** Sun and moon logo and itialis.

SCROGGS, JAMES A
108 Murray Hill Dr, Warrensburg, MO 64093, Phone: 660-747-2568, jscroggsknives@embarqmail.com
Specialties: Straight knives, prefers light weight. **Patterns:** Hunters, hideouts, and fighters. **Technical:** Grinds CPM-154 stainless plus experiments in steel. Prefers handles of walnut in English, bastonge, American black. Also uses myrtle, maple, Osage orange. **Prices:** $200 to $1000. **Remarks:** 1st knife sold in 1985. Full-time maker, no orders taken. **Mark:** SCROGGS in block or script.

SCULLEY, PETER E
340 Sunset Dr, Rising Fawn, GA 30738, Phone: 706-398-0169

SEATON, DAVID D
1028 South Bishop Ave, #237, Rolla, MO 65401, Phone: 573-465-3193, aokcustomknives@gmail.com
Specialties: Gentleman's and Lady's folders. **Patterns:** Liner lock folders of own design and to customer specs, lock backs, slip joints, some stright knives, tactical folders, skinners, fighters, and utility knives. **Technical:** Grinds ATS 34, O1, 1095, 154CM, CPM154, commercial Damascus. Blades are mostly flat ground, some hollow ground. Does own heat treating, tempering, and Nitre Bluing. Prefers natural handle materials such as ivory, mother of pearl, bone, and exotic woods, some use of G10 and micarta on hard use knives. Use gem stones, gold, silver on upscale knives, offers some carving, filework, and engrving. **Prices:** $150 to $600 avg; some to $1500 and up depending on materials and embellishments. **Remarks:** First knife sold in 2002, part-time maker, doing business at AOK Custom Knives. **Mark:** full or last name engraved on blade.

SEIB, STEVE
7914 Old State Road, Evansville, IN 47710, Phone: 812-867-2231, sseib@insightbb.com
Specialties: Working straight knives. **Pattern:** Skinners, hunters, bowies and camp knives. **Technical:** Forges high-carbon and makes own damascus. **Remarks:** Part-time maker. ABS member. **Mark:** Last name.

SELF, ERNIE
950 O'Neill Ranch Rd, Dripping Springs, TX 78620-9760, Phone: 512-940-7134, ernieself@hillcountrytx.net
Specialties: Traditional and working straight knives and folders of his design and in standard patterns. **Patterns:** Hunters, locking folders and slip-joints. **Technical:** Grinds 440C, D2, 440V, ATS-34 and Damascus. Offers fancy filework. **Prices:** $250 to $1000; some to $2500. **Remarks:** Full-time maker; first knife sold in 1982. Also customizes Buck 110's and 112's folding hunters. **Mark:** In oval shape - Ernie Self Maker Dripping Springs TX.

SELLEVOLD, HARALD
PO Box 4134, S Kleivesmau:2, Bergen, NORWAY N5835, Phone: 47 55-310682, haraldsellevold@c2i.net; Web:www.knivmakeren.com
Specialties: Norwegian-styles; collaborates with other Norse craftsmen. **Patterns:** Distinctive ferrules and other mild modifications of traditional patterns; Bowies and friction folders. **Technical:** Buys Damascus blades; blacksmiths his own blades. Semi-gemstones used in handles; gemstone inlay. **Prices:** $350 to $2000. **Remarks:** Full-time maker; first knife sold in 1980. **Mark:** Name and country in logo.

SELZAM, FRANK

Martin Reinhard Str 23, Bad Koenigshofen, GERMANY 97631, Phone: 09761-5980, frankselzam.de

Specialties: Hunters, working knives to customers specs, hand tooled and stitched leather sheaths large stock of wood and German stag horn. **Patterns:** Mostly own design. **Technical:** Forged blades, own Damascus, also stock removal stainless. **Prices:** $250 to $1500. **Remark:** First knife sold in 1978. **Mark:** Last name stamped.

SENTZ, MARK C

4084 Baptist Rd, Taneytown, MD 21787, Phone: 410-756-2018

Specialties: Fancy straight working knives of his design. **Patterns:** Hunters, fighters, folders and utility/camp knives. **Technical:** Forges 1085, 1095, 5160, 5155 and his Damascus. Most knives come with wood-lined leather sheath or wooden presentation sheath. **Prices:** Start at $275. **Remarks:** Full-time maker; first knife sold in 1989. Doing business as M. Charles Sentz Gunsmithing, Inc. **Mark:** Last name.

SERAFEN, STEVEN E

24 Genesee St, New Berlin, NY 13411, Phone: 607-847-6903

Specialties: Traditional working/using straight knives of his design and to customer specs. **Patterns:** Bowies, fighters, hunters. **Technical:** Grinds ATS-34, 440C, high-carbon steel. **Prices:** $175 to $600; some to $1200. **Remarks:** Part-time maker; first knife sold in 1990. **Mark:** First and middle initial, last name in script.

SERVEN, JIM

PO Box 1, Fostoria, MI 48435, Phone: 517-795-2255

Specialties: Highly finished unique folders. **Patterns:** Fancy working folders, axes, miniatures and razors; some straight knives. **Technical:** Grinds 440C; forges his own Damascus. **Prices:** $150 to $800; some to $1500. **Remarks:** Full-time maker; first knife sold in 1971. **Mark:** Name in map logo.

SEVEY CUSTOM KNIFE

94595 Chandler Rd, Gold Beach, OR 97444, Phone: 541-247-2649, sevey@charter.net; Web: www.seveyknives.com

Specialties: Fixed blade hunters. **Patterns:** Drop point, trailing paint, clip paint, full tang, hidden tang. **Technical:** D-2, and ATS-34 blades, stock removal. Heat treatment by Paul Bos. **Prices:** $225 and up depending on overall length and grip material. **Mark:** Sevey Custom Knife.

SEWARD, BEN

471 Dogwood Ln., Austin, AR 72007, Phone: 501-416-1543, sewardsteel@gmail.com

Specialties: Forged blades, mostly bowies and fighters. **Technical:** Forges high-carbon steels such as 1075 and W2. **Remarks:** First knife made in 2005; ABS journeyman smith and member Arkansas Knifemakers Association.

SFREDDO, RODRIGO MENEZES

cep g5 150-000, Rua 15 De Setembro 66, Nova Petropolis, RS, BRAZIL 95150-000, Phone: 011-55-54-303-303-90, www.brazilianbladesmiths.com.br; www.sbccutelaria.org.br

Specialties: Integrals, Bowies, hunters, dirks & swords. **Patterns:** Forges his own Damascus and 52100 steel. **Technical:** Specialized in integral knives and Damascus. **Prices:** From $350 and up. Most around $750 to $1000. **Remarks:** Considered by many to be the Brazil's best bladesmith. ABS SBC Member. **Mark:** S. Sfreddo on the left side of the blade.

SHADLEY, EUGENE W

209 NW 17th Street, Grand Rapids, MN 55744, Phone: 218-999-7197 or 218-244-8628, Fax: call first, ShadleyKnives@hotmail.com

Specialties: Gold frames are available on some models. **Patterns:** Whittlers, stockman, sowbelly, congress, trapper, etc. **Technical:** Grinds ATS-34, 416 frames. **Prices:** Starts at $600, some models up to $15,000. **Remarks:** Full-time maker; first knife sold in 1985. Doing business as Shadley Knives. **Mark:** Last name.

SHADMOT, BOAZ

MOSHAV PARAN D N, Arava, ISRAEL 86835, srb@arava.co.il

SHARP, DAVID

17485 Adobe St., Hesperia, CA 92345, Phone: 520-370-1899, sharpwerks@gmail.com or david@sharpwerks.com; Web: www.sharpwerks.com

Specialties: Fixed blades. **Patterns:** Original and real Loveless pattern utilities, hunters and fighters. **Technical:** Stock removal, tool steel and stainless steel, hollow grind, machine finish, full polish, various handle materials. **Prices:** $300 to $1,500. **Remarks:** Part-time maker, first knife sold in 2011. **Mark:** "Sharpwerks" on original designs; "D. Sharp" on Loveless designs.

SHARRIGAN, MUDD

111 Bradford Rd, Wiscasset, ME 04578-4457, Phone: 207-882-9820, Fax: 207-882-9835

Specialties: Custom designs; repair straight knives, custom leather sheaths. **Patterns:** Daggers, fighters, hunters, crooked knives and seamen working knives; traditional Scandinavian-styles. **Technical:** Forges 1095, 5160, and W2. **Prices:** $50 to $325; some to $1200. **Remarks:** Full-time maker; first knife sold in 1982. **Mark:** Swallow tail carving. Mudd engraved.

SHEEHY, THOMAS J

4131 NE 24th Ave, Portland, OR 97211-6411, Phone: 503-493-2843

Specialties: Hunting knives and ulus. **Patterns:** Own or customer designs. **Technical:** 1095/O1 and ATS-34 steel. **Prices:** $35 to $200. **Remarks:** Do own heat treating; forged or ground blades. **Mark:** Name.

SHEELY, "BUTCH" FOREST

15784 Custar Rd., Grand Rapids, OH 43522, Phone: 419-308-3471, sheelyblades@gmail.com

Specialties: Traditional bowies and pipe tomahawks. **Patterns:** Bowies, hunters, integrals, dirks, axes and hawks. **Technical:** Forges 5160, 52100, 1084, 1095, and Damascus. **Prices:** $150 to $1500; **Remarks:** Full-time bladesmith part-time blacksmith; first knife sold in 1982. ABS Journeysmith, sole author of all knives and hawks including hand sewn leather sheaths, doing business as Beaver Creek Forge. **Mark:** First and last name above Bladesmith.

SHEETS, STEVEN WILLIAM

6 Stonehouse Rd, Mendham, NJ 07945, Phone: 201-543-5882

SHIFFER, STEVE

PO Box 582, Leakesville, MS 39451, Phone: 601-394-4425, aiifish2@yahoo.com; Web: wwwchoctawplantationforge.com

Specialties: Bowies, fighters, hard use knives. **Patterns:** Fighters, hunters, combat/utility knives. Walker pattern LinerLock® folders. Allen pattern scale and bolster release autos. **Technical:** Most work forged, stainless stock removal. Makes own Damascus. O1 and 5160 most used also 1084, 440c, 154cm, s30v. **Prices:** $125 to $1000. **Remarks:** First knife sold in 2000, all heat treatment done by maker. Doing business as Choctaw Plantation Forge. **Mark:** Hot mark sunrise over creek.

SHINOSKY, ANDY

3117 Meanderwood Dr, Canfield, OH 44406, Phone: 330-702-0299, andrew@shinosky.com; Web: www.shinosky.com

Specialties: Collectable folders and interframes. **Patterns:** Drop point, spear point, trailing point, daggers. **Technical:** Grinds ATS-34 and Damascus. Prefers natural handle materials. Most knives are engraved by Andy himself. **Prices:** Start at $800. **Remarks:** Part-time maker/engraver. First knife sold in 1992. **Mark:** Name.

SHIPLEY, STEVEN A

800 Campbell Rd Ste 137, Richardson, TX 75081, Phone: 972-644-7981, Fax: 972-644-7985, steve@shipleysphotography.com

Specialties: Hunters, skinners and traditional straight knives. **Technical:** Hand grinds ATS-34, 440C and Damascus steels. Each knife is custom sheathed by his son, Dan. **Prices:** $175 to $2000. **Remarks:** Part-time maker; like smooth lines and unusual handle materials. **Mark:** S A Shipley.

SHOEMAKER, CARROLL

380 Yellowtown Rd, Northup, OH 45658, Phone: 740-446-6695

Specialties: Working/using straight knives of his design. **Patterns:** Hunters, utility/camp and early American backwoodsmen knives. **Technical:** Grinds ATS-34; forges old files, O1 and 1095. Uses some Damascus; offers scrimshaw and engraving. **Prices:** $100 to $175; some to $350. **Remarks:** Spare-time maker; first knife sold in 1977. **Mark:** Name and city or connected initials.

SHOEMAKER, SCOTT

316 S Main St, Miamisburg, OH 45342, Phone: 513-859-1935

Specialties: Twisted, wire-wrapped handles on swords, fighters and fantasy blades; new line of seven models with quick-draw, multi-carry Kydex sheaths. **Patterns:** Bowies, boots and one-of-a-kinds in his design or to customer specs. **Technical:** Grinds A6 and ATS-34; buys Damascus. Hand satin finish is standard. **Prices:** $100 to $1500; swords to $8000. **Remarks:** Part-time maker; first knife sold in 1984. **Mark:** Angel wings with last initial, or last name.

SHOGER, MARK O

10525 S.W. 161st Ct., Beaverton, OR 97007, Phone: 503-521-1714, mosdds@msn.com

Specialties: Working and using straight knives and folders of his design; fancy and embellished knives. **Patterns:** Hunters, Bowies, daggers and folders. **Technical:** Forges O1, W2, 1084, 5160, 52100 and 1084/15n20 pattern weld. **Remarks:** Spare-time maker. **Mark:** Last name "Shoger" or stamped last initial over anvil.

SHROPSHIRE, SHAWN

PO Box 453, Piedmont, OK 73078, Phone: 405-833-5239, shawn@sdsknifeworks.com; Web: www.sdsknifeworks.com

Specialties: Working straight knives and frontier style period pieces. **Patterns:** Bowies, hunters, skinners, fighters, patch/neck knives. **Technical:** Grinds D2, 154CM and some Damascus, forges 1084, 5160. **Prices:** Starting at $125. **Remarks:** Part-time maker; first knife sold in 1997. Doing business at SDS Knifeworks. **Mark:** Etched "SDS Knifeworks - Oklahoma" in an oval or "SDS" tang stamp.

SHULL, JAMES

5146 N US 231 W, Rensselaer, IN 47978, Phone: 219-866-0436, nbjs@netnitco.net Web: www.shullhandforgedknives.com

Specialties: Working knives of hunting, fillet, Bowie patterns. **Technical:** Forges or uses 1095, 5160, 52100 & O1. **Prices:** $100 to $300. **Remarks:** DBA Shull Handforged Knives. **Mark:** Last name in arc.

SIBERT, SHANE

PO BOX 241, Gladstone, OR 97027, Phone: 503-650-2082, shane.sibert@comcast.net Web: www.sibertknives.com

Specialties: Innovative light weight hiking and backpacking knives for outdoorsman and adventurers, progressive fixed blade combat and fighting knives. One-of-a-kind knives of various configurations. Titanium frame lock folders. **Patterns:** Modern configurations of utility/camp knives, bowies, modified spear points, daggers, tantos, recurves, clip points and spine serrations. **Technical:** Stock removal. Specializes in CPM S30V, CPM S35VN,

CPM D2, CPM 3V, stainless damascus. Micarta, G-10, stabilized wood and titanium. **Prices:** $200 - $1000, some pieces $1500 and up. **Remarks:** Full-time maker, first knife sold in 1994. **Mark:** Stamped "SIBERT" and occasionally uses electro-etch with oval around last name.

SIBRIAN, AARON
4308 Dean Dr, Ventura, CA 93003, Phone: 805-642-6950
Specialties: Tough working knives of his design and in standard patterns. **Patterns:** Makes a "Viper utility"—a kukri derivative and a variety of straight using knives. **Technical:** Grinds 440C and ATS-34. Offers traditional Japanese blades; soft backs, hard edges, temper lines. **Prices:** $60 to $100; some to $250. **Remarks:** Spare-time maker; first knife sold in 1989. **Mark:** Initials in diagonal line.

SIMMONS, H R
1100 Bay City Rd, Aurora, NC 27806, Phone: 252-916-2241
Specialties: Working/using straight knives of his design. **Patterns:** Fighters, hunters and utility/camp knives. **Technical:** Forges and grinds Damascus and L6; grinds ATS-34. **Prices:** $150 and up. **Remarks:** Part-time maker; first knife sold in 1987. Doing business as HRS Custom Knives, Royal Forge and Trading Company. **Mark:** HRS.

SIMONELLA, GIANLUIGI
Via Battiferri 33, Maniago, ITALY 33085, Phone: 01139-427-730350
Specialties: Traditional and classic folding and working/using knives of his design and to customer specs. **Patterns:** Bowies, fighters, hunters, utility/camp knives. **Technical:** Forges ATS-34, D2, 440C. **Prices:** $250 to $400; some to $1000. **Remarks:** Full-time maker; first knife sold in 1988. **Mark:** Wilson.

SINCLAIR, J E
520 Francis Rd, Pittsburgh, PA 15239, Phone: 412-793-5778
Specialties: Fancy hunters and fighters, liner locking folders. **Patterns:** Fighters, hunters and folders. **Technical:** Flat-grinds and hollow grind, prefers hand rubbed satin finish. Uses natural handle materials. **Prices:** $185 to $800. **Remarks:** Part-time maker; first knife sold in 1995. **Mark:** First and middle initials, last name and maker.

SINYARD, CLESTON S
27522 Burkhardt Dr, Elberta, AL 36530, Phone: 334-987-1361, nimoforge1@gulftel.com; Web: www.knifemakersguild
Specialties: Working straight knives and folders of his design. **Patterns:** Hunters, buckskinners, Bowies, daggers, fighters and all-Damascus folders. **Technical:** Makes Damascus from 440C, stainless steel, D2 and regular high-carbon steel; forges "forefinger pad" into hunters and skinners. **Prices:** In Damascus $450 to $1500; some $2500. **Remarks:** Full-time maker; first knife sold in 1980. Doing business as Nimo Forge. **Mark:** Last name, U.S.A. in anvil.

SIROIS, DARRIN
Tactical Combat Tools, 6182 Lake Trail Dr., Fayetteville, NC 28304, Phone: 910-730-0536, knives@tctknives.com; www.tctknives.com
Specialties: Tactical fighters, hunters and camp knives. **Technical:** Stock removal method of blade making, using D2 and 154CM steels. Entire process, including heat treat, done in-house. **Prices:** $80 to $750. **Remarks:** Part-time maker; first knife sold in 2008. **Mark:** Letters TCT surrounded by a triangle, or "Delta Tactical Combat Tools."

SISKA, JIM
48 South Maple St, Westfield, MA 01085, Phone: 413-642-3059, siskaknives@comcast.net
Specialties: Traditional working straight knives, no folders. **Patterns:** Hunters, fighters, Bowies and one-of-a-kinds; folders. **Technical:** Grinds D2, A2, 54CM and ATS-34; buys Damascus. Likes exotic woods. **Prices:** $300 and up. **Remarks:** Part-time. **Mark:** Siska in Old English.

SJOSTRAND, KEVIN
1541 S Cain St, Visalia, CA 93292, Phone: 559-625-5254
Specialties: Traditional and working/using straight knives and folders of his design or to customer specs. **Patterns:** Fixed blade hunters, Bowies, utility/camp knives. **Technical:** Grinds ATS-34, 440C and 1095. Prefers high polished blades and full tang. Natural and stabilized hardwoods, Micarta and stag handle material. **Prices:** $150 to $400. **Remarks:** Part-time maker; first knife sold in 1992. Doing business as Black Oak Blades. **Mark:** SJOSTRAND

SKIFF, STEVEN
SKIFF MADE BLADES, PO Box 537, Broadalbin, NY 12025, Phone: 518-883-4875, skiffmadeblades@hotmail.com; Web: www.skiffmadeblades.com
Specialties: Custom using/collector grade straight blades and LinerLock® folders of maker's design or customer specifications. **Patterns:** Hunters, utility/camp knives, tactical/fancy art folders. **Prices:** Straight blades $225 and up. Folders $450 and up. **Technical:** Stock removal hollow ground ATS-34, 154 CM, S30V, and tool steel. Damascus-Devon Thomas, Robert Eggerling, Mike Norris and Delbert Ealy. Nickel silver and stainless knives heat treating. Handle materials: man made and natural woods (stabilized). Horn shells sheaths for straight blades, sews own leather and uses sheaths by "Tree-Stump Leather." **Remarks:** First knife sold 1997. Started making folders in 2000. **Mark:** SKIFF on blade of straight blades and in inside of backspacer on folders.

SLEE, FRED
9 John St, Morganville, NJ 07751, Phone: 732-591-9047
Specialties: Working straight knives, some fancy, to customer specs. **Patterns:** Hunters, fighters, fancy daggers and folders. **Technical:** Grinds D2, 440C and ATS-34. **Prices:** $285 to $1100. **Remarks:** Part-time maker; first knife sold in 1980. **Mark:** Letter "S" in Old English.

SLOAN, DAVID
PO BOX 83, Diller, NE 68342, Phone: 402-793-5755, sigp22045@hotmail.com
Specialties: Hunters, choppers and fighters. **Technical:** Forged blades of W2, 1084 and Damascus. **Prices:** Start at $225. **Remarks:** Part-time maker, made first knife in 2002, received JS stamp 2010. **Mark:** Sloan JS.

SLOAN, SHANE
4226 FM 61, Newcastle, TX 76372, Phone: 940-846-3290
Specialties: Collector-grade straight knives and folders. **Patterns:** Uses stainless Damascus, ATS-34 and 12C27. Bowies, lockers, slip-joints, fancy folders, fighters and period pieces. **Technical:** Grinds D2 and ATS-34. Uses hand-rubbed satin finish. Prefers rare natural handle materials. **Prices:** $250 to $6500. **Remarks:** Full-time maker; first knife sold in 1985. **Mark:** Name and city.

SLOBODIAN, SCOTT
PO Box 1498, San Andreas, CA 95249, Phone: 209-286-1980, Fax: 209-286-1982, info@slobodianswords.com; Web: www.slobodianswords.com
Specialties: Japanese-style knives and swords, period pieces, fantasy pieces and miniatures. **Patterns:** Small kweikens, tantos, wakazashis, katanas, traditional samurai swords. **Technical:** Flat-grinds 1050, commercial Damascus. **Prices:** Prices start at $1500. **Remarks:** Full-time maker; first knife sold in 1987. **Mark:** Blade signed in Japanese characters and various scripts.

SMALE, CHARLES J
509 Grove Ave, Waukegan, IL 60085, Phone: 847-244-8013

SMALL, ED
Rt 1 Box 178-A, Keyser, WV 26726, Phone: 304-298-4254, coldanvil@gmail.com
Specialties: Working knives of his design; period pieces. **Patterns:** Hunters, daggers, buckskinners and camp knives; likes one-of-a-kinds, very primative bowies. **Technical:** Forges and grinds W2, L6 and his own Damascus. **Prices:** $150 to $1500. **Remarks:** Full-time maker; first knife sold in 1978. **Mark:** Script initials connected.

SMART, STEVE
907 Park Row Cir, McKinney, TX 75070-3847, Phone: 214-837-4216, Fax: 214-837-4111
Specialties: Working/using straight knives and folders of his design, to customer specs and in standard patterns. **Patterns:** Bowies, hunters, kitchen knives, locking folders, utility/camp, fishing and bird knives. **Technical:** Grinds ATS-34, D2, 440C and O1. Prefers mirror polish or satin finish; hollow-grinds all blades. All knives come with sheath. Offers some filework. **Prices:** $95 to $225; some to $500. **Remarks:** Spare-time maker; first knife sold in 1983. **Mark:** Name, Custom, city and state in oval.

SMIT, GLENN
627 Cindy Ct, Aberdeen, MD 21001, Phone: 410-272-2959, wolfsknives@comcast.net; Web: www.facebook.com/Wolf'sKnives
Specialties: Working and using straight and folding knives of his design or to customer specs. Customizes and repairs all types of cutlery. Exclusive maker of Dave Murphy Style knives. **Patterns:** Hunters, Bowies, daggers, fighters, utility/camp, folders, kitchen knives and miniatures, Murphy combat, C.H.A.I.K., Little 88 and Tiny 90-styles. **Technical:** Grinds 440C, ATS-34, O1, A2 also grinds 6AL4V titanium allox for blades. Reforges commercial Damascus and makes cast aluminum handles. **Prices:** Miniatures start at $50; full-size knives start at $100. **Remarks:** Spare-time maker; first knife sold in 1986. Doing business as Wolf's Knives. **Mark:** G.P. SMIT, with year on reverse side, Wolf's Knives-Murphy's way with date.

SMITH, J D
69 Highland, Roxbury, MA 02119, Phone: 617-989-0723, jdsmith02119@yahoo.com
Specialties: Fighters, Bowies, Persian, locking folders and swords. **Patterns:** Bowies, fighters and locking folders. **Technical:** Forges and grinds D2, his Damascus, O1, 52100 etc. and wootz-pattern hammer steel. **Prices:** $500 to $2000; some to $5000. **Remarks:** Full-time maker; first knife sold in 1987. Doing business as Hammersmith. **Mark:** Last initial alone or in cartouche.

SMITH, J.B.
21 Copeland Rd., Perkinston, MS 39573, Phone: 228-380-1851
Specialties: Traditional working knives for the hunter and fisherman. **Patterns:** Hunters, Bowies, and fishing knives; copies of 1800 period knives. **Technical:** Grinds ATS-34, 440C. **Prices:** $100 to $800. **Remarks:** Full-time maker, first knife sold in 1972. **Mark:** J.B. Smith MAKER PERKINSTON, MS.

SMITH, JERRY
JW Smith & Sons Custom Knives, 111 S Penn Ave, Oberlin, KS 67749, Phone: 785-475-2695, jerry@jwsmithandsons.com Web: www.jwsmithandsons.com
Specialties: Fixed blade and folding knives. **Technical:** Steels used D2, A2, O1, 154 CM, 154 CPM. Stock removal, heat treat in house, all leather work in house. **Prices:** $240. **Remarks:** Full-time knifemaker. First knife made in 2004. Slogan: "Cut Like You Mean It"

SMITH, JOHN M
3450 E Beguelin Rd, Centralia, IL 62801, Phone: 618-249-6444, jknife@frontiernet.net
Specialties: Folders. **Patterns:** Folders. **Prices:** $250 to $2500. **Remarks:** First knife sold in 1980. Not taking orders at this time on fixed blade knives. Part-time maker. **Mark:** Etched signature or logo.

SMITH, JOHN W
1322 Cow Branch Rd, West Liberty, KY 41472, Phone: 606-743-3599, jwsknive@mrtc.com; Web: www.jwsmithknives.com
Specialties: Fancy and working locking folders of his design or to customer specs. **Patterns:** Interframes, traditional and daggers. **Technical:** Grinds 530V and his own

Damascus. Offers gold inlay, engraving with gold inlay, hand-fitted mosaic pearl inlay and filework. Prefers hand-rubbed finish. Pearl and ivory available. **Prices:** Utility pieces $375 to $650. Art knives $1200 to $10,000. **Remarks:** Full-time maker. **Mark:** Initials engraved inside diamond.

SMITH, JOSH
Box 753, Frenchtown, MT 59834, Phone: 406-626-5775, joshsmithknives@gmail.com; Web: www.joshsmithknives.com
Specialties: Mosaic, Damascus, LinerLock folders, automatics, Bowies, fighters, etc. **Patterns:** All kinds. **Technical:** Advanced Mosaic and Damascus. **Prices:** $450 and up. **Remarks:** A.B.S. Master Smith. **Mark:** Josh Smith with last two digits of the current year.

SMITH, LACY
PO BOX 188, Jacksonville, AL 36265, Phone: 256-310-4619, sales@smith-knives.com; Web: www.smith-knives.com
Specialties: All styles of fixed-blade knives. **Technical:** Stock removal method of blade making. **Prices:** $100 and up. **Mark:** Circle with three dots and three S's on inside.

SMITH, LENARD C
PO Box D68, Valley Cottage, NY 10989, Phone: 914-268-7359

SMITH, MICHAEL J
1418 Saddle Gold Ct, Brandon, FL 33511, Phone: 813-431-3790, smithknife@hotmail.com; Web: www.smithknife.com
Specialties: Fancy high art folders of his design. **Patterns:** Locking locks and automatics. **Technical:** Uses ATS-34, non-stainless and stainless Damascus; hand carves folders, prefers ivory and pearl. Hand-rubbed satin finish. Liners are 6AL4V titanium. **Prices:** $500 to $3000. **Remarks:** Full-time maker; first knife sold in 1989. **Mark:** Name, city, state.

SMITH, NEWMAN L.
865 Glades Rd Shop #3, Gatlinburg, TN 37738, Phone: 423-436-3322, thesmithshop@aol.com; Web: www.thesmithsshop.com
Specialties: Collector-grade and working knives. **Patterns:** Hunters, slip-joint and lock-back folders, some miniatures. **Technical:** Grinds O1 and ATS-34; makes fancy sheaths. **Prices:** $165 to $750; some to $1000. **Remarks:** Full-time maker; first knife sold in 1984. Partners part-time to handle Damascus blades by Jeff Hurst; marks these with SH connected. **Mark:** First and middle initials, last name.

SMITH, RALPH L
525 Groce Meadow Rd, Taylors, SC 29687, Phone: 864-444-0819, ralph_smith1@charter.net; Web: www.smithhandcraftedknives.com
Specialties: Working knives: straight and folding knives. Hunters, skinners, fighters, bird, boot, Bowie and kitchen knives. **Technical:** Concave Grind D2, ATS 34, 440C, steel hand finish or polished. **Prices:** $125 to $350 for standard models. **Remarks:** First knife sold in 1976. KMG member since 1981. SCAK founding member and past president. **Mark:** SMITH handcrafted knives in SC state outline.

SMITH, RAYMOND L
217 Red Chalk Rd, Erin, NY 14838, Phone: 607-795-5257, Bladesmith@wildblue.net; Web: www.theanvilsedge.com
Specialties: Working/using straight knives and folders to customer specs and in standard patterns; period pieces. **Patterns:** Bowies, hunters, skip-joints. **Technical:** Forges 5160, 52100, 1018, 15N20, 1084, ATS 34. Damascus and wire cable Damascus. Filework. **Prices:** $125 to $1500; estimates for custom orders. **Remarks:** Full-time maker; first knife sold in 1991. ABS Master Smith. Doing business as The Anvils Edge. **Mark:** Ellipse with RL Smith, Erin NY MS in center.

SMITH, RICK
BEAR BONE KNIVES, 1843 W Evans Creek Rd., Rogue River, OR 97537, Phone: 541-582-4144, BearBoneSmith@msn.com; Web: www.bearbone.com
Specialties: Classic, historical style Bowie knives, hunting knives and various contemporary knife styles. **Technical:** Blades are either forged or made by stock removal method depending on steel used. Also forge weld wire Damascus. Does own heat treating and tempering using digital even heat kiln. Stainless blades are sent out for cryogenic "freeze treat." Preferred steels are O1, tool, 5160, 1095, 1084, ATS-34, 154CM, 440C and various high carbon Damascus. **Prices:** $350 to $1500. Custom leather sheaths available for knives. **Remarks:** Full-time maker since 1997. Serial numbers no longer put on knives. Official business name is "Bear Bone Knives." **Mark:** Early maker's mark was "Bear Bone" over capital letters "RS" with downward arrow between letters and "Hand Made" underneath letters. Mark on small knives is 3/8 circle containing "RS" with downward arrow between letters. Current mark since 2003 is "R Bear Bone Smith" arching over image of coffin Bowie knife with two shooting stars and "Rogue River, Oregon" underneath.

SMITH, SHAWN
2644 Gibson Ave, Clouis, CA 93611, Phone: 559-323-6234, kslc@sbcglobal.net
Specialties: Working and fancy straight knives. **Patterns:** Hunting, trout, fighters, skinners. **Technical:** Hollow grinds ATS-34, 154CM, A-2. **Prices:** $150.00 and up. **Remarks:** Part time maker. **Mark:** Shawn Smith handmade.

SMITH, STUART
Smith Hand Forged Knives, 32 Elbon Rd., Blairgowrie, Gauteng, SOUTH AFRICA 2123, Phone: +27 84 248 1324, samuraistu@forgedknives.co.za; Web: www.forgedknives.co.za
Specialties: Hand-forged bowie knives and puukos in high-carbon steel and maker's own damascus. **Patterns:** Bowies, puukos, daggers, hunters, fighters, skinners and swords. **Technical:** Forges 5160, 1070, 52100 and SilverSteel, and maker's own damascus from 5160 and Bohler K600 nickel tool steel. Fitted guards and threaded pommels. Own heat

treating. Wood and bronze carving. Own sheaths and custom sheaths. **Prices:** $150 to $1,500. **Remarks:** Full-time maker since 2004; first knife sold in 2000. **Mark:** Stamped outline of an anvil with SMITH underneath on right side of knife. For 2014, anvil and surname with 10Yrs.

SMOCK, TIMOTHY E
1105 N Sherwood Dr, Marion, IN 46952, Phone: 765-664-0123

SNODY, MIKE
910 W. Young Ave., Aransas Pass, TX 78336, Phone: 361-443-0161, snodyknives@yahoo.com; Web: www.snodygallery.com
Specialties: High performance straight knives in traditional and Japanese-styles. **Patterns:** Skinners, hunters, tactical, Kwaiken and tantos. **Technical:** Grinds BG42, ATS-34, 440C and A2. Offers full or tapered tangs, upgraded handle materials such as fossil ivory, coral and exotic woods. Traditional diamond wrap over stingray on Japanese-style knives. Sheaths available in leather or Kydex. **Prices:** $100 to $1000. **Remarks:** Part-time maker; first knife sold in 1999. **Mark:** Name over knife maker.

SNOW, BILL
4824 18th Ave, Columbus, GA 31904, Phone: 706-576-4390, tipikw@knology.net
Specialties: Traditional working/using straight knives and folders of his design and to customer specs. Offers engraving and scrimshaw. **Patterns:** Bowies, fighters, hunters and folders. **Technical:** Grinds ATS-34, 440V, 440C, 420V, CPM350, BG42, A2, D2, 5160, 52100 and O1; forges if needed. Cryogenically quenches all steels; inlaid handles; some integrals; leather or Kydex sheaths. **Prices:** $125 to $700; some to $3500. **Remarks:** Now also have 530V, 10V and 3V steels in use. Full-time maker; first knife sold in 1958. Doing business as Tipi Knife works. **Mark:** Old English scroll "S" inside a tipi.

SOAPER, MAX H.
2375 Zion Rd, Henderson, KY 42420, Phone: 270-827-8143
Specialties: Primitive Longhunter knives, scalpers, camp knives, cowboy Bowies, neck knives, working knives, period pieces from the 18th century. **Technical:** Forges 5160, 1084, 1095; all blades differentially heat treated. **Prices:** $80 to $800. **Remarks:** Part-time maker since 1989. **Mark:** Initials in script.

SONNTAG, DOUGLAS W
902 N 39th St, Nixa, MO 65714, Phone: 417-693-1640, dougsonntag@gmail.com
Specialties: Working knives; art knives. **Patterns:** Hunters, boots, straight working knives; Bowies, some folders, camp/axe sets. **Technical:** Grinds D2, ATS-34, forges own Damascus; does own heat treating. **Prices:** $225 and up. **Remarks:** Full-time maker; first knife sold in 1986. **Mark:** Etched name in arch.

SONNTAG, JACOB D
14148 Trisha Dr., St. Robert, MO 65584, Phone: 573-336-4082, Jake0372@live.com
Specialties: Working knives; some art knives. **Patterns:** Hunters, bowies, and tomahawks. **Technical:** Grinds D2, ATS34 and Damascus. Forges some Damascus and tomahawks; does own heat treating. **Prices:** $200 and up. **Remarks:** Part-time maker; first knife sold in 2010. **Mark:** Etched name or stamped

SONNTAG, KRISTOPHER D
902 N 39th St, Nixa, MO 65714, Phone: 417-838-8327, kriss@buildit.us
Specialties: Working fixed blades, hunters, skinners, using knives. **Patterns:** Hunters, bowies, skinners. **Technical:** Grinds D2, ATS 34, Damascus. Makes some Damascus; does own heat treating. **Prices:** $200 and up. **Remarks:** Part-time maker; first knife sold in 2010. **Mark:** Etched name or stamped

SONTHEIMER, G DOUGLAS
12604 Bridgeton Dr, Potomac, MD 20854, Phone: 301-948-5227
Specialties: Fixed blade knives. **Patterns:** Whitetail deer, backpackers, camp, claws, fillet, fighters. **Technical:** Hollow Grinds. **Price:** $500 and up. **Remarks:** Spare-time maker; first knife sold in 1976. **Mark:** LORD.

SOPPERA, ARTHUR
Pilatusblick, Oberer Schmidberg, Ulisbach, SWITZERLAND 9631, Phone: 71-988 23 27, Fax: 71-988 47 57, doublelock@hotmail.com; Web: www.sopperaknifeart.ch
Specialties: High-art, high-tech knives of his design. **Patterns:** Locking folders, and fixed blade knives. **Technical:** Grinds ATS-34 and commercial Damascus. Folders have button lock of his own design; some are fancy folders in jeweler's fashion. Also makes jewelry with integrated small knives. **Prices:** $300 to $1500, some $2500 and higher. **Remarks:** Full-time maker; first knife sold in 1986. **Mark:** Stylized initials, name, country.

SORNBERGER, JIM
25126 Overland Dr, Volcano, CA 95689, Phone: 209-295-7819, sierrajs@volcano.net
Specialties: Classic San Francisco-style knives. Collectible straight knives. **Patterns:** Fighters, daggers, bowies, miniatures, hunters, custom canes and LinerLock folders. **Technical:** Grinds 440C, 154CM and ATS-34; engraves, carves and embellishes. **Prices:** $500 to $35,000 in gold with gold quartz inlays. **Remarks:** Full-time maker; first knife sold in 1970. **Mark:** First initial, last name, city and state.

SOWELL, BILL
100 Loraine Forest Ct, Macon, GA 31210, Phone: 478- 994-9863, billsowell@reynoldscable.net
Specialties: Antique reproduction Bowies, forging Bowies, hunters, fighters, and most others. Also folders. **Technical:** Makes own Damascus, using 1084/15N20, also makes own designs in powder metals, forges 5160-1095-1084, and other carbon steels, grinds ATS-34. **Prices:** Starting at $150 and up. **Remarks:** Part-time maker. Sold first knife in 1998. Does own leather work. ABS Master Smith. **Mark:** Iron Horse Forge - Sowell - MS.

SPARKS, BERNARD
PO Box 73, Dingle, ID 83233, Phone: 208-847-1883, dogknifeii@juno.com; Web:

www.sparksknives.com

Specialties: Maker engraved, working and art knives. Straight knives and folders of his own design. **Patterns:** Locking inner-frame folders, hunters, fighters, one-of-a-kind art knives. **Technical:** Grinds 530V steel, 440-C, 154CM, ATS-34, D-2 and forges by special order; triple temper, cryogenic soak. Mirror or hand finish. New Liquid metal steel. **Prices:** $300 to $2000. **Remarks:** Full-time maker, first knife sold in 1967. **Mark:** Last name over state with a knife logo on each end of name. Prior 1980, stamp of last name.

SPICKLER, GREGORY NOBLE
5614 Mose Cir, Sharpsburg, MD 21782, Phone: 301-432-2746

SPINALE, RICHARD
4021 Canterbury Ct, Lorain, OH 44053, Phone: 440-282-1565
Specialties: High-art working knives of his design. **Patterns:** Hunters, fighters, daggers and locking folders. **Technical:** Grinds 440C, ATS-34 and 07; engraves. Offers gold bolsters and other deluxe treatments. **Prices:** $300 to $1000; some to $3000. **Remarks:** Spare-time maker; first knife sold in 1976. **Mark:** Name, address, year and model number.

SPIVEY, JEFFERSON
9244 W Wilshire, Yukon, OK 73099, Phone: 405-371-9304, jspivey5@cox.net
Specialties: The Saber tooth: a combination hatchet, saw and knife. **Patterns:** Built for the wilderness, all are one-of-a-kind. **Technical:** Grinds chromemoly steel. The saw tooth spine curves with a double row of biangular teeth. **Prices:** Start at $275. **Remarks:** First knife sold in 1977. As of September 2006 Spivey knives has resumed production of the Sabertooth knife (one word trademark).**Mark:** Name and serial number.

SPRAGG, WAYNE E
252 Oregon Ave, Lovell, WY 82431, Phone: 307-548-7212
Specialties: Working straight knives, some fancy. **Patterns:** Folders. **Technical:** Forges carbon steel and makes Damascus. **Prices:** $200 and up. **Remarks:** All stainless heat-treated by Paul Bos. Carbon steel in shop heat treat. **Mark:** Last name front side w/s initials on reverse side.

SPROKHOLT, ROB
Burgerweg 5, Gatherwood, NETHERLANDS 1754 KB Burgerbrug, Phone: 0031 6 51230225, Fax: 0031 84 2238446, info@gatherwood.nl; Web: www.gatherwood.nl
Specialties: One-of-a-kind knives. Top materials collector grade, made to use. **Patterns:** Outdoor knives (hunting, sailing, hiking), Bowies, man's surviving companions MSC, big tantos, folding knives. **Technical:** Handles mostly stabilized or oiled wood, ivory, Micarta, carbon fibre, G10. Stiff knives are full tang. Characteristic one row of massive silver pins or tubes. Folding knives have a LinerLock® with titanium or Damascus powdersteel liner thumb can have any stone you like. Stock removal grinder: flat or convex. Steel 440-C, RWL-34, ATS-34, PM damascener steel. **Prices:** Start at 320 euro. **Remarks:** Writer of the first Dutch knifemaking book, supply shop for knife enthusiastic. First knife sold in 2000. **Mark:** Gatherwood in an eclipse etched blade or stamped in an intarsia of silver in the spine.

SQUIRE, JACK
350 W. 7th St., McMinnville, OR 97182-5509, Phone: 503-472-7290

ST. CLAIR, THOMAS K
12608 Fingerboard Rd, Monrovia, MD 21770, Phone: 301-482-0264

STAFFORD, RICHARD
104 Marcia Ct, Warner Robins, GA 31088, Phone: 912-923-6372, Fax: Cell: 478-508-5821, rnrstafford@cox.net
Specialties: High-tech straight knives and some folders. **Patterns:** Hunters in several patterns, fighters, boots, camp knives, combat knives and period pieces. **Technical:** Grinds ATS-34 and 440C. Machine satin finish offered. **Prices:** Starting at $150. **Remarks:** Part-time maker; first knife sold in 1983. **Mark:** R. W. STAFFORD GEORGIA.

STAINTHORP, GUY
4 Fisher St, Brindley Ford, Stroke-on-Trent, ENGLAND ST8 7QJ, Phone: 07946 469 888, guystainthorp@hotmail.com Web: http://stainthorpknives.co.uk/index.html
Specialties: Tactical and outdoors knives to his own design. **Patterns:** Hunting, survival and occasionally folding knives. **Technical:** Grinds RWL-34, O1, S30V, Damasteel. Micarta, G10 and stabilised wood/bone for handles. **Prices:** $200 - $1000. **Remarks:** Full-time knifemaker. **Mark:** Squared stylised GS over "Stainthorp".

STALCUP, EDDIE
PO Box 2200, Gallup, NM 87305, Phone: 505-863-3107, sharon.stalcup@gmail.com
Specialties: Working and fancy hunters, bird and trout. Special custom orders. **Patterns:** Drop point hunters, locking liner and multi blade folders. **Technical:** ATS-34, 154 CM, 440C and CPM 154 and S30V. **Prices:** $150 to $1500. **Remarks:** Scrimshaw, exotic handle material, wet formed sheaths. Membership Arizona Knife Collectors Association. Southern California blades collectors & professional knife makers assoc. **Mark:** E.F. Stalcup, Gallup, NM.

STANCER, CHUCK
62 Hidden Ranch Rd NW, Calgary, AB, CANADA T3A 5S5, Phone: 403-295-7370, stancerc@telusplanet.net
Specialties: Traditional and working straight knives. **Patterns:** Bowies, hunters and utility knives. **Technical:** Forges and grinds most steels. **Prices:** $175 and up. **Remarks:** Part-time maker. **Mark:** Last name.

STANFORD, PERRY
405N Walnut #9, Broken Arrow, OK 74012, Phone: 918-251-7983 or 866-305-5690, stanfordoutdoors@valornet.com; Web: www.stanfordoutdoors.homestead.com
Specialties: Drop point, hunting and skinning knives, handmade sheaths. **Patterns:** Stright, hunting, and skinners. **Technical:** Grinds 440C, ATS-34 and Damascus. **Prices:**

$65 to $275. **Remarks:** Part-time maker, first knife sold in 2007. Knifemaker supplier, manufacturer of paper sharpening systems. Doing business as Stanford Outdoors. **Mark:** Company name and nickname.

STANLEY, JOHN
604 Elm St, Crossett, AR 71635, Phone: 970-304-3005
Specialties: Hand forged fixed blades with engraving and carving. **Patterns:** Scottish dirks, skeans and fantasy blades. **Technical:** Forge high-carbon steel, own Damascus. **Prices** $70 to $500. **Remarks:** All work is sole authorship. Offers engraving and carving services on other knives and handles. **Mark:** Varies.

STAPEL, CHUCK
Box 1617, Glendale, CA 91209, Phone: 213-705-6433, www.stapelknives.com
Specialties: Working knives of his design. **Patterns:** Variety of straight knives, tantos, hunters, folders and utility knives. **Technical:** Grinds D2, 440C and AEB-L. **Prices:** $185 to $12,000. **Remarks:** Full-time maker; first knife sold in 1974. **Mark:** Last name or last name, U.S.A.

STAPLETON, WILLIAM E
BUFFALO 'B' FORGE, 5425 Country Ln, Merritt Island, FL 32953
Specialties: Classic and traditional knives of his design and customer spec. **Patterns:** Hunters and using knives. **Technical:** Forges, O1 and L6 Damascus, cable Damascus and 5160; stock removal on request. **Prices:** $150 to $1000. **Remarks:** Part-time maker, first knife sold 1990. Doing business as Buffalo "B" Forge. **Mark:** Anvil with S initial in center of anvil.

STATES, JOSHUA C
43905 N 16th St, New River, AZ 85087, Phone: 623-826-3809, Web: www.dosgatosforge.com
Specialties: Design and fabrication of forged working and art knives from O1 and my own damascus. Stock removal from 440C and CM154 upon request. Folders from 440C, CM154 and Damascus. Flat and Hollow grinds. Knives made to customer specs and/or design.**Patterns:** Bowies, hunters, daggers, chef knives, and exotic shapes. **Technical:** Damascus is 1095, 1084, O1 and 15N20. Carved or file-worked fittings from various metals including my own mokume gane and Damascus.**Prices:** $150 to $1500. **Remarks:** Part-time maker with waiting list. First knife sold in 2006. **Mark:** Initials JCS inside small oval, or Dos Gatos Forge. Unmarked knives come with certificate of authorship.

STECK, VAN R
260 W Dogwood Ave, Orange City, FL 32763, Phone: 407-416-1723, van@thudknives.com
Specialties: Specializing in double-edged grinds. Free-hand grinds: folders, spears, bowies, swords and miniatures. **Patterns:** Tomahawks with a crane for the spike, tactical merged with nature.**Technical:** Hamon lines, folder lock of own design, the arm-lock! **Prices:** $50 - $1500. **Remarks:** Builds knives designed by Laci Szabo or builds to customer design. Studied with Reese Weiland on folders and automatics. **Mark:** GEISHA holding a sword with initials and THUD KNIVES in a circle.

STEGALL, KEITH
701 Outlet View Dr, Wasilla, AK 99654, Phone: 907-376-0703, kas5200@yahoo.com
Specialties: Traditional working straight knives. **Patterns:** Most patterns. **Technical:** Grinds 440C and 154CM. **Prices:** $100 to $300. **Remarks:** Spare-time maker; first knife sold in 1987. **Mark:** Name and state with anchor.

STEGNER, WILBUR G
9242 173rd Ave SW, Rochester, WA 98579, Phone: 360-273-0937, wilbur@wgsk.net; Web: www.wgsk.net
Specialties: Working/using straight knives and folders of his design. **Patterns:** Hunters and locking folders. **Technical:** Makes his own Damascus steel. **Prices:** $100 to $1000; some to $5000. **Remarks:** Full-time maker; first knife sold in 1979. Google search key words-"STEGNER KNIVES." Best folder awards NWKC 2009, 2010 and 2011. **Mark:** First and middle initials, last name in bar over shield logo.

STEIER, DAVID
7722 Zenith Way, Louisville, KY 40219, Phone: 502-969-8409, umag300@aol.com; Web: www.steierknives.com
Specialties: Folding LinerLocks, Bowies, slip joints, lockbacks, and straight hunters. **Technical:** Stock removal blades of 440C, ATS-34, and Damascus from outside sources like Robert Eggerling and Mike Norris. **Prices:** $150 for straight hunters to $1400 for fully decked-out folders. **Remarks:** First knife sold in 1979. **Mark:** Last name STEIER.

STEIGER, MONTE L
Box 186, Genesee, ID 83832, Phone: 208-285-1769, montesharon@genesee-id.com
Specialties: Traditional working/using straight knives of all designs. **Patterns:** Hunters, utility/camp knives, fillet and chefs. Carving sets and steak knives. **Technical:** Grinds 1095, O1, 440C, ATS-34. Handles of stacked leather, natural wood, Micarta or pakkawood. Each knife comes with right- or left-handed sheath. **Prices:** $110 to $600. **Remarks:** Spare-time maker; first knife sold in 1988. Retired librarian **Mark:** First initial, last name, city and state.

STEIGERWALT, KEN
507 Savagehill Rd, Orangeville, PA 17859, Phone: 570-683-5156, Web: www.steigerwaltknives.com
Specialties: Carving on bolsters and handle material. **Patterns:** Folders, button locks and rear locks. **Technical:** Grinds ATS-34, 440C and commercial Damascus. Experiments with unique filework. **Prices:** $500 to $5000. **Remarks:** Full-time maker; first knife sold in 1981. **Mark:** Kasteigerwalt

STEINAU, JURGEN
Julius-Hart Strasse 44, Berlin, GERMANY 01162, Phone: 372-6452512, Fax: 372-645-2512
Specialties: Fantasy and high-art straight knives of his design. **Patterns:** Boots, daggers and switch-blade folders. **Technical:** Grinds 440B, 2379 and X90 Cr.Mo.V. 78. **Prices:** $1500 to $2500; some to $3500. **Remarks:** Full-time maker; first knife sold in 1984. **Mark:** Symbol, plus year, month day and serial number.

STEINBERG, AL
5244 Duenas, Laguna Woods, CA 92653, Phone: 949-951-2889, lagknife@fea.net
Specialties: Fancy working straight knives to customer specs. **Patterns:** Hunters, Bowies, fishing, camp knives, push knives and high end kitchen knives. **Technical:** Grinds O1, 440C and 154CM. **Prices:** $60 to $2500. **Remarks:** Full-time maker; first knife sold in 1972. **Mark:** Signature, city and state.

STEINBRECHER, MARK W
1122 92nd Place, Pleasant Prairie, WI 53158-4939
Specialties: Working and fancy folders. **Patterns:** Daggers, pocket knives, fighters and gents of his own design or to customer specs. **Technical:** Hollow grinds ATS-34, O1 other makers Damascus. Uses natural handle materials: stag, ivories, mother-of-pearl. File work and some inlays. **Prices:** $500 to $1200, some to $2500. **Remarks:** Part-time maker, first folder sold in 1989. **Mark:** Name etched or handwritten on ATS-34; stamped on Damascus.

STEINGASS, T.K.
194 Mesquite Lane, Hedgesville, WV 25427, Phone: 304-268-1161, tksteingass@frontier.com; Web: http://steingassknives.com
Specialties: Loveless style hunters and fighters and sole authorship knives: Man Knife, Silent Hunter, and Silent Fighter. Harpoon Grind Camp Knife and Harpoon Grind Man Hunter. **Technical:** Stock removal, use CPM 154, S3V and occasionally 1095 or O1 for camp choppers. **Prices:** $200 to $500. **Remarks:** Part-time maker; first knife made in 2010. **Mark:** STEINGASS.

STEKETEE, CRAIG A
871 NE US Hwy 60, Billings, MO 65610, Phone: 417-744-2770, stekknives04@yahoo.com
Specialties: Classic and working straight knives and swords of his design. **Patterns:** Bowies, hunters, and Japanese-style swords. **Technical:** Forges his own Damascus; bronze, silver and Damascus fittings, offers filework. Prefers exotic and natural handle materials. **Prices:** $200 to $4000. **Remarks:** Full-time maker. **Mark:** STEK.

STEPHAN, DANIEL
2201 S Miller Rd, Valrico, FL 33594, Phone: 727-580-8617, knifemaker@verizon.net
Specialties: Art knives, one-of-a-kind.

STERLING, MURRAY
693 Round Peak Church Rd, Mount Airy, NC 27030, Phone: 336-352-5110, Fax: Fax: 336-352-5105, sterck@surry.net; Web: www.sterlingcustomknives.com
Specialties: Single and dual blade folders. Interframes and integral dovetail frames. **Technical:** Grinds ATS-34 or Damascus by Mike Norris and/or Devin Thomas. **Prices:** $300 and up. **Remarks:** Full-time maker; first knife sold in 1991. **Mark:** Last name stamped.

STERLING, THOMAS J
ART KNIVES BY, 120 N Pheasant Run, Coupeville, WA 98239, Phone: 360-678-9269, Fax: 360-678-9269, netsuke@comcast.net; Web: www.bladegallery.com Or www.sterlingsculptures.com
Specialties: Since 2003 Tom Sterling and Dr. J.P. Higgins have created a unique collaboration of one-of-a-kind, ultra-quality art knives with percussion or pressured flaked stone blades and creatively sculpted handles. Their knives are often highly influenced by the traditions of Japanese netsuke and unique fusions of cultures, reflecting stylistically integrated choices of exotic hardwoods, fossil ivories and semi-precious materials, contrasting inlays and polychromed and pyrographed details. **Prices:** $300 to $900. **Remarks:** Limited output ensures highest quality artwork and exceptional levels of craftsmanship. **Mark:** Signatures Sterling and Higgins.

STETTER, J. C.
115 E College Blvd PMB 180, Roswell, NM 88201, Phone: 505-627-0978
Specialties: Fixed and folding. **Patterns:** Traditional and yours. **Technical:** Forged and ground of varied materials including his own pattern welded steel. **Prices:** Start at $250. **Remarks:** Full-time maker, first knife sold 1989. **Mark:** Currently "J.C. Stetter."

STEWART, EDWARD L
4297 Audrain Rd 335, Mexico, MO 65265, Phone: 573-581-3883
Specialties: Fixed blades, working knives some art. **Patterns:** Hunters, Bowies, utility/camp knives. **Technical:** Forging 1095-W-2-l-6-52100 makes own Damascus. **Prices:** $85 to $500. **Remarks:** Part-time maker first knife sold in 1993. **Mark:** First and last initials-last name.

STEYN, PETER
PO Box 76, Welkom, Freestate, SOUTH AFRICA 9460, Phone: 27573522015, Fax: 27573523566, Web:www.petersteynknives.com email:info@petersteynknives.com
Specialties: Fixed blade knives of own design, all with hand-stitched leather sheaths. Folding knives of own design supplied with soft pouches. **Patterns:**Fixed blades: hunters and skinners. Folding knives: friction folders, slip joints and lockbacks. **Technical:**Grinds 12C27 and Damasteel. Blades are bead-blasted in plain or patterned finish. Ceramic wash also available in satin or antiqued finish. Grind syle is convex, concave on the obverse, and convex on the reverse. Works with a wide variety of handle materials, prefers exotic woods and synthetics. **Prices:** $150 to $650. **Remarks:**Full-time maker, first knife sold 2005, member of South African Guild. **Mark:** Letter 'S' in shape of pyramid with full name above and 'Handcrafted' below.

STICE, DOUGLAS W
PO Box 12815, Wichita, KS 67277, Phone: 316-295-6855, doug@sticecraft.com; Web: www.sticecraft.com
Specialties: Working fixed blade knives of own design. **Patterns:** Tacticals, hunters, skinners,utility, and camp knives. **Technical:** Grinds CPM154CM, 154CM, CPM3V, Damascus; uses 18" contact grinds where wheel for hollow grinds, also flat. **Prices:** $100 to $750. **Remarks:** Full-time maker; first professional knife made in 2009. All knives have serial numbers and include certificate of authenticity. **Mark:** Stylized "Stice" stamp.

STIDHAM, DANIEL
3106 Mill Cr. Rd., Gallipolis, Ohio 45631, Phone: 740-446-1673, danstidham@yahoo.com
Specialties: Fixed blades, folders, Bowies and hunters. **Technical:**440C, Alabama Damascus, 1095 with filework. **Prices:** Start at $150. **Remarks:** Has made fixed blades since 1961, folders since 1986. Also sells various knife brands.**Mark:** Stidham Knives Gallipolis, Ohio 45631.

STIMPS, JASON M
374 S Shaffer St, Orange, CA 92866, Phone: 714-744-5866

STIPES, DWIGHT
2651 SW Buena Vista Dr, Palm City, FL 34990, Phone: 772-597-0550, dwightstipes@adelphia.net
Specialties: Traditional and working straight knives in standard patterns. **Patterns:** Boots, Bowies, daggers, hunters and fighters. **Technical:** Grinds 440C, D2 and D3 tool steel. Handles of natural materials, animal, bone or horn. **Prices:** $75 to $150. **Remarks:** Full-time maker; first knife sold in 1972. **Mark:** Stipes.

STOKES, ED
22614 Cardinal Dr, Hockley, TX 77447, Phone: 713-351-1319
Specialties: Working straight knives and folders of all designs. **Patterns:** Boots, Bowies, daggers, fighters, hunters and miniatures. **Technical:** Grinds ATS-34, 440C and D2. Offers decorative butt caps, tapered spacers on handles and finger grooves, nickel-silver inlays, handmade sheaths. **Prices:** $185 to $290; some to $350. **Remarks:** Full-time maker; first knife sold in 1973. **Mark:** First and last name, Custom Knives with Apache logo.

STONE, JERRY
PO Box 1027, Lytle, TX 78052, Phone: 830-709-3042
Specialties: Traditional working and using folders of his design and to customer specs; fancy knives. **Patterns:** Fighters, hunters, locking folders and slip joints. Also make automatics. **Technical:** Grinds 440C and ATS-34. Offers filework. **Prices:** $175 to $1000. **Remarks:** Full-time maker; first knife sold in 1973. **Mark:** Name over Texas star/town and state underneath.

STORCH, ED
RR 4, Mannville, AB, CANADA T0B 2W0, Phone: 780-763-2214, storchkn@telus.net; Web: www.storchknives.com
Specialties: Working knives, fancy fighting knives, kitchen cutlery and art knives. Knifemaking classes. **Patterns:** Working patterns, Bowies and folders. **Technical:** Forges his own Damascus. Grinds ATS-34. Builds friction folders. Salt heat treating. **Prices:** $100 to $500 (U.S.). **Remarks:** Full-time maker; first knife sold in 1984. **Mark:** Last name.

STORMER, BOB
34354 Hwy E, Dixon, MO 65459, Phone: 636-734-2693, bs34354@gmail.com
Specialties: Straight knives, using collector grade. **Patterns:** Bowies, skinners, hunters, camp knives. **Technical:** Forges 5160, 1095. **Prices:** $200 to $500. **Remarks:** Part-time maker, ABS Journeyman Smith 2001. **Mark:** Setting sun/fall trees/initials.

STOUT, CHARLES
RT3 178 Stout Rd, Gillham, AR 71841, Phone: 870-386-5521

STOUT, JOHNNY
1205 Forest Trail, New Braunfels, TX 78132, Phone: 830-606-4067, johnny@stoutknives.com; Web: www.stoutknives.com
Specialties: Folders, some fixed blades. Working knives, some fancy. **Patterns:** Hunters, tactical, Bowies, automatics, liner locks and slip-joints. **Technical:** Grinds stainless and carbon steels; forges own Damascus. **Prices:** $450 to $895; some to $3500. **Remarks:** Full-time maker; first knife sold in 1983. Hosts semi-annual Guadalupe Forge Hammer-in and Knifemakers Rendezvous. **Mark:** Name and city in logo with serial number.

STRAIGHT, KENNETH J
11311 103 Lane N, Largo, FL 33773, Phone: 813-397-9817

STRANDE, POUL
Soster Svenstrup Byvej 16, Viby Sj., Dastrup, DENMARK 4130, Phone: 46 19 43 05, Fax: 46 19 53 19, Web: www.poulstrande.com
Specialties: Classic fantasy working knives; Damasceret blade, Nikkel Damasceret blade, Lamineret: Lamineret blade with Nikkel. **Patterns:** Bowies, daggers, fighters, hunters and swords. **Technical:** Uses carbon steel and 15C20 steel. **Prices:** NA. **Remarks:** Full-time maker; first knife sold in 1985. **Mark:** First and last initials.

STRAUB, SALEM F.
324 Cobey Creek Rd., Tonasket, WA 98855, Phone: 509-486-2627, vorpalforge@hotmail.com Web: www.prometheanknives.com
Specialties: Elegant working knives, fixed blade hunters, utility, skinning knives; liner

locks. Makes own horsehide sheaths. **Patterns:** A wide range of syles, everything from the gentleman's pocket to the working kitchen, integrals, Bowies, folders, check out my website to see some of my work for ideas. **Technical:** Forges several carbon steels, 52100, W1, etc. Grinds stainless and makes/uses own damascus, cable, san mai, stadard patterns. Likes clay quenching, hamons, hand rubbed finishes. Flat, hollow, or convex grinds. Prefers synthetic handle materials. Hidden and full tapered tangs. **Prices:** $150 - $600, some higher. **Remarks:** Full-time maker. Doing what it takes to make your knife ordering and buying experience positive and enjoyable; striving to exceed expectations. All knives backed by lifetime guarantee. **Mark:** "Straub" stamp or "Promethean Knives" etched. Some older pieces stamped "Vorpal" though no longer using this mark. **Other:** Feel free to call or e-mail anytime. I love to talk knives.

STRICKLAND, DALE
1440 E Thompson View, Monroe, UT 84754, Phone: 435-896-8362
Specialties: Traditional and working straight knives and folders of his design and to customer specs. **Patterns:** Hunters, folders, miniatures and utility knives. **Technical:** Grinds Damascus and 440C. **Prices:** $120 to $350; some to $500. **Remarks:** Part-time maker; first knife sold in 1991. **Mark:** Oval stamp of name, Maker.

STRIDER, MICK
STRIDER KNIVES, 120 N Pacific Unit L-7, San Marcos, CA 92069, Phone: 760-471-8275, Fax: 503-218-7069, striderguys@striderknives.com; Web: www.striderknives.com

STRONG, SCOTT
1599 Beaver Valley Rd, Beavercreek, OH 45434, Phone: 937-426-9290
Specialties: Working knives, some deluxe. **Patterns:** Hunters, fighters, survival and military-style knives, art knives. **Technical:** Forges and grinds O1, A2, D2, 440C and ATS-34. Uses no solder; most knives disassemble. **Prices:** $75 to $450; some to $1500. **Remarks:** Spare-time maker; first knife sold in 1983. **Mark:** Strong Knives.

STROYAN, ERIC
Box 218, Dalton, PA 18414, Phone: 717-563-2603
Specialties: Classic and working/using straight knives and folders of his design. **Patterns:** Hunters, locking folders, slip-joints. **Technical:** Forges Damascus; grinds ATS-34, D2. **Prices:** $200 to $600; some to $2000. **Remarks:** Part-time maker; first knife sold in 1968. **Mark:** Signature or initials stamp.

STUART, MASON
24 Beech Street, Mansfield, MA 02048, Phone: 508-339-8236, smasonknives@verizon.net Web: smasonknives.com
Specialties: Straight knives of his design, standard patterns. **Patterns:** Bowies, hunters, fighters and neck knives. **Technical:** Forges and grinds. Damascus, 5160, 1095, 1084, old files. Uses only natural handle material. **Prices:** $350 - 2,000. **Remarks:** Part-time maker. **Mark:** First initial and last name.

STUART, STEVE
Box 168, Gores Landing, ON, CANADA K0K 2E0, Phone: 905-440-6910, stevestuart@xplornet.com
Specialties: Straight knives. **Patterns:** Tantos, fighters, skinners, file and rasp knives. **Technical:** Uses 440C, CPM154, CPMS30V, Micarta and natural handle materials. **Prices:** $60 to $400. **Remarks:** Part-time maker. **Mark:** SS.

STUCKY, DANIEL
37924 Shenandoah Loop, Springfield, OR 97478, Phone: 541-747-6496, stuckyj1@msn.com, www.stuckyknives.com
Specialties: Tactical, fancy and everyday carry folders, fixed-blade hunting knives, trout, bird and fillet knives. **Technical:** Stock removal maker. Steels include but are not limited to damascus, CPM 154, CPM S30V, CPM S35VN, 154CM and ATS-34. **Prices:** Start at $300 and can go to thousands, depending on materials used. **Remarks:** Full-time maker; first knife sold in 1999. **Mark:** Name over city and state.

STYREFORS, MATTIAS
Unbyn 23, Boden, SWEDEN 96193, infor@styrefors.com
Specialties: Damascus and mosaic Damascus. Fixed blade Nordic hunters, folders and swords. **Technical:** Forges, shapes and grinds Damascus and mosaic Damascus from mostly UHB 15N20 and 20C with contrasts in nickel and 15N20. Hardness HR 58. **Prices:** $800 to $3000. **Remarks:** Full-time maker since 1999. International reputation for high end Damascus blades. Uses stabilized Arctic birch and willow burl, horn, fossils, exotic materials and scrimshaw by Viveca Sahlin for knife handles. Hand tools and hand stitches leather sheaths in cow raw hide. Works in well equipped former military forgery in northern Sweden. **Mark:** MS.

SUEDMEIER, HARLAN
762 N 60th Rd, Nebraska City, NE 68410, Phone: 402-873-4372
Patterns: Straight knives. **Technical:** Forging hi carbon Damascus. **Prices:** Starting at $175. **Mark:** First initials & last name.

SUGIHARA, KEIDOH
4-16-1 Kamori-Cho, Kishiwada City, Osaka, JAPAN F596-0042, Fax: 0724-44-2677
Specialties: High-tech working straight knives and folders of his design. **Patterns:** Bowies, hunters, fighters, fishing, boots, some pocket knives and liner-lock folders. **Technical:** Grinds ATS-34, COS-25, buys Damascus and high-carbon steels. Prices $60 to $4000. **Remarks:** Full-time maker, first knife sold in 1980. **Mark:** Initial logo with fish design.

SUGIYAMA, EDDY K
2361 Nagayu, Naoirimachi Naoirigun, Oita, JAPAN, Phone: 0974-75-2050
Specialties: One-of-a-kind, exotic-style knives. **Patterns:** Working, utility and miniatures.

Technical: CT rind, ATS-34 and D2. **Prices:** $400 to $1200. **Remarks:** Full-time maker. **Mark:** Name or cedar mark.

SUMMERS, ARTHUR L
1310 Hess Rd, Concord, NC 28025, Phone: 704-787-9275 Cell: 704-305-0735, arthursummers88@hotmail.com
Specialties: Drop points, clip points, straight blades. **Patterns:** Hunters, Bowies and personal knives. **Technical:** Grinds ATS-34, CPM-D2, CPM-154 and damascus. **Prices:** $250 to $1000. **Remarks:** Full-time maker; first knife sold in 1988. **Mark:** Serial number is the date.

SUMMERS, DAN
2675 NY Rt. 11, Whitney Pt., NY 13862, Phone: 607-692-2391, dansumm11@msn.com
Specialties: Period knives and tomahawks. **Technical:** All hand forging. **Prices:** Most $100 to $400.

SUMMERS, DENNIS K
827 E. Cecil St, Springfield, OH 45503, Phone: 513-324-0624
Specialties: Working/using knives. **Patterns:** Fighters and personal knives. **Technical:** Grinds 440C, A2 and D2. Makes drop and clip point. **Prices:** $75 to $200. **Remarks:** Part-time maker; first knife sold in 1995. **Mark:** First and middle initials, last name, serial number.

SUNDERLAND, RICHARD
Av Infraganti 23, Col Lazaro Cardenas, Puerto Escondido, OA, MEXICO 71980, Phone: 011 52 94 582 1451, sunamerica@prodigy.net.mx7
Specialties: Personal and hunting knives with carved handles in oosic and ivory. **Patterns:** Hunters, Bowies, daggers, camp and personal knives. **Technical:** Grinds 440C, ATS-34 and O1. Handle materials of rosewoods, fossil mammoth ivory and oosic. **Prices:** $150 to $1000. **Remarks:** Part-time maker; first knife sold in 1983. Doing business as Sun Knife Co. **Mark:** SUN.

SUTTON, S RUSSELL
4900 Cypress Shores Dr, New Bern, NC 28562, Phone: 252-637-3963, srsutton@suddenlink.net; Web: www.suttoncustomknives.com
Specialties: Straight knives and folders to customer specs and in standard patterns. **Patterns:** Boots, hunters, interframes, slip joints and locking liners. **Technical:** Grinds ATS-34, 440C and stainless Damascus. **Prices:** $220 to $2000. **Remarks:** Full-time maker; first knife sold in 1992. Provides relief engraving on bolsters and guards. **Mark:** Etched last name.

SWEAZA, DENNIS
4052 Hwy 321 E, Austin, AR 72007, Phone: 501-941-1886, knives4den@aol.com

SWEENEY, COLTIN D
1216 S 3 St W, Missoula, MT 59801, Phone: 406-721-6782

SWENSON, LUKE
SWENSON KNIVES, 1667 Brushy Creek Dr., Lakehills, TX 78063, Phone: 210-722-3227, luke@swensonknives.com; Web: www.swensonknives.com
Specialties: Fixed blades for outdoor/survival or bushcraft use, some tactical and military patterns, and slip-joint folders. **Technical:** Stock-removal method of blade making. Flat grinds A2 tool steel for fixed blades, and hollow grinds CPM 154 for slip-joint folders. Credits Bill Ruple for mentoring him in the making slip joints. **Prices:** $275 to $600. **Remarks:** Part-time maker/full-time firefighter; first knife made in 2003. **Mark:** Name and city where maker lives.

SWYHART, ART
509 Main St, PO Box 267, Klickitat, WA 98628, Phone: 509-369-3451, swyhart@gorge.net; Web: www.knifeoutlet.com/swyhart.htm
Specialties: Traditional working and using knives of his design. **Patterns:** Bowies, hunters and utility/camp knives. **Technical:** Forges 52100, 5160 and Damascus 1084 mixed with either 15N20 or O186. Blades differentially heat-treated with visible temper line. **Prices:** $75 to $250; some to $350. **Remarks:** Part-time maker; first knife sold in 1983. **Mark:** First name, last initial in script.

SYLVESTER, DAVID
465 Sweede Rd., Compton, QC, CANADA, Phone: 819-837-0304, david@swedevilleforge.com Web: swedevilleforge.com
Patterns: I hand forge all my knives and I like to make hunters and integrals and some Bowies and fighters. I work with W2, 1084, 1095, and my damascus. **Prices:** $200 - $1500. **Remarks:** Part-time maker. ABS Journeyman Smith. **Mark:** D.Sylvester

SYMONDS, ALBERTO E
Rambla M Gandhi 485, Apt 901, Montevideo, URUGUAY 11300, Phone: 011 598 27103201, Fax: 011 598 2 7103201, albertosymonds@hotmail.com
Specialties: All kinds including puukos, nice sheaths, leather and wood. **Prices:** $300 to $2200. **Mark:** AESH and current year.

SYSLO, CHUCK
3418 South 116 Ave, Omaha, NE 68144, Phone: 402-333-0647, ciscoknives@cox.net
Specialties: Hunters, working knives, daggers & misc. **Patterns:** Hunters, daggers and survival knives; locking folders. **Technical:** Flat-grinds D2, 440C and 154CM; hand polishes only. **Prices:** $250 to $1000; some to $3000. **Remarks:** Part-time maker; first knife sold in 1978. Uses many natural materials. **Mark:** CISCO in logo.

SZCZERBIAK, MACIEJ
Crusader Forge Knives, PO Box 2181, St. George, UT 84771, Phone: 435-574-2193, crusaderforge@yahoo.com; Web: www.crusaderforge.com

Patterns: Drop-point, spear-point and tanto fixed blades and tactical folders. **Technical:** Stock removal using CPM-S30V and D2 steels. Knives designed with the technical operator in mind, and maintain an amazing balance in the user's hand. **Prices:** $300 to $2,500. **Remarks:** First knife made in 1999.

SZILASKI, JOSEPH
52 Woods Dr, Pine Plains, NY 12567, Phone: 518-398-0309, Web: www.szilaski.com
Specialties: Straight knives, folders and tomahawks of his design, to customer specs and in standard patterns. Many pieces are one-of-a-kind. **Patterns:** Bowies, daggers, fighters, hunters, art knives and early American-styles. **Technical:** Forges A2, D2, O1 and Damascus. **Prices:** $450 to $4000; some to $10,000. **Remarks:** Full-time maker; first knife sold in 1990. ABS Master Smith and voting member KMG. **Mark:** Snake logo.

T

TABER, DAVID E.
51 E. 4th St., Ste. 300, Winona, MN 55987, Phone: 507-450-1918, dtaber@qwestoffice.net
Specialties: Traditional slip joints, primarily using and working knives. **Technical:** Blades are hollow ground on a 20" wheel, ATS-34 and some damascus steel. **Remarks:** Full-time orthodontist, part-time maker; first knife made in January 2011. **Mark:** dr.t.

TABOR, TIM
18925 Crooked Lane, Lutz, FL 33548, Phone: 813-948-6141, taborknives.com
Specialties: Fancy folders, Damascus Bowies and hunters. **Patterns:** My own design folders & customer requests. **Technical:** ATS-34, hand forged Damascus, 1084, 15N20 mosaic Damascus, 1095, 5160 high carbon blades, flat grind, file work & jewel embellishments. **Prices:** $175 to $1500. **Remarks:** Part-time maker, sold first knife in 2003. **Mark:** Last name

TAKACH, ANDREW
1390 Fallen Timber Rd., Elizabeth, PA 15037, Phone: 724-691-2271, a-takach@takachforge.com; Web: www.takachforge.com
Specialties: One-of-a-kind fixed blade working knives (own design or customer's). Mostly all fileworked. **Patterns:** Hunters, skinners, caping, fighters, and designs of own style. **Technical:** Forges mostly 5160, 1090, 01, an down pattern welded Damascus, nickle Damascus, and cable and various chain Damascus. Also do some San Mai. **Prices:** $100 to $350, some over $550. **Remarks:** Doing business as Takach Forge. First knife sold in 2004. **Mark:** Takach (stamped).

TAKAHASHI, MASAO
39-3 Sekine-machi, Maebashi-shi, Gunma, JAPAN 371 0047, Phone: 81 27 234 2223, Fax: 81 27 234 2223
Specialties: Working straight knives. **Patterns:** Daggers, fighters, hunters, fishing knives, boots. **Technical:** Grinds ATS-34 and Damascus. **Prices:** $350 to $1000 and up. **Remarks:** Full-time maker; first knife sold in 1982. **Mark:** M. Takahashi.

TALLY, GRANT
26961 James Ave, Flat Rock, MI 48134, Phone: 313-414-1618
Specialties: Straight knives and folders of his design. **Patterns:** Bowies, daggers, fighters. **Technical:** Grinds ATS-34, 440C and D2. Offers filework. **Prices:** $250 to $1000. **Remarks:** Part-time maker; first knife sold in 1985. Doing business as Tally Knives. **Mark:** Tally (last name).

TAMATSU, KUNIHIKO
5344 Sukumo, Sukumo City, Kochi-ken, JAPAN 788-0000, Phone: 0880-63-3455, ktamatsu@mb.gallery.ne.jp; Web: www.knife.tamatu.net
Specialties: Loveless-style fighters, sub-hilt fighters and hunting knives. **Technical:** Mirror-finished ATS-34, BG-42 and CPM-S30V blades. **Prices:** $400 to $2,500. **Remarks:** Part-time maker, making knives for eight years. **Mark:** Electrical etching of "K. Tamatsu."

TAMBOLI, MICHAEL
12447 N 49 Ave, Glendale, AZ 85304, Phone: 602-978-4308, mnbtamboli@gmail.com
Specialties: Miniatures, some full size. **Patterns:** Miniature hunting knives to fantasy art knives. **Technical:** Grinds ATS-34 & Damascus. **Prices:** $75 to $500; some to $2000. **Remarks:** Full time maker; first knife sold in 1978. **Mark:** Initials, last name, last name city and state, MT Custom Knives or Mike Tamboli in Japanese script.

TASMAN, KERLEY
9 Avignon Retreat, Pt Kennedy, WA, AUSTRALIA 6172, Phone: 61 8 9593 0554, Fax: 61 8 9593 0554, taskerley@optusnet.com.au
Specialties: Knife/harness/sheath systems for elite military personnel and body guards. **Patterns:** Utility/tactical knives, hunters small game and presentation grade knives. **Technical:** ATS-34 and 440C, Damascus, flat and hollow grids. **Prices:** $200 to $1800 U.S. **Remarks:** Will take presentation grade commissions. Multi award winning maker and custom jeweler. **Mark:** Maker's initials.

TAYLOR, BILLY
10 Temple Rd, Petal, MS 39465, Phone: 601-544-0041
Specialties: Straight knives of his design. **Patterns:** Bowies, skinners, hunters and utility knives. **Technical:** Flat-grinds 440C, ATS-34 and 154CM. **Prices:** $60 to $300. **Remarks:** Part-time maker; first knife sold in 1991. **Mark:** Full name, city and state.

TAYLOR, C GRAY
560 Poteat Ln, Fall Branch, TN 37656, Phone: 423-348-8304, graysknives@aol.com; Web: www.cgraytaylor.com
Specialties: Traditonal multi-blade lobster folders, also art display Bowies and daggers. **Patterns:** Orange Blossom, sleeveboard and gunstocks. **Technical:** Grinds. **Prices:** Upscale. **Remarks:** Full-time maker; first knife sold in 1975. **Mark:** Name, city and state.

TAYLOR, SHANE
42 Broken Bow Ln, Miles City, MT 59301, Phone: 406-234-7175, shane@taylorknives.com; Web: www.taylorknives.com
Specialties: One-of-a-kind fancy Damascus straight knives and folders. **Patterns:** Bowies, folders and fighters. **Technical:** Forges own mosaic and pattern welded Damascus. **Prices:** $450 and up. **Remarks:** ABS Master Smith, full-time maker; first knife sold in 1982. **Mark:** First name.

TEDFORD, STEVEN J.
14238 Telephone Rd., Colborne, ON, CANADA K0K 1S0, Phone: 613-689-7569, firebornswords@yahoo.com; Web: www.steventedfordknives.com
Specialties: Handmade custom fixed blades, specialty outdoors knives. **Patterns:** Swept Survival Bowie, large, medium and small-size field-dressing/hunting knives, drop-point skinners, and world-class fillet knives. **Technical:** Exclusively using ATS-34 stainless steel, Japanese-inspired, free-hand ground, zero-point edge blade design. **Prices:** All knives are sold wholesale directly from the shop starting at $150 to $500+. **Remarks:** Tedford Knives; Function is beauty. Every knife is unconditionally guaranteed for life.

TENDICK, BEN
798 Nadine Ave, Eugene, OR 97404, Phone: 541-912-1280, bentendick@gmail.com; Web: www.brtbladeworks.com
Specialties: Hunter/utility, tactical, bushcraft, and kitchen. **Technical:** Preferred steel - L6, 5160, and 15N20. Stock Removal.**Prices:** $130 to $700.**Remarks:** Part-time; has been making knives since early 90's but started seriously making knives in 2010. In business at BRT Bladeworks, no website yet but can be found on Facebook. **Mark:** Initials (BRT) with B backwards and T between the B and R, and also use last name.

TERRILL, STEPHEN
16357 Goat Ranch Rd, Springville, CA 93265, Phone: 559-539-3116, slterrill@yahoo.com
Specialties: Deluxe working straight knives and folders. **Patterns:** Fighters, tantos, boots, locking folders and axes; traditional oriental patterns. **Technical:** Forges 1095, 5160, Damascus, stock removal ATS-34. **Prices:** $300+. **Remarks:** Full-time maker; first knife sold in 1972. **Mark:** Name, city, state in logo.

TERZUOLA, ROBERT
10121 Eagle Rock NE, Albuquerque, NM 87122, Phone: 505-856-7077, terzuola@earthlink.net
Specialties: Working folders of his design; period pieces. **Patterns:** High-tech utility, defense and gentleman's folders. **Technical:** Grinds CPM154, Damascus, and CPM S30V. Offers titanium, carbon fiber and G10 composite for side-lock folders and tactical folders. **Prices:** $550 to $2000. **Remarks:** Full-time maker; first knife sold in 1980. **Mark:** Mayan dragon head, name.

TESARIK, RICHARD
Pisecnik 87, 614 00 Brno, Czech Republic, Phone: 00420-602-834-726, rtesarik@gmail.com; Web: www.tesariknoze.cz
Specialties: Handmade art knives. **Patterns:** Daggers, hunters and LinerLock or back-lock folders. **Technical:** Grinds RWL-34, N690 and stainless or high-carbon damascus. Carves on blade, handle and other parts. I prefer fossil material and exotic wood, don't use synthetic material. **Prices:** $600 to $2,000. **Remarks:** Part-time maker, full-time hobby; first knife sold in 2009. **Mark:** TR.

THAYER, DANNY O
8908S 100W, Romney, IN 47981, Phone: 765-538-3105, dot61h@juno.com
Specialties: Hunters, fighters, Bowies. **Prices:** $250 and up.

THEIS, TERRY
21452 FM 2093, Harper, TX 78631, Phone: 830-864-4438
Specialties: All European and American engraving styles. **Prices:** $200 to $2000. **Remarks:** Engraver only.

THEVENOT, JEAN-PAUL
16 Rue De La Prefecture, Dijon, FRANCE 21000
Specialties: Traditional European knives and daggers. **Patterns:** Hunters, utility-camp knives, daggers, historical or modern style. **Technical:** Forges own Damascus, 5160, 1084. **Remarks:** Part-time maker. ABS Master Smith. **Mark:** Interlocked initials in square.

THIE, BRIAN
13250 150th St, Burlington, IA 52601, Phone: 319-850-2188, thieknives@gmail.com; Web: www.mepotelco.net/web/tknives
Specialties: Working using knives from basic to fancy. **Patterns:** Hunters, fighters, camp and folders. **Technical:** Forges blades and own Damascus. **Prices:** $250 and up. **Remarks:** ABS Journeyman Smith, part-time maker. Sole author of blades including forging, heat treat, engraving and sheath making. **Mark:** Last name hand engraved into the blade, JS stamped into blade.

THILL, JIM
10242 Bear Run, Missoula, MT 59803, Phone: 406-251-5475
Specialties: Traditional and working/using knives of his design. **Patterns:** Fighters, hunters and utility/camp knives. **Technical:** Grinds D2 and ATS-34; forges 10-95-85, 52100, 5160, 10 series, reg. Damascus-mosaic. Offers hand cut sheaths with rawhide lace. **Prices:** $145 to $350; some to $1250. **Remarks:** Full-time maker; first knife sold in 1962. **Mark:** Running bear in triangle.

THOMAS, BOB
Sunset Forge, 3502 Bay Rd., Ferndale, WA 98248, Phone: 360-201-0160, Fax: 360-366-5723, sunsetforge@rockisland.com

THOMAS, DAVID E

8502 Hwy 91, Lillian, AL 36549, Phone: 251-961-7574, redbluff@gulftel.com
  Specialties: Bowies and hunters. **Technical:** Hand forged blades in 5160, 1095 and own Damascus. **Prices:** $400 and up. **Mark:** Stylized DT, maker's last name, serial number.

THOMAS, DEVIN

PO Box 568, Panaca, NV 89042, Phone: 775-728-4363, hoss@devinthomas.com; Web: www.devinthomas.com
  Specialties: Traditional straight knives and folders in standard patterns. **Patterns:** Bowies, fighters, hunters. **Technical:** Forges stainless Damascus, nickel and 1095. Uses, makes and sells mokume with brass, copper and nickel-silver. **Prices:** $300 to $1200. **Remarks:** Full-time maker; first knife sold in 1979. **Mark:** First and last name, city and state with anvil, or first name only.

THOMAS, KIM

PO Box 531, Seville, OH 44273, Phone: 330-769-9906
  Specialties: Fancy and traditional straight knives of his design and to customer specs; period pieces. **Patterns:** Boots, daggers, fighters, swords. **Technical:** Forges own Damascus from 5160, 1010 and nickel. **Prices:** $135 to $1500; some to $3000. **Remarks:** Part-time maker; first knife sold in 1986. Doing business as Thomas Iron Works. **Mark:** KT.

THOMAS, ROCKY

1716 Waterside Blvd, Moncks Corner, SC 29461, Phone: 843-761-7761
  Specialties: Traditional working knives in standard patterns. **Patterns:** Hunters and utility/camp knives. **Technical:** ATS-34 and commercial Damascus. **Prices:** $130 to $350. **Remarks:** Spare-time maker; first knife sold in 1986. **Mark:** First name in script and/or block.

THOMPSON, KENNETH

4887 Glenwhite Dr, Duluth, GA 30136, Phone: 770-446-6730
  Specialties: Traditional working and using knives of his design. **Patterns:** Hunters, Bowies and utility/camp knives. **Technical:** Forges 5168, O1, 1095 and 52100. **Prices:** $75 to $1500; some to $2500. **Remarks:** Part-time maker; first knife sold in 1990. **Mark:** P/W; or name, P/W, city and state.

THOMPSON, LEON

45723 SW Saddleback Dr, Gaston, OR 97119, Phone: 503-357-2573
  Specialties: Working knives. **Patterns:** Locking folders, slip-joints and liner locks. **Technical:** Grinds ATS-34, D2 and 440C. **Prices:** $450 to $1000. **Remarks:** Full-time maker; first knife sold in 1976. **Mark:** First and middle initials, last name, city and state.

THOMPSON, LLOYD

PO Box 1664, Pagosa Springs, CO 81147, Phone: 970-264-5837
  Specialties: Working and collectible straight knives and folders of his design. **Patterns:** Straight blades, lock back folders and slip joint folders. **Technical:** Hollow-grinds ATS-34, D2 and O1. Uses sambar stag and exotic woods. **Prices:** $150 to upscale. **Remarks:** Full-time maker; first knife sold in 1985. Doing business as Trapper Creek Knife Co. **Remarks:** Offers three-day knife-making classes. **Mark:** Name.

THOMPSON, TOMMY

4015 NE Hassalo, Portland, OR 97232-2607, Phone: 503-235-5762
  Specialties: Fancy and working knives; mostly liner-lock folders. **Patterns:** Fighters, hunters and liner locks. **Technical:** Grinds D2, ATS-34, CPM440V and T15. Handles are either hardwood inlaid with wood banding and stone or shell, or made of agate, jasper, petrified woods, etc. **Prices:** $75 to $500; some to $1000. **Remarks:** Part-time maker; first knife sold in 1987. Doing business as Stone Birds. Knife making temporarily stopped due to family obligations. **Mark:** First and last name, city and state.

THOMSEN, LOYD W

25241 Renegade Pass, Custer, SD 57730, Phone: 605-673-2787, loydt@yahoo.com; Web: horseheadcreekknives.com
  Specialties: High-art and traditional working/using straight knives and presentation pieces of his design and to customer specs; period pieces. Hand carved animals in crown of stag on handles and carved display stands. **Patterns:** Bowies, hunters, daggers and utility/camp knives. **Technical:** Forges and grinds 1095HC, 1084, L6, 15N20, 440C stainless steel, nickel 200; special restoration process on period pieces. Makes sheaths. Uses natural materials for handles. **Prices:** $350 to $1000. **Remarks:** Full-time maker; first knife sold in 1995. Doing business as Horsehead Creek Knives. **Mark:** Initials and last name over a horse's head.

THORBURN, ANDRE E.

P.O. Box 1748, Bela Bela, Warmbaths, LP, SOUTH AFRICA 0480, Phone: 27-82-650-1441, Fax: 27-86-750-2765, andrethorburn@gmail.com; Web: www.thorburnknives.co.za
  Specialties: Working and fancy folders of own design to customer specs. **Technical:** Uses RWL-34, Damasteel, CPM steels, Bohler N690, and carbon and stainless damascus. **Prices:** Starting at $350. **Remarks:** Full-time maker since 1996; first knife sold in 1990. Member of South African, Italian, and German guilds. **Mark:** Initials and name in a double circle.

THOUROT, MICHAEL W

T-814 Co Rd 11, Napoleon, OH 43545, Phone: 419-533-6832, Fax: 419-533-3516, mike2row@henry-net.com; Web: wwwsafariknives.com
  Specialties: Working straight knives to customer specs. Designed two-handled skinning ax and limited edition engraved knife and art print set. **Patterns:** Fishing and fillet knives, Bowies, tantos and hunters. **Technical:** Grinds O1, D2, 440C and Damascus. **Prices:** $200 to $5000. **Remarks:** Part-time maker; first knife sold in 1968. **Mark:** Initials.

THUESEN, ED

21211 Knolle Rd, Damon, TX 77430, Phone: 979-553-1211, Fax: 979-553-1211
  Specialties: Working straight knives. **Patterns:** Hunters, fighters and survival knives. **Technical:** Grinds D2, 440C, ATS-34 and Vascowear. **Prices:** $150 to $275; some to $600. **Remarks:** Part-time maker; first knife sold in 1979. Runs knifemaker supply business. **Mark:** Last name in script.

TIENSVOLD, ALAN L

PO Box 355, 3277 U.S. Hwy. 20, Rushville, NE 69360, Phone: 308-360-0613, tiensvoldknives@gpcom.net
  Specialties: Working knives, tomahawks and period pieces, high end Damascus knives. **Patterns:** Random, ladder, twist and many more. **Technical:** Hand forged blades, forges own Damascus. **Prices:** Working knives start at $300. **Remarks:** Received Journeyman rating with the ABS in 2002. Does own engraving and fine work. **Mark:** Tiensvold hand made U.S.A. on left side, JS on right.

TIENSVOLD, JASON

PO Box 795, Rushville, NE 69360, Phone: 308-360-2217, jasontiensvoldknives@yahoo.com
  Specialties: Working and using straight knives of his design; period pieces. Gentlemen folders, art folders. Single action automatics. **Patterns:** Hunters, skinners, Bowies, fighters, daggers, liner locks. **Technical:** Forges own Damascus using 15N20 and 1084, 1095, nickel, custom file work. **Prices:** $200 to $4000. **Remarks:** Full-time maker, first knife sold in 1994; doing business under Tiensvold Custom Knives. **Mark:** J. Tiensvold on left side, MS on right.

TIGHE, BRIAN

12-111 Fourth Ave, Suite 376 Ridley Square, St. Catharines, ON, CANADA L2S 3P5, Phone: 905-892-2734, Web: www.tigheknives.com
  Specialties: Folding knives, bearing pivots. High tech tactical folders. **Patterns:** Boots, daggers and locking. **Technical:** BG-42, RWL-34, Damasteel, 154CM, S30V, CPM 440V and CPM 420V. Prefers natural handle material inlay; hand finishes. **Prices:** $450 to $4000. **Remarks:** Full-time maker; first knife sold in 1989. **Mark:** Etched signature.

TILL, CALVIN E AND RUTH

11 Chadron Creek Trl. Ct., Chadron, NE 69337-6967, Phone: 308-432-6945
  Specialties: Straight knives, hunters, Bowies; no folders **Patterns:** Training point, drop point hunters, Bowies. **Technical:** ATS-34 sub zero quench RC59, 61. **Prices:** $700 to $1200. **Remarks:** Sells only the absolute best knives they can make. Manufactures every part in their knives. **Mark:** RC Till. The R is for Ruth.

TILTON, JOHN

24041 Hwy 383, Iowa, LA 70647, Phone: 337-582-6785, john@jetknives.com
  Specialties: Bowies, camp knives, skinners and folders. **Technical:** All forged blades. Makes own Damascus. **Prices:** $150 and up. **Remarks:** ABS Journeyman Smith. **Mark:** Initials J.E.T.

TINDERA, GEORGE

BURNING RIVER FORGE, 751 Hadcock Rd, Brunswick, OH 44212-2648, Phone: 330-220-6212
  Specialties: Straight knives; his designs. **Patterns:** Personal knives; classic Bowies and fighters. **Technical:** Hand-forged high-carbon; his own cable and pattern welded Damascus. **Prices:** $125 to $600. **Remarks:** Spare-time maker; sold first knife in 1995. Natural handle materials.

TINGLE, DENNIS P

19390 E Clinton Rd, Jackson, CA 95642, Phone: 209-223-4586, dtknives@earthlink.net
  Specialties: Swords, fixed blades: small to medium, tomahawks. **Technical:** All blades forged. **Remarks:** ABS, JS. **Mark:** D. Tingle over JS.

TIPPETTS, COLTEN

4068 W Miners Farm Dr, Hidden Springs, ID 83714, Phone: 208-229-7772, coltentippetts@gmail.com
  Specialties: Fancy and working straight knives and fancy locking folders of his own design or to customer specifications. **Patterns:** Hunters and skinners, fighters and utility. **Technical:** Grinds BG-42, high-carbon 1095 and Damascus. **Prices:** $200 to $1000. **Remarks:** Part-time maker; first knife sold in 1996. **Mark:** Fused initials.

TODD, RICHARD C

375th LN 46001, Chambersburg, IL 62323, Phone: 217-327-4380, ktodd45@yahoo.com
  Specialties: Multi blade folders and silver sheaths. **Patterns:** Jewel setting and hand engraving. **Mark:** RT with letter R crossing the T or R Todd.

TOICH, NEVIO

Via Pisacane 9, Rettorgole di Caldogna, Vincenza, ITALY 36030, Phone: 0444-985065, Fax: 0444-301254
  Specialties: Working/using straight knives of his design or to customer specs. **Patterns:** Bowies, hunters, skinners and utility/camp knives. **Technical:** Grinds 440C, D2 and ATS-34. Hollow-grinds all blades and uses mirror polish. Offers hand-sewn sheaths. Uses wood and horn. **Prices:** $120 to $300; some to $450. **Remarks:** Spare-time maker; first knife sold in 1989. Doing business as Custom Toich. **Mark:** Initials and model number punched.

TOKAR, DANIEL

Box 1776, Shepherdstown, WV 25443
  Specialties: Working knives; period pieces. **Patterns:** Hunters, camp knives, buckskinners, axes, swords and battle gear. **Technical:** Forges L6, 1095 and his

Damascus; makes mokume, Japanese alloys and bronze daggers; restores old edged weapons. **Prices:** $25 to $800; some to $3000. **Remarks:** Part-time maker; first knife sold in 1979. Doing business as The Willow Forge. **Mark:** Arrow over rune and date.

TOMBERLIN, BRION R
ANVIL TOP CUSTOM KNIVES, 825 W Timberdell, Norman, OK 73072, Phone: 405-202-6832, anviltopp@aol.com
Specialties: Handforged blades, working pieces, standard classic patterns, some swords and customer designs. **Patterns:** Bowies, hunters, fighters, Persian and eastern-styles. Likes Japanese blades. **Technical:** Forges 1050, 1075, 1084, 1095, 5160, some forged stainless, also does some stock removal in stainless. Also makes own damascus. **Prices:** $350 to $4,000 or higher for swords and custom pieces. **Remarks:** Part-time maker, ABS master smith. Prefers natural handle materials, hand-rubbed finishes. Likes temper lines. **Mark:** BRION with MS.

TOMEY, KATHLEEN
146 Buford Pl, Macon, GA 31204, Phone: 478-746-8454, ktomey@tomeycustomknives.com; Web: www.tomeycustomknives.com
Specialties: Working hunters, skinners, daily users in fixed blades, plain and embellished. Tactical neck and belt carry. Japanese influenced. Bowies. **Technical:** Grinds O1, ATS-34, flat or hollow grind, filework, satin and mirror polish finishes. High quality leather sheaths with tooling. Kydex with tactical. **Prices:** $150 to $500. **Remarks:** Almost full-time maker. **Mark:** Last name in diamond.

TOMPKINS, DAN
PO Box 398, Peotone, IL 60468, Phone: 708-258-3620
Specialties: Working knives, some deluxe, some folders. **Patterns:** Hunters, boots, daggers and push knives. **Technical:** Grinds D2, 440C, ATS-34 and 154CM. **Prices:** $85 to $150; some to $400. **Remarks:** Part-time maker; first knife sold in 1975. **Mark:** Last name, city, state.

TONER, ROGER
531 Lightfoot Pl, Pickering, ON, CANADA L1V 5Z8, Phone: 905-420-5555
Specialties: Exotic sword canes. **Patterns:** Bowies, daggers and fighters. **Technical:** Grinds 440C, D2 and Damascus. Scrimshaws and engraves. Silver cast pommels and guards in animal shapes; twisted silver wire inlays. Uses semi-precious stones. **Prices:** $200 to $2000; some to $3000. **Remarks:** Part-time maker; first knife sold in 1982. **Mark:** Last name.

TORRES, HENRY
2329 Moody Ave., Clovis, CA 93619, Phone: 559-297-9154, Web: www.htknives.com
Specialties: Forged high-performance hunters and working knives, Bowies, and fighters. **Technical:** 52100 and 5160 and makes own Damascus. **Prices:** $350 to $3000. **Remarks:** Started forging in 2004. Has mastersmith with American Bladesmith Association.

TOSHIFUMI, KURAMOTO
3435 Higashioda, Asakura-gun, Fukuoka, JAPAN, Phone: 0946-42-4470

TOWELL, DWIGHT L
2375 Towell Rd, Midvale, ID 83645, Phone: 208-355-2419
Specialties: Solid, elegant working knives; art knives, high quality hand engraving and gold inlay. **Patterns:** Hunters, Bowies, daggers and folders. **Technical:** Grinds 154CM, ATS-34, 440C and other maker's Damascus. **Prices:** Upscale. **Remarks:** Full-time maker. First knife sold in 1970. Member of AKI. **Mark:** Towell, sometimes hand engraved.

TOWNSEND, ALLEN MARK
6 Pine Trail, Texarkana, AR 71854, Phone: 870-772-8945

TOWNSLEY, RUSSELL
PO BOX 91, Floral, AR 72534-0091, Phone: 870-307-8069, circleTRMtownsley@yahoo.com
Specialties: Using knives of his own design. **Patterns:** Hunters, skinners, folders. **Technical:** Hollow grinds D2 and O1. Handle material - antler, tusk, bone, exotic woods. **Prices:** Prices start at $125. **Remarks:** Arkansas knifemakers association. Sold first knife in 2009. Doing business as Circle-T knives. **Mark:** Encircled T.

TRACE RINALDI CUSTOM BLADES
1470 Underpass Rd, Plummer, ID 83851, Trace@thrblades.com; Web: www.thrblades.com
Technical: Grinds S30V, 3V, A2 and talonite fixed blades. **Prices:** $300-$1000. **Remarks:** Tactical and utility for the most part. **Mark:** Diamond with THR inside.

TRINDLE, BARRY
1660 Ironwood Trail, Earlham, IA 50072-8611, Phone: 515-462-1237
Specialties: Engraved folders. **Patterns:** Mostly small folders, classical-styles and pocket knives. **Technical:** 440 only. Engraves. Handles of wood or mineral material. **Prices:** Start at $1000. **Mark:** Name on tang.

TRISLER, KENNETH W
6256 Federal 80, Rayville, LA 71269, Phone: 318-728-5541

TRITZ, JEAN-JOSE
Pinneberger Chaussee 48, Hamburg, GERMANY 22523, Phone: +49(40) 49 78 21, jeanjosetritz@aol.com; www.tritz-messer.com
Specialties: Scandinavian knives, Japanese kitchen knives, friction folders, swords. **Patterns:** Puukkos, Tollekniven, Hocho, friction folders, swords. **Technical:** Forges tool steels, carbon steels, 52100 Damascus, mokume, San Maj. **Prices:** $200 to $2000; some higher. **Remarks:** Full-time maker; first knife sold in 1989. Does own leatherwork, prefers natural materials. Sole authorship. Speaks French, German, English, Norwegian. **Mark:** Initials in monogram.

TROUT, GEORGE H.
727 Champlin Rd, Wilmington, OH 45177, Phone: 937-382-2331, gandjtrout@msn.com
Specialties: Working knives, some fancy. **Patterns:** Hunters, drop points, Bowies and fighters. **Technical:** Stock removal: ATS-34, 440C Forged: 5160, W2, 1095, O1 Full integrals: 440C, A2, O1. **Prices:** $150 and up. **Remarks:** Makes own sheaths and mosaic pins. Fileworks most knives. First knife 1985. **Mark:** Etched name and state on stock removal. Forged: stamped name and forged.

TRUJILLO, ALBERT M B
2035 Wasmer Cir, Bosque Farms, NM 87068, Phone: 505-869-0428, trujilloscutups@comcast.net
Specialties: Working/using straight knives of his design or to customer specs. **Patterns:** Hunters, skinners, fighters, working/using knives. File work offered. **Technical:** Grinds ATS-34, D2, 440C, S30V. Tapers tangs, all blades cryogenically treated. **Prices:** $75 to $500. **Remarks:** Part-time maker; first knife sold in 1997. **Mark:** First and last name under logo.

TRUNCALI, PETE
2914 Anatole Court, Garland, TX 75043, Phone: 214-763-7127, truncaliknives@yahoo.com Web:www.truncaliknives.com
Specialties: Lockback folders, locking liner folders, automatics and fixed blades. Does business as Truncali Custom Knives.

TSCHAGER, REINHARD
S. Maddalena di Sotto 1a, Bolzano, ITALY 39100, Phone: 0471-975005, Fax: 0471-975005, reinhardtschager@virgilio.it
Specialties: Classic, high-art, collector-grade straight knives of his design. **Patterns:** Jewel knife, daggers, and hunters. **Technical:** Grinds ATS-34, D2 and Damascus. Oval pins. Gold inlay. Offers engraving. **Prices:** $900 to $2000; some to $3000. **Remarks:** Spare-time maker; first knife sold in 1979. **Mark:** Gold inlay stamped with initials.

TUOMINEN, PEKKA
Pohjois-Keiteleentie 20, Tossavanlahti, FINLAND 72930, Phone: 358405167853, puukkopekka@luukku.com; Web: www.puukkopekka.com
Specialties: Puukko knives. **Patterns:** Puukkos, hunters, leukus, and folders. **Technical:** Forges silversteel, 1085, 52100, and makes own Damascus 15N20 and 1095. Grinds RWL-34 and ATS-34. **Prices:** Starting at $300. **Remarks:** Full-time maker. **Mark:** PEKKA; earlier whole name.

TURCOTTE, LARRY
1707 Evergreen, Pampa, TX 79065, Phone: 806-665-9369, 806-669-0435
Specialties: Fancy and working/using knives of his design and to customer specs. **Patterns:** Hunters, kitchen knives, utility/camp knives. **Technical:** Grinds 440C, D2, ATS-34. Engraves, scrimshaws, silver inlays. **Prices:** $150 to $350; some to $1000. **Remarks:** Part-time maker; first knife sold in 1977. Doing business as Knives by Turcotte. **Mark:** Last name.

TURECEK, JIM
12 Elliott Rd, Ansonia, CT 06401, Phone: 203-734-8406, jturecek@sbcglobal.net
Specialties: Exotic folders, art knives and some miniatures. **Patterns:** Trout and bird knives with split bamboo handles and one-of-a-kind folders. **Technical:** Grinds and forges stainless and carbon damascus. All knives are handmade using no computer-controlled machinery. **Prices:** $2,000 to $10,000. **Remarks:** Full-time maker; first knife sold in 1983. **Mark:** Last initial in script, or last name.

TURNBULL, RALPH A
14464 Linden Dr, Spring Hill, FL 34609, Phone: 352-688-7089, tbull2000@bellsouth.net; Web: www.turnbullknives.com
Specialties: Fancy folders. **Patterns:** Primarily gents pocket knives. **Technical:** Wire EDM work on bolsters. **Prices:** $300 and up. **Remarks:** Full-time maker; first knife sold in 1973. **Mark:** Signature or initials.

TURNER, KEVIN
17 Hunt Ave, Montrose, NY 10548, Phone: 914-739-0535
Specialties: Working straight knives of his design and to customer specs; period pieces. **Patterns:** Daggers, fighters and utility knives. **Technical:** Forges 5160 and 52100. **Prices:** $90 to $500. **Remarks:** Part-time maker; first knife sold in 1991. **Mark:** Acid-etched signed last name and year.

TURNER, MIKE
PO BOX 194, Williams, OR 97544, Phone: 541-846-0204, mike@turnerknives.com Web: www.turnerknives.com
Specialties: Forged and stock removed full tang, hidden and thru tang knives. **Patterns:** Hunters, fighters, Bowies, boot knives, skinners and kitchen knives. **Technical:** I make my own damascus. **Prices:** $200 - $1,000. **Remarks:** Part-time maker, sold my first knife in 2008, doing business as Mike Turner Custom Knives. **Mark:** Name, City, & State.

TYRE, MICHAEL A
1219 Easy St, Wickenburg, AZ 85390, Phone: 928-684-9601/602-377-8432, mtyre86@gmail.com; Web: www.mikeytrecustomknives.com
Specialties: Quality folding knives, upscale gents folders, one-of-a-kind collectable models. **Patterns:** Working fixed blades for hunting, kitchen and fancy bowies. Forging my own damascus patterns. **Technical:** Grinds, prefers hand-rubbed satin finishes and uses natural handle materials. **Prices:** $250 to $1,300. **Remarks:** ABS journeyman smith.

TYSER, ROSS
1015 Hardee Court, Spartanburg, SC 29303, Phone: 864-585-7616
Specialties: Traditional working and using straight knives and folders of his design and

in standard patterns. **Patterns:** Bowies, hunters and slip-joint folders. **Technical:** Grinds 440C and commercial Damascus. Mosaic pins; stone inlay. Does filework and scrimshaw. Offers engraving and cut-work and some inlay on sheaths. **Prices:** $45 to $125; some to $400. **Remarks:** Part-time maker; first knife sold in 1995. Doing business as RT Custom Knives. **Mark:** Stylized initials.

U

UCHIDA, CHIMATA
977-2 Oaza Naga Shisui Ki, Kumamoto, JAPAN 861-1204

UPTON, TOM
Little Rabbit Forge, 1414 Feast Pl., Rogers, AR 72758, Phone: 479-636-6755, Web: www.upton-knives.com
Specialties: Working fixed blades. **Patterns:** Hunters, utility, fighters, bowies and small hatchets. **Technical:** Forges 5160, 1084 and W2 blade steels, or stock removal using D2, 440C and 154CM. Performs own heat treat. **Prices:** $150 and up. **Remarks:** Part-time maker; first knife sold in 1977. Member of ABS, Arkansas Knifemakers Association and Knife Group Association. **Mark:** Name (Small Rabbit logo), city and state, etched or stamped.

V

VAGNINO, MICHAEL
PO Box 67, Visalia, CA 93279, Phone: 559-636-0501; cell: 559-827-7802, mike@mvknives.com; Web: www.mvknives.com
Specialties: Folders and straight knives, working and fancy. **Patterns:** Folders--locking liners, slip joints, lock backs, double and single action autos. Straight knives--hunters, Bowies, camp and kitchen. **Technical:** Forges 52100, W2, 15N20 and 1084. Grinds stainless. Makes own damascus and does engraving. **Prices:** $300 to $4,000 and above. **Remarks:** Full-time maker, ABS Mastersmith. **Mark:** Logo, last name.

VAIL, DAVE
554 Sloop Point Rd, Hampstead, NC 28443, Phone: 910-270-4456
Specialties: Working/using straight knives of his own design or to the customer's specs. **Patterns:** Hunters/skinners, camp/utility, fillet, Bowies. **Technical:** Grinds ATS-34, 440c, 154 CM and 1095 carbon steel. **Prices:** $90 to $450. **Remarks:** Part-time maker. Member of NC Custom Knifemakers Guild. **Mark:** Etched oval with "Dave Vail Hampstead NC" inside.

VALLOTTON, BUTCH AND AREY
621 Fawn Ridge Dr, Oakland, OR 97462, Phone: 541-459-2216, Fax: 541-459-7473
Specialties: Quick opening knives w/complicated mechanisms. **Patterns:** Tactical, fancy, working, and some art knives. **Technical:** Grinds all steels, uses others' Damascus. Uses Spectrum Metal. **Prices:** From $350 to $4500. **Remarks:** Full-time maker since 1984; first knife sold in 1981. Co/designer, Applegate Fairbarn folding w/Bill Harsey. **Mark:** Name w/ viper head in the "V."

VALLOTTON, RAINY D
1295 Wolf Valley Dr, Umpqua, OR 97486, Phone: 541-459-0465
Specialties: Folders, one-handed openers and art pieces. **Patterns:** All patterns. **Technical:** Stock removal all steels; uses titanium liners and bolsters; uses all finishes. **Prices:** $350 to $3500. **Remarks:** Full-time maker. **Mark:** Name.

VALLOTTON, SHAWN
621 Fawn Ridge Dr, Oakland, OR 97462, Phone: 503-459-2216
Specialties: Left-hand knives. **Patterns:** All styles. **Technical:** Grinds 440C, ATS-34 and Damascus. Uses titanium. Prefers bead-blasted or anodized finishes. **Prices:** $250 to $1400. **Remarks:** Full-time maker. **Mark:** Name and specialty.

VALLOTTON, THOMAS
621 Fawn Ridge Dr, Oakland, OR 97462, Phone: 541-459-2216
Specialties: Custom autos. **Patterns:** Tactical, fancy. **Technical:** File work, uses Damascus, uses Spectrum Metal. **Prices:** From $350 to $700. **Remarks:** Full-time maker. Maker of ProtŽgé 3 canoe. **Mark:** T and a V mingled.

VAN CLEVE, STEVE
Box 372, Sutton, AK 99674, Phone: 907-745-3038, Fax: 907-745-8770, sucents@mtaonline.net; Web: www.alaskaknives.net

VAN DE MANAKKER, THIJS
Koolweg 34, Holland, NETHERLANDS, Phone: 0493539369, www.ehijsvandemanakker.com
Specialties: Classic high-art knives. **Patterns:** Swords, utility/camp knives and period pieces. **Technical:** Forges soft iron, carbon steel and Bloomery Iron. Makes own Damascus, Bloomery Iron and patterns. **Prices:** $20 to $2000; some higher. **Remarks:** Full-time maker; first knife sold in 1969. **Mark:** Stylized "V."

VAN DEN BERG, NEELS
166 Van Heerdan St., Capital Park, Pretoria, Gauteng, SOUTH AFRICA, Phone: +27(0)12-329-5649 or +27(0)83-451-3105, neels@blackdragonforge.com; Web: http://www.blackdragonforge.com or http://www.facebook.com/neels.vandenberg
Specialties: Handforged damascus and high-carbon steel axes, hunters, swords and art knives. **Patterns:** All my own designs and customer collaborations, from axes, hunters, choppers, bowies, swords and folders to one-off tactical prototypes. **Technical:** Flat and hollow grinding. Handforges high-carbon steel and maker's own damascus. Also works in high-carbon stainless steels. **Prices:** $50 to $1,000. **Remarks:** Part-time maker; first knife sold in Oct. 2009. **Mark:** Stylized capital letter "N" resembling a three-tier mountain, normally hot stamped in forged blades.

VAN DEN ELSEN, GERT
Purcelldreef 83, Tilburg, NETHERLANDS 5012 AJ, Phone: 013-4563200, gvdelsen@home.nl
Specialties: Fancy, working/using, miniatures and integral straight knives of the maker's design or to customer specs. **Patterns:** Bowies, fighters, hunters and Japanese-style blades. **Technical:** Grinds ATS-34 and 440C; forges Damascus. Offers filework, differentially tempered blades and some mokume-gane fittings. **Prices:** $350 to $1000; some to $4000. **Remarks:** Part-time maker; first knife sold in 1982. Doing business as G-E Knives. **Mark:** Initials GE in lozenge shape.

VAN DER WESTHUIZEN, PETER
PO Box 1698, Mossel Bay, SC, SOUTH AFRICA 6500, Phone: 27 446952388, pietvdw@telkomsa.net
Specialties: Working knives, folders, daggers and art knives. **Patterns:** Hunters, skinners, bird, trout and sidelock folders. **Technical:** Sandvik, 12627. Damascus indigenous wood and ivory. **Prices:** From $450 to $5500. **Remarks:** First knife sold in 1987. Full-time since 1996. **Mark:** Initial & surname. Handmade RSA.

VAN DIJK, RICHARD
76 Stepney Ave Rd 2, Harwood Dunedin, NEW ZEALAND, Phone: 0064-3-4780401, Web: www.hoihoknives.com
Specialties: Damascus, Fantasy knives, sgiandubhs, dirks, swords, and hunting knives. **Patterns:** Mostly one-offs, anything from bird and trout to swords, no folders. **Technical:** Forges mainly own Damascus, some 5160, O1, 1095, L6. Prefers natural handle materials, over 40 years experience as goldsmith, handle fittings are often made from sterling silver and sometimes gold, manufactured to cap the handle, use gemstones if required. Makes own sheaths. **Prices:** $300 and up. **Remarks:** Full-time maker, first knife sold in 1980. Doing business as HOIHO KNIVES. **Mark:** Stylized initials RvD in triangle.

VAN EIZENGA, JERRY W
14281 Cleveland, Nunica, MI 49448, Phone: 616-638-2275
Specialties: Hand forged blades, Scagel patterns and other styles. **Patterns:** Camp, hunting, bird, trout, folders, axes, miniatures. **Technical:** 5160, 52100, 1084. **Prices:** Start at $250. **Remarks:** Part-time maker, sole author of knife and sheath. First knife made 1970s. ABS member who believes in the beauty of simplicity. **Mark:** J.S. stamp.

VAN ELDIK, FRANS
Ho Flaan 3, Loenen, NETHERLANDS 3632 BT, Phone: 0031 294 233 095, Fax: 0031 294 233 095
Specialties: Fancy collector-grade straight knives and folders of his design. **Patterns:** Hunters, fighters, boots and folders. **Technical:** Forges and grinds D2, 154CM, ATS-34 and stainless Damascus. **Prices:** Start at $450. **Remarks:** Spare-time maker; first knife sold in 1979. Knifemaker 30 years, 25 year member of Knifemakers Guild. **Mark:** Lion with name and Amsterdam.

VAN HEERDEN, ANDRE
P.O. Box 905-417, Garsfontein, Pretoria, GT, SOUTH AFRICA 0042, Phone: 27 82 566 6030, andrevh@iafrica.com; Web: www.andrevanheerden.com
Specialties: Fancy and working folders of his design to customer specs. **Technical:** Grinds RWL34, 19C27, D2, carbon and stainless Damascus. **Prices:** Starting at $350. **Remarks:** Part-time maker, first knife sold in 2003. **Mark:** Initials and name in a double circle.

VAN REENEN, IAN
6003 Harvard St, Amarillo, TX 79109, Phone: 806-236-8333, ianvanreenen@suddenlink.net Web: www.ianvanreenenknives.com
Specialties: Slipjoints, single and double blades. **Patterns:** Trappers, peanuts, saddle horn trappers. **Technical:** ATS-34 and CPM 154.**Prices:** $400 to $700. **Remarks:** Specializing in slipjoints. **Mark:** VAN REENEN

VAN RYSWYK, AAD
AVR KNIVES, Werf Van Pronk 8, Vlaardingen, NETHERLANDS 3134 HE, Phone: +31 10 4742952, info@avrknives.com; Web: www.avrknives.com
Specialties: High-art interframe folders of his design. **Patterns:** Hunters and locking folders. **Technical:** Uses semi-precious stones, mammoth ivory, iron wood, etc. **Prices:** $550 to $3800. **Remarks:** Full-time maker; first knife sold in 1993.

VANCE, DAVID
2646 Bays Bend Rd., West Liberty, KY 41472, Phone: 606-743-1465 or 606-362-6191, dtvance@mrtc.com; Web: www.facebook.com/ddcutlery
Specialties: Custom hunting or collectible knives, folders and fixed blades, also unique bullet casing handle pins and filework. **Patterns:** Maker's design or made to customers' specifications. **Technical:** Uses stock removal method on 1095 steel. **Remarks:** Part-time maker; first knife made in 2006. **Mark:** Cursive D&D.

VANDERFORD, CARL G
2290 Knob Creek Rd, Columbia, TN 38401, Phone: 931-381-1488
Specialties: Traditional working straight knives and folders of his design. **Patterns:** Hunters, Bowies and locking folders. **Technical:** Forges and grinds 440C, O1 and wire Damascus. **Prices:** $60 to $125. **Remarks:** Part-time maker; first knife sold in 1987. **Mark:** Last name.

VANDERKOLFF, STEPHEN
5 Jonathan Crescent, Mildmay, ON, CANADA N0g 2JO, Phone: 519-367-3401, steve@vanderkolffknives.com; Web: www.vanderkolffknives.com
Specialties: Fixed blades from gent's pocketknives and drop hunters to full sized Bowies and art knives. **Technical:** Primary blade steel 440C, Damasteel or custom made Damascus. All heat treat done by maker and all blades hardness tested. Handle material:

stag, stabilized woods or MOP. **Prices:** $150 to $1200. **Remarks:** Started making knives in 1998 and sold first knife in 2000. Winner of the best of show art knife 2005 Wolverine Knife Show.

VANDEVENTER, TERRY L
3274 Davis Rd, Terry, MS 39170-8719, Phone: 601-371-7414, tvandeventer@comcast.net
Specialties: Bowies, hunters, camp knives, friction folders. **Technical:** 1084, 1095, 15N20 and L6 steels. Damascus and mokume. Natural handle materials. **Prices:** $600 to $3000. **Remarks:** Sole author; makes everything here. First ABS MS from the state of Mississippi. **Mark:** T.L. Vandeventer (silhouette of snake underneath). MS on ricasso.

VANHOY, ED AND TANYA
24255 N Fork River Rd, Abingdon, VA 24210, Phone: 276-944-4885, vanhoyknives@centurylink.net
Specialties: Traditional and working/using straight knives and folders and innovative locking mechanisms. **Patterns:** Fighters, straight knives, folders, hunters, art knives and Bowies. **Technical:** Grinds ATS-34 and carbon/stainless steel Damascus; forges carbon and stainless Damascus. Offers filework and engraving with hammer and chisel. **Prices:** $250 to $3000. **Remarks:** Full-time maker; first knife sold in 1977. Wife also engraves. Doing business as Van Hoy Custom Knives. **Mark:** Acid etched last name.

VARDAMAN, ROBERT
2406 Mimosa Lane, Hattiesburg, MS 39402, Phone: 601-268-3889, rvx222@gmail.com
Specialties: Working straight knives, mainly integrals, of his design or to customer specs. **Patterns:** Mainly integrals, bowies and hunters. **Technical:** Forges 52100, W2 and 1084. Filework. **Prices:** $250 to $1,000. **Remarks:** Part-time maker. First knife sold in 2004. **Mark:** Last name, last name with Mississippi state logo.

VASQUEZ, JOHNNY DAVID
1552 7th St, Wyandotte, MI 48192, Phone: 734-281-2455

VAUGHAN, IAN
351 Doe Run Rd, Manheim, PA 17545-9368, Phone: 717-665-6949

VEIT, MICHAEL
3289 E Fifth Rd, LaSalle, IL 61301, Phone: 815-223-3538, whitebear@starband.net
Specialties: Damascus folders. **Technical:** Engraver, sole author. **Prices:** $2500 to $6500. **Remarks:** Part-time maker; first knife sold in 1985. **Mark:** Name in script.

VELARDE, RICARDO
7240 N Greenfield Dr, Park City, UT 84098, Phone: 435-901-1773, velardeknives@mac.com Web: www.velardeknives.com
Specialties: Investment grade integrals and interframs. **Patterns:** Boots, fighters and hunters; hollow grind. **Technical:** BG on Integrals. **Prices:** $1450 to $5200. **Remarks:** First knife sold in 1992. **Mark:** First initial and last name.

VELICK, SAMMY
3457 Maplewood Ave, Los Angeles, CA 90066, Phone: 310-663-6170, metaltamer@gmail.com
Specialties: Working knives and art pieces. **Patterns:** Hunter, utility and fantasy. **Technical:** Stock removal and forges. **Prices:** $100 and up. **Mark:** Last name.

VENSILD, HENRIK
Gl Estrup, Randersvei 4, Auning, DENMARK 8963, Phone: +45 86 48 44 48
Specialties: Classic and traditional working and using knives of his design; Scandinavian influence. **Patterns:** Hunters and using knives. **Technical:** Forges Damascus. Hand makes handles, sheaths and blades. **Prices:** $350 to $1000. **Remarks:** Part-time maker; first knife sold in 1967. **Mark:** Initials.

VERONIQUE, LAURENT
Avenue du Capricorne, 53, 1200 Bruxelles, BELGIUM, Phone: 0032-477-48-66-73, whatsonthebench@gmail.com
Specialties: Fixed blades and friction folders. **Patterns:** Bowies, camp knives, ladies' knives and maker's own designs. **Technical:** Maker's own San Mai steel with a Blue Paper Steel edge and pure-nickel-and-O1 outer layers, called "Nickwich" (nickel in sandwich), and damascus, numerical milling embellishments and inlays, and hand-fashioned sheaths. **Prices:** Start at $350. **Remarks:** Part-time maker since 2005, ABS journeyman smith since 2013.

VESTAL, CHARLES
26662 Shortsville Rd., Abingdon, VA 24210, Phone: 276-492-3262, charles@vestalknives.com; Web: www.vestalknives.com
Specialties: Hunters and double ground fighters in traditional designs and own designs. **Technical:** Grinds CPM-154, ATS-134, 154-CM and other steels. **Prices:** $300 to $1000, some higher. **Remarks:** First knife sold in 1995.

VIALLON, HENRI
Les Belins, Thiers, FRANCE 63300, Phone: 04-73-80-24-03, Fax: 04 73-51-02-02
Specialties: Folders and complex Damascus **Patterns:** His draws. **Technical:** Forge. **Prices:** $1000 to $5000. **Mark:** H. Viallon.

VICKERS, DAVID
11620 Kingford Dr., Montgomery, TX 77316, Phone: 936-537-4900, jdvickers@gmail.com
Specialties: Working/using blade knives especially for hunters. His design or to customer specs. **Patterns:** Hunters, skinners, camp/utility. **Technical:** Grinds ATS-34, 440C, and D-2. Uses stag, various woods, and micarta for handle material. Hand-stitched sheaths. **Remark:** Full-time maker. **Prices:** $125 - $350. **Mark:** VICKERS

VIELE, H J
88 Lexington Ave, Westwood, NJ 07675, Phone: 201-666-2906, h.viele@verizon.net
Specialties: Folding knives of distinctive shapes. **Patterns:** High-tech folders and one-of-a-kind. **Technical:** Grinds ATS-34 and S30V. **Prices:** Start at $575. **Remarks:** Full-time maker; first knife sold in 1973. **Mark:** Japanese design for the god of war.

VILAR, RICARDO AUGUSTO FERREIRA
Rua Alemada Dos Jasmins NO 243, Parque Petropolis, Mairipora, SP, BRAZIL 07600-000, Phone: 011-55-11-44-85-43-46, ricardovilar@ig.com.br.
Specialties: Traditional Brazilian-style working knives of the Sao Paulo state. **Patterns:** Fighters, hunters, utility, and camp knives, welcome customer design. Specialize in the "true" Brazilian camp knife "Soracabana." **Technical:** Forges only with sledge hammer to 100 percent shape in 5160 and 52100 and his own Damascus steels. Makes own sheaths in the "true" traditional "Paulista"-style of the state of Sao Paulo. **Remark:** Full-time maker. **Prices:** $250 to $600. Uses only natural handle materials. **Mark:** Special designed signature styled name R. Vilar.

VILLA, LUIZ
R. Com. Miguel Calfat 398, Itaim Bibi, SP, BRAZIL 04537-081, Phone: 011-8290649
Specialties: One-of-a-kind straight knives and jewel knives of all designs. **Patterns:** Bowies, hunters, utility/camp knives and jewel knives. **Technical:** Grinds D6, Damascus and 440C; forges 5160. Prefers natural handle material. **Prices:** $70 to $200. **Remarks:** Part-time maker; first knife sold in 1990. **Mark:** Last name and serial number.

VILLAR, RICARDO
Al. dos Jasmins 243, Mairipora, SP, BRAZIL 07600-000, Phone: 011-4851649
Specialties: Straight working knives to customer specs. **Patterns:** Bowies, fighters and utility/camp knives. **Technical:** Grinds D6, ATS-34 and 440C stainless. **Prices:** $80 to $200. **Remarks:** Part-time maker; first knife sold in 1993. **Mark:** Percor over sword and circle.

VILPPOLA, MARKKU
Jaanintie 45, Turku, FINLAND 20540, Phone: +358 (0)50 566 1563, markku@mvforge.fi Web: www.mvforge.fi
Specialties: All kinds of swords and knives. **Technical:** Forges silver steel, CO, 8%, nickel, 1095, A203E, etc. Mokume (sterling silver/brass/copper). Bronze casting (sand casting, lost-wax casting). **Prices:** Starting at $200.

VINING, BILL
9 Penny Lane, Methuen, MA 01844, Phone: 978-688-4729, billv@medawebs.com; Web: www.medawebs.com/knives
Specialties: Liner locking folders. Slip joints & lockbacks. **Patterns:** Likes to make patterns of his own design. **Technical:** S30V, 440C, ATS-34. Damascus from various makers. **Prices:** $450 and up. **Remarks:** Part-time maker. **Mark:** VINING or B. Vining.

VISTE, JAMES
EDGE WISE FORGE, 9745 Dequindre, Hamtramck, MI 48212, Phone: 313-587-8899, grumblejunky@hotmail.com
Mark: EWF touch mark.

VISTNES, TOR
, Svelgen, NORWAY N-6930, Phone: 047-57795572
Specialties: Traditional and working knives of his design. **Patterns:** Hunters and utility knives. **Technical:** Grinds Uddeholm Elmax. Handles made of rear burls of different Nordic stabilized woods. **Prices:** $300 to $1100. **Remarks:** Part-time maker; first knife sold in 1988. **Mark:** Etched name and deer head.

VITALE, MACE
925 Rt 80, Guilford, CT 06437, Phone: 203-457-5591, Web: www.laurelrockforge.com
Specialties: Hand forged blades. **Patterns:** Hunters, utility, chef, Bowies and fighters. **Technical:** W2, 1095, 1084, L6. Hand forged and finished. **Prices:** $100 to $1000. **Remarks:** American Bladesmith Society, Journeyman Smith. Full-time maker; first knife sold 2001. **Mark:** MACE.

VOGT, DONALD J
9007 Hogans Bend, Tampa, FL 33647, Phone: 813-973-3245, vogtknives@verizon.net
Specialties: Art knives, folders, automatics. **Technical:** Uses Damascus steels for blade and bolsters, filework, hand carving on blade bolsters and handles. Other materials used: jewels, gold, mother-of-pearl, gold-lip pearl, black-lip pearl, ivory. **Prices:** $4,000 to $10,000. **Remarks:** Part-time maker; first knife sold in 1997. **Mark:** Last name.

VOGT, PATRIK
Kungsvagen 83, Halmstad, SWEDEN 30270, Phone: 46-35-30977
Specialties: Working straight knives. **Patterns:** Bowies, hunters and fighters. **Technical:** Forges carbon steel and own Damascus. **Prices:** From $100. **Remarks:** Not currently making knives. **Mark:** Initials or last name.

VOORHIES, LES
14511 Lk Mazaska Tr, Faribault, MN 55021, Phone: 507-332-0736, lesvor@msn.com; Web: www.lesvoorhiesknives.com
Specialties: Steels. **Patterns:** Liner locks & autos. **Technical:** ATS-34 Damascus. **Prices:** $250 to $1200. **Mark:** L. Voorhies.

VOSS, BEN
2212 Knox Rd. 1600 Rd. E, Victoria, IL 61485-9644, Phone: 309-879-2940
Specialties: Fancy working knives of his design. **Patterns:** Bowies, fighters, hunters, boots and folders. **Technical:** Grinds 440C, ATS-34 and D2. **Prices:** $35 to $1200. **Remarks:** Part-time maker; first knife sold in 1986. **Mark:** Name, city and state.

VOTAW, DAVID P
305 S State St, Pioneer, OH 43554, Phone: 419-737-2774
Specialties: Working knives; period pieces. **Patterns:** Hunters, Bowies, camp knives, buckskinners and tomahawks. **Technical:** Grinds O1 and D2. **Prices:** $100 to $200; some to $500. **Remarks:** Part-time maker; took over for the late W.K. Kneubuhler. Doing business as W-K Knives. **Mark:** WK with V inside anvil.

W

WACHOLZ, DOC
95 Anne Rd, Marble, NC 28905, Phone: 828-557-1543, killdrums@aol.com; web: rackforge.com
Specialties: Forged tactical knives and tomahawks. **Technical:** Use 52100 and 1084 high carbon steel; make own Damascus; design and dew own sheaths. Grind up and down fashion on a 3" wheel.**Prices:** $300 to $800. **Remarks:** Part-time maker; started forging in 1999, with ABS master Charles Ochs.. **Mark:** Early knives stamped RACK, newer knives since 2005 stamped WACHOLZ.

WADA, YASUTAKA
2-6-22 Fujinokidai, Nara City, Nara, JAPAN 631-0044, Phone: 0742 46-0689
Specialties: Fancy and embellished one-of-a-kind straight knives of his design. **Patterns:** Bowies, daggers and hunters. **Technical:** Grinds ATS-34. All knives hand-filed and flat grinds. **Prices:** $400 to $2500; some higher. **Remarks:** Part-time maker; first knife sold in 1990. **Mark:** Owl eyes with initial and last name underneath or last name.

WAGAMAN, JOHN K
107 E Railroad St, Selma, NC 27576, Phone: 919-965-9659, Fax: 919-965-9901
Specialties: Fancy working knives. **Patterns:** Bowies, miniatures, hunters, fighters and boots. **Technical:** Grinds D2, 440C, 154CM and commercial Damascus; inlays mother-of-pearl. **Prices:** $110 to $2000. **Remarks:** Part-time maker; first knife sold in 1975. **Mark:** Last name.

WAIDE, RUSTY
Triple C Knives, PO Box 499, Buffalo, MO 65622, Phone: 417-345-7231, Fax: 417-345-1911, wrrccc@yahoo.com; Web: www.triplecknives.com
Specialties: Custom-designed hunting knives and cowboy working knives in high-carbon and damascus steels. **Prices:** $150 to $450. **Remarks:** Part-time maker; first knife sold in 2010. **Mark:** Name.

WAITES, RICHARD L
PO Box 188, Broomfield, CO 80038, Phone: 303-465-9970, Fax: 303-465-9971, dickknives@aol.com
Specialties: Working fixed blade knives of all kinds including "paddle blade" skinners. Hand crafted sheaths, some upscale and unusual. **Technical:** Grinds 440C, ATS 34, D2. **Prices:** $100 to $500. **Remarks:** Part-time maker. First knife sold in 1998. Doing business as R.L. Waites Knives. **Mark:** Oval etch with first and middle initial and last name on top and city and state on bottom. Memberships; Professional Knifemakers Association and Rocky Mountain Blade Collectors Club.

WALKER, BILL
431 Walker Rd, Stevensville, MD 21666, Phone: 410-643-5041

WALKER, DON
2850 Halls Chapel Rd, Burnsville, NC 28714, Phone: 828-675-9716, dlwalkernc@gmail.com

WALKER, JIM
22 Walker Ln, Morrilton, AR 72110, Phone: 501-354-3175, jwalker46@att.net
Specialties: Period pieces and working/using knives of his design and to customer specs. **Patterns:** Bowies, fighters, hunters, camp knives. **Technical:** Forges 5160, O1, L6, 52100, 1084, 1095. **Prices:** Start at $450. **Remarks:** Full-time maker; first knife sold in 1993. **Mark:** Three arrows with last name/MS.

WALKER, MICHAEL L
925-A Paseo del, Pueblo Sur Taos, NM 87571, Phone: 505-751-3409, Fax: 505-751-3417, metalwerkr@msn.com
Specialties: Innovative knife designs and locking systems; titanium and SS furniture and art. **Patterns:** Folders from utility grade to museum quality art; others upon request. **Technical:** State-of-the-art materials: titanium, stainless Damascus, gold, etc. **Prices:** $3500 and above. **Remarks:** Designer/MetalCrafts; full-time professional knifemaker since 1980; four U.S. patents; invented LinerLock® and was awarded registered U.S. trademark no. 1,585,333. **Mark:** Early mark MW, Walker's Lockers by M.L. Walker; current M.L. Walker or Michael Walker.

WALL, GREG
4753 Michie Pebble Hill Rd., Michie, TN 38357, Phone: 662-415-2909, glwall36@hotmail.com, www.wallhandmadeknives.com
Specialties: Working straight knives. **Patterns:** Classic hollow-handle survival knives, Ek-style fighters, drop-point hunters and big 7's models. **Technical:** Stock removal method of blade making, convex and flat grinds, using O1 tool steels and 440C stainless steel. **Prices:** $295 to $395. **Remarks:** First knife made and sold in 1983.

WALLINGFORD JR., CHARLES W
9024 Old Union Rd, Union, KY 41091, Phone: 859-384-4141, Web: www.cwknives.com
Specialties: 18th and 19th century styles, patch knives, rifleman knives. **Technical:** 1084 and 5160 forged blades. **Prices:** $125 to $300. **Mark:** CW.

WARD, CHUCK
PO Box 2272, 1010 E North St, Benton, AR 72018-2272, Phone: 501-778-4329, chuckbop@aol.com
Specialties: Traditional working and using straight knives and folders of his design. **Technical:** Grinds 440C, D2, A2, ATS-34 and O1; uses natural and composite handle materials. **Prices:** $90 to $400, some higher. **Remarks:** Part-time maker; first knife sold in 1990. **Mark:** First initial, last name.

WARD, J J
7501 S R 220, Waverly, OH 45690, Phone: 614-947-5328
Specialties: Traditional and working/using straight knives and folders of his design. **Patterns:** Hunters and locking folders. **Technical:** Grinds ATS-34, 440C and Damascus. Offers handmade sheaths. **Prices:** $125 to $250; some to $500. **Remarks:** Spare-time maker; first knife sold in 1980. **Mark:** Etched name.

WARD, KEN
1125 Lee Roze Ln, Grants Pass, OR 97527, Phone: 541-956-8864
Specialties: Working knives, some to customer specs. **Patterns:** Straight, axes, Bowies, buckskinners and miniatures. **Technical:** Grinds ATS-34, Damascus. **Prices:** $100 to $700. **Remarks:** Part-time maker; first knife sold in 1977. **Mark:** Name.

WARD, RON
PO BOX 21, Rose Hill, VA 24281, Phone: 276-445-4757
Specialties: Classic working and using straight knives, fantasy knives. **Patterns:** Bowies, hunter, fighters, and utility/camp knives. **Technical:** Grinds 440C, 154CM, ATS-34, uses composite and natural handle materials. **Prices:** $50 to $750. **Remarks:** Part-time maker, first knife sold in 1992. Doing business as Ron Ward Blades. **Mark:** RON WARD BLADES.

WARD, W C
817 Glenn St, Clinton, TN 37716, Phone: 615-457-3568
Specialties: Working straight knives; period pieces. **Patterns:** Hunters, Bowies, swords and kitchen cutlery. **Technical:** Grinds O1. **Prices:** $85 to $150; some to $500. **Remarks:** Part-time maker; first knife sold in 1969. He styled the Tennessee Knife Maker. **Mark:** TKM.

WARDELL, MICK
20 Clovelly Rd, Bideford, N Devon, ENGLAND EX39 3BU, wardellknives@hotmail.co.uk Web: www.wardellscustomknives.com
Specialties: Spring back folders and a few fixed blades. **Patterns:** Locking and slip-joint folders, Bowies. **Technical:** Grinds stainless Damascus and RWL34. Heat-treats. **Prices:** $300 to $2500. **Remarks:** Full-time maker; first knife sold in 1986. Takes limited Comissions. **Mark:** Wardell.

WARDEN, ROY A
275 Tanglewood Rd, Union, MO 63084, Phone: 314-583-8813, rwarden@yhti.net
Specialties: Complex mosaic designs of "EDM wired figures" and "stack up" patterns and "lazer cut" and "torch cut" and "sawed" patterns combined. **Patterns:** Mostly "all mosaic" folders, automatics, fixed blades. **Technical:** Mosaic Damascus with all tool steel edges. **Prices:** $100 to $1000. **Remarks:** Part-time maker; first knife sold in 1987. **Mark:** WARDEN stamped or initials connected.

WARE, J.D.
Calle 40 #342 x 47 y 49, Colonia Benito Juarez Norte, Merida, Yucatan, MEXICO 97119, jdware@jdwareknives.com; Web: www.jdwareknives.com
Specialities: Coin knives, slip-joint folders, chef's knives and hunting/camping/fishing knives. **Technical:** Practices stock-removal and forging methods of blade making using O1, 440C and D2 blade steels. **Prices:** Start at $200. **Remarks:** Full-time maker; first knife made in 1976. **Mark:** Usually etched "JD Ware, Artesano, Merida Yucatan, Hecho a Mano, Mexico."

WARE, TOMMY
158 Idlewilde, Onalaska, TX 77360, Phone: 936-646-4649
Specialties: Traditional working and using straight knives, folders and automatics of his design and to customer specs. **Patterns:** Hunters, automatics and locking folders. **Technical:** Grinds ATS-34, 440C and D2. Offers engraving and scrimshaw. **Prices:** $425 to $650; some to $1500. **Remarks:** Full-time maker; first knife sold in 1990. Doing business as Wano Knives. **Mark:** Last name inside oval, business name above, city and state below, year on side.

WARREN
1423 Sante Fe Circle, Roseville, CA 95678, Phone: 916-257-5904, Fax: 215-318-2945, al@warrenknives.com; Web: www.warrenknives.com
Specialties: Working straight knives and folders, some fancy. **Patterns:** Hunters, Bowies, fillets, lockback, folders & multi blade. **Technical:** Grinds ATS-34 and S30V.440V. **Prices:** $225 to $2,500.**Remarks:** Full-time maker; first knife sold in 1978. **Mark:** First and middle initials, last name.

WARREN, ALAN AND CARROLL
6605 S.E. 69th Ave., Portland, OR 97206, Phone: 503-788-6863 or 503-926-3559, alanwarrenknives@yahoo.com
Specialties: Mostly one-of-a-kind straight knives, bird & trout knives, skinners, fighters, bowies, daggers and short swords. My designs or custom. **Technical:** Hollow and flat grinds 154CM, ATS-34, CPM-S30V, O1, and others. Uses just about all handle materials available. Makes custom-to-fit, hand-tooled and hand stitched leather sheaths, some with skin inlays or hard inlays to match knife handle materials such as G-10, Micarta, ironwood, ivory, stag, etc. **Prices:** $200 to $1,800, some to $3,595. **Remarks:** Full-time maker for nine years; first knife sold in 1998. **Mark:** Name, city, state.

custom knifemakers

WARREN, DANIEL
571 Lovejoy Rd, Canton, NC 28716, Phone: 828-648-7351
Specialties: Using knives. **Patterns:** Drop point hunters. **Prices:** $200 to $500. **Mark:** Warren-Bethel NC.

WASHBURN, ARTHUR D
ADW CUSTOM KNIVES, 211 Hinman St / PO Box 625, Pioche, NV 89043, Phone: 775-962-5463, knifeman@lcturbonet.com; Web: www.adwcustomknives.com
Specialties: Locking liner folders. **Patterns:** Slip joint folders (single and multiplied), lock-back folders, some fixed blades. Do own heat-treating; Rockwell test each blade. **Technical:** Carbon and stainless Damascus, some 1084, 1095, AEBL, 12C27, S30V. **Prices:** $200 to $1000 and up. **Remarks:** Sold first knife in 1997. Part-time maker. **Mark:** ADW enclosed in an oval or ADW.

WASHBURN JR., ROBERT LEE
1929 Lava Flow Dr., St. George, UT 84790, Phone: 435-619-4432, Fax: 435-574-8554, rlwashburn@excite.com; Web: www.washburnknives.net
Specialties: Hand-forged period, Bowies, tactical, boot and hunters. **Patterns:** Bowies, tantos, loot hunters, tactical and folders. **Prices:** $100 to $2500. **Remarks:** All hand forged. 52100 being his favorite steel. **Mark:** Washburn Knives W.

WATANABE, MELVIN
1297 Kika St., Kailua, HI 96734, Phone: 808-261-2842, meltod808@yahoo.com
Specialties: Fancy folding knives. Some hunters. **Patterns:** Liner-locks and hunters. **Technical:** Grinds ATS-34, stainless Damascus. **Prices:** $350 and up. **Remarks:** Part-time maker; first knife sold in 1985. **Mark:** Name and state.

WATANABE, WAYNE
PO Box 3563, Montebello, CA 90640, wwknives@yahoo.com
Specialties: Straight knives in Japanese-styles. One-of-a-kind designs; welcomes customer designs. **Patterns:** Tantos to katanas, Bowies. **Technical:** Flat grinds A2, O1 and ATS-34. Offers hand-rubbed finishes and wrapped handles. **Prices:** Start at $200. **Remarks:** Part-time maker. **Mark:** Name in characters with flower.

WATERS, GLENN
11 Doncaster Place, Hyland Park, NSW, AUSTRALIA 2448, Phone: 172-33-8881, watersglenn@hotmail.com; Web: www.glennwaters.com
Specialties: One-of-a-kind collector-grade highly embellished art knives. Folders, fixed blades, and automatics. **Patterns:** Locking liner folders, automatics and fixed art knives. **Technical:** Grinds blades from Damasteel, and selected Damascus makers, mostly stainless. Does own engraving, gold inlaying and stone setting, filework, and carving. Gold and Japanese precious metal fabrication. Prefers exotic material, high karat gold, silver, Shyaku Dou, Shibu Ichi Gin, precious gemstones. **Prices:** Upscale. **Remarks:** Designs and makes some-of-a-kind highly embellished art knives often with fully engraved handles and blades. A jeweler by trade for 20 years before starting to make knives. Full-time since 1999, first knife sold in 1994. **Mark:** Glenn Waters maker Japan, G. Waters or Glen in Japanese writing.

WATSON, BERT
9315 Meade St., Westminster, CO 80031, Phone: 303-587-3064, watsonbd21960@q.com
Specialties: Working/using straight knives of his design and to customer specs. **Patterns:** Hunters, utility/camp knives. **Technical:** Grinds O1, ATS-34, 440C, D2, A2 and others. **Prices:** $150 to $800. **Remarks:** Full-time maker. **Mark:** GTK and/or Bert.

WATSON, BILLY
440 Forge Rd, Deatsville, AL 36022, Phone: 334-365-1482, hilldweller44@att.net
Specialties: Working and using straight knives and folders of his design; period pieces. **Patterns:** Hunters, Bowies and utility/camp knives. **Technical:** Forges and grinds his own Damascus, 1095, 5160 and 52100. **Prices:** $40 to $1500. **Remarks:** Full-time maker; first knife sold in 1970. **Mark:** Last name.

WATSON, DANIEL
350 Jennifer Ln, Driftwood, TX 78619, Phone: 512-847-9679, info@angelsword.com; Web: http://www.angelsword.com
Specialties: One-of-a-kind knives and swords. **Patterns:** Hunters, daggers, swords. **Technical:** Hand-purify and carbonize his own high-carbon steel, pattern-welded Damascus, cable and carbon-induced crystalline Damascus. Teehno-Wootz™ Damascus steel, heat treats including cryogenic processing. European and Japanese tempering. **Prices:** $125 to $25,000. **Remarks:** Full-time maker; first knife sold in 1979. **Mark:** "Angel Sword" on forged pieces; "Bright Knight" for stock removal. Avatar on Techno-Wootz™ Damascus. Bumon on traditional Japanese blades.

WATSON, PETER
66 Kielblock St, La Hoff, NW, SOUTH AFRICA 2570, Phone: 018-84942
Specialties: Traditional working and using straight knives and folders of his design. **Patterns:** Hunters, locking folders and utility/camp knives. **Technical:** Sandvik and 440C. **Prices:** $120 to $250; some to $1500. **Remarks:** Part-time maker; first knife sold in 1989. **Mark:** Buffalo head with name.

WATSON, TOM
1103 Brenau Terrace, Panama City, FL 32405, Phone: 850-785-9209, tom@tomwatsonknives.com; Web: www.tomwatsonknives.com
Specialties: Utility/tactical LinerLocks and flipper folders. **Patterns:** Various patterns. **Technical:** Grinds D2 and CPM-154. **Prices:** $375 and up. **Remarks:** In business since 1978. **Mark:** Name and city.

WATTELET, MICHAEL A
PO Box 649, 125 Front, Minocqua, WI 54548, Phone: 715-356-3069, redtroll@frontier.com
Specialties: Working and using straight knives of his design and to customer specs; fantasy knives. **Patterns:** Daggers, fighters and swords. **Technical:** Grinds 440C and L6; forges and grinds O1. Silversmith. **Prices:** $75 to $1000; some to $5000. **Remarks:** Full-time maker; first knife sold in 1966. Doing business as M and N Arts Ltd. **Mark:** First initial, last name.

WATTS, JOHNATHAN
9560 S Hwy 36, Gatesville, TX 76528, Phone: 254-487-2866
Specialties: Traditional folders. **Patterns:** One and two blade folders in various blade shapes. **Technical:** Grinds ATS-34 and Damascus on request. **Prices:** $120 to $400. **Remarks:** Part-time maker; first knife sold in 1997. **Mark:** J Watts.

WATTS, RODNEY
Watts Custom Knives, 1100 Hwy. 71 S, Hot Springs, SD 57747, Phone: 605-890-0645, wattscustomknives@yahoo.com; www.wattscustomknives.com
Specialties: Fixed blades and some folders, most of maker's own designs, some Loveless and Johnson patterns. **Technical:** Stock removal method of blade making, using CPM 154 and ATS-34 steels. **Prices:** $450 to $1,100. **Remarks:** Part-time maker; first knife made in 2007. Won "Best New Maker" award at the 2011 BLADE Show. **Mark:** Watts over Custom Knives.

WATTS, WALLY
9560 S Hwy 36, Gatesville, TX 76528, Phone: 254-223-9669
Specialties: Unique traditional folders of his design. **Patterns:** One- to five-blade folders and single-blade gents in various blade shapes. **Technical:** Grinds ATS-34; Damascus on request. **Prices:** $150 to $400. **Remarks:** Full-time maker; first knife sold in 1986. **Mark:** Last name.

WEBSTER, BILL
58144 West Clear Lake Rd, Three Rivers, MI 49093, Phone: 269-244-2873, wswebster_5@msn.com Web: www.websterknifeworks.com
Specialties: Working and using straight knives, especially for hunters. His patterns are custom designed. **Patterns:** Hunters, skinners, camp knives, Bowies and daggers. **Technical:** Hand-filed blades made of D2 steel only, unless other steel is requested. Preferred handle material is stabilized and exotic wood and stag. Sheaths are made by Green River Leather in Kentucky. Hand-sewn sheaths by Bill Dehn in Three Rivers, MI. **Prices:** $75 to $500. **Remarks:** Part-time maker, first knife sold in 1978. **Mark:** Originally WEB stamped on blade, at present, Webster Knifeworks Three Rivers, MI laser etched on blade.

WEEKS, RYAN
PO Box 1101, Bountiful, UT 84001, Phone: 801-755-6789, ryan@ryanwknives.com; Web: www.ryanwknives.com
Specialties: Military and Law Enforcement applications as well as hunting and utility designs. **Patterns:** Fighters, bowies, hunters, and custom designs, I use man made as well as natural wood and exotic handle materials. **Technical:** Make via forge and stock removal methods, preferred steel includes high carbon, CPM154 CM and ATS34, Damascus and San Mai. **Prices:** $160 to $750. **Remarks:** Part-time maker; Business name is "Ryan W. Knives." First knife sold in 2009. **Mark:** Encircled "Ryan" beneath the crossed "W" UTAH, USA.

WEEVER, JOHN
1162 Black Hawk Trl., Nemo, TX 76070, Phone: 254-898-9595, john.weever@gmail.com; Web: WeeverKnives.com
Specialties: Traditional hunters (fixed blade, slip joint, and lockback) and tactical. **Patterns:** See website. **Technical:** Types of steel: S30V, Damascus or customer choice. Handles in mammoth ivory, oosic, horn, sambar, stag, etc. Sheaths in exotic leathers. **Prices:** $400 to $1200. **Remarks:** Stock removal maker full-time; began making knives in 1985. Member of knifemakers guild. **Mark:** Tang stamp: head of charging elephant with ears extended and WEEVER curved over the top.

WEHNER, RUDY
297 William Warren Rd, Collins, MS 39428, Phone: 601-765-4997
Specialties: Reproduction antique Bowies and contemporary Bowies in full and miniature. **Patterns:** Skinners, camp knives, fighters, axes and Bowies. **Technical:** Grinds 440C, ATS-34, 154CM and Damascus. **Prices:** $100 to $500; some to $850. **Remarks:** Full-time maker; first knife sold in 1975. **Mark:** Last name on Bowies and antiques; full name, city and state on skinners.

WEILAND JR., J REESE
PO Box 2337, Riverview, FL 33568, Phone: 813-671-0661, RWPHIL413@verizon.net; Web: www.reeseweilandknives.com
Specialties: Hawk bills; tactical to fancy folders. **Patterns:** Hunters, tantos, Bowies, fantasy knives, spears and some swords. **Technical:** Grinds ATS-34, 154CM, 440C, D2, O1, A2, Damascus. Titanium hardware on locking liners and button locks. **Prices:** $150 to $4000. **Remarks:** Full-time maker, first knife sold in 1978. Knifemakers Guild member since 1988.

WEINAND, GEROME M
14440 Harpers Bridge Rd, Missoula, MT 59808, Phone: 406-543-0845
Specialties: Working straight knives. **Patterns:** Bowies, fishing and camp knives, large special hunters. **Technical:** Grinds O1, 440C, ATS-34, 1084, L6, also stainless Damascus, Aebl and 304; makes all-tool steel Damascus; Dendritic D2 from powdered steel. Heat-treats. **Prices:** $30 to $100; some to $500. **Remarks:** Full-time maker; first knife sold in 1982. **Mark:** Last name.

WEINSTOCK, ROBERT
PO Box 170028, San Francisco, CA 94117-0028, Phone: 415-731-5968, robertweinstock@att.net
Specialties: Folders, slip joins, lockbacks, autos. **Patterns:** Daggers, folders. **Technical:** Grinds A2, O1 and 440C. Chased and hand-carved blades and handles. Also using various Damascus steels from other makers. **Prices:** $3000 to 7000. **Remarks:** Full-time maker; first knife sold in 1994. **Mark:** Last name carved in steel.

WEISS, CHARLES L
PO BOX 1037, Waddell, AZ 85355, Phone: 623-935-0924, weissknife@live.com
Specialties: High-art straight knives and folders; deluxe period pieces. **Patterns:** Daggers, fighters, boots, push knives and miniatures. **Technical:** Grinds 440C, 154CM and ATS-34. **Prices:** $300 to $1200; some to $2000. **Remarks:** Full-time maker; first knife sold in 1975. **Mark:** Name and city.

WELLING, RONALD L
15446 Lake Ave, Grand Haven, MI 49417, Phone: 616-846-2274
Specialties: Scagel knives of his design or to customer specs. **Patterns:** Hunters, camp knives, miniatures, bird, trout, folders, double edged, hatchets, skinners and some art pieces. **Technical:** Forges Damascus 1084 and 1095. Antler, ivory and horn. **Prices:** $250 to $3000. **Remarks:** Full-time maker. ABS Journeyman maker. **Mark:** First initials and or name and last name. City and state. Various scagel kris (1or 2).

WELLING, WILLIAM
Up-armored Knives, 5437 Pinecliff Dr., West Valley, NY 14171, Phone: 716-942-6031, uparmored@frontier.net; Web: www.up-armored.com
Specialties: Innovative tactical fixed blades each uniquely coated in a variety of Up-armored designed patterns and color schemes.Convexed edged bushcraft knives for the weekend camper, backpacker, or survivalist. Knives developed specifically for tactical operators. Leather- and synthetic-suede-lined Kydex sheaths. **Patterns:** Modern samples of time tested designs as well as contemporary developed cutting tools. **Technical:** Stock removal specializing in tested 1095CV and 5160 steels. **Prices:** $200 to $500. **Remarks:** Part-time maker; first knife sold in 2010. **Mark:** Skull rounded up by Up-Armored USA.

WERTH, GEORGE W
5223 Woodstock Rd, Poplar Grove, IL 61065, Phone: 815-544-4408
Specialties: Period pieces, some fancy. **Patterns:** Straight fighters, daggers and Bowies. **Technical:** Forges and grinds O1, 1095 and his Damascus, including mosaic patterns. **Prices:** $200 to $650; some higher. **Remarks:** Full-time maker. Doing business as Fox Valley Forge. **Mark:** Name in logo or initials connected.

WESCOTT, CODY
5330 White Wing Rd, Las Cruces, NM 88012, Phone: 575-382-5008
Specialties: Fancy and presentation grade working knives. **Patterns:** Hunters, locking folders and Bowies. **Technical:** Hollow-grinds D2 and ATS-34; all knives file worked. Offers some engraving. Makes sheaths. **Prices:** $110 to $500; some to $1200. **Remarks:** Full-time maker; first knife sold in 1982. **Mark:** First initial, last name.

WEST, CHARLES A
1315 S Pine St, Centralia, IL 62801, Phone: 618-532-2777
Specialties: Classic, fancy, high tech, period pieces, traditional and working/using straight knives and folders. **Patterns:** Bowies, fighters and locking folders. **Technical:** Grinds ATS-34, O1 and Damascus. Prefers hot blued finishes. **Prices:** $100 to $1000; some to $2000. **Remarks:** Full-time maker; first knife sold in 1963. Doing business as West Custom Knives. **Mark:** Name or name, city and state.

WESTBERG, LARRY
305 S Western Hills Dr, Algona, IA 50511, Phone: 515-295-9276
Specialties: Traditional and working straight knives of his design and in standard patterns. **Patterns:** Bowies, hunters, fillets and folders. **Technical:** Grinds 440C, D2 and 1095. Heat-treats. Uses natural handle materials. **Prices:** $85 to $600; some to $1000. **Remarks:** Part-time maker; first knife sold in 1987. **Mark:** Last name-town and state.

WHEELER, GARY
351 Old Hwy 48, Clarksville, TN 37040, Phone: 931-552-3092, LR22SHTR@charter.net
Specialties: Working to high end fixed blades. **Patterns:** Bowies, Hunters, combat knives, daggers and a few folders. **Technical:** Forges 5160, 1095, 52100 and his own Damascus. **Prices:** $125 to $2000. **Remarks:** Full-time maker since 2001, first knife sold in 1985 collaborates/works at B&W Blade Works. ABS Journeyman Smith 2008. **Mark:** Stamped last name.

WHEELER, NICK
140 Studebaker Rd., Castle Rock, WA 98611, Phone: 360-967-2357, merckman99@yahoo.com
Specialties: Bowies, integrals, fighters, hunters and daggers. **Technical:** Forges W2, W1, 1095, 52100 and 1084. Makes own damascus, from random pattern to complex mosaics. Also grinds stainless and other more modern alloys. Does own heat-treating and leather work. Also commissions leather work from Paul Long. **Prices:** Start at $250. **Remarks:** Full-time maker; ABS member since 2001. Journeyman bladesmith. **Mark:** Last name.

WHEELER, ROBERT
289 S Jefferson, Bradley, IL 60915, Phone: 815-932-5854, b2btaz@brmemc.net

WHETSELL, ALEX
PO Box 215, Haralson, GA 30229, Phone: 770-599-8012, www.KnifeKits.com
Specialties: Knifekits.com, a source for fold locking liner type and straight knife kits. These kits are industry standard for folding knife kits. **Technical:** Many selections of colored G10 carbon fiber and wood handle material for kits, as well as bulk sizes for the

custom knifemaker, heat treated folding knife pivots, screws, bushings, etc.

WHIPPLE, WESLEY A
1002 Shoshoni St, Thermopolis, WY 82443, Phone: 307-921-2445, wildernessknife@yahoo.com
Specialties: Working straight knives, some fancy. **Patterns:** Hunters, Bowies, camp knives, fighters. **Technical:** Forges high-carbon steels, Damascus, offers relief carving and silver wire inlay and checkering. **Prices:** $300 to $1400; some higher. **Remarks:** Full-time maker; first knife sold in 1989. A.K.A. Wilderness Knife and Forge. **Mark:** Last name/JS.

WHITE, BRYCE
1415 W Col Glenn Rd, Little Rock, AR 72210, Phone: 501-821-2956
Specialties: Hunters, fighters, makes Damascus, file work, handmade only. **Technical:** L6, 1075, 1095, O1 steels used most. **Patterns:** Will do any pattern or use his own. **Prices:** $200 to $300. Sold first knife in 1995. **Mark:** White.

WHITE, CALEB A.
502 W. River Rd. #88, Hooksett, NH 03106, Phone: 603-210-1271, caleb@calebwhiteknives.com; www.calebwhiteknives.com
Specialties: Hunters, tacticals, dress knives, daggers and utilitarian pieces. **Patterns:**7.5" Gentleman's model, 8" Firefly model, both dress/semi-field knives meant for everyday carry and hard use. **Technical:** Stock-removal knifemaker preferring 52100 blade steel, also 1084 and ATS-34 stainless. Ninety percent are full-tang pieces, with hidden tangs on daggers. **Prices:** $150 to $600, or up for daggers and art knives. **Remarks:** Full-time maker. **Mark:** Derivation of maker's last name, replacing the "T" with a symbol loosely based on the Templars' cross and shield.

WHITE, DALE
525 CR 212, Sweetwater, TX 79556, Phone: 325-798-4178, dalew@taylortel.net
Specialties: Working and using knives. **Patterns:** Hunters, skinners, utilities and Bowies. **Technical:** Grinds 440C, offers file work, fancy pins and scrimshaw by Sherry Sellers. **Prices:** From $45 to $300. **Remarks:** Sold first knife in 1975. **Mark:** Full name, city and state.

WHITE, GARRETT
871 Sarijon Rd, Hartwell, GA 30643, Phone: 706-376-5944
Specialties: Gentlemen folders, fancy straight knives. **Patterns:** Locking liners and hunting fixed blades. **Technical:** Grinds 440C, S30V, and stainless Damascus. **Prices:** $150 to $1000. **Remarks:** Part-time maker. **Mark:** Name.

WHITE, JOHN PAUL
231 S Bayshore, Valparaiso, FL 32580, Phone: 850-729-9174, johnwhiteknives@gmail.com
Specialties: Forged hunters, fighters, traditional Bowies and personal carry knives with handles of natural materials and fittings with detailed file work. **Technical:** Forges carbon steel and own Damascus. **Prices:** $1,200 to $5,000. **Remarks:** Master Smith, American Bladesmith Society. **Mark:** First initial, last name.

WHITE, LOU
7385 Red Bud Rd NE, Ranger, GA 30734, Phone: 706-334-2273

WHITE, RICHARD T
359 Carver St, Grosse Pointe Farms, MI 48236, Phone: 313-881-4690

WHITE, ROBERT J
RR 1 641 Knox Rd 900 N, Gilson, IL 61436, Phone: 309-289-4487
Specialties: Working knives, some deluxe. **Patterns:** Bird and trout knives, hunters, survival knives and locking folders. **Technical:** Grinds A2, D2 and 440C; commercial Damascus. Heat-treats. **Prices:** $125 to $250; some to $600. **Remarks:** Full-time maker; first knife sold in 1976. **Mark:** Last name in script.

WHITE JR., ROBERT J BUTCH
RR 1, Gilson, IL 61436, Phone: 309-289-4487
Specialties: Folders of all sizes. **Patterns:** Hunters, fighters, boots and folders. **Technical:** Forges Damascus; grinds tool and stainless steel. **Prices:** $500 to $1800. **Remarks:** Spare-time maker; first knife sold in 1980. **Mark:** Last name in block letters.

WHITENECT, JODY
, Halifax County, Elderbank, NS, CANADA B0N 1K0, Phone: 902-384-2511
Specialties: Fancy and embellished working/using straight knives of his design and to customer specs. **Patterns:** Bowies, fighters and hunters. **Technical:** Forges 1095 and O1; forges and grinds ATS-34. Various filework on blades and bolsters. **Prices:** $200 to $400; some to $800. **Remarks:** Part-time maker; first knife sold in 1996. **Mark:** Longhorn stamp or engraved.

WHITESELL, J. DALE
P.O. Box 455, Stover, MO 65078, Phone: 573-569-0753, dalesknives@yahoo.com; Web: whitesell-knives.webs.com
Specialties: Fixed blade working knives,a nd some collector pieces. **Patterns:** Hunting and skinner knives, camp knives, and kitchen knives. **Technical:** Blades ground from O1, 1095, and 440C in hollow, flat and saber grinds. Wood, bone, deer antler, and G10 are basic handle materials. **Prices:** $100 to $450. **Remarks:** Part-time maker, first knife sold in 2003. Doing business as Dale's Knives. All knives have serial number to indicate steel (since June 2010).**Mark:** Whitesell on the left side of the blade.

WHITLEY, L WAYNE
1675 Carrow Rd, Chocowinity, NC 27817-9495, Phone: 252-946-5648

WHITLEY, WELDON G
4308 N Robin Ave, Odessa, TX 79764, Phone: 432-530-0448, Fax: 432-530-0448,

wgwhitley@juno.com

Specialties: Working knives of his design or to customer specs. **Patterns:** Hunters, folders and various double-edged knives. **Technical:** Grinds 440C, 154CM and ATS-34. **Prices:** $150 to $1250. **Mark:** Name, address, road-runner logo.

WHITTAKER, ROBERT E

PO Box 204, Mill Creek, PA 17060

Specialties: Using straight knives. Has a line of knives for buckskinners. **Patterns:** Hunters, skinners and Bowies. **Technical:** Grinds O1, A2 and D2. Offers filework. **Prices:** $35 to $100. **Remarks:** Part-time maker; first knife sold in 1980. **Mark:** Last initial or full initials.

WHITTAKER, WAYNE

2900 Woodland Ct, Metamore, MI 48455, Phone: 810-797-5315, lindorwayne@yahoo.com

Specialties: Liner locks and autos. **Patterns:** Folders. **Technical:** Damascus, mammoth, ivory, and tooth. **Prices:** $500 to $1500. **Remarks:** Full-time maker. **Mark:** Inside of backbar.

WICK, JONATHAN P.

5541 E. Calle Narcisco, Hereford, AZ 85615, Phone: 520-227-5228, vikingwick@aol.com

Specialties: Fixed blades, pocketknives, neck knives, hunters, bowies, fighters, Roman-style daggers with full tangs, stick tangs and some integrals, and leather-lined, textured copper sheaths. **Technical:** Forged blades and own damascus and mosaic damascus, along with shibuichi, mokume, lost wax casting. **Prices:** $250 - $1800 and up. **Remarks:** Full-time maker, ABS member, sold first knife in 2008. **Mark:** J P Wick, also on small blades a JP over a W.

WICKER, DONNIE R

2544 E 40th Ct, Panama City, FL 32405, Phone: 904-785-9158

Specialties: Traditional working and using straight knives of his design or to customer specs. **Patterns:** Hunters, fighters and slip-joint folders. **Technical:** Grinds 440C, ATS-34, D2 and 154CM. Heat-treats and does hardness testing. **Prices:** $90 to $200; some to $400. **Remarks:** Part-time maker; first knife sold in 1975. **Mark:** First and middle initials, last name.

WIGGINS, BILL

105 Kaolin Lane, Canton, NC 28716, Phone: 828-226-2551, wncbill@bellsouth.net Web: www.wigginsknives.com

Specialties: Forged working knives. **Patterns:** Hunters, Bowies, camp knives and utility knives of own design or will work with customer on design. **Technical:** Forges 1084 and 52100 as well as making own Damascus. **Prices:** $250 - $1500. **Remarks:** Part-time maker. First knife sold in 1989. ABS board member. **Mark:** Wiggins

WILBURN, AARON

2521 Hilltop Dr., #364, Redding, CA 96002, Phone: 530-227-2827, wilburnforge@yahoo.com; Web: www.wilburnforge.com

Patterns: Daggers, bowies, fighters, hunters and slip-joint folders. **Technical:** Forges own damascus and works with high-carbon steel. **Prices:** $500 to $5,000. **Remarks:** Full-time maker and ABS master smith. **Mark:** Wilburn Forge.

WILCHER, WENDELL L

RR 6 Box 6573, Palestine, TX 75801, Phone: 903-549-2530

Specialties: Fantasy, miniatures and working/using straight knives and folders of his design and to customer specs. **Patterns:** Fighters, hunters, locking folders. **Technical:** Hand works (hand file and hand sand knives), not grind. **Prices:** $75 to $250; some to $600. **Remarks:** Part-time maker; first knife sold in 1987. **Mark:** Initials, year, serial number.

WILKINS, MITCHELL

15523 Rabon Chapel Rd, Montgomery, TX 77316, Phone: 936-588-2696, mwilkins@consolidated.net

WILLEY, WG

14210 Sugar Hill Rd, Greenwood, DE 19950, Phone: 302-349-4070, Web: www.willeyknives.com

Specialties: Fancy working straight knives. **Patterns:** Small game knives, Bowies and throwing knives. **Technical:** Grinds 440C and 154CM. **Prices:** $350 to $600; some to $1500. **Remarks:** Part-time maker; first knife sold in 1975. Owns retail store. **Mark:** Last name inside map logo.

WILLIAMS, JASON L

PO Box 67, Wyoming, RI 02898, Phone: 401-539-8353, Fax: 401-539-0252

Specialties: Fancy and high tech folders of his design, co-inventor of the Axis Lock. **Patterns:** Fighters, locking folders, automatics and fancy pocket knives. **Technical:** Forges Damascus and other steels by request. Uses exotic handle materials and precious metals. Offers inlaid spines and gemstone thumb knobs. **Prices:** $1000 and up. **Remarks:** Full-time maker; first knife sold in 1989. **Mark:** First and last initials on pivot.

WILLIAMS, MICHAEL

333 Cherrybark Tr., Broken Bow, OK 74728, Phone: 580-420-3051, hforge@pine-net.com

Specialties: Functional, personalized, edged weaponry. Working and collectible art. **Patterns:** Bowies, hunters, camp knives, daggers, others. **Technical:** Forges high carbon steel and own forged Damascus. **Prices:** $500 - $12000. **Remarks:** Full-time ABS Master Smith. **Mark:** Williams MS.

WILLIAMS, ROBERT

15962 State Rt. 267, East Liverpool, OH 43920, Phone: 203-979-0803, wurdmeister@gmail.com; Web: www.customstraightrazors.com

Specialties: Custom straight razors with a philosophy that form must follow function, so shaving performance drives designs and aesthetics. **Technical:** Stock removal and forging, working with 1095, O1 and damascus. Natural handle materials and synthetics, accommodating any and all design requests and can incorporate gold inlays, scrimshaw, hand engraving and jewel setting. All work done in maker's shop, sole-source maker shipping worldwide. **Remarks:** Full-time maker; first straight razor in 2005. **Mark:** Robert Williams - Handmade, USA with a hammer separating the two lines.

WILLIAMS JR., RICHARD

1440 Nancy Circle, Morristown, TN 37814, Phone: 615-581-0059

Specialties: Working and using straight knives of his design or to customer specs. **Patterns:** Hunters, dirks and utility/camp knives. **Technical:** Forges 5160 and uses file steel. Hand-finish is standard; offers filework. **Prices:** $80 to $180; some to $250. **Remarks:** Spare-time maker; first knife sold in 1985. **Mark:** Last initial or full initials.

WILLIAMSON, TONY

Rt 3 Box 503, Siler City, NC 27344, Phone: 919-663-3551

Specialties: Flint knapping: knives made of obsidian flakes and flint with wood, antler or bone for handles. **Patterns:** Skinners, daggers and flake knives. **Technical:** Blades have width/thickness ratio of at least 4 to 1. Hafts with methods available to prehistoric man. **Prices:** $58 to $160. **Remarks:** Student of Errett Callahan. **Mark:** Initials and number code to identify year and number of knives made.

WILLIS, BILL

RT 7 Box 7549, Ava, MO 65608, Phone: 417-683-4326

Specialties: Forged blades, Damascus and carbon steel. **Patterns:** Cable, random or ladder lamented. **Technical:** Professionally heat treated blades. **Prices:** $75 to $600. **Remarks:** Lifetime guarantee on all blades against breakage. All work done by maker; including leather work. **Mark:** WF.

WILLUMSEN, MIKKEL

Nyrnberggade 23, S Copenhagen, DENMARK 2300, Phone: 4531176333, mw@willumsen-cph.com Web: www.wix.com/willumsen/urbantactical

Specialties: Folding knives, fixed blades, and balisongs. Also kitchen knives. **Patterns:** Primarily influenced by design that is function and quality based. Tactical style knives inspired by classical designs mixed with modern tactics. **Technical:** Uses CPM 154, RW 134, S30V, and carbon fiber titanium G10 for handles. **Prices:** Starting at $600.

WILSON, CURTIS M

PO Box 383, Burleson, TX 76097, Phone: 817-295-3732, cwknifeman2026@att.net; Web: www.cwilsonknives.com

Specialties: Traditional working/using knives, fixed blade, folders, slip joint, LinerLock® and lock back knives. Art knives, presentation grade Bowies, folder repair, heat treating services. Sub-zero quench. **Patterns:** Hunters, camp knives, military combat, single and multi-blade folders. Dr's knives large or small or custom design knives. **Technical:** Grinds ATS-34, 440C 52100, D2, S30V, CPM 154, mokume gane, engraves, scrimshaw, sheaths leather of kykex heat treating and file work. **Prices:** $150-750. **Remarks:** Part-time maker since 1984. Sold first knife in 1993. **Mark:** Curtis Wilson in ribbon or Curtis Wilson with hand made in a half moon.

WILSON, JAMES G

PO Box 4024, Estes Park, CO 80517, Phone: 303-586-3944

Specialties: Bronze Age knives; Medieval and Scottish-styles; tomahawks. **Patterns:** Bronze knives, daggers, swords, spears and battle axes; 12-inch steel Misericorde daggers, sgian dubhs, "his and her" skinners, bird and fish knives, capers, boots and daggers. **Technical:** Casts bronze; grinds D2, 440C and ATS-34. **Prices:** $49 to $400; some to $1300. **Remarks:** Part-time maker; first knife sold in 1975. **Mark:** WilsonHawk.

WILSON, MIKE

1416 McDonald Rd, Hayesville, NC 28904, Phone: 828-389-8145

Specialties: Fancy working and using straight knives of his design or to customer specs, folders. **Patterns:** Hunters, Bowies, utility knives, gut hooks, skinners, fighters and miniatures. **Technical:** Hollow grinds 440C, 1095, D2, XHP and CPM-154. Mirror finishes are standard. Offers filework. **Prices:** $130 to $600. **Remarks:** Full-time maker; first knife sold in 1985. **Mark:** Last name.

WILSON, P.R. "REGAN"

805 Janvier Rd., Scott, LA 70583, Phone: 504-427-1293, pat71ss@cox.net; www.acadianawhitetailtaxidermy.com

Specialties: Traditional working knives. **Patterns:** Old-school working knives, trailing points, drop points, hunters, boots, etc. **Technical:** 440C, ATS-34 and 154CM steels, all hollow ground with mirror or satin finishes. **Prices:** Start at $175 with sheath. **Remarks:** Mentored by Jim Barbee; first knife sold in 1988; lessons and guidance offered in maker's shop. **Mark:** Name and location with "W" in center of football-shaped logo.

WILSON, PHILIP C

SEAMOUNT KNIFEWORKS, PO Box 846, Mountain Ranch, CA 95246, Phone: 209-754-1990, seamount@bigplanet.com; Web: www.seamountknifeworks.com

Specialties: Working knives; emphasis on salt water fillet knives and utility hunters of his design. **Patterns:** Fishing knives, hunters, utility knives. **Technical:** Grinds CPM10V, S-90V, CPMS110V, K390, K294, CPM154, M-390, ELMAX. Heat-treats and Rockwell tests all blades. **Prices:** Start at $400. **Remarks:** First knife sold in 1985. Doing business as Sea-Mount Knife Works. **Mark:** Signature.

WILSON, RON

2639 Greenwood Ave, Morro Bay, CA 93442, Phone: 805-772-3381
Specialties: Classic and fantasy straight knives of his design. **Patterns:** Daggers, fighters, swords and axes, mostly all miniatures. **Technical:** Forges and grinds Damascus and various tool steels; grinds meteorite. Uses gold, precious stones and exotic wood. **Prices:** Vary. **Remarks:** Part-time maker; first knives sold in 1995. **Mark:** Stamped first and last initials.

WILSON, RW

PO Box 2012, Weirton, WV 26062, Phone: 304-723-2771, rwknives@hotmail.com
Specialties: Working straight knives; period pieces. **Patterns:** Bowies, tomahawks and patch knives. **Technical:** Grinds 440C; scrimshaws. **Prices:** $85 to $175; some to $1000. **Remarks:** Part-time maker; first knife sold in 1966. Knifemaker supplier. Offers free knife-making lessons. **Mark:** Name in tomahawk.

WILSON, STAN

8931 Pritcher Rd, Lithia, FL 33547, Phone: 727-461-1992, swilson@stanwilsonknives.com; Web: www.stanwilsonknives.com
Specialties: Fancy folders and automatics of his own design. **Patterns:** Locking liner folders, single and dual action autos, daggers. **Technical:** Stock removal, uses Damascus, stainless and high carbon steels, prefers ivory and pearl, Damascus with blued finishes and filework. **Prices:** $400 and up. **Remarks:** Member of Knifemakers Guild and Florida Knifemakers Association. Full-time maker will do custom orders. **Mark:** Name in script.

WILSON, VIC

9130 Willow Branch Dr, Olive Branch, MS 38654, Phone: 901-591-6550, vdubjr55@earthlink.net; Web: www.knivesbyvic.com
Specialties: Classic working and using knives and folders. **Patterns:** Hunters, boning, utility, camp, my patterns or customers. **Technical:** Grinds O1 and D2. Also does own heat treating. Offer file work and decorative liners on folders. Fabricate custom leather sheaths for all knives. **Prices:** $150 to $400. **Remarks:** Part-time maker, first knife sold in 1989. **Mark:** Etched V over W with oval circle around it, name, Memphis, TN.

WINGO, GARY

240 Ogeechee, Ramona, OK 74061, Phone: 918-536-1067, wingg_2000@yahoo.com; Web: www.geocities.com/wingg_2000/gary.html
Specialties: Folder specialist. Steel 440C, D2, others on request. Handle bone-stag, others on request. **Patterns:** Trapper three-blade stockman, four-blade congress, single- and two-blade barlows. **Prices:** 150 to $400. **Mark:** First knife sold 1994. Steer head with Wingo Knives or Straight line Wingo Knives.

WINGO, PERRY

22 55th St, Gulfport, MS 39507, Phone: 228-863-3193
Specialties: Traditional working straight knives. **Patterns:** Hunters, skinners, Bowies and fishing knives. **Technical:** Grinds 440C. **Prices:** $75 to $1000. **Remarks:** Full-time maker; first knife sold in 1988. **Mark:** Last name.

WINKLER, DANIEL

PO Box 2166, Blowing Rock, NC 28605, Phone: 828-295-9156, danielwinkler@bellsouth.net; Web: www.winklerknives.com
Specialties: Forged cutlery styled in the tradition of an era past as well as producing a custom-made stock removal line. **Patterns:** Fixed blades, friction folders, lock back folders, and axes/tomahawks. **Technical:** Forges, grinds, and heat treats carbon steels, specialty steels, and his own Damascus steel. **Prices:** $350 to $4000+. **Remarks:** Full-time maker since 1988. Exclusively offers leatherwork by Karen Shook. ABS Master Smith; Knifemakers Guild voting member. **Mark:** Hand forged: Dwinkler; Stock removal: Winkler Knives

WINN, MARVIN

Maxcutter Custom Knives, 587 Winn Rd., Sunset, LA 70584, Phone: 214-471-7012, maxcutter03@yahoo.com Web: www.maxcutterknives.com
Patterns: Hunting knives, some tactical and some miniatures. **Technical:** 1095, 5160, 154 CM, 12C27, CPM S30V, CPM 154, CTS-XHP and CTS-40CP blade steels, damascus or to customer's specs. Stock removal. **Prices:** $200 to $2,000. **Remarks:** Part-time maker. First knife made in 2002. **Mark:** Name and state.

WINN, TRAVIS A.

558 E 3065 S, Salt Lake City, UT 84106, Phone: 801-467-5957
Specialties: Fancy working knives and knives to customer specs. **Patterns:** Hunters, fighters, boots, Bowies and fancy daggers, some miniatures, tantos and fantasy knives. **Technical:** Grinds D2 and 440C. Embellishes. **Prices:** $125 to $500; some higher. **Remarks:** Part-time maker; first knife sold in 1976. **Mark:** TRAV stylized.

WINSTON, DAVID

1671 Red Holly St, Starkville, MS 39759, Phone: 601-323-1028
Specialties: Fancy and traditional knives of his design and to customer specs. **Patterns:** Bowies, daggers, hunters, boot knives and folders. **Technical:** Grinds 440C, ATS-34 and D2. Offers filework; heat-treats. **Prices:** $40 to $750; some higher. **Remarks:** Part-time maker; first knife sold in 1984. Offers lifetime sharpening for original owner. **Mark:** Last name.

WIRTZ, ACHIM

Mittelstrasse 58, Wuerselen, GERMANY 52146, Phone: 0049-2405-462-486, wootz@web.de
Specialties: Medieval, Scandinavian and Middle East-style knives. **Technical:** Forged blades only, Damascus steel, Wootz, Mokume. **Prices:** Start at $200. **Remarks:** Part-time maker. First knife sold in 1997. **Mark:** Stylized initials.

WISE, DONALD

304 Bexhill Rd, St Leonardo-On-Sea, East Sussex, ENGLAND TN3 8AL
Specialties: Fancy and embellished working straight knives to customer specs. **Patterns:** Hunters, Bowies and daggers. **Technical:** Grinds Sandvik 12C27, D2 D3 and O1. Scrimshaws. **Prices:** $110 to $300; some to $500. **Remarks:** Full-time maker; first knife sold in 1983. **Mark:** KNIFECRAFT.

WOLF, BILL

4618 N 79th Ave, Phoenix, AZ 85033, Phone: 623-910-3147, bwcustomknives143@gmail.com; Web: www.billwolfcustomknives.com
Specialties: Investment grade knives. **Patterns:** Own designs or customer's. **Technical:** Grinds stainless and all steels. **Prices:** $400 to ? **Remarks:** First knife made in 1988. **Mark:** WOLF

WOLF JR., WILLIAM LYNN

4006 Frank Rd, Lagrange, TX 78945, Phone: 409-247-4626

WOOD, ALAN

Greenfield Villa, Greenhead, Brampton, ENGLAND CA8 7HH, info@alanwoodknives.com; Web: www.alanwoodknives.com
Specialties: High-tech working straight knives of his design. **Patterns:** Hunters, utility/camp and bushcraft knives. **Technical:** Grinds 12C27, RWL-34, stainless Damascus and O1. Blades are cryogenic treated. **Prices:** $200 to $800; some to $1,200. **Remarks:** Full-time maker; first knife sold in 1979. Not currently taking orders. **Mark:** Full name with stag tree logo.

WOOD, OWEN DALE

6492 Garrison St, Arvada, CO 80004-3157, Phone: 303-456-2748, wood.owen@gmail.com; Web: www.owenwoodknives.net
Specialties: Folding knives and daggers. **Patterns:** Own Damascus, specialties in 456 composite blades. **Technical:** Materials: Damascus stainless steel, exotic metals, gold, rare handle materials. **Prices:** $1000 to $9000. **Remarks:** Folding knives in art deco and art noveau themes. Full-time maker from 1981. **Mark:** OWEN WOOD.

WOOD, WEBSTER

22041 Shelton Trail, Atlanta, MI 49709, Phone: 989-785-2996, mainganikan@src-milp.com
Specialties: Works mainly in stainless; art knives, Bowies, hunters and folders. **Remarks:** Full-time maker; first knife sold in 1980. Retired guild member. All engraving done by maker. **Mark:** Initials inside shield and name.

WORLEY, JOEL A.

PO BOX 64, Maplewood, OH 45340, Phone: 937-638-9518, j.a.worleyknives@woh.rr.com
Specialties: Bowies, hunters, fighters, utility/camp knives also period style friction folders. **Patterns:** Classic styles, recurves, his design or customer specified. **Technical:** Most knives are fileworked and include a custom made leather sheath. Forges 5160, W2, Cru forge V, files own Damascus of 1080 and 15N20. **Prices:** $250 and up. **Remarks:** Part-time maker. ABS member. First knife sold in 2005. **Mark:** First name, middle initial and last name over a shark incorporating initials.

WRIGHT, KEVIN

671 Leland Valley Rd W, Quilcene, WA 98376-9517, Phone: 360-765-3589, kevinw@ptpc.com
Specialties: Fancy working or collector knives to customer specs. **Patterns:** Hunters, boots, buckskinners, miniatures. **Technical:** Forges and grinds L6, 1095, 440C and his own Damascus. **Prices:** $75 to $500; some to $2000. **Remarks:** Part-time maker; first knife sold in 1978. **Mark:** Last initial in anvil.

WRIGHT, L.T.

130b Warren Ln., Wintersville, OH 43953, Phone: 740-317-1404, lt@ltwrightknives.com; Web: www.ltwrightknives.com
Specialties: Hunting and tactical knives. **Patterns:** Drop point hunters, bird, trout and tactical. **Technical:** Grinds D2, 440C and O1. **Remarks:** Full-time maker.

WRIGHT, RICHARD S

PO Box 201, 111 Hilltop Dr, Carolina, RI 02812, Phone: 401-364-3579, rswswitchblades@hotmail.com; Web: www.richardswright.com
Specialties: Bolster release switchblades, tactical automatics. **Patterns:** Folding fighters, gents pocket knives, one-of-a-kind high-grade automatics. **Technical:** Reforges and grinds various makers Damascus. Uses a variety of tool steels. Uses natural handle material such as ivory and pearl, extensive file-work on most knives. **Prices:** $850 and up. **Remarks:** Full-time knifemaker with background as a gunsmith. Made first folder in 1991. **Mark:** RSW on blade, all folders are serial numbered.

WRIGHT, ROBERT A

21 Wiley Bottom Rd, Savannah, GA 31411, Phone: 912-598-8239; Cell: 912-656-9085, maker@robwrightknives.com; Web: www.RobWrightKnives.com
Specialties: Hunting, skinning, fillet, fighting and tactical knives. **Patterns:** Custom designs by client and/or maker. **Technical:** All types of steel, including CPM-S30V, D2, 440C, O1 tool steel and damascus upon request, as well as exotic wood and other high-quality handle materials. **Prices:** $200 and up depending on cost of steel and other materials. **Remarks:** Full-time maker, member of The Knifemakers' Guild and Georgia Custom Knifemaker's Guild. **Mark:** Etched maple leaf with maker's name: R.A. Wright.

WRIGHT, TIMOTHY

PO Box 3746, Sedona, AZ 86340, Phone: 928-282-4180
Specialties: High-tech folders and working knives. **Patterns:** Interframe locking folders, non-inlaid folders, straight hunters and kitchen knives. **Technical:** Grinds BG-42, AEB-L,

K190 and Cowry X; works with new steels. All folders can disassemble and are furnished with tools. **Prices:** $150 to $1800; some to $3000. **Remarks:** Full-time maker; first knife sold in 1975. **Mark:** Last name and type of steel used.

WUERTZ, TRAVIS
2487 E Hwy 287, Casa Grande, AZ 85222, Phone: 520-723-4432

WULF, DERRICK
25 Sleepy Hollow Rd, Essex, VT 05452, Phone: 802-777-8766, dickwulf@yahoo.com Web: www.dicksworkshop.com
Specialties: Makes predominantly forged fixed blade knives using carbon steels and his own Damascus.**Mark:** "WULF".

WYATT, WILLIAM R
Box 237, Rainelle, WV 25962, Phone: 304-438-5494
Specialties: Classic and working knives of all designs. **Patterns:** Hunters and utility knives. **Technical:** Forges and grinds saw blades, files and rasps. Prefers stag handles. **Prices:** $45 to $95; some to $350. **Remarks:** Part-time maker; first knife sold in 1990. **Mark:** Last name in star with knife logo.

WYLIE, TOM
Peak Knives, 2 Maun Close, Sutton-In-Ashfield, Notts, England NG17 5JG, tom@peakknives.com
Specialties: Knives for adventure sports and hunting, mainly fixed blades. **Technical:** Damasteel or European stainless steel used predominantly, handle material to suit purpose, embellished as required. Work can either be all handmade or CNC machined. **Prices:** $450+. **Remarks:** Pro-Am maker. **Mark:** Ogram "tinne" in circle of life, sometimes with addition of maker's name.

Y

YASHINSKI, JOHN L
207 N Platt, PO Box 1284, Red Lodge, MT 59068, Phone: 406-446-3916
Specialties: Indian knife sheaths, beaded, tacked, painted rawhide sheaths, antiqued to look old, old beads and other parts, copies of originals. Write with color copies to be made. **Prices:** $100 to $600. Call to discuss price variations.

YEATES, JOE A
730 Saddlewood Circle, Spring, TX 77381, Phone: 281-367-2765, joeyeates291@cs.com; Web: www.yeatesBowies.com
Specialties: Bowies and period pieces. **Patterns:** Bowies, toothpicks and combat knives. **Technical:** Grinds 440C, D2 and ATS-34. **Prices:** $600 to $2500. **Remarks:** Full-time maker; first knife sold in 1975. **Mark:** Last initial within outline of Texas; or last initial.

YESKOO, RICHARD C
76 Beekman Rd, Summit, NJ 07901

YONEYAMA, CHICCHI K.
5-19-8 Nishikicho, Tachikawa-City, Tokyo, JAPAN 190-0022, Phone: 081-1-9047449370, chicchi.ky1007@gmail.com; Web: https://sites.google.com/site/chicchiyoneyama/
Specialties: Folders, hollow ground, lockback and slip-joint folders with interframe handles. **Patterns:** Pocketknives, desk and daily-carry small folders. **Technical:** Stock-removal method on ATS-34, 440C, V10 and SG2/damascus blade steels. **Prices:** $300 to $1,000 and up. **Remarks:** Full-time maker; first knife sold in 1999. **Mark:** Saber tiger mark with logos/Chicchi K. Yoneyama.

YORK, DAVID C
PO Box 3166, Chino Valley, AZ 86323, Phone: 928-636-1709, dmatj@msn.com
Specialties: Working straight knives and folders. **Patterns:** Prefers small hunters and skinners; locking folders. **Technical:** Grinds D2. **Prices:** $75 to $300; some to $600. **Remarks:** Part-time maker; first knife sold in 1975. **Mark:** Last name.

YOSHIHARA, YOSHINDO
8-17-11 Takasago Katsushi, Tokyo, JAPAN

YOSHIKAZU, KAMADA
540-3 Kaisaki Niuta-cho, Tokushima, JAPAN, Phone: 0886-44-2319

YOSHIO, MAEDA
3-12-11 Chuo-cho tamashima, Kurashiki-city, Okayama, JAPAN, Phone: 086-525-2375

YOUNG, BUD
Box 336, Port Hardy, BC, CANADA V0N 2P0, Phone: 250-949-6478
Specialties: Fixed blade, working knives, some fancy. **Patterns:** Drop-points to skinners. **Technical:** Hollow or flat grind, 5160, 440C, mostly ATS-34, satin finish. Using supplied damascus at times. **Prices:** $150 to $2000 CDN. **Remarks:** Spare-time maker; making knives since 1962; first knife sold in 1985. Not taking orders at this time, sell as produced. **Mark:** Name.

YOUNG, CLIFF
Fuente De La Cibeles No 5, Atascadero, San Miguel De Allende, GJ, MEXICO 37700, Phone: 011-52-415-2-57-11
Specialties: Working knives. **Patterns:** Hunters, fighters and fishing knives. **Technical:** Grinds all; offers D2, 440C and 154CM. **Prices:** Start at $250. **Remarks:** Part-time maker; first knife sold in 1980. **Mark:** Name.

YOUNG, GEORGE
713 Pinoak Dr, Kokomo, IN 46901, Phone: 765-457-8893
Specialties: Fancy/embellished and traditional straight knives and folders of his design

and to customer specs. **Patterns:** Hunters, fillet/camp knives and locking folders. **Technical:** Grinds 440C, CPM440V, and stellite 6K. Fancy ivory, black pearl and stag for handles. Filework: all stellite construction (6K and 25 alloys). Offers engraving. **Prices:** $350 to $750; some $1500 to $3000. **Remarks:** Full-time maker; first knife sold in 1954. Doing business as Young's Knives. **Mark:** Last name integral inside Bowie.

YOUNG, JOHN
483 E. 400 S, Ephraim, UT 84627, Phone: 435-340-1417 or 435-283-4555
Patterns: Fighters, hunters and bowies. **Technical:** Stainless steel blades, including ATS-34, 440C and CTS-40CP. **Prices:** $800 to $5,000. **Remarks:** Full-time maker since 2006; first knife sold in 1997. **Mark:** Name, city and state.

YOUNG, RAYMOND L
CUTLER/BLADESMITH, 2922 Hwy 188E, Mt. Ida, AR 71957, Phone: 870-867-3947
Specialties: Cutler-Bladesmith, sharpening service. **Patterns:** Hunter, skinners, fighters, no guard, no ricasso, chef tools. **Technical:** Edge tempered 1095, 516C, mosaic handles, water buffalo and exotic woods. **Prices:** $100 and up. **Remarks:** Federal contractor since 1995. Surgical steel sharpening. **Mark:** R.

YURCO, MICKEY
PO Box 712, Canfield, OH 44406, Phone: 330-533-4928, shorinki@aol.com
Specialties: Working straight knives. **Patterns:** Hunters, utility knives, Bowies and fighters, push knives, claws and other hideouts. **Technical:** Grinds 440C, ATS-34 and 154CM; likes mirror and satin finishes. **Prices:** $20 to $500. **Remarks:** Part-time maker; first knife sold in 1983. **Mark:** Name, steel, serial number.

Z

ZACCAGNINO JR., DON
2256 Bacom Point Rd, Pahokee, FL 33476-2622, Phone: 561-985-0303, zackknife@gmail.com Web: www.zackknives.com
Specialties: Working knives and some period pieces of their designs. **Patterns:** Heavy-duty hunters, axes and Bowies; a line of light-weight hunters, fillets and personal knives. **Technical:** Grinds 440C and 17-4 PH; highly finished in complex handle and blade treatments. **Prices:** $165 to $500; some to $2500. **Remarks:** Part-time maker; first knife sold in 1969 by Don Zaccagnino Sr. **Mark:** ZACK, city and state inside oval.

ZAFEIRIADIS, KONSTANTINOS
Dionyson Street, Marathon Attiki, GREECE 19005, Phone: 011-30697724-5771 or 011-30697400-6245, info@kzknives.com; Web: www.kzknives.com
Specialties: Fixed blades, one-of-a-kind swords with bronze fittings made using the lost wax method. **Patterns:** Ancient Greek, central Asian, Viking, bowies, hunting knives, fighters, daggers. **Technical:** Forges 5160, O1 and maker's own damascus. **Prices:** $1,100 and up. **Remarks:** Full-time maker; first knife sold in 2010. **Mark:** (backward K) ZK.

ZAHM, KURT
488 Rio Casa, Indialantic, FL 32903, Phone: 407-777-4860
Specialties: Working straight knives of his design or to customer specs. **Patterns:** Daggers, fancy fighters, Bowies, hunters and utility knives. **Technical:** Grinds D2, 440C; likes filework. **Prices:** $75 to $1000. **Remarks:** Part-time maker; first knife sold in 1985. **Mark:** Last name.

ZAKABI, CARL S
PO Box 893161, Mililani Town, HI 96789-0161, Phone: 808-626-2181
Specialties: User-grade straight knives of his design, cord wrapped and bare steel handles exclusively. **Patterns:** Fighters, hunters and utility/camp knives. **Technical:** Grinds 440C and ATS-34. **Prices:** $90 to $400. **Remarks:** Spare-time maker; first knife sold in 1988. Doing business as Zakabi's Knifeworks LLC. **Mark:** Last name and state inside a Hawaiian sharktooth dagger.

ZAKHAROV, GLADISTON
Rua Pernambuca, 175-Rio Comprido (Long River), Jacaret-SP, BRAZIL 12302-070, Brazil, Phone: 55 12 3958 4021, Fax: 55 12 3958 4103, arkhip@terra.com.br; Web: www.arkhip.com.br
Specialties: Using straight knives of his design. **Patterns:** Hunters, kitchen, utility/camp and barbecue knives. **Technical:** Grinds his own "secret steel." **Prices:** $30 to $200. **Remarks:** Full-time maker. **Mark:** Arkhip Special Knives.

ZBORIL, TERRY
5320 CR 130, Caldwell, TX 77836, Phone: 979-535-4157, tzboril@tconline.net
Specialties: ABS Journeyman Smith.

ZEMBKO III, JOHN
140 Wilks Pond Rd, Berlin, CT 06037, Phone: 860-828-3503, johnzembko@hotmail.com
Specialties: Working knives of his design or to customer specs. **Patterns:** Likes to use stabilized high-figured woods. **Technical:** Grinds ATS-34, A2, D2; forges O1, 1095; grinds Damasteel. **Prices:** $50 to $400; some higher. **Remarks:** First knife sold in 1987. **Mark:** Name.

ZEMITIS, JOE
14 Currawong Rd, Cardiff Heights, NSW, AUSTRALIA 2285, Phone: 0249549907, jjvzem@bigpond.com
Specialties: Traditional working straight knives. **Patterns:** Hunters, Bowies, tantos, fighters and camp knives. **Technical:** Grinds O1, D2, W2 and 440C; makes his own Damascus. Embellishes; offers engraving. **Prices:** $150 to $3000. **Remarks:** Full-time maker; first knife sold in 1983. **Mark:** First initial, last name and country, or last name.

ZERMENO, WILLIAM D.

9131 Glenshadow Dr, Houston, TX 77088, Phone: 281-726-2459, will@wdzknives.com Web: www.wdzknives.com

Specialties: Tactical/utility folders and fixed blades. **Patterns:** Frame lock and liner lock folders the majority of which incorporate flippers and utility fixed blades. **Technical:** Grinds CPM 154, S30V, 3V and stainless Damascus. **Prices:** $250 - $600. **Remarks:** Part-time maker, first knife sold in 2008. Doing business as www.wdzknives.com. **Mark:** WDZ over logo.

ZIMA, MICHAEL F

732 State St, Ft. Morgan, CO 80701, Phone: 970-867-6078, Web: http://www.zimaknives.com

Specialties: Working and collector quality straight knives and folders. **Patterns:** Hunters, lock backs, LinerLock®, slip joint and automatic folders. **Technical:** Grinds Damascus, 440C, ATS-34 and 154CM. **Prices:** $200 and up. **Remarks:** Full-time maker; first knife sold in 1982. **Mark:** Last name.

ZINKER, BRAD

BZ KNIVES, 1591 NW 17 St, Homestead, FL 33030, Phone: 305-216-0404, bzinker@gmail.com

Specialties: Fillets, folders and hunters. **Technical:** Uses ATS-34 and stainless Damascus. **Prices:** $200 to $600. **Remarks:** Voting member of Knifemakers Guild and Florida Knifemakers Association. **Mark:** Offset connected initials BZ.

Neustrasse 15, Niederkail, GERMANY 54526, Phone: 0049 6575 1371, r.zirbes@freenet.de Web: www.zirbes-knives.com www.zirbes-messer.de

Specialties: Fancy embellished knives with engraving and self-made scrimshaw (scrimshaw made by maker). High-tech working knives and high-tech hunters, boots, fighters and folders. All knives made by hand. **Patterns:** Boots, fighters, folders, hunters. **Technical:** Uses only the best steels for blade material like CPM-T 440V, CPM-T 420V, ATS-34, D2, C440, stainless Damascus or steel according to customer's desire. **Prices:** Working knives and hunters: $200 to $600. Fancy embellished knives with engraving and/or scrimshaw: $800 to $3000. **Remarks:** Part-time maker; first knife sold in 1991. Member of the German Knifemaker Guild. **Mark:** Zirbes or R. Zirbes.

ZOWADA, TIM

4509 E Bear River Rd, Boyne Falls, MI 49713, Phone: 231-8 81-5056, tim@tzknives.com Web: www.tzknives.com

Specialties: Working knives and straight razors. **Technical:** Forges O1, L6, his own Damascus and smelted steel "Michi-Gane". **Prices:** $200 to $2500; some to $5000. **Remarks:** Full-time maker; first knife sold in 1980. **Mark:** Gothic, lower case "TZ"

ZSCHERNY, MICHAEL

1840 Rock Island Dr, Ely, IA 52227, Phone: 319-848-3629, zschernyknives@aol.com

Specialties: Quality folding knives. **Patterns:** Liner-lock and lock-back folders in titanium, working straight knives. **Technical:** Grinds ATS-34 and commercial Damascus, prefers natural materials such as pearls and ivory. **Prices:** Starting at $500. **Remarks:** Full-time maker, first knife sold in 1978. **Mark:** Last name, city and state; folders, last name with stars inside folding knife.

AK

Barlow, Jana Poirier	Anchorage
Brennan, Judson	Delta Junction
Breuer, Lonnie	Wasilla
Broome, Thomas A	Kenai
Chamberlin, John A	Anchorage
Cornwell, Jeffrey	Anchorage
Dempsey, Gordon S	N. Kenai
Desrosiers, Adam	Petersburg
Desrosiers, Haley	Petersburg
Dufour, Arthur J	Anchorage
England, Virgil	Anchorage
Flint, Robert	Anchorage
Gouker, Gary B	Sitka
Grebe, Gordon S	Anchor Point
Harvey, Mel	Nenana
Hibben, Westley G	Anchorage
Hook, Bob	North Pole
Kelsey, Nate	Anchorage
Knapp, Mark	Fairbanks
Lance, Bill	Eagle River
Lance, Lucas	Wasilla
Malaby, Raymond J	Juneau
Mcfarlin, Eric E	Kodiak
Miller, Nate	Fairbanks
Miller, Terry	Healy
Mirabile, David	Juneau
Moore, Marve	Willow
Parrish Iii, Gordon A	North Pole
Stegall, Keith	Wasilla
Van Cleve, Steve	Sutton

AL

Alverson, Tim (R.V.)	Arab
Batson, James	Madison
Baxter, Dale	Trinity
Bell, Tony	Woodland
Bowles, Chris	Reform
Brothers, Dennis L.	Oneonta
Coffman, Danny	Jacksonville
Conn Jr., C T	Attalla
Daniels, Alex	Town Creek
Dark, Robert	Oxford
Daughtery, Tony	Loxley
Durham, Kenneth	Cherokee
Elrod, Roger R	Enterprise
Gilbreath, Randall	Dora
Golden, Randy	Montgomery
Grizzard, Jim	Oxford
Hammond, Jim	Arab
Howard, Durvyn M.	Hokes Bluff
Howell, Keith A.	Oxford
Howell, Len	Opelika
Howell, Ted	Wetumpka
Huckabee, Dale	Maylene
Hulsey, Hoyt	Attalla
Mccullough, Jerry	Georgiana
Mcnees, Jonathan	Northport
Militano, Tom	Jacksonville
Morris, C H	Frisco City
Pardue, Melvin M	Repton
Ploppert, Tom	Cullman
Roe Jr., Fred D	Huntsville
Russell, Tom	Jacksonville
Sinyard, Cleston S	Elberta
Smith, Lacy	Jacksonville
Thomas, David E	Lillian
Watson, Billy	Deatsville

AR

Anders, David	Center Ridge
Ardwin, Corey	North Little Rock
Barnes Jr., Cecil C.	Center Ridge
Brown, Jim	Little Rock
Browning, Steven W	Benton
Bullard, Benoni	Bradford
Bullard, Tom	Flippin
Chambers, Ronny	Beebe
Cook, James R	Nashville
Copeland, Thom	Nashville
Cox, Larry	Murfreesboro
Crawford, Pat And Wes	West Memphis
Crotts, Dan	Elm Springs
Crowell, James L	Mtn. View
Dozier, Bob	Springdale
Duvall, Fred	Benton
Echols, Rodger	Nashville
Edge, Tommy	Cash
Ferguson, Lee	Hindsville
Fisk, Jerry	Nashville
Fitch, John S	Clinton
Flournoy, Joe	El Dorado
Foster, Ronnie E	Morrilton
Foster, Timothy L	El Dorado
Frizzell, Ted	West Fork
Gadberry, Emmet	Hattieville
Greenaway, Don	Fayetteville
Herring, Morris	Dyer
Hutchinson, Alan	Conway
Kirkes, Bill	Little Rock
Koster, Daniel	Bentonville
Krein, Tom	Gentry
Lawrence, Alton	De Queen
Lemoine, David C	Mountain Home
Livesay, Newt	Siloam Springs
Lunn, Gail	Mountain Home
Lunn, Larry A	Mountain Home
Lynch, Tad	Beebe
Maringer, Tom	Springdale
Martin, Bruce E	Prescott
Martin, Hal W	Morrilton
Massey, Roger	Texarkana
Newberry, Allen	Lowell
Newton, Ron	London
Nolte, Barbie	Lowell
Nolte, Steve	Lowell
Olive, Michael E	Leslie
Passmore, Jimmy D	Hoxie
Pearce, Logan	De Queen
Perry, Jim	Hope
Perry, John	Mayflower
Peterson, Lloyd (Pete) C	Clinton
Polk, Clifton	Van Buren
Polk, Rusty	Van Buren
Quattlebaum, Craig	Beebe
Randow, Ralph	Greenbrier
Red, Vernon	Conway
Reeves, J.R.	Texarkana
Rhea, Lin	Prattsville
Richards, Ralph (Bud)	Bauxite
Roberts, T. C. (Terry)	Siloam Springs
Seward, Ben	Austin
Stanley, John	Crossett
Stout, Charles	Gillham
Sweaza, Dennis	Austin
Townsend, Allen Mark	Texarkana
Townsley, Russell	Floral
Upton, Tom	Rogers
Walker, Jim	Morrilton
Ward, Chuck	Benton
White, Bryce	Little Rock
Young, Raymond L	Mt. Ida

AZ

Allan, Todd	Glendale
Ammons, David C	Tucson
Bennett, Glen C	Tucson
Birdwell, Ira Lee	Congress
Boye, David	Dolan Springs
Cheatham, Bill	Laveen
Choate, Milton	Somerton
Clark, R W	Surprise
Dawson, Barry	Prescott Valley
Dawson, Lynn	Prescott Valley
Deubel, Chester J.	Tucson
Dodd, Robert F	Camp Verde
Fuegen, Larry	Prescott
Goo, Tai	Tucson
Hancock, Tim	Scottsdale
Hoel, Steve	Pine
Holder, D'Alton	Wickenburg
Karp, Bob	Phoenix
Kiley, Mike And Jandy	Chino Valley
Kopp, Todd M	Apache Jct.
Lampson, Frank G	Chino Valley
Lee, Randy	St. Johns
Mcfall, Ken	Lakeside
Mcfarlin, J W	Lake Havasu City
Miller, Michael	Kingman
Montell, Ty	Thatcher
Mooney, Mike	Queen Creek
Newhall, Tom	Tucson
Purvis, Bob And Ellen	Tucson
Robbins, Bill	Sierra Vista
Rybar Jr., Raymond B	Camp Verde
States, Joshua C	New River
Tamboli, Michael	Glendale
Tyre, Michael A	Wickenburg
Weiss, Charles L	Waddell
Wick, Jonathan P.	Hereford
Wolf, Bill	Phoenix
Wright, Timothy	Sedona
Wuertz, Travis	Casa Grande
York, David C	Chino Valley

CA

Abegg, Arnie	Huntington Beach
Adkins, Richard L	Mission Viejo
Andrade, Don Carlos	Los Osos
Athey, Steve	Riverside
Barnes, Gregory	Altadena
Barron, Brian	San Mateo
Begg, Todd M.	Petaluma
Benson, Don	Escalon
Berger, Max A.	Carmichael
Bolduc, Gary	Corona
Bost, Roger E	Palos Verdes
Boyd, Francis	Berkeley
Breshears, Clint	Manhattan Beach
Brooks, Buzz	Los Angles
Brous, Jason	Goleta
Browne, Rick	Upland
Bruce, Richard L.	Yankee Hill
Butler, Bart	Ramona
Cabrera, Sergio B	Wilmington
Cantrell, Kitty D	Ramona
Caston, Darriel	Folsom
Caswell, Joe	Newbury
Clinco, Marcus	Venice
Coffey, Bill	Clovis
Coleman, John A	Citrus Heights
Connolly, James	Oroville
Cucchiara, Matt	Fresno
Davis, Charlie	Lakeside
De Maria Jr., Angelo	Carmel Valley
Dion, Greg	Oxnard
Dobratz, Eric	Laguna Hills
Doolittle, Mike	Novato
Driscoll, Mark	La Mesa
Dwyer, Duane	San Marcos
Ellis, William Dean	Sanger
Emerson, Ernest R	Harbor City
English, Jim	Jamul
Ernest, Phil (Pj)	Whittier
Essegian, Richard	Fresno
Felix, Alexander	Torrance
Ferguson, Jim	Lakewood
Forrest, Brian	Descanso
Fraley, D B	Dixon
Fred, Reed Wyle	Sacramento
Freeman, Matt	Fresno
Freer, Ralph	Seal Beach
Fulton, Mickey	Willows
Girtner, Joe	Brea
Guarnera, Anthony R	Quartzhill
Hall, Jeff	Paso Robles
Hardy, Scott	Placerville
Harris, Jay	Redwood City
Harris, John	Riverside
Helton, Roy	San Diego
Herndon, Wm R "Bill"	Acton
Hink Iii, Les	Stockton
Hoy, Ken	North Fork
Humenick, Roy	Rescue
Jacks, Jim	Covina

Jackson, David	Lemoore
Jensen, John Lewis	Pasadena
Johnson, Randy	Turlock
Kazsuk, David	Anza
Kelly, Dave	Los Angeles
Keyes, Dan	Chino
Kilpatrick, Christian A	Citrus Hieghts
Koster, Steven C	Huntington Beach
Larson, Richard	Turlock
Leland, Steve	Fairfax
Lin, Marcus	Rolling Hills Estates
Lockett, Sterling	Burbank
Luchini, Bob	Palo Alto
Maccaughtry, Scott F.	Camarillo
Mackie, John	Whittier
Massey, Ron	Joshua Tree
Mata, Leonard	San Diego
Maxwell, Don	Clovis
Mcabee, William	Colfax
Mcclure, Michael	Menlo Park
Mcgrath, Patrick T	Westchester
Melin, Gordon C	La Mirada
Meloy, Sean	Lemon Grove
Montano, Gus A	San Diego
Morgan, Jeff	Santee
Moses, Steven	Santa Ana
Mutz, Jeff	Rancho Cucamonga
Naten, Greg	Bakersfield
Orton, Rich	Covina
Osborne, Donald H	Clovis
Palm, Rik	San Diego
Panchenko, Serge	Citrus Heights
Pendleton, Lloyd	Volcano
Perry, Chris	Fresno
Pfanenstiel, Dan	Modesto
Pitt, David F	Anderson
Quesenberry, Mike	Blairsden
Randall, Patrick	Newbury Park
Rozas, Clark D	Wilmington
Schmitz, Raymond E	Valley Center
Schneider, Herman J.	Apple Valley
Schroen, Karl	Sebastopol
Sharp, David	Hesperia
Sibrian, Aaron	Ventura
Sjostrand, Kevin	Visalia
Slobodian, Scott	San Andreas
Smith, Shawn	Clouis
Sornberger, Jim	Volcano
Stapel, Chuck	Glendale
Steinberg, Al	Laguna Woods
Stimps, Jason M	Orange
Strider, Mick	San Marcos
Terrill, Stephen	Springville
Tingle, Dennis P	Jackson
Torres, Henry	Clovis
Vagnino, Michael	Visalia
Velick, Sammy	Los Angeles
Warren, Al	Roseville
Watanabe, Wayne	Montebello
Weinstock, Robert	San Francisco
Wilburn, Aaron	Redding
Wilson, Philip C	Mountain Ranch
Wilson, Ron	Morro Bay

CO

Anderson, Mark Alan	Denver
Anderson, Mel	Hotchkiss
Booco, Gordon	Hayden
Brock, Kenneth L	Allenspark
Burrows, Chuck	Durango
Corich, Vance	Morrison
Dannemann, Randy	Hotchkiss
Davis, Don	Loveland
Dennehy, John D	Loveland
Dill, Robert	Loveland
Fairly, Daniel	Bayfield
Fredeen, Graham	Colorado Springs
Fronefield, Daniel	Peyton
Graham, Levi	Greeley
Hackney, Dana A.	Monument
High, Tom	Alamosa
Hockensmith, Dan	Berthoud
Hughes, Ed	Grand Junction
Hughes, Tony	Littleton
Irie, Michael L	Colorado Springs
Kitsmiller, Jerry	Montrose
Leck, Dal	Hayden
Mcwilliams, Sean	Carbondale
Miller, Hanford J	Cowdrey
Miller, M A	Northglenn
Ott, Fred	Durango
Owens, John	Nathrop
Rexford, Todd	Woodland Park
Roberts, Chuck	Golden
Rollert, Steve	Keenesburg
Ronzio, N. Jack	Fruita
Sanders, Bill	Mancos
Thompson, Lloyd	Pagosa Springs
Waites, Richard L	Broomfield
Watson, Bert	Westminster
Wilson, James G	Estes Park
Wood, Owen Dale	Arvada
Zima, Michael F	Ft. Morgan
Redd, Bill	Broomfield

CT

Buebendorf, Robert E	Monroe
Chapo, William G	Wilton
Cross, Kevin	Portland
Framski, Walter P	Prospect
Jean, Gerry	Manchester
Loukides, David E	Cheshire
Meyer, Christopher J	Tolland
Plunkett, Richard	West Cornwall
Putnam, Donald S	Wethersfield
Rainville, Richard	Salem
Turecek, Jim	Ansonia
Vitale, Mace	Guilford
Zembko Iii, John	Berlin

DE

Willey, Wg	Greenwood

FL

Adams, Les	Hialeah
Alexander,, Oleg, And Cossack Blades	Wellington
Anders, Jerome	Miramar
Angell, Jon	Hawthorne
Atkinson, Dick	Wausau
Bacon, David R.	Bradenton
Barry Iii, James J.	West Palm Beach
Beers, Ray	Lake Wales
Benjamin Jr., George	Kissimmee
Blackwood, Neil	Lakeland
Bosworth, Dean	Key Largo
Bradley, John	Pomona Park
Bray Jr., W Lowell	New Port Richey
Brown, Harold E	Arcadia
Butler, John	Havana
Chase, Alex	DeLand
D'Andrea, John	Citrus Springs
Davis Jr., Jim	Zephyrhills
Dietzel, Bill	Middleburg
Dintruff, Chuck	Seffner
Doggett, Bob	Brandon
Dotson, Tracy	Baker
Ellerbe, W B	Geneva
Ellis, Willy B	Tarpon Springs
Enos Iii, Thomas M	Orlando
Ferrara, Thomas	Naples
Fowler, Charles R	Ft McCoy
Gamble, Roger	Newberry
Gardner, Robert	West Palm Beach
Ghio, Paolo	Pensacola
Goers, Bruce	Lakeland
Granger, Paul J	Largo
Greene, Steve	Intercession City
Griffin Jr., Howard A	Davie
Grospitch, Ernie	Orlando
Harris, Ralph Dewey	Brandon
Heaney, John D	Haines City
Heitler, Henry	Tampa
Hodge Iii, John	Palatka
Hostetler, Larry	Fort Pierce
Hostetter, Wally	San Mateo
Humphreys, Joel	Lake Placid
Hunter, Richard D	Alachua
Hytovick, Joe "Hy"	Dunnellon
Jernigan, Steve	Milton
Johanning Custom Knives, Tom	Sarasota
Johnson, John R	Plant City
King, Bill	Tampa
Krapp, Denny	Apopka
Levengood, Bill	Tampa
Lewis, Mike	DeBary
Long, Glenn A	Dunnellon
Lovestrand, Schuyler	Vero Beach
Lozier, Don	Ocklawaha
Lyle Iii, Ernest L	Chiefland
Mandt, Joe	St. Petersburg
Mason, Bill	Hobe Sound
Mcdonald, Robert J	Loxahatchee
Miller, Ronald T	Largo
Miller, Steve	Clearwater
Newton, Larry	Jacksonville
Ochs, Charles F	Largo
Owens, Donald	Melbourne
Parker, Cliff	Zephyrhills
Partridge, Jerry D.	DeFuniak Springs
Pattay, Rudy	Citrus Springs
Pendray, Alfred H	Williston
Piergallini, Daniel E	Plant City
Randall Made Knives,	Orlando
Reed, John M	Port Orange
Renner, Terry	Palmetto
Robinson, Calvin	Pace
Robinson Iii, Rex R	Leesburg
Rodkey, Dan	Hudson
Romeis, Gordon	Fort Myers
Russ, Ron	Williston
Schwarzer, Lora Sue	Crescent City
Schwarzer, Stephen	Crescent City
Smith, Michael J	Brandon
Stapleton, William E	Merritt Island
Steck, Van R	Orange City
Stephan, Daniel	Valrico
Stipes, Dwight	Palm City
Straight, Kenneth J	Largo
Tabor, Tim	Lutz
Turnbull, Ralph A	Spring Hill
Vogt, Donald J	Tampa
Watson, Tom	Panama City
Weiland Jr., J Reese	Riverview
White, John Paul	Valparaiso
Wicker, Donnie R	Panama City
Wilson, Stan	Lithia
Zaccagnino Jr., Don	Pahokee
Zahm, Kurt	Indialantic
Zinker, Brad	Homestead

GA

Arrowood, Dale	Sharpsburg
Ashworth, Boyd	Powder Springs
Barker, John	Cumming
Barker, Robert G.	Bishop
Bentley, C L	Albany
Bish, Hal	Jonesboro
Brach, Paul	Cumming
Bradley, Dennis	Blairsville
Buckner, Jimmie H	Putney
Busbie, Jeff	Bloomingdale
Cambron, Henry	Dallas
Chamblin, Joel	Concord
Cole, Welborn I	Athens
Crockford, Jack	Chamblee
Daniel, Travis E	Thomaston
Davidson, Scott	Alto
Davis, Steve	Powder Springs
Dunn, Charles K	Shiloh
Fowler, Stephan	Kennesaw
Frost, Dewayne	Barnesville
Gaines, Buddy	Commerce
Gatlin, Steve	Leesburg
Glover, Warren D	Cleveland
Greene, David	Covington
Hammond, Hank	Leesburg

Hammond, Ray	Buford
Hardy, Douglas E	Franklin
Hawkins, Rade	Fayetteville
Hensley, Wayne	Conyers
Hewitt, Ronald "Cotton"	Adel
Hinson And Son, R	Columbus
Hoffman, Kevin L	Savannah
Hossom, Jerry	Duluth
Kimsey, Kevin	Cartersville
King, Fred	Cartersville
Knott, Steve	Guyton
Landers, John	Newnan
Lockett, Lowell C.	Canton
Lonewolf, J Aguirre	Demorest
Mathews, Charlie And Harry	Statesboro
Mcgill, John	Blairsville
Mitchell, James A	Columbus
Moncus, Michael Steven	Smithville
Parks, John	Jefferson
Peters, Daniel	Columbus
Poole, Marvin O	Commerce
Powell, Robert Clark	Smarr
Prater, Mike	Flintstone
Price, Timmy	Blairsville
Pridgen Jr., Larry	Fitzgerald
Ragsdale, James D	Ellijay
Roghmans, Mark	LaGrange
Rosenfeld, Bob	Hoschton
Sculley, Peter E	Rising Fawn
Snow, Bill	Columbus
Sowell, Bill	Macon
Stafford, Richard	Warner Robins
Thompson, Kenneth	Duluth
Tomey, Kathleen	Macon
Whetsell, Alex	Haralson
White, Garrett	Hartwell
White, Lou	Ranger
Wright, Robert A	Savannah

HI

Evans, Vincent K And Grace	Keaau
Gibo, George	Hilo
Lui, Ronald M	Honolulu
Mann, Tim	Honokaa
Matsuoka, Scot	Mililani
Mayo Jr., Tom	Waialua
Mitsuyuki, Ross	Honolulu
Onion, Kenneth J	Kaneohe
Ouye, Keith	Honolulu
Salter, Gregg	Waikoloa
Watanabe, Melvin	Kailua
Zakabi, Carl S	Mililani Town

IA

Brooker, Dennis	Chariton
Brower, Max	Boone
Clark, Howard F	Runnells
Cockerham, Lloyd	Denham Springs
Helscher, John W	Washington
Lainson, Tony	Council Bluffs
Lewis, Bill	Riverside
Mckiernan, Stan	Lamoni
Miller, James P	Fairbank
Thie, Brian	Burlington
Trindle, Barry	Earlham
Westberg, Larry	Algona
Zscherny, Michael	Ely

ID

Alderman, Robert	Sagle
Bair, Mark	Firth
Bloodworth Custom Knives,	Meridian
Burke, Bill	Boise
Eddy, Hugh E	Caldwell
Hawk, Grant And Gavin	Idaho City
Hogan, Thomas R	Boise
Horton, Scot	Buhl
Howe, Tori	Athol
Mann, Michael L	Spirit Lake
Metz, Greg T	Cascade
Patton, Dick And Rob	Nampa
Quarton, Barr	McCall
Reeve, Chris	Boise
Rohn, Fred	Coeur d'Alene
Sawby, Scott	Sandpoint
Sparks, Bernard	Dingle
Steiger, Monte L	Genesee
Tippetts, Colten	Hidden Springs
Towell, Dwight L	Midvale
Trace Rinaldi Custom Blades,	Plummer

IL

Bloomer, Alan T	Maquon
Camerer, Craig	Chesterfield
Cook, Louise	Ozark
Cook, Mike	Ozark
Detmer, Phillip	Breese
Deyong, Clarence	Geneva
Dicristofano, Anthony P	Melrose Park
Eaker, Allen L	Paris
Fiorini, Bill	Grayville
Hall, Scott M.	Geneseo
Hawes, Chuck	Weldon
Heath, William	Bondville
Hill, Rick	Maryville
Knuth, Joseph E	Rockford
Kovar, Eugene	Evergreen Park
Leone, Nick	Pontoon Beach
Markley, Ken	Sparta
Meers, Andrew	Carbondale
Meier, Daryl	Carbondale
Myers, Paul	Wood River
Myers, Steve	Springfield
Nowland, Rick	Waltonville
Pellegrin, Mike	Troy
Pritchard, Ron	Dixon
Roosevelt, Russell	Albion
Rosenbaugh, Ron	Crystal Lake
Rossdeutscher, Robert N	Arlington Heights
Rzewnicki, Gerald	Elizabeth
Schneider, Craig M	Claremont
Smale, Charles J	Waukegan
Smith, John M	Centralia
Todd, Richard C	Chambersburg
Tompkins, Dan	Peotone
Veit, Michael	LaSalle
Voss, Ben	Victoria
Werth, George W	Poplar Grove
West, Charles A	Centralia
Wheeler, Robert	Bradley
White, Robert J	Gilson
White Jr., Robert J Butch	Gilson

IN

Ball, Ken	Mooresville
Barkes, Terry	Edinburgh
Barrett, Rick L. (Toshi Hisa)	Goshen
Bose, Reese	Shelburn
Bose, Tony	Shelburn
Chaffee, Jeff L	Morris
Claiborne, Jeff	Franklin
Cramer, Brent	Wheatland
Crowl, Peter	Waterloo
Curtiss, David	Granger
Damlovac, Sava	Indianapolis
Darby, Jed	Greensburg
Fitzgerald, Dennis M	Fort Wayne
Fraps, John R	Indianapolis
Good, D.R.	Tipton
Harding, Chad	Solsberry
Hunt, Maurice	Brownsburg
Imel, Billy Mace	New Castle
Johnson, C E Gene	Chesterton
Kain, Charles	Indianapolis
Keeslar, Steven C	Hamilton
Keeton, William L	Laconia
Kinker, Mike	Greensburg
Largin, Ken	Connersville
Mayville, Oscar L	Marengo
Minnick, Jim & Joyce	Middletown
Patton, Phillip	Yoder
Quakenbush, Thomas C	Ft Wayne
Robertson, Leo D	Indianapolis
Seib, Steve	Evansville

KS

Bradburn, Gary	Wichita
Burrows, Stephen R	Humboldt
Chard, Gordon R	Iola
Craig, Roger L	Topeka
Culver, Steve	Meriden
Darpinian, Dave	Olathe
Dawkins, Dudley L	Topeka
Dick, Dan	Hutchinson
Evans, Phil	Columbus
Hegwald, J L	Humboldt
Herman, Tim	Olathe
Keranen, Paul	Tacumseh
King Jr., Harvey G	Alta Vista
Kraft, Steve	Abilene
Lamb, Curtis J	Ottawa
Magee, Jim	Salina
Petersen, Dan L	Auburn
Smith, Jerry	Oberlin
Stice, Douglas W	Wichita

KY

Addison, Kyle A	Hazel
Baskett, Barbara	Eastview
Baskett, Lee Gene	Eastview
Bybee, Barry J	Cadiz
Carson, Harold J "Kit"	Vine Grove
Carter, Mike	Louisville
Downing, Larry	Bremen
Dunn, Steve	Smiths Grove
Edwards, Mitch	Glasgow
Finch, Ricky D	West Liberty
Fister, Jim	Simpsonville
France, Dan	Cawood
Frederick, Aaron	West Liberty
Greco, John	Greensburg
Hibben, Daryl	LaGrange
Hibben, Gil	LaGrange
Hibben, Joleen	LaGrange
Hoke, Thomas M	LaGrange
Holbrook, H L	Sandy Hook
Keeslar, Joseph F	Almo
Pease, W D	Ewing
Pierce, Harold L	Louisville
Rados, Jerry F	Columbia
Richerson, Ron	Greenburg
Rigney Jr., Willie	Bronston
Smith, John W	West Liberty
Soaper, Max H.	Henderson
Steier, David	Louisville
Vance, David	West Liberty
Wallingford Jr., Charles W	Union

LA

Barker, Reggie	Springhill
Blaum, Roy	Covington
Caldwell, Bill	West Monroe
Calvert Jr., Robert W (Bob)	Rayville
Capdepon, Randy	Carencro
Capdepon, Robert	Carencro
Chauvin, John	Scott
Dake, C M	New Orleans
Dake, Mary H	New Orleans
Durio, Fred	Opelousas
Faucheaux, Howard J	Loreauville
Fontenot, Gerald J	Mamou
Gorenflo, James T (Jt)	Baton Rouge
Graves, Dan	Shreveport
Johnson, Gordon A.	Choudrant
Ki, Shiva	Baton Rouge
Laurent, Kermit	LaPlace
Lemaire, Ryan M.	Abbeville
Leonard, Randy Joe	Sarepta
Mitchell, Max Dean And Ben	Leesville
Phillips, Dennis	Independence
Potier, Timothy F	Oberlin
Primos, Terry	Shreveport

IL (Idaho section — additional top entries)

Shull, James — Rensselaer
Smock, Timothy E — Marion
Thayer, Danny O — Romney
Young, George — Kokomo

Provenzano, Joseph D — Ponchatoula
Randall Jr., James W — Keithville
Reggio Jr., Sidney J — Sun
Sanders, Michael M — Ponchatoula
Tilton, John — Iowa
Trisler, Kenneth W — Rayville
Wilson, P.R. "Regan" — Scott
Winn, Marvin — Sunset

MA

Banaitis, Romas — Medway
Cooper, Paul — Woburn
Dailey, G E — Seekonk
Dugdale, Daniel J. — Walpole
Entin, Robert — Boston
Gedraitis, Charles J — Holden
Grossman, Stewart — Clinton
Hinman, Theodore — Greenfield
Jarvis, Paul M — Cambridge
Khalsa, Jot Singh — Millis
Klein, Kevin — Boston
Kubasek, John A — Easthampton
Lapen, Charles — W. Brookfield
Little, Larry — Spencer
Martin, Randall J — Bridgewater
Mcluin, Tom — Dracut
Moore, Michael Robert — Lowell
Rebello, Indian George — New Bedford
Rizzi, Russell J — Ashfield
Rua, Gary — Fall River
Saviano, James — Douglas
Siska, Jim — Westfield
Smith, J D — Roxbury
Stuart, Mason — Mansfield
Vining, Bill — Methuen

MD

Bagley, R. Keith — White Plains
Barnes, Aubrey G. — Hagerstown
Barnes, Gary L. — New Windsor
Cohen, N J (Norm) — Baltimore
Dement, Larry — Prince Fredrick
Fuller, Jack A — New Market
Gossman, Scott — Whiteford
Hart, Bill — Pasadena
Heard, Tom — Waldorf
Hendrickson, E Jay — Frederick
Hendrickson, Shawn — Knoxville
Kreh, Lefty — "Cockeysville"
Mccarley, John — Taneytown
Mcgowan, Frank E — Sykesville
Merchant, Ted — White Hall
Nicholson, R. Kent — Phoenix
Nuckels, Stephen J — Hagerstown
Presti, Matt — Union Bridge
Sentz, Mark C — Taneytown
Smit, Glenn — Aberdeen
Sontheimer, G Douglas — Potomac
Spickler, Gregory Noble — Sharpsburg
St. Clair, Thomas K — Monrovia
Walker, Bill — Stevensville

ME

Bohrmann, Bruce — Yarmouth
Ceprano, Peter J. — Auburn
Coombs Jr., Lamont — Bucksport
Gray, Daniel — Brownville
Hillman, Charles — Friendship
Leavitt Jr., Earl F — E. Boothbay
Oyster, Lowell R — Corinth
Sharrigan, Mudd — Wiscasset

MI

Ackerson, Robin E — Buchanan
Alcorn, Douglas A. — Chesaning
Andrews, Eric — Grand Ledge
Arms, Eric — Tustin
Behnke, William — Kingsley
Booth, Philip W — Ithaca
Buckbee, Donald M — Grayling
Carr, Tim — Muskegon
Carroll, Chad — Grant

Casey, Kevin — Hickory Corners
Cashen, Kevin R — Hubbardston
Cook, Mike A — Portland
Cousino, George — Onsted
Cowles, Don — Royal Oak
Dilluvio, Frank J — Prudenville
Doyle, John — Gladwin
Ealy, Delbert — Indian River
Erickson, Walter E. — Atlanta
Gordon, Larry B — Farmington Hills
Gottage, Dante — Clinton Twp.
Gottage, Judy — Clinton Twp.
Haas, Randy — Marlette
Harm, Paul W — Attica
Harrison, Brian — Cedarville
Hartman, Arlan (Lanny) — Baldwin
Hoffman, Jay — Munising
Hughes, Daryle — Nunica
Krause, Roy W — St. Clair Shores
Lankton, Scott — Ann Arbor
Lark, David — Kingsley
Logan, Iron John — Leslie
Lucie, James R — Fruitport
Marsh, Jeremy — Ada
Mills, Louis G — Ann Arbor
Morris, Michael S. — Yale
Nevling, Mark — Owosso
Noren, Douglas E — Springlake
Parker, Robert Nelson — Royal Oak
Repke, Mike — Bay City
Rose Ii, Doun T. — Fife Lake
Sakmar, Mike — Howell
Sandberg, Ronald B — Brownstown
Serven, Jim — Fostoria
Tally, Grant — Flat Rock
Van Eizenga, Jerry W — Nunica
Vasquez, Johnny David — Wyandotte
Viste, James — Hamtramck
Webster, Bill — Three Rivers
Welling, Ronald L — Grand Haven
White, Richard T — Grosse Pointe Farms
Whittaker, Wayne — Metamore
Wood, Webster — Atlanta
Zowada, Tim — Boyne Falls

MN

Andersen, Karl B. — Warba
Burns, Robert — Carver
Davis, Joel — Albert Lea
Hagen, Doc — Pelican Rapids
Hansen, Robert W — Cambridge
Hebeisen, Jeff — Hopkins
Johnson, Jerry L — Worthington
Johnson, Keith R. — Bemidji
Johnson, R B — Clearwater
Knipschield, Terry — Rochester
Leblanc, Gary E — Little Falls
Maines, Jay — Wyoming
Mesenbourg, Nick — Inver Grove Heights
Metsala, Anthony — Princeton
Mickley, Tracy — North Mankato
Ritchie, Adam — Bloomington
Rydbom, Jeff — Annandale
Shadley, Eugene W — Grand Rapids
Taber, David E. — Winona
Voorhies, Les — Faribault

MO

Abernathy, Lance — Platte City
Allred, Elvan — St. Charles
Andrews, Russ — Sugar Creek
Betancourt, Antonio L. — St. Louis
Braschler, Craig W. — Zalma
Buxton, Bill — Kaiser
Chinnock, Daniel T. — Union
Cover, Jeff — Potosi
Cover, Raymond A — Mineral Point
Davis, W C — El Dorado Springs
Dippold, Al — Perryville
Duncan, Ron — Cairo
Eaton, Frank L Jr — Farmington
Ehrenberger, Daniel Robert — Mexico

Engle, William — Boonville
Hanson Iii, Don L. — Success
Harrison, Jim (Seamus) — St. Louis
Jones, John A — Holden
Kinnikin, Todd — Pacific
Knickmeyer, Hank — Cedar Hill
Knickmeyer, Kurt — Cedar Hill
Krause, Jim — Farmington
Lee, Ethan — Sturgeon
Martin, Tony — Arcadia
Mccrackin, Kevin — House Spings
Mccrackin And Son, V J — House Springs
Mosier, David — Independence
Mulkey, Gary — Branson
Muller, Jody — Goodson
Newcomb, Corbin — Moberly
Ramsey, Richard A — Neosho
Rardon, A D — Polo
Rardon, Archie F — Polo
Riepe, Richard A — Harrisonville
Robbins, Howard P — Flemington
Robbins, Landon — Crane
Royer, Kyle — Mountain View
Scroggs, James A — Warrensburg
Seaton, David D — Rolla
Sonntag, Douglas W — Nixa
Sonntag, Jacob D — St. Robert
Sonntag, Kristopher D — Nixa
Steketee, Craig A — Billings
Stewart, Edward L — Mexico
Stormer, Bob — Dixon
Waide, Rusty — Buffalo
Warden, Roy A — Union
Whitesell, J. Dale — Stover
Willis, Bill — Ava

MS

Black, Scott — Picayune
Boleware, David — Carson
Cohea, John M — Nettleton
Davis, Jesse W — Coldwater
Davison, Todd A. — Kosciusko
Evans, Bruce A — Booneville
Flynt, Robert G — Gulfport
Jones, Jack P. — Ripley
Lamey, Robert M — Biloxi
Lebatard, Paul M — Vancleave
May, Charles — Aberdeen
Mayo Jr., Homer — Biloxi
Nichols, Chad — Blue Springs
Phillips, Donavon — Morton
Pickett, Terrell — Lumberton
Provost, J.C. — Laurel
Roberts, Michael — Clinton
Robinson, Chuck — Picayune
Shiffer, Steve — Leakesville
Smith, J.B. — Perkinston
Taylor, Billy — Petal
Vandeventer, Terry L — Terry
Vardaman, Robert — Hattiesburg
Wehner, Rudy — Collins
Wilson, Vic — Olive Branch
Wingo, Perry — Gulfport
Winston, David — Starkville

MT

Barnes, Jack — Whitefish
Barnes, Wendell — Clinton
Barth, J.D. — Alberton
Beam, John R. — Kalispell
Beaty, Robert B. — Missoula
Bell, Don — Lincoln
Bizzell, Robert — Butte
Brooks, Steve R — Walkerville
Caffrey, Edward J — Great Falls
Campbell, Doug — McLeod
Carlisle, Jeff — Simms
Christensen, Jon P — Stevensville
Colter, Wade — Colstrip
Conklin, George L — Ft. Benton
Crowder, Robert — Thompson Falls
Curtiss, Steve L — Eureka

Dunkerley, Rick	Lincoln
Eaton, Rick	Broadview
Ellefson, Joel	Manhattan
Fassio, Melvin G	Lolo
Forthofer, Pete	Whitefish
Fritz, Erik L	Forsyth
Gallagher, Barry	Lewistown
Harkins, J A	Conner
Hill, Howard E	Polson
Hintz, Gerald M	Helena
Hulett, Steve	West Yellowstone
Kajin, Al	Forsyth
Kauffman, Dave	Montana City
Kelly, Steven	Bigfork
Luman, James R	Anaconda
Mcguane Iv, Thomas F	Bozeman
Mckee, Neil	Stevensville
Moyer, Russ	Havre
Nedved, Dan	Kalispell
Olson, Joe	Geyser
Parsons, Pete	Helena
Patrick, Willard C	Helena
Peele, Bryan	Thompson Falls
Peterson, Eldon G	Whitefish
Pursley, Aaron	Big Sandy
Rodewald, Gary	Hamilton
Ruana Knife Works,	Bonner
Smith, Josh	Frenchtown
Sweeney, Coltin D	Missoula
Taylor, Shane	Miles City
Thill, Jim	Missoula
Weinand, Gerome M	Missoula
Yashinski, John L	Red Lodge

NC

Baker, Herb	Eden
Barefoot, Joe W.	Wilmington
Best, Ron	Stokes
Bisher, William (Bill)	Denton
Brackett, Jamin	Fallston
Britton, Tim	Winston-Salem
Busfield, John	Roanoke Rapids
Craddock, Mike	Thomasville
Crist, Zoe	Flat Rock
Drew, Gerald	Mill Spring
Gaddy, Gary Lee	Washington
Gingrich, Justin	Wade
Goode, Brian	Shelby
Greene, Chris	Shelby
Gross, W W	Archdale
Hall, Ken	Waynesville
Hege, John B.	Danbury
Johnson, Tommy	Troy
Livingston, Robert C	Murphy
Maynard, William N.	Fayetteville
Mcghee, E. Scott	Clarkton
Mclurkin, Andrew	Raleigh
Mcnabb, Tommy	Bethania
Mcrae, J Michael	Mint Hill
Nichols, Calvin	Raleigh
Parrish, Robert	Weaverville
Patrick, Chuck	Brasstown
Patrick, Peggy	Brasstown
Randall, Steve	Lincolnton
Rapp, Steven J	Marshall
Santini, Tom	Pikeville
Scholl, Tim	Angier
Simmons, H R	Aurora
Sirois, Darrin	Fayetteville
Sterling, Murray	Mount Airy
Summers, Arthur L	Concord
Sutton, S Russell	New Bern
Vail, Dave	Hampstead
Wacholz, Doc	Marble
Wagaman, John K	Selma
Walker, Don	Burnsville
Warren, Daniel	Canton
Whitley, L Wayne	Chocowinity
Wiggins, Bill	Canton
Williamson, Tony	Siler City
Wilson, Mike	Hayesville
Winkler, Daniel	Blowing Rock

ND

Kommer, Russ	Fargo
Pitman, David	Williston

NE

Archer, Ray And Terri	Omaha
Hielscher, Guy	Alliance
Jokerst, Charles	Omaha
Marlowe, Charles	Omaha
Moore, Jon P	Aurora
Mosier, Joshua J	Deshler
Sloan, David	Diller
Suedmeier, Harlan	Nebraska City
Syslo, Chuck	Omaha
Tiensvold, Alan L	Rushville
Tiensvold, Jason	Rushville
Till, Calvin E And Ruth	Chadron

NH

Hitchmough, Howard	Peterborough
Hudson, C Robbin	Rummney
Jonas, Zachary	Wilmot
Macdonald, John	Raymond
Philippe, D A	Cornish
Saindon, R Bill	Goshen
White, Caleb A.	Hooksett

NJ

Fisher, Lance	Pompton Lakes
Grussenmeyer, Paul G	Cherry Hill
Knowles, Shawn	Great Meadows
Lesswing, Kevin	Bayonne
Licata, Steven	Boonton
Mccallen Jr., Howard H	So Seaside Park
Nadeau, Brian	Stanhope
Pressburger, Ramon	Howell
Sheets, Steven William	Mendham
Slee, Fred	Morganville
Viele, H J	Westwood
Yeskoo, Richard C	Summit

NM

Black, Tom	Albuquerque
Burnley, Lucas	Albuquerque
Chavez, Ramon	Belen
Cherry, Frank J	Albuquerque
Cordova, Joey	Bernalillo
Cordova, Joseph G	Bosque Farms
Cumming, Bob	Cedar Crest
Digangi, Joseph M	Los Ojos
Duran, Jerry T	Albuquerque
Dyess, Eddie	Roswell
Fisher, Jay	Clovis
Garner, George	Albuquerque
Goode, Bear	Navajo Dam
Gunter, Brad	Tijeras
Hartman, Tim	Albuquerque
Hethcoat, Don	Clovis
Hume, Don	Albuquerque
Kimberley, Richard L.	Santa Fe
Leu, Pohan	Rio Rancho
Lewis, Tom R	Carlsbad
Lynn, Arthur	Galisteo
Macdonald, David	Los Lunas
Meshejian, Mardi	Santa Fe
Reid, Jim	Albuquerque
Rogers, Richard	Magdalena
Schaller, Anthony Brett	Albuquerque
Stalcup, Eddie	Gallup
Stetter, J. C.	Roswell
Terzuola, Robert	Albuquerque
Trujillo, Albert M B	Bosque Farms
Walker, Michael L	Pueblo Sur Taos
Wescott, Cody	Las Cruces

NV

Barnett, Van	Reno
Beasley, Geneo	Wadsworth
Bingenheimer, Bruce	Spring Creek
Cameron, Ron G	Logandale
Dellana,	Reno

George, Tom	Henderson
Hrisoulas, Jim	Henderson
Kreibich, Donald L.	Reno
Nishiuchi, Melvin S	Las Vegas
Thomas, Devin	Panaca
Washburn, Arthur D	Pioche

NY

Baker, Wild Bill	Boiceville
Castellucio, Rich	Amsterdam
Davis, Barry L	Castleton
Farr, Dan	Rochester
Faust, Dick	Rochester
Gregory, Matthew M.	Glenwood
Hobart, Gene	Windsor
Johnson, Mike	Orient
Johnston, Dr. Robt	Rochester
Levin, Jack	Brooklyn
Loos, Henry C	New Hyde Park
Ludwig, Richard O	Maspeth
Lupole, Jamie G	Kirkwood
Manaro, Sal	Holbrook
Maragni, Dan	Georgetown
Mccornock, Craig	Willow
Meerdink, Kurt	Barryville
Page, Reginald	Groveland
Rachlin, Leslie S	Elmira
Rappazzo, Richard	Cohoes
Rotella, Richard A	Niagara Falls
Scheid, Maggie	Rochester
Schippnick, Jim	Sanborn
Serafen, Steven E	New Berlin
Skiff, Steven	Broadalbin
Smith, Lenard C	Valley Cottage
Smith, Raymond L	Erin
Summers, Dan	Whitney Pt.
Szilaski, Joseph	Pine Plains
Turner, Kevin	Montrose
Welling, William	West Valley

OH

Bendik, John	Olmsted Falls
Busse, Jerry	Wauseon
Coffee, Jim	Norton
Collins, Lynn M	Elyria
Coppins, Daniel	Cambridge
Cottrill, James I	Columbus
Crews, Randy	Patriot
Downing, Tom	Cuyahoga Falls
Downs, James F	Powell
Etzler, John	Grafton
Francis, John D	Ft. Loramie
Franklin, Mike	Aberdeen
Gittinger, Raymond	Tiffin
Glover, Ron	Mason
Greiner, Richard	Green Springs
Hinderer, Rick	Shreve
Humphrey, Lon	Newark
Imboden Ii, Howard L.	Dayton
Johnson, Wm. C. "Bill"	Enon
Jones, Roger Mudbone	Waverly
Kiefer, Tony	Pataskala
Longworth, Dave	Felicity
Maienknecht, Stanley	Sardis
Marshall, Rex	Wilmington
Mcdonald, Rich	Hillboro
Mcgroder, Patrick J	Madison
Mercer, Mike	Lebanon
Messer, David T	Dayton
Morgan, Tom	Beloit
Munjas, Bob	Waterford
O'Machearley, Michael	Wilmington
Panak, Paul S	Andover
Potter, Billy	Dublin
Roddy, Roy "Tim"	Hubbard
Rose, Derek W	Gallipolis
Rowe, Fred	Amesville
Salley, John D	Tipp City
Schuchmann, Rick	Cincinnati
Sheely, "Butch" Forest	Grand Rapids
Shinosky, Andy	Canfield
Shoemaker, Carroll	Northup

Shoemaker, Scott — Miamisburg
Spinale, Richard — Lorain
Strong, Scott — Beavercreek
Summers, Dennis K — Springfield
Thomas, Kim — Seville
Thourot, Michael W — Napoleon
Tindera, George — Brunswick
Trout, George H. — Wilmington
Votaw, David P — Pioneer
Ward, J J — Waverly
Williams, Robert — East Liverpool
Worley, Joel A. — Maplewood
Wright, L.T. — Wintersville
Yurco, Mickey — Canfield
Stidham, Daniel — Gallipolis

OK

Baker, Ray — Sapulpa
Berg, Lee — Ketchum
Carrillo, Dwaine — Moore
Coye, Bill — Tulsa
Crenshaw, Al — Eufaula
Crowder, Gary L — Sallisaw
Damasteel Stainless Damascus, — Norman
Darby, David T — Cookson
Dill, Dave — Bethany
Duff, Bill — Poteau
Dunlap, Jim — Sallisaw
Gepner, Don — Norman
Heimdale, J E — Tulsa
Johns, Rob — Enid
Kennedy Jr., Bill — Yukon
Kirk, Ray — Tahlequah
Lairson Sr., Jerry — Ringold
Martin
Martin, John Alexander — Okmulgee
Mcclure, Jerry — Norman
Menefee, Ricky Bob — Blawchard
Midgley, Ben — Wister
Miller, Michael E — Chandler
Parsons, Larry — Mustang
Shropshire, Shawn — Piedmont
Spivey, Jefferson — Yukon
Stanford, Perry — Broken Arrow
Tomberlin, Brion R — Norman
Williams, Michael — Broken Bow
Wingo, Gary — Ramona

OR

Bell, Gabriel — Coquille
Bell, Michael — Coquille
Bochman, Bruce — Grants Pass
Brandt, Martin W — Springfield
Buchanan, Thad — Powell Butte
Buchanan, Zac — Eugene
Buchner, Bill — Idleyld Park
Busch, Steve — Oakland
Carter, Murray M — Hillsboro
Clark, Nate — Yoncalla
Coon, Raymond C — Damascus
Crowner, Jeff — Cottage Grove
Davis, Terry — Sumpter
Dixon Jr., Ira E — O'Brien
Frank, Heinrich H — Dallas
Gamble, Frank — Salem
Goddard, Wayne — Eugene
Harsey, William H — Creswell
Horn, Jess — Eugene
House, Cameron — Salem
Kelley, Gary — Aloha
Lake, Ron — Eugene
Little, Gary M — Broadbent
Magruder, Jason — Talent
Martin, Gene — Williams
Martin, Walter E — Williams
Ochs, Eric — Sherwood
Olson, Darrold E — McMinnville
Pruyn, Peter — Grants Pass
Richard, Raymond — Gresham
Richards, Chuck — Salem
Rider, David M — Eugene
Sarganis, Paul — Jacksonville

Scarrow, Wil — Gold Hill
Schoeningh, Mike — North Powder
Schrader, Robert — Bend
Sevey Custom Knife, — Gold Beach
Sheehy, Thomas J — Portland
Shoger, Mark O — Beaverton
Sibert, Shane — Gladstone
Smith, Rick — Rogue River
Squire, Jack — McMinnville
Stucky, Daniel — Springfield
Tendick, Ben — Eugene
Thompson, Leon — Gaston
Thompson, Tommy — Portland
Turner, Mike — Williams
Vallotton, Butch And Arey — Oakland
Vallotton, Rainy D — Umpqua
Vallotton, Shawn — Oakland
Vallotton, Thomas — Oakland
Ward, Ken — Grants Pass
Warren, Alan And Carroll — Portland

PA

Anderson, Gary D — Spring Grove
Anderson, Tom — Manchester
Appleby, Robert — Shickshinny
Bennett, Brett C — Reinholds
Besedick, Frank E — Monongahela
Blystone, Ronald L. — Creekside
Candrella, Joe — Warminster
Clark, D E (Lucky) — Johnstown
Corkum, Steve — Littlestown
Darby, Rick — Levittown
Evans, Ronald B — Middleton
Frey Jr., W Frederick — Milton
Godlesky, Bruce F. — Apollo
Goldberg, David — Ft Washington
Gottschalk, Gregory J — Carnegie
Harner Iii, "Butch" Lloyd R. — Littlestown
Heinz, John — Upper Black Eddy
Hudson, Rob — Northumberland
Johnson, John R — New Buffalo
Malloy, Joe — Freeland
Marlowe, Donald — Dover
Mensch, Larry C — Milton
Miller, Rick — Rockwood
Moore, Ted — Elizabethtown
Morett, Donald — Lancaster
Nealy, Bud — Stroudsburg
Neilson, J — Wyalusing
Ogden, Bill — Avis
AVIS
Parker, J E — Clarion
Root, Gary — Erie
Rose, Bob — Wagontown
Rupert, Bob — Clinton
Sass, Gary N — Sharpsville
Scimio, Bill — Spruce Creek
Sinclair, J E — Pittsburgh
Steigerwalt, Ken — Orangeville
Stroyan, Eric — Dalton
Takach, Andrew — Elizabeth
Vaughan, Ian — Manheim
Whittaker, Robert E — Mill Creek

RI

Dickison, Scott S — Portsmouth
Jacques, Alex — East Greenwich
Mchenry, William James — Wyoming
Olszewski, Stephen — Coventry
Williams, Jason L — Wyoming
Wright, Richard S — Carolina

SC

Beatty, Gordon H. — Seneca
Branton, Robert — Awendaw
Brend, Walter — Ridge Springs
Cox, Sam — Gaffney
Denning, Geno — Gaston
Estabrook, Robbie — Conway
Frazier, Jim — Wagener
Gainey, Hal — Greenwood
George, Harry — Aiken

Gregory, Michael — Belton
Hendrix, Jerry — Clinton
Hendrix, Wayne — Allendale
Hucks, Jerry — Moncks Corner
Kay, J Wallace — Liberty
Knight, Jason — Harleyville
Kreger, Thomas — Lugoff
Langley, Gene H — Florence
Lutz, Greg — Greenwood
Manley, David W — Central
Miles Jr., C R "Iron Doctor" — Lugoff
Odom Jr., Victor L. — North
O'Quinn, W. Lee — Elgin
Page, Larry — Aiken
Parler, Thomas O — Charleston
Peagler, Russ — Moncks Corner
Perry, Johnny — Inman
Smith, Ralph L — Taylors
Thomas, Rocky — Moncks Corner
Tyser, Ross — Spartanburg

SD

Boley, Jamie — Parker
Boysen, Raymond A — Rapid Ciy
Ferrier, Gregory K — Rapid City
Thomsen, Loyd W — Custer
Watts, Rodney — Hot Springs

TN

Accawi, Fuad — Clinton
Adams, Jim — Cordova
Bailey, Joseph D. — Nashville
Blanchard, G R (Gary) — Dandridge
Breed, Kim — Clarksville
Burris, Patrick R — Athens
Byrd, Wesley L — Evensville
Canter, Ronald E — Jackson
Casteel, Dianna — Monteagle
Casteel, Douglas — Monteagle
Claiborne, Ron — Knox
Clay, Wayne — Pelham
Conley, Bob — Jonesboro
Coogan, Robert — Smithville
Corby, Harold — Johnson City
Elishewitz, Allen — Lenoir City
Ewing, John H — Clinton
Hale, Lloyd — Pulaski
Harley, Larry W — Bristol
Harley, Richard — Bristol
Heflin, Christopher M — Nashville
Hughes, Dan — Spencer
Hurst, Jeff — Rutledge
Hutcheson, John — Chattanooga
Johnson, David A — Pleasant Shade
Johnson, Ryan M — Signal Mountain
Kemp, Lawrence — Ooltewah
Levine, Bob — Tullahoma
Marshall, Stephen R — Mt. Juliet
Mccarty, Harry — Blaine
Mcdonald, W.J. "Jerry" — Germantown
Moulton, Dusty — Loudon
Raley, R. Wayne — Collierville
Ridge, Tim — Crossville
Sampson, Lynn — Jonesborough
Smith, Newman L. — Gatlinburg
Taylor, C Gray — Fall Branch
Vanderford, Carl G — Columbia
Wall, Greg — Michie
Ward, W C — Clinton
Wheeler, Gary — Clarksville
Williams Jr., Richard — Morristown

TX

Adams, William D — Burton
Alexander, Eugene — Ganado
Allen, Mike "Whiskers" — Malakoff
Aplin, Spencer — Brazoria
Appleton, Ron — Bluff Dale
Ashby, Douglas — Dallas
Baker, Tony — Allen
Barnes, Marlen R. — Atlanta
Barr, Judson C. — Irving

Batts, Keith — Hooks
Blackwell, Zane — Eden
Blum, Kenneth — Brenham
Bradley, Gayle — Weatherford
Bratcher, Brett — Plantersville
Brewer, Craig — Killeen
Broadwell, David — Wichita Falls
Brooks, Michael — Lubbock
Brown, Douglas — Fort Worth
Budell, Michael — Brenham
Bullard, Randall — Canyon
Burden, James — Burkburnett
Buzek, Stanley — Waller
Callahan, F Terry — Boerne
Carey, Peter — Lago Vista
Carpenter, Ronald W — Jasper
Carter, Fred — Wichita Falls
Champion, Robert — Amarillo
Chase, John E — Aledo
Chew, Larry — Weatherford
Childers, David — W. Spring
Churchman, T W (Tim) — Bandera
Cole, James M — Bartonville
Connor, John W — Odessa
Connor, Michael — Winters
Cornett, Brian — McKinney
Costa, Scott — Spicewood
Crain, Jack W — Granbury
Darcey, Chester L — College Station
Davidson, Larry — New Braunfels
Davis, Vernon M — Waco
De Mesa, John — Lewisville
Dean, Harvey J — Rockdale
Debaud, Jake — Dallas
Delong, Dick — Centerville
Dietz, Howard — New Braunfels
Dominy, Chuck — Colleyville
Dyer, David — Granbury
Eldridge, Allan — Ft. Worth
Epting, Richard — College Station
Eriksen, James Thorlief — Garland
Evans, Carlton — Gainesville
Fant Jr., George — Atlanta
Ferguson, Jim — San Angelo
Fisher, Josh — Murchison
Foster, Al — Magnolia
Foster, Norvell C — Marion
Fowler, Jerry — Hutto
Fritz, Jesse — Slaton
Fry, Jason — Abilene
Fuller, Bruce A — Blanco
Gann, Tommy — Canton
Garner, Larry W — Tyler
George, Les — Corpus Christi
Graham, Gordon — New Boston
Green, Bill — Sachse
Griffin, Rendon, Mark And John — Houston
Grimes, Mark — Bedford
Guinn, Terry — Eastland
Halfrich, Jerry — San Marcos
Halligan, Ed — San Antonio
Hamlet Jr., Johnny — Clute
Hand, Bill — Spearman
Hawkins, Buddy — Texarkana
Hawkins Jr., Charles R. — San Angelo
Haynes, Jerry — Gunter
Hays, Mark — Austin
Hemperley, Glen — Willis
Hicks, Gary — Tuscola
Hill, Steve E — Spring Branch
Horrigan, John — Burnet
Howell, Jason G — Lake Jackson
Hudson, Robert — Humble
Hughes, Lawrence — Plainview
Jackson, Charlton R — San Antonio
Jaksik Jr., Michael — Fredericksburg
Jangtanong, Suchat — Dripping Springs
Johnson, Ruffin — Houston
Keller, Bill — San Antonio
Kern, R W — San Antonio
Kious, Joe — Kerrville
Ladd, Jim S — Deer Park

Ladd, Jimmie Lee — Deer Park
Lambert, Jarrell D — Granado
Laplante, Brett — McKinney
Lay, L J — Burkburnett
Lemcke, Jim L — Houston
Lennon, Dale — Alba
Lister Jr., Weldon E — Boerne
Love, Ed — San Antonio
Lovett, Michael — Mound
Luchak, Bob — Channelview
Luckett, Bill — Weatherford
Majors, Charlie — Montgomery
Martin, Michael W — Beckville
Mcconnell Jr., Loyd A — Marble Falls
Merz Iii, Robert L — Katy
Minchew, Ryan — Midland
Mitchell, Wm Dean — Warren
Moen, Jerry — Dallas
Moore, James B — Ft. Stockton
Neely, Greg — Bellaire
Nolen, Steve — Keller
Oates, Lee — La Porte
O'Brien, Mike J. — San Antonio
Ogletree Jr., Ben R — Livingston
Osborne, Warren — Waxahachie
Ott, Ted — Elgin
Overeynder, T R — Arlington
Ownby, John C — Murphy
Packard, Ronnie — Bonham
Pardue, Joe — Hillister
Patterson, Pat — Barksdale
Pierce, Randall — Arlington
Pollock, Wallace J — Cedar Park
Polzien, Don — Lubbock
Powers, Walter R. — Lolita
Ralph, Darrel — Forney
Ray, Alan W — Lovelady
Richardson Jr., Percy — Pollok
Roberts, Jack — Houston
Robinson, Charles (Dickie) — Vega
Rucker, Thomas — Spring
Ruple, William H — Pleasanton
Ruth, Michael G — Texarkana
Ruth, Jr., Michael — Texarkana
Self, Ernie — Dripping Springs
Shipley, Steven A — Richardson
Sloan, Shane — Newcastle
Smart, Steve — McKinney
Snody, Mike — Aransas Pass
Stokes, Ed — Hockley
Stone, Jerry — Lytle
Stout, Johnny — New Braunfels
Swenson, Luke — Lakehills
Theis, Terry — Harper
Thuesen, Ed — Damon
Truncali, Pete — Garland
Turcotte, Larry — Pampa
Van Reenen, Ian — Amarillo
Vickers, David — Montgomery
Ware, Tommy — Onalaska
Watson, Daniel — Driftwood
Watts, Johnathan — Gatesville
Watts, Wally — Gatesville
Weever, John — Nemo
White, Dale — Sweetwater
Whitley, Weldon G — Odessa
Wilcher, Wendell L — Palestine
Wilkins, Mitchell — Montgomery
Wilson, Curtis M — Burleson
Wolf Jr., William Lynn — Lagrange
Yeates, Joe A — Spring
Zboril, Terry — Caldwell
Zermeno, William D. — Houston

UT

Allred, Bruce F — Layton
Black, Earl — Salt Lake City
Carter, Shayne — Payson
Ence, Jim — Richfield
Ennis, Ray — Ogden
Erickson, L.M. — Ogden
Hunter, Hyrum — Aurora

Johnson, Steven R — Manti
Jorgensen, Carson — Mt Pleasant
Lang, David — Kearns
Maxfield, Lynn — Layton
Nell, Chad — St. George
Nielson, Jeff V — Monroe
Nunn, Gregory — Castle Valley
Palmer, Taylor — Blanding
Peterson, Chris — Salina
Ricks, Kurt J. — Trenton
Strickland, Dale — Monroe
Szczerbiak, Maciej — St. George
Velarde, Ricardo — Park City
Washburn Jr., Robert Lee — St. George
Weeks, Ryan — Bountiful
Winn, Travis A. — Salt Lake City
Young, John — Ephraim
Jenkins, Mitch — Manti
Johnson, Jerry — Spring City

VA

Apelt, Stacy E — Norfolk
Arbuckle, James M — Yorktown
Ball, Butch — Floyd
Ballew, Dale — Bowling Green
Batley, Mark S. — Wake
Batson, Richard G. — Rixeyville
Beverly Ii, Larry H — Spotsylvania
Catoe, David R — Norfolk
Chamberlain, Charles R — Barren Springs
Davidson, Edmund — Goshen
Foster, Burt — Bristol
Goodpasture, Tom — Ashland
Harris, Cass — Bluemont
Hedrick, Don — Newport News
Hendricks, Samuel J — Maurertown
Holloway, Paul — Norfolk
Jones, Barry M And Phillip G — Danville
Jones, Enoch — Warrenton
Kearney, Jarod — Swoope
Martin, Herb — Richmond
Mccoun, Mark — DeWitt
Metheny, H A "Whitey" — Spotsylvania
Mills, Michael — Colonial Beach
Murski, Ray — Reston
Norfleet, Ross W — Providence Forge
Parks, Blane C — Woodbridge
Pawlowski, John R — Barhamsville
Schlueter, David — Madison Heights
Vanhoy, Ed And Tanya — Abingdon
Vestal, Charles — Abingdon
Ward, Ron — Rose Hill

VT

Bensinger, J. W. — Marshfield
Haggerty, George S — Jacksonville
Kelso, Jim — Worcester
Wulf, Derrick — Essex

WA

Amoureux, A W — Northport
Ber, Dave — San Juan Island
Berglin, Bruce — Mount Vernon
Bromley, Peter — Spokane
Brothers, Robert L — Colville
Brown, Dennis G — Shoreline
Brunckhorst, Lyle — Bothell
Bump, Bruce D. — Walla Walla
Butler, John R — Shoreline
Campbell, Dick — Colville
Chamberlain, Jon A — E. Wenatchee
Conti, Jeffrey D — Bonney Lake
Conway, John — Kirkland
Crowthers, Mark F — Rolling Bay
D'Angelo, Laurence — Vancouver
Davis, John — Selah
De Wet, Kobus — Yakima
Diaz, Jose — Ellensburg
Diskin, Matt — Freeland
Erickson, Daniel — Snohomish
Ferry, Tom — Auburn
Gray, Bob — Spokane

Gray, Robb — Seattle
Greenfield, G O — Everett
Hansen, Lonnie — Spanaway
House, Gary — Ephrata
Keyes, Geoff P. — Duvall
Lisch, David K — Seattle
Norton, Don — Port Townsend
O'Malley, Daniel — Seattle
Padilla, Gary — Bellingham
Pedersen, Ole — Monroe
Podmajersky, Dietrich — Seattle
Rader, Michael — Bothell
Roeder, David — Kennewick
Rogers, Ray — Wauconda
Sanford, Dick — Montesano
Schempp, Ed — Ephrata
Schempp, Martin — Ephrata
Stegner, Wilbur G — Rochester
Sterling, Thomas J — Coupeville
Straub, Salem F. — Tonasket
Swyhart, Art — Klickitat
Thomas, Bob — Ferndale
Wheeler, Nick — Castle Rock
Wright, Kevin — Quilcene

WI

Boyes, Tom — West Bend
Brandsey, Edward P — Janesville
Bruner, Fred Jr. — Fall Creek
Carr, Joseph E. — Menomonee Falls
Coats, Ken — Stevens Point
Delarosa, Jim — Janesville
Haines, Jeff — Mayville
Johnson, Richard — Germantown
Kanter, Michael — New Berlin
Kohls, Jerry — Princeton
Kolitz, Robert — Beaver Dam
Lary, Ed — Mosinee
Lerch, Matthew — Sussex
Maestri, Peter A — Spring Green
Martin, Peter — Waterford
Mikolajczyk, Glen — Caledonia
Millard, Fred G — Richland Center
Nelson, Ken — Racine
Niemuth, Troy — Sheboygan
Ponzio, Doug — Beloit
Rabuck, Jason — Springbrook
Revishvili, Zaza — Madison
Ricke, Dave — West Bend
Rochford, Michael R — Dresser
Roush, Scott — Washburn
Schrap, Robert G — Wauwatosa
Steinbrecher, Mark W — Pleasant Prairie
Wattelet, Michael A — Minocqua

WV

Derr, Herbert — St. Albans
Drost, Jason D — French Creek
Drost, Michael B — French Creek
Elliott, Jerry — Charleston
Jeffries, Robert W — Red House
Liegey, Kenneth R — Millwood
Maynard, Larry Joe — Crab Orchard
Morris, Eric — Beckley
Pickens, Selbert — Dunbar
Reynolds, Dave — Harrisville
Small, Ed — Keyser
Steingass, T.K. — Hedgesville
Tokar, Daniel — Shepherdstown
Wilson, Rw — Weirton
Wyatt, William R — Rainelle

WY

Amos, Chris — Riverton
Ankrom, W.E. — Cody
Banks, David L. — Riverton
Barry, Scott — Laramie
Bartlow, John — Sheridan
Deveraux, Butch — Riverton
Draper, Audra — Riverton
Draper, Mike — Riverton
Fowler, Ed A. — Riverton

Friedly, Dennis E — Cody
Kilby, Keith — Cody
Oliver, Todd D — Cheyenne
Rexroat, Kirk — Wright
Reynolds, John C — Gillette
Rodebaugh, James L — Carpenter
Ross, Stephen — Evanston
Spragg, Wayne E — Lovell
Whipple, Wesley A — Thermopolis

ARGENTINA

Ayarragaray, Cristian L. — Parana, Entre Rios
Bertolami, Juan Carlos — Neuquen
Gibert, Pedro — San Martin de los Andes, Neuquen
Kehiayan, Alfredo — Maschwitz, Buenos Aires
Rho, Nestor Lorenzo — Junin, Buenos Aires
Santiago, Abud — Buenos Aires

AUSTRALIA

Barnett, Bruce — Mundaring, WA
Bennett, Peter — Engadine, NSW
Brodziak, David — Albany, WA
Crawley, Bruce R — Croydon, VIC
Cross, Robert — Tamworth, NSW
Del Raso, Peter — Mt. Waverly, VIC
Gerner, Thomas — Walpole, WA
Giljevic, Branko — New South Wales
Green, William (Bill) — View Bank, VIC
Harvey, Max — Western Australia 6149
Hedges, Dee — Bedfordale, WA
Husiak, Myron — Altona, VIC
K B S, Knives — North Castlemaine, VIC
Maisey, Alan — Vincentia, NSW
Mcintyre, Shawn — Hawthornm, E VIC
Phillips, Alistair — Amaroo, ACT
Tasman, Kerley — Pt Kennedy, WA
Waters, Glenn — Hyland Park, NSW
Zemitis, Joe — Cardiff Heights, NSW

BELGIUM

Dox, Jan — Schoten
Monteiro, Victor — Maleves Ste Marie
Veronique, Laurent — 1200 Bruxelles

BRAZIL

Bodolay, Antal — Belo Horizonte, MG
Bossaerts, Carl — Ribeirao Preto, SP
Campos, Ivan — Tatui, SP
Dorneles, Luciano Oliveira — Nova Petropolis, RS
Gaeta, Angelo — Centro Jau, SP
Garcia, Mario Eiras — Caxingui, SP
Ikoma, Flavio — Presidente Prudente, SP
Lala, Paulo Ricardo P And Lala, Roberto P. Presidente Prudente, SP
Neto Jr.,, Nelson And De Carvalho, Henrique M. Braganca Paulista, SP
Paulo, Fernandes R — Lencois Paulista, SP
Petean, Francisco And Mauricio — Birigui, SP
Ricardo Romano, Bernardes — Itajuba MG
Sfreddo, Rodrigo Menezes — Nova Petropolis, RS
Vilar, Ricardo Augusto Ferreira — Mairipora, SP
Villa, Luiz — Itaim Bibi, SP
Villar, Ricardo — Mairipora, SP
Zakharov, Gladiston — Jacaret-SP

CANADA

Arnold, Joe — London, ON
Beauchamp, Gaetan — Stoneham, QC
Beets, Marty — Williams Lake, BC
Bell, Donald — Bedford, NS
Berg, Lothar — Kitchener ON
Beshara, Brent (Besh) — NL
Boos, Ralph — Edmonton, AB
Bourbeau, Jean Yves — Ile Perrot, QC
Bradford, Garrick — Kitchener, ON
Bucharsky, Emil — Alberta
Burke, Dan — Springdale, NL
Dallyn, Kelly — Calgary, AB
Debraga, Jose C. — Trois Rivieres, QC
Debraga, Jovan — Quebec
Deringer, Christoph — Cookshire, QC
Desaulniers, Alain — Cookshire, QC

Diotte, Jeff — LaSalle, ON
Doiron, Donald — Messines, QC
Doucette, R — Brantford, ON
Doussot, Laurent — St. Bruno, QC
Downie, James T — Ontario
Frigault, Rick — Golden Lake, ON
Ganshorn, Cal — Regina, SK
Garvock, Mark W — Balderson, ON
Gilbert, Chantal — Quebec City, QC
Haslinger, Thomas — British Columbia V1B 3G7
Hayes, Wally — Essex, ON
Hindmarch, Garth — Carlyle, SK
Hofer, Louis — Rose Prairie, BC
Jobin, Jacques — Levis, QC
Kaczor, Tom — Upper London, ON
Lambert, Kirby — Regina, SK
Langley, Mick — Qualicum Beach, BC
Lay, R J (Bob) — Logan Lake, BC
Leber, Heinz — Hudson's Hope, BC
Lemelin, Stephanie — Brossard
Lightfoot, Greg — Kitscoty, AB
Linklater, Steve — Aurora, ON
Loerchner, Wolfgang — Bayfield, ON
Lyttle, Brian — High River, AB
Maneker, Kenneth — Galiano Island, BC
Marchand, Rick — Mahone Bay, NS
Marzitelli, Peter — Langley, BC
Massey, Al — Mount Uniacke, NS
Mckenzie, David Brian — Campbell River, BC
Miville-Deschenes, Alain — Quebec
Moeller, Harald — Parksville, BC
Moizis, Stan — Delta, British Columbia (BC)
Nease, William — LaSalle, ON
Niro, Frank — Kamloops, B.C.
O'Hare, Sean — Grand Manan, NB
Olson, Rod — Nanton, AB
Painter, Tony — Whitehorse, YT
Patrick, Bob — S. Surrey, BC
Pepiot, Stephan — Winnipeg, MB
Piesner, Dean — Conestogo, ON
Poirier, Rick — New Brunswick E4V 2W7
Rassenti, Peter — Quebec J7P 4C2
Ridley, Rob — Sundre, AB
Roberts, George A — Whitehorse, YT
Ross, Tim — Thunder Bay, ON
Schoenfeld, Matthew A — Galiano Island, BC
Stancer, Chuck — Calgary, AB
Storch, Ed — Mannville, AB
Stuart, Steve — Gores Landing, ON
Sylvester, David — Compton, QC
Tedford, Steven J. — Colborne, ON
Tighe, Brian — St. Catharines, ON
Toner, Roger — Pickering, ON
Vanderkolff, Stephen — Mildmay, ON
Whitenect, Jody — Elderbank, NS
Young, Bud — Port Hardy, BC

CZECH REPUBLIC

Tesarik, Richard — 614 00 Brno

DENMARK

Andersen, Henrik Lefolii — Fredensborg
Anso, Jens — Sporup
Rafn, Dan C. — Hadsten
Strande, Poul — Dastrup
Vensild, Henrik — Auning
Willumsen, Mikkel — S Copenhagen

ENGLAND

Bailey, I.R. — Colkirk
Barker, Stuart — Wigston, Leicester
Boden, Harry — Derbyshire
Ducker, Brian — Colkirk
Farid, Mehr R — Kent
Harrington, Roger — East Sussex
Nowacki, Stephen R. — Southampton, Hampshire
Orford, Ben — Worcestershire
Penfold, Mick — Tremar, Cornwall
Price, Darrell Morris — Devon
Stainthorp, Guy — Stroke-on-Trent
Wardell, Mick — N Devon
Wise, Donald — East Sussex

Wood, Alan	Brampton

FINLAND
Hankala, Jukka	39580 Riitiala
Palikko, J-T	00190 Helsinki
Ruusuvuori, Anssi	Piikkio
Tuominen, Pekka	Tossavanlahti
Vilppola, Markku	Turku

FRANCE
Bennica, Charles	Moules et Baucels
Chomilier, Alain And Joris	Clermont-Ferrand
Doursin, Gerard	Pernes les Fontaines
Graveline, Pascal And Isabelle	Moelan-sur-Mer
Headrick, Gary	Juan Les Pins
Madrulli, Mme Joelle	Salon De Provence
Regel, Jean-Louis	Saint Leger de Fougeret
Reverdy, Nicole And Pierre	Romans
Thevenot, Jean-Paul	Dijon
Viallon, Henri	Thiers

GERMANY
Balbach, Markus	WeilmŸnster
Becker, Franz	Marktl
Boehlke, Guenter	
Borger, Wolf	Graben-Neudorf
Dell, Wolfgang	Owen-Teck
Drumm, Armin	Dornstadt
Faust, Joachim	Goldkronach
Fruhmann, Ludwig	Burghausen
Greiss, Jockl	Schenkenzell
Hehn, Richard Karl	Dorrebach
Herbst, Peter	Lauf a.d. Pegn.
Joehnk, Bernd	Kiel
Kressler, D F	D-28832 Achim
Rankl, Christian	Munchen
Rinkes, Siegfried	Markterlbach
Selzam, Frank	Bad Koenigshofen
Steinau, Jurgen	Berlin
Tritz, Jean-Jose	Hamburg
Wirtz, Achim	Wuerselen
Zirbes, Richard	Niederkail

GREECE
Filippou, Ioannis-Minas	Athens
Zafeiriadis, Konstantinos	Marathon Attiki

IRELAND
Moore, Davy	Quin, Co Clare

ISRAEL
Shadmot, Boaz	Arava

ITALY
Ameri, Mauro	Genova
Ballestra, Santino	Ventimiglia
Bertuzzi, Ettore	Bergamo
Bonassi, Franco	Pordenone
Esposito, Emmanuel	Buttigliera Alta TO
Fogarizzu, Boiteddu	Pattada
Frizzi, Leonardo	Firenze
Garau, Marcello	Oristano
Giagu, Salvatore And Deroma Maria Rosaria (SS)	Pattada
Ramondetti, Sergio	CHIUSA DI PESIO (CN)
Riboni, Claudio	Truccazzano (MI)
Scordia, Paolo	Roma
Simonella, Gianluigi	Maniago
Toich, Nevio	Vincenza
Tschager, Reinhard	Bolzano

JAPAN
Aida, Yoshihito	Tokyo
Ebisu, Hidesaku	Hiroshima
Fujikawa, Shun	Osaka
Fukuta, Tak	Gifu
Hara, Koji	Gifu
Hirayama, Harumi	Saitama
Hiroto, Fujihara	Hiroshima
Isao, Ohbuchi	Fukuoka
Ishihara, Hank	Chiba
Kagawa, Koichi	Kanagawa
Kanki, Iwao	Hyogo
Kansei, Matsuno	Gifu
Kato, Shinichi	Aichi
Katsumaro, Shishido	Hiroshima
Keisuke, Gotoh	Oita
Koyama, Captain Bunshichi	Aichi
Mae, Takao	Osaka
Makoto, Kunitomo	Hiroshima
Matsuno, Kansei	Gifu-City
Matsusaki, Takeshi	Nagasaki
Michinaka, Toshiaki	Tottori
Narasada, Mamoru	NAGANO
Ryuichi, Kuki	Saitama
Sakakibara, Masaki	Tokyo
Sugihara, Keidoh	Osaka
Sugiyama, Eddy K	Oita
Takahashi, Masao	Gunma
Tamatsu, Kunihiko	Kochi-ken
Toshifumi, Kuramoto	Fukuoka
Uchida, Chimata	Kumamoto
Wada, Yasutaka	Nara
Yoneyama, Chicchi K.	Tokyo
Yoshihara, Yoshindo	Tokyo
Yoshikazu, Kamada	Tokushima
Yoshio, Maeda	Okayama

MEXICO
Scheurer, Alfredo E Faes	Distrito Federal
Sunderland, Richard	Puerto Escondido, OA
Ware, J.D.	Merida, Yucatan
Young, Cliff	San Miguel De Allende, GJ

NETHERLANDS
Brouwer, Jerry	Alkmaar
Sprokholt, Rob	Gatherwood
Van De Manakker, Thijs	Holland
Van Den Elsen, Gert	Tilburg
Van Eldik, Frans	Loenen
Van Ryswyk, Aad	Vlaardingen

NEW ZEALAND
Bassett, David J.	Auckland
Gunther, Eddie	Auckland
Jansen Van Vuuren, Ludwig	Dunedin
Knapton, Chris C.	Henderson, Aukland
Pennington, C A	Kainga Christchurch
Reddiex, Bill	Palmerston North
Ross, D L	Dunedin
Sandow, Brent Edward	Auckland
Sandow, Norman E	Auckland
Sands, Scott	Christchurch 9
Van Dijk, Richard	Harwood Dunedin

NORWAY
Bache-Wiig, Tom	Eivindvik
Sellevold, Harald	Bergen
Vistnes, Tor	Svelgen

NOTTS, ENGLAND
Wylie, Tom	Sutton-In-Ashfield

RUSSIA
Kharlamov, Yuri	Tula

SLOVAKIA
Albert, Stefan	Filakovo 98604
Bojtos, Arpad	98403 Lucenec
Kovacik, Robert	98556 Tomasovce
Mojzis, Julius	98511 Halic
Pulis, Vladimir	96701 Kremnica
Santa, Ladislav "Lasky"	97637 Hrochot

SOUTH AFRICA
Arm-Ko Knives,	Marble Ray , KZN
Baartman, George	Bela-Bela, LP
Bauchop, Robert	Munster, KN
Beukes, Tinus	Vereeniging, GT
Bezuidenhout, Buzz	Malvern, KZN
Boardman, Guy	New Germany, KZN
Brown, Rob E	Port Elizabeth, EC
Burger, Fred	Munster, KZN
Burger, Tiaan	Pretoria, GT
Culhane, Sean K.	Horizon, Roodepoort, 1740
Dickerson, Gavin	Petit, GT
Fellows, Mike	Riversdale 6670
Grey, Piet	Naboomspruit, LP
Harvey, Heather	Belfast, MP
Harvey, Kevin	Belfast, LP
Herbst, Gawie	Akasia, GT
Herbst, Thinus	Akasia, GT
Horn, Des	Onrusrivier, WC
Klaasee, Tinus	George, WC
Kojetin, W	Germiston, GT
Lancaster, C G	Free State
Liebenberg, Andre	Randburg, GT
Mackrill, Stephen	Johannesburg, GT
Mahomedy, A R	Marble Ray, KZN
Mahomedy, Humayd A.R.	Marble Ray, KZN
Naude, Louis	Malmesbury, WC
Oelofse, Tinus	Glenstantia, Pretoria
Owen, David J.A.	Johannesburg
Pienaar, Conrad	Free State
Prinsloo, Theuns	Free State
Rietveld, Bertie	Magaliesburg, GT
Russell, Mick	Port Elizabeth, EC
Schoeman, Corrie	Free State
Schutte, Neill	Bloemfontein
Smith, Stuart	Gauteng
Steyn, Peter	Freestate
Thorburn, Andre E.	Warmbaths, LP
Van Den Berg, Neels	Pretoria, Gauteng
Van Der Westhuizen, Peter	Mossel Bay, SC
Van Heerden, Andre	Pretoria, GT
Watson, Peter	La Hoff, NW

SOUTH AUSTRALIA
Edmonds, Warrick	Adelaide Hills

SPAIN
Cecchini, Gustavo T.	Sao Jose Rio Preto
Goshovskyy, Vasyl	Castellon de la Plana

SWEDEN
Bergh, Roger	Bygdea
Billgren, Per	Soderfors
Eklund, Maihkel	Farila
Embretsen, Kaj	Edsbyn
Hedlund, Anders	Brastad
Henningsson, Michael (Gothenburg)	426 68 Vastra Frolunda
Hogstrom, Anders T	Johanneshov
Johansson, Anders	Grangesberg
Lundstrom, Jan-Ake	Dals-Langed
Lundstrom, Torbjorn (Tobbe)	Are
Nilsson, Jonny Walker	93391 Arvidsjaur
Nordell, Ingemar	FSrila
Persson, Conny	Loos
Styrefors, Mattias	Boden
Vogt, Patrik	Halmstad

SWITZERLAND
Roulin, Charles	Geneva
Soppera, Arthur	Ulisbach

UNITED ARAB EMIRATES
Kukulka, Wolfgang	Dubai

UNITED KINGDOM
Hague, Geoff	Quarley, Hampshire
Heasman, H G	Llandudno, N. Wales
Horne, Grace	Sheffield
Maxen, Mick	Hatfield, Herts

URUGUAY
Gonzalez, Leonardo Williams	Maldonado
Symonds, Alberto E	Montevideo

ZIMBABWE
Burger, Pon	Bulawayo

the knifemakers' guild

2014 membership

a   Les Adams, Douglas A. Alcorn, Mike "Whiskers" Allen

b   Robert K. Bagley, Tony Baker, Robert Ball, Santino and Arlete Ballestra, James J. Barry, III, John Bartlow, Barbara Baskett, Gene Baskett, Michael S. Blue, Arpad Bojtos, Tony Bose, Dennis Bradley, W. Lowell Bray, Jr., Fred Bruner, Jr., John Busfield

c   Harold J. "Kit" Carson, Michael Carter, Dianna Casteel, Douglas Casteel, William Chapo, Daniel Chinnock, Kenneth R. Coats, Bob F. Conley, George Cousino, Colin J. Cox, Pat Crawford, Kevin Cross

d   George Dailey, Alex K. Daniels, Jack Davenport, Edmund Davidson, Scott Davidson, John H. Davis, William C. Davis, Mike Dilluvio, David Dodds, Tom Downing, James Downs, William Duff, Will Dutton

e   Jim Elliott, William B. Ellis, James T. Eriksen, Carlton R. Evans

f   Cliff Fendley, Lee Ferguson, Robert G. Flynt, John R. Fraps, Stanley Fujisaka

g   Steve Gatlin, Warren Glover, Richard R. Golden, Gregory J. Gottschalk

h   Philip (Doc) L. Hagen, Jim Hammond, Ralph Dewey Harris, Rade Hawkins, Earl Jay Hendrickson, Wayne G. Hensley, Gil Hibben, Wesley G. Hibben, R. Hinson, Steven W. Hoel, Kevin Hoffman, Larry Hostetler, Rob Hudson, Roy Humenick, Joseph Hytovick

i   Billy Mace Imel, Michael Irie

j   James T. Jacks, Brad Johnson, Jerry L. Johnson, Ronald B. Johnson, Steven R. Johnson, William "Bill" C. Johnson, Jack Jones, Lonnie L. Jones

k   William L. Keeton, Bill Kennedy, Jr., Bill King, Harvey King, Terry Knipschield

l   Tim "Chops" Lambkin, Ed Lary, Paul M. LeBetard, Gary E. LeBlanc, David C. Lemoine, William S. Letcher, William L. Levengood, Jack Levin, Bob Levine, Ken Linton, Wolfgang Loerchner, Schuyler Lovestrand, Don Lozier, Bill Luckett, Gail Lunn, Ernest Lyle

m   Stephen Mackrill, Riccardo Mainolfi, Joe Malloy, Herbert A. Martin, Charlie B. Mathews, Harry S. Mathews, Ted Merchant, Robert L. Merz, III, Toshiaki Michinaka, James P. Miller, Stephen C. Miller, Jerry Moen, Jeff Morgan, Stephen D. Myers

n   Bud Nealy, Corbin Newcomb, Larry Newton, Ross W Norfleet

o   Clifford W. O'Dell, Charles F. Ochs, III, Ben R. Ogletree, Sean O'Hare, Jr., Warren Osborne, T. R. Overeynder, John E. Owens

p   Larry Page, Cliff Parker, Jerry Partridge, John R. Pawlowski, W. D. Pease, Michael Pellegrin, Alfred Pendray, John W. PerMar, John Perry, Dwight Phillips, Daniel Piergallini, Leon Pittman, Otakar Pok, Larry Pridgen, Jr., Joseph R. Prince,

r   James D. Ragsdale, Steven Rapp, Ron F. Richard, Joseph Calvin Robinson, Michael Rochford, Gordon Romeis, A.G. Russell

s   Michael A. Sakmar, Joseph A. Sangster, Kenneth Savage, Scott W. Sawby, Juergen Schanz, Mike Schirmer, Mark C. Sentz, Eugene W. Shadley, John I Shore, Jim Siska, Steven C. Skiff, Ralph Smith, Arthur Soppera, James Rodney Sornberger, David Steier, Murray Sterling, Douglas W. Stice, Russ Sutton, Charles C. Syslo

t   Leon Thompson, Bobby L. Toole, Reinhard Tschager, Ralph Turnbull

v   Charles Vestal, Donald Vogt

w   George A. Walker, Charles B. Ward, Tom Watson, John S. Weever, Wayne Whittaker, Stan Wilson, Daniel Winkler, Marvin Winn

y   George L. Young, Mike Yurco

z   Brad Zinker

abs master smith listing

a   David Anders, Gary D. Anderson, E. R. Russ Andrews II

b   Gary Barnes, Aubrey G. Barnes Sr., James L. Batson, Jimmie H. Buckner, Bruce D. Bump, Bill Burke, Bill Buxton

c   Ed Caffrey, Murray M. Carter, Kevin R. Cashen, Hsiang Lin (Jimmy) Chin, Jon Christensen, Howard F. Clark, Michael Connor, James R. Cook, Joseph G. Cordova, Jim Crowell, Steve Culver

d   Sava Damlovac, Harvey J. Dean, Christoph Deringer, Adam DesRosiers, Bill Dietzel, Audra L. Draper, Rick Dunkerley, Steve Dunn, Kenneth Durham

e   Dave Ellis

f   Robert Thomas Ferry III, Jerry Fisk, John S. Fitch, Joe Flournoy, Don Fogg—retired, Burt Foster, Ronnie E. Foster, Larry D. Fuegen, Bruce A. Fuller, Jack A. Fuller

g   Bert Gaston, Thomas Gerner, Greg Gottschalk

h   Tim Hancock, Don L. Hanson III, Heather Harvey, Kevin Harvey, Wally Hayes, E. Jay Hendrickson, Don Hethcoat, John Horrigan, Gary House, Rob Hudson

j   Jim L. Jackson—retired

k   Joseph F. Keeslar, Keith Kilby, Ray Kirk, Hank Knickmeyer, Jason Knight, Bob Kramer

l   Jerry Lairson Sr.

m   J. Chris Marks, John Alexander Martin, Roger D. Massey, Victor J. McCrackin, Shawn McIntyre, Hanford J. Miller, Wm Dean Mitchell

n   Greg Neely, J. Neilson, Ron Newton, Douglas E. Noren

o   Charles F. Ochs III

p   Alfred Pendray, Dan Petersen Ph.D., Timothy Potier

r   Michael Rader, J. W. Randall, Kirk Rexroat, Linden W. Rhea, Dickie Robinson, James L. Rodebaugh, Kyle Royer, Raymond B. Rybar Jr.

s   James P. Saviano, Stephen C. Schwarzer, Mark C. Sentz, Rodrigo Menezes Sfreddo, J.D. Smith, Josh Smith, Raymond L. Smith, Bill Sowell, Charles Stout, Joseph Szilaski

t   Shane Taylor, Jean-paul Thevenot, Jason Tiensvold, Brion Tomberlin, P. J. Tomes, Henry Torres

v   Michael V. Vagnino Jr., Terry L. Vandeventer

w   James L. Walker, Daniel Warren, John White, Aaron Michael Wilburn, Michael L. Williams, Daniel Winkler

professional knifemaker's association

Mike Allen, Pat Ankrom, Shane Paul Atwood, Eddie J. Baca, D. Scott Barry, John Bartlow, Donald Bell, Tom Black, Justin Bridges, Kenneth L. Brock, Lucas Burnley, Craig Camerer, Tim S. Cameron, Ken Cardwell, David Clark, Vance Corich, Del Corsi, Culpepper & Co., John Easter, Ray W. Ennis, Lee Ferguson, Chuck Fraley, Graham Fredeen, Bob Glassman, Levi Graham, Bob Ham, Alford "Alf" Hanna, James Helm, Wayne Hensley, Gary Hicks, Guy E. Hielscher, Jay Higgins, Mike L. Irie, Mitch Jenkins, Harvey King, Todd Kopp, Jim Krause, Tom Krein, Scott Kuntz, Tim "Chops" Lambkin, James R. Largent, Ken Linton, Arthur Lynn, Jim Magee, Jerry & Sandy McClure, Mardi Meshejian, Clayton Miller, Michael Miller, Tyree L. Montell, Mike Mooney, Steve Myers, Robert Nash, Fred A. Ott, William Pleins, James L. Poplin, Bill Post, Calvin Powell, Steve Powers, Peter Pruyn, Bill Redd, Jim Reid, Steve Rollert, David Ruana, Dennis "Bud" Ruana, Don Ruana, Walter Scherar, Terry Schreiner, M.L. "Pepper" Seaman, Eugene Solomonik, Eddie F. Stalcup, Craig Steketee, Douglas Stice, Mark Strauss, Kurt Swearingen, James D. Thrash, Ed Thuesen, Albert Trujillo, Pete Truncali, Charles Turnage, Mike Tyre, Dick Waites, James Walton, Al Warren, Rodney Watts, Hans Weinmueller, Harold J. Wheeler, Jacob Wilson, R.W. Wilson, Michael C. Young, Monte Zavatta, Russ Zima, Daniel F. Zvonek

state/regional associations

arizona knife collectors association

Lee Beene, Larry Braasch, Bill Cheatam, Bob Dodd, Gary Fields, Tim Hancock, Bob Haskins, D'Alton Holder, Gerard Hurst, Todd M. Kopp, Mike Mooney, Jim Ort, Brian Quinn, Ray Rybar, Paul Vandine, Jim Yarbrough

arkansas knifemakers association

David Anders, Robert Atkins, Joel Austin, Reggie Barker, James Black, Michael Bond, Benoni Bullard, Bill Buxton, Brad Cartwright, Philip R. Clark, Barry Connell, James Cook, Larry Cox, Gary Crowder, James Crowell, Steve Culver, Brad Cunningham, David Darby, Bill Duff, David Etchieson, Lee Ferguson, Linda Ferguson, Jerry Fisk, Joe and Gwen Flournoy, Dewayne Forrester, Ronnie Foster, Roy Frost, Larry Garner, Art Gilbert, Paul Giller, Don Hanson III, Ryan Hays, B.R. Hughes, Raymon Hunt, Alan Hutchinson, Larry Inman, James H. Jackson, Michael Jacobson, Hershel Janes, Gary Johnson, Kevin Jones, Lacy C. Key, Jack J. King, Ray Kirk, Bill Kirkes, Jerry Lairson Sr., Claude Lambert, Alton Lawrence, David Lemoine, Michael Lewis, Ken Linton, David Lisch, Lewis Lloyd, Greg Lucas, Tad Lynch, Bill Lyons, Herman Martin, Roger Massey, Tom McGinnis, John McKeehan, Robert Melton, Steve Merritt, Ben Midgley, Kurtz Miller, Ron Mobbs, Jim Moore, David Murphy, Keith Murr, Allen Newberry, Ron Newton, Russell L. Nortier, Jimmy Passmore, Logan Pearce, Lloyd "Pete" Peterson, Jerry Petty, Gary Phipps, James E. Powell III, Vernon Red, Ron Reeves, Lin Rhea, Tim Richardson, Kenny Rowe, Kyle Royer, Jimmy Sandusky, James A. Scroggs, Ben Seward, Joe D. Smith, Robert Smith, Hoy Speer, Larry Spurlin, Eric Stanley, R.J. Stanley, Kenneth Staton, Charles Stout, Hubert "Buddy" Thomason, Brion Tomberlin, Tom Upton, Terry Vandeventer, Steven Vuong, James Walker, Chuck Ward, Bryce White, Doug White, Mike Williams, Rick Wilson, Terry Wright, Alvin Zinz

australian knifemakers guild inc.

Peter Bald, Bruce Barnett, Alex Bean, Walter Bidgood, Matt Black, Scott Broad, David Brodziak, Matt Brook, Zac Cheong, Stephen Cooper, Peter Del Raso, Michael Fechner, Keith Fludder, John Foxwell, Alfred Frater, Adam Fromholtz, Thomas Gerner, Branko Giljevic, James Gladstone, Peter Gordon, Karim Haddad, Mal Hannan, Jamie Harrington, Rod Harris, Glenn Michael Henke, Robert Herbert, Joe Kiss, Michael Masion, Maurie, McCarthy, Shawn McIntyre, Will Morrison, Garry Odgers, Adam Parker, Terri Parker, Jeff Peck, Alistair Phillips, Fred Rowley, Wayne Saunders, Doug Timbs, Stewart Townsend, Rob Wakelin, Jason Weightman, Ross Yeats, Joe Zemitis

california knifemakers association

Stewart Anderson, Elmer Art, Anton Bosch, Roger Bost, Clint Breshears, Christian Bryant, Mike Butcher, Joe Caswell, Marcus Clinco, Clow Richard, Mike Desensi, Parker Dunbar, Frank Dunkin, Vern Edler III, Stephanie Engnath, Robert Ewing, Chad Fehmie, Alex Felix, Jim Ferguson, Bob Fitlin, Brian Forrest, Dave Gibson, Joe Girtner, Jerry Goettig, Jeanette Gonzales, Russ Green, Tim Harbert, John Harris, Wm. R. 'Bill' Herndon, Neal A. Hodges, Jerid Johnson, Lawrence Johnson, David Kahn, David Kazsuk, Paul Kelso, Steve Koster, Robert Liguori, Harold Locke, R.W. Loveless, Gerald Lundgren, Gordon Melin, Jim Merritt, Russ Moody, Gerald Morgan, Mike Murphy, Tim Musselman, Jeff Mutz, Aram Nigoghossian, Bruce Oakley, Rich Orton, Barry E. Posner, Pat Randall, E. J. Robison, Valente Rosas, Clark Rozas, H. J. Schneider, Chris Stanko, Bill Stroman, Tyrone Swader, Reinhardt Swanson, Tony Swatton, Billy Traylor, Tru-grit, Larry White, Stephen A. Williams

canadian knifemakers guild

Joe Arnold, Gaetan Beauchamp, Paul Bold, Guillaume Cote, Christoph Deringer, Rob Douglas, James Emmons, Emmanuel Esposito, Paul-Aime Fortier, Rick Frigault, Thomas Haslinger, Wally Hayes, Nathan Knowles, Steve Linklater, Elizabeth Loerchner, Wolfgang Loerchner, Mike Mossington, William Nease, Rod Olson, Simone Raimondi, David Riccardo, Murray St. Amour, Paul Savage, Brian Tighe, Libor Tobolak, Stephen Vanderkolff, Craig Wheatley

florida knifemaker's association

Arizona Custom Knives, James J. Barry III, Terry Betts, Dennis Blaine, Dennis Blankenhem, Dean Bosworth, W. Lowell Bray Jr., Patrick Burris, Lowell Cobb, Jack Davenport, John H. Davis, Jim Elliott, Tom M. Enos, Todd Fischer, Roger Gamble, Paul Granger, Ernie Grospitch, Marshall Hall, Kevin Hoffman, Richard Johnson, Roy Kelleher, Bill King, Bill Levengood, Ernie Lyle, Steve Miller, Martin L. "Les" Murphy, Larry Newton, John Permar, Dan Piergallini, Carlo Raineri, Terry Lee Renner, Ann Sheffield/Sheffield Knifemaker's Supply, Jimmie Smith, Louis M. Vallet, Voodoo Daggers, Donald Vogt, Stan Wilson, Denny Young, Maggie Young, Brad Zinker

georgia custom knifemakers' guild

Don R. Adams, Doug Adams, Adam Andreasen, Joel Atkinson, Paul Brach, Dennis Bradley, Bobby Bragg, Steve Brazeale, Aaron Brewer, Marsha Brewer, Jerry Brinegar, James Brooker, Mike Brown, Robert Busbee, Jeff Busbie, G.H. Caldwell, Henry Cambron, Paul Chastain, Frank Chikey, Jim Collins, John Costa, Jerry Costin, Jesse Crump, Travis Daniel, Robert Dark, Scott Davidson, Charles K. Dunn, Will Dutton, Emory Fennell, Jarrett Fleming, Dylan Fletcher, Stephan Fowler, Dewayne Frost, Dean Gates, Steve Gatlin, Grady Gentles, Warren Glover, Jim Hamer, Hank Hammond, George Hancox, Rade Hawkins, Wayne Hensley, Ronald Hewitt, Kevin Hoffman, Anton Holstrom, Jack Jackson, Henry Johnson, Frank Jones, Davin Kates, Dale Kilby, Raley Lane, Rick Lowe, Damon Lusky, Larry Martin, Dan Masson, Charlie Mathews, Harry Mathews, Leroy Mathews, Vince McDowell, Larry McEachern, Russell McNabb, David McNeal, Dan Mink, James Mitchell, Ralph Mitchell, Sandy Morrisey, Dan Moye, Jerry Partridge, Dan Peters, James Poplin, Joan Poythress, Carey Quinn, Jim Ragsdale, Eddie Ray, Carl Rechsteiner, Adam Reese, David Roberts, Joseph Robinson, Andy Roy, Joe Sangster, Jamey Saunders, Craig Schneeberger, Randy Scott, John Shore, Ken Simmons, Nelson Simmons, Jim Small, Dave Smith, Johnny

Smith, Bill Snow, Luke Snyder, Brian Sorensen, Tim Spry, Charles Taylor, Cliff Thrower, Don Tommey, Alex Whetsel, Gerald White, Jerry Wiley, Chris Wilkes, Mike Wilson, Patrick & Hilary Wilson, Robert A. Wright

kansas custom knifemakers association
Roger Ball, James W. "Jim" Bevan, Gary Bradburn, Claude Campbell, Roger Craig, Steve Culver, Mike Curran, Dave Darpinian, Richard Davis, Dan Dick, Ed Day, Laural "Shorty" Ediger, Phil Evans, Andy Garrett, Jim Glines, Ernie Grospitch, Jim Haller Jr., Jim Haller Sr., Steve Hansen, Billy Helton, Jon Finley, Ross Jagears, Carolyn Kaberline, Paul Keranen, Harvey King, Ray Kirk, Doug Klaus, Troy Klaus, Knives N' Such (Tom and Susie Durham), Tom Lyles, Bill Lyons, Matt Manley, Gilbert Masters, Bruce Miller, Channing "Red" Morford, Joe O'Neill, Dan L. Peterson, Lister Potter, John Sandy, Robert Schornick, M.L. "Pepper" Seaman, Joe Skupa, David Sloane, Eric Showalter, Greg Steinert, Douglas Stice, Frank Weiss, Jeff Wells, Kevin Werth, Jim Wharton, Wesley Workman, Roy C. Young III, Tony Zanussi

knife group association of oklahoma
Mike "Whiskers" Allen, Howard Allman, David Anders, Rocky Anderson, Dale Atkerson, Richard Barchenger, Roy Brinsfield, Troy Brown, Tom Buchanan, F. L. Clowdus, Charles Conner, Bill Coye, Gary Crowder, Steve Culver, Marc Cullip, David Darby, Voyne Davis, Dan Dick, Lynn Drury, Bill Duff, Steve Elmenhorst, Beau Erwin, David Etchieson, Harry Fentress, Lee Ferguson, Linda Ferguson, Gary Gloden, Steve Hansen, Paul Happy, Calvin Harkins, Billy Helton, Ed Hites, Tim Johnston, Les Jones, Jim Keen, Bill Kennedy, Stew Killiam, Andy Kirk, Ray Kirk, Nicholas Knack, Jerry Lairson, Sr., Al Lawrence, Ken Linton, Newt Livesay, Ron Lucus, Matt Manley, John Martin, Jerry McClure, Sandy McClure, Jim McGuinn, Gary McNeill, Rick Menefee, Ben Midgley, Michael E. Miller, Roy Miller, Ray Milligan, Gary Mulkey, Allen Newberry, Jerald Nickels, Jerry Parkhurst, Chris Parson, Larry Parsons, Jerry Paul, Paul Piccola, Cliff Polk, Ron Reeves, Lin Rhea, Mike Ruth, Dan Schneringer, Terry Schreiner, Allen Shafer, Shawn Shropshire, Randell Sinnett, Clifford Smith, Doug Sonntag, Perry Stanford, Jeremy Steely, Douglas Stice, Mike Stott, Michael Tarango, Don Thompson, Brian Tomberlin, Tom Upton, Chuck Ward, Jesse Webb, Brett Wheat-Simms, Jesse Webb, Rob Weber, Joe Wheeler, Bill Wiggins, Joe Wilkie, Daniel Zvonek

knifemakers' guild of southern africa
Jeff Angelo, John Arnold, George Baartman, Francois Basson, Rob Bauchop, George Beechey, Arno Bernard, Buzz Bezuidenhout, Harucus Blomerus, Chris Booysen, Thinus Bothma, Ian Bottomley, Peet Bronkhorst, Rob Brown, Fred Burger, Sharon Burger, Trevor Burger, William Burger, Brian Coetzee, Rucus Coetzee, Jack Connan, Larry Connelly, Andre de Beer, André de Villiers, Melodie de Witt, Gavin Dickerson, Roy Dunseith, Johan Ellis, Bart Fanoy, Mike Fellows, Werner Fourie, Andrew Frankland, Brian Geyer, Ettoré Gianferrari, Dale Goldschmidt, Stan Gordon, Nick Grabe, John Grey, Piet Grey, Heather Harvey, Kevin Harvey, Dries Hattingh, Gawie Herbst, Thinus Herbst, Greg Hesslewood, Rupert Holtshausen, Des Horn, Oubaas Jordaan, Nkosilathi Jubane, Billy Kojetin, Mark Kretschmer, Andre Lesch, Steven Lewis, Garry Lombard, Steve Lombard, Ken Madden, Abdur-Rasheed Mahomedy, Peter Mason, Shelley Mason, Francois Massyn, Edward Mitchell, George Muller, Günther Muller, Deon Nel, Tom Nelson, Andries Olivier, Christo Oosthuizen, Johan Oosthuysen, Cedric Pannell, Willie Paulsen, Nico Pelzer, Conrad Pienaar, David Pienaar, Jan Potgieter, Lourens Prinsloo, Theuns Prinsloo, Hilton Purvis, Derek Rausch, Chris Reeve, Martin Reeves, Bertie Rietveld, Melinda Rietveld, Dean Riley, John Robertson, Neels Roos, Corrie Schoeman, Eddie Scott, Harvey Silk, Mike Skellern, Toi Skellern, Carel Smith, Stuart Smith, Ken Smythe, Graham Sparks, Kosie Steenkamp, Willem Steenkamp, Peter Steyn, Peter Szkolnik, André Thorburn, Hennie Van Brakel, Fanie Van Der Linde, Johan van der Merwe, Van van der Merwe, Lieben Van Der Sandt, Marius Van der Vyver, Louis Van der Walt, Johann Van Deventer, Cor Van Ellinckhuijzen, Andre van Heerden, Ben Venter, Willie Venter, Gert Vermaak, René Vermeulen, Erich

Vosloo, Jan Wahl, Desmond, Waldeck, Albie Wantenaar, Henning Wilkinson, John Wilmot, Wollie Wolfaardt, Owen Wood

montana knifemaker's association
Peter C. Albert, Gordon Alcorn, Chet Allinson, Marvin Allinson, Tim & Sharyl Alverson, Bill Amoureux, Wendell Barnes, Jim & Kay Barth, Bob & Marian Beaty, Donald Bell, Brett Bennett, Raymond Bernier, Bruce Bingenheimer, Robert Bizzell, BladeGallery, Chuck Bragg, Frederick Branch, Peter Bromley, Emil Bucharksky, Thomas and Linda Buckner, Bruce & Kay Bump, Chuck and Brenda Bybee, Jim & Kate Carroll, Rocco Chicarilli & Linda McNeese, Clayton Christofferson, Seth Coughlin, Bob Crowder, John Davis, John Doyal, Rich & Jacque Duxbury, Kevin Easley, Arnold Erhardt, Daniel Erickson, Mel & Darlene Fassio, E.V. Ford, Stephen & Kathy Garger, Chris & Jolene Giarde, Robb & Brandis Gray, Dana & Sandy Hackney, Doc & Lil Hagen, Gary & Betsy Hannon, Tedd Harris, Roger & Diane Hatt, Cal Heinrich, Sam & Joy Hensen, Gerald & Pamela Hintz, Tori Howe, Kevin Hutchins, Karl Jermunson, Keith Johnson, Don Kaschmitter, Steven Kelly, Jay Kemble, Dan & Penny Kendrick, Monte Koppes, Sheridan Lee, David Lisch, James Luman, Robert Martin, Neil McKee, Larry McLaughlin, Mac & Nancy McLaughlin, Phillip Moen, Daniel O'Malley, Tim Olds, Joe Olson, Collin Paterson, James Petri, Tim & Becca Pierce, Riley Pitchford, James Poling, Richard Prusz, Greg Rabatin, Jim Raymond, Darren Reeves, Tom Rickard and Cathy Capps, Ryan Robison, Ruana Knifeworks, Dean Schroeder, Rachel Slade, Gordon St. Clair, Terry Steigers, George Stemple, Dan & Judy Stucky, Art & Linda Swyhart, Jim Thill, James & Sharon Thompson, Dennis & Dora VanDyke, Bill & Lori Waldrup, Jonathan & Doris Walther, Michael Wattelet, Gerome & Darlene Weinand, Walter Wengrzynek, Daniel & Donna Westlind, Richard Wheeler, Sheldon & Edna Wickersham, Dave Wilkes, Randy Williams, R.W. Wilson, Mike & Seana Young

new england bladesmiths guild
Rick Barrett, Kevin Cashen, Mike Davis, Don Fogg, Burt Foster, Ric Furrer, Brian Lyttle, Bill McGrath, W.D. Pease, Jake Powning, Jim Siska, Tim Zowada

north carolina custom knifemakers' guild
Joe Aker, Dr. James Batson, Wayne Bernauer, Tom Beverly, William "Bill" Bisher, Jamin Brackett, William P. Brixon, Jr., Mark Carey, Barry Clodfelter, Travis Daniel, Jeffrey W. Foster, Jimmy Freeman, Russell Gardner, Anthony Griffin, Ken Hall, Mark Hall, Ed Halligan, Koji Hara, John B. Hege, Terrill Hoffman, Jesse Houser, B.R. Hughes, Dan Johnson, Tommy Johnson, Barry and Phillip Jones, Frank Joyce, Robert Knight, Michael Lamb, Dr. Jim Lucie, Stuart Maynard, William Morris, Ron Newton, Calvin Nichols, Victor L. Odom Jr., J.D. Palmer Jr., Howard Peacock, James Poplin, Anthony Prudhomme, Murphy Ragsdale, Steve Randall, Bruce Ryan, Joel Sandifer, Tim Scholl, Darrin Sirois, Gene Smith, Charles E. Staples Jr., Arthur Summers, Russell Sutton, Bruce Turner, Ed & Tanya Van Hoy, Christopher M. Williams, Michael Wilson, Daniel Winkler.

ohio knifemakers association
Raymond Babcock, Van Barnett, Steve Bottorff, Harold A. Collins, Larry Detty, Tom Downing, Jim Downs, Patty Ferrier, Jeff Flannery, James Fray, Bob Foster, Raymond Guess, Scott Hamrie, Rick Hinderer, Curtis Hurley, Ed Kalfayan, Michael Koval, Judy Koval, Gene Loro, Larry Lunn, Stanley Maienknecht, Dave Marlott, Mike Mercer, David Morton, Patrick McGroder, Charles Pratt, Darrel Ralph, Roy Roddy, Michael Sheppard, Carroll Shoemaker, John Smith, Clifton Smith, Jerry Smith, Art Summers, Jan Summers, Donald Tess, Dale Warther, John Wallingford, Earl Witsaman, Joanne Yurco, Mike Yurco

saskatchewan knifemakers guild
Dennis Allenback, Vern Alton, Jason Balfour, Clarence Broeksma, Irv Brunas, Jim Clow, Bob Crowder, Kevin Donald, Brian Drayton, Ray Fehler, Cal Ganshorn, Brandon Gray, Gary Greer, Wayne Hamilton, Robert Hazell, Bryan Hebb, Donald Kreuger, Ryan

Kreuger, Paul Laronge, Michael Lenaghan, Chris Mathie, Len Meeres, Ron Nelson, Morris Nesdole, Parker Neuls, Bryan Olafson, Ben Parry, Blaine Parry, Matt Parry, Greg Penner, Gary Peterson, Nick Petruic, Barry Popick, Jim Quickfall, Rob Ridley, Robert Robson, Robert Sainsbury, Darrel Selinger, Kim Senft, Carter Smyth, Don Spasoff, Ed Storch, Jim Takenaka, Tim Vanderwekken, Dan Westlind, Trevor Whitfield

scandinavian knifemakers guild

André Andersson, Michael Andersson, Jens Ansø, Magnus Axelson, Laszlo Balatoni, Mats Bjurman, Ulf Brandt, Vladic Daniluk, Alfred Dobner, Maihkel Eklund, Tommy Eklund, Greger Forselius, Anders Forsell, Roger Fält, Johan Gustafsson, Jukka Hankala, Anders Hedlund, Stefan Hermansson, Jonas Holmberg, Michael Holmström, Anders Högström, Pasi Jaakonaho, Jano knives, Anders Johansson, Tony Karlsson, Arto Liukko, Claes Löfgren, Thomas Löfgren, Anders

Nilsson, Ingemar Nordell, Ulf Nygårdh, Erik Nylund, Jakob Nylund, Simon Nylund, Conny Pearson, JT Pälikkö, Teuvo Sorvari, Pekka Tuominen, Henrik Ussing, Rauno Vainionpää, Kay Vikström, Markku Vilppula, Jesper Voxnaes, Stig Wallman, Bjarne Widheden

south carolina association of knifemakers

Douglas Bailey, Ken Black, Dick Brainard, Bobby Branton, Richard Bridwell, Dan Cannady, Rodger Casey, Robert L. Davis, Geno Denning, Charlie Douan, Eddy T. Elsmore, Robert D. Estabrook, Lewis A. Fowler, Jim Frazier, Wayne Hendrix, T.J. Hucks, Johnny Johnson, Lonnie Jones, John Keaton, Col. Thomas Kreger, Gene Langley, David Manley, C.R. Miles, Gene Miller, Barry L. Myers, Paul G. Nystrom, Lee O'Quinn, Victor Odom Jr., Larry Page, Johnny L. Perry, James Rabb, Ricky Rankin, Jerry Riddle, Rick Rockwood, John Sarratt, Ralph L. Smith, David Stroud, Rocky Thomas, Justin Walker, Mickey Walker, H. Syd Willis Jr.

photo index

The firms listed here are special in the sense that they make or market special kinds of knives made in facilities they own or control either in the U.S. or overseas. Or they are special because they make knives of unique design or function. The second phone number listed is the fax number.

sporting cutlers

A.G. RUSSELL KNIVES INC
2900 S. 26th St
Rogers, AR 72758-8571
800-255-9034
fax 479-631-0130
ag@agrussell.com; www.agrussell.com
The oldest knife mail-order company, highest quality. Free catalog available. In these catalogs you will find the newest and the best. If you like knives, this catalog is a must

AL MAR KNIVES
PO Box 2295
Tualatin, OR 97062-2295
503-670-9080; fax 503-639-4789
www.almarknives.com
Featuring our Ultralight™ series of knives. Sere 2000™ Shrike, Sere™, Operator™, Nomad™ and Ultraligh series™

ATLANTA CUTLERY CORP.
2147 Gees Mill Rd., Box 839
Conyers, GA 30013
770-922-7500; fax 770-918-2026
www.atlantacutlery.com
Outdoor sporting and hunting knives, mail order

BARK RIVER KNIVES
6911 County Road 426 M.5 Road
Escanaba, MI 49829
906-789-1801
jacquie@barkriverknives.com
www.barkriverknifetool.com
Family-owned business producing bushcraft, hunting, Canadian, deluxe game, professional guide, search & rescue and EDC knives

BEAR & SON CUTLERY, INC.
111 Bear Blvd. SW
Jacksonville, AL 36265
256-435-2227; fax 256-435-9348
www.bearandsoncutlery.com
Bear Jaws®, three sizes of multi-tools, cutlery, hunting and pocketknives in traditional and innovative patterns and designs

BECK'S CUTLERY & SPECIALTIES
51 Highland Trace Ln.
Benson, NC 27504
919-902-9416
beckscutlery@ebarqmail.com;
www.beckscutleryonline.com

BENCHMADE KNIFE CO. INC.
300 Beavercreek Rd
Oregon City, OR 97045
800-800-7427
info@benchmade.com;
www.benchmade.com
Sports, utility, law enforcement, military, gift and semi custom

BERETTA U.S.A. CORP.
17601 Beretta Dr.
Accokeek, MD 20607
301-283-2191
www.berettausa.com
Full range of hunting & specialty knives

BLACKHAWK PRODUCTS GROUP
6160 Commander Pkwy.
Norfolk, VA 23502
757-436-3101; fax 757-436-3088
cs@blackhawk.com
www.blackhawk.com
Leading manufacturer of tactical sheaths and knives

BLADE-TECH INDUSTRIES
5530 184th St. E, Ste. A
Puyallup, WA 98375
253-655-8059; fax 253-655-8066
tim@blade-tech.com
www.blade-tech.com

BLIND HORSE KNIVES
130b Warren Ln.
Wintersville, OH 43953
740-219-1141
blindhorseknives@yahoo.com
www.blindhorseknives.com
Quality working knives

BLUE GRASS CUTLERY, INC.
20 E Seventh St, PO Box 156
Manchester, OH 45144
937-549-2602; 937-549-2709 or 2603
sales @bluegrasscutlery.com;
www.bluegrasscutlery.com
Manufacturer of Winchester Knives, John Primble Knives and many contract lines

BOKER USA INC
1550 Balsam St.
Lakewood, CO 80214-5917
800-992-6537; 303-462-0668
sales@bokerusa.com; www.bokerusa.com
Wide range of fixed-blade and folding knives for hunting, military, tactical and general use

BROWNING
One Browning Place
Morgan, UT 84050
800-333-3504; Customer Service:
801-876-2711 or 800-333-3288
www.browning.com
Outdoor hunting & shooting products

BUCK KNIVES INC.
660 S Lochsa St
Post Falls, ID 83854-5200
800-326-2825; Fax: 800-733-2825
www.buckknives.com
Sports cutlery

BULLDOG BRAND KNIVES
P.O. Box 23852
Chattanooga, TN 37422
423-894-5102; fax 423-892-9165
Fixed blade and folding knives for hunting and general use

BUSSE COMBAT KNIFE CO.
11651 Co Rd 12
Wauseon, OH 43567
419-923-6471; 419-923-2337
www.bussecombat.com
Simple & very strong straight knife designs for tactical & expedition use

CAMILLUS CUTLERY CO.
60 Round Hill Rd.
Fairfield, CT 06824
800-835-2263
info@camillusknives.com
www.camillusknives.com

CANAL STREET CUTLERY
30 Canal St.
Ellenville, NY 12428
845-647-5900
info@canalstreetcutlery.com
www.canalstreetcutlery.com
Manufacturers of pocket and hunting knives finished to heirloom quality

CAS HANWEI
650 Industrial Blvd
Sale Creek, TN 37373
800-635-9366
www.cashanwei.com
Extensive variety of fixed-blade and folding knives for hunting, diving, camping, military and general use. Japanese swords and European knives

CASE, W.R. & SONS CUTLERY CO.
50 Owens Way
Bradford, PA 16701
800-523-6350; Fax: 814-368-1736
consumer-relations@wrcase.com
www.wrcase.com
Folding pocket knives

CHRIS REEVE KNIVES
2949 S. Victory View Way
Boise, ID 83709-2946
208-375-0367; Fax: 208-375-0368
crknifo@chrisreeve.com;
www.chrisreeve.com
Makers of the Sebenza, Umnumzaan and Mnandi folding knives, the legendary Green Beret knife and other military knives

COAST CUTLERY CO
8033 N.E. Holman
Portland, OR 97218
800-426-5858; Fax: 503-234-4422
www.coastportland.com
Variety of fixed-blade and folding knives and multi-tools for hunting, camping and general use

COLD STEEL INC
6060 Nicolle St.
Ventura, CA 93003
800-255-4716 or 805-642-9727
sales@coldsteel.com
www.coldsteel.com
Wide variety of folding lockbacks and fixed-blade hunting, fishing and neck knives, as well as bowies, kukris, tantos, throwing knives, kitchen knives and swords

COLONIAL KNIFE, A DIVISION OF COLONIAL CUTLERY INT.
61 Dewey Ave.
Warwick, RI 02886
401-421-6500; Fax: 401-737-0054
stevep@colonialknifecorp.com
www.colonialknifecorp.com
Collectors edition specialty knives. Special promotions. Old cutler, barion, trappers, military knives. Industrial knives-electrician.

CONDOR™ TOOL & KNIFE
7557 W. Sand Lake Rd., #106
Orlando, FL 32819
407-354-3488; Fax: 407-354-3489
rtj@att.net

CRAWFORD KNIVES, LLC
205 N Center
West Memphis, AR 72301
870-732-2452
www.crawfordknives.com
Folding knives for tactical and general use

CRKT
18348 SW 126th Place
Tualatin, OR 97062
800-891-3100; fax 503-682-9680
info@crkt.com; www.crkt.com
Complete line of sport, work and tactical knives

CUTCO CORPORATION
1116 E. State St.
Olean, NY 14760
716-372-3111
www.cutco.com
Household cutlery / sport knives

DPX GEAR INC.
2321 Kettner Blvd.
San Diego, CA 92101
619-780-2600; fax: 619-780-2605
www.dpxgear.com
Hostile environment survival knives and tools

EMERSON KNIVES, INC.
1234 254th St.
Harbor City, CA 90710
310-539-5633; fax: 310-539-5609
www.emersonknives.com
Hard use tactical knives; folding & fixed blades

ESEE KNIVES
POB 99
Gallant, AL 35972
256-613-0372
www.eseeknives.com
Survival and tactical knives

EXTREMA RATIO
Mauro Chiostri/Maurizio Castrati
Via Tourcoing 40/p
Prato (PO) 59100
ITALY
0039 0576 584639; fax: 0039 0576 584312
info@extremaratio.com
Tactical/military knives and sheaths, blades and sheaths to customers specs

FALLKNIVEN
Granatvägen 8
S-961 43 Boden
SWEDEN
46-(0)-921 544 22; Fax: 46-(0)-921 544 33
info@fallkniven.se; www.fallkniven.com
High quality stainless knives

FAMARS USA
2091 Nooseneck Hill Rd., Ste. 200
Coventry, RI 02816
855-FAMARS1 (326-2771)
www.famarsusa.com
FAMARS has been building guns for over 50 years. Known for innovative design, quality and craftsmanship. New lines of gentleman's knives, tactical fixed blades and folders, hunters and utility pieces.

FOX KNIVES USA
9918 162nd St. Ct. E, Ste. 14
Puyallup, WA 98375
303-263-2468
www.foxknivesusa.com
Designer, manufacturer and distributor of high-quality cutlery

FROST CUTLERY CO
PO Box 22636
Chattanooga, TN 37422
800-251-7768
www.frostcutlery.com
Wide range of fixed-blade and folding knives with a multitude of handle materials

GATCO SHARPENERS/TIMBERLINE
PO Box 600
Getzville, NY 14068
716-646-5700; fax: 716-646-5775
gatco@gatcosharpeners.com;
www.gatcosharpeners.com
Manufacturer of the GATCO brand of knife sharpeners and Timberline brand of knives

GERBER LEGENDARY BLADES
14200 SW 72nd Ave
Portland, OR 97223
503-639-6161; fax: 307-857-4702
www.gerbergear.com
Knives, multi-tools, axes, saws, outdoor products

GINSU OUTDOORS
118 E. Douglas Rd.
Walnut Ridge, AR 72476
800-982-5233; fax: 870-886-9162
www.douglasquikut.com
Hunting and fishing knives

GROHMANN KNIVES
PO Box 40
116 Water St
Pictou, Nova Scotia B0K 1H0
CANADA
888-7KNIVES; Fax: 902-485-5872
www.grohmannknives.com
Fixed-blade belt knives for hunting and fishing, folding pocketknives for hunting and general use. Household cutlery.

H&B FORGE CO.
235 Geisinger Rd
Shiloh, OH 44878
419-895-1856
www.hbforge.com
Special order hawks, camp stoves, fireplace accessories, muzzleloading accroutements

HALLMARK CUTLERY
POB 220
Kodak, TN 37764
866-583-3912; fax: 901-405-0948
www.hallmarkcutlery.com
Traditional folders, tactical folders and fixed blades, multi-tools, shotgun shell knives, Bad Blood, Robert Klaas and Chief brand knives, and Super Premium care products

HISTORIC EDGED WEAPONRY
1021 Saddlebrook Dr
Hendersonville, NC 28739
828-692-0323; fax: 828-692-0600
histwpn@bellsouth.net
Antique knives from around the world; importer of puukko and other knives from Norway, Sweden, Finland and Lapland; also edged weaponry book "Travels for Daggers" by Eiler R. Cook

JOY ENTERPRISES-FURY CUTLERY
Port Commerce Center III
1862 M.L. King Jr. Blvd
Riviera Beach, FL 33404
800-500-3879; fax: 561-863-3277
mail@joyenterprises.com;
www.joyenterprises.com;
www.furycutlery.com
Fury™ Mustang™ extensive variety of fixed-blade and folding knives for hunting, fishing, diving, camping, military and general use; novelty key-ring knives. Muela Sporting Knives. KA-BAR KNIVES INC. Fury Tactical, Muela of Spain, Mustang Outdoor Adventure

KA-BAR KNIVES INC
200 Homer St
Olean, NY 14760
800-282-0130; fax: 716-790-7188
info@ka-bar.com; www.ka-bar.com

KAI USA LTD.
18600 S.W. Teton Ave.
Tualatin, OR 97062
800-325-2891; fax 503-682-7168
info@kershawknives.com
www.kershawknives.com
Manufacturer of high-quality, lifetime-guaranteed knives. Kai USA brands include Kershaw Knives for everyday carrying, hunting, fishing and other outdoor use; Zero Tolerance Knives for professional use; and Shun Cutlery, providing premium-quality kitchen knives

KATZ KNIVES, INC.
10924 Mukilteo Speedway #287
Mukilteo, WA 98275
480-786-9334; fax 460-786-9338
katzkn@aol.com; www.katzknives.com

KELLAM KNIVES WORLDWIDE
P.O. Box 3438
Lantana, FL 33465
800-390-6918
info@kellamknives.com;
www.kellamknives.com
Largest selection of Finnish knives; handmade & production

KLOTZLI (MESSER KLOTZLI)
Hohengasse 3 CH 3400
Burgdorf
SWITZERLAND
41-(34)-422-23 78; fax 41-(34)-422-76 93
info@klotzli.com; www.klotzli.com
High-tech folding knives for tactical and general use

KNIGHTS EDGE LTD.
5696 N. Northwest Highway
Chicago, IL 60646-6136
773-775-3888; fax 773-775-3339
sales@knightsedge.com;
www.knightsedge.com
Medieval weaponry, swords, suits of armor, katanas, daggers

KNIVES OF ALASKA, INC.
Charles or Jody Allen
3100 Airport Dr
Denison, TX 75020
903-786-7366; fax 903-786-7371
info@knivesofalaska.com;
www.knivesofalaska.com
High quality hunting & outdoorsmen's knives

KNIVES PLUS
2467 Interstate 40 West
Amarillo, TX 79109
800-359-6202
www.knivesplus.com
Retail cutlery and cutlery accessories since 1987; free catalog available

LANSKY KNIFE, TOOL & SHARPENERS
POB 50830
Henderson, NV 89106
716-877-7511; fax 716-877-6955
cfire@lansky.com
www.lansky.com
Knives, mlti-tools, survival axes, sharpeners

LEATHERMAN TOOL GROUP, INC.
12106 N.E. Ainsworth Cir.
Portland, OR 97220-0595
800-847-8665; fax 503-253-7830
info@leatherman.com;
www.leatherman.com
Multi-tools

LONE STAR WHOLESALE
2401 Interstate 40 W
Amarillo, TX 79109
806-836-9540; fax 806-359-1603
sales@lswtexas.com
www.lswtexas.com
Great prices, dealers only, most major brands

MANTIS KNIVES
520 Cameron St.
Placentia, CA 92870
714-996-9673
gwest@mantis.bz
www.mantisknives.com
Manufacturer of utility, karambit, fixed and folding blades, and Neccessikeys

MARBLE ARMS
420 Industrial Park
Gladstone, MI 49837
906-428-3710
info@marblearms.com
www.marblearms.com

MASTER CUTLERY INC
700 Penhorn Ave
Secaucus, NJ 07094
888-227-7229; fax 888-271-7228
www.mastercutlery.com
Largest variety in the knife industry

MEYERCO USA
4481 Exchange Service Dr.
Dallas, TX 75236
214-467-8949; fax 214-467-9241
www.meyercousa.com
Folding tactical,rescue and speed-assisted pocketknives; fixed-blade hunting and fishing designs; multi-function camping tools and machetes

MICROTECH KNIVES
300 Chestnut Street Ext.
Bradford, PA 16701
814-363-9260; Fax: 814-362-7069
info@microtechknives.com
www.microtechknives.com
Manufacturers of the highest quality production knives

MISSION KNIVES
13771 Newhope St.
Garden Grove, CA 92843
714-638-4692; fax 714-638-4621
info@missionknives.com
www.missionknives.com
Manufacturer of titanium and steel knives and tools with over 20 years in business. Tactical, combat, military, law enforcement, EOD units, survivalist, diving, recreational straight blades, folding blades and mine probes, and more.

MOKI KNIFE COMPANY LTD.
15 Higashisenbo
Seki City GIFU
Pref JAPAN
575-22-4185; fax 575-24-5306
information@moki.co.jp
www.moki.co.jp
Pocketknives, folders, fixed-blade knives and gent's knives

MUSEUM REPLICAS LTD.
P.O. Box 840, 2147 Gees Mill Rd
Conyers, GA 30012
800-883-8838; fax: 770-388-0246
www.museumreplicas.com
Historically accurate & battle-ready swords & daggers

NEMESIS KNIVES, LLC
179 Niblick Rd., #180
Paso Robles, CA 93446
562-594-4740
info@nemesis-knives.com
www.nemesis-knives.com
Semi-custom and production kinves

ONTARIO KNIFE CO.
26 Empire St.
Franklinville, NY 14737
800-222-5233; fax 716-676-5535
knifesales@ontarioknife.com
www.ontarioknife.com
Fixed blades, tactical folders, military & hunting knives, machetes

OUTDOOR EDGE CUTLERY CORP.
9500 W. 49th Ave., #A-100
Wheat Ridge, CO 80033
800-447-3343; 303-530-7667
moreinfo@outdooredge.com;
www.outdooredge.com

PACIFIC SOLUTION MARKETING, INC.
1220 E. Belmont St.
Ontario, CA 91761
Tel: 877-810-4643
Fax: 909-930-5843
sales@pacificsolution.com
www.pacificsolution.com
Wide range of folding pocket knives, hunting knives, tactical knives, novelty knives, medieval armors and weapons as well as hand forged samurai swords and tantos.

PRO-TECH KNIVES LLC
17115 Alburtis Ave.
Artesia, CA 90701-2616
562-860-0678
service@protechknives.com
www.protechknives.com
Manufacturer specializing in automatic knives for police, military and discriminating collectors

QUEEN CUTLERY COMPANY
507 Chestnut St.
Titusville, PA 16354
814-827-3673; fax: 814-827-9693
jmoore@queencutlery.com
www.queencutlery.com
Pocket knives, collectibles, Schatt & Morgan, Robeson, club knives

RANDALL MADE KNIVES
4857 South Orange Blossom Trail
Orlando, FL 32839
407-855-8075; fax 407-855-9054
grandall@randallknives.com;
www.randallknives.com
Handmade fixed-blade knives for hunting, fishing, diving, military and general use

REMINGTON ARMS CO., INC.
870 Remington Drive
Madison, NC 27025-0700
800-243-9700
www.remington.com

RUKO LLC.
PO Box 38
Buffalo, NY 14207-0038
800-611-4433; fax 905-826-1353
info@rukoproducts.com
www.rukoproducts.com

SANTA FE STONEWORKS
3790 Cerrillos Rd.
Santa Fe, NM 87507
800-257-7625
knives@rt66.com
www.santafestoneworks.com
Gem stone handles

SARCO KNIVES LLC
449 Lane Dr
Florence AL 35630
256-766-8099; fax 256-766-7246
www.TriEdgeKnife.com
*Etching and engraving services, club knives, etc.
New knives, antique-collectible knives*

SARGE KNIVES
2720 E. Phillips Rd.
Greer, SC 29650
800-454-7448; fax 864-331-0752
cgaines@sargeknives.com
www.sargeknives.com
*High-quality, affordable pocketknives, hunting,
fishing, camping and tactical. Custom engraving for
promotional knives or personalized gifts*

SOG SPECIALTY KNIVES & TOOLS, INC.
6521 212th St SW
Lynnwood, WA 98036
425-771-6230; fax 425-771-7689
sogsales@sogknives.com
www.sogknives.com
*SOG assisted technology, Arc-Lock, folding knives,
specialized fixed blades, multi-tools*

SPARTAN BLADES, LLC
POB 620
Aberdeen, NC 28315
910-757-0035
contact@spartanbladesusa.com
www.spartanbladesusa.com
Tactical, combat, fighter, survival and field knives

SPYDERCO, INC.
820 Spyderco Way
Golden, CO 80403
800-525-7770; fax 303-278-2229
sales@spyderco.com
www.spyderco.com
Knives, sharpeners and accessories

STONE RIVER GEAR
75 Manor Rd.
Red Hook, NY 12571
203-470-2526; fax 866-258-7202
info@stonerivergear.com
www.stonerivergear.com
*Fighters, tactical, survival and military knives,
household cutlery, hunting knives, pocketknives,
folders and utility tools*

SWISS ARMY BRANDS INC.
15 Corporate Dr.
Orangeburg, NY 10962
800-431-2994
customer.service@swissarmy.com
www.swissarmy.com
*Folding multi-blade designs and multi-tools for
hunting, fishing, camping, hiking, golfing and
general use. One of the original brands (Victorinox)
of Swiss Army Knives*

TAYLOR BRANDS LLC
1043 Fordtown Road
Kingsport, TN 37663
800-251-0254; fax 423-247-5371
info@taylorbrandsllc.com
www.taylorbrandsllc.com
*Smith & Wesson Knives, Old Timer, Uncle Henry
and Schrade.*

TIMBERLINE KNIVES
7223 Boston State Rd.
Boston, NY 14075
800-liv-sharp; fax 716-646-5775
www.timberlineknives.com
*High technology production knives for
professionals, sporting, tradesmen & kitchen use*

TRU-BALANCE KNIFE CO.
PO Box 140555
Grand Rapids, MI 49514
616-647-1215
Manufacturing and sale of throwing knives

UNITED CUTLERY
475 U.S. Hwy. 319 S
Moultrie, GA 31768
800-548-0835; fax 229-551-0182
customerservice@unitedcutlery.com
www.unitedcutlery.com
*Wholesale only; pocket, sportsman knives, licensed
movie knives, swords, exclusive brands*

WILLIAM HENRY STUDIO
3200 NE Rivergate St
McMinnville, OR 97128
503-434-9700; Fax: 503-434-9704
www.williamhenrystudio.com
Semi-production, handmade knives

WUU JAU CO. INC
2600 S Kelly Ave
Edmond, OK 73013
405-359-5031; fax 405-340-5965
mail@wuujau.com; www.wuujau.com
*Wide variety of imported fixed-blade and folding
knives for hunting, fishing, camping, and general
use. Wholesale to knife dealers only*

XIKAR INC
PO Box 025757
Kansas City MO 64102
888-266-1193; fax 917-464-6398
info@xikar.com; www.xikar.com
Gentlemen's cutlery and accessories

importers

A.G. RUSSELL KNIVES INC
2900 S. 26th St.
Rogers, AR 72758-8571
800-255-9034
fax 479-631-0130
ag@agrussell.com; www.agrussell.com
*The oldest knife mail-order company, highest
quality. Free catalog available. In these catalogs you
will find the newest and the best. If you like knives,
this catalog is a must. Celebrating over 40 years in
the industry*

ADAMS INTERNATIONAL KNIFEWORKS
8710 Rosewood Hills
Edwardsville, IL 62025
Importers & foreign cutlers

AITOR-BERRIZARGO S.L.
P.I. Eitua PO Box 26
48240 Berriz Vizcaya
SPAIN
946826599; 94602250226
info@aitor.com; www.aitor.com
Sporting knives

ATLANTA CUTLERY CORP.
P.O.Box 839
Conyers, Ga 30012
770-922-7500; Fax: 770-918-2026
custserve@atlantacutlery.com;
www.atlantacutlery.com
Exotic knives from around the world

BAILEY'S
PO Box 550
Laytonville, CA 95454
800-322-4539; 707-984-8115
baileys@baileys-online.com;
www.baileys-online.com

BELTRAME, FRANCESCO
Fratelli Beltrame F&C snc Via dei Fabbri
15/B-33085 MANIAGO (PN)
ITALY
39 0427 701859
www.italianstiletto.com

BOKER USA, INC.
1550 Balsam St
Lakewood, CO 80214-5917
303-462-0662; 303-462-0668
sales@bokerusa.com; www.bokerusa.com
Ceramic blades

CAMPOS, IVAN DE ALMEIDA
R. Stelio M. Loureiro, 205
Centro, Tatui
BRAZIL
00-55-15-33056867
www.ivancampos.com

C.A.S. HANWEI, INC.
650 Industrial Blvd
Sale Creek, TN 37373
423-332-4700; fax 423-332-7248
info@cashanwei.com; www.cashanwei.com

CAS/HANWEI, MUELA
Catoctin Cutlery
PO Box 188
Smithsburg, MD 21783

CLASSIC INDUSTRIES
1325 Howard Ave, Suite 408
Burlingame, CA 94010

COAST CUTLERY CO.
POB 5821
Portland, OR 97228
800-426-5858
staff@coastcutlery.com;
www.coastcutlery.com

COLUMBIA PRODUCTS CO.
PO Box 1333
Sialkot 51310
PAKISTAN

COLUMBIA PRODUCTS INT'L
PO Box 8243
New York, NY 10116-8243
201-854-3054; Fax: 201-854-7058
nycolumbia@aol.com;
http://www.columbiaproducts.homestead.
com/cat.html
Pocket, hunting knives and swords of all kinds

COMPASS INDUSTRIES, INC.
104 E. 25th St
New York, NY 10010
800-221-9904; Fax: 212-353-0826
jeff@compassindustries.com;
www.compassindustries.com
Imported pocket knives

CONAZ COLTELLERIE
Dei F.Lli Consigli-Scarperia
Via G. Giordani, 20
50038 Scarperia (Firenze)
ITALY
36 55 846187; 39 55 846603
conaz@dada.it; www.consigliscarperia.it
*Handicraft workmanship of knives of the ancient
Italian tradition. Historical and collection knives*

CONSOLIDATED CUTLERY CO., INC.
696 NW Sharpe St
Port St. Lucie, FL 34983
772-878-6139

CRAZY CROW TRADING POST
PO Box 847
Pottsboro, TX 75076
800-786-6210; Fax: 903-786-9059
info@crazycrow.com; www.crazycrow.com
Solingen blades, knife making parts & supplies

DER FLEISSIGEN BEAVER
(The Busy Beaver)
Harvey Silk
PO Box 1166
64343 Griesheim
GERMANY
49 61552231; 49 6155 2433
Der.Biber@t-online.de
Retail custom knives. Knife shows in Germany & UK

EXTREMA RATIO
Mauro Chiostri; Mavrizio Castrati
Via Tourcoing 40/p
59100 Prato (PO)
ITALY
0039 0576 58 4639; fax 0039 0576 584312
info@extremarazio.com;
www.extremaratio.com
Tactical & military knives manufacturing

FALLKNIVEN
Granatvagen 8
S-961 43 Boden
SWEDEN
+46 (0) 921 544 22; fax +46 (0) 921 544 33
info@fallkniven.se
www.fallkniven.se
High quality knives

FREDIANI COLTELLI FINLANDESI
Via Lago Maggiore 41
I-21038 Leggiuno
ITALY

**GIESSER MESSERFABRIK GMBH,
 JOHANNES**
Raiffeisenstr 15
D-71349 Winnenden
GERMANY
49-7195-1808-29
info@giesser.de; www.giesser.de
Professional butchers and chef's knives

HIMALAYAN IMPORTS
3495 Lakeside Dr
Reno, NV 89509
775-825-2279
unclebill@himalayan-imports.com; www.
himilayan-imports.com

**IVAN DE ALMEIDA CAMPOS-KNIFE
 DEALER**
R. Xi De Agosto
107, Centro, Tatui, Sp 18270
BRAZIL
55-15-251-8092; 55-15-251-4896
campos@bitweb.com.br
Custom knives from all Brazilian knifemakers

JOY ENTERPRISES
1862 Martin Luther King Jr. Blvd.
Riviera Beach, FL 33404
561-863-3205; fax 561-863-3277
mail@joyenterprises.com;
www.joyenterprises.com
Fury™, Mustang™, Hawg Knives, Muela

KELLAM KNIVES WORLDWIDE
POB 3438
Lantana, FL 33465
561-588-3185 or 800-390-6918
info@kellamknives.com;
www.kellamknives.com
Knives from Finland; own line of knives

KNIFE IMPORTERS, INC.
11307 Conroy Ln
Manchaca, TX 78652
512-282-6860, Fax: 512-282-7504
Wholesale only

KNIGHTS EDGE LTD.
5696 N Northwest Hwy
Chicago, IL 60646
773-775-3888; fax 773-775-3339
www.knightsedge.com
*Exclusive designers of our Rittersteel, Stagesteel
and Valiant Arms and knightedge lines of weapon*

LEISURE PRODUCTS CORP.
PO Box 1171
Sialkot-51310
PAKISTAN

L. C. RISTINEN
Suomi Shop
17533 Co Hwy 38
Frazee MN 56544
218-538-6633; 218-538-6633
icrist@wcta.net
*Scandinavian cutlery custom antique, books and
reindeer antler*

LINDER, CARL NACHF.
Erholungstr. 10
D-42699 Solingen
GERMANY
212 33 0 856; Fax: 212 33 71 04
info@linder.de; www.linder.de

MARTTIINI KNIVES
PO Box 44 (Marttiinintie 3)
96101 Rovaniemi
FINLAND

MATTHEWS CUTLERY
POB 2768
Moultrie, GA 31776
800-251-0123; fax 877-428-3599
www.matthewscutlery.com
Wholesale of major brands

MESSER KLÖTZLI
PO Box 104
Hohengasse 3, Ch-3402 Burgdorf
SWITZERLAND
034 422 2378; 034 422 7693
info@klotzli.com; www.klotzli.com

MUSEUM REPLICAS LIMITED
2147 Gees Mill Rd
Conyers, GA 30012
800-883-8838; fax 770-388-0246
mrw@museumreplicas.com
www.museumreplicas.com
*Subsidiary of Atlanta Cutlery. Battle-ready swords
and other historic edged weapons, as well as
clothing, jewelry and accessories.*

NICHOLS CO.
Pomfret Rd
South Pomfret, VT 05067
*Import & distribute knives from EKA (Sweden), Helle
(Norway), Brusletto (Norway), Roselli (Finland). Also
market Zippo products, Snow, Nealley axes and
hatchets and snow & Neally axes*

NORMARK CORP.
Craig Weber
10395 Yellow Circle Dr
Minnetonka, MN 55343

PRODUCTORS AITOR, S.A.
Izelaieta 17
48260 Ermua
SPAIN
943-170850; 943-170001
info@aitor.com
Sporting knives

PROFESSIONAL CUTLERY SERVICES
9712 Washburn Rd
Downey, CA 90241
562-803-8778; 562-803-4261
*Wholesale only. Full service distributor of domestic
& imported brand name cutlery. Exclusive U.S.
importer for both Marto Swords and Battle Ready
Valiant Armory edged weapons*

SVORD KNIVES
Smith Rd., RD 2
Waiuku, South Auckland
NEW ZEALAND
64 9 2358846; fax 64 9 235648
www.svord.com

SWISS ARMY BRANDS INC.
15 Corporate Dr.
Orangeburg, NY 10962
800-431-2994 or 914-425-4700
customer.service@swissarmy.com
www.swissarmy.com
Importer and distributor of Victorinox's Swiss Army brand

TAYLOR BRANDS, LLC
1043 Fordtown Road
Kingsport, TN 37663
800-251-0254; fax 423-247-5371
info@taylorbrandsllc.com;
www.taylorbrandsllc.com
Fixed-blade and folding knives for tactical, rescue, hunting and general use. Also provides etching, engraving, scrimshaw services.

UNITED CUTLERY
475 U.S. Hwy. 319 S
Moultrie, GA 31768
800-548-0835 or 229-890-6669; fax 229-551-0182
customerservice@unitedcutlery.com
www.unitedcutlery.com
Harley-Davidson ® Colt ® , Stanley ®, U21 ®, Rigid Knives ®, Outdoor Life ®, Ford ®, hunting, camping, fishing, collectible & fantasy knives

WENGER N. A.
15 Corporate Dr
Orangeburg, NY 10962
800-431-2996; fax 914-425-4700
marketing@wengerna.com
www.wengerna.com
Wenger Genuine Swiss Army Knives and Wenger Swiss Watches

WORLD CLASS EXHIBITION KNIVES
Cary Desmon
941-504-2279
www.withoutequal.com
Carries an extensive line of Pius Lang knives

ZWILLING J.A. HENCKELS USA
171 Saw Mill River Rd
Hawthorne, NY 10532
914-747-0300; fax 914-747-1850
info@jahenckels.com;
www.jahenckels.com
Zwilling, Henckels International, Miyabi, Staub, Demeyere kitchen cutlery, scissors, shears, gadgets, cookware, flatware

knife making supplies

AFRICAN IMPORT CO.
Alan Zanotti
22 Goodwin Rd
Plymouth, MA 02360
508-746-8552; 508-746-0404
africanimport@aol.com
Ivory

ALABAMA DAMASCUS STEEL
PO Box 54
WELLINGTON, AL 36279
256-310-4619 or 256-282-7988
sales@alabamadamascussteel.com
www.alabamadamascussteel.com
We are a manufacturer of damascus steel billets & blades. We also offer knife supplies. We can custom make any blade design that the customer wants. We can also make custom damascus billets per customer specs.

ALPHA KNIFE SUPPLY
425-868-5880; Fax: 425-898-7715
chuck@alphaknifesupply.com;
www.alphaknifesupply.com
Inventory of knife supplies

AMERICAN SIEPMANN CORP.
65 Pixley Industrial Parkway
Rochester, NY 14624
585-247-1640; Fax: 585-247-1883
www.siepmann.com
CNC blade grinding equipment, grinding wheels, production blade grinding services. Sharpening stones and sharpening equipment

ANKROM EXOTICS
Pat Ankrom
22900 HWY 5
Centerville, IA 52544
641-436-0235
ankromexotics@hotmail.com
www.ankromexotics.com
Stabilized handle material; Exotic burls and hardwoods from around the world; Stabilizing services available

ATLANTA CUTLERY CORP.
P.O.Box 839
Conyers, Ga 30012
770-922-7500; Fax: 770-918-2026
custserve@atlantacutlery.com;
www.atlantacutlery.com

BLADEMAKER, THE
Gary Kelley
17485 SW Phesant Ln
Beaverton, OR 97006
503-649-7867
garykelley@theblademaker.com;
www.theblademaker.com
Period knife and hawk blades for hobbyists & re-enactors and in dendritic D2 steel. "Ferroulithic" steel-stone spear point, blades and arrowheads

BOONE TRADING CO., INC.
PO Box 669
562 Coyote Rd
Brinnon, WA 98320
800-423-1945; Fax: 360-796-4511
bella@boonetrading.com
www.boonetrading.com
Ivory of all types, bone, horns

BORGER, WOLF
Benzstrasse 8
76676 Graben-Neudorf
GERMANY
wolf@messerschmied.de;
www.messerschmied.de

BOYE KNIVES
PO Box 1238
Dolan Springs, AZ 86441-1238
800-853-1617 or 928-767-4273
boye@citlink.net
www.boyeknives.com
Dendritic steel and Dendritic cobalt

BRONK'S KNIFEWORKS
Lyle Brunckhorst
Country Village

23706 7th Ave SE, Suite B
Bothell, WA 98021
425-402-3484
bronks@bronksknifeworks.com;
www.bronksknifeworks.com
Damascus steel

CRAZY CROW TRADING POST
PO Box 847
Pottsboro, TX 75076
800-786-6210; Fax: 903-786-9059
info@crazycrow.com; www.crazycrow.com
Solingen blades, knife making parts & supplies

CULPEPPER & CO.
Joe Culpepper
P.O. Box 690
8285 Georgia Rd.
Otto, NC 28763
828-524-6842; Fax: 828-369-7809
culpepperandco@verizon.net
www.knifehandles.com http://www.knifehandles.com
www.stingrayproducts.com <http://www.stingrayproducts.com>
Mother of pearl, bone, abalone, stingray, dyed stag, blacklip, ram's horn, mammoth ivory, coral, scrimshaw

CUSTOM FURNACES
PO Box 353
Randvaal, 1873
SOUTH AFRICA
27 16 365-5723; 27 16 365-5738
johnlee@custom.co.za
Furnaces for hardening & tempering of knives

DAMASCUS USA
149 Deans Farm Rd
Tyner, NC 27980-9607
252-333-0349
rob@damascususa.com;
www.damascususa.com
All types of damascus cutlery steel, including 100 percent finished damascus blade blanks

DAN'S WHETSTONE CO., INC.
418 Hilltop Rd
Pearcy, AR 71964
501-767-1616; fax 501-767-9598
questions@danswhetstone.com;
www.danswhetstone.com
Natural abrasive Arkansas stone products

DIAMOND MACHINING TECHNOLOGY, INC. DMT
85 Hayes Memorial Dr
Marlborough, MA 01752
800-666-4DMT
dmtcustomercare@dmtsharp.com;
www.dmtsharp.com
Knife and tool sharpeners-diamond, ceramic and easy edge guided sharpening kits

DIGEM DIAMOND SUPPLIERS
7303 East Earll Drive
Scottsdale, Arizona 85251
602-620-3999
eglasser@cox.net
#1 international diamond tool provider. Every diamond tool you will ever need 1/16th of an inch to 11'x9'. BURRS, CORE DRILLS, SAW BLADES, MILLING SHAPES, AND WHEELS

DIXIE GUN WORKS, INC.
1412 West Reelfoot Ave.
Union City, TN 38281
731-885-0700; Fax: 731-885-0440
www.dixiegunworks.com
Knife and knifemaking supplies

EZE-LAP DIAMOND PRODUCTS
3572 Arrowhead Dr
Carson City, NV 89706
775-888-9500; Fax: 775-888-9555
sales@eze-lap.com; www.eze-lap.com
Diamond coated sharpening tools

FINE TURNAGE PRODUCTIONS
Charles Turnage
1210 Midnight Drive
San Antonio, TX 78260
210-352-5660
info@fineturnage.com
www.fineturnage.com
Specializing in stabilized mammoth tooth and bone, mammoth ivory, fossil brain coral, meteorite, etc.

FLITZ INTERNATIONAL, LTD.
821 Mohr Ave
Waterford, WI 53185
800-558-8611; Fax: 262-534-2991
info@flitz.com; www.flitz.com
Metal polish, buffing pads, wax

FORTUNE PRODUCTS, INC.
2010A Windy Terrace
Cedar Park, TX 78613
800-742-7797; Fax: 800-600-5373
www.accusharp.com
AccuSharp knife sharpeners

GALLERY HARDWOODS
Larry Davis, Eugene, OR
www.galleryhardwoods.com
Stabilized exotic burls and woods

GILMER WOOD CO.
2211 NW St Helens Rd
Portland, OR 97210
503-274-1271; Fax: 503-274-9839
www.gilmerwood.com

GIRAFFEBONE KNIFE SUPPLY
3052 Isim Rd.
Norman, OK 73026
888-804-0683
sandy@giraffebone.com;
www.giraffebone.com
Exotic handle materials

GLENDO CORPORATION/GRS TOOLS
D.J. Glaser
900 Overlander Rd.
Emporia, KS 66801
620-343-1084; Fax: 620-343-9640
glendo@glendo.com; www.grstools.com
Engraving, equipment, tool sharpener, books/videos

HALPERN TITANIUM INC.
Les and Marianne Halpern
PO Box 214
4 Springfield St
Three Rivers, MA 01080
888-283-8627; Fax: 413-289-2372
info@halperntitanium.com;
www.halperntitanium.com
Titanium, carbon fiber, G-10, fasteners; CNC milling

HAWKINS KNIFE MAKING SUPPLIES
110 Buckeye Rd
Fayetteville, GA 30214
770-964-1023
Sales@hawkinsknifemakingsupplies.com
www.HawkinsKnifeMakingSupplies.com
All styles

HILTARY INDUSTRIES
6060 East Thomas Road
Scottsdale, AZ 85251
Office: 480-945-0700
Fax: 480-945-3333
usgrc@usgrc.biz, eglasser@cox.net
OEM manufacturer, knife and sword importer, appraiser, metal supplier, diamond products, stag, meteorite, reconstituted gems, exotic wood, leather and bone

HOUSE OF TOOLS LTD.
#54-5329 72 Ave. S.E.
Calgary, Alberta
CANADA T2C 4X
403-640-4594; Fax: 403-451-7006
www.houseoftools.net

INDIAN JEWELERS SUPPLY CO.
Mail Order: 601 E Coal Ave
Gallup, NM 87301-6005
2105 San Mateo Blvd NE
Albuquerque, NM 87110-5148
800-545-6540; fax: 888-722-4172
orders@ijsinc.com; www.ijsinc.com
Handle materials, tools, metals

INTERAMCO INC.
5210 Exchange Dr
Flint, MI 48507
810-732-8181; 810-732-6116
solutions@interamco.com
Knife grinding and polishing

JANTZ SUPPLY / KOVAL KNIVES
PO Box 584
309 West Main
Davis, OK 73030
800-351-8900; 580-369-3082
jantz@jantzusa.com
www.knifemaking.com
Pre shaped blades, kit knives, complete knifemaking supply line

JMD INTERNATIONAL
2985 Gordy Pkwy., Unit 405
Marietta, GA 30066
678-969-9147; Fax: 770-640-9852
knifesupplies@gmail.com;
www.knifesupplies.com
Serving the cutlery industry with the finest selection of India stag, buffalo horn, mother-of-pearl and smooth white bone

JOHNSON, R.B.
I.B.S. Int'l. Folder Supplies, Box 11
Clearwater, MN 55320
320-558-6128; 320-558-6128
www.foldingknifesupplies.com
Threaded pivot pins, screws, taps, etc.

JOHNSON WOOD PRODUCTS
34897 Crystal Rd
Strawberry Point, IA 52076
563-933-6504

K&G FINISHING SUPPLIES
1972 Forest Ave
Lakeside, AZ 85929
928-537-8877; fax: 928-537-8066
csinfo@knifeandgun.com;
www.knifeandgun.com
Full service supplies

KOWAK IVORY
Roland and Kathy Quimby
(April-Sept): PO Box 350
Ester, AK 99725
907-479-9335
(Oct-March)
PO Box 693
Bristow, OK 74010
918-367-2684
sales@kowakivory.com;
www.kowakivory.com
Fossil ivories

LITTLE GIANT POWER HAMMER
Roger Rice
420 4th Corso
Nebraska City, NE 68410
402-873-6603
www.littlegianthammer.com
Rebuilds hammers and supplies parts

LIVESAY, NEWT
3306 S Dogwood St
Siloam Springs, AR 72761
479-549-3356; 479-549-3357
Combat utility knives, titanium knives, sportsmen knives, custom made orders taken on knives and after market Kydex© sheaths for commercial or custom cutlery

M MILLER ORIGINALS
Michael Miller
2960 E Carver Ave
Kingman AZ 86401
928-757-1359
mike@mmilleroriginals.com;
www.mmilleroriginals.com
Supplies stabilized juniper burl blocks and scales, mosaic damascus, damascus

MARKING METHODS, INC.
Sales
301 S. Raymond Ave
Alhambra, CA 91803-1531
626-282-8823; Fax: 626-576-7564
sales@markingmethods.com;
www.markingmethods.com
Knife etching equipment & service

MASECRAFT SUPPLY CO.
254 Amity St
Meriden, CT 06450
800-682-5489; Fax: 203-238-2373
info@masecraftsupply.com;
www.masecraftsupply.com
*Natural & specialty synthetic handle materials &
more*

MEIER STEEL
Daryl Meier
75 Forge Rd
Carbondale, IL 62901
618-549-3234; Fax: 618-549-6239
www.meiersteel.com

NICO, BERNARD
PO Box 5151
Nelspruit 1200
SOUTH AFRICA
011-2713-7440099; 011-2713-7440099
bernardn@iafrica.com

NORRIS, MIKE
Rt 2 Box 242A
Tollesboro, KY 41189
606-798-1217
Damascus steel

NORTHCOAST KNIVES
17407 Puritas Ave
Cleveland, Ohio 44135
www.NorthCoastKnives.com
*Tutorials and step-by-step projects. Entry level
knifemaking supplies.*

OSO FAMOSO
PO Box 654
Ben Lomond, CA 95005
831-336-2343
oso@osofamoso.com;
www.osofamoso.com
Mammoth ivory bark

OZARK CUTLERY SUPPLY
5230 S. MAIN ST.
Joplin, MO 64804
417-782-4998
ozarkcutlery@gmail.com
*28 years in the cutlery business, Missouri's oldest
cutlery firm*

PARAGON INDUSTRIES, INC. L. P.
2011 South Town East Blvd
Mesquite, TX 75149-1122
800-876-4328 or 972-288-7557
info@paragonweb.com;
www.paragonweb.com
Heat treating furnaces for knifemakers

**POPLIN, JAMES / POP'S KNIVES &
SUPPLIES**
1654 S. Smyrna Church Rd.
Washington, GA 30673
706-678-5408
www.popsknifesupplies.com

PUGH, JIM
PO Box 711
917 Carpenter
Azle, TX 76020
817-444-2679; Fax: 817-444-5455
*Rosewood and ebony Micarta blocks,rivets for
Kydex sheaths, 0-80 screws for folders*

RADOS, JERRY
134 Willie Nell Rd.
Columbia, KY 42728
606-303-3334
jerryr@ttlv.net
www.radosknives.com
Damascus steel

REACTIVE METALS STUDIO, INC.
PO Box 890
Clarksdale, AZ 86324
800-876-3434; 928-634-3434; Fax: 928-
634-6734
info@reactivemetals.com; www.
reactivemetals.com

R. FIELDS ANCIENT IVORY
Donald Fields
790 Tamerlane St
Deltona, FL 32725
386-532-9070
donaldfields@aol.com
Selling ancient ivories; Mammoth, fossil & walrus

RICK FRIGAULT CUSTOM KNIVES
1189 Royal Pines Rd.
Golden Lake, Ontario
CANADA K0J 1X0
613-401-2869
jill@mouseworks.net
www.frigault.org
*Selling padded zippered knife pouches with an
option to personalize the outside with the marker,
purveyor, stores-address, phone number, email
web-site or any other information needed. Available
in black cordura, mossy oak camo in sizes 4"x2" to
20"x4.5"*

RIVERSIDE MACHINE
201 W Stillwell Ave.
DeQueen, AR 71832
870-642-7643; Fax: 870-642-4023
uncleal@riversidemachine.net
www.riversidemachine.net

ROCKY MOUNTAIN KNIVES
George L. Conklin
PO Box 902, 615 Franklin
Ft. Benton, MT 59442
406-622-3268; Fax: 406-622-3410
bbgrus@ttc-cmc.net
Working knives

RUMMELL, HANK
10 Paradise Lane
Warwick, NY 10990
845-469-9172
hank@newyorkcustomknives.com;
www.newyorkcustomknives.com

SAKMAR, MIKE
1451 Clovelly Ave
Rochester, MI 48307
248-852-6775; Fax: 248-852-8544
mikesakmar@yahoo.com
Mokume bar stock. Retail & wholesale

SANDPAPER, INC. OF ILLINOIS
P.O. Box 2579
Glen Ellyn, IL 60138
630-629-3320; Fax: 630-629-3324
sandinc@aol.com; www.sandpaperinc.com
Abrasive belts, rolls, sheets & discs

SCHEP'S FORGE
PO Box 395
Shelton, NE 68876-0395

SENTRY SOLUTIONS LTD.
PO Box 214
Wilton, NH 03086
800-546-8049; Fax: 603-654-3003
info@sentrysolutions.com;
www.sentrysolutions.com
Knife care products

**SHEFFIELD KNIFEMAKERS
SUPPLY, INC.**
PO Box 741107
Orange City, FL 32774
386-775-6453; fax: 386-774-5754
email@sheffieldsupply.com;
www.sheffieldsupply.com

SHINING WAVE METALS
PO Box 563
Snohomish, WA 98291
425-334-5569
info@shiningwave.com;
www.shiningwave.com
*A full line of mokume-gane in precious and non-
precious metals for knifemakers, jewelers and other
artists*

SMITH'S
747 Mid-America Blvd.
Hot Springs, AR 71913-8414
501-321-2244; Fax: 501-321-9232
sales@smithsproducts.com
www.smithsproducts.com

SOSTER SVENSTRUP BYVEJ 16
Søster Svenstrup Byvej 16
4130 Viby Sjælland
Denmark
45 46 19 43 05; Fax: 45 46 19 53 19
www.poulstrande.com

STAMASCUS KNIFEWORKS INC.
Ed VanHoy
24255 N Fork River Rd
Abingdon, VA 24210
276-944-4885; Fax: 276-944-3187
stamascus@centurylink.net
www.stamascusknifeworks.com
Blade steels

STOVER, JEFF
PO Box 43
Torrance, CA 90507
310-532-2166
edgedealer1@yahoo.com;
www.edgedealer.com
Fine custom knives, top makers

TEXAS KNIFEMAKERS SUPPLY
10649 Haddington Suite 180
Houston TX 77043
713-461-8632; Fax: 713-461-8221
sales@texasknife.com;
www.texasknife.com
*Complete line of knifemaking supplies, equipment,
and custom heat treating*

TRU-GRIT, INC.
760 E Francis Unit N
Ontario, CA 91761
909-923-4116; Fax: 909-923-9932
www.trugrit.com
*The latest in Norton and 3/M ceramic grinding belts.
Also Super Flex, Trizact, Norax and Micron belts to
3000 grit. All of the popular belt grinders. Buffers
and variable speed motors. ATS-34, 440C, BG-42,
CPM S-30V, 416 and Damascus steel*

WASHITA MOUNTAIN WHETSTONE CO.
PO Box 20378
Hot Springs, AR 71903-0378
501-525-3914; Fax: 501-525-0816
wmw@hsnp

WEILAND, J. REESE
PO Box 2337
Riverview, FL 33568
813-671-0661
rwphil413@verizon.net
Folders, straight knives, etc.

WILSON, R.W.
PO Box 2012
113 Kent Way
Weirton, WV 26062
304-723-2771
rwknives@hotmail.com

WOOD CARVERS SUPPLY, INC.
PO Box 7500
Englewood, FL 34295
800-284-6229
teamwcs@yahoo.com
www.woodcarverssupply.com
Over 2,000 unique wood carving tools

WOOD LAB
Michael Balaskovitz
4393 Van Buren St.
Hudsonville, MI 49426
616-322-5846
woodlabgroup@gmail.com
www.woodlab.biz
Acrylic stabilizing services and materials

**WOOD STABILIZING SPECIALISTS
   INT'L, LLC**
2940 Fayette Ave
Ionia, IA 50645
800-301-9774; 641-435-4746
mike@stabilizedwood.com;
www.stabilizedwood.com
Processor of acrylic impregnated materials

ZOWADA CUSTOM KNIVES
Tim Zowada
4509 E. Bear River Rd
Boyne Falls, MI 49713
231-881-5056
tim@tzknives.com; www.tzknives.com
*Damascus, pocket knives, swords, Lower case
gothic tz logo*

mail order, sales, dealers and purveyors

A.G. RUSSELL KNIVES INC
2900 S. 26th St
Rogers, AR 72758-8571
800-255-9034 or 479-631-0130
fax 479-631-8493
ag@agrussell.com; www.agrussell.com
*The oldest knife mail-order company, highest
quality. Free catalog available. In these catalogs you
will find the newest and the best. If you like knives,
this catalog is a must*

ARIZONA CUSTOM KNIVES
Julie Maguire
3620 U.S. 1 S,
Suite 260-F
St. Augustine, FL 32086
904-460-0009
sharptalk@arizonacustomknives.com;
www.arizonacustomknives.com
Color catalog $5 U.S. / $7 Foreign

ARTKNIVES.COM
Fred Eisen Leather & Art Knives
129 S. Main St.
New Hope, PA 18938
215-862-5988
fredeisen@verizon.net
www.artknives.com
*Handmade knives from over 75 makers/high-quality
manufacturers, leather sheath maker*

ATLANTA CUTLERY CORP.
P.O.Box 839
Conyers, Ga 30012
770-922-7500; Fax: 770-918-2026
custserv@atlantacutlery.com;
www.atlantacutlery.com

**ATLANTIC BLADESMITHS/PETER
   STEBBINS**
50 Mill Rd
Littleton, MA 01460
978-952-6448
*Sell, trade, buy; carefully selected handcrafted,
benchmade and factory knives*

BALLARD CUTLERY
1495 Brummel Ave.
Elk Grove Village, IL 60007
847-228-0070

BECK'S CUTLERY SPECIALTIES
51 Highland Trace Ln.
Benson, NC 27504
919-902-9416
beckscutlery@embarqmail.com;
www.beckscutlery.com
Knives

BLADE HQ
400 S. 1000 E, Ste. E
Lehi, UT 84043
888-252-3347 or 801-768-0232
questions@bladehq.com
www.bladehq.com
*Online destination for knives and gear, specializing
in law enforcement and military, including folders,
fixed blades, custom knives, asisted-opening
folders, automatics, butterfly knives, hunters,
machetes, multi-tools, axes, knife cases, paracord,
sharpeners, sheaths, lubricants and supplies*

BLADEART.COM
14216 S.W. 136 St.
Miami, FL 33186
305-255-9176
sales@bladeart.com
www.bladeart.com
Custom knives, swords and gear

BLADEGALLERY.COM
107 Central Way
Kirkland, WA 98033
425-889-5980 or 877-56BLADE
info@bladegallery.com;
www.bladegallery.com
*Bladegallery.com specializes in hand-made
one-of-a-kind knives from around the world. We
have an emphasis on forged knives and high-end
gentlemen's folders*

BLADEOPS, LLC
1352 W. 7800 S
West Jordan, UT 84088
888-EZ BLAD (392-5233)
trevor@bladeops.com
www.bladeops.com
*Online dealer of all major brands of automatic
knives, butterfly knives, spring-assisted folders,
throwing knives, manual folders, survival and self-
defense knives, sharpeners and paracord*

BLUE RIDGE KNIVES
166 Adwolfe Rd
Marion, VA 24354
276-783-6143; fax 276-783-9298
onestop@blueridgeknives.com;

www.blueridgeknives.com
Wholesale distributor of knives

BOB'S TRADING POST
308 N Main St
Hutchinson, KS 67501
620-669-9441
bobstradingpost@cox.net;
www.bobstradingpostinc.com
*Tad custom knives with Reichert custom sheaths
one at a time, one of a kind*

BOONE TRADING CO., INC.
PO Box 669
562 Coyote Rd
Brinnon, WA 98320
800-423-1945; Fax: 360-796-4511
bella@boonetrading.com
www.boonetrading.com
Ivory of all types, bone, horns

CARMEL CUTLERY
Dolores & 6th
PO Box 1346
Carmel, CA 93921
831-624-6699; 831-624-6780
sanford@carmelcutlery.com;
www.carmelcutlery.com
*Quality custom and a variety of production pocket
knives, swords; kitchen cutlery; personal grooming
items*

CLASSIC CUTLERY
11 Vatcher Road, Ste. 1
Hancock, NH 03449
classiccutlery@earthlink.net
www.classiccutleryusa.com
*Private-label zip-up knife cases and all brands of
production cutlery and outdoor gear*

CUTLERY SHOPPE
3956 E Vantage Pointe Ln
Meridian, ID 83642-7268
800-231-1272; Fax: 208-884-4433
orders@cutleryshoppe.com;
www.cutleryshoppe.com
Discount pricing on top quality brands

CUTTING EDGE, THE
2900 South 26th St
Rogers, AR 72758-8571
800-255-9034; Fax: 479-631-8493
ce_info@cuttingedge.com;
www.cuttingedge.com
*After-market knives since 1968. They offer about
1,000 individual knives for sale each month.*

Subscription by first class mail, in U.S. $20 per year, Canada or Mexico by air mail, $25 per year. All overseas by air mail, $40 per year. The oldest and the most experienced in the business of buying and selling knives. They buy collections of any size, take knives on consignment. Every month there are 4-8 pages in color featuring the work of top makers

DENTON, JOHN W.
703 Hiawassee Estates Dr.
Hiawassee, GA 30546
706-781-8479
jwdenton@windstream.net
www.boblovelessknives.com
Loveless knives

DUNN KNIVES INC.
PO Box 307
1449 Nocatee St.
Intercession City, FL 33848
800-245-6483
s.greene@earthlink.com;
www.dunnknives.com

EDGEDEALER.COM
PO BOX 43
TORRANCE, CA 90507
310-532-2166
edgedealer1@yahoo.com
www.edgedealer.com
Antiques

EPICUREAN EDGE
107 Central Way
Kirkland, WA 98033
425-889-5980
info@epicedge.com
www.epicedge.com
Specializing in handmade and one-of-a-kind kitchen knives from around the world

EXQUISITEKNIVES.COM
770 Sycamore Ave., Ste. 122, Box 451
Vista, CA 92083
760-945-7177
ellis@mastersmith.com;
www.exquisiteknives.com and
www.robertloveless.com
Purveyor of high-end custom knives

FAZALARE INTERNATIONAL ENTERPRISES
PO Box 7062
Thousand Oaks, CA 91359
805-496-2002
ourfaz@aol.com
Handmade multiblades; older Case; Fight'n Rooster; Bulldog brand & Cripple Creek

FROST CUTLERY CO.
PO Box 22636
Chattanooga, TN 37422
800-251-7768
www.frostcutlery.com

GODWIN, INC. G. GEDNEY
PO Box 100
Valley Forge, PA 19481
610-783-0670; Fax: 610-783-6083
sales@gggodwin.com;
www.gggodwin.com
18th century reproductions

GPKNIVES, LLC
2230 Liebler Rd.
Troy, IL 62294
866-667-5965
gpk@gpknives.com
www.gpknives.com
Serving law enforcement, hunters, sportsmen and collectors

GRAZYNA SHAW/QUINTESSENTIAL CUTLERY
POB 296
Clearwater, MN 55320
320-217-9002
gshaw@quintcut.com
www.quintcut.com
Specializing in investment-grade custom knives and early makers

GUILD KNIVES
Donald Guild
320 Paani Place 1A
Paia, HI 96779
808-877-3109
don@guildknives.com;
www.guildknives.com
Purveyor of custom art knives

HOUSE OF BLADES
6451 N.W. Loop 820
Ft. Worth, TX 76135
817-237-7721
sales@houseofblades.com
www.houseofbladestexas.com
Handmades, pocketknives, hunting knives, antique and collector knives, swords, household cutlery and knife-related items.

JENCO SALES, INC. / KNIFE IMPORTERS, INC. / WHITE LIGHTNING
PO Box 1000
11307 Conroy Ln
Manchaca, TX 78652
800-531-5301; fax 800-266-2373
jencosales@sbcglobal.net
Wholesale distributor of domestic and imported cutlery and sharpeners

KELLAM KNIVES WORLDWIDE
POB 3438
Lantana, FL 33465
800-390-6918; 561-588-3185
info@kellamknives.com;
www.kellamknives.com
Largest selection of Finnish knives; own line of folders and fixed blades

KNIFEART.COM
13301 Pompano Dr
Little Rock AR 72211
501-221-1010
connelley@knifeart.com
www.knifeart.com
Large internet seller of custom knives & upscale production knives

KNIFEPURVEYOR.COM LLC
919-295-1283
mdonato@knifepurveyor.com
www.knifepurveyor.com
Owned and operated by Michael A. Donato (full-time knife purveyor since 2002). We buy, sell, trade, and consign fine custom knives. We also specialize in buying and selling valuable collections of fine custom knives. Our goal is to make every transaction a memorable one.

KNIVES PLUS
2467 I 40 West
Amarillo, TX 79109
806-359-6202
salessupport@knivesplus.com
www.knivesplus.com
Retail cutlery and cutlery accessories since 1987

KRIS CUTLERY
2314 Monte Verde Dr
Pinole, CA 94564
510-758-9912 Fax: 510-758-9912
kriscutlery@aol.com; www.kriscutlery.com
Japanese, medieval, Chinese & Philippine

LONE STAR WHOLESALE
2401 Interstate 40 W
Amarillo, TX 79109
806-836-9540; fax 806-359-1603
sales@1swtexas.com
www.1swtexas.com
Nationwide distributor of knives, knife accessories and knife-related tools

MATTHEWS CUTLERY
PO Box 2768
Moultrie, GA 31776
800-251-0123; fax 877-428-3599
www.matthewscutlery.com

MOORE CUTLERY
PO Box 633
Lockport, IL 60441
708-301-4201
www.moorecutlery.com
Owned & operated by Gary Moore since 1991 (a full-time dealer). Purveyor of high quality custom & production knives

MUSEUM REPLICAS LIMITED
2147 Gees Mill Rd
Conyers, GA 30012
800-883-8838
www.museumreplicas.com
Historically accurate and battle ready swords & daggers

NEW GRAHAM KNIVES
560 Virginia Ave.
Bluefield, VA 24605
276-326-1384
mdye@newgraham.com
www.newgraham.com
Wide selection of knives from over 75 manufacturers, knife sharpening and maintenance accessories

NORDIC KNIVES
436 1st St., Ste. 203A
Solvang, CA 93463
805-688-3612; fax 805-688-1635
info@nordicknives.com
www.nordicknives.com
Custom and Randall knives

PARKERS' KNIFE COLLECTOR SERVICE
6715 Heritage Business Court
Chattanooga, TN 37421
423-892-0448; fax 423-892-9165
www.bulldogknives.org
Online and mail order dealer specializing in collectible knives, including Bulldog Knives, Weidmannsheil and Parker Eagle Brand. Parkers' Greatest Knife Show On Earth

PLAZA CUTLERY, INC.
3333 S. Bristol St., Suite 2060
South Coast Plaza
Costa Mesa, CA 92626
866-827-5292; 714-549-3932
dan@plazacutlery.com;
www.plazacutlery.com
*Largest selection of knives on the west coast.
Custom makers from beginners to the best. All
customs, William Henry, Strider, Reeves, Randalls &
others available online, by phone*

ROBERTSON'S CUSTOM CUTLERY
4960 Sussex Dr
Evans, GA 30809
706-650-0252; 706-860-1623
customknives@comcast.net
www.robertsoncustomcutlery.com
*World class custom knives, custom knife
entrepreneur*

SMOKY MOUNTAIN KNIFE WORKS, INC.
2320 Winfield Dunn Pkwy
PO Box 4430
Sevierville, TN 37864
800-564-8374; 865-453-5871
info@smkw.com; www.smkw.com
*The world's largest knife showplace, catalog and
website*

VOYLES, BRUCE
PO Box 22007
Chattanooga, TN 37422
423-238-6753; Fax: 423-238-3960
bruce@jbrucevoyles.com;
www.jbrucevoyles.com
Knives, knife auctions

knife services

appraisers

Levine, Bernard, P.O. Box 2404, Eugene, OR, 97402, 541-484-0294, brlevine@
ix.netcom.com
Russell, A.G., Knives Inc, 2900 S. 26th St., Rogers, AR 72758-8571, phone
800-255-9034 or 479-631-0130, fax 479-631-8493, ag@agrussell.com,
www.agrussell.com
Vallini, Massimo, Via G. Bruno 7, 20154 Milano, ITALY, 02-33614751,
massimo_vallini@yahoo.it, Knife expert

custom grinders

McGowan Manufacturing Company, 4720 N. La Cholla Blvd., #190, Tucson,
AZ, 85705, 800-342-4810, 520-219-0884, info@mcgowanmfg.com, www.
mcgowanmfg.com, Knife sharpeners, hunting axes
Peele, Bryan, The Elk Rack, 215 Ferry St. P.O. Box 1363, Thompson Falls, MT,
59873
Schlott, Harald, Zingster Str. 26, 13051 Berlin, GERMANY, 049 030 9293346,
harald.schlott@T-online.de, Custom grinder, custom handle artisan,
display case/box maker, etcher, scrimshander
Wilson, R.W., P.O. Box 2012, Weirton, WV, 26062

custom handles

Cooper, Jim, 1221 Cook St, Ramona, CA, 92065-3214, 760-789-1097, (760)
788-7992, jamcooper@aol.com
Burrows, Chuck, dba Wild Rose Trading Co, 102 Timber Ln., Durango, CO,
81303, 970-317-5592, chuck@wrtcleather.com, www.wrtcleather.com
Fields, Donald, 790 Tamerlane St, Deltona, FL, 32725, 386-532-9070,
donaldfields@aol.com, Selling ancient ivories; mammoth & fossil walrus
Grussenmeyer, Paul G., 310 Kresson Rd, Cherry Hill, NJ, 08034, 856-428-
1088, 856-428-8997, pgrussentne@comcast.net, www.pgcarvings.com
Holland, Dennis K., 4908-17th Pl., Lubbock, TX, 79416
Imboden II, Howard L., hi II Originals, 620 Deauville Dr., Dayton, OH, 45429
Kelso, Jim, 577 Collar Hill Rd, Worcester, VT, 05682, 802-229-4254, (802)
223-0595
Knack, Gary, 309 Wightman, Ashland, OR, 97520
Marlatt, David, 67622 Oldham Rd., Cambridge, OH, 43725, 740-432-7549
Mead, Dennis, 2250 E. Mercury St., Inverness, FL, 34453-0514
Myers, Ron, 6202 Marglenn Ave., Baltimore, MD, 21206, 410-866-6914
Schlott, Harald, Zingster Str. 26, 13051 Berlin, GERMANY, 049 030 9293346,
harald.schlott@T-online.de, Custom grinder, custom handle artisan,
display case/box maker, etcher, scrimshander
Snell, Barry A., 4801 96th St. N., St. Petersburg, FL, 33708-3740
Vallotton, A., 621 Fawn Ridge Dr., Oakland, OR, 97462
Watson, Silvia, 350 Jennifer Lane, Driftwood, TX, 78619
Wilderness Forge, 315 North 100 East, Kanab, UT, 84741, 435-644-3674,
bhatting@xpressweb.com
Williams, Gary, (GARBO), PO Box 210, Glendale, KY, 42740-2010

display cases and boxes

Bill's Custom Cases, P O Box 603, Montague, CA, 96064, 541-727-7223,
billscustomcases@earthlink.net
Brooker, Dennis, Rt. 1, Box 12A, Derby, IA, 50068
Culpepper & Company / Tomway LLC, 8285 Georgia Rd., Otto, NC, 28763
828-524-6842,info@culpepperco.com, www.tomway.com
Gimbert, Nelson, P.O. Box 787, Clemmons, NC, 27012
McLean, Lawrence, 12344 Meritage Ct, Rancho Cucamonga, CA, 91739, 714-
848-5779, lmclean@charter.net
Miller, Michael K., M&M Kustom Krafts, 28510 Santiam Highway, Sweet
Home, OR, 97386
Miller, Robert, P.O. Box 2722, Ormond Beach, FL, 32176
Retichek, Joseph L., W9377 Co. TK. D, Beaver Dam, WI, 53916
Robbins, Wayne, 11520 Inverway, Belvidere, IL, 61008
S&D Enterprises, 20 East Seventh St, Manchester, OH, 45144, 937-549-2602,
937-549-2602, sales@s-denterprises.com, www.s-denterprises.com,
Display case/ box maker. Manufacturer of aluminum display, chipboard
type displays, wood displays. Silk screening or acid etching for logos on
product
Schlott, Harald, Zingster Str. 26, 13051 Berlin, GERMANY, 049 030 9293346,
harald.schlott@T-online.de, Custom grinder, custom handle artisan,
display case/box maker, etcher, scrimshander

engravers

Adlam, Tim, 1705 Witzel Ave., Oshkosh, WI, 54902, 920-235-4589, www.
adlamengraving.com
Alcorn, Gordon, 10573 Kelly Canyon Rd., Bozeman, MT 59715, 406-586-1350,
alcorncustom@yahoo.com, www.alcornengraving.com
Alfano, Sam, 45 Catalpa Trace, Covington, LA, 70433, alfano@gmail.com,
www.masterengraver.com
Baron, David, Baron Technology Inc., 62 Spring Hill Rd., Trumbull, CT, 06611,
203-452-0515, bti@baronengraving.com, www.baronengraving.com,
Polishing, plating, inlays, artwork
Bates, Billy, 2302 Winthrop Dr. SW, Decatur, AL, 35603, bbrn@aol.com, www.
angelfire.com/al/billybates
Bettenhausen, Merle L., 8300 W. 191st St., Mokena, IL, 60448, 708-532-2179
Blair, Jim, PO Box 64, 59 Mesa Verde, Glenrock, WY, 82637, 307-436-8115,
jblairengrav@msn.com, www.jimblairengraving.com
Booysen, Chris, South Africa, +27-73-284-1493, chris@cbknives.com, www.
cbknives.com
Churchill, Winston G., RFD Box 29B, Proctorsville, VT 05153, www.wchurchill.
com
Collins, Michael, 405-392-2273, info@michaelcollinsart.com, www.
michaelcollinsart.com
Cover, Raymond A., 1206 N. Third St., Festus, MO 63010 314-808-2508
cover@sbcglobal.net, http://rcoverengraving.com
DeLorge, Ed, 6734 W Main St, Houma, LA, 70360, 985-223-0206, delorge@
triparish.net, http://www.eddelorge.com
Dickson, John W., PO Box 49914, Sarasota, FL, 34230, 941-952-1907
Dolbare, Elizabeth, PO Box 502, Dubois, WY, 82513-0502 edolbare@hotmail.
com, http://www.scrimshaw-engraving.com/
Downing, Jim, PO Box 4224, Springfield, MO, 65803, 417-865-5953,
handlebar@thegunengraver.com, www.thegunengraver.com,

Scrimshander

Duarte, Carlos, 108 Church St., Rossville, CA, 95678, 916-782-2617 carlossilver@surewest.net, www.carlossilver.com

Dubber, Michael W., 11 S. Green River Rd., Evansville, IN, 47715, 812-454-0271, m.dubber@firearmsengraving.com, www.firearmsengraving.com

Eaton, Rick, 313 Dailey Rd., Broadview, MT 59015, 406-667-2405, rick@eatonknives.com, www.eatonknives.com

Eklund, Maihkel, Föne Stam V9, S-820 41 Färila, SWEDEN, info@art-knives.com, www.art-knives.com

Eldridge, Allan, 7731 Four Winds Dr., Ft. Worth, TX 76133, 817-370-7778

Ellis, Willy B, Willy B's Customs, 1025 Hamilton Ave., Tarpon Springs, FL, 34689, 727-942-6420, wbflashs@verizon.net, www.willyb.com

Flannery Gun Engraving, Jeff, 11034 Riddles Run Rd., Union, KY, 41091, 859-384-3127, engraving@fuse.net, www.flannerygunengraving.com

Gournet, Geoffroy, 820 Paxinosa Ave., Easton, PA, 18042, 610-559-0710, ggournet@yahoo.com, www.gournetusa.com

Halloran, Tim, 316 Fenceline Dr., Blue Grass, IA 52726 563-260-8464, vivtim@msn.com, http://halloranengraving.com

Hands, Barry Lee, 30608 Fernview Ln., Bigfork, MT 59911, 406-249-4334, barry_hands@yahoo.com, www.barryleehands.com

Holder, Pat, 18910 McNeil Ranch Rd., Wickenburg, AZ 85390, 928-684-2025 dholderknives@commspeed.net, www.dholder.com

Ingle, Ralph W., 151 Callan Dr., Rossville, GA, 30741, 706-858-0641, riengraver@aol.com, Photographer

Johns, Bill, 1716 8th St, Cody, WY, 82414, 307-587-5090, http://billjohnsengraver.com

Kelso, Jim, 577 Coller Hill Rd, Worcester, VT, 05682, 802-229-4254, jimkelsojournal@gmail.com, www.jimkelso.com

Koevenig, Eugene and Eve, Koevenig's Engraving Service, Rabbit Gulch, Box 55, Hill City, SD, 57745-0055

Kostelnik, Joe and Patty, RD #4, Box 323, Greensburg, PA, 15601

Kudlas, John M., 55280 Silverwolf Dr, Barnes, WI, 54873, 715-795-2031, jkudlas@cheqnet.net, Engraver, scrimshander

Lark, David, 6641 Schneider Rd., Kingsley, MI 49649, Phone: 231-342-1076 dblark58@yahoo.com

Larson, Doug, Dragon's Fire Studio, Percival, IA, Phone: 402-202-3703 (cell) dragonsfirestudio@hotmail.com

Limings Jr., Harry, 5793 Nichels Ln., Johnstown, OH, 43031-9576

Lindsay, Steve, 3714 West Cedar Hill, Kearney, NE, 68845, Phone: 308-236-7885 steve@lindsayengraving.com, www.lindsayengraving.com

Lurth, Mitchell, 1317 7th Ave., Marion, IA 52302, Phone: 319-377-1899 www.lurthengraving.com

Lyttle, Brian, Box 5697, High River AB CANADA, T1V 1M7

Lytton, Simon M., 19 Pinewood Gardens, Hemel Hempstead, Hertfordshire HP1 1TN, ENGLAND, 01-442-255542, simonlyttonengraver@virginmedia.com

Markow, Paul, 130 Spinnaker Ridge Dr. SW, B206, Huntsville, AL 35824, 256-513-9790, paul.markow@gmail.com, sites.google.com/site/artistictouch2010/engraving

Mason, Joe, 146 Value Rd, Brandon, MS, 39042, 601-824-9867, masonjoe@bellsouth.net, www.joemasonengraving.com

McCombs, Leo, 1862 White Cemetery Rd., Patriot, OH, 45658

McDonald, Dennis, 8359 Brady St., Peosta, IA, 52068

McLean, Lawrence, 12344 Meritage Ct, Rancho Cucamonga, CA, 91739, 714-848-5779, lmclean@charter.net

Meyer, Chris, 39 Bergen Ave., Wantage, NJ, 07461, 973-875-6299

Minnick, Joyce, 144 N. 7th St., Middletown, IN, 47356

Morgan, Tandie, P.O. Box 693, 30700 Hwy. 97, Nucla, CO, 81424

Morton, David A., 1110 W. 21st St., Lorain, OH, 44052

Moulton, Dusty, 135 Hillview Ln, Loudon, TN, 37774, 865-408-9779

Muller, Jody & Pat, 3359 S. 225th Rd., Goodson, MO, 65663, 417-852-4306/417-752-3260, mullerforge2@hotmail.com, www.mullerforge.com

Nelida, Toniutti, via G. Pasconi 29/c, Maniago 33085 (PN), ITALY

Nilsson, Jonny Walker, Tingsstigen 11, SE-933 33 Arvidsjaur, SWEDEN, +(46) 960-13048, 0960.1304@telia.com, www.jwnknives.com

Nott, Ron, Box 281, Summerdale, PA, 17093

Parke, Jeff, 1365 Fort Pierce Dr. #3, St. George, UT 84790, Phone: 435-421-1692 jeffrey_parke@hotmail.com, www.parkeengraving.com

Parsons, Michael R., McKee Knives, 7042 McFarland Rd, Indianapolis, IN, 46227, 317-784-7943

Patterson, W.H., P.O. Drawer DK, College Station, TX, 77841

Peri, Valerio, Via Meucci 12, Gardone V.T. 25063, ITALY

Pilkington Jr., Scott, P.O. Box 97, Monteagle, TN, 37356, 931-924-3400, scott@pilkguns.com, www.pilkguns.com

Pulisova, Andrea, CSA 230-95, 96701 Kremnica, Slovakia, Phone: 00421 903-340076 vpulis@gmail.com, www.vpulis.host.sk

Rabeno, Martin, Spook Hollow Trading Co, 530 Eagle Pass, Durango, CO, 81301

Raftis, Andrew, 2743 N. Sheffield, Chicago, IL, 60614

Riccardo, David, Riccardo Fine Hand Engraving, Buckley, MI, Phone: 231-269-3028, riccardoengraving@acegroup.cc, www.riccardoengraving.com

Roberts, J.J., 7808 Lake Dr., Manassas, VA, 20111, 703-330-0448, jjrengraver@aol.com, www.jjrobertsengraver.com

Robidoux, Roland J., DMR Fine Engraving, 25 N. Federal Hwy. Studio 5, Dania, FL, 33004

Rosser, Bob, Hand Engraving, 2809 Crescent Ave Ste 20, Birmingham, AL, 35209, www.hand-engravers.com

Rudolph, Gil, 20922 Oak Pass Ave, Tehachapi, CA, 93561, 661-822-4949

Rundell, Joe, 6198 W. Frances Rd., Clio, MI, 48420

Sawby, Marian, 480 Snowberry Ln., Sandpoint, ID 83864, 208-263-4253, http://sawbycustomknives.com

Schönert, Elke, 18 Lansdowne Pl., Central, Port Elizabeth, SOUTH AFRICA

Shaw, Bruce, P.O. Box 545, Pacific Grove, CA, 93950, 831-646-1937, 831-644-0941, shawdogs@aol.com

Simmons, Rick W., 3323 Creek Manor Dr., Kingwood, TX, 77339, 504-261-8450, exhibitiongrade@gmail.com www.hertemple.org/exhibitionengraver.com

Slobodian, Barbara, 4101 River Ridge Dr., PO Box 1498, San Andreas, CA 95249, 209-286-1980, fax 209-286-1982, barbara@dancethetide.com. Specializes in Japanese-style engraving.

Small, Jim, 2860 Athens Hwy., Madison, GA 30650, 706-818-1245, smallengrave@aol.com, www.jimsmallengraving.com

Smith, Ron, 5869 Straley, Ft. Worth, TX, 76114

Smitty's Engraving, 21320 Pioneer Circle, Harrah, OK, 73045, 405-454-6968, mail@smittys-engraving.us, www.smittys-engraving.us

Spode, Peter, Tresaith Newland, Malvern, Worcestershire WR13 5AY, ENGLAND

Swartley, Robert D., 2800 Pine St., Napa, CA, 94558

Takeuchi, Shigetoshi, 21-14-1-Chome kamimuneoka Shiki shi, 353 Saitama, JAPAN

Theis, Terry, 21452 FM 2093, Harper, TX, 78631, 830-864-4438

Valade, Robert B., 931 3rd Ave., Seaside, OR, 97138, 503-738-7672, (503) 738-7672

Waldrop, Mark, 14562 SE 1st Ave. Rd., Summerfield, FL, 34491

Warenski-Erickson, Julie, 590 East 500 N., Richfield, UT, 84701, 435-627-2504, julie@warensikives.com, www.warensikives.com

Warren, Kenneth W., P.O. Box 2842, Wenatchee, WA, 98807-2842, 509-663-6123, (509) 663-6123

Whitehead, James 2175 South Willow Ave. Space 22 Fresno, CA 93725 559-412-4374 jdwmks@yahoo.com

Whitmore, Jerry, 1740 Churchill Dr., Oakland, OR, 97462

Winn, Travis A., 558 E. 3065 S., Salt Lake City, UT, 84106

Zietz, Dennis, 5906 40th Ave., Kenosha, WI, 53144

Zima, Russ, 7291 Ruth Way, Denver, CO, 80221, 303-657-9378, rzima@rzengraving.com, www.rzengraving.com

etchers

Baron Engraving, David Baron, 62 Spring Hill Rd., Trumbull, CT, 06611, 203-452-0515 sales@baronengraving.com, www.baronengraving.com

Fountain Products, 492 Prospect Ave., West Springfield, MA, 01089, 413-781-4651

Hayes, Dolores, P.O. Box 41405, Los Angeles, CA, 90041

Holland, Dennis, 4908 17th Pl., Lubbock, TX, 79416

Kelso, Jim, 577 Coller Hill Rd, Worcester, VT, 05682, 802-229-4254, jimkelsojournal@gmail.com, www.jimkelso.com

Larstein, Francine, Francine Etched Knives, 368 White Rd, Watsonville, CA, 95076, 800-557-1525/831-426-6046, francine@francinetchedknives.com, www.francineetchedknives.com

Lefaucheux, Jean-Victor, Saint-Denis-Le-Ferment, 27140 Gisors, FRANCE

Myers, Ron, 6202 Marglenn Ave., Baltimore, MD, 21206, (acid) etcher

Nilsson, Jonny Walker, Tingsstigen 11, SE-933 33 Arvidsjaur, SWEDEN, +(46) 960-13048, 0960.13048@telia.com, www.jwnknives.com

Schlott, Harald, Zingster Str. 26, 13051 Berlin, GERMANY, 049 030 9293346, harald.schlott@T-online.de, Custom grinder, custom handle artisan, display case/box maker, etcher, scrimshander

Vallotton, A., Northwest Knife Supply, 621 Fawn Ridge Dr., Oakland, OR, 97462

Watson, Silvia, 350 Jennifer Lane, Driftwood, TX, 78619

heat treaters

Bay State Metal Treating Co., 6 Jefferson Ave., Woburn, MA, 01801

Holt, B.R., 1238 Birchwood Drive, Sunnyvale, CA, 94089

Kazou, Okaysu, 12-2 1 Chome Higashi, Ueno, Taito-Ku, Tokyo, JAPAN, 81-33834-2323, 81-33831-3012

Metal Treating Bodycote Inc., 710 Burns St., Cincinnati, OH, 45204

O&W Heat Treat Inc., One Bidwell Rd., South Windsor, CT, 06074, 860-528-9239, (860) 291-9939, owht1@aol.com

Paul Bos Heat Treating c/o Paul Farner, Buck Knives: 660 S. Lochsa St., Post Falls, ID 83854, 208-262-0500, Ext. 211 / fax 800-733-2825, pfarner@ buckknives.com, or contact Paul Bos direct: 928-232-1656, paulbos@ buckknives.com

Progressive Heat Treating Co., 2802 Charles City Rd, Richmond, VA, 23231, 804-545-0010, 804-545-0012

Texas Heat Treating Inc., 303 Texas Ave., Round Rock, TX, 78664

Texas Knifemakers Supply, 10649 Haddington, Suite 180, Houston, TX, 77043

Tinker Shop, The, 1120 Helen, Deer Park, TX, 77536

Valley Metal Treating Inc., 355 S. East End Ave., Pomona, CA, 91766

Wilderness Forge, 315 North 100 East, Kanab, UT, 84741, 435-644-3674, bhatting@xpressweb.com

Wilson, R.W., P.O. Box 2012, Weirton, WV, 26062

leather workers

Abramson, David, 116 Baker Ave, Wharton, NJ, 07885, lifter4him1@aol.com, www.liftersleather.com

Bruner, Rick, 7756 Aster Lane, Jenison, MI, 49428, 616-457-0403

Burrows, Chuck, dba Wild Rose Trading Co, 102 Timber Ln., Durango, CO 81303, 970-317-5592, wrtc@wrtcleather.com, www.wrtcleather.com

Clements' Custom Leathercraft, Chas, 1741 Dallas St., Aurora, CO 80010, Phone: 303-364-0403

Cole, Dave, 620 Poinsetta Dr., Satellite Beach, FL 32937, 321-773-1687, www. dcknivesandleather.blademakers.com. Custom sheath services.

Cooper, Harold, 136 Winding Way, Frankfort, KY, 40601

Cooper, Jim, 1221 Cook St, Ramona, CA, 92065-3214, 760-789-1097, 760-788-7992, jamcooper@aol.com

CowCatcher Leatherworks, 2045 Progress, Raleigh, NC 27608, Phone: 919-833-8262 cowcatcher1@ymail.com, www.cowcatcher.us

Cubic, George, GC Custom Leather Co., 10561 E. Deerfield Pl., Tucson, AZ, 85749, 520-760-0695, gcubic@aol.com

Dawkins, Dudley, 221 N. Broadmoor Ave, Topeka, KS, 66606-1254, 785-235-3871, dawkind@sbcglobal.net, ABS member/knifemaker forges straight knives

Evans, Scott V, Edge Works Mfg, 1171 Halltown Rd., Jacksonville, NC, 28546, 910-455-9834, fax 910-346-5660, support@tacticalholsters.com, www.tacticalholsters.com

Genske, Jay, 283 Doty St, Fond du Lac, WI, 54935, 920-921-8019/Cell Phone 920-579-0144, jaygenske@hotmail.com, http: //genskeknives.weebly.com, Custom Grinder, Custom Handle Artisan

Green River Leather, 1100 Legion Park Road, PO BOX 190, Greensburg, KY, 42743, Phone: 270-932-2212 fax: 270-299-2471 email: info@ greenriverleather.com

Hawk, Ken, Rt. 1, Box 770, Ceres, VA, 24318-9630

Homyk, David N., 8047 Carriage Ln., Wichita Falls, TX, 76306

John's Custom Leather, John R. Stumpf, 523 S. Liberty St, Blairsville, PA, 15717, 724-459-6802, 724-459-5996

Kravitt, Chris, Treestump Leather, 443 Cave Hill Rd., Waltham, ME, 04605-8706, 207-584-3000, sheathmkr@aol.com, www.treestumpleather.com, Reference: Tree Stump Leather

Larson, Richard, 549 E. Hawkeye, Turlock, CA, 95380

Layton, Jim, 2710 Gilbert Avenue, Portsmouth, OH, 45662

Lee, Randy, P.O. Box 1873, 270 N 9th West, St. Johns, AZ, 85936, 928-337-2594, 928-337-5002, randylee.knives@yahoo.com, info@randyleeknives.com, Custom knifemaker; www.randyleeknives.com

Long, Paul, Paul Long Custom Leather, 108 Briarwood Ln. W, Kerrville, TX, 78028, 830-367-5536, PFL@cebridge.net

Lott, Sherry, 1100 Legion Park Rd., Greenburg, KY 42743, phone 270-932-2212, fax 270-299-2471, sherrylott@alltel.net

Mason, Arne, 258 Wimer St., Ashland, OR, 97520, 541-482-2260, (541) 482-7785, www.arnemason.com

McGowan, Liz, 12629 Howard Lodge Dr., Winter Add-2023 Robin Ct Sebring FL 33870, Sykesville, MD, 21784, 410-489-4323

Metheny, H.A. "Whitey", 7750 Waterford Dr., Spotsylvania, VA 22551, 540-582-3228 Cell 540-842-1440, fax 540-582-3095, hametheny@aol.com, http://whitey.methenyknives.com

Miller, Michael K., 28510 Santiam Highway, Sweet Home, OR, 97386

Mobley, Martha, 240 Alapaha River Road, Chula, GA, 31733

Morrissey, Martin, 4578 Stephens Rd., Blairsville, GA, 30512

Niedenthal, John Andre, Beadwork & Buckskin, Studio 3955 NW 103 Dr., Coral Springs, FL, 33065-1551, 954-345-0447, a_niedenthal@hotmail.com

Neilson, Tess, 291 Scouten Rd., Wyalusing, PA, 18853, 570-721-0470, mountainhollow@epix.net, www.mountainhollow.net, Doing business as Neilson's Mountain Hollow

Parsons, Larry, 1038 W. Kyle, Mustang, OK 73064 405-376-9408 s.m.parsons@sbcglobal.net

Parsons, Michael R., McKee Knives, 7042 McFarland Rd, Indianapolis, IN, 46227, 317-784-7943

Poag, James H., RR #1 Box 212A, Grayville, IL, 62844

Red's Custom Leather, Ed Todd, 9 Woodlawn Rd., Putnam Valley, NY, 10579, 845-528-3783

Rowe, Kenny, Rowe's Leather, 3219 Hwy 29 South, Hope, AR, 71801, 870-777-8216, fax 870-777-0935, rowesleather@yahoo.com, www.rowesleather.com

Schrap, Robert G., Custom Leather Knife Sheaths, 7024 W. Wells St., Wauwatosa, WI, 53213, 414-771-6472, fax 414-479-9765, rschrap@aol.com, www.customsheaths.com

Strahin, Robert, 401 Center St., Elkins, WV, 26241, *Custom Knife Sheaths

Turner, Kevin, 17 Hunt Ave., Montrose, NY, 10548

Velasquez, Gil, 7120 Madera Dr., Goleta, CA, 93117

Walker, John, 17 Laber Circle, Little Rock, AR, 72210, 501-455-0239, john.walker@afbic.com

Watson, Bill, #1 Presidio, Wimberly, TX, 78676

Whinnery, Walt, 1947 Meadow Creek Dr., Louisville, KY, 40218

Williams, Sherman A., 1709 Wallace St., Simi Valley, CA, 93065

miscellaneous

Robertson, Kathy, Impress by Design, PO Box 1367, Evans, GA, 30809-1367, 706-650-0982, (706) 860-1623, impressbydesign@comcast.net, Advertising/graphic designer

Strahin, Robert, 401 Center St., Elkins, WV, 26241, 304-636-0128, rstrahin@copper.net, *Custom Knife Sheaths

photographers

Alfano, Sam, 36180 Henery Gaines Rd., Pearl River, LA, 70452

Allen, John, Studio One, 3823 Pleasant Valley Blvd., Rockford, IL, 61114

Bilal, Mustafa, Turk's Head Productions, 908 NW 50th St., Seattle, WA, 98107-3634, 206-782-4164, (206) 782-4164, info@turkshead.com, www.turkshead.com, Graphic design, marketing & advertising

Bogaerts, Jan, Regenweg 14, 5757 Pl., Liessel, HOLLAND

Box Photography, Doug, 1804 W Main St, Brenham, TX, 77833-3420

Brown, Tom, 6048 Grants Ferry Rd., Brandon, MS, 39042-8136

Butman, Steve, P.O. Box 5106, Abilene, TX, 79608

Calidonna, Greg, 205 Helmwood Dr., Elizabethtown, KY, 42701

Campbell, Jim, 7935 Ranch Rd., Port Richey, FL, 34668

Cooper, Jim, Sharpbycoop.com Photography, 9 Mathew Court, Norwalk, CT 06851, jcooper@sharpbycoop.com, www.sharpbycoop.com

Courtice, Bill, P.O. Box 1776, Duarte, CA, 91010-4776

Crosby, Doug, RFD 1, Box 1111, Stockton Springs, ME, 04981

Danko, Michael, 3030 Jane Street, Pittsburgh, PA, 15203

Davis, Marshall B., P.O. Box 3048, Austin, TX, 78764

Earley, Don, 1241 Ft. Bragg Rd., Fayetteville, NC, 28305

Ehrlich, Linn M., 1850 N Clark St #1008, Chicago, IL, 60614, 312-209-2107

Etzler, John, 11200 N. Island Rd., Grafton, OH, 44044

Fahrner, Dave, 1623 Arnold St., Pittsburgh, PA, 15205

Faul, Jan W., 903 Girard St. NE, Rr. Washington, DC, 20017

Fedorak, Allan, 28 W. Nicola St., Amloops BC CANADA, V2C 1J6

Fox, Daniel, Lumina Studios, 6773 Industrial Parkway, Cleveland, OH, 44070, 440-734-2118, (440) 734-3542, lumina@en.com

Freiberg, Charley, PO Box 42, Elkins, NH, 03233, 603-526-2767, charleyfreiberg@tos.net

Gardner, Chuck, 116 Quincy Ave., Oak Ridge, TN, 37830

Gawryla, Don, 1105 Greenlawn Dr., Pittsburgh, PA, 15220

Goffe Photographic Associates, 3108 Monte Vista Blvd., NE, Albuquerque, NM, 87106

Graham, James, 7434 E Northwest Hwy, Dallas, TX, 75231, 214-341-5138, jamie@jamiephoto.com, www.jamiephoto.com, Product photographer

Graley, Gary W., RR2 Box 556, Gillett, PA, 16925

Griggs, Dennis, 118 Pleasant Pt Rd, Topsham, ME, 04086, 207-725-5689

Hanusin, John, Reames-Hanusin Studio, PO Box 931, Northbrook, IL, 60065 0931

Hodge, Tom, 7175 S US Hwy 1 Lot 36, Titusville, FL, 32780-8172, 321-267-7989, egdoht@hotmail.com

Holter, Wayne V., 125 Lakin Ave., Boonsboro, MD, 21713, 301-416-2855, mackwayne@hotmail.com

Hopkins, David W, Hopkins Photography inc, 201 S Jefferson, Iola, KS, 66749, 620-365-7443, nhoppy@netks.net

Kerns, Bob, 18723 Birdseye Dr., Germantown, MD, 20874

LaFleur, Gordon, 111 Hirst, Box 1209, Parksville BC CANADA, V0R 270

Lear, Dale, 6544 Cora Mill Rd, Gallipolis, OH, 45631, 740-245-5482, dalelear@yahoo.com, Ebay Sales

LeBlanc, Paul, No. 3 Meadowbrook Cir., Melissa, TX, 75454

Lester, Dean, 2801 Junipero Ave Suite 212, Long Beach, CA, 90806-2140

Leviton, David A., A Studio on the Move, P.O. Box 2871, Silverdale, WA, 98383, 360-697-3452

Long, Gary W., 3556 Miller's Crossroad Rd., Hillsboro, TN, 37342

Long, Jerry, 402 E. Gladden Dr., Farmington, NM, 87401

Lum, Billy, 16307 Evening Star Ct., Crosby, TX, 77532

Martin, Cory, 4249 Taylor Harbor #7, Mt. Pleasant, WI 53403, 262-352-5392, info@corymartinimaging.com, www.corymartinimaging.com

McCollum, Tom, P.O. Box 933, Lilburn, GA, 30226

Mitch Lum Website and Photography, 22115 NW Imbrie Dr. #298, Hillsboro, OR 97124, mitch@mitchlum.com, www.mitchlum.com, 206-356-6813

Moake, Jim, 18 Council Ave., Aurora, IL, 60504

Moya Inc., 4212 S. Dixie Hwy., West Palm Beach, FL, 33405

Norman's Studio, 322 S. 2nd St., Vivian, LA, 71082

Owens, William T., Box 99, Williamsburg, WV, 24991

Pachi, Francesco, Loc. Pometta 1, Sassello, 17046 (SV) ITALY Tel-fax: 0039 019 72 00 86 www.pachi-photo.com

Palmer Studio, 2008 Airport Blvd., Mobile, AL, 36606

Payne, Robert G., P.O. Box 141471, Austin, TX, 78714

Pigott, John, 9095 Woodprint LN, Mason, OH, 45040

Point Seven, 6450 Weatherfield Ct., Unit 2A, Maumee, OH, 43537, 419-866-8880 pointseven@pointsevenstudios.com, www.pointsevenstudios.com

Rob Andrew Photography, Rob Szjkowski, 7960 Silverton Ave., Ste. 125, San Diego, CA 92126, 760-920-6380, rob@robandrewphoto.com, www.robandrewphoto.com

Professional Medica Concepts, Patricia Mitchell, P.O. Box 0002, Warren, TX, 77664, 409-547-2213, pm0909@wt.net

Rasmussen, Eric L., 1121 Eliason, Brigham City, UT, 84302

Rhoades, Cynthia J., Box 195, Clearmont, WY, 82835

Rice, Tim, PO Box 663, Whitefish, MT, 59937

Richardson, Kerry, 2520 Mimosa St., Santa Rosa, CA, 95405, 707-575-1875, kerry@sonic.net, www.sonic.net/~kerry

Ross, Bill, 28364 S. Western Ave. Suite 464, Rancho Palos Verdes, CA, 90275

Rubicam, Stephen, 14 Atlantic Ave., Boothbay Harbor, ME, 04538-1202

Rush, John D., 2313 Maysel, Bloomington, IL, 61701

Schreiber, Roger, 429 Boren Ave. N., Seattle, WA, 98109

Semmer, Charles, 7885 Cyd Dr., Denver, CO, 80221

Silver Images Photography, 2412 N Keystone, Flagstaff, AZ, 86004

Slobodian, Scott, 4101 River Ridge Dr., P.O. Box 1498, San Andreas, CA, 95249, 209-286-1980, (209) 286-1982, www.slobodianswords.com

Smith, Earl W., 5121 Southminster Rd., Columbus, OH, 43221

Smith, Randall, 1720 Oneco Ave., Winter Park, FL, 32789

Storm Photo, 334 Wall St., Kingston, NY, 12401

Surles, Mark, P.O. Box 147, Falcon, NC, 28342

Third Eye Photos, 140 E. Sixth Ave., Helena, MT, 59601

Thurber, David, P.O. Box 1006, Visalia, CA, 93279

Tighe, Brian, 12-111 Fourth Ave., Ste. 376 Ridley Square, St. Catharines ON CANADA, L0S 1M0, 905-892-2734, www.tigheknives.com

Towell, Steven L., 3720 N.W. 32nd Ave., Camas, WA, 98607, 360-834-9049, sltowell@netscape.net

Verno Studio, Jay, 3030 Jane Street, Pittsburgh, PA, 15203

Ward, Chuck, 1010 E North St, PO Box 2272, Benton, AR, 72018, 501-778-4329, chuckbop@aol.com

Wise, Harriet, 242 Dill Ave., Frederick, MD, 21701

Worley, Holly, Worley Photography, 6360 W David Dr, Littleton, CO, 80128-5708, 303-257-8091, 720-981-2800, hsworley@aol.com, Products, Digital & Film

scrimshanders

Adlam, Tim, 1705 Witzel Ave., Oshkosh, WI, 54902, 920-235-4589, ctimadlam@new.rr.com, www.adlamengraving.com

Alpen, Ralph, 7 Bentley Rd., West Grove, PA, 19390, 610-869-7141

Anderson, Terry Jack, 10076 Birnamwoods Way, Riverton, UT, 84065-9073

Bailey, Mary W., 3213 Jonesboro Dr., Nashville, TN, 37214, Phone: 615-889-3172 mbscrim@aol.com

Baker, Duane, 2145 Alum Creek Dr., Cambridge Park Apt. #10, Columbus, OH, 43207

Barrows, Miles, 524 Parsons Ave., Chillicothe, OH, 45601

Brady, Sandra, Scrimshaw by Sandra Brady, 9608 Monclova Rd., Monclova, OH 43542, 419-866-0435, 419-261-1582 sandy@sandrabradyart.com, www.sandrabradyart.com

Beauchamp, Gaetan, 125 de la Riviere, Stoneham, QC, G3C 0P6, CANADA, 418-848-1914, fax 418-848-6859, knives@gbeauchamp.ca, www.gbeauchamp.ca

Bellet, Connie, PO Box 151, Palermo, ME, 04354 0151, 207-993-2327, phwhitehawk@gwl.net

Benade, Lynn, 2610 Buckhurst Dr, Beachwood, OH, 44122, 216-464-0777, llbnc17@aol.com

Bonshire, Benita, 1121 Burlington Dr., Muncie, IN, 47302

Boone Trading Co. Inc., P.O. Box 669, Brinnon, WA, 98320, 800-423-1945, ww.boonetrading.com

Bryan, Bob, 1120 Oak Hill Rd., Carthage, MO, 64836

Burger, Sharon, Glenwood, Durban KZN, South Africa, cell: +27 83 7891675, scribble@iafrica.com, www.sharonburger-scrimshaw.co.za

Byrne, Mary Gregg, 1018 15th St., Bellingham, WA, 98225-6604

Cable, Jerry, 332 Main St., Mt. Pleasant, PA, 15666

Caudill, Lyle, 7626 Lyons Rd., Georgetown, OH, 45121

Cole, Gary, PO Box 668, Naalehu, HI, 96772, 808-929-9775, 808-929-7371

Collins, Michael, Rt. 3075, Batesville Rd., Woodstock, GA, 30188

Conover, Juanita Rae, P.O. Box 70442, Eugene, OR, 97401, 541-747-1726 or 543-4851, juanitaraeconover@yahoo.com

Courtnage, Elaine, Box 473, Big Sandy, MT, 59520

Cover Jr., Raymond A., 1206 N. 3rd St., Festus, MO, 63010, Phone: 314-808-2508 cover@sbcglobal.net, http://rcoverengraving.com

Cox, J. Andy, 116 Robin Hood Lane, Gaffney, SC, 29340

Dietrich, Roni, Wild Horse Studio, 1257 Cottage Dr, Harrisburg, PA, 17112, 717-469-0587, ronimd@aol

DiMarzo, Richard, 2357 Center Place, Birmingham, AL, 35205

Dolbare, Elizabeth, PO Box 502, Dubois, WY, 82513-0502

Eklund, Maihkel, Föne 1111, S-82041 Färila, SWEDEN, +46 6512 4192, maihkel.eklund@swipnet.se, www.art-knives.com

Eldridge, Allan, 1424 Kansas Lane, Gallatin, TN, 37066

Ellis, Willy B., Willy B's Customs by William B Ellis, Tarpon Springs, FL, 34689, 727-942-6420, wbflashs@verizon.net, www.willyb.com

Fisk, Dale, Box 252, Council, ID, 83612, dafisk@ctcweb.net

Foster Enterprises, Norvell Foster, P.O. Box 200343, San Antonio, TX, 78220

Fountain Products, 492 Prospect Ave., West Springfield, MA, 01089

Gill, Scott, 925 N. Armstrong St., Kokomo, IN, 46901

Halligan, Ed, 14 Meadow Way, Sharpsburg, GA, 30277, ehkiss@bellsouth.net

Hands, Barry Lee, 26192 East Shore Route, Bigfork, MT, 59911

Hargraves Sr., Charles, RR 3 Bancroft, Ontario CANADA, K0L 1C0

Harless, Star, c/o Arrow Forge, P.O. Box 845, Stoneville, NC, 27048-0845

Harrington, Fred A., Summer: 2107 W Frances Rd, Mt Morris MI 48458 8215, Winter: 3725 Citrus, St. James City, FL, 33956, Winter 239-283-0721, Summer 810-686-3008

Hergert, Bob, 12 Geer Circle, Port Orford, OR, 97465, 541-332-3010, hergert@harborside.com, www.scrimshander.com

Hielscher, Vickie, 6550 Otoe Rd, P.O. Box 992, Alliance, NE, 69301, 308-762-4318, g-hielsc@bbcwb.net

High, Tom, 5474 S. 112.8 Rd., Alamosa, CO, 81101, 719-589-2108, info1@rockymountainscrimshaw.com, www.rockymountainscrimshaw.com, Wildlife Artist

Himmelheber, David R., 11289 40th St. N., Royal Palm Beach, FL, 33411

Holland, Dennis K., 4908-17th Place, Lubbock, TX, 79416

Hutchings, Rick "Hutch", 3007 Coffe Tree Ct, Crestwood, KY, 40014, 502-241-2871, baron1@bellsouth.net

Imboden II, Howard L., 620 Deauville Dr., Dayton, OH, 45429, 937-439-1536,

Guards by the "Last Wax Technic"

Johnson, Corinne, W3565 Lockington, Mindora, WI, 54644

Johnston, Kathy, W. 1134 Providence, Spokane, WA, 99205

Karst Stone, Linda, 903 Tanglewood Ln, Kerrville, TX, 78028-2945, 830-896-4678, 830-257-6117, linda@karstone.com, www.karstone.com

Kelso, Jim, 577 Coller Hill Rd, Worcester, VT, 05682

Kirk, Susan B., 1340 Freeland Rd., Merrill, MI, 48637

Koevenig, Eugene and Eve, Koevenig's Engraving Service, Rabbit Gulch, Box 55, Hill City, SD, 57745-0055

Kostelnik, Joe and Patty, RD #4, Box 323, Greensburg, PA, 15601

Lemen, Pam, 3434 N. Iroquois Ave., Tucson, AZ, 85705

Martin, Diane, 28220 N. Lake Dr., Waterford, WI, 53185

McDonald, René Cosimini-, 14730 61 Court N., Loxahatchee, FL, 33470

McFadden, Berni, 2547 E Dalton Ave, Dalton Gardens, ID, 83815-9631

McGowan, Frank, 12629 Howard Lodge Dr., Winter Add-2023 Robin Ct Sebring FL 33870, Sykesville, MD, 21784, 863-385-1296

McGrath, Gayle, PMB 232 15201 N Cleveland Ave, N Ft Myers, FL, 33903

McLaran, Lou, 603 Powers St., Waco, TX, 76705

McWilliams, Carole, P.O. Box 693, Bayfield, CO, 81122

Mitchell, James, 1026 7th Ave., Columbus, GA, 31901

Moore, James B., 1707 N. Gillis, Stockton, TX, 79735

Ochonicky, Michelle "Mike", Stone Hollow Studio, 31 High Trail, Eureka, MO, 63025, 636-938-9570, www.stonehollowstudio.com

Ochs, Belle, 124 Emerald Lane, Largo, FL, 33771, 727-536-3827, contact@oxforge.com, www.oxforge.com

Pachi, Mirella, Localita Pometta 1, 17046 Sassello (SV), ITALY, +39 019 72 00 86, www.pachi-photo.com

Parish, Vaughn, 103 Cross St., Monaca, PA, 15061

Peterson, Lou, 514 S. Jackson St., Gardner, IL, 60424

Pienaar, Conrad, 19A Milner Rd., Bloemfontein 9300, SOUTH AFRICA, Phone: 027 514364180 fax: 027 514364180

Poag, James H., RR #1 Box 212A, Grayville, IL, 62844

Polk, Trena, 4625 Webber Creek Rd., Van Buren, AR, 72956

Pulisova, Andrea, CSA 230-95, 96701 Kremnica, Slovakia, Phone: 00421 903-340076 vpulis@gmail.com, www.vpulis.host.sk

Purvis, Hilton, P.O. Box 371, Noordhoek, 7979, SOUTH AFRICA, 27 21 789 1114, hiltonp@telkomsa.net, www.kgsa.co.za/member/hiltonpurvis

Ramsey, Richard, 8525 Trout Farm Rd, Neosho, MO, 64850

Ristinen, Lori, 14256 County Hwy 45, Menahga, MN, 56464, 218-538-6608, lori@loriristinen.com, www.loriristinen.com

Roberts, J.J., 7808 Lake Dr., Manassas, VA, 22111, 703-330-0448, jjrengraver@aol.com, www.angelfire.com/va2/engraver

Rudolph, Gil, 20922 Oak Pass Ave, Tehachapi, CA, 93561, 661-822-4949

Rundell, Joe, 6198 W. Frances Rd., Clio, MI, 48420

Satre, Robert, 518 3rd Ave. NW, Weyburn SK CANADA, S4H 1R1

Schlott, Harald, Zingster Str. 26, 13051 Berlin, +49 030 929 33 46, GERMANY, harald.schlott@web.de, www.gravur-kunst-atelier.de

Schulenburg, E.W., 25 North Hill St., Carrollton, GA, 30117

Schwallie, Patricia, 4614 Old Spartanburg Rd. Apt. 47, Taylors, SC, 29687

Selent, Chuck, P.O. Box 1207, Bonners Ferry, ID, 83805

Semich, Alice, 10037 Roanoke Dr., Murfreesboro, TN, 37129

Shostle, Ben, 1121 Burlington, Muncie, IN, 47302

Smith, Peggy, 676 Glades Rd., #3, Gatlinburg, TN, 37738

Smith, Ron, 5869 Straley, Ft. Worth, TX, 76114

Steigerwalt, Jim, RD#3, Sunbury, PA, 17801

Stuart, Stephen, 15815 Acorn Circle, Tavares, FL, 32778, 352-343-8423, (352) 343-8916, inkscratch@aol.com

Talley, Mary Austin, 2499 Countrywood Parkway, Memphis, TN, 38016, matalley@midsouth.rr.com

Thompson, Larry D., 23040 Ave. 197, Strathmore, CA, 93267

Toniutti, Nelida, Via G. Pascoli, 33085 Maniago-PN, ITALY

Trout, Lauria Lovestrand, 1555 Delaney Dr, No. 1723, Talahassee, FL, 32309, 850-893-8836, mayalaurie@aol.com

Tucker, Steve, 3518 W. Linwood, Turlock, CA, 95380

Tyser, Ross, 1015 Hardee Court, Spartanburg, SC, 29303

Velasquez, Gil, Art of Scrimshaw, 7120 Madera Dr., Goleta, CA, 93117

Wilderness Forge, 475 NE Smith Rock Way, Terrebonne, OR, 97760, bhatting@xpressweb.com

Williams, Gary, PO Box 210, Glendale, KY, 42740, 270-369-6752, scrimbygarbo@gmail.com, scrimshawbygarbo.com

Winn, Travis A., 558 E. 3065 S., Salt Lake City, UT, 84106

Young, Mary, 4826 Storeyland Dr., Alton, IL, 62002

organizations

AMERICAN BLADESMITH SOCIETY
c/o Office Manager, Cindy Sheely; P. O. Box 160, Grand Rapids, Ohio 43522; cindy@americanbladesmith.com; (419) 832-0400; Web: www.americanbladesmith.com

AMERICAN KNIFE & TOOL INSTITUTE
Jan Billeb, Comm. Coordinator, AKTI, 22 Vista View Ln., Cody, WY 82414; 307-587-8296, akti@akti.org; www. akti.org

AMERICAN KNIFE THROWERS ALLIANCE
c/o Bobby Branton; POB 807; Awendaw, SC 29429; akta@ akta-usa.com, www.AKTA-USA.com

ARIZONA KNIFE COLLECTOR'S ASSOCIATION
c/o Mike Mooney, President, 19432 E. Cloud Rd., Quen Creek, AZ 85142; Phone: 480-244-7768, mike@moonblades. com, Web: www.arizonaknifecollectors.org

ART KNIFE COLLECTOR'S ASSOCIATION
c/o Mitch Weiss, Pres.; 2211 Lee Road, Suite 104; Winter Park, FL 32789

BAY AREA KNIFE COLLECTOR'S ASSOCIATION
c/o Larry Hirsch, 5339 Prospect Rd. #129, San Jose, CA 95129, bladeplay@earthlink.net, Web: www.bakcainc.org

ARKANSAS KNIFEMAKERS ASSOCIATION
David Etchieson, 60 Wendy Cove, Conway, AR 72032; Phone: 501-554-2582, arknifeassn@yahoo.com, Web: www. arkansasknifemakers.com

AUSTRALASIAN KNIFE COLLECTORS
PO BOX 149 CHIDLOW 6556 WESTERN AUSTRALIA TEL: (08) 9572 7255; FAX: (08) 9572 7266. International Inquiries: TEL: + 61 8 9572 7255; FAX: + 61 8 9572 7266; akc@knivesaustralia.com.au

CALIFORNIA KNIFEMAKERS ASSOCIATION
c/o Clint Breshears, Membership Chairman; 1261 Keats St; Manhattan Beach CA 90266; 310-372-0739; breshears@ mindspring.com
Dedicated to teaching and improving knifemaking

CANADIAN KNIFEMAKERS GUILD
c/o Wolfgang Loerchner; PO Box 255, Bayfield, Ont., CANADA N0M 1G0; 519-565-2196; info@canadianknifemakersguild.com, www. canadianknifemakersguild.com

CUSTOM KNIFE COLLECTORS ASSOCIATION
c/o Kevin Jones, PO Box 5893, Glen Allen, VA 23058-5893; E-mail: customknifecollectorsassociation@yahoo.com; Web: www.customknifecollectorsassociation.com
The purpose of the CKCA is to recognize and promote the artistic significance of handmade knives, to advnace their collection and conservation, and to support the creative expression of those who make them. Open to collectors, makers purveyors, and other collectors. Has members from eight countries. Produced a calednar which features custom knives either owned or made by CKCA members.

CUTTING EDGE, THE
2900 S. 26th St., Rogers, AR 72758; 479-631-0130; 800-255-9034; ce_info@cuttingedge.com, www.cuttingedge.com
After-market knives since 1968. We offer about 1,000 individual knives each month. The oldest and the most experienced in the business of buying and selling knives. We buy collections of any size, take knives on consignment or we will trade. Web: www.cuttingedge.com

FLORIDA KNIFEMAKERS ASSOCIATION
c/o President Terry Renner, 707 13th Ave. Cir. W, Palmetto, Florida, 34221 (941) 545-6320; terrylmusic@gmail.com, Web: www.floridaknifemakers.org

JAPANESE SWORD SOCIETY OF THE U.S.
PO Box 712; Breckenridge, TX 76424

KNIFE COLLECTORS CLUB INC, THE
2900 S. 26th St, Rogers, AR 72758; 479-631-0130; 800-255-9034; ag@agrussell.com; Web: www.agrussell.com/kcc-one-year-membership-usa-/p/KCC/
The oldest and largest association of knife collectors. Issues limited edition knives, both handmade and highest quality production, in very limited numbers. The very earliest was the CM-1, Kentucky Rifle

KNIFEMAKERS' GUILD, THE
c/o Gene Baskett, Knifemakers Guild, Box 13, La Grange, KY 40031; 502-222-1397; Web: www.knifemakersguild.com

KNIFEMAKERS GUILD OF SOUTHERN AFRICA, THE
c/o Andre Thorburn; PO Box 1748; Bela Bela, Warmbaths, LP, SOUTH AFRICA 0480; +27 14 740 0528 andrethorburn@gmail.com; Web: www.kgsa.co.za

MONTANA KNIFEMAKERS' ASSOCIATION, THE
1439 S. 5th W, Missoula, MT 59801; 406-728-2861; cayley51@msn.com, Web: www.montanaknifemakers.com
Annual book of custom knife makers' works and directory of knife making supplies; $19.99

NATIONAL KNIFE COLLECTORS ASSOCIATION
PO Box 21070; Chattanooga, TN 37424; 423-892-5007; 423-667-8199; nkcalisa@hotmail.com; Web: www.nkcalisa.wix.com/nkca-website-2

NEO-TRIBAL METALSMITHS
PO Box 1854, Cortaro, AZ 85652-1854; Phone: 520-744-9777, taigoo@msn.com, Web: www.neo-tribalmetalsmiths.com

NEW ENGLAND CUSTOM KNIFE ASSOCIATION
Vickie Gray, Treasurer, 686 Main Rd, Brownville, ME 04414; Phone: 207-965-2191, Web: www.necka.net

NORTH CAROLINA CUSTOM KNIFEMAKERS GUILD
c/o Chris Williams, President, 7198 Henry Smith Rd., Sain Pauls, NC 28384 (910) 391-6573, blindhogg@aol.com, Web: www.ncknifeguild.org

NORTH STAR BLADE COLLECTORS
PO Box 20523, Bloomington, MN 55420; info@nsbc.us, Web: www.nsbc.us

OHIO KNIFEMAKERS ASSOCIATION
c/o Jerry Smith, Anvils and Ink Studios, P.O. Box 151, Barnesville, Ohio 43713; jerry_smith@anvilsandinkstudios.com, Web: www.oocities.org/ohioknives/

OREGON KNIFE COLLECTORS ASSOCIATION
Web: www.oregonknifeclub.org

ROCKY MOUNTAIN BLADE COLLECTORS ASSOCIATION
Mike Moss. Pres., P.O. Box 324, Westminster, CO 80036; rmbladecollectors@gmail.com, Web: www.rmbladecollectors.org

SOUTH CAROLINA ASSOCIATION OF KNIFEMAKERS
c/o Col. Tom Kreger, President, (803) 438-4221; tdkreger@bellsouth.net, Web: www.southcarolinaassociationofknifemakers.org

SOUTHERN CALIFORNIA BLADES KNIFE COLLECTORS CLUB
SC Blades, PO Box 231112, Encinitas, CA 92023-1112; Phone: 619-417-4329, scblades@att.net, Web: www.scblades.org

THE WILLIAM F. MORAN JR. MUSEUM & FOUNDATION
4204 Ballenger Creek Pike, Frederick, MD 21703, 301-663-6923

publications

AUTOMATIC KNIFE RESOURCE
c/o Lantama Cutlery, POB 721, Montauk, NY 11954; 631-668-5995; info@latama.net, Web: www.thenewsletter.com,
Unique compilation and archive for the switchblade/automatic knife fan. Sheldon Levy's Newsletter was first published in 1992, and was a labor of love from its inception and has remained informative and insightful.

BLADE AND BLADE'S COMPLETE KNIFE GUIDE
700 E. State St., Iola, WI 54990-0001; 715-445-4612; Web: www.blademag.com, www.KnifeForums.com, www.ShopBlade.com, facebook.com/blademag
The world's No. 1 knife magazine. The most indepth knife magazine on the market, covering all aspects of the industry, from knifemaking to production knives and handmade pieces. With 13 issues per year, BLADE® boasts twice the distribution of its closest competitor.

CUTLERY NEWS JOURNAL (BLOG)
http://cutlerynewsjournal.wordpress.com
Covers significant happenings from the world of knife collecting, in addition to editorials, trends, events, auctions, shows, cutlery history, and reviews

KNIFE WORLD
PO Box 3395, Knoxville, TN 37927; Phone: 865-397-1955, knifepub@knifeworld.com, www.knifeworld.com
Since 1977, a monthly knife publication covering all types of knives

KNIVES ILLUSTRATED
22840 Savi Ranch Pkwy. #200, Yorba Linda, CA 92887; Phone: 714-200-1963; bmiller@beckett.com; Web: www.knivesillustrated.com
All encompassing publication focusing on factory knives, new handmades, shows and industry news

THE LEATHER CRAFTERS & SADDLERS JOURNAL
222 Blackburn St., Rhinelander, WI 54501; Phone: 715-362-5393; info@leathercraftersjournal.com, Web: www.leathercraftersjournal.com
Bi-monthly how-to leathercraft magazine